PRAISE FOR OTHER AMERICA'S TEST KITCHEN TITLES

"This tome definitely raises the bar for all-in-one, basic, must-have cookbooks. . . . Kimball and his company have scored another hit." Portland Oregonian on *The America's Test Kitchen Family Cookbook*

"A foolproof, go-to resource for everyday cooking." Publishers Weekly on *The America's Test Kitchen Family Cookbook*

"If you're hankering for old-fashioned pleasures, look no further." People Magazine on *America's Best Lost Recipes*

"A time-saving tome." The Chicago Tribune on *834 Kitchen Quick Tips*

"For anyone looking for a lighter way of cooking, this book and its 300 recipes would be a most valuable resource." Providence Journal on *The Best Light Recipe*

"Further proof that practice makes perfect, if not transcendent. . . . If an intermediate cook follows the directions exactly, the results will be better than takeout or mom's." The New York Times on *The New Best Recipe*

"Exceptional renditions with thorough instruction…" Publishers Weekly on *Cooking at Home with America's Test Kitchen*

"Like a mini-cooking school, the detailed instructions and illustrations ensure that even the most inexperienced cook can follow these recipes with success." Publishers Weekly on *Best American Side Dishes*

"Makes one-dish dinners a reality for average cooks, with honest ingredients and detailed make-ahead instructions." The New York Times on *The Best Cover & Bake Recipes*

"*The Best Meat Recipes* conquers every question one could have about all things meat." The San Francisco Chronicle on *The Best Meat Recipes*

"The best instructional book on baking this reviewer has seen." Library Journal (starred review) on *Baking Illustrated*

"A must-have for anyone into our nation's cooking traditions—and a good reference, too." Los Angeles Daily News on *The Best American Classics*

"If you've always wanted to make real Italian dishes as close to the Italian way as we can make them in America, here's a cookbook that shows you how." Pittsburgh Post-Gazette on *The Best Italian Classics*

"*Cook's Illustrated* to the rescue. . . . *The Best Vegetable Recipes* belongs on every cooking reference shelf. Here's to our health." Pittsburgh Tribune-Review on *The Best Vegetable Recipes*

AMERICA'S TEST KITCHEN
17 Station Street, Brookline, MA 02445

Library of Congress Cataloging-in-Publication Data
The Editors at America's Test Kitchen

THE BEST OF AMERICA'S TEST KITCHEN 2009:
The Year's Best Recipes, Equipment Reviews, and Tastings

1st Edition

Hardcover: $35 US/$38 CAN
ISBN-13: 978-1-933615-33-2   ISBN-10: 1-933615-33-8
1. Cooking. 1. Title
2008

Manufactured in the United States of America

10 9 8 7 6 5 4 3 2 1

Distributed by America's Test Kitchen
17 Station Street, Brookline, MA 02445

EDITORIAL DIRECTOR: Jack Bishop
EXECUTIVE EDITOR: Elizabeth Carduff
ASSOCIATE EDITORS: Elizabeth Emery and Rachel Toomey
CONTRIBUTING EDITOR: Matthew Card
EDITORIAL ASSISTANT: Elizabeth Pohm
DESIGN DIRECTOR: Amy Klee
ART DIRECTOR: Greg Galvan
DESIGNERS: Erica Lee and Matthew Warnick
FRONT COVER PHOTOGRAPH: Carl Tremblay
COVER STYLING: Marie Piraino
STAFF PHOTOGRAPHER: Daniel J. van Ackere
ADDITIONAL PHOTOGRAPHERS: Keller + Keller, Peter Tannenbaum, and Carl Tremblay
FOOD STYLING: Marie Piraino and Mary Jane Sawyer
PRODUCTION DIRECTOR: Guy Rochford
SENIOR PRODUCTION MANAGER: Jessica Quirk
TRAFFIC AND PROJECT MANAGER: Alice Cummiskey
COLOR AND IMAGING SPECIALIST: Andrew Mannone
PRODUCTION AND IMAGING SPECIALIST: Lauren Pettapiece
COPYEDITOR: Evie Righter
PROOFREADER: Jeffrey Schier
INDEXER: Elizabeth Parson

PICTURED ON THE FRONT COVER: Tiramisù (page 276)

THE BEST OF

America's
TEST KITCHEN

THE YEAR'S BEST RECIPES, EQUIPMENT REVIEWS, AND TASTINGS

2009

BY THE EDITORS AT
AMERICA'S TEST KITCHEN

CONTENTS

INTRODUCTION

A YEAR IS A LONG TIME. IN OUR SMALL TOWN, the sap ran better than it had in decades, a drunk turkey stumbled into Sherman's store, our neighbor Rick unexpectedly came across and then shot a wild boar, our firehouse won the Woodchuck Challenge, it was a great year for rabbit hunting, Tom and Nancy built a small home down the valley, black bears have been raiding bird feeders all over town, the apple harvest was abundant, and our daughter Caroline led the Harvest Festival Parade with her cow in tow.

Here in the test kitchen, a year is equally eventful and productive. We develop recipes for our two magazines, *Cook's Illustrated* and *Cook's Country*, as well as our two television shows (based on the magazines) and a plethora of cookbooks.

Like most of us here at America's Test Kitchen, I taste some but not all of the food produced by the kitchen. That would be a Herculean and belly busting undertaking. So I am usually reduced to asking Erin, our test kitchen director, which recipes she recommends the most, for a picnic, a fancy dinner party, Tuesday night supper, or a cookout. She is my personal "Best of America's Test Kitchen."

Even better is having one cookbook with all of our favorite recipes produced throughout the year. Perhaps my favorite is the French Onion Soup, which is based on a visit by a French friend of ours, Henri, who made an impromptu lunch using nothing more than onions and a little white wine. It was superb. We borrowed his basic notion and the resulting recipe is contained in this volume. For would-be bakers who really don't want to spend hours in the kitchen, the Drop Biscuits are just the thing—a simple, no-roll biscuit recipe without the need to cut in butter or shortening. (The recipe contains a secret technique that we stumbled across in our testing.) Other favorites include the Skillet-Barbecued Pork Chops, the fabulous Poached Salmon with Herb and Caper Vinaigrette (the fish is really steamed, not poached, to preserve flavor and juiciness), the Rustic Plum Cake, and one of my all-time favorite recipes, the Foolproof Pie Dough made with vodka (no alcohol remains in the crust after baking). It is a snap to roll out and it works every time.

We have also included our favorite illustrated techniques as well as a year's worth of tastings and testings, everything from Parmesan cheese to supermarket tea, dark chocolate, vegetable broth, and potato chips. You will also get specific brand suggestions for garlic presses, cast-iron skillets, cutting boards, baking sheets—the list goes on and on.

In editing and collecting the recipes for this book, one comes to realize that the "best" is not always the most complicated. As corny as it sounds, simpler is often better. The best taste experience of my year was at a small café in southern France after my wife, Adrienne, and I had spent four hours hiking out of a deep gorge in the Pyrenees, having become utterly lost, reduced to "following the river back to civilization." Upon arrival, we ordered two beers each and quaffed them down in seconds. I still remember the slightly bitter aftertaste, the shock of the cold liquid on the back of the throat, and a deep appreciation for modern refrigeration. (So much for Rousseau and the "natural man" who walks nobly through the wilderness. Another beer, please!)

I hope you enjoy the best of our year in the test kitchen. It was a very good year and these are our very best recipes.

CHRISTOPHER KIMBALL
Founder and Editor,
Cook's Illustrated and *Cook's Country*
Host, *America's Test Kitchen* and
Cook's Country from America's Test Kitchen

STARTERS
& SALADS

EGGPLANT CAVIAR **4**

Eggplant Caviar with Roasted
Red Peppers

RESTAURANT-STYLE HUMMUS **5**

Artichoke-Lemon Hummus

Hummus with Smoked Paprika

Roasted Garlic Hummus

Roasted Red Pepper Hummus

Ultimate Hummus

SHEET PAN CRACKERS **9**

Cheesy Sheet Pan Crackers

SCALLION PANCAKES **11**

Scallion Pancakes with Scallion
Dipping Sauce

SPANISH-STYLE GARLIC SHRIMP **13**

FRIED CHICKEN WINGS **16**

Buffalo Sauce

Honey-Mustard Sauce

Spicy Chili-Garlic Sauce

Sweet Soy-Garlic Sauce

VENEZUELAN STUFFED
CORN CAKES **19**

Chicken and Avocado
Corn Cake Filling

Black Bean and Cheese
Corn Cake Filling

ROASTED VEGETABLE SALADS **21**

Roasted Fennel and Mushroom
Salad with Radishes

Roasted Beet and Carrot Salad
with Watercress

Roasted Green Bean and
Potato Salad with Radicchio

PEAR SALADS **24**

Pan-Roasted Pear Salad with
Watercress, Parmesan, and Pecans

Pan-Roasted Pear Salad with
Radicchio, Blue Cheese, and Walnuts

Pan-Roasted Pear Salad with
Frisée, Goat Cheese, and Almonds

24-HOUR PICNIC SALAD **25**

MEMPHIS CHOPPED COLESLAW **28**

CAESAR SALAD **29**

EGGPLANT CAVIAR

EGGPLANT CAVIAR IS A STAPLE IN both Russian and Georgian households and is traditionally known as poor man's caviar because the tiny seeds in the eggplant resemble caviar eggs. Eggplant caviar is a savory spread typically served with hearty brown bread as an hors d'oeuvre. It has a simple, earthy flavor that concentrates on the pure richness of the eggplant.

After poring over a number of recipes from Russian and Georgian cookbooks, I found the ingredient lists to be fairly consistent: eggplant, garlic, onion, olive oil, either lemon juice or red wine vinegar, and finally, some type of tomato product. After making a few batches of eggplant caviar I realized the key to success would be the cooking of the eggplant. I was after smooth and silky eggplant caviar, with balanced acidity, and one that allowed the eggplant to remain the star ingredient.

The authentic recipes we found either roasted the eggplant in the oven or cooked it on the stovetop. I started by testing three cooking methods: roasting, broiling, and sautéing diced eggplant. Tasters liked the effect of roasting the best; broiling the eggplant charred the edges before the interior was done, and sautéing was somewhat better, but the method took far too long and the flavor seemed lackluster. Roasting, however, intensified the eggplant flavor and gave the vegetable a silky consistency.

I had been roasting the eggplant whole; however, in our research we found that some recipes cut the eggplants in half lengthwise, scored the flesh side, and roasted them flesh side down. I did a side-by-side test of these two methods, and also roasted a diced eggplant to see if we could cut down on the cooking time. The diced eggplant did not work well; cooking toughened the edges, leaving chewy bits in the spread. Although eggplant roasted whole was fine, even better was the eggplant that was cut in half and scored. Eggplant prepared this way released its liquid more quickly during the roasting process and thereby concentrated the eggplant flavor. The slight caramelizing effect added a bit of depth, too. With a few more tests, I settled on cooking the eggplant in a 400-degree oven for about one hour until the skin was shriveled. I then scooped out the hot, soft interior that now resembled pulp and let it drain to get rid of excess liquid.

With my eggplant cooked to perfection, I now turned to the other flavoring ingredients in the dish. Many recipes I reviewed fold in raw garlic and onion, but tasters found their harsh bite out of place in this smooth, silky dip. Instead, I sautéed both to mellow their flavor.

Tomatoes also showed up as a flavoring in a number of recipes I consulted; they lent a sweet, meaty dimension of flavor to the eggplant. I tested fresh tomatoes against canned diced tomatoes. Even with out-of-season tomatoes, tasters preferred the fresh to canned. The only problem was that the tomatoes made the mixture watery. I tried salting and draining the tomatoes, but this seemed like too much of a hassle. That's when I thought of tomato paste. This was exactly what my eggplant needed—just 1 teaspoon of intensely flavored paste deepened and sweetened the eggplant flavor without harming the texture of the creamy, silky spread. To finish, I stirred in some olive oil for further richness and fresh lemon juice and fresh dill to brighten the flavors. For a variation, I incorporated roasted red peppers, which are included in many Russian recipes, and which tasters enjoyed.

—SUZANNAH MCFERRAN, *America's Test Kitchen Books*

EGGPLANT CAVIAR

MAKES ABOUT 1½ CUPS

Serve on small slices of brown bread. Russian brown bread has a substantial texture and a somewhat tangy flavor, much like German brown bread. If you are unable to find authentic Russian (or German) brown bread, cocktail pumpernickel is a good substitute.

- 1 **large eggplant (about 1½ pounds), unpeeled and halved lengthwise**
- 6 **tablespoons extra-virgin olive oil**
   Salt and pepper
- 1 **small onion, minced (about ¾ cup)**

3 garlic cloves, minced

1 teaspoon tomato paste

1 tablespoon fresh lemon juice

1 teaspoon minced fresh dill

1. Adjust an oven rack to the middle position and heat the oven to 400 degrees. Line a rimmed baking sheet with foil. Score the cut sides of the eggplant about 1 inch deep. Drizzle the scored sides of the eggplant with 2 tablespoons of the olive oil and season with salt and pepper.

2. Lay the eggplant cut side down on the prepared baking sheet and roast until the eggplant is very soft, the skin is shriveled and shrunken, and a knife piercing the flesh meets no resistance, about 1 hour. Let the eggplant cool until able to handle, about 5 minutes.

3. Set a small colander over a bowl (or in the sink). Use a spoon to scoop the hot eggplant pulp out of the skins into the colander; discard the skins. Scrape up any eggplant that has stuck to the foil and add it to the colander. Let the pulp drain for 30 minutes. Transfer the eggplant pulp to a cutting board and chop coarse; transfer the chopped eggplant to a bowl and set aside.

4. Meanwhile, heat 2 more tablespoons of the olive oil in a 10-inch nonstick skillet over medium heat until shimmering. Add the onion and cook until softened, 5 to 7 minutes. Stir in the garlic and cook until fragrant, about 30 seconds. Stir in the tomato paste and cook until the mixture deepens in color slightly, about 3 minutes. Stir in the chopped eggplant and cook until warmed through, about 2 minutes longer.

5. Transfer the eggplant mixture to a serving bowl. Stir in the remaining 2 tablespoons olive oil and the lemon juice and season with salt and pepper to taste. Cover and refrigerate until chilled, at least 1 hour or up to 2 days. Stir in the dill and season again with salt and pepper before serving.

VARIATION

EGGPLANT CAVIAR WITH ROASTED RED PEPPERS

Follow the recipe for Eggplant Caviar, adding ¼ cup jarred roasted red peppers, drained, rinsed, and patted dry, chopped fine, with the oil and lemon juice in step 5.

RESTAURANT-STYLE HUMMUS

LIKE MANY TIME-PRESSED COOKS, I often purchase hummus at the supermarket rather than make it myself. The dip is usually unremarkable but serves its purpose as a quick snack or appetizer. A version I recently tasted at a restaurant, however, opened my eyes to how great hummus can actually be. This hummus had a light, silky-smooth texture and memorable flavor: a careful balance of pureed chickpeas, bean cooking liquid, tahini (ground sesame paste), lemon juice, garlic, and a drizzle of extra-virgin olive oil.

My efforts to re-create the restaurant hummus in the test kitchen started with an investigation of chickpeas, known as *hummus* in Arabic and *garbanzo* in Spanish. In Middle Eastern cuisine, hummus is traditionally made with dried beans, but it can also be made with canned. I made batches with each type and found that, although the flavor of the dried-bean hummus was superior to the canned-bean version, canned beans produced perfectly acceptable results. Given their convenience, I decided to go with canned. I patched together a working recipe that included a few tablespoons each of water (to stand in for the bean cooking liquid), extra-virgin olive oil, tahini, fresh lemon juice, and a clove of garlic. With this ingredient list in hand, I was ready to tackle texture.

The biggest stumbling block to a creamy, airy consistency was the chickpeas' tough outer skins, so my first thought was to remove them. I tried a ricer, then a food mill, and even rubbed the beans against a colander in my efforts to leave the fibrous skins behind—all to no avail. Perhaps I could achieve a better texture simply by pulverizing the entire bean (including the skin) and all the other ingredients in a food processor. Unfortunately, no matter how long I processed, the hummus retained a certain amount of coarse graininess. I turned to the blender, which can often produce a smoother consistency than a food processor, but the results were inconsistent.

It was time to regroup. I thought back to the silky-smooth consistency of the restaurant hummus I was so fond of. Mayonnaise gets its rich silkiness through the creation of an emulsion: a blend of two or more

RESTAURANT-STYLE HUMMUS

liquids that normally don't mix in which one is present as tiny droplets dispersed throughout the other. Would emulsifying the oil and water give my hummus the silky texture I was after?

I started out by making the chickpea puree as creamy as possible. I discovered that grinding the chickpeas alone and then slowly adding a small amount of water and lemon juice produced a smoother puree than processing everything at once. Then, instead of adding the olive oil and tahini separately as most recipes recommend, I whisked the two together and slowly added the mixture to the puree in a slow drizzle while processing, creating the emulsion right in the hummus. At last, a smooth, silky, light hummus was born.

With the technique settled, it was time to fine-tune the flavors of the dip. Tahini brands vary significantly in fat as well as flavor, with some carrying bitter off-tastes. With a good tahini, tasters liked a hefty 6 tablespoons, three times the amount usually found in homemade recipes, appreciating the nutty flavor it lent to the dip.

Garlic, lemon juice, spices, and olive oil are also keys to good hummus, but too much or too little of any one can throw the whole recipe off-kilter. After much trial and error, I settled on 3 tablespoons of lemon juice and modest amounts of garlic and olive oil. Cumin is common in Middle Eastern cooking, and tasters liked the earthy undertone it added, along with the subtle heat from a pinch of cayenne. Garnishing the dip with a sprinkle of fresh cilantro, a drizzle of olive oil, and a smattering of whole chickpeas added visual and textural interest.

Finally, I spent some time working on flavor variations. I came up with garlic, roasted red pepper, smoked paprika, and artichoke-lemon versions that far surpassed anything similar I could buy at the supermarket. With recipes so quick and easy to make, I doubt I'll ever buy hummus again.

—MATTHEW HERRON, *Cook's Illustrated*

RESTAURANT-STYLE HUMMUS

MAKES ABOUT 2 CUPS

Both tahini and chickpeas vary widely from brand to brand. See page 8 for our recommendations. The hummus can be refrigerated in an airtight container for 5 days. If you do not plan on serving it immediately, refrigerate the hummus and garnishes separately. When ready to serve, stir in approximately 1 tablespoon of warm water if the texture is too thick and garnish as directed. Serve with wedges of pita bread.

3 tablespoons fresh lemon juice
¼ cup water
6 tablespoons tahini, stirred well (see note)
2 tablespoons extra-virgin olive oil,
   plus extra for drizzling
1 (14-ounce) can chickpeas, drained and rinsed (see note)
1 garlic clove, minced
½ teaspoon salt
¼ teaspoon ground cumin
   Pinch cayenne pepper
1 tablespoon minced fresh cilantro or parsley

1. Combine the lemon juice and water in a small bowl or measuring cup. Whisk together the tahini and 2 tablespoons of the oil in a second small bowl or measuring cup. Set aside 2 tablespoons of the chickpeas for garnish.

2. Process the remaining chickpeas, garlic, salt, cumin, and cayenne in a food processor until almost fully ground, about 15 seconds. Scrape down the bowl with a rubber spatula. With the machine running, add the lemon juice–water mixture in a steady stream through the feed tube. Scrape down the bowl and continue to process for 1 minute. With the machine running, add the oil-tahini mixture in a steady stream through the feed tube; continue to process until the hummus is smooth and creamy, about 15 seconds, scraping down the bowl as needed.

3. Transfer the hummus to a serving bowl, sprinkle the reserved chickpeas and the cilantro over the surface, cover with plastic wrap, and chill until the flavors meld, at least 30 minutes. Drizzle with olive oil; serve cold or at room temperature.

VARIATIONS
ARTICHOKE-LEMON HUMMUS

Rinse and pat dry 1 cup canned or jarred artichoke hearts packed in water. Chop ¼ cup artichoke hearts and set aside for the garnish. Follow the recipe for Restaurant-Style Hummus, increasing the lemon juice to 4 tablespoons and omitting the cumin. Process the entire can of chickpeas (do not reserve 2 tablespoons) along with the remaining ¾ cup artichokes and ¼ teaspoon grated lemon zest in step 2. Garnish the hummus with the reserved artichokes, 2 teaspoons chopped fresh parsley or mint, and olive oil.

HUMMUS WITH SMOKED PAPRIKA

Follow the recipe for Restaurant-Style Hummus, processing the entire can of chickpeas (do not reserve 2 tablespoons) in step 2 and substituting 1 teaspoon smoked paprika for the cumin. Omit the cilantro or parsley. Garnish the hummus with 1 tablespoon thinly sliced scallion greens, 2 tablespoons toasted pine nuts, and olive oil.

ROASTED GARLIC HUMMUS

Cut the top quarter off 2 heads of garlic and discard. Wrap the garlic in foil and roast in a 350-degree oven until browned and very tender, about 1 hour. Meanwhile, heat 2 tablespoons olive oil and 2 thinly sliced garlic cloves in a small skillet over medium-low heat. Cook, stirring occasionally, until golden brown, about 15 minutes. Using a slotted spoon, transfer the garlic slices to a paper towel–lined plate and set aside; reserve the oil. Once the roasted garlic is cool, squeeze the cloves from their skins (you should have about ¼ cup). Follow the recipe for Restaurant-Style Hummus, substituting the garlic cooking oil for the olive oil in step 1 and omitting the cumin. Process the entire can of chickpeas (do not reserve 2 tablespoons) along with the roasted garlic in step 2. Garnish the hummus with the garlic slices, 2 teaspoons chopped fresh parsley, and olive oil.

ROASTED RED PEPPER HUMMUS

Follow the recipe for Restaurant-Style Hummus, omitting the water and cumin. Process the entire can of chickpeas (do not reserve 2 tablespoons), along with ¼ cup jarred roasted red peppers that have been dried thoroughly with paper towels, in step 2. Garnish the hummus with 2 tablespoons toasted sliced almonds, 2 teaspoons chopped fresh parsley, and olive oil.

ULTIMATE HUMMUS

Pick through and rinse ½ cup dried chickpeas. Cover the beans with 1 quart water and soak overnight. Drain. Bring the beans, ⅛ teaspoon baking soda, and 1 quart water to a boil. Reduce to a gentle simmer and cook, stirring occasionally, until the beans are tender, 1½ to 2 hours. Drain, reserving ¼ cup of the bean cooking water, and cool. Continue with the recipe for Restaurant-Style Hummus, replacing the tap water with the reserved cooking water.

NOTES FROM THE TEST KITCHEN

THE BEST TAHINI

Tahini is a thick paste made from ground sesame seeds that is most often used to flavor Middle Eastern dishes such as hummus or as a condiment for falafel. We tasted five supermarket brands, both straight from the jar and blended into our Restaurant-Style Hummus recipe. Some brands were alarmingly bitter, but both **Joyva Sesame Tahini** (left), $5.80 for 15 ounces, and **Krinos Tahini** (right), $5.49 for 16 ounces, were pleasantly "tangy," "nutty," and "buttery."

THE BEST CANNED CHICKPEAS

We sampled six brands of canned chickpeas, both plain—drained and rinsed—and pureed in our Restaurant-Style Hummus recipe. None of our tasters could tolerate a bland bean, especially when eaten straight from the can. Low-sodium samples (with less than 250 milligrams of salt per ½ cup) were bland and dull, while others had a distinctly metallic, bitter flavor that couldn't be masked by the assertive ingredients in the hummus. Our favorite chickpeas were the ones from **Pastene,** 79 cents for 14 ounces; tasters loved the creamy yet firm texture and their clean, slightly salty flavor.

SHEET PAN CRACKERS

THERE IS A BROAD CATEGORY of simple flatbreads and crackers topped with all manner of flavorings that are ostensibly based on Armenian cracker bread. Wheaty flavored, crisp as can be, and highly addictive, they are the perfect accompaniment to cheeses, dips, spreads, and charcuterie. Most gourmet markets and some supermarkets carry them and, despite their inexpensive ingredients and seemingly simple preparation, crackers of this sort cost a pretty penny. I wanted to figure out how to make them at home.

The recipes I found for these crackers are similar and all include flour, yeast, salt, water, and a topping such as seeds, spices, or toasted garlic. Some expanded on the basics by adding fat—usually olive oil—and a sweetener. Essentially, the dough is like any basic bread or pizza dough. Unsurprisingly, those I tried all tasted fairly alike aside from the toppings. The bigger issue was texture, which ranged from almost flaky and tender to ultra-crunchy. The best of the bunch were quite thin and crisp with just a hint of crunch and enough structure to scoop a sturdy dip. To a certain degree, the texture of the cracker was due to the dough's consistency: stiff, intractable dough was virtually impossible to roll thin enough to bake up crisp; slacker dough fared far better.

With that in mind, I set to work developing a supple, flavorful dough that could be easily rolled. For flour, I favored all-purpose because I knew it would produce a softer, less glutinous dough. Salt and a moderate amount of yeast went in with the flour and I used water for the liquid component—dairy made the crackers too soft. The doughs I tested that included olive oil were the easiest to work with, so I stirred in a tablespoon. Sweetener also helped to make the dough easy to manipulate, so I added a bit of honey, which also improved the cracker's flavor and browning. (Honey is largely composed of fructose, a very effective browning agent.)

Once the dough came together, I kneaded it to various extents to gauge elasticity. The longer the dough was kneaded, the more supple and elastic it became. In the end, I couldn't see any improvement in the dough past 8 minutes. Eight minutes it was.

While the dough was pretty slack, it wasn't nearly as easy to roll as I had hoped. The more I stretched and pulled at it, the faster the elastic dough snapped back. If I'd wanted a pizza crust, things would have been fine, but I wanted the dough to be as thin as possible for the crispest texture.

The ultimate solution finally dawned on me: Roll the dough directly out on a rimless (or inverted rimmed) baking sheet. At first the dough stuck a bit, but lightly oiling the baking sheet reduced the friction, and it was quick work to roll it as thin as I wanted. While some recipes employed high heat to crisp the cracker quickly, I found that this resulted in uneven browning. Instead, a moderate 350-degree setting baked and colored the crackers evenly.

I'd achieved the flavorful base and crisp texture I had hoped for, but had yet to test toppings. Some of the recipes I tried had kept the topping to a light dusting of sesame or poppy seeds and salt; others added so many flavorings that the crackers looked like an "everything" bagel. I opted for a moderate approach, including poppy, sesame, rye, and flax seeds as well as a generous sprinkle of crunchy kosher salt. To be honest, however, the crackers tasted fine with just salt, or any one of the toppings independently. Broken into ragged, rustic shards, these sheet pan crackers looked every bit as good as those sold at my local gourmet market, and tasted far better and fresher.

—MEGAN WYCOFF, *America's Test Kitchen Books*

SHEET PAN CRACKERS

MAKES TWO 18 BY 13-INCH CRACKERS

You will need about 1 tablespoon of oil to brush over the crackers before baking. You can make this dough in a food processor but it will be harder to stretch it as thin as called for in this recipe; when made in a standing mixer, this dough is more elastic.

1¾–2	cups (8¾ to 10 ounces) unbleached all-purpose flour, plus extra for the work surface
1	tablespoon extra-virgin olive oil, plus extra for brushing
1	tablespoon honey
½	teaspoon instant or rapid-rise yeast
½	teaspoon table salt
½	cup warm water (110 degrees)
2	teaspoons poppy, sesame, rye, and/or flax seeds (optional)
	Coarse sea salt or kosher salt, for sprinkling

1. Combine 1¾ cups of the flour, the oil, honey, yeast, and table salt in a standing mixer fitted with the dough hook. With the mixer on low speed, add the water and mix until the dough comes together, about 2 minutes.

2. Increase the speed to medium-low and knead until the dough is smooth and elastic, about 8 minutes. (If after 4 minutes more flour is needed, add the remaining ¼ cup flour, 1 tablespoon at a time, until the dough clears the sides of the bowl but sticks to the bottom.)

3. Turn the dough out onto a lightly floured work surface and knead by hand to form a smooth, round ball. Place the dough in a lightly oiled bowl and wrap tightly with greased plastic wrap. Let rise in a warm place until doubled in size, 1 to 1½ hours.

4. Lightly coat two 18 by 13-inch rimless (or inverted) baking sheets with vegetable oil spray. Turn the dough out onto a lightly floured surface, divide it into 2 equal pieces, and cover with greased plastic wrap. Working with one piece of dough at a time (keep the other piece covered), press the dough into a small rectangle, then transfer to one of the prepared baking sheets. Using a rolling pin and your hands, roll and stretch the dough evenly to the edges of the baking sheet following the photos. Cover the dough with a clean kitchen towel and let rest 10 to 20 minutes. Repeat with the remaining dough.

5. Adjust the oven racks to the upper- and lower-middle positions and heat the oven to 350 degrees. Brush the crackers with oil and sprinkle with the seeds, if desired, and coarse sea salt. Bake until golden brown, about 20 minutes, switching and rotating the baking sheets halfway through baking.

6. Let the crackers cool on the baking sheets for at least 15 minutes, then break into large pieces and serve.

VARIATION

CHEESY SHEET PAN CRACKERS

Since the cheese itself is salty, use a light hand when sprinkling the coarse salt over the crackers before baking.

Sprinkle ¼ cup grated Parmesan or Asiago cheese over the top of each cracker before baking.

NOTES FROM THE TEST KITCHEN

MAKING SHEET PAN CRACKERS

1. Press each piece of dough into a rough rectangle, then transfer to an inverted, lightly greased baking sheet. Roll the dough out as far as you can to the edges of the pan.

2. Using your fingers, gently stretch the dough to the edge of the pan. If the dough snaps back from the edge, let it rest for a few minutes and try again.

3. Brush the dough lightly with olive oil and sprinkle with seeds (if using) and coarse sea salt.

4. After the crackers have been baked and cooled, gently break them into large, rustic pieces.

HANDLING THE DOUGH FOR SHEET PAN CRACKERS

The key to crisp crackers is getting the dough very thin, yet we kept ruining this paper-thin dough every time we tried to transfer it to a baking sheet—it would stick together or tear. Using parchment paper (our standard solution for sticky or delicate doughs) also didn't work—the superthin dough and parchment simply stuck together and became wrinkly. Our final solution? Roll the dough out right on the baking sheet. It is important to use a rimless or inverted baking sheet, and greasing the pan lightly helps prevent the dough from sticking.

SCALLION PANCAKES

A TRULY GREAT SCALLION PANCAKE IS THIN—about ¼ inch thick—with multiple, paper-thin layers laced with scallions and just a hint of sesame. Unfortunately, this staple of Chinese takeout is often greasy, bland, and sadly lacking in scallion flavor. With bunches of scallions and recipes in hand, I headed into the test kitchen to develop an exemplary version of this addictive treat.

Scallion pancakes, called *cong you bing* in Chinese, consist of a few simple ingredients—flour, water, scallions, and sometimes sesame oil. They are more akin to a flatbread than a pancake and thus the ingredients, when mixed, form a soft dough rather than a pourable batter. It didn't take long to come up with flour and water amounts—1½ cups flour to ½ cup water—so I quickly turned to building flavor.

I wanted these pancakes to have a strong scallion flavor, unlike the bland versions I've had in the past. I tested varying amounts of scallions until I finally settled on ½ cup (or 2 tablespoons of minced scallions for each of the four pancakes). Any more than this and the pancakes became difficult to roll. Some recipes I consulted contained herbs, such as parsley and cilantro, in addition to the scallions. Parsley was fine, but in terms of flavor, it didn't make much of an impact. Cilantro, on the other hand, infused the pancakes with its distinctive herbal flavor—and tasters were hooked.

My last addition to these pancakes was sesame oil, a common ingredient in the more complex recipes found in our research. Most versions simply brushed the oil onto the pancake before rolling it out, but I felt adding it directly into the dough would be better. Unfortunately, it made the dough sticky and difficult to work with. So I simply brushed a thin layer directly onto the flattened pancake before sprinkling on the scallions and herbs.

At last, it was time to roll—a step that is crucial to the outcome of scallion pancakes. If rolled properly, not only are the scallions incorporated more evenly into the pancake, but the thin layers that remain from rolling the dough create the intricate layering of scallions and dough that define this dish. I knew from my research that just kneading the scallions into the dough, then rolling it into a disk, would form a heavy, dense pancake with no layers. Instead, I turned to the methods found in our library of Chinese cookbooks.

I started with the dough portioned into four balls and rested (the Chinese recipes were virtually identical to this point, so I followed suit). The most common method calls for rolling the pancake into a thin disk, then sprinkling the flavorings onto the dough and rolling it into a log. From there, the log is coiled around itself like a snake. Then the coiled patty is rolled (and flattened) into a pancake and ready to cook. While this method might sound fussy, I had mastered it by my second pancake. And with just a little effort, I was rewarded with tender layers and evenly incorporated scallions.

Finally, it was time to cook. Scallion pancakes are traditionally cooked in a generous amount of oil, but the grease factor was a chief complaint among tasters. I reduced the amount of oil down to just a couple of tablespoons, but by the time the fourth pancake was added to the pan, the others had soaked up all the oil and the resulting pancakes were soft, with little crispness. Instead, I increased the amount of oil at tablespoon increments until I settled on 4 tablespoons, or ¼ cup. But to keep the "deep-fry" effect at bay, I split the 4 tablespoons among the pancakes, and cooked them one at a time, with just 1 tablespoon of oil per pancake—enough to produce crispy scallion pancakes without the grease.

—SARAH WILSON, *America's Test Kitchen Books*

SCALLION PANCAKES WITH SCALLION DIPPING SAUCE

MAKES 4 PANCAKES, SERVING 4 TO 6

If serving these pancakes without the dipping sauce, sprinkle with salt to taste before serving. Mirin is a Japanese sweet cooking wine found in most supermarkets. If you cannot find it, substitute 2 tablespoons dry white wine or sake mixed with 1 teaspoon sugar.

SAUCE

¼ cup soy sauce
2 tablespoons rice vinegar
2 tablespoons mirin (see note)
2 tablespoons water
1 scallion, sliced thin on the bias
1 teaspoon chili oil (optional)
½ teaspoon toasted sesame oil

PANCAKES

- 1½ cups (7½ ounces) unbleached all-purpose flour, plus extra for the work surface
- 1 teaspoon salt
- ½ cup water, at room temperature, plus extra if needed
- ¼ cup vegetable oil, plus extra for brushing
- 2 teaspoons toasted sesame oil
- 6 scallions, minced (about ½ cup)
- 2 tablespoons minced fresh cilantro

1. FOR THE SAUCE: Combine all of the ingredients in a serving bowl and set aside. (The sauce can be refrigerated in a covered container for up to 6 hours.)

2. FOR THE PANCAKES: Whisk the flour and salt together in a medium bowl. Add the ½ cup water and mix with a dinner fork until combined. (If there are any floury bits left in the bottom of the bowl, add additional water, 1 teaspoon at a time, until the dough comes together.) Turn the dough out onto a lightly floured work surface and knead until it is smooth and satiny, about 5 minutes, adding extra flour to the work surface or to your hands as needed to prevent sticking. Transfer the dough to a clean bowl, brush with a thin layer of vegetable oil, and let it rest at room temperature for 30 minutes.

3. Divide the dough into 4 equal pieces and keep covered with plastic wrap. Working with one piece of dough at a time, roll into a 7-inch circle about ⅛ inch thick on a lightly floured work surface. Brush the dough round lightly with sesame oil, then sprinkle with 2 tablespoons of the scallions and 1½ teaspoons of the cilantro.

4. Following the photos, roll the dough into a cylinder, then coil the cylinder into a round, tucking the tail end underneath. Then roll into a 5-inch pancake, about ¼ inch thick. Set aside and cover with plastic wrap while repeating with the remaining dough pieces, scallions, and cilantro.

5. Heat 1 tablespoon of the vegetable oil in a 12-inch nonstick skillet over medium heat until shimmering. Swirl the oil to coat the skillet, then add a dough round and cook until golden brown on both sides, 1½ to 2 minutes per side. Transfer the pancake to a cutting board, tent with foil, and repeat three more times with the remaining 3 tablespoons oil and remaining 3 dough rounds. Slice the cooked pancakes into wedges and serve with the Scallion Dipping Sauce.

NOTES FROM THE TEST KITCHEN

ROLLING AND FORMING SCALLION PANCAKES

1. After rolling each piece of dough into a 7-inch circle about ⅛ inch thick, brush with sesame oil, then sprinkle with 2 tablespoons of the scallions and 1½ teaspoons of the cilantro.

2. Roll the round into a tight cylinder, brushing away any clumps of flour that have stuck to the bottom of the dough.

3. Coil the cylinder into a tight round, tucking the end under.

4. Using a rolling pin, roll the round into a 5-inch pancake about ¼ inch thick, flouring the work surface as needed to prevent sticking.

MIRIN

Mirin is a tawny, sweetened Japanese rice wine that is used in many Asian recipes, such as sauces, marinades, and various glazes where it adds sheen and luster to foods. Mirin comes in two varieties: hon mirin, which is brewed in the traditional method using glutinous rice, malted rice, and distilled alcohol and requires over a year to brew and mature; and aji mirin, which is simply sake fortified with sugar to mimic the flavor and syrupy consistency of hon mirin. Hon mirin is more expensive and difficult to find while aji mirin is more widely available.

SPANISH-STYLE GARLIC SHRIMP

IF THERE IS ONE THING that can catch attention in a Spanish tapas restaurant, it's the heady aroma wafting up from a dish of *gambas al ajillo*—little shrimp sizzling in a pool of olive oil and garlic. When properly prepared, the shrimp is wonderfully sweet and tender and infused with deep garlic flavor. A large quantity of oil is heated along with sliced garlic, Spanish chiles, and bay leaves in a *cazuela* (an earthenware ramekin) until lightly sizzling. The shrimp are added, heated until just barely cooked through, and served directly out of the cooking vessel. The dish is always accompanied by crusty bread to soak up all the leftover garlic- and shrimp-flavored oil.

As perfect as the dish is, it needs some adjustments to work as an appetizer served at home. Since most home cooks are going to prepare only a single appetizer, the dish needs to be more substantial. I settled on a pound of large shrimp (rather than the smaller shrimp that are typical of this dish) as the ideal portion size for six people.

Traditional recipes for gambas al ajillo call for completely submerging the shrimp in oil, where they can be heated evenly and gently at a low temperature. But to fully submerge a pound of large shrimp, I'd need nearly 2 cups of oil—far more than I'd need for six people. I wanted to find a way to reduce the amount (to about half a cup) but still maintain the juiciness and garlic flavor that are the hallmarks of this dish.

Since a smaller pan size means deeper oil, I tried using an 8-inch saucepan. But the oil still only covered about half of the shrimp. The results? Tough, overcooked shrimp on the bottom and raw shrimp on top.

My shrimp were partially overcooking because they were heating unevenly—some were closer to the heat source than others. When I switched to a 12-inch skillet, the oil provided only a thin coating beneath the shrimp, but at least I could fit them in a single layer. This single-layer method meant that I would have to turn the shrimp halfway through cooking. But with this many shrimp, I was afraid that by the time I had turned the last shrimp, the first ones would be overcooked. Keeping the heat at medium-low was the solution, giving me plenty of time to turn each shrimp individually. But with only a thin layer of oil in the pan, the shrimp were not absorbing enough garlic flavor. I increased the garlic from four thinly sliced cloves to eight, which provided the right proportion of shrimp to garlic, but the slices were still acting more like a garnish than a fully integrated part of the dish. I had to find a different way to get more garlic flavor into the shrimp.

I smashed four garlic cloves before heating them in a fresh batch of olive oil, then allowed them to brown and impart a sweet roasted flavor to the oil. After discarding the smashed cloves, I added the shrimp. They were better, but still not great.

Then I tried marinating the shrimp in a simple mixture of oil, salt, and raw garlic. After 30 minutes, I cooked the marinated shrimp and sliced garlic in the oil in which I had previously browned the smashed cloves. It was a resounding success.

By adding the garlic to the pan in three forms and at three different stages (minced raw garlic to provide pungency in the marinade, crushed and browned garlic to infuse sweetness into the oil, and slow-cooked sliced garlic to add mild garlic flavor), I finally had juicy shrimp that were deeply flavored with garlic in a robust and complex sauce.

The traditional additions of bay leaf and red chile were deemed essential to the recipe. Heating the aromatics in the pan along with the sliced garlic allowed them to flavor the oil. While most recipes call for a splash of dry sherry or brandy, I found that sherry vinegar and chopped parsley were better suited to rounding out the flavors; they provided a jolt of brightness that cut through the richness of the olive oil.

As a finishing touch, I realized I could recapture some of the restaurant spirit by transferring the dish to a small cast-iron skillet that I'd heated on the stove. Placed on a trivet on the table, the shrimp and garlic continued to sizzle until my eager tasters downed the last one.

—J. KENJI ALT, *Cook's Illustrated*

SPANISH-STYLE GARLIC SHRIMP

SERVES 6

Serve the shrimp with crusty bread for dipping in the richly flavored olive oil. We prefer the slightly sweet flavor of dried chiles in this recipe, but ¼ teaspoon sweet paprika can be substituted. If sherry vinegar is unavailable, use 2 teaspoons dry sherry and 1 teaspoon white vinegar.

- 14 garlic cloves
- 1 pound large shrimp (31 to 40 per pound), peeled and deveined
- 8 tablespoons olive oil
- ½ teaspoon salt
- 1 bay leaf
- 1 (2-inch) piece mild dried chile, such as New Mexico, roughly broken, seeds included (see note)
- 1½ teaspoons sherry vinegar (see note)
- 1 tablespoon chopped fresh parsley

1. Mince 2 of the garlic cloves with a chef's knife or garlic press. Toss the minced garlic with the shrimp, 2 tablespoons of the olive oil, and salt in a medium bowl. Let the shrimp marinate at room temperature for 30 minutes.

2. Meanwhile, using the flat side of a chef's knife, smash 4 garlic cloves. Heat the smashed garlic with the remaining 6 tablespoons olive oil in a 12-inch skillet over medium-low heat, stirring occasionally, until the garlic is light golden brown, 4 to 7 minutes. Remove the pan from the heat and allow the oil to cool to room temperature. Using a slotted spoon, remove the smashed garlic from the skillet and discard.

3. Thinly slice the remaining 8 garlic cloves. Return the skillet to low heat and add the sliced garlic, bay leaf, and chile. Cook, stirring occasionally, until the garlic is tender but not browned, 4 to 7 minutes. (If the garlic has not begun to sizzle after 3 minutes, increase the heat to medium-low.) Increase the heat to medium-low; add the shrimp with the marinade to the pan in a single layer. Cook the shrimp, undisturbed, until the oil starts to gently bubble, about 2 minutes. Using tongs, flip the shrimp and continue to cook until almost cooked through, about 2 minutes longer. Increase the heat to high and add the sherry vinegar and parsley. Cook, stirring constantly, until the shrimp are cooked through and the oil is bubbling vigorously, 15 to 20 seconds. Serve immediately.

NOTES FROM THE TEST KITCHEN

CHOOSING THE RIGHT CHILE

AUTHENTIC CHOICE
The slightly sweet cascabel chile is the traditional choice for gambas al ajillo.

BEST SUBSTITUTE
New Mexico chile (aka California chile, chile Colorado, or dried Anaheim chile) is far more widely available and has the same bright freshness as the cascabel.

GETTING THE MOST GARLIC FLAVOR
We imparted garlic flavor to the shrimp in three different ways for three different effects, resulting in a dish with multilayered garlic complexity.

1. The minced garlic in the marinade gets cooked briefly with the shrimp, maintaining a hint of raw-garlic pungency.

2. Gently browning smashed whole garlic cloves infuses the olive oil with a sweet roasted-garlic flavor.

3. Sliced garlic cooked gently in low-temperature olive oil loses its harsh flavor, becoming soft and mellow.

SPANISH-STYLE GARLIC SHRIMP

FRIED CHICKEN WINGS

WHEN PEOPLE THINK OF FRIED CHICKEN WINGS, they inevitably think of Buffalo wings. Conceived at the Anchor Bar in Buffalo, New York, in the 1960s, Buffalo wings are now found throughout the country at any bar or Super Bowl party worth its salt. The odd combination of chicken wings slathered with hot sauce is actually a harmonious union. The sauce's bright heat is tamed by the soothing, creamy dip.

Because wings are such perfect party food and beloved by many, I set out to develop a variety of sauces for our wings—why not give Buffalo wings a bit of competition? But first I had to find the best way to cook the wings; I was after a light, crispy skin.

For fried chicken wings, the raw chicken wing itself is almost always cut in two segments, and the relatively meatless wingtip is removed. The wings come packaged as whole wings or already cut into pieces affectionately referred to as "drumettes." I found that precut wings were often poorly cut and unevenly sized, so I chose to buy whole wings and butcher them myself, which was easy and economical.

While the wings were easy to butcher, cooking them proved a little trickier because of their high fat content. Wings are typically deep-fried, but that can be a daunting project in a home kitchen, with hot fat splattering about. I found that if I used a deep Dutch oven and kept the oil at a constant 350 degrees, splattering oil was minimal.

The test kitchen's standard way of frying wings has always been to dredge the wings in cornstarch, which provides a thin and brittle coating, and to fry them for about 10 minutes. However, we had recently developed a recipe for Korean Fried Chicken, in which we discovered a new method for frying that ensured supercrispy skin. The chicken is twice-fried, which entails frying the chicken pieces for an initial period of five minutes, followed by a five-minute rest, and concluding with an additional three to five minutes of frying until the chicken is cooked. Twice-frying, as it turns out, slows down the cooking process to allow more moisture to evaporate and more fat to render, leaving a perfectly crisp, thin skin. Sure enough, this technique worked perfectly here, producing crispier, thinner-skinned chicken wings.

The other discovery we made pertained to the coating. The ideal coating involved first dredging the chicken in a thin layer of cornstarch and then dipping it into a cornstarch batter before adding it to the hot oil. This worked like a charm for our chicken wings.

I could now shift my attention to the sauces. Most recipes I found agreed that authentic Buffalo wing sauce is nothing but Frank's Louisiana Hot Sauce and butter or margarine, blended in a 2-to-1 ratio. Most recipes also suggest intensifying the sauce's heat with a bit of Tabasco or other hot sauce because, on its own, Frank's is not quite spicy enough. While tasters liked this simple sauce, they wanted something a little more dynamic. I included brown sugar to round out the flavors, and a little cider vinegar to balance out the sugar and add a pleasing sharpness.

Next I developed a honey mustard sauce. I wanted to fashion one that was not as spicy as its Buffalo counterpart. I started off with the basics, a combination of honey, Dijon mustard, butter, and Worcestershire sauce, and then added some whole grain mustard to balance the sweetness of the honey.

My final two sauces were Asian inspired. The sweet soy-garlic sauce was made by combining sugar, soy sauce, water, and garlic in a saucepan and reducing it to a glaze. I balanced the sauce with a splash of rice vinegar and a shot of hot sauce. The chili-garlic sauce was also quite simple, comprising sugar, ketchup, chili-garlic sauce, and a touch of lemon juice. These variations were a huge hit and, dare I say, were favored by many over the Buffalo wings.

—SUZANNAH MCFERRAN, *America's Test Kitchen Books*

FRIED CHICKEN WINGS

SERVES 6 TO 8

The chicken wings must be fried in two batches. Make sure to stir the chicken once it has been added to the oil so that the wings do not stick together.

3–4   quarts peanut or vegetable oil
1½   cups cornstarch
3½   pounds chicken wings, wingtips discarded and wings split (see page 18)
    Salt and pepper
1   cup cold water
1   recipe sauce (recipes follow)

1. Adjust an oven rack to the middle position and heat the oven to 200 degrees. Measure 2 inches of the oil into a large Dutch oven and heat over medium-high heat to 350 degrees. (Use an instant-read thermometer that registers high temperatures or clip a candy/deep-fat thermometer onto the side of the pan.)

2. Sift ½ cup of the cornstarch into a shallow dish. Set a large mesh strainer over a large bowl. Pat the chicken dry with paper towels and season with salt and pepper. Working with several pieces of chicken at a time, coat the chicken thoroughly with the cornstarch, then transfer to the strainer and shake vigorously to remove all but a thin coating of cornstarch. Transfer the chicken to a wire rack set over a rimmed baking sheet.

3. Whisk the remaining 1 cup cornstarch, the water, and 1 teaspoon salt together in a large bowl to form a smooth batter. When the oil is hot, finish coating the chicken by adding half of the chicken to the batter and turn to coat well. Using tongs, remove the chicken from the batter, one piece at a time, allowing any excess batter to drip back into the bowl, and add to the hot oil.

4. Fry the chicken, stirring to prevent the pieces from sticking together and adjusting the heat as necessary to maintain an oil temperature of 350 degrees, until the chicken begins to crisp and turn slightly golden, about 5 minutes. Transfer the fried chicken wings to a clean wire rack set over a rimmed baking sheet and set aside for about 5 minutes. Meanwhile, batter and fry the remaining chicken.

5. Return the oil to 350 degrees (if necessary) over medium-high heat. Return the first batch of fried chicken wings to the oil and continue to fry until the exterior is very crisp and deep golden brown, 3 to 5 minutes. Drain briefly on a paper towel–lined plate, then transfer to a wire rack set over a rimmed baking sheet and keep warm in a 200-degree oven. Repeat with the second batch. (The unsauced fried chicken wings can be held for up to an hour in a 200-degree oven.)

6. Transfer all of the chicken wings to a large bowl, drizzle with the sauce, and gently toss until evenly coated. Transfer the chicken wings to a platter and serve.

BUFFALO SAUCE

MAKES ABOUT 1 CUP

Frank's Louisiana Hot Sauce is not terribly spicy. We like to combine it with a more potent hot sauce to bring up the heat. Serve with blue cheese dressing, along with carrot and celery sticks.

4   tablespoons (½ stick) unsalted butter
½   cup Frank's Louisiana Hot Sauce
1–2   tablespoons hot sauce, plus more to taste
1   tablespoon dark brown sugar
2   teaspoons cider vinegar

Melt the butter in a small saucepan over low heat. Whisk in the hot sauces, brown sugar, and vinegar until combined; set aside until needed. (The sauce can be refrigerated in an airtight container for up to 24 hours. Rewarm and whisk to recombine before using.)

HONEY-MUSTARD SAUCE

MAKES ABOUT 1 CUP

We like to garnish these wings with minced fresh parsley.

4   tablespoons (½ stick) unsalted butter
1   garlic clove, minced
⅓   cup honey
2   tablespoons Dijon mustard
2   tablespoons whole-grain mustard
2   tablespoons Worcestershire sauce

Melt the butter with the garlic in a small saucepan over low heat. Whisk in the honey, mustards, and Worcestershire until combined; set aside until needed. (The sauce can be refrigerated in an airtight container for up to 24 hours. Rewarm and whisk to recombine before using.)

SPICY CHILI-GARLIC SAUCE

MAKES ABOUT 1 CUP

We like to garnish these wings with thinly sliced scallion and minced fresh cilantro. Be sure to use chili-garlic sauce in this recipe and not chili-garlic paste, which is much hotter. For more heat, add the greater amount of chili-garlic sauce.

⅓	cup sugar
⅓	cup ketchup
3–4	tablespoons Asian chili-garlic sauce (see note)
2	teaspoons fresh lemon juice

Whisk all of the ingredients together in a small bowl; set aside until needed. (The sauce can be refrigerated in an airtight container for up to 24 hours. Bring to room temperature and whisk to recombine before using.)

SWEET SOY-GARLIC SAUCE

MAKES ABOUT 1 CUP

We like to garnish these wings with thinly sliced scallion and minced fresh cilantro.

½	cup sugar
¼	cup soy sauce
¼	cup water
3	garlic cloves, minced
1	tablespoon rice vinegar
1	teaspoon Asian chili paste

Simmer all of the ingredients in a small saucepan over medium heat until syrupy, 5 to 6 minutes; set aside until needed. (The sauce can be refrigerated in an airtight container for up to 24 hours. Bring to room temperature and whisk to recombine before using.)

NOTES FROM THE TEST KITCHEN

CUTTING UP CHICKEN WINGS

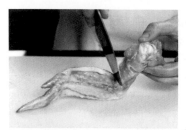

1. With a chef's knife, cut into the skin between the larger sections of the wing until you hit the joint.

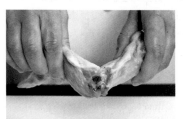

2. Bend back the two sections to pop and break the joint.

3. Cut through the skin and flesh to completely separate the two meaty portions.

4. Hack off the wing-tip and discard.

ASIAN CHILI-GARLIC SAUCE

Sriracha is the generic name for this Southeast Asian hot sauce from Thailand. It is named after the seaside town Si Racha, where it was first produced in small batches as a local product. It is made from sun-ripened chile peppers, vinegar, garlic, sugar, and salt, and has a consistency like slightly chunky ketchup.

VENEZUELAN STUFFED CORN CAKES

STUFFED CORN CAKES, or *Arepas,* are popular in Venezuela and Colombia, and in recent years they have even made their way to cosmopolitan areas in the United States. Although the arepas in Venezuela and Colombia are very similar—both have a polenta-like texture and subtle corn flavor—they are typically served in different ways. Venezuelan-style arepas are split open and stuffed with a filling—anything from meat and cheese to eggs, corn, beans, and even fish—much like a sandwich. In Colombia, they tend to be eaten more like bread, simply spread with butter or topped with cheese, though sometimes they are stuffed and fried to be eaten as more of a meal. I decided to develop a recipe for Venezuelan arepas, as their sandwich-style was greatly appealing.

Arepas are made using a flour called *masarepa* (also called *harina precocida* and *masa al instante*), which is a precooked white or yellow cornmeal. The white variety, or *masarepa blanca,* is most often used in Venezuela, so I chose to use it in my recipe. Water, salt, and sometimes eggs, milk, or cheese are added to the flour to make a dough, and the arepas are then shaped into rounds that are typically anywhere from ¼ to 1 inch thick. The shaped arepas are browned on a griddle until a crust is formed, and then transferred to the oven to bake.

Many of the recipes I found in my research recommended using equal parts masarepa and hot water; however, we found that this ratio produced a dry and crumbly arepa. I was working with 2 cups of masarepa, so I made batches of arepas using 2½ and 3 cups of warm water and compared them side by side. The arepas made with 3 cups of water were difficult to shape because the dough was so wet, and they fell apart when I cooked them. The batch made with 2½ cups of water was much better—these arepas were easy to shape, cooked up nicely, and were moist and tender—though some tasters thought they were a little dense. I remedied that by adding just 1 teaspoon of baking powder—not a traditional ingredient, but welcomed nonetheless for the subtle lightness that it gave to the arepas.

Now I was ready to fine-tune the shaping and cooking

process. I got the shaping right pretty quickly—3-inch rounds about ½ inch thick were our favorite size. Any thinner, and they were difficult to split open and stuff; any thicker, and the ratio of cake to filling was too high.

Instead of using a grill or griddle as many recipes do, I simply browned my arepas in a nonstick skillet with a little vegetable oil. Once they were golden and a crust had formed on both sides, I transferred them to a baking sheet and into a 400-degree oven to bake through in the center. The arepas were now ready to be split open and stuffed, so it was time to turn my attention to the fillings.

I decided to limit the fillings to simple ingredients that could be easily combined: chicken and avocado; and black bean and cheese. I used the typical additions of scallions, cilantro, lime juice, and a little chili powder to provide a balanced flavor base for both and then worked in the main ingredients.

To make the chicken and avocado filling, a classic combination in Venezuela, we bound tender shredded chicken together with chunks of rich avocado. The bean and cheese filling got its velvety texture not only from the cheese, but also from mashed beans. I could fit a generous 3 tablespoons of filling into each arepa, which is plenty, considering that one arepa is perfect for a snack or light lunch, and two make a suitable dinner portion.

—RACHEL TOOMEY, *America's Test Kitchen Books*

VENEZUELAN STUFFED CORN CAKES

MAKES 8 CORN CAKES

Masarepa, a precooked corn flour that is also called *harina precocida* and *masa al instante,* is available in specialty Latin markets, and can often be found in the Latin American aisle at supermarkets. While we had the best results with masarepa, we found that white cornmeal can be substituted.

- 2 cups (10 ounces) masarepa blanca (see note)
- 1 teaspoon salt
- 1 teaspoon baking powder
- 2½ cups warm water
- ¼ cup vegetable oil
- 1 recipe filling (recipes follow)

1. Adjust an oven rack to the middle position and heat the oven to 400 degrees. Whisk the masarepa, salt, and baking powder together in a medium bowl. Gradually add the water and stir to form a dough. Using a generous ⅓ cup of dough, form eight 3-inch rounds, each about ½ inch thick.

2. Heat 2 tablespoons of the oil in a 12-inch nonstick skillet over medium-high heat until shimmering. Add 4 of the corn cakes and cook until golden on both sides, about 4 minutes total. Transfer to a parchment paper–lined baking sheet and repeat with the remaining 2 tablespoons oil and the remaining 4 corn cakes. (The corn cakes can be cooled and refrigerated for up to 3 days, or frozen for up to 1 month in a zipper-lock bag.)

3. Bake until the corn cakes sound hollow when tapped on the bottom, about 10 minutes. (If frozen, increase the baking time to 20 minutes.) Split the hot corn cakes open using a paring knife or fork as if they were English muffins, and stuff each with a generous 3 tablespoons filling. Serve immediately.

CHICKEN AND AVOCADO CORN CAKE FILLING

MAKES ENOUGH FOR 8 CORN CAKES

The filling can be made while the corn cakes are in the oven.

- 1 cup cooked chicken, shredded into bite-sized pieces
- 1 ripe avocado, halved, pitted, and cut into ½-inch chunks
- 2 tablespoons minced fresh cilantro
- 2 scallions, sliced thin
- 1 tablespoon fresh lime juice
- ¼ teaspoon chili powder
  Salt and pepper

Mix all of the ingredients together and season with salt and pepper to taste. Cover with plastic wrap and refrigerate until needed. (The filling can be refrigerated for up to 2 days.)

BLACK BEAN AND CHEESE CORN CAKE FILLING

MAKES ENOUGH FOR 8 CORN CAKES

The filling can be made while the cork cakes are in the oven.

- 1 (15-ounce) can black beans, rinsed and drained
- 4 ounces Monterey Jack cheese, shredded (about 1 cup)
- 2 tablespoons minced fresh cilantro
- 2 scallions, sliced thin
- 1 tablespoon fresh lime juice
- ¼ teaspoon chili powder
  Salt and pepper

Using a potato masher or fork, mash the beans in a medium bowl until most are broken. Stir in the remaining ingredients and season with salt and pepper to taste. Cover with plastic wrap and refrigerate until needed. (The filling can be refrigerated for up to 2 days.)

NOTES FROM THE TEST KITCHEN

MAKING THE CORN CAKES

1. Cook the corn cakes in two batches until golden on both sides, about 2 minutes per side.

2. Using a fork (or paring knife), split the corn cakes open as you would an English muffin. (You may want to use a dish towel to hold the corn cakes as they will be very hot.)

3. Stuff each corn cake with a generous 3 tablespoons of filling.

ROASTED VEGETABLE SALADS

FRESH-FROM-THE-FARM PRODUCE needs little adulteration—a quick steam or sauté and a drizzle of extra-virgin olive oil will suffice. But the reality is that most of us have to make do with ordinary supermarket vegetables, especially in the winter.

The good news is that roasting can transform tired produce through the development of hundreds of new flavor compounds. But while roasting is straightforward for individual vegetables, roasting a few veggies together, as I wanted to do for a light side salad, can be tricky. To begin, I sketched out some combinations, taking color, flavor, and texture into account. I took advantage of the test kitchen's experience to determine the best approach to roasting. First I tossed my selections with a little olive oil and seasoned them with salt and pepper, plus a pinch of sugar to aid in caramelization. To guarantee maximum browning—a crucial requirement—I placed them on a baking sheet I had heated in a 500-degree oven. By the time I put the sheet back into the oven, the vegetables were sizzling.

Twenty-five minutes later, the results were in. I quickly eliminated porous vegetables like eggplant and zucchini from the lineup, because they were simply too limp and soggy to even consider tossing with dressing for a salad. Winning combos were beets and carrots, cremini mushrooms and fennel, and potatoes and green beans. These particular pairings maintained their structure after roasting and, thanks to the care I had taken to cut them into same-sized pieces, they cooked to a similarly firm yet tender consistency.

Now to figure out the dressing. Using just a tablespoon of oil kept the salads from being greasy, and a similarly light hand with the vinegar (or lemon juice) let the sweetness of the vegetables dominate. Tossing the vegetables with the vinaigrette while they were still hot allowed them to better absorb its flavors.

To make roasted vegetables a proper salad, I went back to the produce aisle for inspiration and decided that something crisp and raw was the missing link. Added to the cooled roasted vegetables, slightly bitter radicchio, spicy radishes, and peppery watercress each contributed the freshness and vibrancy that every self-respecting salad needs.

—REBECCA HAYS, *Cook's Illustrated*

ROASTED FENNEL AND MUSHROOM SALAD WITH RADISHES

SERVES 4

If fennel fronds (the delicate greenery attached to the fennel stems) are unavailable, substitute 1 to 2 tablespoons chopped fresh tarragon leaves. If you are using a dark-colored nonstick baking sheet, line the pan with aluminum foil to prevent scorching.

- 2 fennel bulbs (about 1½ pounds), quartered, cored, and cut crosswise into ½-inch-thick slices; ⅓ cup fronds reserved and chopped (see note)
- 20 ounces cremini mushrooms, quartered if large or halved if medium
- 3 tablespoons extra-virgin olive oil
  Salt and pepper
- ¼ teaspoon sugar
- 2 tablespoons fresh lemon juice
- 1 teaspoon Dijon mustard
- 4–6 radishes, cut in half and sliced thin

1. Adjust an oven rack to the lowest position, place a large rimmed baking sheet on the rack, and heat the oven to 500 degrees. Toss the fennel and mushrooms with 2 tablespoons of the oil, ½ teaspoon salt, ¼ teaspoon pepper, and sugar in a large bowl. Remove the baking sheet from the oven and, working quickly, carefully transfer the fennel and mushrooms to the sheet and spread in an even layer. (Do not wash the bowl.) Roast until the vegetables are tender and well browned on one side, 20 to 25 minutes (do not stir during roasting).

2. Meanwhile, whisk the remaining 1 tablespoon oil, lemon juice, mustard, ¼ teaspoon salt, and ⅛ teaspoon pepper in the now-empty bowl.

3. Toss the hot vegetables with the vinaigrette and let cool to room temperature, about 30 minutes. Stir in the radishes and reserved fennel fronds, transfer to a serving platter, and serve.

ROASTED BEET AND CARROT SALAD WITH WATERCRESS

SERVES 4

If using a dark-colored nonstick baking sheet, line the pan with aluminum foil to prevent scorching.

- 1 pound beets, peeled and cut into ½-inch-thick wedges, wedges cut in half crosswise if beets are large
- 1 pound carrots, peeled and cut on the bias into ¼-inch-thick slices
- 3 tablespoons extra-virgin olive oil
  Salt and pepper
- ¼ teaspoon sugar
- 2 tablespoons white wine vinegar
- 1 teaspoon honey
- 1 shallot, minced (about 3 tablespoons)
- 6 ounces watercress, washed and trimmed (about 4 cups)

1. Adjust an oven rack to the lowest position, place a large rimmed baking sheet on the rack, and heat the oven to 500 degrees. Toss the beets and carrots with 2 tablespoons of the oil, ½ teaspoon salt, ¼ teaspoon pepper, and sugar in a large bowl. Remove the baking sheet from the oven and, working quickly, carefully transfer the beets and carrots to the sheet and spread in an even layer. (Do not wash the bowl.) Roast until the vegetables are tender and well browned on one side, 20 to 25 minutes (do not stir during roasting).

2. Meanwhile, whisk the remaining 1 tablespoon oil, vinegar, honey, shallot, ¼ teaspoon salt, and ⅛ teaspoon pepper in the now-empty bowl.

3. Toss the hot vegetables with the vinaigrette and let cool to room temperature, about 30 minutes. Stir in the watercress, transfer to a serving platter, and serve.

ROASTED GREEN BEAN AND POTATO SALAD WITH RADICCHIO

SERVES 4

If using a dark-colored nonstick baking sheet, line the pan with aluminum foil to prevent scorching.

- 1 pound green beans, trimmed and cut into 1½-inch pieces
- 1 pound Red Bliss potatoes (about 4 medium), cut into ½-inch pieces
- 3 tablespoons extra-virgin olive oil
  Salt and pepper
- ¼ teaspoon sugar
- 2 tablespoons red wine vinegar
- 1 garlic clove, minced
- 1 small head radicchio (about 6 ounces), washed and cut into 2- by ¼-inch slices (about 4 cups)

1. Adjust an oven rack to the lowest position, place a large rimmed baking sheet on the rack, and heat the oven to 500 degrees. Toss the beans and potatoes with 2 tablespoons of the oil, ½ teaspoon salt, ¼ teaspoon pepper, and sugar in a large bowl. Remove the baking sheet from the oven and, working quickly, carefully transfer the beans and potatoes to the sheet and spread in an even layer. (Do not wash the bowl.) Roast until the vegetables are tender and well browned on one side, 20 to 25 minutes (do not stir during roasting).

2. Meanwhile, whisk the remaining 1 tablespoon oil, vinegar, garlic, ¼ teaspoon salt, and ⅛ teaspoon pepper in the now-empty bowl.

3. Toss the hot vegetables with the vinaigrette and let cool to room temperature, about 30 minutes. Stir in the radicchio, transfer to a serving platter, and serve.

NOTES FROM THE TEST KITCHEN

BEATING BEET STAINS

Prepping the beets can leave a cutting board with dark stains that discolor other foods you put on it. Instead of stopping to wash the board between uses, give its surface a light coat of nonstick cooking spray before chopping. This thin coating adds no discernible slickness under the knife and allows you to quickly wipe the board clean with a paper towel before proceeding with the next task.

ROASTED GREEN BEAN AND POTATO SALAD WITH RADICCHIO

PEAR SALADS

ADDING SLICES OF PERFECTLY RIPE, juicy pear to a salad is a hit when using peak-season fruit. But what are you supposed to do the other 11 months of the year? Cooking mediocre supermarket pears until their exteriors caramelize is a great way to boost their flavor. Whether roasted in the oven or seared on the stovetop, heat heightens the pears' subtle complexity and intensifies their sweetness.

Most pear salad recipes offer complicated roasting instructions that yield overly soft pears better suited for a dessert. I wanted a simple technique for caramelizing pears that wouldn't overcook the fruit. Pan-roasting the pears on the stovetop, where I could easily control the heat and check the pears constantly, seemed like the way to go.

I heated a large skillet with oil over medium-high heat, added an even layer of ½-inch-thick pear slices, and cooked them on each side until brown. The cooked pears were OK when tossed with spicy greens, cheese, toasted nuts, and dressing. However, the slices continually turned out limp, no matter how I adjusted the heat. The texture improved when I cut the pears bigger—into quarters. The exteriors still browned, but now the interiors weren't overcooked. Tossing the pears with sugar before cooking encouraged even better browning. After the pears cooled, I sliced each quarter crosswise to form bite-sized pieces.

As beautiful as the pears turned out, tasters complained that the fruit was still lacking presence in the salad. Up to this point, I had been using balsamic vinegar in my vinaigrette. Its mellow, fruity flavor worked perfectly to accentuate the perfumed essence of the pears. I wondered if the vinegar had a role outside the dressing. After caramelizing another batch of pears, I added a couple of extra tablespoons of straight balsamic vinegar to the hot pan. Almost immediately, the vinegar reduced to form a glazy coating on the pears. When cooled, sliced, and tossed with the other salad ingredients, there was no doubt: These pears deserved top billing in the recipe title.

—CHARLES KELSEY, *Cook's Illustrated*

PAN-ROASTED PEAR SALAD WITH WATERCRESS, PARMESAN, AND PECANS
SERVES 4 TO 6

The test kitchen prefers Bartlett pears for this recipe, but Bosc pears can also be used. With either variety, the pears should be ripe but firm; check the flesh at the neck of the pear—it should give slightly when pressed gently with a finger. If using Bartletts, look for pears that are starting to turn from green to yellow. Romaine lettuce may be substituted for green leaf.

- 3 ripe but firm pears (about 1½ pounds), quartered and cored (see note)
- 2½ teaspoons sugar
  Salt and pepper
- 2 teaspoons olive oil, plus 2 tablespoons
- 4 tablespoons balsamic vinegar
- 1 small shallot, minced (about 1 tablespoon)
- ½ medium head green leaf lettuce, washed, dried, and torn into 1-inch pieces (about 4 cups)
- 2 small bunches watercress, washed, dried, and stemmed (about 4 cups)
- 4 ounces Parmesan cheese, shaved into thin slices with a vegetable peeler
- ¾ cup pecans, toasted and chopped

1. Toss the pears, 2 teaspoons of the sugar, ¼ teaspoon salt, and ⅛ teaspoon pepper in a medium bowl. Heat the 2 teaspoons oil in a large skillet over medium-high heat until just smoking. Add the pears cut side down in a single layer and cook until golden brown, 2 to 4 minutes. Using a small spatula or fork, tip each pear onto its second cut side; continue to cook until the second side is light brown, 2 to 4 minutes longer. Turn off the heat, leave the skillet on the burner, and add 2 tablespoons of the vinegar; gently stir until the vinegar becomes glazy and coats the pears, about 30 seconds. Transfer the pears to a large plate and let cool to room temperature, about 45 minutes. Cut each pear quarter crosswise into ½-inch pieces.

2. Whisk the remaining 2 tablespoons oil, remaining 2 tablespoons vinegar, remaining ½ teaspoon sugar, and shallot together in a large bowl; season with salt and pepper. Add the lettuce, watercress, and cooled pears to the bowl; toss and adjust the seasonings with salt and pepper to taste. Divide the salad among individual plates; top each with portions of the cheese and nuts. Serve immediately.

VARIATIONS

PAN-ROASTED PEAR SALAD WITH RADICCHIO, BLUE CHEESE, AND WALNUTS

Follow the recipe for Pan-Roasted Pear Salad with Watercress, Parmesan, and Pecans, substituting 1 large head radicchio, quartered, cored, and cut crosswise into ½-inch pieces (about 4 cups), for the watercress, 4 ounces crumbled Gorgonzola or Stilton cheese (1 cup) for the Parmesan, and ¾ cup toasted and chopped walnuts for the pecans.

PAN-ROASTED PEAR SALAD WITH FRISÉE, GOAT CHEESE, AND ALMONDS

Follow the recipe for Pan-Roasted Pear Salad with Watercress, Parmesan, and Pecans, substituting 1 head frisée, torn into 1-inch pieces (about 4 cups), for the watercress, 4 ounces crumbled goat cheese (1 cup) for the Parmesan, and ¾ cup toasted sliced almonds for the pecans.

NOTES FROM THE TEST KITCHEN

PAN-ROASTING PEARS
To maximize caramelization, arrange the pear quarters so that one of the cut sides is flush with the hot skillet. Once the first side is lightly browned, simply use a fork or small spatula to tip the pears over onto their uncooked cut side.

24-HOUR PICNIC SALAD

AT A RECENT BARBECUE, I discovered this strange salad, sitting alongside the baked beans, chips, and potato salad. It featured layers of iceberg lettuce, peas, hard-cooked egg, shredded cheddar cheese, and bacon, all neatly arranged in a huge glass bowl. On top was a layer of iceberg coated with what looked like mayonnaise spread to the edges, like frosting on a cake. The hostess confirmed that it had been fully assembled a day in advance—what a great idea! After she tossed the salad together, I took the first scoop and was surprised that the lettuce and other vegetables were still crisp after a day in the bowl. The creamy dressing brought all the flavors together.

Determined to re-create this salad, I found a handful of recipes online and prepared them in the test kitchen. All shared the concept of layering the ingredients, but unlike the one I'd had at the barbecue, most of these were overdressed with thick, bland, and sweet dressings (mostly just sugar and mayonnaise) that didn't properly coat the salad. I had a lot of work to do.

I tried using other lettuces, but iceberg retained the most crunch after sitting with the dressing for a day. I found that soft ingredients like mushrooms, spinach, and scallions wilted into mush, while crunchy ones like celery, bell pepper, cucumber, and red onion stayed crisp. My tasters preferred assertive blue cheese over the mild flavor of cheddar, especially when I layered the dressing and blue cheese together, which allowed the flavors to mingle overnight.

For the dressing, my first step was to cut back on the sugar and add tart cider vinegar and hot sauce for brightness and depth. The flavor was great, but the dressing was still too thick to blend into the salad. Thinning it out caused the dressing to run down through the ingredients overnight, resulting in soggy vegetables.

Then I remembered one recipe I had found (and quickly dismissed) that called for salting the layers of lettuce. I dutifully prepared the recipe, and the next day found a pool of water sitting in the bottom of the bowl—I was sure I had made a mistake. I tossed the salad together anyway and was pleasantly surprised that the thick dressing combined with the water to coat the salad beautifully. I had the perfect make-ahead salad.

—DIANE UNGER, *Cook's Country*

24-HOUR PICNIC SALAD

SERVES 12

Frank's is our favorite brand of hot sauce. If using a hotter brand, such as Tabasco, reduce the amount to 1 tablespoon.

SALAD

- 1 head iceberg lettuce, cored and chopped rough (about 6 cups)
- 1 teaspoon salt
- ½ red onion, sliced thin
- 6 hard-cooked eggs, peeled and chopped
- 1½ cups frozen peas
- 4 celery ribs, sliced thin
- 1 red bell pepper, stemmed, seeded, and chopped
- 1 cucumber, halved, seeded, and sliced thin
- 1 pound bacon, cooked until crisp and crumbled
- 5 ounces blue cheese, crumbled (about 1¼ cups)

DRESSING

- 1½ cups mayonnaise
- 3 tablespoons cider vinegar
- 2 tablespoons hot sauce (see note)
- 2 teaspoons sugar
- 1½ teaspoons pepper

1. FOR THE SALAD: Place half of the lettuce in a large serving bowl and sprinkle with ½ teaspoon of the salt. Rinse the onion under cold water; pat dry with paper towels. Layer the onion, eggs, peas, celery, bell pepper, and cucumber over the lettuce. Add the remaining lettuce to the bowl, sprinkle with the remaining ½ teaspoon salt, and top with the bacon and cheese.

2. FOR THE DRESSING: Combine all of the ingredients in a bowl and spread the dressing evenly over the top of the salad. Cover with plastic wrap and refrigerate at least 8 hours or up to 24 hours. Remove the plastic wrap and toss until the salad is evenly coated with the dressing. Serve.

NOTES FROM THE TEST KITCHEN

PREPARING BELL PEPPERS

1. Slice ¼ inch from the top and bottom of each pepper and then gently remove the stem from the top lobe.

2. Pull the core out of the pepper. Make a slit down one side of the pepper and lay it flat, skin-side down, in one long strip.

3. Slide a sharp knife along the inside of the pepper to remove all the ribs and seeds. Cut into strips and chop.

A MULTITASKING SALAD SPINNER

To show off the multiple layers of our 24-Hour Picnic Salad, we like to serve it in a clear bowl. If you don't have a big glass bowl, you might have a suitable substitute on hand without even knowing it: The bowl from our top-rated **OXO Good Grips Salad Spinner** works perfectly in this recipe.

A FLAVORFUL HOT SAUCE

To avoid a searingly hot salad, we recommend using the test kitchen's favorite brand of hot sauce, **Frank's Red Hot,** which has mellow heat and deep flavor. Some brands of hot sauce, such as Tabasco and La Preferida, are nearly twice as hot as Frank's, so if using one of those start with half the amount and add more to taste.

24-HOUR PICNIC SALAD

MEMPHIS CHOPPED COLESLAW

STUDDED WITH CELERY SEEDS and crunchy green pepper, Memphis Chopped Coleslaw is tossed with an unapologetically sugary mustard dressing that's balanced by a bracing hit of vinegar. With its bold, brash flavors, this bright yellow slaw is a perfect match for even the spiciest and smokiest barbecue.

When I started researching recipes, I was intrigued that many called for a combination of refrigerator staples (yellow mustard, mayonnaise, sour cream, and ketchup) to give the dressing complex flavor. Tasters told me the complexity was there, but some felt the dressing lacked punch. Switching from ketchup to garlicky chili sauce helped, as did adding shredded onion. Using spicy jalapeño (instead of green bell pepper) and brown sugar (instead of white) gave just the right mix of savory and sweet.

But even though the dressing had the bold tastes I wanted, the flavors still seemed somehow divergent. To help the flavors meld, one recipe I found simmered the sauce before pouring it over the cabbage. While this sounded promising, I feared the heat of the sauce might cook the cabbage and make it soft and soggy. I couldn't have been more wrong. Although the cabbage did absorb some of the hot dressing, it remained crunchy and was seasoned from the inside out. Finally, I had a bold, crisp slaw that was packed with flavor and not waterlogged. Now all I needed was some barbecue.

—JEREMY SAUER, *Cook's Country*

MEMPHIS CHOPPED COLESLAW

SERVES 8 TO 10

In step 1, the salted, rinsed, and dried cabbage mixture can be refrigerated in a zipper-lock plastic bag for up to 24 hours.

- 1 medium head green cabbage, cored and shredded
- 1 jalapeño chile, stemmed, seeded, and minced
- 1 carrot, peeled and shredded on a box grater
- 1 small onion, shredded on a box grater (about ¾ cup)
- 2 teaspoons salt
- ¼ cup yellow mustard
- ¼ cup chili sauce
- ¼ cup mayonnaise
- ¼ cup sour cream
- ¼ cup cider vinegar
- 1 teaspoon celery seeds
- ⅔ cup packed light brown sugar

1. Toss the cabbage, jalapeño, carrot, onion, and salt in a colander set over a medium bowl. Let stand until wilted, about 1 hour. Rinse the cabbage mixture under cold water, drain, dry well with paper towels, and transfer to a large bowl.

2. Bring the mustard, chili sauce, mayonnaise, sour cream, vinegar, celery seeds, and sugar to a boil in a saucepan over medium heat. Pour over the cabbage and toss to coat. Cover with plastic wrap and refrigerate 1 hour or up to 1 day. Serve.

NOTES FROM THE TEST KITCHEN

HOW TO SHRED CABBAGE

1. Cut the cabbage into quarters, then trim and discard the hard core.

2. Separate the cabbage into small stacks of leaves that flatten when pressed.

3. Use a chef's knife to cut each stack of cabbage leaves into thin shreds.

CAESAR SALAD

DUMPING A POTENT MIXTURE of anchovies, garlic, and Worcestershire sauce over romaine lettuce doesn't sound appealing, but those ingredients (along with raw egg, olive oil, lemon juice, mustard, croutons, and Parmesan cheese) are the foundation of Caesar salad. In most Caesar recipes, the forceful flavors run out of control, resulting in a dressing that tastes fishy, too garlicky, or just plain sour. Good Caesar dressing demands a delicate balance of these strongly flavored ingredients.

Traditional Caesars are thickened with an emulsion of raw egg and oil; for food safety reasons, I wanted to find a replacement for the egg. Mayonnaise, which is made from eggs and oil and comes already emulsified, was the obvious choice, and it worked perfectly when thinned with olive oil. Extra-virgin olive oil was too strong; my tasters preferred the milder flavor of regular olive oil.

To keep the flavors in balance, I decreased the lemon juice from the ¼ cup called for in most recipes to 1 tablespoon. When fortified with 1 tablespoon each of white wine vinegar, Worcestershire sauce, and Dijon mustard, the dressing had the right balance of acidity and pungency. A mere two anchovies (some recipes use up to five) provided a welcome depth and complexity. And mixing everything together in a blender ensured a stable dressing that didn't separate.

I had one last ingredient to deal with: garlic. Most Caesar recipes go way overboard. I used just one raw garlic clove in the dressing to keep its sharpness at bay, but added another layer of mellow garlic flavor by tossing cubes of fresh bread with garlic oil and baking them to make croutons. Parmesan cheese in both the dressing and the finished salad provided a classic touch. Tasters agreed that this was a Caesar truly worth hailing.

—KELLEY BAKER, *Cook's Country*

CAESAR SALAD

SERVES 6 TO 8

Two 10-ounce bags of chopped romaine lettuce can be substituted for the hearts.

- ½ cup olive oil
- 2 garlic cloves, minced
- 1 (12-inch) piece French baguette, cut into ½-inch cubes (about 4 cups)
- Salt and pepper
- ½ cup mayonnaise
- ¼ cup finely grated Parmesan cheese, plus 1 cup shredded
- 2 anchovy fillets, rinsed and patted dry
- 1 tablespoon fresh lemon juice
- 1 tablespoon white wine vinegar
- 1 tablespoon Worcestershire sauce
- 1 tablespoon Dijon mustard
- 3 romaine hearts, torn into bite-sized pieces (about 12 cups) (see note)

1. Adjust an oven rack to the middle position and heat the oven to 350 degrees. Whisk the oil and garlic in a large bowl. Reserve half of the oil mixture. Toss the bread cubes with the remaining oil mixture and season with salt and pepper. Bake the croutons on a rimmed baking sheet until golden, about 20 minutes. Cool completely. (The croutons and dressing can be made up to 2 days in advance. Store the croutons at room temperature and refrigerate the dressing.)

2. Process the mayonnaise, grated Parmesan, anchovies, lemon juice, vinegar, Worcestershire, mustard, ½ teaspoon salt, and ½ teaspoon pepper in a blender until smooth. With the blender running, slowly add the reserved oil mixture until incorporated.

3. Toss the romaine, shredded Parmesan, and dressing in a large bowl. Toss in the croutons and serve.

NOTES FROM THE TEST KITCHEN

ANCHOVY PASTE
Made from pulverized anchovies, vinegar, salt, and water, anchovy paste promises all the flavor of oil-packed anchovies without the mess of draining, drying, and chopping the whole fillets. After a head-to-head tasting of our recipe prepared with equal amounts of anchovy paste and anchovy fillets, we found little difference. Though a few astute tasters felt that the paste had a "saltier" and "slightly more fishy" flavor, in such small quantities it was deemed an acceptable substitute. For dishes that use just a touch of anchovy, the squeeze-and-go convenience of the tube can't be beat.

SOUPS & STEWS

FRENCH ONION SOUP

THE IDEAL FRENCH ONION SOUP combines a satisfying broth redolent of sweet caramelized onions with a slice of toasted baguette and melted cheese. But the reality is that most of the onion soup you find isn't very good. Once you manage to dig through the layer of congealed cheese to unearth a spoonful of broth, it just doesn't taste like onions.

The good news is that I already knew of a terrific recipe introduced to the test kitchen by a friend visiting from France. Henri Pinon patiently cooked 3 pounds of onions in butter over very low heat until they were golden brown, then deglazed the pot with water. Nothing unusual there—deglazing is common in onion soup recipes. What followed, however, was something entirely new. Henri allowed the onions to recaramelize, and then he deglazed the pan again. And again. He repeated this process several more times, finally finishing the soup by simmering the onions with water, white wine, and a sprig of thyme. He garnished the soup in the traditional way, with a slice of crusty toasted baguette and a very modest amount of shredded Gruyère, passing the crocks under the broiler to melt the cheese. How did it taste? Beyond compare—the broth was impossibly rich, with deep onion flavor that burst through the tanginess of the Gruyère and bread.

I couldn't wait to give this recipe a try. But before I started cooking, I pondered the technique. When onions caramelize, a complex series of chemical reactions takes place. Heat causes water molecules to separate from the onions' sugar molecules. As they cook, the dehydrated sugar molecules react with each other to form new molecules that produce new colors, flavors, and aromas. Each time Henri deglazed the pan and allowed the onions to recaramelize, he was ratcheting up the flavor of the soup in a big way.

Back in the test kitchen, I started cooking, and a long while later, the soup was on. It was as delicious as when Henri had made it, yet after standing at the stove for more than two hours, I barely had the energy to enjoy it. Was there a way to borrow Henri's technique while cutting down on the active cooking time?

I needed steady heat that wouldn't cause scorching—why not use the oven? I cooked as many sliced onions as I could squeeze into a Dutch oven (4 pounds), and the results were promising—the onions cooked slowly and evenly, building flavor all the while. After some trial and error, I finally settled on a method in which I cooked the onions covered in a 400-degree oven for an hour, then continued cooking with the lid ajar for another hour and a half.

With my new hands-off method, the onions emerged from the oven golden, soft, and sweet, and a nice *fond* had begun to collect on the bottom of the pot. Even better, I'd only had to tend to them twice in 2½ hours. Next, I continued the caramelization process on the stovetop. Because of their head start in the oven, deglazing only three or four times was sufficient. Once the onions were as dark as possible, I poured in a few splashes of dry sherry, which tasters preferred to sweet sherry, white wine, Champagne, red wine, and vermouth.

Settling on a type of onion from standard supermarket varieties was a snap. I quickly dismissed red onions—they bled out to produce a dingy-looking soup. White onions were too mild, and Vidalia onions made the broth too sweet. Yellow onions, on the other hand, offered just the sweet and savory notes I was after.

Henri had used only water for his soup, but after making batches with water, chicken broth, and beef broth alone and in combination, I decided the soup was best with all three.

At last, I could focus on the soup's crowning glory: bread and cheese. Toasting the bread before floating a slice on the soup warded off sogginess. As for the cheese, a modest sprinkling of nutty Gruyère was a grand, gooey finish to a great soup.

—REBECCA HAYS, *Cook's Illustrated*

FRENCH ONION SOUP

SERVES 6

Sweet onions, such as Vidalia or Walla Walla, will make this recipe overly sweet. Use broiler-safe crocks and keep the rim of the bowls 4 to 5 inches from the heating element to obtain a proper gratinée of melted, bubbly cheese. If using ordinary soup bowls, sprinkle the toasted bread slices with Gruyère and return them to the broiler until the cheese melts, then float them on

FRENCH ONION SOUP

top of the soup. For the best flavor, make the soup a day or two in advance. Alternatively, the onions can be prepared through step 1, cooled in the pot, and refrigerated for up to 3 days before proceeding with the recipe.

SOUP

3 tablespoons unsalted butter, cut into 3 pieces
6 large yellow onions (about 4 pounds), halved and cut pole to pole into ¼-inch-thick slices (see page 35)
  Salt
2 cups water, plus extra for deglazing
½ cup dry sherry
4 cups low-sodium chicken broth
2 cups beef broth
6 sprigs fresh thyme, tied with kitchen twine
1 bay leaf
  Pepper

CROUTONS

1 small baguette, cut on the bias into ½-inch slices
8 ounces Gruyère, shredded (about 2½ cups)

1. FOR THE SOUP: Adjust an oven rack to the lower-middle position and heat the oven to 400 degrees. Generously spray the inside of a heavy-bottomed large (at least 7-quart) Dutch oven with nonstick cooking spray. Place the butter in the pot and add the onions and 1 teaspoon salt. Cook, covered, 1 hour (the onions will be moist and slightly reduced in volume). Remove the pot from the oven and stir the onions, scraping the bottom and sides of the pot. Return the pot to the oven with the lid slightly ajar and continue to cook until the onions are very soft and golden brown, 1½ to 1¾ hours longer, stirring the onions and scraping the bottom and sides of the pot after 1 hour.

2. Carefully remove the pot from the oven and place over medium-high heat. Using oven mitts to handle the pot, cook the onions, stirring frequently and scraping the bottom and sides of the pot, until the liquid evaporates and the onions brown, 15 to 20 minutes, reducing the heat to medium if the onions are browning too quickly. Continue to cook, stirring frequently, until the pot bottom is coated with dark crust, 6 to 8 minutes,

adjusting the heat as necessary. (Scrape any fond that collects on the spoon back into the onions.) Stir in ¼ cup water, scraping the pot bottom to loosen the crust, and cook until the water evaporates and another dark crust has formed on the pot bottom, 6 to 8 minutes. Repeat the process of deglazing 2 or 3 more times, until the onions are very dark brown. Stir in the sherry and cook, stirring frequently, until the sherry evaporates, about 5 minutes.

3. Stir in both broths, 2 cups water, thyme, bay leaf, and ½ teaspoon salt, scraping up any final bits of browned crust on the bottom and sides of the pot. Increase the heat to high and bring to a simmer. Reduce the heat to low, cover, and simmer 30 minutes. Remove and discard the herbs, then season with salt and pepper to taste.

4. FOR THE CROUTONS: While the soup simmers, arrange the baguette slices in a single layer on a baking sheet and bake in a 400-degree oven until the bread is dry, crisp, and golden at the edges, about 10 minutes. Set aside.

5. To serve, adjust an oven rack 6 inches from the broiler element and heat the broiler. Set individual broiler-safe crocks on a baking sheet and fill each with about 1¾ cups soup. Top each bowl with 1 or 2 baguette slices (do not overlap slices) and sprinkle evenly with Gruyère. Broil until the cheese is melted and bubbly around the edges, 3 to 5 minutes. Let cool 5 minutes before serving.

VARIATION

QUICKER FRENCH ONION SOUP

This variation uses a microwave for the initial cooking of the onions, which dramatically reduces the cooking time. The soup's flavor, however, will not be quite as deep as with the stovetop method. If you don't have a microwave-safe bowl large enough to accommodate all of the onions, cook in a smaller bowl in 2 batches.

Follow the recipe for French Onion Soup, combining the onions and 1 teaspoon salt in a large microwave-safe bowl and covering with a large microwave-safe plate (the plate should completely cover the bowl and not rest on the onions). Microwave on high power for 20 to

25 minutes until the onions are soft and wilted, stirring halfway through cooking. (Use oven mitts to remove the bowl from the microwave and remove the plate away from you to avoid steam burn.) Drain the onions (about ½ cup liquid should drain off) and proceed with step 2, melting the butter in the Dutch oven before adding the wilted onions.

NOTES FROM THE TEST KITCHEN

GOLDEN ONIONS WITHOUT THE FUSS

Forget constant stirring on the stovetop. Cooking onions in the oven takes time but requires little attention.

1. RAW: The raw onions nearly fill a large Dutch oven.

2. AFTER 1 HOUR IN OVEN: The onions are starting to wilt and release moisture.

3. AFTER 2½ HOURS IN OVEN: The onions are golden, wilted, and significantly reduced in volume.

SLICING ONIONS THIN

Halve the onion through the root end and then peel. Place the flat side of the onion on the work surface, then slice it from pole to pole into ¼-inch-thick slices.

GARDEN MINESTRONE

MINESTRONE, LITERALLY "BIG SOUP" in Italian, is a broth- and tomato-based soup packed with vegetables, beans, herbs, and either pasta or rice. I wanted to create a light, lively minestrone that could showcase a windfall of summer vegetables.

I began building flavor by sautéing onions and carrots in olive oil. For fresher flavor, I skipped the traditional canned tomatoes and used chopped fresh tomatoes instead. My tasters preferred the mild flavor of chicken broth as a base, rather than heavier beef broth or flavorless water. I added garlic, green beans, canned beans, summer squash, and pasta and let the soup cook until everything was tender.

This soup was lighter, all right—so light it didn't taste like much. For bolder tomato flavor, I cooked some of the tomatoes—seeded to concentrate their flavor more quickly—with the onions and carrots until they broke down and began to resemble a fresher, sweeter tomato paste. A little white wine added a bright note of acidity, and fresh thyme lent a welcome herbal quality. When I added the chicken broth and more raw tomatoes (for another layer of garden-fresh flavor), my soup base was much improved.

In addition to the washed-out flavors, my tasters had complained about the slimy texture of the summer squash (both yellow squash and zucchini). To correct the texture of the squash, I removed its watery seeds and browned the squash—with lots of garlic—right in the pot before starting the soup; I set this mixture aside so that I could add it back at the end of cooking, thus preserving its texture. I also reserved some of the raw tomatoes for the end, which gave the soup another layer of garden-fresh flavor and texture.

Many minestrone recipes call for hearty greens like cabbage or kale. For a lighter, more summery feel, I tried fresh spinach, but its mild flavor faded quickly. Since some recipes offer a pesto garnish, I wondered if fresh basil leaves could serve double duty as an herb and a "vegetable." Tasters loved the bold herbal flavor and vegetal texture a full four cups of roughly chopped basil added. To further lighten the soup, I eliminated the pasta altogether and chose small white navy beans for their creamy texture and delicate flavor. Now this was a soup that tasted like summer.

—KELLEY BAKER, *Cook's Country*

GARDEN MINESTRONE

SERVES 6 TO 8

Zucchini or yellow summer squash can be used alone
or in combination here. If desired, serve minestrone
with grated Parmesan cheese and a splash of extra-virgin
olive oil.

- ¼ cup extra-virgin olive oil
- 3 summer squash, seeded and chopped (see note)
- 6 garlic cloves, minced
- 1 onion, minced (about 1 cup)
- 1 carrot, peeled and chopped
- 6 tomatoes, cored, seeded, and chopped
    Salt and pepper
- ½ cup white wine
- 8 ounces green beans, trimmed and cut into
    1-inch pieces
- 2 teaspoons minced fresh thyme
- 8 cups low-sodium chicken broth
- 2 (15-ounce) cans navy beans, drained and rinsed
- 4 cups loosely packed basil leaves, bruised and chopped

1. Heat 2 tablespoons of the oil in a large Dutch oven
over medium-high heat until shimmering. Cook the
squash until golden and just tender, about 5 minutes.
Add half of the garlic and cook until fragrant, about
30 seconds. Transfer to a plate and tent with foil.

2. Add the remaining 2 tablespoons oil, onion, and
carrot to the now-empty Dutch oven and cook until the
onion is golden, about 8 minutes. Add half of the tomatoes, ½ teaspoon salt, and ½ teaspoon pepper and cook,
stirring occasionally, until the juices have evaporated
and the tomatoes begin to brown, 5 to 7 minutes. Add
the remaining garlic and cook until fragrant, about
30 seconds. Add the wine and simmer, scraping up any
browned bits, until slightly thickened, about 2 minutes.
Add the green beans, thyme, broth, navy beans, and
remaining tomatoes and bring to a boil. Reduce the heat
to medium-low and simmer until the green beans are
tender, about 15 minutes. (At this point, the soup can
be refrigerated in an airtight container for up to 2 days
with the squash reserved separately. When ready to serve,
bring the soup to a simmer and proceed with the recipe.)

3. Stir in the reserved squash and basil and simmer
until heated through, about 1 minute. Season with salt
and pepper to taste. Serve.

NOTES FROM THE TEST KITCHEN

PUTTING THE GARDEN INTO MINESTRONE

Many minestrone recipes settle for overcooked vegetables
and dull broth, but it only takes a few easy steps to pack your
soup with garden-fresh flavor.

1. Brown the seeded
squash (with plenty
of garlic) at the
onset of cooking,
remove it from the
pot, and then add it
back to the soup just
prior to serving.

2. To add body to
the soup without
making it too heavy,
make a fresh
"tomato paste" by
cooking half of the
seeded tomatoes
until they begin to
brown.

3. To add a bright
herbal flavor and
leafy texture, stir in
freshly chopped
basil just before
serving.

TEST KITCHEN WORKHORSE

So what should you consider when selecting a Dutch oven?
Look for a Dutch oven that is roughly twice as wide as it is tall,
with a minimum capacity of six quarts, though seven is even
better. The bottom should be thick—so that it maintains moderate heat and prevents food from scorching—and the lid
should fit tightly to prevent excessive moisture loss.

Our test kitchen is stocked with many of our two favorites,
made by All-Clad and Le Creuset, but some of us are reluctant
to shell out over $200 to buy one. So we tested Dutch ovens
in the under $100 range and came up with an alternative to
the expensive brands. The **Tramontina
6.5-Quart Cast Iron Dutch
Oven** is comparable
in size to the All-
Clad and Le Creuset
ovens and performs
nearly as well. Better yet,
at $40 it costs a fraction
of the price of either.

GARDEN MINESTRONE

VIETNAMESE RICE NOODLE SOUP

THIS DEEPLY FLAVORED SOUP, known as *Pho* (pronounced "fuh") is perhaps the best-recognized rice noodle soup from Southeast Asia. It begins with a stock made from beef bones, which is flavored with spices and sauces. The stock is rich but not heavy and is poured over rice noodles, meat, scallion slices, crisp bean sprouts, and an abundance of fresh herbs such as Thai basil and cilantro leaves. This mix of raw and cooked, hot and cold, creates a unique and satisfying soup.

Since this soup relies heavily upon the quality of the broth, I started there. But after some initial tests, I kept running into the inescapable fact that a full-flavored broth of this caliber (one that needs to simmer slowly for 5 hours or more) is impractical for most cooks today. Faced with this dilemma in the past here in the test kitchen, we have found it possible to punch up the otherwise mild flavor of store-bought chicken broth with extra aromatics to create a quick alternative.

I began to build my base by sautéing onions, garlic, and lemongrass, then adding chicken broth and some water and simmering the mixture briefly to allow the flavors to meld. This was a good start, but I thought I could further enhance my broth. Soy and fish sauces added much-needed body and depth of flavor. Soy sauce lent a meatiness that homemade beef stock would normally contribute, while fish sauce added just the right combination of salt and musky sweetness. Cloves and star anise are common components of this soup and tasters unanimously welcomed their addition.

Satisfied with the broth, I turned my attention to the noodles. I found that boiled noodles had a tendency to turn mushy and—if left in the hot soup for any length of time—break apart. Ultimately, I settled on soaking the noodles in water that had been brought to a boil and then removed from the heat; the slightly cooler temperature did not overcook them. I drained the noodles when they had softened to the point that they were tender but still had a little chew and then let them finish cooking in the hot broth until they softened through.

I next looked at what meat to add and how it should be cooked. Beef filet, sirloin steak, tripe, meatballs, chicken, and chicken organs are all common additions, but I decided to focus on two meats that would be the simplest to prepare and find: thinly sliced beef and shredded chicken. Traditionally the beef is sliced paper-thin and is added to the individual soup bowls raw (the idea is that it cooks directly in the broth). I had trouble getting the broth to cook the beef fully every time, so I opted for cooking the beef in the simmering broth before serving it. I tested a variety of steaks, and concluded that beef tenderloin—the authentic choice for this soup—was indeed the best because it was naturally lean (no bits of fat to turn rubbery in the soup) yet extremely tender and flavorful. The finishing touch for this soup is a generous garnish of bean sprouts, fresh herbs, lime, and some sliced chile for heat.

—MEGAN WYCOFF, *America's Test Kitchen Books*

VIETNAMESE RICE NOODLE SOUP WITH BEEF

SERVES 4

To make slicing the steak easier, freeze it for 15 minutes. Be ready to serve the soup immediately after cooking the beef in step 5; if the beef sits in the hot broth for too long it will become tough. If you cannot find Thai basil, substitute regular basil.

BROTH

- 2 teaspoons vegetable oil
- 2 onions, minced (about 2 cups)
- 4 garlic cloves, minced
- 1 lemongrass stalk, bottom 5 inches only, trimmed and sliced thin (see page 39)
- ⅓ cup fish sauce
- 8 cups low-sodium chicken broth
- 2 cups water
- 2 tablespoons soy sauce
- 2 tablespoons sugar
- 4 star anise pods
- 4 whole cloves

NOODLES, MEAT, AND GARNISH

- 8 ounces (¼-inch-wide) dried flat rice noodles
- 2 cups bean sprouts
- 1 cup loosely packed fresh Thai basil (see note)
- 1 cup loosely packed fresh cilantro
- 2 scallions, sliced thin on the bias
- 1 fresh Thai, serrano, or jalapeño chile, stemmed, seeded, and sliced thin

1   lime, cut into wedges, for serving

12 ounces beef tenderloin (about 2 filets mignons), sliced in half lengthwise, then sliced crosswise into ¼-inch-thick pieces

1. FOR THE BROTH: Heat the oil in a large saucepan over medium heat until just shimmering. Add the onions, garlic, lemongrass, and 1 tablespoon of the fish sauce and cook, stirring frequently, until just softened but not browned, 2 to 5 minutes.

2. Stir in the remaining fish sauce, broth, water, soy sauce, sugar, star anise, and cloves and bring to a simmer. Cover, reduce the heat to low, and simmer until the flavors have blended, about 10 minutes. Pour the broth through a fine-mesh strainer, discarding the solids in the strainer. (At this point, the soup can be refrigerated in an airtight container for up to 1 day.)

3. FOR THE NOODLES, MEAT, AND GARNISH: Bring 4 quarts of water to a boil in a large pot. Remove the boiling water from the heat, add the rice noodles, and let stand, stirring occasionally, until the noodles are tender but still chewy, about 10 minutes.

4. Drain the noodles, divide them evenly among 4 individual serving bowls, and top each with ½ cup of bean sprouts; set aside. Arrange the basil, cilantro, scallions, chile, and lime wedges attractively on a large serving platter; set aside.

5. Return the strained soup to a clean saucepan, bring to a simmer over medium-high heat, then reduce the heat to low. Add the beef and cook until no longer pink, about 1 minute (do not overcook). Remove the soup from the heat. Ladle the soup over the noodles and serve, passing the platter of garnishes separately.

VARIATION

VIETNAMESE RICE NOODLE SOUP WITH CHICKEN

Follow the recipe for Vietnamese Rice Noodle Soup with Beef, substituting 12 ounces boneless, skinless chicken breasts (about 2 medium breasts) for the beef. Add the chicken breasts to the broth in step 2 with the all of the remaining broth ingredients and simmer as directed until the thickest part of the chicken breast registers 160 degrees on an instant-read thermometer, 10 to 15 minutes. Remove the breasts from the broth before straining and shred into bite-sized pieces using two forks. Return the shredded chicken to the strained broth and reheat for 1 to 2 minutes over medium heat before serving as directed in step 5.

NOTES FROM THE TEST KITCHEN

MINCING LEMONGRASS

1. Trim and discard all but the bottom 5 inches of the lemongrass stalk.

2. Remove the tough outer sheath from the stalk. If the lemongrass is particularly thick or tough, remove several layers until you reveal the tender inner portion.

3. Cut the trimmed and peeled stalk in half lengthwise, then slice it thin crosswise.

FISH SAUCE

Fish sauce is a salty, amber-colored liquid made from salted, fermented fish. It is used both as an ingredient and a condiment in Southeast Asia. It has a very concentrated flavor, and adds a salty complexity to dishes that is impossible to replicate. Color correlates with flavor in fish sauce; the lighter the sauce, the lighter the flavor. If you are a fan of fish sauce and use it often, you might want to make a special trip to an Asian market to buy a rich, dark sauce that is suitably pungent (we particularly like **Tiparos** fish sauce, left). Most supermarkets don't carry a wide selection of fish sauce, we recommend buying whatever is available. That will most likely be **Thai Kitchen** (right), an Americanized brand found in most grocery stores, which was the lightest colored (and flavored) brand we tasted. Fish sauce will keep indefinitely without refrigeration.

QUICKER BEEF AND VEGETABLE SOUP

QUICKER BEEF VEGETABLE SOUP

GIVEN ENOUGH MEAT, BONES, AND TIME, a great beef soup isn't all that hard to make. But I often don't have the time, so when I want beef and vegetable soup in a hurry, I usually open a can of soup and complain about its lackluster flavor. But is this all-or-nothing approach really necessary? Could I collapse the two separate steps of making stock and then soup into one and develop bold beef flavor in just 60 minutes?

To get my bearings, I prepared several traditional recipes along with a handful of quick recipes. While every classic recipe yielded intense flavor, the quick soups were uniformly disappointing and lacked any real beef flavor. Most used either cubes of "stew meat"—a butcher's catchall for any relatively chunky scraps of beef—or more tender cuts like strip steak or rib eye. Although stew meat contributed a pleasant beefy flavor, it was barely chewable after simmering for half an hour. The strip and rib eye, though more tender, tasted livery and had a chalky, dry texture. My first and most important goal was to find a cut of meat that could give a quick beef and vegetable soup the same texture and flavor as one that cooked for hours.

Tasters praised the fall-apart tenderness of the shin meat in one of the recipes we tried, but it took hours to break down those tougher muscle fibers into anything remotely tender. I cooked through various cuts, hoping to find one with the same textural characteristics of the shin meat that would cook in a quarter of the time. I discovered that cuts with a loose, open grain—including hanger steak, flank steak, sirloin tip steak (or flap meat), and blade steak—had a shredded texture that fooled tasters into thinking I had cooked the meat for hours.

Of these four cuts, sirloin tip steaks offered the best balance of meaty flavor and tenderness. I just had to be careful how I cut the steaks—too large, and my soup seemed more like a stew; too small, and it resembled a watery chili. For six generous bowls of soup, I needed 1 pound of sirloin tip steaks cut into ½-inch pieces.

With the cut of beef settled, I now turned my attention to finding a way to fortify the flavor of store-bought broth. I tried reducing the broth, but when simmered by half, it turned ultrasalty. It was time to look to the vegetables for an answer.

Up to this point, I had been sticking to the basics: onions, carrots, and celery. Then I remembered that many recipes for French onion soup rely on mountains of caramelized onions to up the meaty flavor of the broth. The liquid and sugars released by the onions leave a rich brown coating on the pan, contributing a depth of flavor that onions simply simmered in the broth can't attain. When I tested this idea, tasters praised the added complexity and sweetness, but I still had a long way to go.

It was time to do some research into what constitutes beefy flavor. I discovered that beef flavor is accentuated by naturally occurring compounds called glutamates, which are found in numerous foods. Like salt, glutamates stimulate receptors on the tongue, making food taste richer and meatier. Mushrooms, it turns out, are high in glutamates—thinking they might help, I prepared soups with white button, portobello, cremini, and porcini mushrooms. Portobellos imparted an overly murky flavor, and earthy porcinis overwhelmed any beef flavor I had already developed. Utilitarian white buttons were OK but a bit bland. Cremini mushrooms were perfect, providing mushroom intensity without being obtrusive.

I wondered what other ingredients high in glutamates could do. Worcestershire sauce, Parmesan cheese rinds, and miso paste competed with the beefiness of the dish. Less-intense tomato paste and red wine boosted the soup's meaty notes, especially when I browned the tomato paste with the meat and then deglazed the caramelized pan drippings with the red wine.

Though soy sauce is especially high in glutamates, I feared it might overpower the soup. But, to my surprise, it enhanced the beef flavor. When I marinated the beef cubes with soy sauce for just 15 minutes, tasters commented on the improved flavor of the meat and also its softer texture.

I had now replicated the beef flavor of long-simmered soups but not the mouth-coating richness. This can only be created when collagen, the tough proteins in the meat and bones, breaks down into gelatin. Could I cheat and just add powdered gelatin instead? A tablespoon of gelatin softened in cold water and stirred into the finished soup provided the viscosity of traditional broths. This was an unlikely finish to a recipe that can stand up to soups that take hours to cook.

—DAVID PAZMIÑO, *Cook's Illustrated*

QUICKER BEEF AND VEGETABLE SOUP

SERVES 6

Choose whole sirloin tip steaks over ones that have been cut into small pieces for stir-fries. If sirloin tip steaks are unavailable, substitute blade or flank steak, removing any hard gristle or excess fat. Button mushrooms can be used in place of the cremini mushrooms, with some trade-off in flavor. Our preferred brand of beef broth is Pacific. If you like, add 1 cup of frozen peas, frozen corn, or frozen cut green beans during the last 5 minutes of cooking.

1   pound sirloin tip steaks, trimmed of excess fat and cut into ½-inch pieces (see note)

2   tablespoons soy sauce

1   teaspoon vegetable oil

1   pound cremini mushrooms, quartered

1   large onion, chopped (about 1½ cups)

2   tablespoons tomato paste

1   garlic clove, minced

½   cup red wine

4   cups beef broth (see note)

1¾   cups low-sodium chicken broth

4   carrots, peeled and cut into ½-inch pieces

2   celery ribs, cut into ½-inch pieces

1   bay leaf

1   tablespoon unflavored powdered gelatin

½   cup cold water

2   tablespoons minced fresh parsley

   Salt and pepper

1. Combine the beef and soy sauce in a medium bowl; set aside for 15 minutes.

2. Heat the oil in a large Dutch oven over medium-high heat until just smoking. Cook the mushrooms and onion, stirring frequently, until the onion pieces are brown and dark bits form on the pan bottom, 8 to 12 minutes. Transfer the vegetables to a bowl.

3. Add the beef to the Dutch oven and cook, stirring occasionally, until the liquid evaporates and the meat starts to brown, 6 to 10 minutes. Add the tomato paste and garlic; cook, stirring constantly, until aromatic, about 30 seconds. Add the wine, scraping the pan bottom with a wooden spoon to loosen any browned bits, and cook until syrupy, 1 to 2 minutes.

4. Add both broths, the carrots, celery, bay leaf, and browned mushrooms and onion; bring to a boil. Reduce the heat to low, cover, and simmer until the vegetables and meat are tender, 25 to 30 minutes. (At this point, the soup can be refrigerated in an airtight container for up to 2 days. When ready to serve, bring the soup to a simmer and proceed with the recipe.) While the soup is simmering, sprinkle the gelatin over the cold water and let stand.

5. When the soup is finished, turn off the heat. Remove the bay leaf. Add the gelatin mixture and stir until completely dissolved. Stir in the parsley. Season with salt and pepper to taste, and serve.

NOTES FROM THE TEST KITCHEN

BUILDING MEATY FLAVOR QUICKLY
These four glutamate-rich ingredients boosted meaty flavors in our quick soup.

MUSHROOMS
Sautéed cremini mushrooms begin to build flavor.

TOMATO PASTE
Thick tomato paste caramelizes in the pot to create more flavor.

RED WINE
Red wine helps loosen flavorful browned bits from the pan bottom.

SOY SAUCE
Strips of beef are marinated in soy sauce before being browned.

CREATING THE FLAVOR BASE

Brown the onions and cremini mushrooms before adding the beef, stirring frequently until the onions are really brown and dark bits form on the pan bottom.

MULLIGATAWNY

LITERALLY TRANSLATED to mean "pepper water," Mulligatawny is a pureed vegetable soup that is mildly spicy with a faint sweetness, usually from coconut, and is sometimes garnished with chicken or lamb. Unfortunately, this soup often falls far short of expectations, with poorly incorporated, raw-tasting spices, and an overly thin base.

In my quest to reclaim this velvety and flavorful soup, I started with its liquid base. My research indicated that chicken broth, lamb broth, beef broth, vegetable broth, and water were all possible choices. Tasters found vegetable broth too sweet and vegetal and beef broth too strong, even a bit sour. Lamb broth was overpowering and I ruled it out because of the work involved in making it. In the end, I decided that chicken broth was the ideal base for the wide range of spices and vegetables. Water made a tasty vegetarian soup that was not quite as rich as the versions made with chicken broth, but still acceptable.

Curry powder, a blend of spices sold in this country, is a central ingredient in most mulligatawny soups. After experimenting with several store-bought curry powders, I found the end product to be muted and muddy-tasting, so I decided to make my own. After a little tinkering, I found great results with a blend of garam masala, cumin, coriander, and turmeric.

I focused next on the aromatics—garlic and ginger—and on the coconut. After testing various amounts of garlic and ginger, I noted that equal amounts of both worked best. As for the coconut, some recipes called for coconut milk, others for fresh coconut meat, and still others added dried coconut. The coconut milk gave the soup a silky consistency, but the flavor tended to dominate the dish, while fresh coconut was not flavorful enough. Dried coconut was the best option, adding enough flavor to the soup without taking it over.

With the aromatics and spices under control it was time to focus on the vegetables. I tested onions, carrots, celery, cauliflower, spinach, and peas. I found that onions were a must, while carrots added color and sweetness and the celery provided a cool flavor that contrasted nicely with the hot spices. Cauliflower was rejected for the cabbage-like flavor it gave to the soup. Spinach and peas did little to enhance the soup's flavor and imparted an undesirable color when pureed.

Several recipes suggested using pureed rice or lentils to thicken the soup, and while tasters didn't oppose these flavors, they didn't like the thick, porridge-like texture they produced when pureed. I found that sprinkling a little flour over the sautéed aromatics gave the soup a thickened yet velvety consistency—silky and substantial but not heavy. Although a few sources said that pureeing the soup was optional, we think that mulligatawny must be mostly smooth, perhaps punctuated by a small amount of lentils, chicken, or lamb.

Returning to the idea of adding lentils to the soup—leaving them whole rather than pureeing them as a thickener—I experimented with adding them after the soup was pureed and tested several lentil varieties. Chana dal, also known as yellow split peas, imparted an overly earthy, vegetal flavor that didn't meld with the flavor of the soup. Red lentils all but disintegrated in the soup, leaving a grainy texture. I finally settled on standard brown lentils (or green French lentils), which held their shape when cooked and readily absorbed the surrounding flavors. A dollop of yogurt and shower of cilantro was all that was needed to finish this deeply flavorful and elegant soup.

—BRYAN ROOF, *America's Test Kitchen Books*

MULLIGATAWNY

SERVES 4 TO 6

Do not use red lentils because they turn very soft when cooked and will disintegrate into the soup.

- 2½ teaspoons garam masala
- 1½ teaspoons ground cumin
- 1½ teaspoons ground coriander
- 1 teaspoon ground turmeric
- 3 tablespoons unsalted butter
- 2 onions, minced (about 2 cups)
- ½ cup sweetened shredded or flaked coconut
- 4 garlic cloves, minced
- 4 teaspoons grated or minced fresh ginger
- 1 teaspoon tomato paste
- ¼ cup unbleached all-purpose flour
- 7 cups low-sodium chicken broth
- 2 carrots, peeled and chopped
- 1 celery rib, chopped
- ½ cup brown lentils, rinsed and picked over (see note)
  Salt and pepper
- 2 tablespoons minced fresh cilantro
  Plain yogurt, for serving

1. Combine the spices in a small bowl and set aside. Melt the butter in a large Dutch oven over medium heat. Sauté the spices until fragrant, about 10 seconds. Add the onions and coconut and cook until softened, 5 to 7 minutes. Stir in the garlic, ginger, and tomato paste and cook until fragrant, about 30 seconds. Stir in the flour until evenly combined, about 1 minute. Gradually whisk in the broth.

2. Stir in the carrots and celery, increase the heat to medium-high, and bring to a boil. Cover, reduce the heat to low, and simmer until the vegetables are tender, 20 to 25 minutes.

3. Puree the soup in a blender in batches until smooth and return to a clean pot. Add the lentils and return to a simmer over medium-high heat. Cover, reduce the heat to medium-low, and cook until the lentils are tender, about 40 minutes. (The soup can be refrigerated in an airtight container for up to 2 days.)

4. Season with salt and pepper to taste. Ladle the soup into individual bowls, sprinkle with the cilantro, and dollop with yogurt before serving.

VARIATIONS

MULLIGATAWNY WITH CHICKEN

Follow the recipe for Mulligatawny, adding 1½ pounds boneless, skinless chicken breasts, trimmed, to the pot with the vegetables in step 2 and simmer until cooked through, 20 to 25 minutes. With tongs, transfer the cooked chicken to a carving board, cool slightly, and cut crosswise into ¼-inch slices. Continue with the recipe, returning the sliced chicken to the pureed soup to reheat before seasoning in step 4.

MULLIGATAWNY WITH LAMB

You will need to buy 2 pounds leg of lamb in order to yield approximately 1½ pounds of trimmed lamb for the soup.

Follow the recipe for Mulligatawny, adding 1½ pounds trimmed boneless leg of lamb, cut into 1 by 1½-inch chunks, to the soup along with the lentils in step 3; simmer until both the lentils and lamb are tender, 40 to 45 minutes.

NOTES FROM THE TEST KITCHEN

GRATING GINGER SAFELY

Peel a small section of a large piece of ginger. Then grate the peeled portion, using the rest of the ginger as a handle.

BLOOMING SPICES

Blooming whole or ground spices in hot butter (or oil) for a few seconds not only deepens the flavor of the spices, as toasting does, but it also flavors the butter in which all the remaining ingredients will be cooked. To bloom spices, heat butter in a nonstick skillet over medium-high heat until the foaming subsides (or if using oil, heat until shimmering) and add all the spices together. Cook the spices while stirring or shaking the pan, until they become fragrant and their color turns a shade darker, about 10 seconds.

HEARTY TUSCAN BEAN STEW

WHEN I SET OUT TO MAKE a heartier stew version of Tuscany's classic white bean soup, I started with the most hotly contested issue in dried bean cookery: how long to soak beans before cooking. Some recipes swear that a lengthy soak leads to beans with a more tender, uniform texture. Others insist that a quick soak—an hour-long rest off the stove covered in just-boiled water—is best. In the past, our recipes have maintained that no soak at all can be the way to go.

I cooked up batches of beans using all three approaches. To my surprise, I found relatively minor differences. The biggest difference was in cooking time: The no-soak beans took 45 minutes longer to soften fully than the other two methods. But I was seeking perfection. And since the beans soaked overnight were, in fact, the most tender and evenly cooked of the bunch and had the least number of exploded beans, that's the method I settled on. But while the beans' interiors were creamy, their skins remained tough.

HEARTY TUSCAN BEAN STEW

Like length of soaking, when to add salt is another much-debated topic in bean cookery. The conventional wisdom is that salt added to beans at the beginning of cooking will prevent them from ever fully softening. Paradoxically, other advice maintains that salting beans too early can create a mushy texture. When I added salt to a batch of beans at the outset of cooking, I found it made some of the beans mealy. As beans cook, their starch granules swell with water, softening to a creamy texture and eventually bursting. The presence of salt in the cooking water causes the starch granules to swell less, so that fewer reach the point of bursting. The result: beans that have a lot of starch granules still intact. To me, the texture of such beans is mealy; others may call the same effect gritty.

Though the texture of the beans was now inferior, their skins were exactly what I wanted: soft and pliable. Was there a different way to use salt to get the same effect? My thoughts turned to brining, which we use in the test kitchen to help meat trap water and remain moist during cooking. I made a brine by dissolving a few tablespoons of salt in water and left the beans to soak overnight in the solution. The next day, I rinsed the beans thoroughly before proceeding with the recipe. My experiment was a success: The cannellini now boasted tender skins and buttery soft interiors. Why the change? When beans are soaked in salted water, rather than being cooked in it, not as much salt enters the beans. Its impact is confined mainly to the skins, where sodium ions interact with the cells to create a softer texture.

Although tasters were impressed with this technique, I knew that no Tuscan would stand for the number of exploded beans in the pot. I would need to simmer the beans very gently—with no perceptible bubbling and no stirring. I wondered if I might simply try cooking my beans in a 250-degree oven. I brought the beans and water to a simmer on the stovetop, then covered the pot and placed it in the oven. The result? Perfectly cooked beans that stayed intact.

With tender, creamy beans in my pot, it was time to work on the stew's other flavors. Salt-cured Italian bacon, or pancetta, is traditional in Tuscan white bean stew, lending depth and flavor. I still needed a few more ingredients to transform the dish into a one-pot meal. My tasters and I settled on chewy, earthy-tasting kale,

another Tuscan favorite, along with canned diced tomatoes, carrots, celery, onion, and lots of garlic. For extra richness, I replaced some of the water in the stew with chicken broth.

I sautéed all the vegetables (except the kale and tomatoes) with the pancetta, added the beans and water, and placed the stew in the oven. The acid in tomatoes can toughen beans, so I waited until the beans were sufficiently softened, about 45 minutes, before adding the tomatoes to the pot, along with the kale.

—CHARLES KELSEY, *Cook's Illustrated*

HEARTY TUSCAN BEAN STEW

SERVES 8

We prefer the creamier texture of beans soaked overnight for this recipe. If you're short on time, quick-soak them: Place the rinsed beans in a large heat-resistant bowl. Bring 2 quarts of water and 3 tablespoons of salt to a boil. Pour the water over the beans and let them sit for 1 hour. Drain and rinse the beans well before proceeding with step 2. If pancetta is unavailable, substitute 4 ounces of bacon (about 4 slices). For a more substantial dish, serve the stew over toasted bread.

Salt
1 pound dried cannellini beans (about 2 cups), rinsed and picked over
1 tablespoon extra-virgin olive oil, plus extra for drizzling
6 ounces pancetta, cut into ¼-inch pieces (see note)
1 large onion, chopped (about 1½ cups)
2 celery ribs, cut into ½-inch pieces
2 carrots, peeled and cut into ½-inch pieces
8 garlic cloves, peeled and crushed
4 cups low-sodium chicken broth
3 cups water
2 bay leaves
1 bunch kale or collard greens (about 1 pound), stems trimmed and leaves chopped into 1-inch pieces
1 (14.5-ounce) can diced tomatoes, drained and rinsed
1 sprig fresh rosemary
Pepper
8 slices country white bread, each 1¼ inches thick, broiled until golden brown on both sides and rubbed with a garlic clove (optional)

1. Dissolve 3 tablespoons salt in 4 quarts cold water in a large bowl or container. Add the beans and soak at room temperature for at least 8 hours and up to 24 hours. Drain and rinse well.

2. Adjust an oven rack to the lower-middle position and heat the oven to 250 degrees. Heat the oil and pancetta in a large Dutch oven over medium heat. Cook, stirring occasionally, until the pancetta is lightly browned and the fat has rendered, 6 to 10 minutes. Add the onion, celery, and carrots. Cook, stirring occasionally, until the vegetables are softened and lightly browned, 10 to 16 minutes. Stir in the garlic and cook until fragrant, about 1 minute. Stir in the broth, water, bay leaves, and soaked beans. Increase the heat to high and bring to a simmer. Cover the pot, transfer it to the oven, and cook until the beans are almost tender (the very center of the beans will still be firm), 45 minutes to 1 hour.

3. Remove the pot from the oven and stir in the greens and tomatoes. Return the pot to the oven and continue to cook until the beans and greens are fully tender, 30 to 40 minutes longer.

4. Remove the pot from the oven and submerge the rosemary sprig in the stew. Cover and let stand 15 minutes. Discard the bay leaves and rosemary sprig and season the stew with salt and pepper to taste. If desired, use the back of a spoon to press some of the beans against the side of the pot to thicken the stew. Serve over toasted bread, if desired, and drizzle with olive oil.

VARIATION

HEARTY TUSCAN BEAN STEW WITH SAUSAGE AND CABBAGE

This variation has much more meat and is made with crinkly Savoy cabbage.

Follow the recipe for Hearty Tuscan Bean Stew, substituting 1½ pounds sweet Italian sausage, casings removed, for the pancetta; ½ medium head Savoy cabbage, cut into 1-inch pieces, for the kale; and 1 sprig fresh oregano for the rosemary. Cook the sausage in the oil in step 2, breaking the meat into small pieces with a wooden spoon until it loses its raw color, about 8 minutes. Transfer the sausage to a paper towel–lined plate and place in the refrigerator. Proceed with the recipe as directed, stirring the sausage and cabbage into the stew along with the tomatoes in step 3.

NOTES FROM THE TEST KITCHEN

SIMMER DOWN

The bubbling action of stew simmered on the stovetop caused our beans to fall apart. Cooking the beans at a near-simmer in a covered pot in a 250-degree oven kept them intact.

SIMMERED ON THE STOVETOP	**NEAR-SIMMERED IN THE OVEN**

THE KEYS TO TENDER, FLAVORFUL BEANS

1. A SALTWATER SOAK: Soaking the beans in salt water overnight helps them cook up creamy, with tender skins.

2. A LOW-TEMPERATURE OVEN: Cooking the beans at a near-simmer in a 250-degree oven leads to fewer exploded beans in the finished stew.

3. WAIT TO ADD TOMATOES: The acid in tomatoes can interfere with the beans' tender texture. Add them toward the end of cooking, when the beans have softened.

THE SCIENCE OF BRINING BEANS

Why does soaking dried beans in salted water make them cook up with softer skins? It has to do with how the sodium ions in salt interact with the cells of the bean skins. As the beans soak, the sodium ions replace some of the calcium and magnesium ions in the skins. Because sodium ions are weaker than mineral ions, they allow more water to penetrate into the skins, leading to a softer texture. During soaking, the sodium ions will only filter partway into the beans, so their greatest effect is on the cells in the outermost part of the beans.

CALDO VERDE

CALDO VERDE

MY FAVORITE PORTUGUESE DISH is *caldo verde,* a thick, garlicky stew of greens and potatoes studded with spicy sausage. It's as simple as can be, but therein lies its appeal: Each flavor comes through loud and clear. But my own attempts at caldo verde at home never turn out very well. The greens taste tired, the garlic takes a backseat, and the sausage lacks the necessary kick. How do you make such a simple stew taste great?

Caldo verde is nothing without hearty greens. Traditionally, the green of choice is the deep forest green-colored *couve gallego,* a Galician cabbage native to the Iberian Peninsula. But since it's hard to find, I limited my tests to more available options: turnip greens, collard greens, Swiss chard, and kale. I added all the greens toward the end of the cooking process, hoping to avoid the bitter taste that can result from overcooking.

Turnip greens fared the worst. The characteristically tender leaves nearly fell apart and became slimy during their short bath in the broth. In addition, they imparted an unpleasant sour flavor that was impossible to ignore. Collard greens are somewhat less tender than turnip greens, and I predicted that they would perform better in the stew, but no such luck—no matter how I cut or cooked them. Tasters unanimously disliked tender swiss chard for its spinach-like flavor and texture, which seemed out of place in this stew.

And then there was the kale. With a coarser, more substantial texture than the other greens, it resisted wilting and provided a more forgiving window of time in which it could cook. The tender but by no means mushy greens also imparted a lovely sweet cabbage flavor to the stew that tasters loved.

I wanted a stew that didn't take all day to prepare, so using store-bought chicken broth as a base (well flavored with sautéed onions and garlic) was a given. But chicken broth and kale are only half the stew; I'd yet to tackle the sausage and potatoes. Caldo verde is defined by the inclusion of Portugal's trademark linguiça, a spicy, garlic-heavy pork sausage. But since it can be somewhat tricky to find, I wanted to find suitable alternatives. The closest options I could think of were chorizo (cured Spanish sausage links) and smoked Polish kielbasa. Tasted in the stew, the chorizo was right at home, providing plenty of deep, paprika-rich flavor. In fact, the stew made with a combination of earthy kale and hot, pungent chorizo won more praise than the stew prepared with linguiça! Caldo verde made with kielbasa was surprisingly good as well. Not quite as rich and full flavored as the other two options perhaps, but perfectly suitable.

Up to this point, I had been sautéing the sausage prior to adding it to the stew. I wondered if perhaps this muted the meat's flavor and unnecessarily toughened the meat. I was right: The stew tasted far better and the meat's texture was much more tender when I simply simmered it in the stew.

I turned my attention to the potatoes, which serve to thicken the otherwise brothy stew. Once the potatoes become tender, a portion—if not all—of them are mashed with the back of a spoon to create a hearty consistency. After tasting partially thickened and fully thickened versions, everybody most liked versions in which the potatoes were only partly smashed, leaving some chunks whole. Low-starch boiling potatoes, such as Red Bliss, worked best—even after vigorous boiling and coarse mashing, the potatoes held together. A number of recipes left the potatoes unpeeled, but I found that the soggy peels inevitably found their way onto a disappointed taster's spoon. Cutting the peeled potatoes into 1-inch chunks kept the cooking time to a minimum.

The stew now tasted great, but the short ingredient list made me think I had to have missed something. I reviewed all the recipes I had found and they were as brief as mine, though I did find a few that included herbs like bay leaves, thyme, oregano, and savory. I dutifully tested each, and tasters preferred the faint mint flavor of the savory (with oregano as a backup) but thought it became overpowering as they ate more of the stew. Instead of mincing the herb, I tried simmering a sprig of savory in the stew along with the sausage. After just 15 minutes, when the savory had given up just the right amount of flavor, I removed the sprig. My final recipe for caldo verde produced a stew that was simple, easy, and flavorful—what's not to love?

—BRIDGET LANCASTER, *America's Test Kitchen Books*

CALDO VERDE

SERVES 6

Using the right potatoes makes a tremendous difference in this recipe, so make sure to use Red Bliss potatoes.

- 2 tablespoons extra-virgin olive oil, plus extra for drizzling (optional)
- 1 onion, chopped (about 1 cup)
- 4 garlic cloves, minced
- 6 cups low-sodium chicken broth
- 1 pound Red Bliss potatoes (about 4 medium), peeled and cut into 1-inch pieces
  Salt
- 8 ounces chorizo, linguiça, or smoked kielbasa sausage, halved lengthwise and cut crosswise into ¼-inch pieces
- 1 sprig fresh savory or oregano
- 6 ounces kale, stems removed and leaves cut crosswise into ¼-inch strips (about 4½ packed cups)
  Pepper

1. Heat the oil in a large stockpot or Dutch oven over medium heat until shimmering. Add the onion and cook, stirring frequently, until softened, about 5 minutes. Add the garlic and cook until fragrant, about 30 seconds.

2. Add 3 cups of the broth, potatoes, and ½ teaspoon salt. Increase the heat to medium-high and bring to a boil. Reduce the heat and simmer until the potatoes are tender, about 15 minutes. (At this point, the soup can be refrigerated in an airtight container for up to 2 days. When ready to serve, bring the soup to a simmer and proceed with the recipe.) Remove the pot from the heat and mash the potatoes in the liquid with a potato masher until no large chunks remain and the potatoes thicken the stew slightly.

3. Return the pot to medium-high heat. Add the remaining 3 cups broth, sausage, and savory and bring to a boil. Reduce the heat to medium-low, cover, and simmer to blend the flavors, about 15 minutes.

4. Remove and discard the savory. Stir in the kale and simmer until just tender, about 5 minutes. Adjust the seasonings with salt and pepper to taste. Serve immediately, drizzling each portion with olive oil, if desired.

NOTES FROM THE TEST KITCHEN

SAUSAGE FOR CALDO VERDE
We taste-tested three types of sausage for caldo verde. Each has a different flavor profile, but all are acceptable.

LINGUIÇA
The Portuguese favorite; rich and garlicky

KIELBASA
Smoky and garlicky; less spicy

CHORIZO
Spicy and pungent; big paprika flavor

HANDLING KALE

1. Hold the stem of each leaf over a bowl filled with water and slash the leafy portion from either side of the thick stem. Discard the stems, then wash and dry the leaves.

2. Stack some leaves in a short pile, roll the leaves into a tight cylinder, and slice crosswise into strips ¼ inch wide.

CHILI CON CARNE

CHILI CON CARNE is a signature Tex-Mex stew that features large, tender chunks of beef, complex chile flavor and heat, a silky broth, and no beans. I wanted to create a simple, authentic-tasting version of this dish using supermarket ingredients.

I prepared an assortment of streamlined recipes (avoiding those that called for ground beef), and I was disheartened by the results. Most of these recipes simply threw chili powder and beef (or chicken) broth over browned meat, and the results were predictably watery and bland. I was going to have to start at the bottom—with the meat.

After some preliminary testing, I settled on using chuck; the test kitchen prefers this affordable cut for stews because its substantial marbling provides rich flavor and tender texture after prolonged cooking. To add a smoky meatiness to the chili, I browned the beef in bacon fat instead of plain oil.

Specialty dried chiles were out. Dumping in store-bought chili powder made for meek and dusty chili, but cooking the chili powder in the bacon fat brought out its complexity and richness. A little cumin, oregano, and garlic balanced out the flavors. I added fresh jalapeño for brightness and heat and minced chipotle (canned smoked jalapeño) for smoky, spicy depth. Surprisingly, my tasters preferred plain water to beef or chicken broth, as the broths muted the complex spice flavor. Although chili purists—especially in Texas—might disapprove, we found that modest amounts of onion and tomato were welcome additions.

The chili tasted great, but the texture wasn't thick and silky enough. Traditional recipes often call for stirring in corn flour (also known as masa harina) at the end of cooking to tighten the texture and add flavor, but I wanted to find a more readily available ingredient. Cornstarch thickened the chili but didn't add flavor. Cornmeal added flavor but lent a gritty texture. Softened and pureed corn tortillas tasted good but were a little grainy.

I scoured the grocery store shelves for another corn thickener before I finally saw it: corn muffin mix. Stirring the mix into some chili broth and cooking the mix-and-broth combination in the microwave produced a perfectly smooth and silky broth with plenty of fire and flavor in every bite.

—CALI RICH, *Cook's Country*

CHILI CON CARNE

SERVES 6 TO 8

If the bacon does not render a full 3 tablespoons of fat in step 1, supplement it with vegetable oil.

- 1 (14.5-ounce) can diced tomatoes
- 2 teaspoons minced canned chipotle chile in adobo sauce
- 4 slices bacon, chopped fine
- 1 (3½- to 4-pound) boneless beef chuck-eye roast, trimmed and cut into 1-inch pieces
  Salt and pepper
- 1 onion, minced (about 1 cup)
- 1 jalapeño chile, stemmed, seeded, and minced
- 3 tablespoons chili powder
- 1½ teaspoons ground cumin
- ½ teaspoon dried oregano
- 4 garlic cloves, minced
- 4 cups water
- 1 tablespoon brown sugar
- 2 tablespoons yellow corn muffin mix

1. Process the tomatoes and chipotle in a food processor until smooth. Cook the bacon in a Dutch oven over medium heat until crisp, about 8 minutes. Transfer the bacon to a paper towel–lined plate and reserve 3 tablespoons bacon fat.

2. Pat the beef dry with paper towels and season with salt and pepper. Heat 1 tablespoon of the reserved bacon fat in the now-empty Dutch oven over medium-high heat until just smoking. Brown half of the beef, about 8 minutes. Transfer to a bowl and repeat with an additional tablespoon bacon fat and the remaining beef.

3. Add the remaining 1 tablespoon bacon fat, onion, and jalapeño to the empty Dutch oven and cook until softened, about 5 minutes. Stir in the chili powder, cumin, oregano, and garlic and cook until fragrant, about 30 seconds. Stir in the water, pureed tomato mixture, bacon, browned beef, and sugar and bring to a boil. Reduce the heat to low and simmer, covered, for 1 hour. Skim the fat and continue to simmer uncovered until the meat is tender, 30 to 45 minutes.

4. Ladle 1 cup of the chili liquid into a medium bowl and stir in the muffin mix; cover with plastic wrap. Microwave until the mixture is thickened, about 1 minute. Slowly whisk the mixture into the chili and simmer until the chili is slightly thickened, 5 to 10 minutes. Season with salt and pepper to taste. Serve. (The chili can be refrigerated in an airtight container for up to 3 days.)

VEGETABLES & SIDE DISHES

GARLICKY OVEN FRIES

WHEN A PLATE OF FRENCH FRIES arrives at my table in a restaurant, I immediately pounce on the darkest morsels. Why? Because fries become darker when the sugar in the potato caramelizes and produces sweeter, more complex flavors. As an avowed garlic lover, I wanted to find a way to infuse dark, crunchy, homemade French fries with the nutty flavor of garlic.

Deep-frying at home is daunting and messy, so I turned to the test kitchen's recipe for making oven fries. Our method calls for oven-frying the cut potatoes on a well-oiled pan in a hot oven. For the first five minutes, the potatoes are cooked covered with foil to steam; then the foil is removed so the exterior can crisp up and the interior can cook through.

I tossed raw potatoes with fresh minced garlic and then followed this procedure, but the garlic burned by the time the fries cooked. Garlic added halfway through the cooking didn't provide enough flavor, and garlic added at the end was too harsh. How was I going to get rich, nutty garlic flavor into these fries?

I went to the spice rack in search of alternatives to fresh garlic. I tried sprinkling garlic salt, dehydrated garlic, and garlic powder on the fries before cooking. Predictably, the garlic salt was too salty and lent little garlic flavor, and the dehydrated garlic had an unpleasant texture. But the garlic powder showed promise: Although it didn't contribute enough fresh garlic flavor, it was at least making the potatoes subtly garlicky.

Looking to bump up the garlic flavor, I tried infusing the cooking oil with potent fresh garlic. I put a handful of minced garlic in a bowl, poured the oil on top, and heated it in the microwave to allow the garlic to perfume the oil. When I cooked the next batch in the infused oil, I was disappointed that the fries still didn't have the nutty, garlicky kick I was looking for.

But using the microwave to flavor the oil gave me an idea. Instead of covering the potatoes for the first part of baking, could I toss them with some of the infused oil and steam them in the microwave to achieve stronger garlic flavor (and get a jump start on the cooking)? I placed the raw cut potatoes in a bowl with some of the garlic oil, covered the bowl with plastic wrap, and microwaved them for five minutes. The potatoes emerged slightly softened and deeply enriched with garlic flavor. After tossing the spuds with garlic powder (and a little cornstarch for extra crunch) and baking them, the finished fries were as dark and crispy as deep-fried fries—with the added bonus of rich, nutty garlic flavor.

—GREG CASE, *Cook's Country*

GARLICKY OVEN FRIES

SERVES 4

Be sure to use potatoes of a similar size and cut them into even wedges so all of the pieces cook at the same rate. Traditional-finish and nonstick baking sheets both work well for this recipe.

- 6 **garlic cloves, minced**
- 6 **tablespoons vegetable oil**
- 3 **russet potatoes (about 8 ounces each), each cut into 12 wedges**
- 2 **tablespoons cornstarch**
- 1½ **teaspoons salt**
- ¾ **teaspoon pepper**
- ½ **teaspoon garlic powder**

1. Adjust an oven rack to the lowest position and heat the oven to 475 degrees. Combine the garlic and oil in a large bowl and microwave until the garlic is fragrant, about 1 minute. Transfer 5 tablespoons of the oil (leaving the garlic in the bowl) to a rimmed baking sheet, turning the sheet to coat.

2. Add the potatoes to the bowl with the remaining oil mixture and toss to coat. Wrap tightly with plastic wrap and microwave on high power until the potatoes are translucent around the edges, 3 to 6 minutes, shaking the bowl to redistribute the potatoes halfway through cooking.

3. Combine the cornstarch, salt, pepper, and garlic powder in a small bowl. Sprinkle over the hot potatoes and toss to coat. Arrange the potatoes in a single layer on the prepared baking sheet and bake, turning once, until deep golden brown and crisp, 30 to 40 minutes. Serve.

NOTES FROM THE TEST KITCHEN

GETTING GREAT GARLIC FLAVOR
We use this three-step process to give our crunchy oven fries maximum garlic flavor.

1. Make a garlic-infused oil by microwaving minced garlic and oil until fragrant.

2. Pour 5 tablespoons of the garlic oil onto a baking sheet and reserve. Toss the potato wedges with the remaining garlic-oil mixture and microwave until tender.

3. For a final layer of garlic flavor, toss the potato wedges with garlic powder (and cornstarch for extra crispness) before baking.

SWEET POTATO FRIES

UNTIL RECENTLY, I've been a French fry purist and never understood the appeal of trendier sweet potato fries. That changed about a year ago when a friend invited me to lunch at her neighborhood pub. Upon sitting down, she ordered her favorite "hot and sweets," and minutes later a basket arrived, piled high with orange fries tossed in a seasoned salt. The combination of the sweet, creamy interior and spicy crust was irresistible. And while my previous encounters with sweet potato fries had ended in soggy disappointment, these were really crisp.

Sweet potatoes obviously have more sugar than regular potatoes, but they also have more moisture, which creates steam—the enemy of crispness. What was the secret to those memorable pub fries?

To create my own recipe, I began with the classic French fry method, wherein the potatoes are first fried in 325-degree oil to gently cook them through without browning. The fries are then removed from the pot and rested for 10 minutes; during this rest, the natural starches in the potato form a thin film on the fries. When the potatoes are fried again at a more aggressive 375 degrees, the starchy coating browns and turns into a crisp, crunchy exterior. Sweet potato fries prepared this way emerged from the oil slightly crisp, but turned soggy by the time I could serve them.

Hoping to rid the sweet potatoes of excess water, I tried dehydrating them for up to an hour in a low-temperature oven before frying. This step only worked to toughen the fries and added no crispness. Instead of trying to remove moisture, what about adding a coating that would crisp during frying and stand up to the potatoes' moisture-rich interior?

Most of the coatings I tried yielded a greasy, thick exterior that masked the sweet potato flavor and looked odd. A tempura-style batter with water, egg, and cornstarch was a step in the right direction, but the coating was still too thick and flaked off easily. Wanting something lighter and less easily detected, I omitted the egg and replaced the water with club soda. The bubbles in the carbonated water kept the cornstarch from clumping and helped to create a starchy coating similar to what forms on French fries between frying sessions. What about the finished fries? They were crisp, and no one could detect any taste other than sweet potato. Even more important, the crust stayed unbelievably crisp for up to 15 minutes while I rounded up tasters.

I had one last test. Did I need to stick with double-frying—the standard method for making regular fries—or did my cornstarch coating make this step unnecessary? I was pleasantly surprised to find that there was no benefit to double-frying here. When combined with my cornstarch coating, a straightforward single fry at 375 degrees produced perfectly cooked, crisp fries.

I wanted to create a spicy salt to accentuate the sweetness of the potatoes. After a little trial and error, I concocted a mixture of chili powder, garlic powder, cayenne, and salt that had my tasters battling for every last fry.

—CALI RICH, *Cook's Country*

CRISPY SWEET POTATO FRIES

CRISPY SWEET POTATO FRIES

SERVES 4

To prevent the sweet potatoes from turning brown, do not cut them until ready to use. In step 2, place a layer of paper towels under the wire rack to collect any drippings; alternatively, place the wire rack over the sink. The sweet potatoes are fried in two batches to prevent overcrowding the pot, which can lead to a reduction in oil temperature and uneven cooking. To make ahead, follow the recipe through step 2 and freeze the coated sweet potatoes on a wire rack set over a rimmed baking sheet until just set, about 15 minutes. Transfer to a zipper-lock storage bag for up to 1 month. When ready to serve, proceed with step 3 (the fries might take a minute or two more to become golden brown and crisp).

- 1 teaspoon salt
- ½ teaspoon chili powder
- ½ teaspoon garlic powder
- ½ teaspoon cayenne pepper
- 2 quarts peanut or vegetable oil
- 1 cup cornstarch
- ¾ cup club soda, chilled
- 2 pounds sweet potatoes (about 3 medium), peeled and cut into ½-inch by ¼-inch lengths

1. Adjust an oven rack to the middle position and heat the oven to 200 degrees. Combine the salt, chili powder, garlic powder, and cayenne in a large bowl.

2. Heat the oil in a large Dutch oven over high heat to 375 degrees. While the oil is heating, whisk the cornstarch and club soda in a medium bowl. Working in small batches, dip the sweet potatoes in the cornstarch mixture, allowing the excess to drip back into the bowl, and transfer to a wire rack.

3. When the oil is ready, fry half of the sweet potatoes, stirring occasionally, until golden brown and crisp, 6 to 8 minutes. Drain the fries on a paper towel–lined baking sheet and transfer to the oven. Return the oil to 375 degrees and repeat with the remaining fries. Transfer the crisp fries to the bowl with the spice mixture and toss to coat. Serve.

NOTES FROM THE TEST KITCHEN

CUTTING THE SWEET POTATOES

For evenly cut fries, we first cut the sweet potato into slices and then cut the slices into thin fries. Because sweet potatoes are irregularly shaped, some of the edge pieces will invariably be smaller and will crisp faster in the oil; this adds welcome textural contrast to the fries.

1. To stabilize the sweet potato for slicing, cut a ¼-inch piece from the bottom of each sweet potato so that it stands flat.

2. Cut the sweet potatoes into ½-inch-thick planks.

3. Cut each plank into ¼-inch-thick fries.

BAKED POTATO FANS

BAKED POTATO FANS were popularized as Hasselback potatoes, the namesake dish of the restaurant at the Hasselbacken Hotel in Stockholm, Sweden. American recipes stay true to the original concept by combining the fluffy interior of a baked potato with the crisp, golden exterior of an oven fry—all with that distinctive, fanned-out presentation.

The fanning is accomplished by slicing almost all the way through a whole potato crosswise along its length at ¼-inch intervals, leaving the bottom of the potato intact and allowing the slices to gently fan open like an accordion as the potato bakes. The skin crisps while the fans create openings into which seasonings, cheese, and breadcrumbs can be sprinkled before a final pass in the oven.

Most recipes would have you believe that baked potato fans can be made with any type of potato. I learned that was definitely not the case after trying waxy red potatoes, which dried out in the oven, and Yukon Golds, which were better but still too dry. The russet, or Idaho, potato was the right choice here, as its starchy flesh translated into a fluffy texture when baked.

Working with the russets, I cut ¼-inch crosswise slices down the length of each potato, trying to leave the bottom intact to hold the slices together. This was hard to do if the bottom of the potato wasn't almost perfectly flat. Following the lead of one astute recipe, I sliced the bottom from each potato, which gave me a flat surface to work with, and placed a chopstick on either side to prevent my knife from slicing all the way through. I brushed the potatoes with oil and baked them. But after all that work, they barely fanned out. The slices were stuck together. The skin had also developed a leathery texture by the time the inside was cooked through. I tackled the sticky fans first. Excess starch exposed to the oven heat was creating a tacky seal and causing the fans to stick together. I found that taking the time to rinse the potatoes of that surface starch after they were sliced prevented them from sticking together. Even better, taking a slice off each end of the potato gave the remaining slices more room to fan out as they baked, allowing even more heat to penetrate and crisp their surfaces.

I was pleased that my potatoes now looked like little accordions; it was time to fix the tough, overcooked exteriors. Rather than relying entirely on the dry and sometimes punishing heat of the oven, I precooked the potatoes in the microwave and then moved them to the oven to finish cooking through and crisp up their skins. Brushing the potatoes with seasoned oil before baking not only added flavor, but it also helped crisp their skins further.

Most recipes sprinkle the potatoes with a topping of grated cheese, breadcrumbs, and seasonings during the last few minutes of baking. Cheddar cheese was too greasy, but a combination of Parmesan (for nutty flavor) and Monterey Jack (because it melts well) was perfect.

Store-bought breadcrumbs were too sandy, but home-made crumbs stayed moist in the oven, especially with a little melted butter added. Fresh garlic didn't have enough time to cook and mellow, but garlic powder (mixed with some sweet paprika) worked nicely. As a final step, I broiled the potatoes to make the topping irresistibly crunchy.

—KELLEY BAKER, *Cook's Country*

BAKED POTATO FANS

SERVES 4

To ensure that the potatoes fan out evenly, look for uniformly shaped potatoes. If desired, sprinkle with chives before serving.

BREADCRUMB TOPPING

- 1 slice high-quality white sandwich bread, torn into pieces
- 4 tablespoons (½ stick) unsalted butter, melted
- 2 ounces Monterey Jack cheese, shredded (about ½ cup)
- ¼ cup grated Parmesan cheese
- 1 teaspoon paprika
- ½ teaspoon garlic powder
   Salt and pepper

POTATO FANS

- 4 russet potatoes
- 2 tablespoons extra-virgin olive oil
   Salt and pepper

1. FOR THE BREADCRUMB TOPPING: Adjust an oven rack to the middle position and heat the oven to 200 degrees. Pulse the bread in a food processor to coarse crumbs. Transfer the crumbs to a baking sheet and bake until light golden and crisp, about 20 minutes. Let cool 5 minutes, then combine the crumbs, butter, cheeses, paprika, garlic powder, ¼ teaspoon salt, and ¼ teaspoon pepper in a large bowl. (The breadcrumb topping can be refrigerated in a zipper-lock bag for 2 days.)

2. FOR THE POTATO FANS: Heat the oven to 450 degrees. Following the photos on page 59, cut ¼ inch from the bottom and ends of the potatoes, then slice the potatoes crosswise at ¼-inch intervals, leaving ¼ inch of the potato intact. Gently rinse the potatoes under running water, let drain, and transfer, sliced-side down, to a plate. Microwave until slightly soft to the touch, 6 to 12 minutes, flipping the potatoes halfway through cooking.

3. Arrange the potatoes, sliced-side up, on a foil-lined baking sheet. Brush the potatoes all over with the oil and season with salt and pepper. Bake until the skin is crisp and the potatoes are beginning to brown, 25 to 30 minutes. Remove the potatoes from the oven and heat the broiler.

4. Carefully top the potatoes with the reserved topping mixture, pressing gently to adhere. Broil until the breadcrumbs are deep golden brown, about 3 minutes. Serve.

VARIATION

BAKED POTATO FANS WITH BLUE CHEESE AND BACON

Follow the recipe for Baked Potato Fans substituting ⅓ cup crumbled blue cheese for the Monterey Jack. In step 4, sprinkle 4 slices bacon, cooked until crisp and crumbled, over the potatoes just prior to serving.

NOTES FROM THE TEST KITCHEN

PREPPING BAKED POTATO FANS

These potatoes may look difficult to make, but we found a few simple, no-fuss tricks ensure perfect potato fans every time.

1. Trim ¼-inch slices from the bottom and ends of each potato to allow them to sit flat and to give the slices extra room to fan out during baking.

2. Chopsticks provide a foolproof guide for slicing the potato petals without cutting all the way through the potato.

3. Gently flex the fans open while rinsing under cold running water; this rids the potatoes of excess starch that can impede fanning.

GRILLED POTATOES

THE TEST KITCHEN'S ESTABLISHED TECHNIQUE for grilling potatoes needs no improvement: Halve and skewer small red potatoes, parboil them, brush them with olive oil, and then quickly place them on the hot grill. Besides yielding perfectly cooked potatoes—charred (not burnt) exteriors, smooth and creamy interiors, and plenty of smoky flavor—the skewers hold them together, allowing for hassle-free transfer from pot to grill to serving platter.

Seeing as there are no finer complements for potatoes than garlic and rosemary, I decided to see if I could incorporate this combination into our recipe. Coating the potatoes with oil, garlic, and rosemary prior to grilling seemed too easy, and it was: The garlic burned and became bitter, and the rosemary charred. I tried tossing the potatoes in the oil after they came off the grill, but the raw garlic was too harsh. Tasters winced.

Clearly, this was going to take some experimenting. One of my first ideas was to add crushed garlic cloves and rosemary sprigs to the water in which the potatoes were parboiled, hoping the potatoes would drink up their flavors. Hardly.

Switching gears, I decided to precook the skewered potatoes in the microwave. I brushed the potatoes with oil to prevent sticking, seasoned them with salt, microwaved them, and threw them on the grill. Although their texture was firmer and their skins saltier than when parboiled, the interiors remained unseasoned. Piercing each potato prior to microwaving encouraged the salt on the skin to migrate to the inside.

Now all I needed was to find a bold way to deliver the garlic and rosemary flavors. I slowly cooked 9 cloves of garlic and 1 teaspoon of rosemary in ¼ cup of oil, then brushed the potatoes with this mixture prior to microwaving. But I didn't stop there. I brushed them with the infused oil again before grilling, and I tossed the potatoes with the garlic-and-rosemary oil yet again before serving. This repeated contact resulted in the potent flavor I was searching for.

—KEITH DRESSER, *Cook's Illustrated*

GRILLED POTATOES WITH GARLIC AND ROSEMARY

SERVES 4

This recipe allows you to grill an entree while the hot coals burn down in step 1. Once that item is done, start grilling the potatoes. This recipe works best with small potatoes that are about 1½ inches in diameter. If using medium potatoes, 2 to 3 inches in diameter, cut the potatoes into quarters. If the potatoes are larger than 3 inches in diameter, cut each potato into eighths. Since the potatoes are cooked in the microwave, use wooden skewers.

Vegetable oil for the cooking grate
4 tablespoons olive oil
9 garlic cloves, minced
1 teaspoon chopped fresh rosemary
Kosher salt
2 pounds small Red Bliss potatoes (about 18), halved and skewered (see note)
Pepper
Disposable 13 by 9-inch aluminum roasting pan
2 tablespoons chopped fresh chives

1. Light a large chimney starter filled with charcoal briquettes (about 100 briquettes) and allow it to burn until all the charcoal is covered with a layer of fine gray ash, about 20 minutes. Empty the coals into the grill; build a two-level fire by arranging two-thirds of the coals over half of the grill and arranging the remaining coals in a single layer over the other half. Position the cooking grate over the coals, cover the grill, and heat the grate until hot, about 5 minutes; scrape the grate clean with a grill brush. Remove the lid and let the coals burn until the fire on the hotter part of the grill is medium (you can hold your hand 5 inches above the grate for 5 to 6 seconds), about 10 minutes. Dip a wad of paper towels in vegetable oil; holding the wad with tongs, wipe the cooking grate.

2. Meanwhile, heat the olive oil, garlic, rosemary, and ½ teaspoon salt in a small skillet over medium heat until sizzling, about 3 minutes. Reduce the heat to medium-low and continue to cook until the garlic is light blond, about 3 minutes. Pour the mixture through a fine-mesh strainer into a small bowl; press on the solids. Measure 1 tablespoon of the solids and 1 tablespoon oil into a large bowl and set aside. Discard the remaining solids but reserve the remaining oil.

3. Place the skewered potatoes in a single layer on a large microwave-safe plate and poke each potato several times with a skewer. Brush with 1 tablespoon strained oil and season liberally with salt. Microwave on high power until the potatoes offer slight resistance when pierced with the tip of a paring knife, about 8 minutes, turning them halfway through the cooking time. Transfer the potatoes to a baking sheet coated with 1 more tablespoon strained oil. Brush with the remaining tablespoon strained oil; season with salt and pepper to taste.

4. Place the potatoes on the hotter side of the grill. Cook, turning once, until grill marks appear, about 4 minutes. Move the potatoes to the cooler side of the grill; cover with the disposable pan and continue to cook until a paring knife slips in and out of the potatoes easily, 5 to 8 minutes longer. Remove the potatoes from the skewers and transfer to a bowl with the reserved garlic-oil mixture; add the chives and toss until thoroughly coated. Serve immediately.

VARIATION

POTATOES WITH GARLIC AND ROSEMARY ON A GAS GRILL

Follow the recipe for Grilled Potatoes with Garlic and Rosemary, skipping step 1. Turn all the burners to high, cover, and heat the grill until very hot, about 15 minutes. Use a grill brush to scrape the grill clean; oil the cooking grate. Proceed with the recipe from step 2, leaving the primary burner on high and reducing the other burner(s) to medium. Grill the potatoes, omitting the disposable pan, with the lid down.

NOTES FROM THE TEST KITCHEN

SKEWERING POTATOES FOR THE GRILL

Place the potato half cut-side down on the work surface and pierce through the center with a skewer. Repeat, holding already-skewered potatoes for better leverage.

GRILLED POTATOES WITH GARLIC AND ROSEMARY

MASHED POTATO CASSEROLE

THE APPEAL OF A CASSEROLE made with mashed potatoes is considerable, with the promise of fluffy, buttery, creamy potatoes nestled under a savory golden crust. And with all the mashing and mixing done beforehand, it's the perfect convenience dish during the holiday season—you can prepare this casserole a day in advance and just pop it in the oven before mealtime. But upon making several existing recipes, I found that most simply threw mashed potatoes into a casserole dish and baked them in the oven. The results were bland, gluey, dense potatoes that were definitely not worth the convenience.

To fix this recipe, I focused first on the choice of potato. I prepared casseroles with russet, Yukon Gold, and all-purpose potatoes and determined that russets were the least heavy of the lot. Heavy cream was much too rich for this dish, but whole milk tasted too lean. I split the difference with half-and-half, which helped to lighten the dish, but tasters weren't happy until I cut the half-and-half with chicken broth, which kept the potatoes moist and provided an even lighter texture.

Taking a cue from shepherd's pie (another recipe where mashed potatoes are baked), I tried beating eggs into the potato mixture. An egg or two helped a little, but it wasn't until I added four that I achieved the fluffy, airy texture I wanted. And since the potatoes were rising in the dish, the top crust was browning even better than before.

We usually like to mash potatoes with a potato ricer to guarantee a uniform, lump-free consistency, but since I had broken out my hand-held mixer to beat the eggs into the potatoes, I wondered if I could simplify things by using it to mash the potatoes. In the past, the test kitchen has found that hand-held mixers make mashed potatoes gluey, but that wasn't an issue here, because the eggs gave the casserole an airy lift.

Some recipes season the mashed potatoes with ingredients like dried mustard and thyme, but we preferred the sharpness of Dijon mustard and fresh garlic. Not only was this dish easy to make ahead of time, but my tasters agreed that these potatoes—with their creamy, light interior and crisp, brown crust—were now the star of the holiday table.

—MEREDITH BUTCHER, *Cook's Country*

MASHED POTATO CASSEROLE

SERVES 6 TO 8

The casserole may also be baked in a 13 by 9-inch pan. The baking dish with the potatoes can be covered with plastic and refrigerated for up to 24 hours. When ready to bake, let the casserole sit at room temperature for 1 hour. Increase the baking time by 10 minutes.

- 4 pounds russet potatoes (about 8 medium), peeled and cut into 1-inch chunks
- ½ cup half-and-half
- ½ cup low-sodium chicken broth
- 12 tablespoons (1½ sticks) unsalted butter, cut into pieces
- 1 garlic clove, minced
- 2 teaspoons Dijon mustard
- 2 teaspoons salt
- 4 large eggs
- ¼ cup finely chopped fresh chives

1. Adjust an oven rack to the upper-middle position and heat the oven to 375 degrees. Bring the potatoes and water to cover by 1 inch to a boil in a large pot over high heat. Reduce the heat to medium and simmer until the potatoes are tender, about 20 minutes.

2. Heat the half-and-half, broth, butter, garlic, mustard, and salt in a saucepan over medium-low heat until smooth, about 5 minutes. Keep warm.

3. Drain the potatoes and transfer them to a large bowl. With an electric mixer on medium-low speed, beat the potatoes, slowly adding the half-and-half mixture until smooth and creamy, about 1 minute. Scrape down the bowl; beat in the eggs 1 at a time until incorporated, about 1 minute. Fold in the chives.

4. Transfer the potato mixture to a greased 2-quart baking dish. Bake until the potatoes rise and begin to brown, about 35 minutes. Let cool 10 minutes. Serve.

ROASTED BROCCOLI

WHILE I'M A FAN of the concentrated flavor and dappled browning that roasting lends vegetables, I'd never considered broccoli a suitable candidate. Its awkward shape, tough stems, and shrubby florets seemed ill suited for cooking via high, dry heat; moist cooking methods better accommodate its idiosyncrasies. However, there are plenty of people who do consider broccoli fit for roasting and wax poetic about the results.

Though skeptical, I roasted a bunch, following one of the recipes I had collected for the task. It tasted good—good enough to eat straight from the sizzling pan. That said, this recipe and the others I tried still had their flaws. First of all, none clearly addressed how best to prepare the broccoli for roasting. How big, for example, should you cut florets from the crown, and what should be done with the stalk to ensure that it cooked at the same rate? Second, except for the broccoli in direct contact with the baking sheet, browning was spotty. And last, the florets tended to char and taste bitter.

If contact with the baking sheet was the key to browning, I thought I'd try to cut the broccoli in a fashion that maximized this contact. I tackled the crown first, lopping it off the stalk, flipping it on its base, and cutting it crosswise into slabs. The cross sections fell apart into a jumble of odd-sized pieces that cooked unevenly. Perhaps wedges would work. I sliced another crown in half, then cut each half into uniform wedges that lay flat on the baking sheet—much more promising. Turning my attention to the stalk, I sliced off the tough exterior, then cut the stalk into rectangular pieces slightly smaller than the more delicate wedges to help promote even cooking of both parts.

The most successful recipes from my initial survey dressed the broccoli simply, with salt, pepper, and a splash of extra-virgin olive oil. A 500-degree oven delivered the best browning, but it also increased the risk of charred florets. A couple of recipes blanched or steamed the broccoli before roasting, but I found these batches tasted bland, as if the flavor had been washed away. Eventually, I discovered that a preheated baking sheet cooked the broccoli in half the time and crisped the florets without any charring.

But despite the blazing heat and the fact that I had solved the problem of charred florets, the broccoli still wasn't as browned as I'd hoped. Would a little sugar help the cause? I tossed a scant ½ teaspoon of sugar over the broccoli along with the salt and pepper, and the results were the best yet: blistered, bubbled, and browned stems that were sweet and full, along with crispy-tipped florets that tasted even better, especially when dressed with a spritz of lemon juice.

—MATTHEW CARD, *Cook's Illustrated*

ROASTED BROCCOLI

SERVES 4

Trim away the outer peel from the broccoli stalk, otherwise it will turn tough when cooked. For Roasted Broccoli with Garlic, stir 1 tablespoon minced garlic into the olive oil before drizzling it over the broccoli.

- 1 large head broccoli (about 1¾ pounds)
- 3 tablespoons extra-virgin olive oil
- ½ teaspoon salt
- ½ teaspoon sugar
- Pepper
- Lemon wedges, for serving

1. Adjust an oven rack to the lowest position, place a large rimmed baking sheet on the rack, and heat the oven to 500 degrees. Cut the broccoli at the juncture of the florets and stems; remove the outer peel from the stalk. Cut the stalk into 2- to 3-inch lengths and each length into ½-inch-thick pieces. Cut the crowns into 4 wedges if 3 to 4 inches in diameter, or 6 wedges if 4 to 5 inches in diameter. Place the broccoli in a large bowl; drizzle with the oil and toss well until evenly coated. Sprinkle with the salt, sugar, and pepper to taste and toss to combine.

2. Working quickly, remove the baking sheet from the oven. Carefully transfer the broccoli to the baking sheet and spread it into an even layer, placing it flat sides down. Return the baking sheet to the oven and roast until the stalks are well browned and tender and the florets are lightly browned, 9 to 11 minutes. Transfer to a serving dish and serve immediately with lemon wedges.

VARIATIONS

ROASTED BROCCOLI WITH OLIVES, GARLIC, OREGANO, AND LEMON

- 1 recipe Roasted Broccoli
- 2 tablespoons extra-virgin olive oil
- 5 garlic cloves, sliced thin
- ½ teaspoon red pepper flakes
- 2 tablespoons minced pitted black olives
- 1 teaspoon minced fresh oregano
- 2 teaspoons fresh lemon juice

Follow the recipe for Roasted Broccoli, omitting the pepper. While the broccoli roasts, heat the oil, garlic, and pepper flakes in an 8-inch skillet over medium-low heat. Cook, stirring frequently, until the garlic is soft and beginning to turn light golden brown, 5 to 7 minutes. Remove the skillet from the heat; stir in the olives, oregano, and lemon juice. Toss the roasted broccoli with the olive mixture and serve immediately.

ROASTED BROCCOLI WITH SHALLOTS, FENNEL SEEDS, AND PARMESAN

- 1 recipe Roasted Broccoli
- 1 tablespoon extra-virgin olive oil
- 2 large shallots, halved and sliced thin lengthwise (about ½ cup)
- 1 teaspoon fennel seeds, roughly chopped
- 1 ounce Parmesan, shaved (about ½ cup)

Follow the recipe for Roasted Broccoli. While the broccoli roasts, heat the oil in an 8-inch skillet over medium heat until just shimmering. Add the shallots and cook, stirring frequently, until soft and beginning to turn light golden brown, 5 to 6 minutes. Add the fennel seeds and continue to cook until the shallots are golden brown, 1 to 2 minutes longer. Remove the skillet from the heat. Toss the roasted broccoli with the shallots, sprinkle with the Parmesan, and serve immediately.

NOTES FROM THE TEST KITCHEN

FLAVOR BOOST FOR BROCCOLI
Tossing the broccoli with a little sugar before roasting helps it brown more evenly and taste even better.

ROASTED BROCCOLI

BRAISED VEGETABLES

BRAISING WORKS WELL either with vegetables that are too fibrous to eat raw or, more typically, with hearty vegetables such as leeks, fennel, or endive that won't fall apart when cooked. At their best, braised vegetables are sweet and tender, with a deeply caramelized exterior. Unfortunately, as with just about every simple dish, bad versions of braised vegetables abound. Leeks that have been cooked too long, until mushy, or caramelized too aggressively, leaving behind a bitter flavor, are common. I set out to avoid these pitfalls, starting first with the goal of developing a recipe for braised leeks that would also work for braised endive and fennel.

Here in the United States, leeks are usually reserved for soup or building a flavor base for other dishes. But their unique, onion-like sweetness makes them a delicious side dish and in France they are often braised (a dish known as *poireaux braise*), which enhances their delicate flavor. Looking like giant scallions, leeks are related to both garlic and onion, though their flavor and fragrance are milder and more subtle.

My first action was to better acquaint myself with the best leeks for braising. Leeks come in all sizes (larger ones are more suitable to braising), but in most stores they are bundled together without regard to size. To ensure even cooking times, I made my own bundles of same-size leeks. I also tried to buy the leeks with the longest white stems, the most tender and useable part of a leek.

Don't be fooled by supermarkets that sell leeks that are already trimmed down to the lighter base part. While this may seem like a good deal because you aren't paying for the upper leaves, which are discarded anyway, the truth is that the actual purpose of this procedure is to trim away aging leaves and make tough, old leeks look fresher to the unwary consumer. The bottom line: hand-select your leeks and try to find a store that sells them untrimmed. Once you get them home, trimming is essential because it is the only way to expose the many layers of the leek and clean it properly. Instead of following the often-recommended technique of slicing off the leaves right where they lighten into the white base of the leek, I found I could move about 2 inches upward into the leaves, to the point at which the light green part turns dark green.

Next I focused on technique. I browned both the cut side and the rounded side of all our leek halves and proceeded with the braise. The resulting braise was flavorful, but handling the leeks so much made them much more vulnerable to falling apart and I wanted them to remain whole for a nice presentation. To avoid handling them so much, I then tried browning the leeks on the cut side only, pouring the braising liquid over the leeks once browned. To compensate for only browning one side, I tried sprinkling a little sugar into the pan before adding the leeks to help the caramelization and this worked—the leeks caramelized to a deeper brown, which resulted in a sauce with richer flavor.

I continued my testing by exploring braising liquids. Water, a common choice, had few supporters among our tasters. Cream was too rich and cider too seasonal for a year-round recipe. White wine made the dish too acidic, and while chicken broth tasted deep and round, it obscured the flavor of the leeks. The ideal balance turned out to be a mixture of equal parts white wine and chicken broth, which produced deep yet brightly flavored leeks that retained a hint of oniony flavor. I added some fresh thyme leaves and then reduced the braising liquid to make a light sauce after the leeks finished cooking.

However, the delicate leeks suffered in the blast of high heat necessary to reduce the braising liquid, so I removed them once they were finished cooking and tented them with foil to keep them warm. With the leeks safely on the serving platter, I was able to crank up the heat and reduce the braising liquid, which came together in just a couple of minutes. A tablespoon of butter and a little lemon juice rounded out the flavors of the sauce and minced parsley added color. Less than 30 minutes of effort resulted in an elegant and satisfying side dish.

—SARAH WILSON, *America's Test Kitchen Books*

BRAISED LEEKS

SERVES 4

We prefer to use large leeks for this recipe; the diameter of each leek should be about 1 inch and you should trim it to be about 6 inches in length in order to fit easily in the skillet. When prepping the leeks, be sure to trim only the dangling roots from the root end, leaving the rest of the root intact to hold the layers together. To check the browning progress, grasp the root ends gingerly with tongs and peek underneath the cut side. You will need a skillet with a tight-fitting lid for this recipe.

- 3 tablespoons unsalted butter
- ½ teaspoon sugar
- Salt
- 4 large leeks, white and light green parts only, root ends trimmed (see note) and halved lengthwise
- ¼ cup dry white wine
- ¼ cup low-sodium chicken broth
- ½ teaspoon minced fresh thyme
- 1 tablespoon minced fresh parsley (optional)
- 1 teaspoon fresh lemon juice
- Pepper

1. Melt 2 tablespoons of the butter in a 12-inch non-stick skillet over medium-high heat. Sprinkle the sugar and ¼ teaspoon salt evenly over the bottom of the skillet and add the leeks, cut side down, in a single layer. Cook, shaking the skillet occasionally, until golden brown, about 5 minutes, adjusting the heat as needed if browning too quickly.

2. Add the wine, broth, and thyme. Reduce the heat to low, cover, and simmer until the leeks lose their vibrant color, turn translucent, and a paring knife inserted into the root end meets little resistance, about 10 minutes.

3. Gently transfer the leeks to a warmed serving platter, leaving the liquid in the skillet; cover the leeks and set aside. Return the liquid to a simmer over medium high heat and cook until it has a syrupy sauce consistency, 1 to 2 minutes. Off the heat, whisk in the remaining tablespoon butter, parsley (if using), and lemon juice and season with salt and pepper to taste. Spoon the sauce over the leeks and serve immediately.

VARIATIONS
BRAISED ENDIVE
Both red and green endive work well here.

Follow the recipe for Braised Leeks, increasing the amount of sugar to 1 teaspoon and reducing the amount of lemon juice to ½ teaspoon. Substitute 4 heads endive, trimmed and halved lengthwise, for the leeks; increase the covered cooking time in step 2 to 12 to 15 minutes.

BRAISED FENNEL
Don't core the fennel bulb before cutting it into wedges; the core will help hold the layers of fennel together during cooking.

Follow the recipe for Braised Leeks, substituting 2 fennel bulbs, trimmed of stalks, halved, and each half cut into 4 wedges, for the leeks; increase the browning time in step 1 to about 10 minutes and the covered cooking time in step 2 to 15 to 18 minutes.

NOTES FROM THE TEST KITCHEN

CLEANING LEEKS
When braising leeks, we like to cut the leeks lengthwise in half, but we always find dirt nestled between the layers. To clean them, hold the leek under cold, running water, carefully pulling the leaves apart to allow the dirt to wash away. Then gently pat dry with a paper towel.

STUFFED EGGPLANT

ONE OF THE MORE WELL-KNOWN specialties of Turkish cuisine, stuffed eggplant or *imam bayildi*, has also become popular in Greece and throughout the Middle East. At its best, stuffed eggplant consists of tender eggplant filled with onions and garlic and scented with warm spices and fruity olive oil. Unfortunately, many recipes I tried featured oil-saturated eggplant and bland, watery fillings. I wanted a recipe with creamy, earthy eggplant, and a hearty, flavorful filling that would make a satisfying side dish or an interesting vegetarian entrée.

I began my testing with the long, slender Japanese or Asian eggplants, but I quickly found that they did not have enough flesh, which made stuffing them difficult. Large (sometimes called globe) eggplants, on the other hand, had too much flesh. The smaller variety of eggplant—sometimes labeled Italian—however, worked great. Smaller than the globes, but not as thin as the Japanese eggplants, these were ideal for stuffing. (I had the best results with firm eggplants that weigh about 10 ounces each.) Their flesh cooks up creamy, with an earthy flavor that is not at all bitter—a trait often associated with eggplant.

With the type of eggplant resolved, I had to figure out the best cooking method. I started by cutting the eggplants in half lengthwise, as opposed to leaving them whole as many recipes do, under the logic that one half was the perfect serving for a side dish, and two halves made a suitable entrée portion. I started by sautéing the eggplants in a skillet on the stovetop in some olive oil. The cut sides of the eggplants caramelized beautifully, which intensified the flavor of the eggplant.

I found that flipping the eggplants in the skillet caused the skin to break, which prevented the eggplants from holding the filling. But by leaving them cut side down the entire time, the previously caramelized exterior became just plain burnt by the time the eggplants were tender. As a solution, after browning the eggplants (and without flipping them), I reduced the heat, covered the pan, and continued to cook the eggplant until tender. This part-sauté, part-steam combination method was almost seamless, except for the fact that I had to cook the eggplants in two batches.

Hoping to avoid multiple batches, I turned to the oven. I brushed the eggplant halves with oil and seasoned them with salt and pepper, then I arranged them cut side down on a preheated baking sheet, and covered them with foil. After less than an hour in a 400-degree oven, the eggplant emerged golden brown and tender. Pleased with the results, I turned my attention to the filling.

To start, I tried using a simple combination of onion, which I caramelized slightly, garlic, and grated Pecorino Romano cheese (a substitution for the Greek cheese typically used, *kefalotyri*, which is hard to find). Tasters liked the flavor but wanted something more substantial, a filling that would hold its own against the meaty eggplant. I tried bread cubes and breadcrumbs, but both resulted in a mushy texture. I found several recipes that called for green bell peppers, but tasters thought they were too bitter. The combination of diced tomatoes and toasted pine nuts, however, was a perfect fit. The tomatoes added substance without making the filling mushy or adding too much moisture, and also imparted a sweetness that was the perfect complement to the eggplant. The nuts, aside from imparting richness and flavor, also added a pleasant, lightly crunchy texture to the filling.

Now I just had to round out the flavors. I seasoned the filling with oregano, cinnamon, and a little cayenne for heat. After stirring in some red wine vinegar to brighten the overall flavor of the dish and balance the sweetness of the onions, I was ready to stuff the eggplants.

I simply opened up the center of each eggplant by pushing the flesh to the sides using two forks. I then mounded a generous amount (about ¼ cup) of filling into each opening, and sprinkled extra grated cheese over the top of each eggplant half. Just five minutes in a 400-degree oven was all the eggplant and filling needed to heat through. A sprinkling of fresh parsley for color and freshness was all it took to finish things off.

—RACHEL TOOMEY, *America's Test Kitchen Books*

STUFFED EGGPLANT

SERVES 4 AS A MAIN COURSE, OR 8 AS A SIDE DISH

Serve with Greek-style yogurt if desired. This dish can be served hot or at room temperature.

- 4 Italian eggplants (about 10 ounces each), halved lengthwise
- ¼ cup olive oil
  Salt and pepper
- 1 onion, minced (about 1 cup)
- 3 garlic cloves, minced
- 2 teaspoons minced fresh oregano or ½ teaspoon dried
- ¼ teaspoon ground cinnamon
- ⅛ teaspoon cayenne pepper
- 1 pound plum tomatoes (3 to 4 tomatoes), cored, seeded, and chopped medium
- 2 ounces Pecorino Romano cheese, grated (about 1 cup)
- ¼ cup pine nuts, toasted
- 1 tablespoon red wine vinegar
- 2 tablespoons minced fresh parsley

1. Adjust two oven racks to the upper-middle and lowest positions, place a rimmed baking sheet on the lowest rack, and heat the oven to 400 degrees.

2. Brush the cut sides of the eggplant with 2 tablespoons of the oil and season with salt and pepper. Set the eggplant cut side down on the hot baking sheet and, using oven mitts, carefully cover with foil. Roast until the eggplant is golden brown and tender, 50 to 55 minutes. Carefully transfer the eggplant to a paper towel–lined baking sheet and let drain. Do not turn off the oven.

3. Meanwhile, heat the remaining 2 tablespoons oil in a 12-inch skillet over medium heat until shimmering. Add the onion and ½ teaspoon salt and cook until softened and browned, about 10 minutes. Stir in the garlic, oregano, cinnamon, and cayenne and cook until fragrant, about 30 seconds. Stir in the tomatoes, ¾ cup of the cheese, nuts, and vinegar and cook until warmed through, about 1 minute. Season with salt and pepper to taste and set aside.

4. Return the roasted eggplant cut side up to the rimmed baking sheet (or use a large casserole dish). Using two forks, gently push the flesh to the sides of each eggplant half to make room for the filling. Mound about ¼ cup of the filling into each eggplant. (At this point, the eggplants can be covered and refrigerated for up to 24 hours.)

5. Sprinkle with the remaining ¼ cup cheese and bake on the upper-middle rack until the cheese is melted, 5 to 10 minutes. (If refrigerated, increase the baking time to 8 to 12 minutes.) Sprinkle with the parsley and serve warm or at room temperature.

NOTES FROM THE TEST KITCHEN

PREPARING EGGPLANT FOR STUFFING

Using two forks, gently push the flesh to the sides of each eggplant half to make room for the filling.

THE BEST GARLIC PRESSES

A defiantly sticky and undeniably stinky job, hand-mincing garlic is a chore many cooks avoid by pressing the cloves through a garlic press. The question for us was not whether garlic presses work, but which of the many available models works best. After squeezing our way through 12 different models, the unanimous winner was **Kuhn Rikon's 2315 Epicurean Garlic Press** (left), $34.95. Solidly constructed of stainless steel, it has ergonomically curved handles that are comfortable to squeeze and a hopper that smoothly and automatically lifts out for cleaning as you open the handles. It passed all our kitchen tests with flying colors. Also doing well in our tests was the **Trudeau Garlic Press** (right)—with a solid construction, it is sturdy and easy to use, and is our best buy at a reasonable $11.99. (See page 332 for more information about our testing results.)

MEXICAN STREET CORN

MEXICAN STREET CORN

IN MEXICO, STREET VENDORS SELL corn on the cob from carts like vendors in the U.S. sell hotdogs. The corn is served coated with either melted butter, chili powder, and lime juice, or a creamy, cheesy mixture consisting of *crema* (a tangy cultured sour cream) or mayonnaise mixed with chili powder and garlic. The mixture is slathered over the corn and then sprinkled with a crumbly Mexican cheese such as *queso anejo* or *queso fresco*. The cheese-coated corn piqued my interest, so I set out to duplicate this Mexican market delicacy in our test kitchen. First, I focused on the cooking method for the corn and turned to grilling.

Removing all but the last layer of husk, I grilled the corn until it was lightly charred and the kernels were crisp-tender. I removed the corn and brushed the ears with the spiced mayonnaise mixture, which I then sprinkled with cheese. (After some debate, I decided to forgo crema in favor of mayonnaise—it's easier to find and almost as traditional in Mexico as crema.) As for the cheese, I tried queso fresco, a crumbly white cheese, which can be found in Latin markets and some supermarkets; if you can't find it in your area, crumbled farmer's cheese or feta makes a reasonable substitute. Tasters raved about this corn, as every bite was rewarded with a mouthful of creamy chili flavor. However, they commented that the cheese, which was merely sprinkled on top, tended to fall off when eaten. To solve this problem, I ended up making two decisions: first I mixed the cheese in with the mayonnaise, and second, I set aside our grill in favor of the broiler.

This time I fully husked the corn, drizzled it with a tablespoon of olive oil, and transferred it to a foil-lined baking sheet. Caramelizing the corn under the broiler took longer than on the grill, about 10 minutes per side. When the corn was nicely browned, I slathered on the cheese and mayonnaise mixture, and put it back under the broiler for one minute. This final minute under the broiler made a real difference. The mayonnaise began to lightly brown and bubble and the cheese melted just enough to stick to the corn. A squeeze of lime was all the corn needed at that point to send it over the top, and when compared to the grilled corn, tasters actually preferred the flavor of the broiled corn.

—BRYAN ROOF, *America's Test Kitchen Books*

MEXICAN STREET CORN
SERVES 6

If possible, leave the stalks of the corn attached; they make nice handles when cooking and eating.

- 6 large ears fresh corn, husks and silk removed
- 1 tablespoon olive oil
- ½ cup mayonnaise
- 2 tablespoons minced fresh cilantro
- 1 tablespoon fresh lime juice
- 1 garlic clove, minced
- 1 teaspoon chili powder
- Salt
- 1 ounce queso fresco, farmer's cheese, or feta, crumbled (about ¼ cup)
- Pepper
- 1 lime, cut into wedges, for serving

1. Adjust an oven rack 5 inches from the broiler element and heat the broiler. Brush the corn on all sides with the olive oil and transfer to a foil-lined baking sheet. Broil the corn until well browned on one side, about 10 minutes. Turn the corn over and broil until browned on the opposite side, about 10 minutes longer.

2. While the corn broils, stir the mayonnaise, cilantro, lime juice, garlic, chili powder, and ¼ teaspoon salt together until uniform. Stir in the cheese and set aside.

3. Remove the corn from the oven and brush the corn on all sides with the mayonnaise mixture. Return to the broiler and broil the coated corn until the cheese coating is warm and slightly browned on top, about 1 minute. Season with salt and pepper to taste. Serve with the lime wedges and any remaining mayonnaise mixture.

NOTES FROM THE TEST KITCHEN

QUESO FRESCO
Queso fresco is a fresh cow's milk cheese with a moist, crumbly texture and a lightly salty, milky flavor. Queso fresco does not readily melt and is usually sprinkled on bean dishes, stuffed into quesadillas or enchiladas, or used to make street corn. If you don't have access to queso fresco, farmer's cheese or feta makes a good substitute.

SAUTÉED SPINACH

WE'VE ALWAYS SAID NO TO SAUTÉING BABY SPINACH. Like bigger, more mature flat-leaf spinach, this tender young vegetable releases a lot of liquid when it hits a hot pan, which turns it into a waterlogged mess. But given how convenient it is (no stems to remove or grit to rinse out), we thought it was time to give cooking baby spinach another try.

In the past, we've solved the water problem of the baby green's grownup cousin by wilting it first in a pan, squeezing it with tongs in a colander to remove liquid, and then returning it to the skillet. This tactic failed miserably with the baby version. As soon as the pressed spinach was put back in the pan, it exuded even more juices, which watered down the other ingredients in the dish.

Blanching or steaming the baby spinach first to release liquid, a technique we found successful with sturdier curly-leaf spinach, was also out. Besides the hassle of another pot to wash, why add water to something that you know will get even wetter?

How about microwaving? I placed the leaves in a large glass bowl and covered it with a plate. After six minutes, the spinach was warm but still not sufficiently wilted. I was loath to do it—but would adding just a little water (¼ cup) help speed things up? Eureka! After three minutes, the spinach was softened, having extruded a great deal of liquid. Yet a nagging problem remained: Pressing the spinach against the colander didn't remove enough of the liquid or strengthen its tissue-like texture.

I remembered other recipes calling for precooking before sautéing. A few had advocated chopping the wilted vegetable as a way to remove liquid. Taking up a new batch of spinach, I microwaved, pressed, and then roughly chopped it on a cutting board. Not only was the mushy texture gone, but the chopping had released even more of the water pooling around the spinach. With victory in sight, I threw the greens back in the colander for a second squeeze. This chopped and double-pressed spinach was just right: tender, sweet, and ready to be paired with other ingredients. When all was said and done, I had managed to turn a vegetable usually destined for the salad bowl into a delicious side dish with nary a stem to pick.

—DAVID PAZMIÑO, *Cook's Illustrated*

SAUTÉED SPINACH WITH ALMONDS AND GOLDEN RAISINS
SERVES 4

If you don't have a microwave-safe bowl large enough to accommodate the entire amount of spinach, cook it in a smaller bowl in 2 batches. Reduce the water to 2 tablespoons per batch and cook the spinach for about 1½ minutes.

- 3 (6-ounce) bags baby spinach
- ¼ cup water
- 2 tablespoons extra-virgin olive oil, plus 2 teaspoons for drizzling
- 4 garlic cloves, sliced thin crosswise
- ¼ teaspoon red pepper flakes
- ½ cup golden raisins
- Salt
- 2 teaspoons sherry vinegar
- ⅓ cup slivered almonds, toasted

1. Place the spinach and water in a large microwave-safe bowl. Cover the bowl with a large dinner plate (the plate should completely cover the bowl and not rest on the spinach). Microwave on high power until the spinach is wilted and decreased in volume by half, 3 to 4 minutes. Using potholders, remove the bowl from the microwave and keep covered for 1 minute. Carefully remove the plate and transfer the spinach to a colander set in the sink. Using the back of a rubber spatula, gently press the spinach against the colander to release excess liquid. Transfer the spinach to a cutting board and roughly chop it. Return it to the colander and press it a second time.

2. Heat the 2 tablespoons oil, garlic, pepper flakes, and raisins in a 10-inch skillet over medium-high heat. Cook, stirring constantly, until the garlic is light golden brown and beginning to sizzle, 3 to 6 minutes. Add the spinach to the skillet, using tongs to stir and coat with the oil. Sprinkle with ¼ teaspoon salt and continue stirring with the tongs until the spinach is uniformly wilted and glossy green, about 2 minutes. Sprinkle with the vinegar and almonds; stir to combine. Drizzle with the remaining 2 teaspoons oil and season with salt to taste. Serve immediately.

VARIATIONS
SAUTÉED SPINACH WITH PECANS AND FETA

- 3 (6-ounce) bags baby spinach
- ¼ cup water
- 2 tablespoons extra-virgin olive oil, plus 2 teaspoons for drizzling
- 3 large shallots, sliced thin crosswise (about 1 cup)
  Salt
- 2 teaspoons red wine vinegar
- ⅓ cup chopped pecans, toasted
- 1½ ounces feta cheese, crumbled (about ¼ cup)

Follow the recipe for Sautéed Spinach with Almonds and Golden Raisins through step 1. Heat the 2 tablespoons oil and shallots in a 10-inch skillet over medium-high heat. Cook, stirring constantly, until the shallots are golden brown, 3 to 5 minutes. Add the spinach, using tongs to stir and coat with the oil. Sprinkle with ¼ teaspoon salt and continue stirring with the tongs until the spinach is uniformly wilted and glossy green, about 2 minutes. Sprinkle with the vinegar and pecans; stir to combine. Drizzle with the remaining 2 teaspoons oil and sprinkle with the feta. Season with salt to taste. Serve immediately.

SAUTÉED SPINACH WITH LEEKS AND HAZELNUTS

- 3 (6-ounce) bags baby spinach
- ¼ cup water
- 2 tablespoons unsalted butter
- 2 small leeks, white and light-green parts halved lengthwise, washed, and sliced thin
  Salt
- ½ teaspoon grated lemon zest
- ⅛ teaspoon ground nutmeg
- 1 tablespoon fresh lemon juice
- 2 tablespoons heavy cream
- ⅓ cup chopped hazelnuts, toasted

Follow the recipe for Sautéed Spinach with Almonds and Golden Raisins through step 1. Heat the butter in a 10-inch skillet over medium heat until the foaming subsides. Add the leeks and cook, stirring occasionally, until

softened, 10 to 15 minutes, adding 1 teaspoon water to the skillet if the leeks begin to color. Add the spinach, using tongs to stir and coat with the butter. Sprinkle with ¼ teaspoon salt, lemon zest, and nutmeg; continue stirring with the tongs until the spinach is uniformly wilted and glossy green, about 2 minutes. Drizzle with the lemon juice and cream; stir to combine. Sprinkle with the hazelnuts and season with salt to taste. Serve immediately.

NOTES FROM THE TEST KITCHEN

MICROWAVE MAGIC
Wilting the baby spinach in a large glass bowl in the microwave before sautéing it makes it easy to squeeze out excess water and reduces the spinach so that it fits easily in a skillet.

PLUMPED UP   DOWNSIZED

SAAG PANEER

IN THE NORTHERN STATE OF PUNJAB in India, one of the most widely popular delicacies is *saag paneer*, fresh homemade cheese (paneer) with spinach sauce (saag). The spinach sauce is a mixture of pureed and coarsely chopped spinach with a buttery texture, redolent of garlic, ginger, cinnamon, and cumin. The cheese is added to the spinach sauce just before serving, and offers a mild counterpoint to the pungent sauce.

I began with the cheese, and all of my research turned up very similar and equally simple methods for making it. In short, boil milk, add an acid to form curds, strain the mixture through cheesecloth, and press. The main variation in these recipes was the type of acid used, usually lemon juice or distilled white vinegar. I tested both and found that they worked equally well, forming similar amounts of curds. The curds were then strained through cheesecloth, squeezed of as much liquid as possible, and finally pressed for about 30 minutes to form the finished cheese.

The cheese made with the lemon juice, not surprisingly, took on a strong but pleasant lemon flavor. While it was perfect on its own smothered in olive oil, its flavor was too prominent in our heavily spiced sauce. The cheese made with the vinegar tasted clean and fresh and didn't overwhelm the spinach sauce.

Many of the recipes I found prepared the cheese in one of three ways before adding it to the sauce. Some left the cheese curds unpressed and crumbled, others pressed the curds for 30 minutes then cubed the finished cheese, and still others fried the pressed cheese cubes. The method of preparation had no bearing on the flavor of the final product, but tasters disliked the way the unpressed, crumbled cheese disintegrated into the sauce. While the appearance of the fried cheese was the most attractive, frying made the cheese tough. Tasters' top choice was actually the pressed, unfried cheese—they thought it absorbed more of the flavor from the sauce while retaining enough structure to remain distinct in the finished dish.

Moving along, I turned my attention to the spinach sauce. Based on my research, I developed a working recipe that began by blooming the spices in oil, then adding the aromatics, and finally adding the spinach, tomatoes, and liquid. A portion of this mixture was then pureed to develop a mostly smooth sauce that still retained some of the texture from the unpureed spinach and tomatoes. But before I could go any further, I first needed to determine which type of spinach to use.

I tested the three types available in most supermarkets: baby spinach, crinkly leaf spinach, and frozen spinach. When cooked, both varieties of fresh spinach initially took on a bright green hue that led us to believe I was on the right track. Although they did release significant amounts of liquid, I hoped this would play in our favor when it came time to puree a portion of the mixture. But after pureeing the fresh spinach in the blender, both the baby and crinkly leaf varieties developed an algae-like appearance and texture that tasters vehemently disliked.

The frozen spinach, however, having been squeezed of all excess liquid in a clean kitchen towel prior to cooking, performed admirably. After it was pureed in the blender, there was none of the noticeable sliminess that was so problematic in the fresh spinach.

After having firmly established my spinach preference, I needed to determine how much of the sauce should be pureed. Pureeing the entire batch left a texturally boring sauce that was essentially too smooth. Pureeing one quarter of the sauce was hardly noticeable while half was slightly too much. Settling on pureeing one third of the sauce gave me the combination of textures I was looking for—not too smooth, not too coarse.

Final adjustments to the dish entailed tweaking the spices to include garam masala, cumin, cinnamon, and cayenne. And to increase the richness of the sauce I added 2 tablespoons of butter to the blender when I pureed the spinach. This resulted in a final product that was a deep green concoction of heavily spiced spinach contrasted by soft, lightly salted cheese cubes.

—BRYAN ROOF, *America's Test Kitchen Books*

SAAG PANEER

SERVES 4 TO 6

We prefer the richer flavor of cheese made with whole milk; however, low-fat milk can be substituted. Do not substitute nonfat milk. When pressing the cheese in step 2, be sure to use two plates that nestle together nicely; do not invert the top plate, or use a bottom plate with a big rim that will get in the way of squeezing the cheese. Be sure to use a blender to puree the spinach in step 4; a food processor simply won't produce the same smooth, creamy texture. Serve with rice.

CHEESE

3   quarts whole milk (see note)
2¼ teaspoons salt
5   tablespoons white vinegar

SPICES

1   teaspoon garam masala
½   teaspoon ground cumin
¼   teaspoon ground cinnamon
    Pinch cayenne pepper

SPINACH

- 2 tablespoons vegetable oil
- 1 onion, minced (about 1 cup)
  Salt
- 3 garlic cloves, minced
- 1½ teaspoons minced or grated fresh ginger
- 2 (10-ounce) packages frozen spinach, thawed and squeezed dry
- 1 large tomato, cored, seeded, and chopped fine
- 3 cups water
- 2 tablespoons unsalted butter
  Pepper

1. FOR THE CHEESE: Line a colander with a triple layer of cheesecloth and set in the sink. Bring the milk and salt to a boil in a large saucepan over medium-high heat. Stir in the vinegar, reduce the heat to low, and cook until the milk curdles, about 30 seconds. Following the photos, pour the milk mixture through the cheesecloth and let the curds drain for 10 minutes.

2. Pull the edges of the cheesecloth together to form a pouch and twist the pouch to squeeze out as much liquid as possible from the cheese curds. Place the taut, twisted cheese pouch between 2 large plates and weigh down the top plate with a heavy Dutch oven. Set aside at room temperature until the cheese is firm and set, about 30 minutes. When the cheese is a firm block, cut it into 1-inch cubes. (At this point, the cheese can be refrigerated in an airtight container for up to 1 day.)

3. FOR THE SPICES AND SPINACH: Combine the garam masala, cumin, cinnamon, and cayenne in a small bowl. Heat the oil in a 12-inch nonstick skillet over medium-high heat until shimmering. Add the spices and toast until fragrant, about 10 seconds. Stir in the onion and ½ teaspoon salt and cook until softened, 5 to 7 minutes. Stir in the garlic and ginger and cook until fragrant, about 30 seconds. Stir in the spinach, tomato, and 2 cups of the water. Cover and cook until the tomatoes begin to break down, 5 to 7 minutes.

4. Transfer one-third of the spinach mixture, butter, and remaining 1 cup water to a blender and puree until smooth, 10 to 15 seconds. Return the pureed spinach to the pan and continue to simmer until the mixture is no longer watery, 5 to 7 minutes. Gently fold in the cheese cubes, season with salt and pepper to taste, and serve.

NOTES FROM THE TEST KITCHEN

MAKING THE CHEESE FOR SAAG PANEER

1. Pour the curdled milk into the cheese-cloth-lined colander and allow it to drain and cool for 10 minutes.

2. Pull the edges of the cheesecloth together to form a pouch and twist the pouch to squeeze out as much liquid as possible from the cheese curds.

3. Place the cheese pouch between 2 plates and weigh down the top plate with a heavy Dutch oven. Set the cheese aside at room temperature until firm and set.

4. Unwrap the cheese and slice it into 1-inch strips. Slice the strips into 1-inch cubes.

OUR FAVORITE GARAM MASALA

Concocting this complex spice blend at home can add a great deal of time to recipe preparation. In search of a good-tasting commercial garam masala, we tested a few of the top brands. Tasters' favorite was **McCormick Gourmet Collection** garam masala for its ability to both assimilate into dishes and also round out their acidic and sweet notes. Tasters also liked the slightly pungent hits of coriander and the subtle warmth of cardamom, cinnamon, and cloves. Widely available in supermarkets, McCormick won praise from tasters for adding a mellow, well-balanced aroma to most dishes.

CHINESE-STYLE STICKY RICE

STICKY RICE

CHINESE-STYLE RICE should be just soft enough to soak up savory sauces and just sticky enough to be easily eaten with chopsticks. While I was expecting to use starchy short-grain rice, my research revealed that this dish is typically made with regular long-grain rice. While the basic test kitchen recipe for long-grain rice yields separate fluffy grains, I found plenty of Chinese-style recipes that promised to turn the same rice into sticky clumps I could grab with my chopsticks.

Many of these recipes employ the absorption method, in which rice and water are brought to a boil, covered, and left on low heat to steam and absorb liquid. The test kitchen's ratio for perfect fluffy rice using this cooking method is 1½ cups water to 1 cup of long-grain rice. For my sticky rice, I tried using both more and less water; more made the rice mushy, and less prevented the rice from cooking through. I was going to have to find another cooking method.

I found a few recipes that call for letting the rice boil uncovered until the water in the pot drops below the level of the rice; then the heat is turned to low and the pot is covered to allow the rice to steam and absorb the remaining liquid. When I gave this a try, the initial uncovered rapid boil produced two interesting results. First, the boiling water agitated the rice, helping release its starch; when the water was fully absorbed, the released starch made the rice very sticky. Second, when the escaping steam formed tiny holes in the surface of the rice, I had a reliable visual cue that it was time to cover the pot and let the rice finish cooking over low heat. Now I had a recipe for perfectly cooked rice that would clump on my chopsticks every time.

—KELLEY BAKER, *Cook's Country*

CHINESE-STYLE STICKY RICE

SERVES 4 TO 6

Do not stir the rice as it cooks. The finished rice can stand off the heat, covered, for up to 15 minutes.

- 2 cups long-grain white rice
- 3 cups water
- ½ teaspoon salt

1. Place the rice in a fine-mesh strainer set over a bowl. Rinse under running water, swishing with your hands until the water runs clear. Drain thoroughly.

2. Bring the rinsed rice, water, and salt to a boil in a saucepan over medium-high heat. Cook, uncovered, until the water level drops below the surface of the rice and small holes form, about 5 minutes.

3. Reduce the heat to low, cover, and cook until the rice is tender and the water is fully absorbed, about 15 minutes. Serve.

OVEN-BAKED BROWN RICE

BROWN RICE AND WHITE RICE are cut from the same cloth, so to speak—white rice being a permutation of processed brown rice. The difference is that each grain of brown rice still has the bran attached, a nutrient-rich coating, brown in color. Healthy by design, brown rice is a good source of fiber and is considered a whole grain. I wondered why brown rice wasn't on my dinner plate nearly as much as white rice, so I headed into the kitchen to find out.

The first thing I learned is that the bran, while dense with nutrients, also complicates the cooking of brown rice. The tough bran makes it difficult for liquid to permeate the grain, which in turn causes unevenly cooked rice. At its worst, brown rice can be a wet, dense, sticky mess of unevenly cooked grains. Yet, when done right, perfectly cooked brown rice results in a fluffy pillow of nutty grains that have a slightly sticky texture with a hint of chew. I wanted the ideal brown rice every time, and I knew that the right cooking technique would be crucial in achieving this goal.

Brown rice takes roughly twice as long to cook as white, and most cooks make the mistake (born of impatience) of cranking up the flame in an effort to hurry along the slow-cooking grains, which inevitably leads to a burnt pot and crunchy rice. Adding plenty of water isn't the remedy, either; excess liquid swells the rice into a gelatinous, wet mass.

I used a heavy-bottomed pot with a tight-fitting lid,

fiddled with the traditional absorption method (cooking the rice with just enough water), and eventually landed on a workable recipe. Yet when I tested the recipe with less-than-ideal equipment—namely, a flimsy pan with an ill-fitting lid—I was back to burnt, underdone rice. I wanted a surefire method that would work for every cook, no matter the equipment.

I thought a microwave might work well in this instance, given that it cooks food indirectly, without a burner. Sadly, it delivered inconsistent results, with one batch turning brittle and another, prepared in a different microwave, too sticky. A rice cooker yielded flawless brown rice on the first try, but many cooks don't own one.

I then began to consider the merits of cooking the rice in the oven. I'd have more precise temperature control, and I figured that the oven's encircling heat would eliminate the risk of scorching. My first try yielded extremely promising results: With the pan tightly covered in aluminum foil, the rice steamed to near perfection. Fine-tuning the amount of water, I settled on a ratio similar to that used for our white rice recipe: 2⅓ cups of water to 1½ cups of rice, falling well short of the 2:1 water-to-rice ratio advised by most rice producers and nearly every recipe I consulted.

My next task was to spruce up the recipe by bringing out the nutty flavor of the rice. Adding a small amount (1 tablespoon) of oil to the cooking liquid added mild flavor while keeping the rice fluffy. To reduce what was a long baking time of 90 minutes at 350 degrees, I tried starting with boiling water instead of cold tap water and raising the oven temperature to 375 degrees. These steps reduced the baking time to a reasonable one hour. (A hotter oven caused some of the fragile grains to explode.)

I was successful in clearing brown rice's bad reputation for being sticky, wet, and dense by creating a recipe that yielded light and fluffy grains. And everyone was pleased that I had developed a foolproof cooking method that didn't take up extra space on the stovetop. My final objective, however, was to jazz things up a bit by creating a couple of bold flavor variations. I turned to flavorful low-fat ingredients that pair well with the subtle nuttiness of the rice. Tasters favored a combination of Parmesan, lemon, and fresh herbs, commenting that the dish's flavor seemed versatile enough to serve alongside almost any main course. And for a more assertively flavored rice, I settled on a mix of curry, tomatoes, and peas—easily a meal in itself.

—REBECCA HAYS, *Cook's Illustrated*

OVEN-BAKED BROWN RICE

SERVES 6

To minimize any loss of water through evaporation, cover the saucepan as the water is heating, and use the water as soon as it reaches a boil. If you own an 8-inch ceramic baking dish with a lid, use it instead of the glass baking dish and foil. To double the recipe, use a 13 by 9-inch baking dish; the baking time need not be increased.

1½	cups long-, medium-, or short-grain brown rice
2⅓	cups water
1	tablespoon olive oil
½	teaspoon salt

1. Adjust an oven rack to the middle position and heat the oven to 375 degrees. Spread the rice in an 8-inch-square glass baking dish.

2. Bring the water and oil to a boil, covered, in a medium saucepan. Once the water is boiling, immediately stir in the salt and pour the water over the rice. Cover the baking dish tightly with a double layer of foil and bake until the rice is tender, about 1 hour.

3. Remove the baking dish from the oven, uncover, and fluff the rice with a fork. Cover the dish with a clean kitchen towel and let stand for 5 minutes. Uncover and let the rice stand for 5 minutes longer before serving.

VARIATIONS

OVEN-BAKED BROWN RICE WITH PARMESAN, LEMON, AND HERBS

We strongly suggest avoiding dried herbs here, as fresh herbs really make this dish.

1½	cups long-, medium-, or short-grain brown rice
1	small onion, minced (about ½ cup)
1	tablespoon olive oil

½ teaspoon salt

2⅓ cups low-sodium chicken broth

1 ounce Parmesan cheese, grated (about ½ cup)

¼ cup minced fresh parsley

¼ cup minced fresh basil

1 teaspoon grated lemon zest

½ teaspoon fresh lemon juice

⅛ teaspoon pepper

1. Adjust an oven rack to the middle position and heat the oven to 375 degrees. Spread the rice in an 8-inch-square glass baking dish.

2. Combine the onion, oil, and salt in a medium saucepan. Cover and cook over medium-low heat, stirring occasionally, until the onion is softened, 8 to 10 minutes. Stir in the broth and bring to a boil, covered. Once the broth is boiling, immediately pour it over the rice. Cover the baking dish tightly with a double layer of foil and bake until the rice is tender, about 1 hour.

3. Remove the dish from the oven, uncover, and fluff the rice with a fork. Stir in the Parmesan, parsley, basil, lemon zest, lemon juice, and pepper. Cover the dish with a clean kitchen towel and let stand for 5 minutes. Uncover and let the rice stand for 5 minutes longer before serving.

OVEN-BAKED CURRIED BROWN RICE WITH TOMATOES AND PEAS

This is a hearty dish and makes for a nice light main course. If hot curry powder is too spicy, regular works just fine.

1½ cups long-, medium-, or short-grain brown rice

1 small onion, chopped (about ½ cup)

1 tablespoon grated fresh ginger

1 garlic clove, minced

1 tablespoon olive oil

1½ teaspoons hot curry powder (see note)

½ teaspoon salt

1 (14.5-ounce) can diced tomatoes, drained

2⅓ cups low-sodium vegetable broth

½ cup frozen peas, thawed

1. Adjust an oven rack to the middle position and heat the oven to 375 degrees. Spread the rice in an 8-inch-square glass baking dish.

2. Combine the onion, ginger, garlic, oil, curry powder, and salt in a medium saucepan. Cover and cook over medium-low heat, stirring occasionally, until the onion is softened, 8 to 10 minutes. Stir in the tomatoes and cook until heated through, about 2 minutes. Stir in the broth and bring to a boil, covered. Once the broth is boiling, immediately pour it over the rice and cover the baking dish tightly with a double layer of foil. Bake the rice until tender, about 1 hour.

3. Remove the dish from the oven, uncover, and fluff the rice with a fork. Stir in the peas, cover the dish with a clean kitchen towel, and let stand for 5 minutes. Uncover and let the rice stand for 5 minutes longer before serving.

NOTES FROM THE TEST KITCHEN

BROWN RICE: GETTING THE TEXTURE RIGHT
We found that following the directions on the back of the bag usually results in wet, porridge-like rice (top). Many recipes call for too much heat, and, unless you use a very heavy pot, the rice will scorch (center). By using less water than is typical and taking advantage of the even heat of the oven, you can turn out perfectly cooked brown rice every time (bottom).

PROBLEM:
WET & SOUPY

PROBLEM:
BURNT & CRUNCHY

PERFECT:
FLUFFY & CHEWY

BREAKFAST & BREADS

FLUFFY DINER-STYLE OMELETS

WHILE A TYPICAL OMELET can make a fine breakfast or light dinner, the omelets at my local diner can satisfy the biggest of appetites. They're impossibly tall and fluffy and loaded with cheese and other fillings. But the recipes I've tried for these huge omelets have left me with flat and flabby eggs. How do those short-order cooks do it?

Most omelet recipes call for the eggs to be quickly beaten with a fork or whisk, but a peek behind the counter at the diner revealed a drastically different mixing method: using a milkshake blender. Many diners use these blenders (or a similar tool) to incorporate air into the eggs until they've tripled in volume, which results in tall and fluffy cooked omelets. Using five eggs (for a hearty omelet that would serve two), I got the eggs to triple in volume in just a few minutes with my mixer, and the resulting omelet cooked up huge and light—but lacking in richness.

Many omelet recipes add milk or cream to the whipped eggs for richness and stability. My tasters liked the flavor of cream, but when I added it to the whipped eggs, the cooked omelet lost its fluffiness and height. Combining the cream and eggs before whipping didn't work either—the mixture refused to increase in volume, as the fat in the cream was making it impossible to whip air into the eggs. I had much better results when I whipped the cream to soft peaks and then folded the whipped cream into the whipped eggs. The resulting omelet had rich flavor, creamy texture, and that tall and fluffy diner-style height.

My final task was to find the perfect cooking technique. Since I was using such a large volume of eggs, the bottom of the omelet was overcooking by the time the top was set. Flipping the big mass of egg was messy and dangerous, so I turned to a method we often use when pan-searing meats: Start the cooking on the stove and finish it in the oven. After letting the bottom of the omelet set on the stovetop, I popped the skillet into a preheated oven, and six minutes later the omelet came

out puffy, fluffy, and cooked to perfection. All I had to do was fold it in half and I had a diner-style omelet as thick as any I'd ever seen.

—MEREDITH BUTCHER, *Cook's Country*

FLUFFY DINER-STYLE CHEESE OMELET

SERVES 2

Although this recipe will work with any electric mixer, a handheld mixer makes quick work of whipping such a small amount of cream. If using a standing mixer in step 1, transfer the whipped cream to a separate bowl, wipe out the mixing bowl, and then beat the eggs in the clean bowl. To help some of the filling integrate into the eggs, add half of the cooked filling to the omelet right before it goes into the oven, then add the remaining half right when the omelet comes out, prior to folding.

- 3 tablespoons heavy cream, chilled
- 5 large eggs, at room temperature
- ¼ teaspoon salt
- 2 tablespoons unsalted butter
- 2 ounces shredded extra-sharp cheddar cheese (about ½ cup)
- 1 recipe omelet filling (recipes follow) (optional)

1. Adjust an oven rack to the middle position and heat the oven to 400 degrees. With an electric mixer on medium-high speed, beat the cream to soft peaks, about 2 minutes. Set the whipped cream aside. Beat the eggs and salt in a clean bowl on high speed until frothy and the eggs have tripled in volume, about 2 minutes. Gently fold the whipped cream into the eggs.

2. Melt the butter in a 10-inch ovensafe nonstick skillet over medium-low heat, swirling the pan to completely coat the bottom and sides with the melted butter. Add the egg mixture and cook until the edges are nearly set, 2 to 3 minutes. Sprinkle with ¼ cup of the cheese (and half of the filling, if using) and transfer to the oven. Bake until the eggs are set and the edges are beginning to brown, 6 to 8 minutes.

3. Carefully remove the pan from the oven (the handle

will be very hot). Sprinkle with the remaining ¼ cup cheese (and remaining filling, if using) and let sit, covered, until the cheese begins to melt, about 1 minute. Tilt the pan and, using a rubber spatula, push half of the omelet onto a cutting board. Then tilt the skillet so that the omelet folds over itself to form a half-moon. Cut the omelet in half. Serve.

SAUSAGE AND PEPPER OMELET FILLING

- 4 ounces bulk sausage meat
- 1 tablespoon unsalted butter
- 1 small onion, chopped (about ½ cup)
- ½ red bell pepper, stemmed, seeded, and chopped
  Salt and pepper

Cook the sausage in a nonstick skillet over medium heat, breaking up any clumps with a wooden spoon, until browned, about 6 minutes. Transfer to a paper towel–lined plate. Add the butter, onion, and bell pepper to the now-empty skillet and cook until softened, about 10 minutes. Stir in the sausage and season with salt and pepper to taste.

LOADED BAKED POTATO OMELET FILLING

- 1 large Yukon Gold potato, peeled and cut into ½-inch pieces
- 4 slices bacon, chopped
- 2 scallions, sliced thin
  Salt and pepper

Microwave the potatoes on high power, covered, in a large bowl until just tender, 2 to 5 minutes. Cook the bacon in a nonstick skillet over medium heat until crisp, about 8 minutes. Transfer the bacon to a paper towel–lined plate and pour off all but 1 tablespoon bacon fat. Cook the potatoes in the bacon fat until golden brown, about 6 minutes. Transfer the potatoes to a bowl, add the cooked bacon, and stir in the scallions. Season with salt and pepper to taste.

NOTES FROM THE TEST KITCHEN

DOUBLE YOUR PLEASURE
To make two omelets, double this recipe and cook the omelets simultaneously in two skillets. If you have only one skillet, prepare a double batch of ingredients and set half aside for the second omelet. Be sure to wipe out the skillet in between omelets.

IT'S IN THE MIX
Most recipes call for using a whisk to gently beat the eggs and dairy; we found this produced a flat omelet. We use an electric mixer to incorporate air into the eggs and cream, which results in a tall, fluffy omelet.

FLAT OMELET
Whisked eggs and cream yield a flat omelet.

OUR FAVORITE EXTRA-SHARP CHEDDAR CHEESE
After sampling eight extra-sharp cheddar cheeses plain and in melted cheese sandwiches, one thing became clear: Tasters liked the older sharper cheddars best. Our three top-rated cheeses—Cabot Private Stock, Cabot Extra Sharp, and Grafton Village—are all aged at least 12 months, and tasters rated them the three sharpest. The texture of the aged cheddar was also preferred for its dense, crumbly bite. The winner? Tasters liked **Cabot Private Stock Cheddar Cheese,** $7.98 per pound, the best for its well-rounded sharpness and depth of flavor. (See page 328 for more information about our testing results.)

SMOKED SALMON AND LEEK TART

MORE THAN A BAGEL AND CREAM CHEESE SIDEKICK, smoked salmon is found in many dishes throughout the British Isles, from egg dishes like quiches and scrambled eggs to pastas and even pizza. Scots utilize their abundance of smoked salmon in several ways, but perhaps one of the tastiest is the smoked salmon and leek tart. The tart is similar to quiche in that the filling is built on a custard base, but it differs from quiche in the amount of custard—the tart contains just enough to bind the ingredients together, so the end result is a bit lighter than quiche, with the flavor of salmon at the fore. Each bite contains a trio of flavors and textures: flaky pastry, creamy custard, and briny, rich salmon. We set out to develop our own interpretation of this Scottish favorite.

I tried several tarts based on my research of Scottish cuisine. They ranged from the extremely simple and disappointingly flavorless to the horrendously complicated and confusing. Some tarts added various cheeses to the custard for richness and flavor (or replaced the custard altogether with cheese) while others stuck to a simple egg and cream custard. Some recipes folded the salmon into the custard and others arranged the salmon across the top of the tart. Leeks and onions and herbs were a common thread among the many versions, while the crusts couldn't have been more varied. I chose to start my testing from the ground up, with the pastry crust.

I love the flavor of an all-butter crust, but getting an all-butter dough into a tart shell in one piece is time-consuming and stressful—and often requires patching torn dough back together while going in and out of the refrigerator to keep the dough from getting too soft and difficult to handle. To cut out the steps of rolling out and repeatedly chilling the dough, I turned to testing pat-in-the-pan-style crusts.

I tried several recipes, which included everything from shortening to eggs and even cream cheese, but they all produced crusts that were too cookie-like and crumbly—and more importantly, the intense butter flavor I wanted in this tart was lost. Simply patting our all-butter dough into the pan didn't work either. The pieces of cold butter that typically get smeared in the dough during rolling remained in chunks that melted in the oven, leaving unsightly holes and cracks in their place. I then had the idea of cutting the butter completely into the flour.

(Up to this point, I'd been partially cutting in the butter.) I used a food processor to speed things up and ensure that the butter was evenly cut throughout. This worked like a charm—the dough was firm enough to press into the pan and baked evenly as a traditional rolled tart dough. Even better, it tasted as buttery as I'd imagined.

In the testing of fillings, no one liked the tarts that either omitted the custard in favor of a cheese filling or enriched the custard with cheese—these tarts were simply too rich and lacked the delicacy of the simple custard tarts. So, I focused on getting our custard base just right. I tried four eggs and 1 cup of cream, but that turned out to be too much custard for our crust—and too rich as well. When I reduced the eggs to three and swapped in ¾ cup half-and-half for the cream, some tasters commented that the tart tasted too eggy. I finally settled on two eggs and ½ cup half-and-half. With the addition of some fresh dill, the custard was flavorful and delicate.

Moving along, the focus of my testing shifted to the leeks. I found that a quick sauté in a hot pan resulted in brown, bitter leeks that were stringy and tough. Experimenting with the opposite end of the spectrum, I tried cooking them slowly over low heat. This was a marked improvement in both texture and taste, but some bits and pieces were still getting too brown, so I covered the pan to sweat the leeks. Sweating allowed the leeks to cook to a meltingly tender state with deep, sweet flavor.

Next, I focused on incorporating the salmon into the tart. Many of the recipes I researched folded the salmon into the custard. But the once subtle flavor of the salmon turned unpleasantly fishy, overwhelming the other flavors in the filling. Not good at all. Placing the salmon over the custard didn't work well either. The salmon sunk down into the custard, again throwing all the flavors off balance. And the pieces of salmon that didn't become immersed in custard turned dry and chewy once baked. I then wondered whether we should even be cooking the smoked salmon. After all, the smoking process "cooks" the salmon. So after the leek custard had been baked and cooled, I simply scattered chopped salmon over the top. Tasters now raved about the distinct flavorful contrast between the delicate custard and the rich smoky salmon, a contrast that previously had been lost when the salmon was incorporated into the custard. At last, a perfect slice of Scotland.

—BRYAN ROOF, *America's Test Kitchen Books*

SMOKED SALMON AND LEEK TART

SERVES 4 TO 6

You will need a 9-inch fluted tart pan with a removable bottom for this recipe. Since this is a thin tart, be sure to press the dough only ¾ inch up the sides of the pan. Buy smoked salmon that looks bright and glossy and avoid salmon that looks milky and dry. This tart can be served chilled or at room temperature—it makes an excellent choice for brunch.

TART SHELL

- 1¼ cups (6¼ ounces) unbleached all-purpose flour
- 1 tablespoon sugar
- ½ teaspoon salt
- 8 tablespoons (1 stick) unsalted butter, cut into ½-inch cubes and chilled
- 3 tablespoons ice water

FILLING

- 1 tablespoon unsalted butter
- 1 pound leeks, white and light green parts only, halved lengthwise, sliced thin, and rinsed thoroughly
  Salt
- 2 large eggs
- ½ cup half-and-half
- 1 tablespoon minced fresh dill
  Pepper
- 6 ounces thinly sliced smoked salmon, cut into ¼-inch pieces
- 1 tablespoon extra-virgin olive oil
- 1 tablespoon minced fresh chives
- 1 lemon, cut into wedges, for serving

1. FOR THE TART SHELL: Pulse the flour, sugar, and salt together in a food processor until combined, about 4 pulses. Scatter the butter pieces over the flour mixture and pulse until the mixture resembles coarse sand, about 15 pulses. Add 2 tablespoons of the ice water and continue to process until large clumps of dough form and no powdery bits remain, about 5 seconds. If the dough doesn't clump, add the remaining tablespoon water and pulse to incorporate, about 4 pulses.

2. Spray a 9-inch tart pan with a removable bottom with vegetable oil spray. Following the photos on page 89, tear the dough into walnut-sized pieces and pat it into the prepared tart pan, pressing it ¾ inch up the sides of the pan. Lay plastic wrap over the dough and smooth out any bumps using your palm. Leaving the plastic on top of the dough, place the tart pan on a large plate and freeze the tart shell until firm, about 30 minutes.

3. Adjust an oven rack to the middle position and heat the oven to 375 degrees. Set the tart pan on a large baking sheet. Press a large piece of foil into the tart shell and over the edges of the pan and fill with pie weights. Bake until the edges of the tart shell begin to brown and the surface of the dough under the foil no longer looks wet, about 30 minutes, rotating the baking sheet halfway through baking.

4. Carefully remove the foil and weights from the tart shell, and continue to bake the tart shell until golden, 5 to 10 minutes. Transfer the baking sheet to a wire rack and let the tart shell cool while making the filling. (Leave the oven on at 375 degrees.)

5. FOR THE FILLING: Meanwhile, melt the butter in a 10-inch skillet over medium heat. Add the leeks and ½ teaspoon salt and cook, covered, stirring occasionally, until the leeks are softened, about 10 minutes. Remove the pan from the heat, remove the lid, and let the leeks cool for 5 minutes.

6. Whisk the eggs, half-and-half, dill, and ¼ teaspoon pepper together in a large bowl. Stir in the leeks until just incorporated. Spread the leek mixture evenly into the baked tart shell. Bake the tart on the baking sheet until the filling has set and the center feels firm to the touch, 20 to 25 minutes, rotating the baking sheet halfway through baking. Transfer the baking sheet to a wire rack and let the tart cool completely, about 2 hours.

7. Toss the salmon with the oil and chives and season with salt and pepper to taste. Sprinkle the salmon evenly over the cooled tart. To serve, remove the outer metal ring of the tart pan, slide a thin metal spatula between the tart and the tart pan bottom, and carefully slide the tart onto a serving platter or cutting board. Serve with the lemon wedges.

CAMEMBERT, BACON, AND POTATO TART

TARTIFLETTE IS A HOMEY FRENCH CASSEROLE of bacon, onions, and potatoes topped with a thick blanket of Reblochon cheese, a soft, pungent cow's milk cheese produced in the Savoie region. The tart may sound like traditional artery-clogging bistro fare, but it's not: the Reblochon producer's trade union invented the dish in the 1980s in hopes of boosting the sales of their cheese. Their campaign worked, and the casserole has become a classic, especially up high in the French mountains where a quick fix of fat and carbohydrates comes in handy for staying warm and energized before or after skiing.

Bacon, cheese, onions, and potatoes? What's not to love? Tartiflette may taste great, but it certainly doesn't always look the part. I wanted to take the flavors and make a tidier dish—a tartiflette tart as it were.

While the test kitchen has developed a handful of different types of tart dough through the years, my current favorite is a recently created savory press-in dough. As easy as can be, the crust is essentially a butter cookie dough—with far less sugar—that is blended in the food processor, patted in pieces into the tart pan, and smoothed down with plastic wrap—there is no rolling whatsoever. Once the tart bakes (lined with pie weights to prevent shrinkage), the dough evens out and looks every bit as flat and tidy as rolled dough, and it is quite rich, tender, and buttery. The secret to the dough is a high fat-to-flour ratio and a fairly minimal amount of water, which prevents the dough from toughening as it is processed or fitted into the tart.

In traditional tartiflette, the onions are sautéed in fat rendered from the crisped bacon, then tossed with boiled waxy potatoes (like Yukon Golds) before being topped with cheese and baked. In the case of my tart, the first half of that equation made good sense and worked well, but boiled potatoes bombed: they tasted bland and had a wet, moist texture that clashed with that of the crisp crust. I next tried sliding thin-sliced raw potatoes into the cooked onion and bacon mixture with the hope that they would cook through in the time it took the tart to bake, but no such luck—they were crunchy.

Something obvious then occurred to me: why not cook the potatoes with the onions? Theoretically, it could maximize the potatoes' flavor and minimize the effort—and dishes—required for the filling. I slid thin-sliced potatoes into the cooked onion mixture and sautéed them until browned, not unlike a batch of hash browns. While promising, the rendered bacon fat in the pan wasn't abundant enough to prevent the potatoes from sticking to the pan, much less provide a rich enough flavor; adding a couple of tablespoons of butter fixed that. (Tartiflette is an unrepentantly rich dish and I couldn't see sweating any more fat or calories at this point.) Chopped thyme and plenty of salt and pepper went far in boosting the filling's flavor. Within ten minutes or so, the potatoes browned attractively and were tender and ready for the tart once I stirred in the bacon.

Before I could bake the tart, I had to find the right cheese and the best way to top the tart. Reblochon cheese can be hard to find outside specialty stores, and is usually quite expensive, so I opted to find a more readily available, cheaper option. After testing a few other cheeses, including Brie (which lacked the intensity of flavor traditional in this tart), I settled on Camembert, which had as strong a personality and as good melting properties as the Reblochon at a fraction of the price.

For traditional tartiflette, the round of cheese is cut crosswise and thick semicircle slabs of cheese are draped over the filling—it looks messy. Wanting a tidier appearance, and much less uniform coverage over the filling, I cut the cheese in a variety of different configurations until I figured out the easiest approach, which simply involved halving the Camembert round widthwise and cutting the rounds into wedges that could be decoratively placed over the filling. Baked in a reasonably hot oven (375 degrees), the tart emerged with cheese melted smoothly and, serendipitously, with its exposed rind having turned crisp, which accented the otherwise gooey cheese. Far more attractive than the original casserole, the tart had all the flavor of the original plus the added taste and textural contrast of a pastry crust.

—MEGAN WYCOFF, *America's Test Kitchen Books*

CAMEMBERT, BACON, AND POTATO TART

CAMEMBERT, BACON, AND POTATO TART

SERVES 4 TO 6

This tart relies on the Camembert to melt into the crevices and hold everything together. If you can't find a wheel of Camembert, look for wedges that you can slice in half.

TART SHELL

- 1¼ cups (6¼ ounces) unbleached all-purpose flour
- 1 tablespoon sugar
- ½ teaspoon salt
- 8 tablespoons (1 stick) unsalted butter, cut into ¼-inch cubes and chilled
- 3 tablespoons ice water

FILLING

- 6 slices bacon, chopped
- 2 tablespoons unsalted butter
- 1 onion, halved and sliced ¼ inch thick
- 1 pound (2 to 3 medium) Yukon Gold potatoes, peeled and sliced ¼ inch thick
- 2 teaspoons minced fresh thyme
- ½ teaspoon salt
- ¼ teaspoon pepper
- 1 (8-ounce) wheel Camembert cheese (see note)

1. FOR THE TART SHELL: Pulse the flour, sugar, and salt together in a food processor until combined, about 4 pulses. Scatter the butter pieces over the flour mixture and pulse until the mixture resembles coarse sand, about 15 pulses. Add 2 tablespoons of the ice water and continue to process until large clumps of dough form and no powdery bits remain, about 5 seconds. If the dough doesn't clump, add the remaining tablespoon water and pulse to incorporate, about 4 pulses.

2. Spray a 9-inch tart pan with a removable bottom with vegetable oil spray. Following the photos on page 89, tear the dough into walnut-sized pieces and pat it into the prepared tart pan, pressing it up the sides of the pan. Lay plastic wrap over the dough and smooth out any bumps using your palm. Leaving the plastic on top of the dough, place the tart pan on a large plate and freeze the tart shell until firm, about 30 minutes.

3. Adjust an oven rack to the middle position and heat the oven to 375 degrees. Set the tart pan on a large baking sheet. Press a large piece of foil into the tart shell and over the edges of the pan and fill with pie weights. Bake until the edges of the tart shell begin to brown and the surface of the dough under the foil no longer looks wet, about 30 minutes, rotating the baking sheet halfway through baking. Transfer the baking sheet to a wire rack and carefully remove the weights and foil from the tart shell. Let the tart shell cool while making the filling. (Leave the oven on at 375 degrees.)

4. FOR THE FILLING: Meanwhile, cook the bacon and 1 tablespoon of the butter together in a medium nonstick skillet over medium heat until the bacon is crisp, about 8 minutes. Transfer the bacon to a paper towel–lined plate, leaving the bacon fat in the skillet.

5. Add the onion to the fat left in the skillet and cook over medium heat, stirring often, until golden brown, about 10 minutes. Stir in the remaining tablespoon butter, potatoes, thyme, salt, and pepper. Increase the heat to medium-high and continue to cook, stirring occasionally, until the potatoes are tender and lightly browned, about 10 minutes. Stir in the crisp bacon.

6. Spread the potato mixture evenly into the baked tart shell. Following the photos on page 89, cut the Camembert wheel in half through the middle (to make two thin wheels), then cut each half into 4 wedges. Arrange the wedges of cheese, cut-side down, over the top of the tart.

7. Bake the tart on the baking sheet until golden and the cheese is melted and bubbling, about 35 minutes, rotating the baking sheet halfway through baking. Transfer the baking sheet to a wire rack and let the tart cool for 10 minutes. To serve, remove the outer metal ring of the tart pan, slide a thin metal spatula between the tart and the tart pan bottom, and carefully slide the tart onto a serving platter or cutting board. Serve.

CUTTING THE CAMEMBERT

1. Cut the wheel of Camembert in half horizontally to form two rounds.

2. Cut each round into 4 equal wedges.

MAKING A TART SHELL

1. Sprinkle walnut-sized clumps of dough into the tart pan.

2. Working outward from the center, press the dough into an even layer, then press it up the sides and into the fluted edges.

3. Use your thumb to level off the top edge. Use this excess dough to patch any holes.

4. Lay plastic wrap over the dough and smooth out any bumps using your palm.

SUNDAY BRUNCH FRENCH TOAST

I ALWAYS LOOK FORWARD TO THE FRENCH TOAST my dad makes for holiday brunch. He soaks sandwich bread in a creamy egg custard and fries eight pieces at a time to a crisp golden brown on a griddle he inherited from Grandma. We all sit down together to toast that is light and fluffy, with a crunchy exterior. But I don't own a griddle, so cooking French toast for brunch guests is tricky: Since my skillet holds only two pieces at a time, I have to either try to keep the toast warm in the oven (which makes it soggy and limp) or feed everyone in stages. If I was going to make eight slices of French toast without Grandma's griddle, I was going to have to try to cook them in the oven.

I soaked eight slices of hearty white sandwich bread in a mixture of milk and eggs until the bread was wet and heavy, put them on a buttered baking sheet, and popped them into the oven. The results of this first test were discouraging, as the French toast came out of the oven mushy and falling apart. Drying the bread in the oven before the soak gave it enough structure to withstand a long, deep bath in the custard (to ensure a custardy center) without falling apart. To ensure the best possible texture, I found that it was necessary to soak the bread for 30 seconds on each side and then let the slices rest briefly on an elevated rack so that any excess surface custard could drain away, thus preventing a soggy exterior. As I fine-tuned the flavor, my tasters let me know they preferred the richness of half-and-half to milk, especially when I added a little lemon juice to mimic the tang of buttermilk—a familiar flavor in many breakfast dishes such as pancakes and waffles.

The French toast was now custardy and holding together well, but it wasn't browning or getting crisp. In the test kitchen, we oven-fry potato wedges by coating a baking sheet with vegetable oil and preheating it in a hot oven. Using this technique, I placed the soaked bread slices on the sizzling, oiled sheet and flipped them halfway through cooking. After about 15 minutes, the toast came out crisp and golden on the outside and creamy and custardy inside. Now that I wasn't slaving over the stovetop for several skillet batches, I had some time to

SUNDAY BRUNCH FRENCH TOAST

think about how I could dress up this French toast for guests.

Since I serve my French toast with powdered sugar and maple syrup, I wondered if I could incorporate these flavors as a topping in the oven. I made a paste of powdered sugar and maple syrup and brushed it on the toast after I flipped it. While the powdered sugar became gummy, the maple syrup brought welcome moisture, flavor, and sweetness (and allowed me to eliminate the sugar in the custard). Swapping out the powdered sugar for brown sugar helped the maple topping caramelize into a delectable candied crust that my tasters loved.

—LYNN CLARK, *Cook's Country*

SUNDAY BRUNCH FRENCH TOAST

SERVES 4

Be sure to use a firm-textured bread such as Arnold Country Classic White or Pepperidge Farm Farmhouse Hearty White here.

- 8 slices high-quality white sandwich bread (see note)
- 6 large eggs
- ¾ cup half-and-half
- 1 tablespoon vanilla extract
- 2 teaspoons fresh lemon juice
- ¼ teaspoon salt
- ¼ cup vegetable oil
- 6 tablespoons light brown sugar
- 1 tablespoon maple syrup
- ½ teaspoon ground cinnamon

1. Adjust an oven rack to the lower-middle position and heat the oven to 300 degrees. Bake the bread on a rimmed baking sheet until dry, about 8 minutes per side. Let the bread cool 5 minutes. Increase the oven temperature to 475 degrees.

2. Whisk the eggs, half-and-half, vanilla, lemon juice, and salt in a 13 by 9-inch pan. Soak 4 slices of the bread in the egg mixture until just saturated, about 30 seconds

per side. Transfer to a wire rack and repeat with the remaining 4 slices bread.

3. Pour the oil onto a rimmed baking sheet, turning the sheet to coat. Transfer to the oven and heat until just smoking, about 4 minutes. Using a fork, stir the brown sugar, maple syrup, and cinnamon in a small bowl until the mixture resembles wet sand.

4. Arrange the soaked bread on the hot baking sheet and bake until golden brown on the first side, about 10 minutes. Flip the bread and sprinkle evenly with the sugar mixture. Bake until the sugar is deep brown and bubbling, about 6 minutes. Cool the toast on the wire rack for 2 minutes. Serve.

NOTES FROM THE TEST KITCHEN

MAKING OVEN-FRIED FRENCH TOAST
Follow these steps for French toast that is light and crispy, with a maple and brown sugar crust.

1. After a dip in the custard, resting the bread on a wire rack gives the custard time to penetrate the interior while preventing the exterior from becoming oversaturated.

2. Placing the bread on a preheated baking sheet coated with oil creates a crisp coating on the exterior of the bread.

3. Sprinkling the toast with a mixture of brown sugar, maple syrup, and cinnamon gives it a caramelized, golden exterior.

BISCUITS AND SAUSAGE GRAVY

I GOT MY FIRST TASTE OF BISCUITS AND GRAVY at a busy diner just off the Blue Ridge Parkway in North Carolina. Having been raised far north of the Mason-Dixon line, I was surprised to see "Biscuits and Gravy" on the breakfast menu, as gravy to me was the concentrated brown sauce I ladled onto my Thanksgiving turkey. I took a flier and ordered it; minutes later, a bowl was plunked down in front of me. In it sat a huge, tangy biscuit smothered in a sausage-studded white cream gravy. After one bite, I knew that this was my new favorite breakfast.

Since then I've eaten my share of biscuits and gravy, but none as good as that first serving. Wanting to create my own version, I started by digging up some biscuit recipes. Identifying the right biscuit for the job—flaky, crumbly, or fluffy—was as simple as baking up a batch of each. Flaky breakfast biscuits might be great with butter and jam, but they didn't soak up the gravy properly. Crumbly cream biscuits were too rich and dense for a gravy with similar characteristics. Fluffy buttermilk biscuits, however, provided a substantial tang that complemented the gravy, and they were sturdy enough to absorb some gravy without turning to mush.

I wanted big biscuits—biscuits and gravy is not a dainty meal—so I upped the flour from the standard 2 cups to 3 cups, which allowed me to bake off eight big, 3-inch biscuits. To ensure a sturdy, hearty texture and buttery flavor, I used a 2-to-1 ratio of butter to shortening—the butter provided the flavor while the shortening made the biscuits sturdy. I found that briefly kneading the dough yielded biscuits with better structure. I also increased the baking powder and baking soda to provide maximum lift in the oven. Now I had sturdy, tender, and buttery biscuits that were perfect for the meaty gravy.

Traditional Southern cream gravy recipes cook a pound of bulk pork sausage and then sprinkle it with flour, which combines with the sausage fat to form a thickening roux. Dairy is added (my tasters much preferred milk to half-and-half or cream, which were too heavy) and the gravy is brought to a simmer. One recurring problem was the quantity of flour: Too little flour and the gravy was watery, but too much and it was pasty. I arrived at ¼ cup flour to 3 cups milk for a perfect, creamy texture. Bumping up the amount of sausage to 1½ pounds ensured plenty of meat in every bite.

With all these rich ingredients, the gravy was a little bland. I discovered that I could augment the sausage's flavor by adding ground fennel and sage, both seasonings typically found in pork sausage. The extra herbs, paired with enough black pepper to give the gravy some serious heat, made this version the best I've ever eaten.

—KELLEY BAKER, *Cook's Country*

BISCUITS AND SAUSAGE GRAVY

SERVES 8

If you don't have buttermilk on hand, powdered buttermilk added according to package instructions or clabbered milk can be used instead. To make clabbered milk, mix 1¼ cups milk with 1 tablespoon lemon juice and let stand 10 minutes.

BISCUITS

- 3 cups (15 ounces) unbleached all-purpose flour, plus extra for the work surface and cutter
- 1 tablespoon sugar
- 1 tablespoon baking powder
- ½ teaspoon baking soda
- 1 teaspoon salt
- 8 tablespoons (1 stick) unsalted butter, cut into ½-inch pieces and chilled
- 4 tablespoons vegetable shortening, cut into ½-inch pieces and chilled
- 1¼ cups buttermilk (see note)

SAUSAGE GRAVY

- ¼ cup unbleached all-purpose flour
- 1 teaspoon ground fennel
- 1 teaspoon ground sage
- 1½ teaspoons pepper
- 1½ pounds bulk pork sausage
- 3 cups whole milk
- Salt

1. FOR THE BISCUITS: Adjust an oven rack to the middle position and heat the oven to 450 degrees. Line a baking sheet with parchment paper. Pulse the flour, sugar, baking powder, baking soda, salt, butter, and shortening in a food processor until the mixture resembles coarse meal. Transfer to a large bowl. Stir in the buttermilk until combined.

2. On a lightly floured work surface, knead the dough until smooth, 8 to 10 kneads. Pat the dough into a 9-inch circle, about ¾ inch thick. Using a 3-inch biscuit cutter dipped in flour, cut out rounds of dough and arrange on the prepared baking sheet. Gather the remaining dough, pat into a ¾-inch-thick circle, and cut out the remaining biscuits. (You should have 8 biscuits in total.)

3. Bake until the biscuits begin to rise, about 5 minutes, then rotate the pan and reduce the oven temperature to 400 degrees. Bake until golden brown, 12 to 15 minutes. Transfer to a wire rack and let cool.

4. FOR THE SAUSAGE GRAVY: Combine the flour, fennel, sage, and pepper in a small bowl. Cook the sausage in a large nonstick skillet over medium heat, breaking up the meat with a wooden spoon, until no longer pink, about 8 minutes. Sprinkle the flour mixture over the sausage and cook, stirring constantly, until the flour has been absorbed, about 1 minute. Slowly stir in the milk and simmer until the sauce has thickened, about 5 minutes. Season with salt to taste. Serve the gravy over split biscuits.

NOTES FROM THE TEST KITCHEN

STAMP BUT DON'T TWIST
Twisting the cutter when stamping out biscuits pinches the dough, resulting in an uneven rise. Using a well-floured cutter and pressing down with equal pressure on both sides of the cutter (and not twisting) ensures that the biscuits will rise evenly.

TWISTED
Crooked biscuit with pinched edges that was stamped while twisting the cutter.

STAMPED
Properly cut biscuit with straight rise.

BEST DROP BISCUITS

MY FAVORITE STYLE OF BISCUIT is the simple but often forgotten drop biscuit with its crisp and craggy golden-brown exterior full of hills and valleys and a tender, fluffy interior. Unlike fairly pale, flat-topped, uniformly tender baking-powder biscuits that are split in half and buttered, drop biscuits are meant to be broken apart and eaten as is, piece by buttery piece.

While both types of biscuit use the same handful of ingredients and are quick to prepare, drop biscuits don't rely on any of the finicky steps rolled biscuits require to get them just right. There's no need to cut super-cold butter into the dry ingredients. Kneading and rolling are not necessary, so you don't have to worry about overworking the dough. And there's no fussy biscuit cutter or rerolling of the scraps. Drop biscuits barely require a recipe. Flour, leavener, and salt are combined in a bowl; the wet ingredients (milk or buttermilk and either melted butter or vegetable oil) are stirred together in a measuring cup; the wet ingredients are stirred into the dry ingredients; and the resulting batter is scooped up and dropped onto a baking sheet.

I headed into the kitchen to try a sampling of drop biscuit recipes. The techniques were as simple as I'd expected, but the texture of the biscuits often fell short, and the flavor was uninspiring. If they weren't dense, gummy, and doughy, my test biscuits were lean and dry. The generous amounts of leavener in most recipes gave the biscuits a bitter, metallic flavor. But the recipes that called for less than 1 tablespoon of baking powder produced biscuits that were heavy and squat. Evidently, you need a lot of leavener to compensate for the lack of cold chunks of butter that produce steam and assist with the rise in classic rolled biscuits.

Still, I had made some progress during this first round of testing. Oil-based biscuits were easy to work with but lacked the most important element: buttery flavor. So butter was a must. I'd also come to some conclusions about the flour.

While some rolled biscuits use softer, low-protein Southern brands of flour or a mixture of cake and all-purpose flours to achieve a light, cottony-soft texture, neither of these improved the texture of the drop biscuits. Instead, because the dough isn't kneaded—and therefore not much gluten development occurs—these softer flours made the biscuits too delicate and unable to form a substantial crust. I stuck with regular all-purpose flour, which provided the structure the drop biscuits needed.

My working recipe contained 2 cups of flour, 1 tablespoon of baking powder, ¾ teaspoon of salt, ¾ cup of milk, and 6 tablespoons of melted butter. Once the wet and dry ingredients were just combined, I used a ¼-cup dry measure to scoop the batter onto a parchment-lined baking sheet and baked the biscuits in a 475-degree oven. While this was definitely better than some of the recipes I'd tried early on, these biscuits weren't quite buttery enough and still tasted of leavener.

Increasing the butter to 8 tablespoons answered my tasters' demand for deeper butter flavor, but something was still missing. Since milk didn't seem to be adding much flavor, I was tempted to try other dairy products in its place. Yogurt provided a tangy complexity, but at the price of unwanted gumminess. Sour cream made the biscuits way too rich. Buttermilk offered the best of both worlds: biscuits that had a rich, buttery tang and were also texturally appealing—crisper on the exterior and fluffier on the interior. Increasing the amount of buttermilk to a full cup amplified these effects.

Although one might think that more liquid would make the biscuits heavier and less crisp, just the opposite was happening. Discussions with several scientists cleared up the confusion. The more liquid I added to the dough, the more steam was created in the hot oven. This steam acts as a powerful leavener, which, in conjunction with the chemical leaveners, lightens the texture of the biscuits. And just as water sprayed on rustic bread dough helps crisp its crust, the additional steam was making the exterior of my biscuits seriously craggy, almost crunchy.

Switching to buttermilk meant that baking soda (not just baking powder) was now an option, as the soda would react with the acid in the buttermilk. After trying various combinations of baking soda and baking powder, I settled on what ended up being a fairly standard ratio for traditional rolled buttermilk biscuits: 2 teaspoons of baking powder to ½ teaspoon of baking soda. I knew I'd succeeded when the biscuits rose properly and I could no longer taste any metallic bitterness. As an added bonus, the baking soda aided browning, giving the biscuits a darker, more attractive crust.

There was just one aspect of my recipe that continued to bother me: the need to wait for the buttermilk to come to room temperature and for the melted butter to cool—in order for them to emulsify properly. But whenever I tried to get away with combining the melted butter with straight-from-the-refrigerator buttermilk, the butter would start to form clumps. In most cases, lumpy buttermilk is considered a mistake, but I wondered what would happen if I actually tried to use this mixture. To find out, I made one batch of biscuits with a completely smooth buttermilk mixture and another with lumpy buttermilk. Compared side by side, the biscuits made with the lumpy buttermilk rose slightly higher and had a more distinct textural contrast between interior and exterior than did the batch made with the smooth buttermilk mixture.

A "mistake" turned out to be the final secret to my recipe. The lumps of butter turned to steam in the oven and helped create more rise. The clumpy buttermilk seemed to mimic the positive effects of making biscuits the old-fashioned way—with bits of cold butter left in the dough—but this method was better on two counts: It was more reliable and less messy. The only hard part was having the patience to wait for the biscuits to cool down before grabbing one to eat.

—SANDRA WU, *Cook's Illustrated*

BEST DROP BISCUITS

MAKES 12

If you don't have buttermilk on hand, powdered buttermilk added according to package instructions or clabbered milk can be used instead. To make clabbered milk, mix 1 cup milk with 1 tablespoon lemon juice and let stand 10 minutes. A ¼-cup (#16) portion scoop can be used to portion the batter. To refresh day-old biscuits, heat them in a 300-degree oven for 10 minutes.

- 2   **cups (10 ounces) unbleached all-purpose flour**
- 2   **teaspoons baking powder**
- ½   **teaspoon baking soda**
- 1   **teaspoon sugar**
- ¾   **teaspoon salt**
- 1   **cup cold buttermilk**
- 8   **tablespoons (1 stick) unsalted butter, melted and cooled slightly (about 5 minutes), plus 2 tablespoons melted butter for brushing biscuits**

BEST DROP BISCUITS

1. Adjust an oven rack to the middle position and heat the oven to 475 degrees. Line a rimmed baking sheet with parchment paper. Whisk the flour, baking powder, baking soda, sugar, and salt in a large bowl. Combine the buttermilk and 8 tablespoons melted butter in a medium bowl, stirring until the butter forms small clumps.

2. Add the buttermilk mixture to the dry ingredients and stir with a rubber spatula until just incorporated and the batter pulls away from the sides of the bowl. Using a greased ¼-cup dry measure, scoop a level amount of batter and drop onto the prepared baking sheet (the biscuits should measure about 2¼ inches in diameter and 1¼ inches high). Repeat with the remaining batter, spacing the biscuits about 1½ inches apart. Bake until the tops are golden brown and crisp, 12 to 14 minutes.

3. Brush the biscuit tops with the remaining 2 tablespoons melted butter. Transfer to a wire rack and let cool 5 minutes before serving.

VARIATIONS

BLACK PEPPER AND BACON DROP BISCUITS

Cut 6 strips bacon in half lengthwise and then crosswise into ¼-inch pieces; fry in a 10-inch nonstick skillet over medium heat until crisp, 5 to 7 minutes. Using a slotted spoon, transfer the bacon to a paper towel–lined plate and cool to room temperature. Follow the recipe for Best Drop Biscuits, adding the crisp bacon and 1 teaspoon coarsely ground black pepper to the flour mixture in step 1.

CHEDDAR AND SCALLION DROP BISCUITS

Follow the recipe for Best Drop Biscuits, adding ½ cup shredded cheddar cheese and ¼ cup thinly sliced scallions to the flour mixture in step 1.

ROSEMARY AND PARMESAN DROP BISCUITS

Follow the recipe for Best Drop Biscuits, adding ¾ cup grated Parmesan cheese and ½ teaspoon minced fresh rosemary to the flour mixture in step 1.

NOTES FROM THE TEST KITCHEN

REUSABLE PAN LINERS

Reusable nonstick baking-pan liners are relatively new and the choices are growing. We baked biscuits, ultrathin lace cookies, and berry-filled tarts on five nonstick liners made from various grades of silicone, silicone-reinforced woven fiberglass, and nonstick fiberglass to see if any could impress us more than a sheet of basic parchment paper.

The liners fell into two classes: lightweights and heavyweights. Baked goods made on lighter liners had bottoms with spotty browning. These liners can be cut to fit any pan, a definite plus, but the flimsy materials creased easily when washed by hand.

Heavier mats imparted plastic and chemical flavors to the cookies and biscuits. DeMarle's Silpat, $16.99, was clearly the best reusable liner we tested. However, these mats stain over time and can transfer flavors from previous uses. Also, unlike parchment, Silpat mats cannot be cut to fit specific pan sizes. Bottom line: We prefer parchment.

CAN TRANSFER OFF-FLAVORS

INEXPENSIVE AND VERSATILE

CLUMPY BUTTER IS GOOD BUTTER

When you stir slightly cooled melted butter into cold buttermilk, the butter will clump. Although this might look like a mistake, it's one of the secrets to this recipe. The clumps of butter are similar to the small bits of cold butter in biscuits prepared according to the traditional method and help guarantee a light and fluffy interior.

BLUEBERRY SCONES

REAL BRITISH SCONES ARE LIKE BRITISH HUMOR— steeped in tradition, dry as a bone, and often tasteless. A distant relative of the crumpet and the English muffin, the first scones were cooked without the aid of an oven; they were prepared on a cast-iron griddle, like thick pancakes. With the addition of baking soda in Victorian times, scones in England took on the role of customizable teatime accompaniments. The dry, bland biscuits were rendered palatable by the addition of plenty of butter, clotted cream, or jam.

Americans, however, are used to having breakfast quickly and on the move. We like our pastries ready to go in single servings with the sweetness, richness, and fruit built in. We've been gradually remodeling scones to fit this image. These days, coffee shop samplings run the gamut from misshapen muffinlike objects to big-as-your-head cakes. It seemed like it was time to redefine the American scone.

Rather than reworking just one style, I decided to try to bring together the best qualities from the sweetness of a coffeehouse confection; the moist freshness of a muffin; the richness and fruit of clotted cream and jam; and the superflaky crumb of a good biscuit. I wanted scones light enough to be eaten on the go, and with a healthy dose of fresh blueberries.

Traditional scone recipes call for a minimal amount of sugar and 2 to 3 tablespoons of butter per cup of flour. I found that a full 4 tablespoons of butter per cup of flour was ideal—any more and the dough became difficult to work with and baked up greasy. Adding ¼ cup sugar per cup of flour gave the scones subtle sweetness without being cloying, and a combination of sour cream and milk offered a contrasting tang.

Unfortunately, with all the added richness and sweetness, my scones were turning out heavy and underrisen. I was using the biscuit mixing method common to most scone recipes: cutting the cold butter into the dry ingredients with my fingertips and then quickly mixing in the wet ingredients. If I was going to capture the light flakiness I was after, my technique was going to need an overhaul.

I took a hint from puff pastry, where the power of steam is used to separate superthin layers of dough into striated flakes. In a standard puff pastry recipe, a piece of dough will be turned, rolled, and folded about five times. With each fold, the number of layers of butter and dough increases exponentially. Upon baking, steam forces the layers apart and then escapes, causing the dough to puff up and crisp. I wasn't after the 768 layers produced by the standard five-turn puff pastry recipe, but adding a few quick folds to my recipe allowed the scones to gently rise and puff. Tasters appreciated that the scones were now much lighter, but I wondered if I could lighten them even more.

A good light pastry depends on distinct pieces of butter distributed throughout the dough that melt during baking and leave behind pockets of air. For this to happen, the butter needs to be as cold and solid as possible until baking. The problem with trying to cut butter into the flour with your fingers or a food processor is that the butter gets too warm during the distribution process. I tried every alternative form of butter incorporation I could think of before discovering that freezing a stick of butter and grating it on the large holes of a box grater works best. The butter could then be quickly and homogenously cut into the flour while remaining cold. This new method of distributing the butter kept the interior of the scones tender and moist without being dense.

Now that I'd made the ultimate plain scone, it was time to move on to adding the blueberries. Many recipes call for mixing blueberries in with the flour and butter and then adding the wet ingredients to form a dough. The results: scones that have been dyed blue by bludgeoned berries. What if I incorporated the berries into the already-mixed dough? No dice. I had to knead the dough an extra 10 to 12 times, which introduced friction and heat. The butter I'd taken such care to add in small flakes was melting into a homogenous mass that wreaked havoc on the texture of the finished scones.

Low on ideas, I was running through a list of other foods that attempt a seamless marriage of distinct elements (sandwiches, napoleons, and sushi) when inspiration finally struck—cinnamon rolls. What if I were to distribute the berries evenly over a large, thin square of dough, roll the whole thing up like a cinnamon roll, and then flatten the log into a rectangle before cutting the scones out of it?

This worked even better than I had hoped. Rolling the blueberries and dough into a log not only distributed the berries much better but also created more flaky layers. My technique had captured the best elements from several styles of scone—sweet, moist, rich, flaky, tender, crisp, and full of fruit. Now I really might have a reason to take a break for tea every afternoon.

—J. KENJI ALT, *Cook's Illustrated*

BLUEBERRY SCONES

MAKES 8

An equal amount of frozen blueberries (do not defrost) can be substituted. The butter should be frozen solid before grating. It is important to work the dough as little as possible and use cold ingredients; if the weather is particularly hot or humid, chill the flour mixture and bowls too. The cut, unbaked berry scones can be covered and refrigerated for up to 24 hours; bake as directed. They can also be frozen for up to 1 month; cover and freeze the scones until frozen solid, about 6 hours, then transfer to a large zipper-lock bag. Bake the frozen scones (do not thaw) as directed, reducing the oven temperature to 375 degrees and increasing the baking time to 25 to 30 minutes.

16 tablespoons (2 sticks) unsalted butter, frozen whole (see note)
1½ cups (7½ ounces) fresh blueberries (see note)
½ cup whole milk
½ cup sour cream
2 cups (10 ounces) unbleached all-purpose flour, plus extra for the work surface
½ cup (3½ ounces) granulated sugar, plus extra for sprinkling
2 teaspoons baking powder
1 teaspoon grated lemon zest
½ teaspoon salt
¼ teaspoon baking soda

1. Adjust an oven rack to the middle position and heat the oven to 425 degrees. Line a baking sheet with parchment paper.

2. Score and remove half of the wrapper from each stick of butter. Grate the unwrapped ends on the large holes of a box grater (you should grate a total of 8 tablespoons). Place the grated butter in the freezer until needed. Melt 2 tablespoons of the remaining ungrated butter and set aside. Save the remaining 6 tablespoons butter for another use. Place the berries in the freezer until needed. Whisk the milk and sour cream together in a medium bowl and refrigerate until needed.

3. Whisk the flour, ½ cup sugar, baking powder, lemon zest, salt, and baking soda together in a medium bowl. Add the frozen, grated butter and toss with your fingers until thoroughly coated. Fold in the chilled milk mixture with a rubber spatula until just combined (do not overmix).

4. Turn the dough and any floury bits out onto a well-floured work surface. Lightly flour your hands and the dough and knead the dough gently 6 to 8 times until it just holds together in a ragged ball, adding additional flour as needed to prevent sticking.

5. Roll the dough out into a 12-inch square. Following the photos on page 99, fold the top, bottom, then sides of the dough over the center to form a 4-inch square. Transfer the dough to a lightly floured plate and chill in the freezer for 5 minutes (do not overchill).

6. Transfer the dough to a lightly floured work surface and roll again into a 12-inch square. Sprinkle the berries evenly over the dough, and press them lightly into the dough. Loosen the dough from the surface with a bench scraper (or thin metal spatula), roll into a tight log, and pinch the seam closed. Lay the dough seam side down and press into a 12 by 4-inch rectangle. Using a floured chef's knife, slice the dough crosswise into 4 equal rectangles, then slice each rectangle on the diagonal into 2 triangles.

7. Place the scones on the prepared baking sheet. Brush with the melted butter and sprinkle lightly with sugar. Bake until the scone tops are lightly golden brown, 18 to 25 minutes, rotating the pan halfway through baking. Transfer to a wire rack and let cool for at least 10 minutes. Serve warm or at room temperature.

MAKING BLUEBERRY SCONES

1. Roll the dough out into a 12-inch square on a lightly floured work surface. Fold the top and bottom of the dough over the center (like a business letter).

2. Fold up the sides of the dough to form a 4-inch square. Transfer the dough to a lightly floured plate and chill in the freezer for 5 minutes.

3. Roll the chilled dough out again into a 12-inch square on a lightly floured counter. Sprinkle the berries evenly over the dough and press them lightly into the dough.

4. Roll the dough up into a tight log and pinch the seam closed.

5. Lay the log seam-side down, then press into a 12 by 4-inch rectangle.

6. With a floured knife, cut the dough crosswise into 4 rectangles, and then cut each rectangle into 2 triangular scones.

SOUTHERN-STYLE SKILLET CORN BREAD

UNLIKE SWEET AND CAKEY NORTHERN VERSIONS of corn bread that are better suited to the dessert table, Southern corn bread contains neither sugar nor flour, making it savory enough to join the main course. I wanted to make a proper Southern corn bread with hearty corn flavor, a sturdy, moist crumb, and a dark brown crust that would win Northern allegiance.

When making Southern skillet corn bread, the batter is poured into the hot greased skillet and cooked in the oven until golden and crusty. After whipping up a spread of existing recipes, I realized this wasn't going to be easy. One corn bread was flat as a pancake, another was dripping in grease, and most were sorely lacking in flavor. Since corn flavor is absolutely essential to good Southern-style skillet corn bread, I figured I'd work through flavor issues first and fix the texture later.

I moved forward using the least offensive recipe of the lot, which was made with flavorful whole-grain stone-ground cornmeal. Subsequent testing, however, exposed the stone-ground cornmeal as too gritty, even when I tried grinding it down further in a food processor. I made my next batch with widely available and finely ground Quaker cornmeal. The texture of this corn bread was certainly better, but now the corn flavor was very mild—not really a surprise, since the germ is removed from this cornmeal during processing. Hoping that toasting would intensify its flavor, I spread the finely ground cornmeal on a baking sheet and threw it into the oven. The corn bread now had big corn flavor, with minimal grit.

Increasing the buttermilk, which my tasters preferred to milk, added a sharp tang that worked well with the corn. When it came to fat selection, my tasters rejected bacon drippings, shortening, and lard, saying that each had a distinct flavor that took away from the corn; a combination of butter (for flavor) and vegetable oil (which can withstand high heat without burning) worked much better. The flavor was now on track, but the texture was too crumbly.

One corn bread recipe I'd seen made a cornmeal mush by softening raw cornmeal with boiling water to moisten the bread's texture. Using the same principle, I mixed the hot toasted cornmeal with the buttermilk. The cornmeal softened in just a few minutes; then I mixed the batter and put the skillet into the oven. Now this was the corn bread I remembered—crisp, slightly moist, cohesive and not crumbly, and with bold corn flavor. But would it win over my coworkers? I sliced up fat wedges and listened with satisfaction as each taster grudgingly admitted that when it comes to corn bread, the South just might be onto something.

—CALI RICH, *Cook's Country*

SOUTHERN-STYLE SKILLET CORN BREAD

SERVES 12

While any 10-inch oven-safe skillet will work here, our first choice (for both tradition and function) is a cast-iron skillet. Avoid coarsely ground cornmeal, as it will make the corn bread gritty.

- 2¼ cups (11¼ ounces) cornmeal (see note)
- 2 cups buttermilk
- ¼ cup vegetable oil
- 4 tablespoons (½ stick) unsalted butter, cut into pieces
- 1 teaspoon baking powder
- 1 teaspoon baking soda
- ¾ teaspoon salt
- 2 large eggs

1. Adjust the oven racks to the lower-middle and middle positions and heat the oven to 450 degrees. Heat a 10-inch oven-safe skillet on the middle rack for 10 minutes. Bake the cornmeal on a rimmed baking sheet set on the lower-middle rack until fragrant and the color begins to deepen, about 5 minutes. Transfer the hot cornmeal to a large bowl and whisk in the buttermilk; set aside.

2. Add the oil to the hot skillet and continue to heat until the oil is just smoking, about 5 minutes. Remove the skillet from the oven and add the butter, carefully swirling the pan until the butter is melted. Pour all but 1 tablespoon of the oil mixture into the cornmeal mixture, leaving the remaining fat in the pan. Whisk the baking powder, baking soda, salt, and eggs into the cornmeal mixture.

3. Pour the cornmeal mixture into the hot skillet and bake until the top begins to crack and the sides are golden brown, 12 to 16 minutes. Let cool in the pan 5 minutes, then turn out onto a wire rack. Serve.

NOTES FROM THE TEST KITCHEN

SECRETS TO SOUTHERN-STYLE CORN BREAD

1. Toasting the cornmeal gives the bread richer corn flavor.

2. Combining the hot cornmeal and buttermilk softens the cornmeal, resulting in a tender, sturdy, slightly moist crumb.

3. A greased and thoroughly heated pan creates a crisp crust.

THE BEST CAST-IRON SKILLETS

A cast-iron pan can combine the best traits of both nonstick and traditional cookware: Its material and weight give it excellent heat retention for high-heat cooking techniques such as frying and searing. You can use it on the stovetop or bake with it in the oven. Its durability is legendary and cast-iron pans actually improve with time and heavy use. Preseasoned cast iron comes close to nonstick, especially with repeated use. We ran eight cast-iron skillets through many tests, and, in the end, we preferred the classic design—with straight (rather than sloped) sides—and roomy interior of the preseasoned **Lodge Logic Skillet** (left), $29.95 for a 12-inch skillet and $19.95 for a 10-inch skillet. It performed well in all our cooking tests, its surface gained seasoning in the course of testing, and it will last for generations. If you don't mind a truly heavy pan, the preseasoned **Camp Chef Skillet** (right) is a solid performer for only $24.99 for a 12-inch skillet and $16.99 for a 10-inch skillet. (See page 339 for more information about our testing results.)

SOUTHERN-STYLE SKILLET CORN BREAD

BEER-BATTER CHEESE BREAD

NOTHING WARMS UP THE HOUSE like the smell of baking bread—but making a yeasted loaf from scratch can take half the day. Luckily, there are quick breads, like beer-batter cheese bread, that can be on the table in less than an hour. The basic recipe for this bread is simple: Just stir together flour, sugar, cheese, salt, beer, and baking powder; scrape the batter into a loaf pan; pour melted butter on top (to create a rich and craggy crust); and bake. There are no long rises, kneading, or hassle. Best of all, the beer gives this bread a hearty flavor.

Unfortunately, there were a lot of problems with the recipes I found. Many loaves tasted sour, like stale beer, while others had negligible cheese flavor. And some breads were so greasy that I had to pass out extra napkins at each tasting. I wanted a lighter loaf of bread enhanced with the yeasty flavor of beer and a big hit of cheese. And I wanted it to be as easy as advertised. To test beer flavor, I made two loaves, using an inexpensive American lager in one and a dark ale in the other. The dark ale tasted great in a glass, but its strong flavor turned bitter when baked in the bread. The mild domestic lager (Budweiser and Miller Genuine Draft were our favorites in a later tasting) provided a clean, subtle grainy flavor without any sourness at all.

Mild cheddar is typically the cheese of choice in this recipe, but no matter how much I used—up to 3 cups for a single loaf—the flavor was, well, mild. I turned to more assertive cheeses like Gruyère, and extra-sharp cheddar. The bolder cheeses let me get away with using less (about 2 cups per loaf), so the bread was less greasy. Since my tasters professed a preference for biting into pockets of cheese in the bread, I shredded half the cheese and diced the rest for added texture.

While some of the greasiness was gone, the loaves still felt too stodgy and heavy. Increasing the amount of baking powder helped lighten the crumb a little, but I knew that pouring melted butter over the batter before baking—which creates the beautiful crust—was part of the problem. Cutting back the butter from a full stick to half a stick made the loaf considerably lighter while still producing that craggy crust. I finally had a beer-batter cheese bread that was as easy to eat as it was to make.

—DIANE UNGER, *Cook's Country*

BEER-BATTER CHEESE BREAD
MAKES ONE 9-INCH LOAF

Insert the toothpick in a few spots when testing for doneness; it may hit a pocket of cheese, which resembles uncooked batter on the toothpick. Strongly flavored beers make the bread bitter, so mild American lagers, like Budweiser, work best here.

- 8   ounces Gruyère cheese, 4 ounces shredded and 4 ounces cut into ¼-inch cubes
- 3   cups (15 ounces) unbleached all-purpose flour
- 3   tablespoons sugar
- 4   teaspoons baking powder
- 1½ teaspoons salt
- ½   teaspoon pepper
- 1   (12-ounce) bottle light-bodied beer (see note)
- 4   tablespoons (½ stick) unsalted butter, melted

1. Adjust an oven rack to the middle position and heat the oven to 375 degrees. Grease a 9 by 5-inch loaf pan.

2. Combine the shredded and cubed cheese, flour, sugar, baking powder, salt, and pepper in a large bowl. Stir in the beer and mix until well combined. Pour the batter into the prepared loaf pan, spreading it to the corners. Drizzle the melted butter evenly over the top of the batter.

3. Bake until the loaf is deep golden brown and a toothpick inserted into the center comes out clean, 45 to 50 minutes. Cool the bread in the pan for 5 minutes, then turn it out onto a rack. Cool completely and slice as desired. (Although this bread can be kept in an airtight container at room temperature for up to 3 days, after the second day the bread is best toasted.)

VARIATION

BEER-BATTER BREAD WITH CHEDDAR AND JALAPEÑO

Follow the recipe for Beer-Batter Cheese Bread, substituting 8 ounces extra-sharp cheddar for the Gruyère. Stir 2 stemmed, seeded, and minced jalapeño chiles into the bowl with the cheese.

ALMOST NO-KNEAD BREAD

IN NOVEMBER 2006, *New York Times* writer Mark Bittman published a recipe developed by Jim Lahey of the Sullivan Street Bakery in Manhattan that did the seemingly impossible. The recipe, which instantly won legions of followers, was exceedingly simple: Mix a few cups of flour, a tiny amount of yeast, and a little salt together in a bowl; stir in some water until the ingredients just come together; and leave the dough to rise. After 12 to 18 hours, the dough is turned a couple of times, shaped, risen, and baked in a Dutch oven. An hour later, out comes the most beautiful-looking loaf most people have ever baked at home—and all with no kneading.

But amid all the praise, threads on our bulletin board and other websites turned out some complaints. I decided to give the existing recipe to five inexperienced bakers in order to see what (if any) issues arose. While all were beautifully browned and crisp, the loaves varied wildly in size and shape. And though the crusts were extraordinary, the flavor of the crumb fell flat. It simply did not capture the complex yeasty, tangy flavor of a true artisanal loaf.

I decided to tackle the problem of shape first. Thanks to the ingenious use of a Dutch oven, the bread always acquired a dark, crisp crust but the loaves took on a disconcertingly broad range of forms. After observing testers make the recipe a few times, I realized the problem: The wetness of the dough was making it too delicate to handle. Though it was well risen before baking, it was deflating on its way into the pot. In addition, because of its high moisture content, the dough was spreading out over the bottom of the pot before it could firm up properly. I analyzed the no-knead recipe and found that its dough is 85 percent hydrated—meaning that for every 10 ounces of flour, there are 8.5 ounces of water. Most rustic breads, on the other hand, max out at around 80 percent hydration, and standard sandwich breads hover between 60 percent and 75 percent hydration.

To find out what would happen if I reduced the water, I made a batch of dough in which I cut the hydration to 70 percent. Sure enough, this dough was much easier to handle and emerged from the oven well risen and perfectly shaped. But unfortunately, the texture was ruined. Instead of an open, airy crumb structure, it was dense and chewy, with rubbery pockets of unleavened flour. So more moisture led to an open but

squat loaf, and less moisture led to a high but dense loaf. Was there a way to reconcile these two extremes?

Many bread recipes call for a rest period after adding water to the flour but before kneading. This rest is called "autolysis" (although most bakers use the French term *autolyse*). In most recipes, autolysis is just 20 to 30 minutes, but the no-knead bread calls for something completely out of the ordinary: a 12-hour rest. Was there something in the mechanics of such a lengthy autolysis that could help me solve the textural problem? The most common explanation for the autolysis process is simply that it allows time for the flour to hydrate and rest, making the dough easier to manipulate later on. But the word "autolysis" technically refers to the destruction of cells or proteins through enzymatic action. I decided to have a closer look at what really happens to the dough during the process.

The ultimate goal of making bread dough is to create gluten, a strong network of cross-linked proteins that traps air bubbles and stretches as the dough bakes, creating the bubbly, chewy crumb structure that is the signature of any good loaf. In order to form these cross-links, the proteins in the flour need to be aligned next to each other. Imagine the proteins as bundled-up balls of yarn you are trying to tie together into one longer piece, which you'll then sew together into a wider sheet. In their balled-up state, it's not possible to tie them together; first you have to untangle and straighten them out. This straightening out and aligning is usually accomplished by kneading.

But untangling and stretching out short pieces of yarn is much easier than untangling entire balls. This is where autolysis comes in. As the dough autolyzes, enzymes naturally present in wheat act like scissors, cutting the balled-up proteins into smaller segments that are easier to straighten during kneading. This is why dough that has undergone autolysis requires much less kneading than freshly made dough. And here's where the hydration level comes in: The more water there is, the more efficiently the cut-and-link process takes place.

So this was the explanation for how the no-knead bread recipe published in the *New York Times* worked. With 85 percent hydration and a 12-hour rest, the dough was so wet and had autolyzed for so long that the enzymes had broken the proteins down into extremely small pieces. These pieces were so small that, even without kneading, they could stretch out and cross-link during fermentation and the brief turning step. At 70 percent hydration, there simply was not enough water in my dough for the enzymes to act as efficiently as they had in the original recipe. As a result, many of the proteins in my finished bread were still in a semi-balled-up state, giving my bread the overly chewy texture.

What if the secret to making a better no-knead bread was actually adding in some kneading? I knew that even at a relatively dry 70 percent hydration, the proteins in my dough had already been broken down significantly by the long 12- to 18-hour autolysis. All they probably needed was a little kneading to untangle and create an airy, light crumb. I took the dough that I had resting from the day before and turned it out onto my board. I gave the dough the bare minimum of kneads—adding just 15 extra seconds to the no-knead recipe—and continued exactly as I had before. The dough emerged from the oven as beautifully browned and perfectly shaped as any I'd made so far. After letting it cool, I cut into it to reveal an ideal crumb structure: large pockets of air and stretched sheets of gluten. Not only that, I found that since such a small amount of kneading could develop gluten in a such a forceful manner, I could actually reduce the minimum time of the rest period from 12 hours to 8. That 15 seconds of kneading had reaped huge benefits.

Now I turned my attention to the loaf's lackluster taste. Most rustic breads make use of a fermented starter and because a starter contains a much more varied assortment of yeasts than the ones found in a packet, it yields more complex flavor. How could I get the flavors that a starter produces without actually having to create one—a multiday process? Turning first to vinegar as a possible way to introduce tanginess (since most bottled vinegars are 5 percent solutions of the same acid produced by bacteria during dough fermentation), I experimented with different amounts of distilled white vinegar before settling on a single tablespoon.

My bread now had tang, but it lacked complexity and a deep yeasty flavor. As I racked my brain, I realized that beyond bread, there is another commonly available substance that relies on yeast for flavor: beer. I started my testing with dark ales, thinking their rich taste would lead to better flavor. The resulting bread had a strange spicy, fruity aftertaste and smelled like beer. Then I tried a light American-style lager. This time, the loaf came out with a distinct "bready" versus "beery" aroma that could fool anyone who had not seen the lager go into the dough. It turns out that the yeast in lagers is treated in a way that closely resembles the way yeast acts in dough, resulting in the production of similar flavor compounds.

Through the simplest of tweaks—less hydration, the addition of vinegar and beer, and a few seconds of kneading—I had a loaf of bread that both looked and tasted incredible.

—J. KENJI ALT, *Cook's Illustrated*

ALMOST NO-KNEAD BREAD

MAKES 1 LARGE ROUND LOAF

This bread bakes best in a heavy enameled cast-iron Dutch oven with a tight-fitting lid, but it will work in any Dutch oven. Take note of the knobs on your Dutch oven lid as not all are ovensafe at 500 degrees; look for inexpensive replacement knobs from the manufacturer of your Dutch oven (or try using a metal drawer handle from a hardware store). For the best flavor, use a mild-flavored beer, like Budweiser, Stella Artois, or Heineken; a mild nonalcoholic beer also works well.

3 cups (15 ounces) unbleached all-purpose flour, plus extra for the work surface
¼ teaspoon rapid-rise or instant yeast
1 teaspoon salt
¾ cup water, at room temperature
½ cup mild-flavored beer (see note), at room temperature
1 tablespoon white vinegar
Vegetable oil spray

1. Whisk the flour, yeast and salt together in a large bowl. Fold in the water, beer, and vinegar with a rubber spatula until the dough comes together and looks shaggy. Cover the bowl with plastic wrap and let sit at room temperature for at least 8 hours, or up to 18 hours.

2. Lay an 18 by 12-inch sheet of parchment paper inside a 10-inch skillet and spray with vegetable oil spray. Turn the dough out onto a lightly floured work surface and knead by hand to form a smooth, round ball, 10 to 15 times. Following the photos on page 105, shape the dough into a ball by pulling the edges into the middle with floured hands. Transfer the dough, seam-side down, to the prepared skillet.

3. Mist the dough with vegetable oil spray and cover loosely with plastic wrap. Let rise at room temperature until doubled in size and the dough barely springs back when poked with a knuckle, about 2 hours.

4. About 30 minutes before baking, adjust an oven rack to the lowest position, place a large, covered Dutch oven on the rack, and heat the oven to 500 degrees.

5. Lightly flour the top of the dough and score the top of the loaf with a razor blade or sharp knife. Carefully remove the pot from the oven and remove the lid. Pick up the parchment and dough and carefully lower them into the hot pot, letting any excess parchment hang over the edge. Cover the pot.

6. Place the pot in the oven, reduce the oven temperature to 425 degrees, and bake covered for 30 minutes. Remove the lid and continue to bake until the center of the loaf registers 210 degrees on an instant-read thermometer and the crust is deep golden brown, 20 to 30 minutes. Carefully remove the bread from the pot, transfer to a wire rack, and cool to room temperature, about 2 hours, before serving.

VARIATIONS

ALMOST NO-KNEAD BREAD WITH OLIVES, ROSEMARY, AND PARMESAN
Follow the recipe for Almost No-Knead Bread, whisking 2 cups grated Parmesan and 1 tablespoon minced fresh rosemary into the flour mixture and adding ½ cup chopped, pitted green olives with the water in step 1.

ALMOST NO-KNEAD SEEDED RYE BREAD
Follow the recipe for Almost No-Knead Bread, substituting 1⅛ cups rye flour for 1⅜ cups of the all-purpose flour. Whisk 2 tablespoons caraway seeds into the flour mixture in step 1.

ALMOST NO-KNEAD WHOLE-WHEAT BREAD
Follow the recipe for Almost No-Knead Bread, substituting 1 cup whole-wheat flour for 1 cup of the all-purpose flour. Stir 2 tablespoons of honey into the water before adding it to the flour mixture in step 1.

ALMOST NO-KNEAD CRANBERRY-PECAN BREAD
Follow the recipe for Almost No-Knead Bread, adding ½ cup dried cranberries and ½ cup toasted pecan halves to the flour mixture in step 1.

NOTES FROM THE TEST KITCHEN

MAKING ALMOST NO-KNEAD BREAD

1. Fold the wet ingredients into the dry with a rubber spatula. Cover the bowl with plastic wrap and let sit at room temperature for at least 8 hours, or up to 18 hours.

2. Turn the dough out onto a lightly floured work surface and knead by hand to form a smooth, round ball, 10 to 15 times.

3. After kneading the loaf, shape the dough into a ball by pulling the edges into the middle.

4. Transfer the dough, seam-side down, to a parchment-lined 10-inch skillet.

5. Heat up a large heavy Dutch oven with a tight-fitting lid on the lowest rack of a 500-degree oven; then, using the parchment, transfer the bread to the hot pot to bake.

6. Cover and bake the bread for 30 minutes, then remove the lid and bake until the center of the loaf registers 210 degrees on an instant-read thermometer.

SCOOP-AND-BAKE DINNER ROLLS

AFTER THE MIXING, kneading, rising, shaping, rising again, and baking, homemade dinner rolls can make the turkey seem like the simple part of a holiday meal. But there is one glimmer of hope: batter-style dinner rolls.

The ingredients for batter-style rolls (flour, yeast, milk, eggs, shortening, salt, and sugar) are simply stirred together into a pancake-batter consistency, briefly risen in the same bowl, and scooped into a muffin tin to bake without ever touching the work surface or your hands.

After testing a handful of recipes, I learned that batter-style rolls really are a snap to put together—I was able to turn them out in minutes, not hours. However, these rolls have a pungent yeast flavor, as the quick rise doesn't give the yeast time to mellow. Just as worrisome, the recipes I tried baked up squat and heavy.

Fixing the flavor was my first challenge. Shortening was the fat of choice in most recipes, but my tasters wanted butter, and they weren't happy until the amount stood at 6 tablespoons. The richness of the butter also helped temper the strong yeast flavor, but it made the batter heavier and the rolls flatter. Most recipes call for two eggs, but cutting back to one and switching from milk to water helped to lighten the batter and give the rolls more lift. But it still wasn't enough.

I turned my attention to the mixing method. Standard yeast doughs are kneaded to develop gluten in the flour, which builds structure and height in the rolls. Kneading my thin batter was out of the question, but what about beating? My hand mixer did the job—and then some—leaving me with rolls that were tall but too tough (from too much gluten). Looking for a more gentle approach that would work—but not overwork—the batter, I beat the batter mixture with a whisk for a few minutes. It worked like a charm, producing the extra lift needed to make these rolls tall but without a trace of toughness.

—CALI RICH, *Cook's Country*

SCOOP-AND-BAKE DINNER ROLLS

MAKES 12

After being covered with greased plastic wrap in step 3, the batter can be refrigerated in the muffin tin for up to 24 hours. When ready to bake, let the batter sit at room temperature for 30 minutes before proceeding with the recipe.

- 2¼ cups (11¼ ounces) unbleached all-purpose flour
- ¼ cup (1¾ ounces) sugar
- 1 teaspoon salt
- 1 envelope (2¼ teaspoons) rapid-rise or instant yeast
- 1 cup warm water (110 degrees)
- 6 tablespoons unsalted butter, softened
- 1 large egg

1. Adjust an oven rack to the middle position and heat the oven to 200 degrees. Maintain the temperature for 10 minutes, then turn off the oven. Grease the muffin tin.

2. Whisk 1¼ cups of the flour, sugar, salt, and yeast in a large bowl. Whisk in the water, butter, and egg until very smooth, about 2 minutes. Add the remaining 1 cup flour and mix with a rubber spatula until just combined. Cover the bowl with greased plastic wrap and place in the warm oven until the batter has doubled in size, about 30 minutes.

3. Remove the batter from the oven and heat the oven to 375 degrees. Punch the dough down. Scoop the batter evenly into the prepared muffin tin using an ice cream scoop. Cover with the greased plastic wrap and let rise at room temperature until the batter nearly reaches the rims of the muffin cups, about 15 minutes. Remove the plastic wrap and bake until the rolls are golden, 14 to 18 minutes. Serve. (The rolls can be stored in an airtight container at room temperature for 3 days.)

NOTES FROM THE TEST KITCHEN

MIX, REST, AND SCOOP
Follow these simple steps for quick batter-style rolls.

1. Whisk the batter until smooth to develop structure and then stir in the last cup of flour until just combined. Cover with plastic wrap and let rise until doubled in size.

2. Scoop the batter into a greased muffin tin (the batter will fill the cups halfway) and let it continue to rise for 15 minutes at room temperature before baking.

CROISSANTS

FOR MOST HOME BAKERS, croissants fall into that category of baked goods best left to the professionals. Did they need to be hard? Could I develop a foolproof method for preparing authentic croissants at home?

Croissants are prepared from a type of dough professionally referred to as "laminated," or composed of multiple layers. The layers are formed by first wrapping a sheet of dough around a solid sheet of butter. The package is next rolled into a thin rectangle, and then folded into thirds, like a business letter, a process called making "turns." The dough is given a chance to rest (to relax the highly elastic gluten) before the "turns" are repeated time and time again. The turning process develops layers exponentially and, depending on the amount of turns made, the finished dough consists of hundreds of layers (laminates) of dough alternated with butter. When the croissants are baked, the water within the butter converts to steam, which pushes and separates the layers from one another, creating the desired flakiness. All this takes time—and lots of it. I hoped to trim away some of that time, but first I needed to tackle the dough itself.

Most of the recipes I had gathered shared a fairly similar ingredient list: flour, water or milk, yeast, sugar, salt, and a little bit of butter. Texturally speaking, croissants fall somewhere in between bread and pastry. I assumed the type of flour I used would affect the texture and a couple of tests proved my assumption correct. High-protein bread flour yielded very elastic dough that was tricky to roll out, and low-protein cake flour made for weak dough lacking integrity. Commonplace all-purpose flour yielded the flakiest, most tender results.

As for the liquid component, water-based doughs produced leaner, blander croissants, while milk-based doughs were significantly fuller tasting, making the choice clear. Moderate amounts of sugar and salt brought out the best flavor, and a full tablespoon of yeast was necessary to provide lift.

Recipes divided on whether they added butter to the dough or not; those that did claimed it made the dough more tender and those that didn't argued that it made the dough harder to handle and less elastic. I made both and couldn't tell much difference so opted to exclude it. There would be more than enough butter in the butter square around which the dough is folded.

The butter square is just that: a solid sheet of butter. Reconfiguring sticks of butter into a thin, uniform layer without melting it, however, is easier said than done. We found it easiest to lay sticks of butter side by side between pieces of parchment and gently pound them together into a solid block with a rolling pin. Dusting the butter with flour—a common trick—made the butter a bit more pliant, easier to handle, and less inclined to melt. I rolled out the dough, folded it up around the butter square, and felt ready to tackle the folding and proofing.

How many turns are really necessary? I tried batches of croissants with as few as three turns and as many as six, which most professionals consider the ideal number. Three turns made for a bready-textured croissant lacking the requisite layers; six was fine, though a bit fragile. Splitting the difference—four turns—provided the perfect amount of flakiness and tenderness.

After following the photographs provided by one recipe I had found, my first attempts at shaping croissants yielded pudgy semicircles with little resemblance at all to the precisely curled, thin-edged crescents sold at my local bakery. Revisiting my collection of recipes, I saw that most recipes suggested stretching the dough taut when shaping, which certainly helped, but it wasn't the whole solution. A couple of the recipes suggested cutting a notch into the shortest side of the triangle—what becomes the interior center of the croissant, which allows the dough to stretch more freely and be rolled more tightly. It worked like a charm and my homemade croissants looked pretty professional.

I liked how my recipe was coming together, but the finished croissants were greasy and a bit flat. I had seen some recipes where the second rising takes place in the refrigerator over a long period of time. We gave this a try and found that chilling the butter eliminated the greasy (and flat) problem—the butter stays in the dough and doesn't leach out. This method also had the advantage of being more convenient: you can shape these croissants, refrigerate them overnight, and bake them off first thing in the morning.

Virtually every recipe I used for research baked the croissants at 400 degrees and after testing a couple of batches at different temperatures, I had to agree. The golden-brown, fresh-as-can-be croissants easily measured up to those from any bakery in town and were made, by me in my own kitchen, just in time for breakfast.

—SARAH WILSON, *America's Test Kitchen Books*

CROISSANTS

CROISSANTS

MAKES 12

If the dough becomes too warm and sticky to work with, cover it with plastic wrap and let it chill in the refrigerator until firm. The croissant dough, wrapped tightly in plastic wrap, can be refrigerated for up to 1 day or frozen for up to 1 month. If frozen, let the dough thaw completely in the refrigerator, about 12 hours, before using. Once shaped and risen in step 9, the croissants can be frozen until firm, about 1 hour, then transferred to a zipper-lock bag and frozen for up to 1 month. Let frozen croissants thaw at room temperature for 30 minutes, then bake as directed.

DOUGH

- 3 cups (15 ounces) unbleached all-purpose flour, plus extra for the work surface
- ¼ cup (1¾ ounces) sugar
- 1 tablespoon rapid-rise or instant yeast
- 1½ teaspoons salt
- 1¼ cups warm whole milk (110 degrees)

BUTTER SQUARE

- 3 sticks unsalted butter, chilled
- 2 tablespoons unbleached all-purpose flour

- 1 large egg, lightly beaten, for brushing

1. FOR THE DOUGH: Combine 2¾ cups of the flour, the sugar, yeast, and salt in a standing mixer fitted with the dough hook. With the mixer on low speed, add the milk and mix until the dough comes together, about 2 minutes.

2. Increase the mixer speed to medium-low and knead the dough until it forms a sticky ball and becomes elastic, about 8 minutes. If after 5 minutes the dough appears overly sticky and doesn't come together into a ball, add the remaining ¼ cup flour, 1 tablespoon at a time. Scrape the dough into a lightly greased bowl, cover with greased plastic wrap, and refrigerate until chilled, about 1 hour.

3. FOR THE BUTTER SQUARE: Lay the 3 sticks of butter side by side on a sheet of parchment paper. Sprinkle the flour over the butter and cover with a second sheet of parchment paper. Pound the butter with a rolling pin until the butter is softened and the flour is fully incorporated, then roll it into an 8-inch square. Wrap the butter square in plastic wrap and refrigerate until chilled, about 1 hour.

4. Turn the dough out onto a lightly floured counter and roll into an 11-inch square. Following the photos on page 110, place the chilled butter square diagonally in the center of the dough. Fold the corners of the dough up over the butter square so that the corners meet in the middle, and pinch the dough seams to seal.

5. Using a rolling pin, gently tap the dough, starting from the center and working outward, until the square becomes larger and the butter begins to soften. Gently roll the dough into a 14-inch square, adding extra flour as needed to prevent sticking. Fold the dough into thirds to form a rectangle, then fold the rectangle in thirds to form a square. Wrap the dough in plastic wrap and let rest in the refrigerator for 2 hours.

6. Repeat step 5 and let the dough rest in the refrigerator for 2 more hours before using.

7. FOR THE CROISSANTS: Line 2 large baking sheets with parchment paper. Roll the chilled dough into a 20-inch square on a lightly floured counter. Following the photos on page 110, cut the dough in half.

8. Cut each piece of dough crosswise into 3 small rectangles and cut each small rectangle on the diagonal into 2 triangles (you will have a total of 12 triangles). Gently stretch each triangle of dough to lengthen it slightly and even out the sides. Cut a 1-inch-long slit in the center of the wide end, then fold the dough on either side of the slit outward.

9. Gently roll up the dough, from the wide end to the tip, gently stretching it as you go. Lay the croissants on the prepared baking sheets, with the pointed end facing down, and bend the ends of each croissant around to form a crescent shape. Cover loosely with greased plastic wrap and let rise slowly in the refrigerator, 10 to 16 hours.

10. Adjust the oven racks to the upper-middle and lower-middle positions and heat the oven to 400 degrees. Brush the croissants with the egg and bake until golden brown, 18 to 22 minutes, rotating and switching the baking sheets halfway through baking. Transfer the croissants to a wire rack and cool slightly. Serve warm or at room temperature.

VARIATION
ALMOND CROISSANTS

Almond paste is available in the baking aisle of most large supermarkets.

Cut one 7-ounce tube almond paste evenly into 12 pieces and roll each piece into a 2-inch-long log. Place a log across the wide end of each triangle before rolling and shaping the croissants. Before baking, brush the croissants with egg as directed, then sprinkle with a few slivered or sliced almonds (you will need ¼ cup almonds in total). Bake as directed.

NOTES FROM THE TEST KITCHEN

FORMING THE CROISSANT DOUGH

1. Roll out the dough into an 11-inch square and place the chilled butter square diagonally in the center of the dough.

2. Fold the corners of the dough up over the butter square so that the corners meet in the middle, and pinch the dough seams to seal.

3. After gently tapping the dough to make the square larger (and to soften the butter), roll the dough into a 14-inch square then fold it into thirds like a business letter.

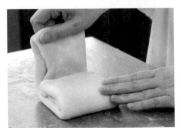

4. Fold the ends of the dough rectangle over the center to form a square. Wrap the dough in plastic wrap and let rest in the refrigerator for 2 hours before repeating steps 3 and 4.

SHAPING CROISSANTS

1. Roll the chilled dough into a 20-inch square on a lightly floured work surface, then cut the dough in half.

2. Cut each dough half crosswise into 3 small rectangles, and cut each small rectangle on the diagonal into 2 triangles (you will have a total of 12 triangles).

3. Gently stretch each triangle of dough to lengthen it slightly and even out the sides.

4. Cut a 1-inch-long slit in the center of the triangle's wide end, then fold the dough on either side of the slit outward.

5. Gently roll up the triangle of dough from the wide end to the tip, gently stretching it as you go.

6. Lay the croissants on the prepared baking sheets with the pointed end facing down, and bend the ends of each croissant around to form a crescent shape.

BABKA

A DIMINUTIVE OF THE POLISH WORD *baba*, meaning "grandmother," babka is a rich and decadent coffeecake-style bread that is traditionally reserved for Easter Sunday in eastern Europe. Made with eggs, sugar, and butter and filled with cinnamon, sugar, nuts, and sometimes raisins, traditional babka is characterized by its round shape (sometimes with a hole in the middle), caramelized exterior, butter-rich flavor, and gooey filling.

We decided to start our testing with the dough and attend to the filling later. The first ingredient up for examination was the flour. We tried both all-purpose flour and bread flour. All-purpose flour was the clear winner, giving the babka a fluffier, more tender crumb. Tasters quickly settled on ½ cup sugar as the right amount for the dough, which made the bread sweet without it tasting cloying. A little vanilla extract added complexity to the dough.

One of the hallmarks of babka is its eggy flavor. Because we wanted our babka to be tender and rich, we started by using just yolks. To our surprise, the all-egg-yolk babka was dry and heavy. We tried various yolk and whole-egg combinations and found that the lightest, most tender babka was made with three whole eggs.

As for liquids, we tried water, milk, and sour cream. Sour cream produced the best results, giving the babka a richer flavor than either milk or water. We tried yeast amounts ranging from 1 teaspoon to 2 tablespoons and got the best results with 1 package (2¼ teaspoons).

Babka just wouldn't be babka without butter—it is usually in the dough and in the filling. But how much should we add to the dough? We tried amounts as little as 4 tablespoons and as much as a whopping 20 tablespoons. As we expected, more butter made the bread taste better and gave it a richer texture. However, there was a limit. Sixteen tablespoons of butter did the trick; the loaves made with more than that became leaden and greasy.

Babka is traditionally allowed to ferment in a cool place overnight. What would happen if the dough were allowed to rise in a warm place? We let one loaf rise at room temperature for two hours and put it up against another that had risen in the refrigerator overnight. The room-temperature babka had a strong yeasty flavor, oily texture, and uneven crumb; the refrigerator babka had a clean, mild flavor with a delicate, even texture. Allowing the dough to rise in the refrigerator accomplishes two things: The lower temperature keeps the butter from melting, and it lets the yeast develop slowly, resulting in a fine, tender crumb. After experimenting with fermentation times, we found that a stay of at least 10 hours in the refrigerator was necessary.

With our dough ready, we turned our attention to the filling, which came together easily. Cinnamon was a given and our tasters preferred a modest 2 teaspoons—after all, this was babka, not cinnamon rolls. Butter was also necessary to make the filling rich and moist. We tested granulated sugar as well as light and dark brown sugar in the filling. Granulated sugar was too dry and added little flavor. Dark brown sugar proved too wet and turned syrupy, like the filling for a sticky bun. And the strong molasses flavor detracted from the cinnamon. Light brown sugar proved the best sweetener, adding moisture and a lighter molasses flavor that complemented the cinnamon. With the addition of nuts and raisins, our filling was complete.

As for shaping, instead of making one large babka in a Bundt or tube pan, we decided to stray from tradition and make two loaves. (This way we could eat one and freeze one.) The soft dough gracefully yielded to a light touch under the rolling pin as we rolled it out. We then sprinkled it with the filling and rolled it up slowly and tightly into a cylinder. Although some babka recipes simply place the cylinder of dough into the pan, we found it best to slice up the cylinder which resulted in a craggy and crunchy top that tasters preferred.

We knew we wanted an initial blast of high heat to give the loaves a proper rise and a nicely browned crust. To determine the best baking temperature, we tried baking the babka at temperatures ranging from 300 to 425 degrees. After much testing, we determined that placing the bread in a 450-degree oven, then immediately turning the temperature down to 350 degrees for the duration of the baking gave us an evenly baked bread with a uniformly browned exterior. Now for the most difficult part of the recipe—waiting for the babka to cool before eating it!

—RACHEL TOOMEY, *America's Test Kitchen Books*

BABKA

MAKES TWO 9-INCH LOAVES

Because of all the butter in this dough, we don't recommend kneading it by hand or in a food processor. After mixing for the final 15 minutes, the dough should be very soft and slightly sticky, but not wet. You will know that you have added enough flour in step 2 if, when you touch the finished dough, it pulls away from your fingers. This is a rustic bread, so do not worry about slicing the raw dough in step 6 into perfect rounds, or even if you are a few rounds short.

DOUGH

- 5½ cups (27½ ounces) unbleached all-purpose flour, plus extra for the work surface
- 1 package (2¼ teaspoons) rapid-rise or instant yeast
- 1 cup sour cream
- ½ cup (3½ ounces) granulated sugar
- 3 large eggs
- ¼ cup water
- 4 teaspoons vanilla extract
- 1 teaspoon salt
- 16 tablespoons (2 sticks) unsalted butter, cut into 16 pieces and softened but still cool

FILLING

- 1½ cups (10½ ounces) packed light brown sugar
- 1 cup walnuts, toasted and chopped coarse
- 1 cup raisins (optional)
- 8 tablespoons (1 stick) unsalted butter, melted
- 2 teaspoons ground cinnamon
- Pinch salt

GLAZE

- 1 tablespoon granulated sugar
- ¼ teaspoon ground cinnamon
- 1 large egg
- 1 tablespoon water

1. FOR THE DOUGH: In a medium bowl, whisk together 4½ cups of the flour and the yeast; set aside. In the bowl of a standing mixer, whisk together the sour cream, granulated sugar, eggs, water, vanilla, and salt. Add the flour mixture (do not stir in) and, using the dough hook, knead the mixture on low speed until the ingredients are evenly combined, about 3 minutes. Increase the mixer speed to medium-low and continue to knead until the dough becomes smooth, about 8 minutes longer, stopping to scrape down the sides of the bowl occasionally. (The dough will be very wet.)

2. With the mixer running on medium-low, slowly add the butter, 1 piece at a time, waiting about 15 seconds between additions. After the butter has been added, scrape down the sides of the bowl and continue to knead the dough on medium-low until the dough forms a very soft ball, about 15 minutes longer. Add the remaining 1 cup flour, 2 tablespoons at a time, until the dough is no longer wet and it clears the sides but sticks to the bottom of the bowl. (You may not need all the flour; the dough should be very soft and sticky.)

3. Scrape the dough into a large, lightly oiled bowl. Cover with plastic wrap and refrigerate for 10 to 24 hours. (Because of the high butter content, the dough will rise only slightly.)

4. FOR THE FILLING: Mix all of the ingredients together; set aside. Spray two 9-inch loaf pans with vegetable oil spray, then line with overhanging strips of parchment paper following the photo on page 113. Spray the parchment paper with vegetable oil spray and set aside.

5. Turn the cold dough onto a lightly floured work surface. Use a rolling pin to roll the dough into a 24 by 18-inch rectangle, about ¹⁄₁₆ inch thick, with the long side facing you. Following the photos on page 113, sprinkle the filling evenly over the dough, leaving a ½-inch border at the far edge. Using both hands, roll the dough into a long, taut cylinder. Brush the seam with water and pinch closed to secure.

6. Lightly dust the roll with flour and pat into a uniform, 24-inch-long cylinder. Using a serrated knife, slice the roll into ¾-inch-thick slices (you should have about 32 slices). Arrange the slices in 2 long rows in each of the prepared loaf pans (about 16 slices per pan). Loosely cover the pans with plastic wrap and let rise at room temperature until almost doubled in size, 2 to 2½ hours.

7. FOR THE GLAZE AND TO BAKE: Adjust an oven rack to the lower-middle position and heat the oven to 450 degrees. Mix the granulated sugar and cinnamon together. In a separate bowl, beat the egg with the water. Brush the loaves gently with the egg mixture, then sprinkle with the cinnamon-sugar mixture. Place the loaf pans in the oven and reduce the temperature to 350 degrees. Bake the loaves until browned and an instant-read thermometer inserted into the side of the loaf reads 190 degrees, 50 to 60 minutes, rotating the pans halfway through the baking time. (If the tops of the loaves look like they are getting too dark, tent the pans loosely with foil.)

8. Transfer the loaf pans to a wire rack and let cool for 15 minutes. Using the overhanging parchment as a grip, remove the babka from the loaf pans. Let the loaves cool completely on the rack before slicing and serving. (The cooled loaves can be wrapped tightly in plastic wrap and stored at room temperature for up to 3 days or frozen for up to 1 month. If frozen, let thaw completely at room temperature, then refresh briefly in a 350-degree oven until lightly warmed before serving.)

NOTES FROM THE TEST KITCHEN

THE BEST SERRATED KNIVES

Serrated knives are an indispensable part of any cook's kitchen arsenal, but do you really need a bread knife, a tomato knife, a sandwich knife, and a cake splitter? In our search for one all-purpose serrated knife, we tested 12 serrated knives, using them to split cake layers, slice bread and ripe tomatoes, and cut sticky-bun dough and club sandwiches. **Wüsthof's Classic Bread Knife, 10-Inches** (top), $79.95, edged out the competition as the best all-purpose serrated knife, and the **Victorinox Forschner 10¼-Inch Curved Blade Bread Knife with Black Fibrox Handle** (bottom), $24.95, performed almost as well for about a third of the price and was easier on large-handed testers. We found that both of these knives boast three traits necessary for a great all-purpose tool: a slightly flexible blade between 10 and 12 inches long, with serrations that are both uniformly spaced and moderate in length. (See page 336 for more information about our testing results.)

SHAPING BABKA

1. After rolling the dough into a 24 by 18-inch rectangle, sprinkle the filling evenly over the dough, leaving ½ inch at the far end.

2. Loosen the dough from the counter using a bench scraper, then roll the dough into a long, taut cylinder; brush the seam with water and pinch to secure.

3. Dust the roll with flour and gently pat the roll into a uniform 24-inch-long roll. Slice the roll into ¾-inch-thick slices (you should have about 32 slices).

4. Arrange the dough slices in two rows (about 8 slices per row) in each loaf pan. Cover the pans loosely with plastic wrap and let rise at room temperature.

QUICK RELEASE FOR BREAD

1. Grease a loaf pan, then line it width-wise with a piece of parchment paper, letting excess paper hang over the edges. Grease the paper.

2. To remove the loaf from the pan, use the overlap as a handy grip and lift the bread out gently.

PASTA

PASTITSIO

EVERY GREEK COOKBOOK HAS A RECIPE for pastitsio, a layered casserole consisting of a ground meat and tomato sauce, pasta, a creamy béchamel, and a sprinkling of cheese. In Greek, the word pastitsio means "made from pasta." When well prepared, it is comfort food at its finest, but often recipes for pastitsio yield a mishmash of overseasoned lamb filling, soggy, overcooked pasta, and thick, gluey béchamel. I aimed to make a pastitsio worthy of serving to our friends from Greece—one that would bring them back to their grandmother's kitchen.

Some of the recipes I found called for ground beef or veal, while others called for ground lamb. Testing my way through these recipes, I found that those made with beef were dry and those made with veal lacked depth of flavor. Lamb, on the other hand, was rich and moist and it contributed a gaminess that we have come to associate with Greek cuisine. But ground lamb can be incredibly fat-laden, making the casserole greasy. To remedy this, I browned the ground lamb and then drained the excess fat off before adding the other ingredients.

Onion and garlic were a given, but getting the spices set proved to be more of a puzzle. Several recipes called for showering the ground lamb with a whole array of spices, including cumin, coriander, cardamom, cinnamon, nutmeg, and cloves. But tasters found the abundance of spices overpowering. A simple combination of cinnamon, oregano, and nutmeg did the trick.

Next, I had to decide on the type of tomato product to use. Diced tomatoes were acceptable, but tasters did not care for the overly assertive chunks of tomato, which did not blend with the other ingredients in the sauce. Tasters preferred the even distribution of crushed tomatoes, but felt that the tomato flavor was not quite bold enough. I fortified the crushed tomatoes with ¼ cup of tomato paste, which provided the perfect backbone of flavor. After simmering the lamb and tomato mixture for only five minutes, the meat sauce was thickened slightly and intensely flavored. The addition of ½ cup of Pecorino Romano (a substitute for the Greek cheese *kefalotyri*, which is hard to find) enriched the sauce, while intensifying the flavor of the lamb.

With one major component of the dish resolved, I turned to the béchamel, a creamy sauce made from milk that is thickened with a *roux* (a paste made from flour and hot fat). Testing sauce amounts, I found that two, three, four, and even five cups of sauce produced dry casseroles. I was surprised by the amount of sauce required, but the pasta absorbed a good deal of the sauce in the oven, and we wanted a creamy casserole. Tasters were finally satisfied with the consistency of the casserole when made with six cups of béchamel!

Many of the recipes I came across called for the addition of eggs in the béchamel to help hold the sauce together during baking so I thought I'd give this a try. To prevent the eggs from coagulating when I combined them with the sauce, I used a common kitchen technique called tempering, in which some of the hot milk mixture is whisked into the eggs before adding it to the rest of the béchamel. This prevented the eggs from scrambling immediately; however, they scrambled as the casserole baked in the oven. To prevent this, I reduced the baking time from 50 minutes in a 350-degree oven to 30 minutes in a 400-degree oven. This allowed the top to brown while keeping the sauce smooth and creamy. Lastly, to enhance the flavor, I added sautéed onion, a healthy bit of garlic, Pecorino Romano cheese, and a touch of nutmeg.

Next it was time to test the pasta. While many recipes call for long pasta such as perciatelli or spaghetti, tasters complained that they were difficult to eat in a casserole. Penne and ziti bulked up the size of the dish with unnecessary air pockets, thus eliminating the desired compact layers. They also produced a pasta-heavy casserole that didn't have the creaminess we were after. Large macaroni was a definite improvement, but smaller elbow macaroni maximized the structure of the casserole, and gave tasters multiflavored bites with every spoonful. Now all our pastitsio needed was a light sprinkling of Pecorino Romano.

—MEGAN WYCOFF, *America's Test Kitchen Books*

PASTITSIO

SERVES 6 TO 8

The baking dish is very full when it goes into the oven. Just in case it overflows, bake it on a foil-lined baking sheet. Do not substitute low-fat or nonfat milk in the sauce.

2 pounds ground lamb

2 onions, minced (about 2 cups)

Salt

¼ cup tomato paste

9 garlic cloves, minced

1 tablespoon minced fresh oregano or 1 teaspoon dried

1 teaspoon ground cinnamon

½ teaspoon fresh grated nutmeg

1 (28-ounce) can crushed tomatoes

3 ounces Pecorino Romano cheese, grated (about 1½ cups)

Pepper

12 ounces elbow macaroni (3 cups)

4 tablespoons (½ stick) unsalted butter

⅓ cup unbleached all-purpose flour

6 cups whole milk

1 large egg

1. Adjust an oven rack to the middle position and heat the oven to 400 degrees. Cook the lamb in a 12-inch skillet over medium-high heat, breaking the meat into small pieces with a wooden spoon, until no longer pink and the fat has rendered, about 5 minutes. Strain the lamb through a fine-mesh strainer, reserving the drippings.

2. Return 2 tablespoons of the reserved lamb drippings, half of the onions, and ½ teaspoon salt to the skillet and cook over medium heat until softened, 5 to 7 minutes. Stir in the tomato paste, 2 tablespoons of the garlic, oregano, cinnamon, and ¼ teaspoon of the nutmeg and cook until fragrant, about 30 seconds. Stir in the drained lamb and crushed tomatoes. Bring to a simmer and cook over medium-low heat until the sauce has thickened, about 5 minutes. Off the heat, stir in ½ cup of the cheese and season with salt and pepper; set aside.

3. Meanwhile, bring 4 quarts water to a boil in a large Dutch oven. Stir in the macaroni and 1 tablespoon salt and cook, stirring often, until just al dente, about 5 minutes. Drain the pasta, rinse under cool water until cold, and leave in the colander.

4. Wipe out the Dutch oven, add the butter, and return to medium heat until melted. Add the remaining onion and ½ teaspoon salt and cook until softened, 5 to

7 minutes. Stir in the remaining garlic and cook until fragrant, about 30 seconds. Stir in the flour and cook, stirring constantly, for 1 minute. Gradually whisk in the milk. Bring to a simmer and cook, whisking often, until the sauce thickens and no longer tastes of flour, about 10 minutes.

5. Off the heat, whisk in ½ cup more of the cheese and the remaining ¼ teaspoon nutmeg. Season with salt and pepper to taste. Crack the egg into a small bowl. Whisk about ½ cup of the béchamel into the egg to temper, then slowly whisk the egg mixture back into the sauce. Stir in the cooked macaroni until evenly coated with the sauce.

6. Spread half of the macaroni into a 13 by 9-inch baking dish, then spread the lamb mixture evenly over the top. Spread the remaining macaroni evenly over the lamb and sprinkle with the remaining ½ cup of the cheese. (At this point, the casserole can be covered and refrigerated for up to 2 days.)

7. Place the baking dish on a foil-lined baking sheet and bake until the edges are bubbling and the top is lightly golden, about 30 minutes. (If refrigerated, cover the dish with foil and bake for 30 to 40 minutes, then uncover and continue to bake for 15 to 20 minutes.) Let stand for 10 minutes before serving.

NOTES FROM THE TEST KITCHEN

THE BEST ELBOW MACARONI

This pasta has become a staple in such distinctly American recipes as macaroni salad and macaroni and cheese. But with so many brands of elbow macaroni on the market, which one should you buy? Are they all the same? To find out, we rounded up eight contenders and tasted them simply dressed with vegetable oil, and in our recipe for classic macaroni and cheese. What did we discover? **Barilla**, an Italian brand that makes pasta for the American market at their plant in Ames, Iowa, won our tasting by a large margin. Our tasters praised this pasta for its "wheaty," "buttery" flavor and "firm texture," and they especially liked that these elbows have small ridges and a slight twist that "holds sauce well."

LASAGNA WITH MEATBALLS

CARNIVALE IS AN ITALIAN FESTIVAL that takes place just before Lent, the period of time before Easter during which Roman Catholics do not eat meat. Traditionally, Carnivale was a time to consume all of the meat that remained in the village before the fast, but these days, it is a great public celebration that entails dressing up in costumes, wearing decorative masks, and partying all day and night. In Naples, a city in southern Italy, a lasagna with tiny meatballs, tomato sauce, and mozzarella cheese (*lasagna di Carnivale*) is traditionally made to celebrate this festival.

I have eaten more than my share of lasagna, which is often nothing more than mushy noodles swimming in a sea of red sauce and cheese. I wanted to try the Neapolitan style of lasagna, with its distinct layers, moderate amount of deeply flavored sauce, and tender meatballs, but I would never make it at home—it contains 25 ingredients and takes an entire day to prepare. Starting from the true Italian premise that less sauce and more pasta is better, I set out to devise a recipe with these classic tastes but without the backbreaking labor.

First, I tried to make sense of the cheese component. Various Italian recipes call for mozzarella, ricotta (sometimes mixed with whole eggs or egg yolks), and a hard grating cheese (usually Parmesan, but sometimes Pecorino Romano). After trying the various combinations, I realized that ricotta was responsible for what we call "lasagna meltdown"—the loss of shape and distinct layering. Even with the addition of whole eggs or yolks as a thickener, I found that ricotta is too watery to use in lasagna that includes meatballs, and usually leads to a sloppy mess.

Mozzarella provides plenty of creaminess, and its stringiness binds the layers to each other and helps keep them from slipping apart when served. Fresh mozzarella, however, has too much moisture to be effective. When it melts, it releases so much liquid that the lasagna becomes mushy and watery. In addition, the delicate flavor of expensive fresh mozzarella is lost in the baking. After a few disastrous attempts with fresh mozzarella, I turned to its shrink-wrapped cousin, whole-milk mozzarella, and had much better results. I also found that a small amount of either Parmesan or Pecorino Romano provides a pleasantly sharp contrast to the somewhat mild-tasting mozzarella.

With the cheese question resolved, I focused on the meatballs. Here again I looked to traditional Italian recipes for inspiration, then tried to simplify. I seasoned ground beef with herbs, cheese, egg yolks, and breadcrumbs. However, instead of rolling out real meatballs, which would be too large to rest snugly between the layers of pasta, I pinched off small bits of the mixture. I tried pinching them off directly into hot oil, which worked fine, but required standing over the oil frying for upwards of four batches. Instead, I placed the meatballs on a baking sheet and after just eight minutes in a 450-degree oven, they were done.

To keep things simple, I decided to add the meatballs to a quick-cooking tomato sauce made with crushed tomatoes. Many traditional recipes simmer whole tomatoes or tomato puree for hours to make a rich, complex sauce. However, since lasagna has so many competing elements, little was gained by this lengthy process. Simmering canned, crushed tomatoes just long enough to make a sauce—about 10 minutes—was sufficient.

Next I focused my attention on the choice of noodles and layering tricks. Here in the test kitchen, we often make lasagna with no-boil noodles. I made our working recipe with no-boil noodles, only to find out that they did not work—they emerged from the oven with a tough, cardboardlike texture. Thinking that soaking the noodles in hot water would help them to soften, I gave it a try. No luck. My lightly sauced lasagna simply did not have enough moisture for the noodles to absorb and become tender as the lasagna cooked. This type of lasagna requires a more traditional type of noodle.

Many Italian lasagna recipes call for fresh pasta. Tasters liked the thinness of the fresh noodles, but voted unanimously against making them from scratch—after all, we were trying to simplify our lasagna-making process, not complicate it. I then tried several brands of fresh pasta from our local markets but they varied dramatically, not only in thickness and dimensions, but also in quality. Traditional dried lasagna noodles—the type that require being boiled before assembling the lasagna—turned out to be our favorite, in part because they were the most reliable, but also because tasters were happiest with the lasagna they produced.

In terms of the actual layering procedure, I spread a small amount of tomato sauce (without any meatballs) over the pan to moisten the bottom layer of pasta, and added the first layer of noodles. After that, I spread the sauce and meatballs evenly over the noodles, covered them with shredded mozzarella, then sprinkled on grated Parmesan. I then built more layers by this same process. Since the meatballs tended to dry out when not covered by pasta, I fashioned a final, top layer of pasta, then dusted it with both cheeses, which browned up nicely during baking for an attractive appearance.

After just 20 minutes in a 400-degree oven, the lasagna was ready to eat (although we do recommend letting it cool for 5 minutes before serving). This lasagna is certainly just as satisfying as traditional Neapolitan versions, and quicker to assemble. The best part is that you don't have to wait for Carnivale to enjoy it!

—RACHEL TOOMEY, *America's Test Kitchen Books*

LASAGNA WITH MEATBALLS

SERVES 8

Do not substitute no-boil lasagna noodles; they do not work in this dish. The size of the noodles will depend on the brand; if the noodles are short (such as DeCecco) you will need to layer them crosswise in the dish, but if they are long (such as Barilla and Ronzoni) layer them lengthwise in the dish. Regardless of which brand of noodle you are using, there should be 3 noodles per layer.

MEATBALLS AND SAUCE

    1   pound 85 percent lean ground beef
    2   ounces Parmesan or Pecorino Romano cheese, grated
        (about 1 cup)
    ½   cup store-bought plain dried breadcrumbs
    2   large eggs, lightly beaten
    ½   cup minced fresh basil or parsley
        Salt and pepper
    3   tablespoons olive oil
    2   garlic cloves, minced
    1   (28-ounce) can crushed tomatoes

NOODLES AND CHEESE

    1   tablespoon salt
   12   dried lasagna noodles (see note)
    1   pound whole-milk mozzarella cheese, shredded
        (about 4 cups)
    4   ounces Parmesan or Pecorino Romano cheese, grated
        (about 2 cups)

1. FOR THE MEATBALLS AND SAUCE: Adjust an oven rack to the middle position and heat the oven to 450 degrees. Spray a rimmed baking sheet with vegetable oil spray; set aside. Mix the beef, cheese, breadcrumbs, eggs, 5 tablespoons of the basil, 1 teaspoon salt, and ½ teaspoon pepper together until uniform. Pinch off scant 1 teaspoon–sized pieces of the mixture (about the size of a small grape), roll into small balls, and arrange on the prepared baking sheet. Bake the meatballs until just cooked through and lightly browned, 8 to 10 minutes. Transfer the meatballs to a paper towel–lined platter and set aside.

2. Heat the oil and garlic in a medium saucepan over medium heat until the garlic starts to sizzle, about 2 minutes. Stir in the tomatoes, bring to a simmer, and cook until the sauce thickens slightly, 10 to 15 minutes. Off the heat, stir in the remaining 3 tablespoons basil and season with salt and pepper to taste. Stir the meatballs into the sauce and cover to keep warm until needed.

3. FOR THE NOODLES AND CHEESE: Meanwhile, bring 4 quarts water to a boil in a stockpot. Stir in the salt and noodles and cook, stirring often, until the pasta is al dente. Drain the noodles and rinse them under cold water until cool. Spread the noodles out in a single layer over clean kitchen towels. (Do not use paper towels; they will stick to the pasta.)

4. Spray a 13 by 9-inch baking dish with vegetable oil spray. Smear 3 tablespoons of the tomato sauce (without any meatballs) over the bottom of the pan. Line the pan with a layer of pasta, making sure that the noodles touch but do not overlap. Spread about 1½ cups of the tomato sauce with meatballs evenly over the pasta. Sprinkle evenly with 1 cup of the mozzarella and ½ cup of the Parmesan. Repeat the layering of pasta, tomato sauce with meatballs, and cheeses 2 more times. For the fourth and final layer, cover the pasta with the remaining 1 cup mozzarella and sprinkle with the remaining ½ cup Parmesan. (At this point, the lasagna can be wrapped tightly with plastic wrap and refrigerated for up to 2 days; let the lasagna sit at room temperature for 1 hour before baking.)

5. Adjust an oven rack to the middle position and heat the oven to 400 degrees. Bake until the cheese on top turns golden brown in spots and the sauce is bubbling, 20 to 25 minutes. Let the lasagna rest for 5 to 10 minutes before cutting and serving.

SIMPLE ITALIAN-STYLE MEAT SAUCE

SIMPLE ITALIAN-STYLE MEAT SAUCE

IN ITALY, COOKING A MEATY PASTA SAUCE is an all-day affair. Whether using ground meat for a *ragù alla Bolognese* or chunks of meat for a rustic sauce, one thing is for sure: These sauces simmer slowly—for three or four hours, or even longer.

In America, though, "Italian meat sauce" has typically come to mean a shortcut version in which ground beef, onions, garlic, and canned tomatoes are thrown together in a pot and cooked for half an hour. Could I develop a rich and flavorful meat sauce to make on a weeknight that tasted as if it had been simmering if not all day, at least for a good portion of it?

My search started with analyzing Bolognese recipes, and I discovered right away that the best ones don't brown the meat. Instead, they call for cooking the ground meat until it loses its raw color, then adding the liquid ingredients one by one, slowly reducing each and building flavor before adding the next. The first liquid in the pot is usually some form of dairy, a Bolognese sauce's signature ingredient that imparts a sweet creaminess to the dish. Most American meat sauces, on the other hand, brown the beef first—a step that certainly adds flavor, but toughens the meat. They also skip the dairy in favor of tomato sauce, which doesn't provide the butterfat or the same layers of complex flavor.

Would eliminating the browning step and adding milk work better? After sautéing onion and garlic, I stirred in a pound of ground beef, breaking it up with a wooden spoon. As soon as it started to lose its raw color, I immediately added ½ cup milk, and then simmered the sauce for 30 minutes or so. The results were disappointing: While some of the meat was tender and moist, most was tough and mealy. And, despite the milk, the sauce lacked flavor overall. If anything, without sufficient time to reduce, the milk actually overpowered the meat flavor in the sauce. It occurred to me that in order for the milk to develop the new flavor compounds that are its key contribution to a Bolognese sauce, a lengthy simmer was necessary. Would cooking the sauce a little longer—45 minutes instead of 30—help? Not enough to notice. Furthermore, the extra 15 minutes of simmering had little impact on the meat, which was still more rubbery than not.

It was time to look beyond Bolognese for ways to improve my simple weeknight sauce. Meat tenderizer seemed like an obvious place to start. A few teaspoons did soften the beef, but also made it spongy. Would soy sauce work? Soy sauce is a base ingredient in many of our steak marinades, where it acts much like a brine, tenderizing meat by helping it retain moisture. But I quickly discovered that while soy minimizes moisture loss in large pieces of meat, such as steak, it has virtually no impact on tiny bits of ground beef. After a little research I found out why: Bigger pieces of meat contain more water, which takes a longer time to evaporate during cooking. The relatively miniscule amount of water in small pieces of ground meat, on the other hand, evaporates almost immediately, and not even soy sauce can help prevent this.

Then a colleague suggested a trick that hadn't occurred to me: mixing in a *panade*. This paste of bread and milk is often blended into meatballs and meatloaf to help them hold their shape and retain moisture during cooking. It was worth a try. Using a fork, I mashed up a piece of bread with some milk until I had a smooth paste, and mixed it into the ground beef until well combined. I then proceeded as usual with the rest of the recipe: stirring the beef mixture into the sautéed onions and garlic, adding the tomatoes, and simmering. I noticed a difference in the sauce even before I ladled it over pasta for tasters. The meat looked moister and, sure enough, tasters confirmed that it was. It turns out that starches from the bread absorb liquid from the milk to form a gel that coats and lubricates the meat much in the same way as fat. But all was not perfect. Tasters were pleased with the meat's tenderness but complained that the sauce was too chunky and resembled chili. No problem. I pulsed the meat and panade together in a food processor to create fine pieces of supple, juicy meat.

With the meat issue solved, it was time to turn my attention to flavor. Without browning or a lengthy simmer to concentrate and build new layers of flavor, complexity and depth were noticeably lacking from my sauce. Could the type of ground beef I used enhance flavor? I bought four different kinds—ground round, chuck, and sirloin, as well as meat labeled "ground beef" (a mix of various beef cuts and trimmings)—and made four sauces. The ground round was bland and spongy, but tasters liked each of the other three equally well. Eighty-five percent lean beef proved to have just the right degree of leanness, adding richness without making the sauce greasy. Still, tasters were pressing,

"Where's the beef (flavor)?"

Next, I tested a range of ingredients that are the usual suspects when trying to boost meaty flavor. Beef broth ended up imparting a tinny off-flavor to the sauce. Worcestershire and steak sauce overwhelmed it with their potent flavorings, and red wine lent a sour taste. Finally, I tried mushrooms—and, at last, I had a winner. The mushrooms brought a real beefiness to the sauce. After experimenting with different types, I discovered that plain white mushrooms worked just fine. The key was browning them. I minced a judicious amount (about 4 ounces) and added them to the pan with the onions. Browning concentrated their flavor but left them tender and supple, allowing them to add complexity without otherwise letting their presence be known.

When it came to other components of the sauce, tasters liked a mix of diced and crushed tomatoes. The diced tomatoes brought chunky texture, while the crushed provided a smooth foundation. I reserved a small amount of juice from the drained diced tomatoes to deglaze the pan after browning the mushrooms. This little trick gave the sauce's tomato flavor a boost, as did a tablespoon of tomato paste. Earlier, I had ruled against milk in the sauce (except for the couple of tablespoons in the panade), but I reinstated dairy in the form of a handful of grated Parmesan, which brought a welcome tanginess. With a dash of red pepper flakes and some fresh oregano, I now had a sauce with meltingly tender meat that was as complex and full-bodied as any sauce simmered for under an hour could be.

—CHARLES KELSEY, *Cook's Illustrated*

SIMPLE ITALIAN-STYLE MEAT SAUCE

MAKES ABOUT 6 CUPS

Except for ground round (which tasters found spongy and bland), this recipe will work with most types of ground beef, as long as it is 85 percent lean. (Eighty percent lean beef will turn the sauce greasy; 90 percent will make it gritty.) Use high-quality crushed tomatoes; our favorite brands are Tuttorosso, Muir Glen, and Hunt's Organic. If using dried oregano, add the entire amount with the canned tomato liquid in step 2. The sauce makes enough for nearly 2 pounds of pasta. Left-over sauce can be refrigerated in an airtight container for up to 3 days or frozen for up to 1 month.

4 ounces white mushrooms, broken into rough pieces
1 slice high-quality white sandwich bread, torn into quarters
2 tablespoons whole milk
  Salt and pepper
1 pound 85 percent lean ground beef (see note)
1 tablespoon olive oil
1 large onion, minced (about 1½ cups)
6 garlic cloves, minced
¼ teaspoon red pepper flakes
1 tablespoon tomato paste
1 (14.5-ounce) can diced tomatoes, drained, ¼ cup liquid reserved
1 tablespoon minced fresh oregano or 1 teaspoon dried (see note)
1 (28-ounce) can crushed tomatoes (see note)
½ ounce grated Parmesan cheese (about ¼ cup)

1. Pulse the mushrooms in a food processor until finely chopped, about eight 1-second pulses, scraping down the sides of the bowl as needed; transfer to a medium bowl. Add the bread, milk, ½ teaspoon salt, and ½ teaspoon pepper to the now-empty bowl and pulse until a paste forms, about eight 1-second pulses. Add the beef and pulse until the mixture is well combined, about six 1-second pulses.

2. Heat the oil in a large saucepan over medium-high heat until just smoking. Add the onion and mushrooms; cook, stirring frequently, until the vegetables are browned and dark bits form on the pan bottom, 6 to 12 minutes. Stir in the garlic, pepper flakes, and tomato paste; cook until fragrant and the tomato paste starts to brown, about 1 minute. Add the ¼ cup reserved tomato liquid and 2 teaspoons of the fresh oregano (if using dried, add the full amount), scraping the bottom of the pan with a wooden spoon to loosen the browned bits. Add the meat mixture and cook, breaking the meat into small pieces with the wooden spoon, until the beef loses its raw color, 2 to 4 minutes, making sure that the meat does not brown.

3. Stir in the crushed and drained diced tomatoes and bring to a simmer; reduce the heat to low and gently simmer until the sauce has thickened and the flavors have blended, about 30 minutes. Stir in the cheese and remaining 1 teaspoon fresh oregano. Season with salt and pepper to taste. Serve.

THE POWER OF PANADE

A paste of milk and bread, *panade* in French, is responsible for keeping the ground beef in our meat sauce moist and tender. Because panades are typically used to help foods like meatballs and meatloaf hold their shape (and moisture), adding a panade to a meat sauce where the beef is crumbled seemed like an odd idea. Wouldn't the mashed-up milk and bread just dissolve into the sauce? We were left scratching our heads when the panade worked.

Our science editor explained what was happening: Starches from the bread absorb liquid from the milk to form a gel that coats and lubricates the protein molecules in the meat, much in the same way as fat, keeping them moist and preventing them from linking together to form a tough matrix. Mixing the beef and panade in a food processor helps to ensure that the starch is well dispersed so that all the meat reaps its benefits.

KEYS TO GREAT FLAVOR

Eliminating browning of the meat in our recipe produced a sauce with tender beef, but also one lacking in deep flavor. To compensate and build a rich and complex-tasting sauce, we browned minced mushrooms in oil. A spoonful of tomato paste and a sprinkle of Parmesan cheese added complexity.

MUSHROOMS

TOMATO PASTE

PARMESAN CHEESE

SKILLET-BAKED SPAGHETTI WITH MEAT SAUCE

BAKED SPAGHETTI WITH MEAT SAUCE is as simple as it sounds: Spaghetti and meat sauce are topped with mozzarella and baked into a melted, cheese-crusted casserole. The reality of this dish, however, is that boiling pasta, making a meat sauce, transferring it to a casserole dish, and baking it requires too many pots and too much time for a weeknight meal. More important, most versions that I tried were bland and boring. I set out to make a skillet spaghetti casserole that was quick and flavorful, and required as little cleanup as possible.

I decided to employ the test kitchen's technique of cooking the pasta in the skillet along with the sauce. When using this method, we add a few cups of water to the mixture to help the pasta cook more evenly and to keep the sauce from drying out. This works well with smaller pasta shapes, but my skillet was filled to the rim with sauce and water, and the spaghetti was floating on the top. Breaking the spaghetti into 2-inch pieces helped the pasta cook more evenly, and I could fit more of it (a full half-pound) in the skillet.

I made a quick meat sauce using ground beef, crushed tomatoes, garlic, and spices. But the flavors became diluted when I added the water. Using less water meant the pasta didn't cook evenly in the thick sauce, and adding more beef didn't provide enough flavor. I had better results by swapping out some of the beef for Italian sausage, which gave the sauce extra seasoning and a long-simmered complexity. To add even deeper, richer flavor (and to make the pasta mixture more cohesive), I mixed a small amount of heavy cream and some of the mozzarella into the pasta before tackling the cheese topping.

Since I didn't want to dirty a baking dish for the cheesy baked crust, I decided to melt the mozzarella right in the skillet. I topped the pasta and sauce with mozzarella and covered the skillet to try to melt the cheese on the stovetop, but it became rubbery. Baking the spaghetti mixture in the skillet melted the cheese and created a decent crust, but it wasn't as fast—and it didn't create as nice a crust—as running it under a hot broiler. Replacing the straight mozzarella with a packaged blend that contained sharper cheeses like Parmesan and asiago

SKILLET-BAKED SPAGHETTI WITH MEAT SAUCE

as well as mozzarella provided a welcome contrast of flavors and textures.

With a finishing hit of fresh basil, I had a flavorful skillet pasta casserole with a substantial cheesy crust. And best of all, cleanup consisted of only one pan.

—LYNN CLARK, *Cook's Country*

SKILLET-BAKED SPAGHETTI WITH MEAT SAUCE

SERVES 4 TO 6

You will need either 1 large or 2 small links of Italian sausage for this recipe. If using hot Italian sausage, use just ⅛ teaspoon of red pepper flakes.

12	ounces 90 percent lean ground beef
4	ounces hot or sweet Italian sausage (see note), casings removed
4	garlic cloves, minced
¼	teaspoon red pepper flakes
¼	teaspoon dried oregano
1	(28-ounce) can crushed tomatoes
8	ounces spaghetti, broken into rough 2-inch pieces
2	cups water
1½	teaspoons salt
¼	cup heavy cream
6	tablespoons chopped fresh basil
4	ounces shredded Italian cheese blend (about 1 cup)

1. Adjust an oven rack to the upper-middle position and heat the broiler. Cook the beef and sausage in a large ovensafe nonstick skillet over medium heat, breaking up the meat with a wooden spoon, until no longer pink, about 5 minutes. Drain the meat on a paper towel–lined plate and pour off the fat from the skillet. Return the meat to the skillet. Add the garlic, pepper flakes, and oregano and cook until fragrant, about 1 minute.

2. Stir in the tomatoes, spaghetti, water, and salt. Cover and cook, stirring often, until the spaghetti begins to soften, about 7 minutes. Reduce the heat to medium-low and continue to simmer, covered, until the spaghetti is al dente, about 7 minutes.

3. Stir in the cream, basil, and ⅓ cup of the cheese. Sprinkle with the remaining ⅔ cup cheese and broil until the surface is spotty brown, about 3 minutes. Let cool 5 minutes. Serve.

NOTES FROM THE TEST KITCHEN

SPAGHETTI BREAKDOWN

1. Place spaghetti in a large zipper-lock bag and, grasping both ends of the pasta, press the spaghetti firmly against the edge of the countertop.

2. Continue pressing smaller pieces of pasta against the edge of the countertop until it has been broken down into rough 2-inch pieces.

THE BEST 12-INCH NONSTICK SKILLET

We've always recommended buying inexpensive nonstick skillets, because with regular use the nonstick coating inevitably scratches, chips off, or becomes ineffective. Why spend big bucks on a pan that will only last a year or two? Since our testing of inexpensive 12-inch nonstick skillets in 2006, several new pans have come on the market. We rounded up eight models priced under $60 and pitted them against our gold standard, the $135 nonstick skillet from All-Clad, to see how they measure up.

We sautéed onions and carrots, cooked thin fillets of sole, made omelets, and fried eggs (with no added fat) in each pan. We found that they all did an acceptable job cooking and releasing these foods. There were noticeable differences in sauté speed, but most home cooks know if their cookware runs a bit fast or slow and adjust accordingly. To gauge durability, we cooked 12-egg frittatas while doing several things that manufacturers specifically forbid in each pan: broiling, cutting with a sharp knife, removing the slices with a metal pie server, and washing with an abrasive metal scrubber. And the results? Although the $135 All-Clad is still the best pan out there, our favorite among the group of less-expensive pans was the **Weaver Premium Hard Anodized 12-Inch Nonstick Skillet,** $28, which not only performed well, but was also preferred for its light weight and comfortable handle. (See page 340 for more information about our testing results.)

PASTA WITH CREAMY TOMATO SAUCE

THE BEST CREAMY TOMATO SAUCES balance the acidity of fruity tomatoes with the unctuousness of rich dairy; the worst deliver instant heartburn and make you wish the two components had never met. What's the best way to merge these seemingly incompatible ingredients in a sauce that brings out the best in each?

While digging through stacks of Italian cookbooks, I found everything from simple *salsa rosate*, which took just minutes and a single pot to prepare, to long-simmered, *ragù*-like sauces that required the better part of a day to pull together. There were no winners among the lot, but there were plenty of thought-provoking methods and ingredients to test.

Traditional Italian sauces (as well as most Italian soups and stews) are built upon *soffrito*, a blend of aromatics, such as onion, carrot, celery, garlic, and parsley, stewed in lots of fat. For the richest-flavored sauce, I assumed that more was more and started with the full list of classic ingredients. As testing progressed, however, I couldn't shake the criticism that the sauce tasted too vegetal. Perhaps in this case, less was more. I cooked a batch of soffrito without celery, and tasters unanimously approved. Next I eliminated carrot, and the reaction was again positive. Left with just garlic and onion, I decided to omit long-cooked garlic in favor of a few quickly sautéed minced cloves, which packed a brighter, cleaner punch.

My goal was a smooth sauce I could make year-round, so fresh tomatoes didn't make much sense. Whole and diced canned tomatoes wouldn't do, either, even when pureed before being blended with the soffrito, because many producers douse them with calcium chloride, a firming agent that prevents the tomatoes from fully softening, regardless of whether they are ground in a processor. Crushed and pureed canned tomatoes, however, each yielded smooth sauce, with tasters preferring the brighter flavor of the crushed. The smoothest kind of canned tomatoes, tomato sauce, failed to impress anyone.

But tasters demanded still more tomato flavor. To develop deep flavor in tomato sauces and soups, the test kitchen has taken whole, drained canned tomatoes, dusted them with sugar, and then roasted them before combining them with the other ingredients. But when I tried adding tomatoes prepared with this technique, the sauce was too sweet, even when I omitted the sugar. Roasting also toughened the tomatoes' texture, which made the finished sauce decidedly pulpy.

For another of the test kitchen's pasta sauces, tomatoes are browned in a saucepan to generate a flavorful *fond*, which is deglazed and incorporated into the sauce. But when I tried this method with my working recipe, the fond had more undertones of caramel than tomato. There's a time and a place for the deep, caramel flavors that thorough browning can provide, but this wasn't it.

After sifting through a list of options and testing the most promising, I landed on sun-dried tomatoes, whose sunny flavor enlivened the sauce and cut through the palate-deadening cream. A pinch of red pepper flakes, and a stiff shot of wine—added prior to the crushed tomatoes and cooked down to evaporate the bitter alcohol—further intensified the sauce's flavor and kept the sweetness of the sauce in check.

In my initial survey, I'd tried a recipe that included pancetta. Though the meat lent the sauce an undeniable body and depth, I had ruled it out as too assertive. Thinking that perhaps milder prosciutto might work, I minced a few paper-thin slices and added it to the pan along with the onion. This sauce was easily the best yet. I liked how the sun-dried tomatoes had softened and the sauce's flavors had unified after half an hour of slow simmering, but I wondered if perhaps it tasted too homogeneous. A splash of wine helped a lot. Then I decided to try adding a bit of raw crushed tomatoes at the last minute, too. Like the wine, the raw tomatoes contributed some needed acidity, and the combination of the two cut through the dairy and brought the sauce's ingredients into sharp relief.

Now for the dairy. From the start, I had assumed that heavy cream was the best dairy product for the job, but a few of the recipes I found used clotted cream, pureed ricotta, or mascarpone cheese instead. I quickly ruled out the clotted cream (very, very odd here), and the ricotta came across as grainy, no matter how long I processed it. I liked the flavor of the mascarpone, but its ultrathick texture turned the sauce gummy.

Heavy cream, then, contributed the clearest creamy flavor, but what was the best way to blend it with the tomato base? I thought the sauce tasted best and most balanced when I simply stirred the cream into the finished tomato mixture and brought it up to temperature before tossing it with the pasta. I found that half a cup

PASTA WITH CREAMY TOMATO SAUCE

was the ideal amount to make the sauce taste rich without overpowering the tomatoes.

Up to this point, I had pureed each of the finished sauces to a velvety texture, thinking that smoothness was the best way to highlight creaminess. And my sauce did taste good when smooth, but it was one-dimensional. On a whim, I left a batch unpureed, and tasters loved the bits of chewy sun-dried tomatoes, soft minced onion, and pulpy crushed tomato that punctuated the otherwise silky consistency. This was finally it: a dynamic sauce in which tomatoes and cream boosted each other's flavors and packed enough complexity to keep you coming back for more.

—MATTHEW CARD, *Cook's Illustrated*

PASTA WITH CREAMY TOMATO SAUCE

SERVES 4

This sauce is best served with short pasta, such as ziti, penne, or fusilli.

- 3 tablespoons unsalted butter
- 1 ounce prosciutto, minced (about 2 tablespoons)
- 1 small onion, minced (about ¾ cup)
- 1 bay leaf
  Pinch red pepper flakes
  Salt
- 3 garlic cloves, minced
- 2 tablespoons tomato paste
- 2 ounces oil-packed sun-dried tomatoes, drained, rinsed, patted dry, and chopped (about 3 tablespoons)
- ¼ cup plus 2 tablespoons dry white wine
- 2 cups plus 2 tablespoons crushed tomatoes (from one 28-ounce can)
- 1 pound pasta (see note)
- ½ cup heavy cream
  Pepper
- ¼ cup chopped fresh basil
  Grated Parmesan cheese, for serving

1. Melt the butter in a medium saucepan over medium heat. Add the prosciutto, onion, bay leaf, pepper flakes, and ¼ teaspoon salt; cook, stirring occasionally, until the onion is very soft and beginning to turn light gold, 8 to 12 minutes. Increase the heat to medium-high, add the garlic, and cook until fragrant, about 30 seconds. Stir in the tomato paste and sun-dried tomatoes and cook, stirring constantly, until slightly darkened, 1 to 2 minutes. Add the ¼ cup wine and cook, stirring frequently, until the liquid has evaporated, 1 to 2 minutes.

2. Add the 2 cups crushed tomatoes and bring to a simmer. Reduce the heat to low, partially cover, and cook, stirring occasionally, until the sauce is thickened (a spoon should leave a trail when dragged through the sauce), 25 to 30 minutes.

3. Meanwhile, bring 4 quarts water to a boil in a stockpot. Add the pasta and 1 tablespoon salt and cook until al dente. Reserve ½ cup of the cooking water; drain the pasta, and transfer it back to the cooking pot.

4. Remove the bay leaf from the sauce and discard. Stir the cream, remaining 2 tablespoons crushed tomatoes, and remaining 2 tablespoons wine into the sauce; season with salt and pepper to taste. Add the sauce to the cooked pasta, adjusting the consistency with up to ½ cup reserved pasta cooking water. Stir in the basil and serve immediately, passing the cheese separately.

NOTES FROM THE TEST KITCHEN

THE BEST WOODEN SPOONS

Is there any real difference between one wooden spoon and another? In a word, yes. We used 10 models to brown beef and stir pots of thick vegetable curry. To test durability, we also tried snapping each in half. Here's what we liked: thin edges (which scrape more effectively than thick); a handle that's strong but not too bulky; and a broad bowl that covers a lot of surface area and can reach into the corners of a pot. Our favorite was the **Mario Batali 13-Inch Wooden Spoon,** $4.95, which we found to be strong but lightweight, with a comfortable grip and a broad, thin-edged bowl.

TASTING SUPERMARKET PARMESAN CHEESE

Can domestic Parmesan really stand up to imported Parmigiano-Reggianos? Simply put, no, it cannot. Our tasters effortlessly picked out the imports in our lineup of eight supermarket cheeses. The two genuine Parmigiano-Reggianos, sold by Boar's Head and Il Villaggio, were the clear favorites, with **Boar's Head Parmigiano-Reggiano,** $17.17 per pound, deemed "best in show" by tasters. The domestic cheeses, all made in Wisconsin, presented a wide range of flavors and textures from quite good to rubbery, salty, and bland. (See page 323 for more information about our testing results.)

PASTA CAPRESE

LEGEND HAS IT THAT THE POPULAR CAPRESE TRIO of garden tomatoes, fresh mozzarella, and basil leaves was introduced in the 1950s at Trattoria Da Vincenzo, a beachside restaurant on the Italian island of Capri. According to creator Margherita Cosentino, the red, white, and green salad of local produce and cheese allowed ladies to "have a nice lunch while still fitting into their bikinis." Swimsuit season or not, the combination became so popular that cooks everywhere took to mixing it with hot pasta, minced garlic, and extra-virgin olive oil for a 15-minute entrée that captures the flavors of summer.

Truth be told, I was skeptical that a recipe would really be required for such a clear-cut dish. Still, I gathered a representative sampling and went into the kitchen. The outcome? Instead of collecting the praise I had expected from my colleagues, I joined them for a few chuckles. The tomatoes, pasta, and basil weren't problems, but the cheese was. In each recipe, it had clumped into an intractable softball-sized wad in the bottom of the pasta bowl. After wrestling a serving out of the dish, things only got worse. The tangles of mozzarella bubble gum were difficult to chew, never mind swallow. The mozzarella was a classic case of Dr. Jekyll and Mr. Hyde: likable and tender at one moment, monstrously tough the next.

For these first tests, I had purchased fresh mozzarella—the kind that comes immersed in plastic tubs of water and is shaped into irregular-sized balls—at the supermarket. What if I used regular block-style mozzarella (the low-moisture version often shredded for pizza) instead? It melted nicely and didn't turn chewy, but this inauthentic substitution cheated the dish of its star ingredient, and tasters complained about blandness.

For my next test, I took a big step in the opposite direction and tried water buffalo–milk mozzarella (*mozzarella di bufala*) from a specialty cheese shop. Much softer than the commercial fresh cheese, this handmade mozzarella melted into tender pillows when combined with the pasta—there were no rubbery bits to be found. In addition to the lovely consistency, tasters praised its flavor, which was dripping with milkiness and tang. The next day, I prepared pasta Caprese using handmade cow's-milk mozzarella and achieved the same impressive results.

So my problem was solved, as long as I had time to go to the cheese store and was willing to pay the big bucks for handmade cheese, which can easily top $9 per pound. Everyone in the test kitchen agreed this wasn't an acceptable solution. I needed to find a way to use fresh mozzarella from the supermarket.

My first thought was to thoroughly coat diced mozzarella cubes with olive oil before adding the steaming pasta. This was a step in the right direction, with the oil preventing sticking . . . initially. After a few minutes, however, the nasty clumping problem reemerged.

I wondered what would happen if I put the diced supermarket cheese in the freezer for a few minutes before combining it with the pasta. Could chilling the cheese keep it from melting fully and clumping into wads of bubble gum? I gave this approach a trial run, dicing the mozzarella and chilling it in the freezer for 10 minutes. I then proceeded as usual, combining the firmed-up cheese with the pasta and tomatoes. Success: When added to hot pasta, the cheese softened but did not fully melt, making the unattractive elastic ropes a thing of the past. It turns out that the proteins in fresh mozzarella begin to melt at about 130 degrees. As the temperature climbs past 130 degrees, the proteins clump together. Freezing the cheese kept it from overheating when tossed with the hot pasta.

With the cheese conundrum solved, I fine-tuned the rest of the recipe, starting with the tomatoes. Juicy, garden-ripe beauties need no adornment, but a sprinkle of sugar can replace the gentle sweetness that is often missing in less-than-perfect specimens. And while Italians would never add an acidic component to a true Caprese recipe, a squirt of fresh lemon juice (favored over all types of vinegar) did a great job of boosting the flavor of lackluster tomatoes.

In recipes that use raw olive oil, the fruity and spicy nuances of extra-virgin oil make a difference, and this dish is no exception. I added a healthy drizzle of the test kitchen's favorite extra-virgin olive oil, then stirred in a minced shallot, a sprinkle of salt, and a few twists of black pepper. Allowing the tomatoes and mozzarella to marinate while the pasta cooked infused them with fruity and subtle garlic flavors. Lengthy marinating times aren't recommended, however, as more than 45 minutes yielded mealy, broken-down tomatoes. Freshly chopped basil was the finishing touch to pasta that tasted just like summer.

—REBECCA HAYS, *Cook's Illustrated*

PASTA CAPRESE

PASTA CAPRESE

SERVES 4 TO 6

This dish will be very warm, not hot. The success of this recipe depends on high-quality ingredients, including ripe, in-season tomatoes and a fruity olive oil (the test kitchen prefers Columela Extra-Virgin). Don't skip the step of freezing the mozzarella, as freezing prevents it from turning chewy when it comes in contact with the hot pasta. If handmade buffalo- or cow's-milk mozzarella is available (it's commonly found in gourmet and cheese shops packed in water), we highly recommend using it, but skip the step of freezing. Additional lemon juice or up to 1 teaspoon sugar can be added at the end to taste, depending on the ripeness of the tomatoes.

- ¼ cup extra-virgin olive oil
- 2–4 teaspoons fresh lemon juice (see note)
- 1 garlic clove, minced
- 1 small shallot, minced (about 2 tablespoons)
  Salt and pepper
- 1½ pounds ripe tomatoes, cored, seeded, and cut into ½-inch dice
- 12 ounces fresh mozzarella cheese, cut into ½-inch cubes (see note)
- 1 pound short tubular or curly pasta, such as penne, fusilli, or campanelle
- ¼ cup chopped fresh basil
- 1 teaspoon sugar (see note)

1. Whisk the oil, 2 teaspoons of the lemon juice, garlic, shallot, ½ teaspoon salt, and ¼ teaspoon pepper together in a large bowl. Add the tomatoes and gently toss to combine; set aside. Do not marinate the tomatoes for longer than 45 minutes.

2. While the tomatoes are marinating, place the mozzarella on a plate and freeze until slightly firm, about 10 minutes. Bring 4 quarts water to a boil in a stockpot. Add the pasta and 1 tablespoon salt and cook until al dente. Drain well.

3. Add the pasta and mozzarella to the tomato mixture and gently toss to combine. Let stand 5 minutes. Stir in the basil; adjust the seasonings with salt and pepper to taste and additional lemon juice or sugar, if desired. Serve immediately.

SPICY SICHUAN NOODLES

DAN DAN MIAN, OR SPICY SICHUAN NOODLES, is a dish that is both substantial and satisfying—a meal in a bowl. By all accounts it is street food in China, the equivalent of sausage and onions from a curbside cart in New York City. To make this dish, you top Chinese noodles with a rich, savory sauce—a mélange of browned ground pork, aromatic ginger and garlic, salty soy sauce, and nutty peanut butter in a chicken broth base. All this is set ablaze by the heat of chiles and finished with a sprinkling of sliced scallions and bean sprouts.

The sauce for spicy Sichuan noodles is built simply. Ground pork, marinated briefly in soy sauce and Chinese rice cooking wine (or sherry), is browned either by sautéing it in a skillet with just a little oil or by deep-frying it in a cup or so of oil. The pork is then removed from the skillet, the oil drained off, and the ginger and garlic briefly cooked. Next the chicken broth is added, then peanut butter or sesame paste. In a simpler rendition, the ginger and garlic are omitted and the other sauce ingredients are simmered right in the skillet with the pork. In both versions, the mixture of pork and sauce is simply poured over noodles and served. I quickly determined that deep-frying the pork was not worth the trouble or waste of oil. Browning could be accomplished easily in only a tablespoon of oil.

Next I concluded that once the pork was browned, there was no need to remove it from the skillet. It was fine to build the sauce on top of it. Having decided on these two simplifications, I began weeding through the different ingredients called for in different recipes. I had one clear goal in mind—to create a rich, complex sauce in which the powerful flavors of garlic, ginger, and soy were well balanced. Fresh ginger and garlic spike the dish with aromatic piquancy, but in equal amounts their potencies vied for dominance and the pairing was not harmonious. Tasters voted garlic to the fore, relegating ginger to second position. Soy sauce brought a savory quality, while oyster sauce added a depth and sweetness that rounded out the flavors. Rice vinegar cut the richness of the sauce and livened things up.

Asian sesame paste (not the same as Middle Eastern tahini) is typically called for in spicy Sichuan noodle recipes, with peanut butter a recommended substitute. I first tried peanut butter because of its availability and it produced perfectly good results. Two tablespoons, the amount recommended in many recipes, was too little to contribute much flavor or to thicken the amount of chicken broth needed to coat a pound of cooked fresh noodles. I doubled the amount to four tablespoons, enough to add rich, nutty flavor and to adequately thicken the sauce. Any more and the sauce became intolerably rich as well as overly thick.

Then I tried Asian sesame paste in place of peanut butter. Its flavor is mysterious, and it yields an intriguing sauce with an earthy, smoky flavor. If your supermarket carries Asian sesame paste or if an Asian grocer is nearby, I recommend seeking it out. The consistency varies from brand to brand—some are thin and pourable, like honey, while others are spreadable—so I found it necessary to compensate by making minor adjustments in the amount of chicken broth in the sauce. While you're shopping for sesame paste, look for Sichuan peppercorns. These berries are from a prickly ash tree native to Asia and bring to the dish a woodsy flavor, with a hint of star anise.

Chinese grocery stores are stocked with a dizzying array of noodles, fresh as well as dried. A couple of recipes recommended fresh egg noodles, so I thought that this is where I would begin. In the refrigerator sections of the major Chinatown markets, the only fresh noodles I found that would qualify as egg noodles (because they listed eggs in their ingredient lists) were "wonton" noodles. Cooked and sauced, these noodles were clearly not right. They were far too delicate. As a result, they wilted under the weight of the sauce, clumped together into a ball, and ended up as listless as a pile of wet rags.

Back in the refrigerated-food aisle, I chose two more types of fresh noodles, lo mein and the descriptively named "plain noodles." I purchased from our local supermarket—for nearly twice the cost—a few packages of fresh "Asian-style noodles" in wide-cut and narrow-cut versions. Cooked, these three types of noodles were different from one another, but all were a better match for the sauce than the wonton noodles. The spaghetti-shaped lo mein didn't give the sauce much noodle surface to cling to and their very yielding texture was unremarkable. The plain noodles, shaped like fat, squared-off strands of spaghetti, were as soft and gummy as a piece of Bazooka; this pleased some and annoyed others. The wide-cut supermarket noodles had good chew, too, but to a lesser degree. Their fettuccine-like shape was perfect for the sauce; the broad surfaces were easily sauced and could buoy up bits of pork.

Fresh noodles are not always an option, so I also looked into dried. I focused on flat noodles with a width between linguine and fettuccine. What was true of fresh noodles was also true of dried: the egg and the imitation egg noodles were too delicate for the sauce. Sturdier non-egg noodles, with their chewy and more substantial presence, were a superior match. In fact, for those who prefer noodles with a lesser "mush" quotient, dried noodles are better than fresh. And if neither fresh nor dried Asian noodles are available, dried linguine is an acceptable substitute.

Noodles for dan dan mian look and hold up better when simply divided among bowls, ladled with sauce, and then sprinkled with a garnish. It is then up to the diner to toss, swirl, and slurp down the noodles with chopsticks . . . or a fork.

—DAWN YANAGIHARA, *Cook's Illustrated*

SPICY SICHUAN NOODLES WITH GROUND PORK

SERVES 4

For this recipe, we prefer fresh Chinese noodles with a width between linguine and fettuccine. If you are using Asian sesame paste that has a pourable rather than spreadable consistency, use only 1 cup of chicken broth.

- 8 ounces ground pork
- 3 tablespoons soy sauce
- 2 tablespoons Chinese rice wine or dry sherry
  Pepper
- 2 tablespoons oyster sauce
- ¼ cup Asian sesame paste or smooth peanut butter
- 1 tablespoon rice vinegar
- 1–1¼ cups low-sodium chicken broth (see note)
- 1 tablespoon vegetable oil
- 6 garlic cloves, minced
- 1 tablespoon minced or grated fresh ginger
- ¾ teaspoon red pepper flakes
- 1 tablespoon toasted sesame oil
- 1 pound fresh Chinese noodles or 12 ounces dried linguine
- 3 scallions, sliced thin on the bias
- 2 cups bean sprouts (optional)
- 1 tablespoon Sichuan peppercorns, toasted and ground (optional)

1. Bring 6 quarts water to a boil in a large stockpot for the noodles.

2. Meanwhile, toss the pork with 1 tablespoon of the soy sauce, rice wine, and a pinch of pepper to combine and set aside. In a separate bowl, whisk the remaining 2 tablespoons soy sauce, oyster sauce, sesame paste, vinegar, and a pinch of pepper together until smooth, then whisk in the broth; set aside.

3. Heat the vegetable oil in a 12-inch skillet over high heat until shimmering. Add the pork mixture and cook, breaking up the meat with a wooden spoon, until the pork is in small, well-browned bits, about 5 minutes. Stir in the garlic, ginger, and pepper flakes and cook until fragrant, about 30 seconds. Stir in the broth mixture, bring to a boil, then reduce to a simmer over medium-low heat and cook until slightly thickened, about 3 minutes. Off the heat, stir in the sesame oil; cover and set aside.

4. While the sauce simmers, stir the noodles into the boiling water and cook, stirring constantly, until the noodles are tender, about 4 minutes for fresh noodles or 10 minutes for dried linguine. Drain the noodles, divide them among individual bowls, then ladle a portion of the sauce over the top. Sprinkle with the scallions, and the bean sprouts and ground Sichuan peppercorns, if using, and serve.

VARIATION

SPICY SICHUAN NOODLES WITH GROUND PORK AND DRIED SHIITAKE MUSHROOMS

Soak 8 small dried shiitake mushrooms in 1 cup boiling water until softened, 15 to 20 minutes; drain, reserving ½ cup of the soaking liquid. Trim and discard the stems, then slice the mushrooms ¼ inch thick and set aside. Follow the recipe for Spicy Sichuan Noodles with Ground Pork, substituting the reserved mushroom liquid for an equal amount of the chicken broth and stirring the sliced mushrooms into the sauce along with the sesame oil in step 3.

NOTES FROM THE TEST KITCHEN

FRESH CHINESE NOODLES
A key ingredient in Chinese cuisine, noodles come in many forms—fresh, dried, wheat, rice, cellophane, hand-pulled, or flash-fried. They're eaten hot, cold, boiled, steamed, stir-fried, and deep-fried. Many varieties of fresh Chinese noodles are available in local supermarkets, though the selection is vaster in an Asian market. Some noodles are cut thin (below left), while others are cut slightly wider (below right).

Their texture is a bit more starchy and chewy than dried noodles and their flavor is cleaner (less wheaty) than Italian pasta, making them an excellent match to potent, highly seasoned sauces. You can substitute dried Italian pasta, such as linguine or spaghetti, but we think these fresh noodles—often called Chinese noodles or Asian-style noodles—are worth tracking down.

Fresh Chinese noodles cook quickly, usually for no more than 3 to 4 minutes in boiling water. Adding salt to the water is not always necessary—many Chinese noodle sauces are rich in soy sauce, which is high in sodium.

THIN

WIDE

VIETNAMESE RICE NOODLE SALAD

ONE OF MY FAVORITE VIETNAMESE DISHES is *bun*, or rice noodle salad. Light yet satisfying, this multilayered salad is piled in a bowl with shredded lettuce at the bottom, followed by pickled carrots and cucumbers, fresh herbs, rice noodles, and grilled meat or seafood. It is garnished with a sprinkle of chopped roasted peanuts and dressed with *nuoc cham*, a sweet-tart and mildly spicy sauce. While it is often found in Vietnamese restaurants, it is relatively simple for home cooks to prepare. Most of the ingredients are meant to be served at room temperature and can be prepared ahead of time, leaving only the cooking of the meat for the last minute.

Starting with the protein, I found recipes made with shrimp, beef, and pork—and sometimes a combination of these. To keep this recipe simple, I chose to just use pork in our recipe (though shrimp and beef would be great as well). I tested pork shoulder, chops, loin, and tenderloin. While the shoulder had a lot of flavor, it also had a lot of fat and tasters thought this cut was too gristly for the salad. The pork chops offered great flavor, but the meat was a little tough for this dish. The loin and the tenderloin were both winning options, but the tenderloin is our top pick—at about one pound, it provides just the right amount of meat for this recipe.

The pork is typically sliced thin, immersed in a salty-sweet marinade, and then broiled or grilled to achieve caramelized crispy-charred edges. The marinades I came across all consisted of the same basic combination of fish sauce, vegetable oil, and sugar. From there they deviated, with some also calling for soy sauce, Vietnamese-style caramel sauce (a simple sugar and water mixture that is cooked until just slightly bitter), and chili paste. We began by testing the sweet element of the sauce. We tried dark brown sugar, light brown sugar, and granulated sugar. Light brown and granulated sugar both failed to caramelize in the short time it took for the meat to cook. Tasters found no discernible difference between the caramel and dark brown sugar and liked both for their deep nutty flavors, so I opted for the less fussy addition of dark brown sugar. Next I tested fish sauce amounts and 2 tablespoons added just the right amount of saltiness to balance the sugar. Three tablespoons of oil was just enough to keep the lean tenderloin meat moist, without making it taste greasy.

The meat was ready, so I turned our attention to the salad dressing, called *nuoc cham*. It appears in a variety of Vietnamese dishes and can be used as a dipping sauce as well as a dressing. The fundamental ingredients are lime juice, fish sauce, sugar, garlic, and chiles, providing a careful balance of tart, sweet, salty, and spicy flavors. Tasters continually requested more dressing, so I decided to use half of it to dress the salad and divided the other half into individual bowls so more sauce could be added as needed while eating.

This salad usually contains a mixture of pickled carrots and daikon radish, a combination that can be found in numerous Vietnamese dishes. Daikon radish can be difficult to find, so I left it out of our version. Because there are so many individual components to prepare in this salad, I opted to streamline this recipe by seasoning the carrots directly in the dressing. I also found the occasional recipe that called for pickling the cucumbers, a method I chose to use since it also ensured that the salad was well flavored. I simply combined the cucumbers with the carrots and let them marinate in the dressing.

To cook the round rice noodles (called *bun*) used for this salad, the best method is to drop them in boiling water that has just been removed from the heat. With that established, I realized that these noodles come in small, medium, large, and extra-large widths. After testing all four sizes, I settled upon the smallest as the best option for the salad—the dressing easily coated the thinner noodles and I got a more even ratio of noodles, meat, and vegetable in every bite.

Finally it was time to add the lettuce. I tried red and green leaf lettuce, Bibb lettuce, and iceberg. Tasters thought that the iceberg lettuce lacked flavor and got lost in the noodles. While the Bibb lettuce was an acceptable option, tasters preferred red or green leaf for the way it held the dressing and for its soft yet crunchy texture. In addition, an abundance of fresh herbs are added, usually mint, Thai basil, cilantro, and red perilla (a minty, citrusy herb). The last in the list is virtually impossible to find, unless you live near a Vietnamese grocery store. I focused on the first three herbs and liked a combination of all three in equal amounts—I settled on a generous ½ cup each.

While each component of this salad is typically layered into individual bowls, and served with the dressing on the side, I opted to toss it all in a large bowl to make the preparation simpler. It is a satisfying meal that you won't soon forget.

—MEGAN WYCOFF, *America's Test Kitchen Books*

VIETNAMESE RICE NOODLE SALAD

SERVES 4 TO 6 AS A MAIN COURSE

To make slicing the pork easier, freeze it for 15 minutes. You can increase the spiciness of this dish by including the minced ribs and seeds from the chiles. We find the trio of fresh cilantro, basil, and mint essential for flavor in this salad; if you cannot find all three, increase the amount of the others to ¾ cup each. Or, if you cannot find Thai basil, substitute regular basil.

PORK

- 3 tablespoons vegetable oil
- 2 tablespoons fish sauce
- 2 tablespoons dark brown sugar
- 1 pork tenderloin (about 1 pound), trimmed and sliced crosswise into ⅛-inch-thick rounds

DRESSING

- ⅔ cup fish sauce
- ½ cup warm water
- 6 tablespoons lime juice from 3 limes
- 5 tablespoons sugar
- 3 fresh Thai, serrano, or jalapeño chiles, seeds and ribs removed, chiles minced (see note)
- 2 garlic cloves, minced

SALAD

- 3 large carrots, peeled and grated on the large holes of a box grater (about 1½ cups)
- 1 large cucumber, peeled, seeded, and sliced into 2-inch-long matchsticks
- ¼ cup chopped unsalted roasted peanuts, plus extra for garnish
- 1 fresh Thai, serrano, or jalapeño chile, seeds and ribs removed, chile minced
- 8 ounces dried rice vermicelli
- 4 cups red or green leaf lettuce, thinly sliced
- ½ cup loosely packed fresh Thai basil (see note)
- ½ cup loosely packed fresh cilantro
- ½ cup loosely packed fresh mint

1. FOR THE PORK: Whisk the oil, fish sauce, and sugar together in a medium bowl until the sugar dissolves. Add the pork and toss to coat evenly. Cover and refrigerate for 30 minutes or up to 24 hours.

2. FOR THE DRESSING: Whisk all of the ingredients together until the sugar dissolves and set aside.

3. FOR THE SALAD: Toss the carrots, cucumber, peanuts, and chile with ¼ cup of the dressing and set aside to marinate while cooking the noodles and pork.

4. Bring 4 quarts water to a boil in a large stockpot. Off the heat, add the rice noodles and let stand, stirring occasionally, until tender, about 10 minutes. Drain the noodles and transfer them to a large bowl. Layer the carrot-cucumber mixture, lettuce, basil, cilantro, and mint on top of the noodles (do not toss), and set aside.

5. Adjust an oven rack 6 inches from the broiler element and heat the broiler. Line a broiler pan bottom with foil and top with a broiler pan top. Remove the pork from the marinade and spread it out over the broiler pan top. Broil the pork until golden on both sides with crisp edges, about 10 minutes, flipping the pork over halfway through the cooking time.

6. Pour half of the remaining dressing over the noodles, carrot-cucumber mixture, lettuce, and herbs and toss to combine. Divide the noodle salad evenly among 4 large individual serving bowls and top with the broiled pork. Sprinkle with additional peanuts and serve, passing the remaining dressing separately.

NOTES FROM THE TEST KITCHEN

RICE NOODLES

In Southeast Asia and regions of China, a delicate pasta made from rice flour and water is used in many dishes including soups, stir-fries, and salads. And these noodles are available in an array of sizes and shapes—from very thin and round to flat (and small or large). For this recipe we use round rice noodles, also called *bun* or rice vermicelli—the smallest size we can get our hands on.

MEAT

FRENCH-STYLE POT ROAST

FRENCH-STYLE POT ROAST

BOEUF À LA MODE—"beef in the latest fashion"—is a classic French recipe that dates to a time when a multiday recipe was the rule rather than the exception. Although boeuf à la mode bears some similarity to American pot roast, this elegant French dish relies heavily on wine for flavor, adds collagen-rich veal and pork parts for body, and has a separately prepared mushroom-onion garnish. After spending days making five classic renditions of this old-fashioned recipe, I understood its allure—and its challenges. It is to pot roast what croissants are to refrigerated crescent rolls and, as such, required up to four days of preparation! To bring boeuf à la mode up to date for the modern home cook—the meats and times have changed, after all—some of the fussy techniques and hard-to-find ingredients would have to go.

Traditionally, this recipe starts with threading strips of seasoned, brandy-soaked salt pork or fatback through the beef roast using a long needle, or *lardoir*. In addition to making up for the lack of marbling in the meat, larding adds flavor. I cut some fatback into thin strips, marinated them in brandy and seasonings, and struggled to pull them through the roast. For the amount of effort these steps took, I was disappointed when tasters felt the payoff wasn't that great. Today's grain-fed beef gets little exercise and has much more marbling than the leaner, grass-fed beef eaten in France when this recipe was created. As long as I chose the right cut (tasters liked a boneless chuck-eye roast best), there was plenty of fat in the meat and larding was just overkill. I was happy to ax this step from my recipe.

In all of the classic recipes I uncovered, the meat was marinated in a mixture of red wine and large-cut *mirepoix* (carrots, onions, and celery) for a significant period of time, up to three days in several cases. Testing various lengths of time, I found the effect superficial unless I was willing to invest at least two full days. Even then, the wine flavor penetrated only the outer part of the meat, and the vegetables didn't really add much. Frankly, the meat picked up so much wine flavor during the hours-long braising time that marinating didn't seem worth the effort.

In fact, some tasters actually complained that the meat was picking up too much wine flavor as it cooked; the beef tasted a bit sour and harsh. I reviewed a Julia Child recipe that called for marinating the roast in a mixture of wine and vegetables and then reducing that marinade by half before adding beef broth and beginning the braising process. I was intrigued. Would cooking the wine before braising the beef in it tame its unpleasant alcoholic punch? I put the wine in a saucepan and reduced it to 2 cups. When I combined the reduced wine with the beef broth and used this mixture as the braising liquid, tasters were much happier. The wine tasted complex and fruity, not sour and astringent.

Most of the vegetable flavor in this dish comes from the garnish of glazed pearl onions and button mushrooms, which is traditionally cooked separately and added just before serving. To speed up the process, I used frozen rather than fresh pearl onions. But the sauce needed some vegetables to balance the wine and meat flavors. Sautéed onion and garlic helped build depth in the early stages of cooking, and tasters liked the sweetness contributed by large chunks of carrots added to the braising liquid later in the cooking process.

I had the wine and vegetables under control, but my recipe didn't seem as rich and meaty as some of the test recipes I had prepared. My first thought was to salt the meat, something we do in the test kitchen to improve the beefy flavor in thick-cut steaks. It works by drawing moisture out of the meat and forming a shallow brine. Over time, the salt migrates back into the meat, seasoning it throughout rather than just on the exterior. Tasters liked the effects of salting the roast overnight, but I was reluctant to make this a two-day recipe. Eventually, I discovered that salting the meat for just an hour was worth the minimal effort. The roast was nicely seasoned and tasted beefier.

Salt pork is traditionally added to the sauce for richness, but tasters preferred the smoky flavor of bacon. I decided to brown the meat in the bacon drippings and then add the bacon bits back to the braising liquid. My sauce was improving.

Compared with regular pot roast braising liquid, which is flavorful but relatively thin and brothy, the sauce that accompanies boeuf à la mode is richer and more akin to a sauce that might be found on a steak at a fine restaurant. Adding some flour to the sautéed onion and garlic helped with the overall consistency, but the sauce still lacked body. I tried adding pork rind, split calves' feet, and veal bones and liked the effect they had on the sauce—the collagen in these animal parts breaks down in the long cooking process and releases plenty of gelatin. But what if I went directly to the source instead?

I tried adding a tablespoon of powdered gelatin rehydrated in ¼ cup of cold water at the beginning of the recipe, but to no effect. The lengthy cooking time and high heat rendered the gelatin ineffective. I decided to try again, adding the gelatin during the sauce reduction stage. This helped, but not enough. It wasn't until I'd added the gelatin after the sauce had finished reducing that I got the results I had been looking for. Finally, it became rich and velvety, on par with the best classic recipe I'd tried at the beginning of my journey. Drizzled with this intense sauce and surrounded by the well-browned mushroom-onion garnish and tender carrots, this old-fashioned pot roast was the best I'd ever tasted.

—SANDRA WU, *Cook's Illustrated*

FRENCH-STYLE POT ROAST

SERVES 6 TO 8

A medium-bodied, fruity red wine such as Côtes du Rhône or Pinot Noir is best for this recipe. If frozen pearl onions are unavailable, use fresh peeled pearl onions and follow the recipe as directed. The gelatin lends richness and body to the finished sauce; don't omit it. To prepare this dish in advance, follow the recipe through step 7, skipping the step of softening and adding the gelatin. Place the meat back into the reduced sauce, cool it to room temperature, cover it, and refrigerate it for up to 2 days. To serve, slice the beef and arrange it in a 13 by 9-inch baking dish. Bring the sauce to a simmer and stir in the gelatin until completely dissolved. Pour the warm sauce over the meat, cover the dish with aluminum foil, and bake it in a 350-degree oven until heated through, about 30 minutes. Serve this dish with boiled potatoes, buttered noodles, or steamed rice.

1 (4 to 5-pound) boneless chuck-eye roast, pulled apart into 2 pieces and fat trimmed (see page 141)
2 teaspoons kosher salt (or 1 teaspoon table salt)
1 bottle (750 ml) medium-bodied red wine (see note)
10 sprigs fresh parsley plus 2 tablespoons minced leaves
2 sprigs fresh thyme
2 bay leaves
Pepper
4 slices bacon, preferably thick-cut, cut crosswise into ¼-inch pieces
1 onion, minced (about 1 cup)
3 garlic cloves, minced
1 tablespoon unbleached all-purpose flour
2 cups beef broth
4 carrots, peeled and cut on the bias into 1½-inch pieces
2 cups frozen pearl onions (see note)
3 tablespoons unsalted butter
2 teaspoons sugar
½ cup water plus ¼ cup cold water to bloom gelatin
10 ounces white mushrooms, halved if small and quartered if large
Table salt
1 tablespoon powdered unflavored gelatin

1. Sprinkle the meat with the kosher salt, place on a wire rack set in a rimmed baking sheet, and let sit at room temperature for 1 hour.

2. Meanwhile, bring the wine to a simmer in a large saucepan over medium-high heat. Cook until reduced to 2 cups, about 15 minutes. Using kitchen twine, tie the parsley sprigs, thyme sprigs, and bay leaves into a bundle.

3. Pat the beef dry with paper towels and season generously with pepper. Tie three pieces of kitchen twine around each piece of meat to keep it from falling apart.

4. Adjust an oven rack to the lower-middle position and heat the oven to 300 degrees. Cook the bacon in a large Dutch oven over medium-high heat, stirring occasionally, until crisp, 6 to 8 minutes. Using a slotted spoon, transfer the bacon to a paper towel–lined plate and reserve. Pour off all but 2 tablespoons of the fat; return the Dutch oven to medium-high heat and heat until the fat begins to smoke. Add the beef to the pot

and brown on all sides, 8 to 10 minutes total. Transfer the beef to a large plate and set aside.

5. Reduce the heat to medium; add the onion and cook, stirring occasionally, until beginning to soften, 2 to 4 minutes. Add the garlic, flour, and reserved bacon; cook, stirring constantly, until fragrant, about 30 seconds. Add the reduced wine, broth, and herb bundle, scraping the bottom of the pan with a wooden spoon to loosen any browned bits. Return the roast and any accumulated juices to the pot; increase the heat to high and bring the liquid to a simmer, then place a large sheet of foil over the pot and cover tightly with the lid. Set the pot in the oven and cook, using tongs to turn the beef every hour, until a dinner fork slips easily in and out of the meat, 2½ to 3 hours, adding the carrots to the pot after 2 hours.

6. While the meat cooks, bring the pearl onions, butter, sugar, and ½ cup water to a boil in a large skillet over medium-high heat. Reduce the heat to medium, cover, and cook until the onions are tender, 5 to 8 minutes. Uncover, increase the heat to medium-high, and cook until all the liquid evaporates, 3 to 4 minutes. Add the mushrooms and ¼ teaspoon table salt; cook, stirring occasionally, until the vegetables are browned and glazed, 8 to 12 minutes. Remove from the heat and set aside. Place the remaining ¼ cup cold water in a small bowl and sprinkle the gelatin on top.

7. Transfer the beef to a cutting board; tent with foil to keep warm. Allow the braising liquid to settle about 5 minutes; then, using a wide, shallow spoon, skim the fat off the surface. Remove the herb bundle and stir in the onion-mushroom mixture. Bring the liquid to a simmer over medium-high heat and cook until the mixture is slightly thickened and reduced to 3¼ cups, 20 to 30 minutes. Season the sauce with salt and pepper to taste. Add the softened gelatin and stir until completely dissolved.

8. Remove the twine from the meat and discard. Using a chef's or carving knife, cut the meat against the grain into ½-inch-thick slices. Divide the meat among warmed bowls or transfer to a platter; arrange the vegetables around the meat, pour the sauce on top, and sprinkle with the minced parsley. Serve.

NOTES FROM THE TEST KITCHEN

ONE ROAST BECOMES TWO
We found that the interior fat of the chuck roast is best trimmed before cooking. Pull the roast apart at the natural seam and trim away large knobs of fat from each half.

TOO FATTY   **GOOD TO GO**

SLOTTED SPOONS
After damaging delicate gnocchi and dropping dozens of green peas as we tested nine models of slotted spoons, we learned that not just any combination of handles and holes would do. Our testers preferred lengthy handles, deep bowls, and enough small slits or punctures to quickly drain water without losing as much as one petite pea. The **OXO Good Grips Nylon Slotted Spoon**, $5.99, met all our demands, as did a stainless steel spoon from Calphalon, $9.95. With its lighter weight and slimmer price tag, OXO just edged out Calphalon for top honors.

THE SECRETS TO MODERNIZING FRENCH POT ROAST

1. SALTING: Instead of the usual 2-day marinade, we improve the flavor of the beef by salting it for just 1 hour.

2. REDUCING: For concentrated wine flavor without harshness or sour notes, we reduce an entire bottle of wine to just 2 cups.

3. GELATIN: Softened gelatin gives our sauce body, eliminating the need for the traditional (and time-consuming) veal bones, calves' feet, and pork rind.

BARBECUED BEEF BRISKET

I BECAME ADDICTED TO THIS TENDER, deeply smoky beef years ago on a trip to the barbecue belt near Austin. I will always remember the image of a sword-sized knife peeling off thin slices of juicy brisket outlined with its signature dark crust. More than anything, that crust—created by the low heat—is what sets Texas-style brisket apart from all others. Its intense, concentrated flavor is brought about by a melding of the meat's juices, smoke, and seasonings.

Most barbecued brisket recipes designed for home cooks call for a backyard smoker—a smaller contraption functioning on the same indirect-heat cooking principles as large, commercial smokers. While a home smoker would be awfully convenient, in the test kitchen we try to avoid developing recipes based on specialized equipment. Besides, a basic kettle grill can do everything a smoker can.

Butchers usually divide the brisket into two cuts. The point cut has substantially more fat than the flat cut, so it was my first choice for barbecuing. Local butchers informed me, however, that they don't usually stock the point cut, as most customers prefer the leaner flat cut. I knew its lean meat was more prone to drying out, so down the line I'd have to find a way to keep it moist.

On the first day of testing I set up my grill to emulate a barbecue pit. I built a medium-sized fire using 3 quarts of charcoal and rubbed a simple salt-and-black-pepper mixture onto a 5-pound flat-cut brisket. I pushed all the coals to one side to create an indirect heat source and topped the coals with some water-soaked wood chunks (soaking causes them to smolder and slowly release smoke) to simulate a fire fueled by hardwood logs. I knew this method worked for barbecuing smaller pieces of meat, such as ribs and chicken, but I was concerned that my charcoal would burn out before the large brisket was cooked.

After placing the cooking grate on, I put my brisket onto the cool side (as far from the fire as possible) and put the lid on. A thermometer tracked the grill's internal temperature, which I planned on maintaining at around 300 degrees by adding handfuls of unlit briquettes. Every hour or so, I removed the lid to refuel the fire, which caused the grill's internal temperature to plunge 100 degrees. Getting it back to 300 degrees took 45 minutes, and 15 minutes later the cycle began

again. After six hours, the fire died. I headed into the test kitchen, where I transferred the underdone brisket to a low-temperature oven for an hour to finish cooking. While some of the meat was chewy and dry, tasters were nevertheless impressed with the brisket's intense beefiness and sweet smoky flavor. But the absence of a discernible crust was a big letdown.

What if I built a bigger, slightly hotter fire, one that wouldn't peter out? The next morning I lit a fire using 4 quarts of charcoal to see how long it would burn without interruption. This meant no refueling and no taking the lid off. According to my thermometer, the grill's internal temperature hovered around 300 degrees (just where I wanted it) until the fourth hour, when it dropped below 200 degrees. After a total of seven hours, the fire burned out and I removed the lid to retrieve the brisket. Though thoroughly cooked, the interior wasn't tender. But all wasn't lost: I learned that constant fueling wasn't necessary and, more important, keeping the lid on established a consistent temperature that created a darker crust.

During my next tests, I discovered that fires made with more than 4 quarts of charcoal caused the brisket to cook too quickly, making for extremely dry meat. About ready to pony up the plane fare to Austin, I had an epiphany of Texas proportions: Fire can burn down as well as up. So what if I laid down a bulk of unlit briquettes and then added 4 quarts of hot coals on top? I pictured the unlit briquettes slowly catching fire as the lit coals burned, creating a time-delayed fire of sorts—a changing of the guard.

To test my theory, I got up before dawn and banked unlit charcoal against one side of a grill, then lit a 4-quart fire in a chimney starter. When the hot coals were ready, I dumped them on the unlit briquettes. Then on went the cooking grate, the brisket, and the lid. As I had hoped, the fire burned consistently in the 300-degree range for about six hours, before dropping too low. I later discovered that throwing 10 unlit briquettes onto the fire about halfway through cooking provided enough extra fuel to render the brisket perfectly tender.

But my brisket needed an even thicker crust. In real Lone Star barbecue, the brisket turns crusty from slow, gentle browning of the meat, as well as from soot. All the salt-and-pepper formula needed was a little sugar, which turned the meat's exterior into a great dark-brown crust.

BARBECUED BEEF BRISKET

A few tricks—like leaving the fat cap intact and making a shield with aluminum foil for part of the cooking time—helped keep the lean flat-cut brisket moist but didn't offer a complete solution. Then I thought about how we usually treat lean proteins—chicken, turkey, and pork—in the test kitchen before grilling: We brine them. I didn't want to add any more time to my recipe, but I thought it would be worth it if it worked. Sure enough, brining the brisket for two hours ensured that each slice was juicy. After barbecuing well over 100 pounds of beef, I had cured my craving with a recipe for homemade barbecued brisket that no Texan could resist.

—CHARLES KELSEY, *Cook's Illustrated*

BARBECUED BEEF BRISKET ON A CHARCOAL GRILL

SERVES 8 TO 10

We prefer hickory wood chunks to smoke our brisket. Pecan, maple, oak, or fruitwoods such as apple, cherry, and peach also work well. It is best to avoid mesquite, which turns bitter during the long process of barbecuing. Use wood chunks that are about the size of a tennis ball. In step 4, be sure to place the brisket as far away from the fire as possible without touching the wall of the grill. A 5- to 6-pound point-cut brisket can be used in the recipe, but because it is a thicker piece of meat it may need to be finished in the oven (see the instructions in step 5 of the recipe). If using the fattier point cut, omit the step of brining. Some of the traditional accompaniments to barbecued brisket include barbecue sauce, sliced white bread or saltines, pickle chips, and thinly sliced onion.

  1 (5 to 6-pound) flat-cut beef brisket (see note)
  ⅔ cup table salt
  ½ cup plus 2 tablespoons sugar
  3 (3-inch) wood chunks (see note)
  3 tablespoons kosher salt (or 1½ tablespoons table salt)
  2 tablespoons pepper
     Disposable 13 by 9-inch aluminum roasting pan

1. Using a sharp knife, cut slits in the fat cap, spaced 1 inch apart, in a crosshatch pattern, being careful to not cut into the meat. Dissolve the table salt and ½ cup of the sugar in 4 quarts cold water in a stockpot or large bucket. Submerge the brisket in the brine and refrigerate for 2 hours.

2. While the brisket brines, soak the wood chunks in water to cover for at least 1 hour; drain. Remove the brisket from the brine and pat dry with paper towels; transfer to a rimmed baking sheet. Combine the kosher salt, pepper, and the remaining 2 tablespoons sugar in a small bowl. Rub the salt mixture over the entire brisket and into the slits.

3. About 20 minutes before grilling, open the top and bottom grill vents halfway and arrange 3 quarts unlit charcoal briquettes (about 50 pieces) banked against one side of the grill. Place the disposable aluminum roasting pan filled with 2 cups of water on the empty side of the grill. Light a large chimney starter filled two-thirds with charcoal briquettes (about 65 pieces) and allow it to burn until the charcoal is partially covered in a thin layer of fine gray ash, about 15 minutes. Spread the coals over one-third of the grill bottom, on top of the unlit briquettes, with the coals steeply banked against the side of the grill. Place the soaked wood chunks on the coals. Set the cooking grate over the coals, cover the grill, and heat until hot, about 5 minutes. Use a grill brush to scrape the cooking grate clean. Lightly dip a wad of paper towels in vegetable oil; holding the wad with tongs, wipe the cooking grate.

4. Lay a 20- by 18-inch piece of heavy-duty foil over the center of the cooking grate covering the hot side and part of the cool side of the grill. Position the brisket, fat-side down, over the cooler side of the grill so that it covers about one-third of the foil. Fold the remaining length of foil back over the top of the brisket, crimping it loosely to tent the meat and provide a protective heat shield from the hot coals. (If the brisket has a pronounced thicker side, position it facing the fire.) Cover the grill, positioning the top vent over the brisket to draw smoke through the grill. Cook the brisket without removing the lid for 3 hours. (The initial temperature of the grill will be about 400 degrees and will drop to about 325 degrees after 3 hours.)

5. Working quickly, add 10 unlit briquettes to the fire and open the bottom vents all the way. Remove and discard the foil shield from the brisket; flip the meat and rotate it so that the side that was closest to the fire is now farthest away. Cover the grill with the top vents over the brisket and cook until tender and an instant-read thermometer inserted into the thickest part of the meat registers 195 degrees, 2 to 4 more hours. (The final temperature of the grill will be about 250 degrees.)

If after 4 hours the meat does not register 195 degrees, remove the brisket from the grill, transfer it to a wire rack set in a rimmed baking sheet lined with foil, and place in a 325-degree oven on the middle rack until the meat comes up to temperature.

6. Transfer the brisket to a cutting board and let rest 30 minutes, tented with foil. Cut the meat across the grain into long, thin slices; serve.

VARIATION
BARBECUED BEEF BRISKET ON A GAS GRILL

It is necessary to divide the wood chips between 2 disposable aluminum pans, one with and one without water. The water in the one pan will delay the smoking of the chips, thus extending the time the brisket is exposed to smoke. In step 2, be sure to place the brisket as far away from the fire as possible without touching the wall of the grill.

1. Follow the recipe for Barbecued Beef Brisket on a Charcoal Grill through step 2, substituting 4 cups wood chips for the wood chunks, soaking them for 30 minutes. Place 2 cups of the wood chips in a small disposable aluminum pan. Place the remaining 2 cups wood chips in another small disposable aluminum pan along with 1 cup water. Position the pans over the primary burner on a gas grill (the burner that will remain on during cooking). Instead of a large aluminum roasting pan, place a 9-inch aluminum pie plate filled with 2 cups water on the other burner(s). Position the cooking grate over the burners. Turn all the burners to high, close the cover, and heat until very hot, about 15 minutes. Use a grill brush to scrape the cooking grate clean. Lightly dip a wad of paper towels in vegetable oil; holding the wad with tongs, wipe the cooking grate. Turn the primary burner to medium-high and turn the remaining burner(s) off.

2. Lay a 20- by 18-inch piece of heavy-duty foil over the center of the cooking grate covering the hot side and part of the cool side of the grill. Position the brisket, fat-side down, over the cooler side of the grill so that it covers about one-third of the foil. Fold the remaining length of foil back over the top of the brisket, crimping it loosely to tent the meat and provide a protective heat shield from the hot coals. (If the brisket has a pronounced thicker side, position it facing the fire.) Cook, without raising the lid, for 3 hours. Transfer the brisket to a wire rack set in a rimmed baking sheet lined with foil.

3. Meanwhile, adjust an oven rack to the middle position and heat the oven to 325 degrees. Roast the brisket until tender and an instant-read thermometer inserted into the thickest part of the meat registers 195 degrees, 1½ to 2 hours. Transfer the brisket to a cutting board and let rest 30 minutes, loosely tented with foil. Cut the brisket across the grain into long, thin slices; serve.

NOTES FROM THE TEST KITCHEN

TWO CUTS OF BRISKET

Cut from the cow's breast section, a whole brisket is a boneless, coarse-grained cut comprised of two smaller roasts: the flat (or first) cut and the point (or second) cut. The knobby point cut (A) overlaps the rectangular flat cut (B). The point cut has more marbling and fat, and the flat cut's meat is lean and topped with a thick fat cap. Our recipe calls for the widely available flat cut (B). Make sure that the fat cap isn't overtrimmed and is ⅓ to ½ inch thick.

WHOLE BRISKET

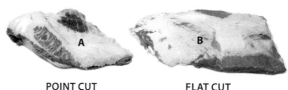

POINT CUT   **FLAT CUT**

TOP THERMOMETER

If your grill doesn't have a built-in thermometer, it's a good idea to buy one so you can monitor the temperature of the fire without opening the grill lid. We tested eight oven and barbecue thermometers and found a surprising range of features and prices—from $7.99 to $99. Our two favorites turned out to be the cheapest models tested: the Weber 9815 Replacement Food Thermometer, $7.99, and the **Polder Stainless Steel Dual Oven/Meat Thermometer**, $10. For a couple dollars more than the Weber, the Polder gives you simultaneous meat and oven temperature readings. On the grill, a heatproof silicone finger-grip under the dial allows you to take the thermometer out of the lid vents and check the temperature of the meat.

PORT-BRAISED SHORT RIBS

SHORT RIBS CAN MAKE FOR A VERY SPECIAL MEAL, but they take a long time to prepare. First the ribs are browned in batches to build flavor and render exterior fat, then the vegetables are sautéed, and then everything is braised for hours in broth flavored with wine and herbs. Unfortunately, when the fat and collagen melt out of the meat, they end up in the sauce. Some recipes go so far as to require refrigerating the cooked ribs in their sauce overnight to make it easier to remove the rendered fat. I wanted to create fork-tender, silky (but not fatty) short ribs with a bold, clean sauce—and I wanted to serve it on the same day I made it.

Starting with a recipe that employed classic braising technique, I browned a batch of short ribs in my Dutch oven and found about three tablespoons of fat left behind in the pot. Not bad, but I knew there was still fat from the ribs' interior to be lost, and I didn't want it to end up in my sauce. Some recipes forgo stovetop browning in favor of roasting the ribs in the oven before braising. I tried this method, and after an hour the ribs had lost plenty of fat—but valuable moisture, too; they looked like beef jerky. For my next test, I covered the ribs with foil to prevent them from drying out while they roasted. After about two hours, I discovered my nicely browned ribs had rendered a whopping cup of fat. It was time for the sauce.

I built a braising sauce on the stovetop using traditional ingredients: onion, carrot, celery, garlic, tomato paste, red wine, and beef broth. I added the roasted ribs, covered the pot, and transferred it to the oven. Moist, tender meat emerged (the defatted ribs had soaked up the braising liquid), but I wanted bolder flavor. I tried replacing the red wine with port, and my tasters loved the rich sweetness it imparted. A little balsamic vinegar added a nice acidity, and a sprig of rosemary lent a welcome herbal flavor. Simply reducing it left me with an overly sticky sauce (the sweet port reduces to syrup) and not nearly enough for serving—only ½ cup. Instead, I decided to add a thickener to the braising liquid at the outset, hoping that by the time the ribs were done the sauce would have the right consistency. Flour and cornstarch made the braising liquid too thick and gravylike. I had better luck with instant tapioca, which imparted no flavor of its own and gave the sauce a smoother, more refined consistency. With a quick skimming and straining of the sauce, I now had short ribs that were perfect every time.

—KELLEY BAKER, *Cook's Country*

PORT-BRAISED SHORT RIBS

SERVES 4 TO 6

Short ribs come in two styles. English-style ribs contain a single rib bone and a thick piece of meat. Flanken-style ribs are cut thinner and have several smaller bones. While either will work here, we prefer the less expensive and more readily available English-style ribs. The ribs and sauce can be refrigerated separately for up to 3 days. When ready to serve, heat the sauce and ribs together over medium heat until the ribs are warmed through.

- 5 pounds beef short ribs (6 to 8 English-style ribs), trimmed of excess fat (see note)
  Salt and pepper
- 1 onion, chopped (about 1 cup)
- 1 carrot, peeled and chopped
- 1 celery rib, chopped
- 4 garlic cloves, minced
- 1 tablespoon tomato paste
- 3 cups low-sodium beef broth
- 1½ cups ruby port
- ¼ cup balsamic vinegar
- ¼ cup Minute Tapioca
- 1 sprig fresh rosemary

1. Adjust an oven rack to the middle position and heat the oven to 375 degrees. Season the ribs with salt and pepper and arrange, bone-side up, in a roasting pan. Cover tightly with aluminum foil and roast until the fat has rendered and the ribs are browned, 1½ to 2 hours. Transfer the ribs to a paper towel–lined plate. Reserve 2 tablespoons of the rendered beef fat and discard the remaining drippings.

2. Reduce the oven temperature to 300 degrees. Heat the reserved fat in a large Dutch oven over medium-high heat until shimmering. Cook the onion, carrot, and celery until lightly browned, about 5 minutes. Add the garlic and tomato paste and cook until fragrant, about 1 minute. Add the broth, port, vinegar, tapioca, rosemary, and ribs to the pot and bring to a simmer.

3. Cover the pot and transfer to the oven. Cook until the sauce is slightly thickened and the ribs are completely tender, about 2 hours. Transfer the ribs to a serving platter. Strain and skim the sauce. Serve, passing the sauce at the table.

NOTES FROM THE TEST KITCHEN

HOW TO ROAST AND RENDER BEFORE YOU BRAISE
The marbling in short ribs gives them great flavor, but it can also make the sauce greasy. Here's how we cut the fat.

1. Trim any visible fat from the exterior of the ribs before cooking.

2. Roast the ribs in a foil-covered pan to render fat from the interior of the meat.

3. Pour off the fat and drippings (there should be at least 1 cup), reserving just 2 tablespoons for building the sauce.

ONION GOGGLES
Chopping and dicing our way through 30 pounds of onions per week in the test kitchen, we're always interested in new methods of eye defense. And while they certainly look a bit goofy, the **R.S.V.P. International Onion Goggles**, $19.99, do help maintain focus on the onions—yellow, Vidalia, red, or otherwise—rather than the tissue box. We found that they block irritating fumes better than sunglasses, and the foam padding around the anti-fog lenses is a more comfortable alternative to swim goggles.

SLOW-ROASTED BEEF

FOR MOST FAMILIES, Sunday roast beef isn't prime rib; it's a lesser cut that's sometimes good, sometimes not. The roasts my parents prepared throughout my childhood were typically tough and dried-out and better suited for sandwiches the next day. But when my grandfather was at the stove, he could take the same inexpensive cut and turn it into something special—tender, rosy, beefy-tasting meat that had everyone asking for seconds. I wanted to work the same kind of wizardry on my own Sunday roast.

First I needed to zero in on the most promising beef. After a week in the kitchen testing a slew of low-cost cuts, I had a clear winner: the eye-round roast. Though less flavorful than fattier cuts from the shoulder (the chuck) and less tender than other meat from the back leg (the round), my eye roast had one key attribute the others lacked: a uniform shape from front to back. This was a roast that would not only cook evenly but look good on the plate as well.

My next challenge was choosing between the two classic methods for roasting meat—high and fast or low and slow. I began with the more common high-heat approach, quickly searing the meat on the stovetop and then transferring it to a 450-degree oven for roasting. The technique works great with more upscale rib and loin cuts but showed its flaws with the leaner eye round, yielding meat that was overcooked and dried-out.

But before heading down the low-temperature path, which normally involves roasting meat in an oven set between 250 and 325 degrees, I wanted to try something more extreme. To extract maximum tenderness from meat, the popular 1960s nutritionist Adelle Davis advocated cooking it at the temperature desired when it was done. For a roast to reach an end temperature of 130 degrees for medium-rare, this process could involve 20 to 30 hours of cooking. Davis's advice wasn't new. Benjamin Thompson, the 18th-century physicist who invented the roasting oven, observed that leaving meat to cook overnight in an oven heated by a dying fire resulted in exceptional tenderness.

Tossing aside practical considerations like food safety and the gas bill, I decided I had to replicate these two experts' findings. I set the one oven in the test kitchen

SLOW-ROASTED BEEF

capable of maintaining such a low temperature to 130 degrees and popped in an eye round. Twenty-four hours later, I pulled out a roast with juicy, meltingly tender meat that tasters likened to beef tenderloin. What special beef magic was going on here?

When I thought back to the test kitchen's discoveries while developing a recipe for Pan-Seared Thick-Cut Strip Steaks, I had my answer: Beef contains enzymes that break down its connective tissues and act as natural tenderizers. These enzymes work faster as the temperature of the meat rises—but just until it reaches 122 degrees, at which point all action stops. Roasting the eye round in an oven set to 130 degrees allowed it to stay below 122 degrees far longer than when cooked in the typical low-temperature roasting range, transforming this lean, unassuming cut into something great.

But given that most ovens don't heat below 200 degrees—and that most home cooks don't want to run their ovens for a full day—how could I expect others to re-create my results? I would have to go as low as I could and see what happened. To accommodate the widest possible range of ovens, I settled on 225 degrees as my lowest starting point. I also decided I would brown the meat first to give it nice color and a crusty exterior. (While tender, my 130-degree roast had an unappetizing gray exterior.) Searing would also help to ensure food safety, since bacteria on roasts are generally confined to the outside.

When I took the roast out of the oven, however, I was disappointed. It was tender, but nothing like the texture of the eye round cooked at 130 degrees. What could I do to keep the meat below 122 degrees longer? A new idea occurred to me: Why not shut off the oven just before the roast reached 122 degrees? As the oven cooled, the roast would continue to cook even more slowly.

Using a meat-probe thermometer to track the internal temperature of the roast, I shut off the oven when the meat reached 115 degrees. Sure enough, the meat stayed below 122 degrees 30 minutes longer, allowing its enzymes to continue the work of tenderizing, before creeping to 130 degrees for medium-rare. Tasters were certainly happy with this roast. It was remarkably tender and juicy for a roast that cost so little.

With the tenderness problem solved, it was time to tackle taste. So far I'd simply sprinkled salt and pepper on the roast just before searing it. Perhaps the flavor would improve if the meat were salted overnight or even brined. Brining—normally reserved for less fatty pork and poultry—certainly pumped more water into the beef and made it very juicy, but it also made it taste bland, watery, and less beefy. Next I tried salting the meat for first four, then 12, and finally 24 hours. As might be expected, the roast benefited most from the longest salting. Because the process of osmosis causes salt to travel from areas of higher to lower concentration, the full 24 hours gave it the most time to penetrate deep into the meat. There was another benefit: Salt, like the enzymes in meat, breaks down proteins to further improve texture.

At last I had tender, flavorful beef for a Sunday roast that even my grandfather would have been proud to serve to his family. The leftovers—if there were any—would have no need for mayonnaise or mustard to taste good.

—DAVID PAZMIÑO, *Cook's Illustrated*

SLOW-ROASTED BEEF WITH HORSERADISH CREAM SAUCE
SERVES 6 TO 8

We don't recommend cooking this roast past medium. Open the oven door as infrequently as possible and remove the roast from the oven while taking its temperature. If the roast has not reached the desired temperature in the time specified in step 3, heat the oven to 225 degrees for 5 minutes, shut it off, and continue to cook the roast to the desired temperature. For a smaller (2½ to 3½-pound) roast, reduce the amount of kosher salt to 3 teaspoons (1½ teaspoons table salt) and black pepper to 1½ teaspoons. For a 4½ to 6-pound roast, cut in half crosswise before cooking to create 2 smaller roasts.

ROAST

1 (3½ to 4½-pound) boneless eye-round roast (see note)

4 teaspoons kosher salt (or 2 teaspoons table salt)

2 teaspoons plus 1 tablespoon vegetable oil

2 teaspoons pepper

HORSERADISH CREAM SAUCE

½ cup heavy cream

½ cup prepared horseradish

1 teaspoon salt

⅛ teaspoon pepper

1. FOR THE ROAST: Sprinkle all sides of the roast evenly with the salt. Wrap with plastic wrap and refrigerate for 18 to 24 hours.

2. Adjust an oven rack to the middle position and heat the oven to 225 degrees. Pat the roast dry with paper towels; rub with 2 teaspoons of the oil and sprinkle all sides evenly with the pepper. Heat the remaining 1 tablespoon oil in a 12-inch skillet over medium-high heat until just smoking. Sear the roast until browned on all sides, 3 to 4 minutes per side. Transfer the roast to a wire rack set in a rimmed baking sheet. Roast until a meat-probe thermometer or an instant-read thermometer inserted into the center of the roast registers 115 degrees for medium-rare, 1¼ to 1¾ hours, or 125 degrees for medium, 1¾ to 2¼ hours.

3. Turn the oven off; leave the roast in the oven, without opening the door, until the meat-probe thermometer or instant-read thermometer inserted into the center of the roast registers 130 degrees for medium-rare, or 140 degrees for medium, 30 to 50 minutes longer. Transfer the roast to a carving board and let rest for 15 minutes.

4. FOR THE SAUCE: Meanwhile, whisk the cream in a medium bowl until thickened but not yet holding soft peaks, 1 to 2 minutes. Gently fold in the horseradish, salt, and pepper. Transfer to a serving bowl and refrigerate for at least 15 minutes before serving.

5. Slice the meat crosswise as thin as possible and serve, passing the horseradish cream at the table.

NOTES FROM THE TEST KITCHEN

LOW-COST LINEUP
Not all bargain cuts have the potential to taste like a million bucks—or look like it when carved and served on a plate.

**OUR FAVORITE:
EYE-ROUND ROAST**
($4.99 per pound)
We singled out this cut not only for its good flavor and relative tenderness but also for its uniform shape that guarantees even cooking and yields nicely shaped slices.

**TOO FATTY:
CHUCK-EYE ROAST**
($3.99 per pound)
While undeniably tender and flavorful, its fat and gristle make this meat better for stew and pot roast than roast beef.

**ODD SHAPE:
TOP-ROUND ROAST**
($3.99 per pound)
A deli staple for sandwiches, this cut comes in irregular shapes that can cook unevenly.

**TOUGH TO CARVE:
BOTTOM-ROUND
RUMP ROAST**
($4.29 per pound)
We ruled out this roast for being both tough and hard to carve against the grain.

MEAT-PROBE THERMOMETERS
Repeatedly opening the oven door to monitor the internal temperature of a roast can throw cooking times off kilter. One solution? Meat-probe thermometers. These remote devices transmit temperature from a long probe left in the meat and attached to a thin cord that snakes out of the oven to a digital console. But don't throw out your instant-read thermometer just yet. We tested 11 models and not one was flawless. The ones that accurately measured temperature sported function buttons that were too slow or too hard to figure out. Others that were user-friendly were also unreliable.

The best of the bunch—the **ThermoWorks Original Cooking Thermometer/Timer,** $19—was great when it worked but has probes that even its manufacturer admits are sometimes defective. Until a better meat probe comes on the market, we recommend this one—with reservations. Check the probe's accuracy by boiling water and taking a reading before trying it with a roast. If the probe doesn't read very close to 212 degrees, ask for a replacement.

GRILLED T-BONE STEAKS

WHEN IT COMES TO FIGURING OUT the best way to cook T-bone and porterhouse steaks, America's finest steakhouses and their heat-blasting broilers might come to mind for some people. But Italy is my first association. During a college semester in Florence, I experienced my first authentic *bistecca alla fiorentina,* a huge T-bone grilled over an oak fire, then sprinkled with sea salt and drizzled with olive oil. Years later, I can still recall that steak's thick, dark crust, smoky aroma, and deep grill flavor.

According to the Florentine T-Bone Steak Academy (yes, there really is such a group), the method for cooking bistecca alla fiorentina hasn't changed in 200 years. The meat, always a thick-cut T-bone from Tuscany's native Chianina steer, is placed about eight inches above the fire and cooked for 5 minutes on each side. Aside from being turned once, the meat is not touched during cooking. And salt never kisses its surface until right before serving.

When I've tried to re-create the thick crust of a Florentine steak on my backyard grill, I've had little success. Two factors have always worked against me: fattier American beef and the hotter fire created by charcoal briquettes. Both variables lead to fat dripping on the coals, causing flare-ups. To keep the flare-ups under control, I move the steaks off and then back on the grill until the meat has a decent sear. Ultimately, it's this back-and-forth dance that prevents the steaks from developing a good crust.

American beef and charcoal briquettes were a given. But could I figure out a way to get results that were at least close to the Florentine method?

From my experience grilling at home, I already knew that cooking over a single-level fire, where the coal is spread in an even layer in the grill, wouldn't work. But what about a two-level fire, where you create hotter and cooler areas by placing more coals on one side of the grill than the other?

I lit a full chimney of coals, and when they were glowing I spread about 90 percent of them in a single layer over half of the grill, arranging the remaining coals on the other side. I replaced the cooking grate and let it heat up for about 5 minutes. The steaks gave off a good hiss when they hit the blazingly hot metal. Quickly, though, the fat melted and the too-familiar flare-ups began. These were small at first, but grew larger by the second. In another minute, my steaks would be on fire.

I pulled the steaks to the grill's cooler half, flipping them once onto their raw sides to finish cooking. That's when I observed how the steaks reacted over a smaller fire. The fat still dripped onto the coals, causing flare-ups, but these flames were small and barely touched the meat. The result? A pretty good crust.

But I knew I could do better. To gain greater control, I varied the amount of charcoal, filling the chimney first one-half, then two-thirds, and finally three-quarters full. Rather than distributing the coals on both sides, I spread them evenly on only half of the grill. This way, I could get a good sear on the grill's hotter side and gently finish cooking the steaks' interiors using indirect heat on the cooler side. The steaks took about 6 minutes per side, and the small flare-ups helped to brown the meat.

One problem remained, however: Tasters found the coveted tenderloin section to be somewhat tough and dry. So I positioned the meat with the tenderloin facing the cooler side of the grill. Now it cooked at a slightly slower rate and stayed tender and juicy.

Now that my grilling technique was nailed down, I had one last question: Would it make any difference if we salted the meat earlier in the process? I'd been following the Florentine protocol of waiting to add salt until the end, but decided to employ the test kitchen's preference for seasoning up to an hour before cooking, which enables the salt to penetrate the meat's interior. A half hour before lighting the coals, I sprinkled the meat with salt. This lengthy exposure boosted the meat's flavor from crust to bone, helping to compensate for American beef's less complex taste. I found it necessary to remove any moisture that accumulated on the surface of the steaks with paper towels; if left in place, this moisture caused the steaks to steam a bit and the crust wasn't as thick.

For a more jazzed-up grilled steak, I brushed on a little herb butter toward the end of cooking. The Florentine T-Bone Steak Academy might not approve of such adornment, but I'm sure it would approve of my steaks' well-browned exteriors, perfectly cooked interiors, and intensely beefy flavor.

—CHARLES KELSEY, *Cook's Illustrated*

CHARCOAL-GRILLED T-BONE STEAKS WITH CHIVE BUTTER

SERVES 4 TO 6

When arranging the lit coals in step 3, make sure that they are in an even layer. If the coals are stacked unevenly, large flare-ups may occur, causing the steaks to blacken. We highly recommend thick steaks, but if cooking thinner steaks (¾ to 1 inch thick), make the following adjustments: Reduce the kosher salt to 1 tablespoon (or 1½ teaspoons table salt) and the pepper to 1½ teaspoons. In step 3, build the fire with a full chimney (about 100 briquettes). Cook the steaks, as directed in step 4, over the hotter part of the grill for about 3 minutes per side for rare to medium-rare, or about 4 minutes per side for medium, but do not transfer them to the cooler side of the grill; they will be fully cooked at this point.

STEAK

- 2 T-bone or porterhouse steaks (about 1¾ pounds each), each 1 to 1½ inches thick (see note)
- 4 teaspoons kosher salt (or 2 teaspoons table salt)
- 2 teaspoons pepper

CHIVE BUTTER

- 4 tablespoons (½ stick) unsalted butter, melted
- ½ shallot, minced (about 1½ tablespoons)
- 1 garlic clove, minced
- 1 tablespoon minced fresh chives
- Pinch salt
- Pinch pepper

1. FOR THE STEAK: Sprinkle the entire surface of each steak evenly with 2 teaspoons of the kosher salt (or 1 teaspoon table salt); let sit at room temperature for 1 hour. Pat the steaks dry with paper towels; sprinkle each evenly with 1 teaspoon of the pepper.

2. FOR THE CHIVE BUTTER: Meanwhile, combine all of the ingredients in a medium bowl.

3. About 20 minutes before grilling, light a large chimney starter filled three-quarters with charcoal briquettes (about 75 pieces) and allow it to burn until the charcoal is partially covered in a thin layer of fine gray ash, about 15 minutes. Spread the coals in an even layer over half of the grill bottom, leaving the other half with no coals. Set the cooking grate over the coals, cover the grill, and heat until hot, about 5 minutes. Use a grill brush to scrape the cooking grate clean. Lightly dip a wad of paper towels in vegetable oil; holding the wad with tongs, wipe the cooking grate. The grill is ready when the coals are medium-hot (you can hold your hand 5 inches above the grate for 3 to 4 seconds).

4. Place the steaks on the grate directly over the coals with the tenderloin sides (smaller side of the T-bone) facing the cooler side of the grill. Grill without moving the steaks until a dark-brown crust forms, about 6 minutes. (Small flare-ups will occur; if the flames become constant, slide the steaks to the cooler side of the grill and mist the fire with water from a spray bottle.) Flip the steaks and turn so that the tenderloin sides are once again facing the cooler side of the grill. Continue to grill until a dark-brown crust forms on the second side, about 6 minutes.

5. Brush the butter over the steaks. Transfer the steaks to the cooler side of the grill with the bone sides facing the fire. Cover the grill and continue cooking until an instant-read thermometer inserted into the center of the steaks registers 120 degrees for rare, about 2 minutes; 125 degrees for medium-rare, about 4 minutes; or 135 degrees for medium, about 6 minutes, flipping the steaks halfway through the cooking time.

6. Transfer the steaks to a cutting board and let rest for 10 minutes. Cut the strip and tenderloin pieces off the bones; cut each piece crosswise into ¼-inch slices. Serve.

VARIATION

GAS-GRILLED T-BONE STEAKS WITH CHIVE BUTTER

If grilling thinner steaks (¾ to 1 inch thick), reduce the kosher salt to 1 tablespoon (or 1½ teaspoons table salt) and the pepper to 1½ teaspoons. Cook the steaks, as directed below, over the hotter part of the grill with the lid down for about 3 minutes per side for rare to medium-rare, or about 4 minutes per side for medium.

Follow the recipe for Charcoal-Grilled T-Bone Steaks through step 2. Turn all the burners to high, close the cover, and heat until very hot, about 15 minutes. Use a grill brush to scrape the cooking grate clean. Lightly dip a wad of paper towels in vegetable oil; holding the wad with tongs, wipe the cooking grate. Leave the primary burner on high and turn the remaining burner(s) to low. Continue with the recipe from step 4, cooking the steaks over the hottest part of the grill with the lid down. For rare steaks (120 degrees), remove the meat from the grill after step 4 and brush with the butter. For medium-rare and medium steaks, brush the butter over the steaks and transfer to the cooler side of the grill, turn the low burner(s) off, and cook with the lid down for about 2 minutes for medium-rare (125 degrees), or about 4 minutes for medium (135 degrees), flipping the steaks halfway through the cooking time.

NOTES FROM THE TEST KITCHEN

TWO TYPES OF T-BONES
Both T-bone and porterhouse steaks contain a strip steak and a tenderloin steak connected by a T-shaped bone. Technically, a T-bone must have a tenderloin portion at least ½ inch across, and a porterhouse's tenderloin must measure at least 1¼ inches across.

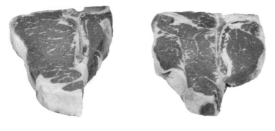

T-BONE　　　　　**PORTERHOUSE**

CREATE TWO HEAT LEVELS
Placing all the coals on one half of the grill and leaving the other half empty creates a hotter side and a cooler side. This will allow you to get a good sear by positioning the steaks on the hotter side first and then finish cooking on the cooler side.

BROILED STEAKS

I USUALLY RELY ON A RED-HOT SKILLET or my grill for putting a crusty sear on steaks, but I wondered if my oven broiler—which throws out a ton of heat—could do the job just as well. The promise of a perfectly cooked steak without a greasy stovetop or a trip outside to the grill was very attractive.

I adjusted my oven rack to the top position, preheated the broiler on "high," and threw a couple of strip steaks on the broiler pan. The results weren't pretty. Though some of the moisture and fat from the steaks drained through the broiler pan slits, much of it sat around the steaks, which caused the meat to steam and turn gray, with absolutely no char or crust. And if that wasn't bad enough, the drippings that made their way through the pan burned, filling the test kitchen with smoke.

Getting some color on the steaks was my first order of business. I quickly discovered that the broiler pan—not the broiler itself—was causing most of the problems. Because broiler pans are only about an inch tall, they don't bring steaks close enough to the broiler element to get a proper sear, even on the top oven rack. To remedy this, I brought in a 3-inch-deep disposable aluminum roasting pan, moved the oven rack down a notch, and set the steaks on a cooling rack placed over the pan. This brought the meat closer to the heat, where it could acquire a good sear. The cooling rack (which is more porous than the broiler-pan rack) also allowed surface moisture to immediately drain away.

Cooking the steaks evenly was another problem. Steaks that went directly from the refrigerator to the broiler had charred exteriors before the centers were done, no matter how many times I flipped them. Letting the steaks sit at room temperature for an hour before cooking helped, but it took too long. Instead, I started the steaks in a moderate oven to take the chill off. I removed them after 6 to 10 minutes, let them rest while the broiler heated, then cooked them as before. This method produced evenly cooked meat every time.

Only one problem remained: the smoke. The fat that was cooking out of the steaks was still burning on the bottom of the pan. To put a stop to the smoke, I tried adding water to the pan, but the steam it produced softened the crust I had worked so hard to create. I tried putting bread in the pan to absorb the grease before it had a chance to burn, but that idea (and bread) went up in smoke. I had much better results by covering the bottom of the pan with salt, which soaked up the grease and greatly minimized the smoke. Finally, I had crusty, charred steaks—and a good reason to use my broiler a lot more often.

—DIANE UNGER, *Cook's Country*

BROILED STEAKS

SERVES 4

To minimize smoking, be sure to trim as much exterior fat and gristle as possible from the steaks before cooking. Try to purchase steaks of a similar size and shape for this recipe. If you like your steaks well done, continue cooking and flipping as directed in step 3 until the steaks reach the desired internal temperature.

- 4 **tablespoons (½ stick) unsalted butter, at room temperature**
- 1 **teaspoon minced fresh thyme**
- 1 **teaspoon Dijon mustard**
  Salt and pepper
  Disposable aluminum pan, 3 inches deep
- 4 **strip steaks, rib-eye steaks, or tenderloin steaks, 1 to 2 inches thick, trimmed (see note)**

1. Adjust the oven racks to the upper-middle and lower-middle positions and heat the oven to 375 degrees. Beat the butter, thyme, mustard, ¼ teaspoon salt, and ¼ teaspoon pepper in a bowl and refrigerate.

2. Spread 2 cups salt over the bottom of the disposable aluminum roasting pan. Pat the steaks dry with paper towels, season with salt and pepper, and transfer to a wire rack. Set the rack over the aluminum roasting pan and transfer to the lower-middle oven rack. Cook 6 to 10 minutes (see the "Perfectly Broiled Steaks" chart, at right), then remove the pan from the oven. Flip the steaks, pat them dry with paper towels, and let rest 10 minutes.

3. Heat the broiler. Transfer the pan to the upper-middle oven rack and broil the steaks, flipping them every 2 to 4 minutes, until an instant-read thermometer inserted into the meat registers 125 to 130 degrees (for medium-rare), 6 to 16 minutes. Transfer the steaks to a platter, top with the chilled butter mixture, and tent with foil. Let rest for 5 minutes. Serve.

NOTES FROM THE TEST KITCHEN

HOW HOT IS YOUR BROILER?

It's good to know if your broiler runs relatively hot, average, or cold. This information allows you to adjust the cooking time for this recipe (and others) accordingly. To see how your broiler stacks up, heat it on high and place a slice of white sandwich bread directly under the heating element on the upper-middle rack. If the bread toasts to golden brown in 30 seconds or less, your broiler runs very hot, and you will need to reduce the cooking time by a minute or two. If the bread toasts perfectly in 1 minute, your broiler runs about average. If the bread takes 2 minutes or longer to toast, your broiler runs cool and you may need to increase the cooking time by a minute or two.

PERFECTLY BROILED STEAKS

The first step to perfectly broiled steaks is knowing exactly how thick your steaks are. Using a ruler, measure each steak and then follow the guidelines below.

STEAK THICKNESS	PREBAKE	BROIL
1 inch	6 minutes	Turn steaks every 2 minutes
1½ inches	8 minutes	Turn steaks every 3 minutes
2 inches	10 minutes	Turn steaks every 4 minutes

BROILER PREP

Since oven-rack positioning varies greatly from model to model, we suggest you ensure correct positioning with a dry run before turning on your oven.

COLD SETUP: Before preheating your oven, and with your oven racks adjusted to the upper-middle and lower-middle positions, place a wire rack on top of a 3-inch-deep disposable aluminum pan and place it on the upper-middle rack. Place the steaks on top of the rack and use a ruler to measure the distance between the top of the steaks and the heating element of the broiler. For optimal searing, there should be ½ inch to 1 inch of space.

MEASURE AND ADJUST: If there is more than 1 inch of space, here's how to close the gap: Elevate the aluminum pan by placing it on an inverted rimmed baking sheet; use a deeper-sided disposable aluminum pan; or stack multiple aluminum pans inside one another. If there's less than ½ inch of space, adjust the oven rack or use a shallower pan.

THE RACK IS RIGHT

A rack set over a deep disposable aluminum pan allows the drippings to fall away from the steak, resulting in a well-developed crust. The salt absorbs the grease and helps control the amount of smoke.

BROILED STEAKS

SLOW-COOKER BARBECUE BEEF SANDWICHES

BARBECUED BEEF SOUNDS LIKE an ideal recipe for the slow cooker, as both outdoor barbecue and slow cookers use slow-and-low heat to tenderize tough cuts of meat. But most of the slow-cooker recipes I found had me simply dumping a few bottles of barbecue sauce over a piece of brisket, turning on the slow cooker, and calling it a day. Eight hours later, the beef was dry, stringy, and chewy. Even worse, the meat tasted more like sour pot roast than barbecue, as the moist heat of the slow cooker washed away the flavor of the sauce.

With smoky, moist, and tender beef cloaked in a tangy sauce as my goal, I started with the meat. My testing proved brisket to be unreliable—too often it was tough and impossible to shred, even after hours of cooking. Flank steak, round steak, and chuck-eye roast worked better, with tasters preferring the chuck for its big, beefy flavor and silky, pull-apart texture.

Although bottled barbecue sauce can be pretty good, I knew I could do better. To create a smoky flavor base, I rendered bacon and cooked onion, chili powder, and paprika in the drippings. Ketchup, brown sugar, and mustard are a must for any barbecue sauce, but my tasters wanted deeper, more complex flavor. Neither beef nor chicken stock added the necessary richness, but a surprise ingredient—coffee—gave the sauce a depth that tasters appreciated (and couldn't identify as coffee).

I poured this sauce over the beef, and after 10 hours of cooking I had tender meat swimming in a watery sauce; as it cooked, the chuck had exuded juice into the sauce, dulling its flavor and thinning its texture. Using only half the sauce for cooking and reserving half for dressing the cooked meat worked well, especially when I reduced the cooking liquid before adding it back to the beef. Splashes of cider vinegar and hot sauce brightened things up, and a teaspoon of liquid smoke gave the dish nice smoky flavor.

After pulling the tender meat into shreds, tossing it with the sauce, and piling it high on a bun, I knew I'd hit the mark. I'd finally made slow-cooker barbecued beef that looked and tasted as if it had come off the grill.

—DIANE UNGER, *Cook's Country*

SLOW-COOKER BARBECUE BEEF SANDWICHES
SERVES 10

Don't shred the meat too fine in step 3; it will break up more when combined with the sauce.

- 1 (5-pound) boneless beef chuck-eye roast, trimmed and cut into 4 pieces
- 4 slices bacon, minced
- 1 onion, minced (about 1 cup)
- 2 tablespoons chili powder
- 1 tablespoon paprika
- 1½ cups brewed coffee
- 1½ cups ketchup
- ¼ cup packed dark brown sugar
- 2 tablespoons brown mustard
- 1 tablespoon hot sauce
- 1 tablespoon cider vinegar
- 1 teaspoon liquid smoke
  Salt and pepper
- 10 sandwich rolls, split

1. Place the beef in the slow-cooker insert. Cook the bacon in a large skillet over medium-high heat until crisp, about 5 minutes. Using a slotted spoon, transfer the bacon to the slow-cooker insert. Pour off all but 2 tablespoons fat from the pan and cook the onion in the remaining fat until softened, about 5 minutes. Add the chili powder and paprika and cook until fragrant, about 30 seconds. Stir in the coffee, ketchup, sugar, and 1 tablespoon of the mustard and simmer until reduced slightly, about 10 minutes. Add half of the sauce to the slow-cooker insert and refrigerate the remaining half. Cover and cook on low until the meat is tender, 9 to 10 hours (or cook on high for 5 to 6 hours).

2. Using a slotted spoon, transfer the meat to a large bowl and cover with foil. Transfer the cooking liquid to a large skillet, skim the fat, and simmer over medium-high heat until reduced to 1 cup, about 10 minutes. Off the heat, stir in the reserved sauce, the remaining 1 tablespoon mustard, hot sauce, vinegar, and liquid smoke.

3. Pull the meat into large chunks, discarding any excess fat or gristle. Toss the meat with 1½ cups of the sauce and let sit, covered, until the meat has absorbed most of the sauce, about 10 minutes. Season with salt and pepper to taste. Serve on the rolls, passing the remaining sauce at the table.

THE RIGHT CUT

We found that a large chuck-eye roast retained its moisture better than other cuts, even after 10 hours in a slow cooker. Here's how we prepare the meat before cooking.

1. Select a well-marbled roast and carefully trim and discard any exterior fat.

2. Slicing from the top of the meat, cut the roast in half (as shown) and then cut each piece in half again.

THE SECRET INGREDIENT

Brewed coffee blends with the other sauce ingredients to add richness without imparting coffee flavor.

THE BEST SLOW COOKERS

Having a slow cooker is a little like having June Cleaver at home—both cook you dinner while you're away. These kitchen helpers have such appeal that they have been steadily rising in cost, as new features are added. We rounded up seven models (all with at least a 6-quart capacity) to test them in action. We found that the best slow cookers had programmable timers, "on" lights, insert handles, and see-through lids. The slow cooker that aced all our tests and had all the features we wanted was the **All-Clad Stainless Steel Slow Cooker**, $149.95. (See page 342 for more information about our testing results.)

JUCY LUCY BURGERS

AS FOR THE ORIGIN OF THIS RECIPE, two Minnesota taverns, Matt's Bar and the 5-8 Club, claim to have created the burger in the 1950s. As the story goes, a customer requested a burger with the cheese sealed in the middle. When he bit in, the hot cheese spurted out and he exclaimed, "That's one juicy lucy!" As for the unusual spelling, that's still a mystery.

Although Jucy Lucys are traditionally fried on a tavern griddle, I wanted to grill them. It seemed simple—seal a slice of American cheese between two burger patties and throw it on the grill. But my burgers, cooked until well done to fully melt the cheese, were dry and tough. Worse still, they had suffered a blowout: The cheese melted through the meat, leaving an empty cavern where the cheese had been. Was there a way to keep this Lucy juicy and hold the cheese inside?

Since a thin slice of American cheese simply disappeared during the long grilling time, I tried sandwiching a chunk of cheese between two patties instead. This improved the odds of keeping the cheese inside, but it was still hit or miss. A co-worker suggested sealing the cheese inside a small patty and then molding a second patty around the first one. This created a double-sealed pocket that kept the cheesy center in place every time.

A hot fire scorched the outside of my burgers and left the cheese unmelted. Grilling the burgers over medium heat worked much better, fully cooking the burger and melting the cheese. The burgers were nearly there, but they still weren't as moist as the ones from the tavern. Then I remembered a meatball trick in which a *pan-ade*—a mixture of bread and milk mashed to a paste—is added to ground beef. This worked, giving me what I had thought was impossible, a tender and juicy well-done burger.

The Jucy Lucys in the Twin Cities are sparsely flavored with salt, pepper, garlic, and Worcestershire sauce. Garlic powder worked better than garlic salt (which was too muted) and minced garlic (too pungent), but I lost the Worcestershire—it made the burgers taste too much like meatloaf. I grilled up a batch of these burgers and, remembering the chin burn, let them cool for a few minutes before diving in. I was rewarded with a warm, melted center of cheese inside an incredible juicy (but not greasy) Lucy.

—LYNN CLARK, *Cook's Country*

CHARCOAL-GRILLED JUCY LUCY BURGERS

SERVES 4

Straight from the grill, the cheesy center of the Jucy Lucy will be molten hot. Be sure to let the burgers rest for at least 5 minutes before serving.

2 slices high-quality white sandwich bread, torn into rough pieces
¼ cup milk
1 teaspoon garlic powder
¾ teaspoon salt
½ teaspoon pepper
1½ pounds 85 percent lean ground beef
1 (½-inch-thick) slice deli American cheese, cut into quarters
4 rolls, for serving

1. Using a potato masher, mash the bread, milk, garlic powder, salt, and pepper in a large bowl until smooth. Add the beef and gently knead until well combined.

2. Divide the meat mixture into 4 equal portions. Following the photos, mold each portion of meat around 1 piece of the cheese. Transfer the patties to a plate, cover with plastic wrap, and refrigerate 30 minutes or up to 24 hours.

3. About 20 minutes before grilling, light a large chimney starter filled with charcoal briquettes (about 100 pieces) and allow it to burn until the charcoal is partially covered in a thin layer of fine gray ash, about 15 minutes. Spread the coals in an even layer over the grill bottom. Set the cooking grate over the coals, cover the grill, and heat until hot, about 5 minutes. Use a grill brush to scrape the cooking grate clean. Lightly dip a wad of paper towels in vegetable oil; holding the wad with tongs, wipe the cooking grate. The grill is ready when the coals are medium-hot (you can hold your hand 5 inches above the grate for 5 to 6 seconds).

4. Grill the burgers until well browned and cooked through, 6 to 8 minutes per side. Transfer to a plate, tent with foil, and let rest for 5 minutes. Serve on the rolls.

VARIATIONS
GAS-GRILLED JUCY LUCY BURGERS

Follow the recipe for Charcoal-Grilled Jucy Lucy Burgers through step 2. Turn all the burners to high, close the cover, and heat until very hot, about 15 minutes. Use a grill brush to scrape the cooking grate clean. Lightly dip a wad of paper towels in vegetable oil; holding the wad with tongs, wipe the cooking grate. Turn the burners down to medium. Continue with the recipe from step 4, grilling with the lid down.

STOVETOP JUCY LUCY BURGERS

Prepare Charcoal-Grilled Jucy Lucy Burgers through step 2. Heat 2 teaspoons vegetable oil in a large nonstick skillet over medium heat until just smoking. Add the patties and cook until well browned, about 6 minutes. Flip the burgers, cover the skillet, and continue cooking until cooked through, about 6 minutes. Transfer to a plate, tent with foil, and let rest for 5 minutes. Serve on the rolls.

NOTES FROM THE TEST KITCHEN

HOW TO FORM A JUCY LUCY
To avoid a burger blowout, it's essential to completely seal in the cheese. Don't worry about overworking the meat—adding milk and bread to the ground beef ensures tender, juicy burgers every time.

1. Using half of each portion of meat, encase the cheese to form a mini burger patty.

2. Mold the remaining half-portion of meat around the mini patty and seal the edges to form a ball.

3. Flatten the ball with the palm of your hand, forming a ¾-inch-thick patty.

CHARCOAL-GRILLED JUCY LUCY BURGERS

SMOKEHOUSE BURGERS

SMOKEHOUSES CONSTANTLY FEED their cooking fires with hardwood logs, permeating the grill with the unmistakable aroma of smoke. Burgers cooked in these covered grill-smokers have no choice but to pick up great flavor. Plus, most are highly seasoned with spices.

The test kitchen's method for cooking with smoke on a standard gas or charcoal grill is to make a fire with both a hot side and a cool side, wrap soaked hardwood chips in a foil packet, and set the packet directly over the fire until it starts to smoke. Then the meat, typically a large cut like a pork shoulder or rack of ribs, is set on the cool side of the grill and cooked (with the lid on) for several hours.

Using this setup, I wrapped soaked hickory chips in foil and tossed the packet on the fire until it started smoking. Since burgers need a good crusty sear, I knew that "low and slow" wasn't going to work here, so I placed my patties over the hot part of grill, put on the lid to trap the smoke, and cooked them for about 6 minutes per side. These burgers were overwhelmingly smoky. To temper the harshness of the smoke flavor, I tried slowing down the process by searing the burgers for only 4 minutes per side on the hot, smoky side of the grill, and then letting them finish cooking on the cooler, less smoky side. These burgers had the mellow, smoky flavor I was after, but my tasters were calling for more aggressive seasoning both inside and out.

I tried stirring all sorts of ingredients into my burger mixture: Worcestershire sauce, ketchup, mustard, dried herbs, and even soy sauce before it hit me—why not add barbecue sauce to these "barbecued" burgers? Sure enough, just 3 tablespoons of bottled barbecue sauce seasoned the meat perfectly, carrying that slightly sweet smoky flavor all the way through the burgers.

Good smokehouses typically use "secret" spice rubs to flavor large cuts of meats before the lengthy smoking process. Would a spice rub help round out the flavors in my quick-cooking burgers? A great deal of trial and error helped me eliminate spices that tasted harsh (like paprika and dry mustard) when seared onto the surface of the meat, leaving me with a simple rub of salt, pepper, garlic powder, and onion powder. I now had burgers with a subtle smoky flavor as well as a potent spice rub to seal the deal.

—DIANE UNGER, *Cook's Country*

CHARCOAL-GRILLED SMOKEHOUSE BURGERS

SERVES 4

Bull's-Eye is our preferred brand of barbecue sauce, but feel free to substitute your favorite. Making large burgers enables the meat to absorb more smoke and seasoning; these big patties fit better on bulkie or Kaiser rolls than on standard hamburger buns. In step 3, do not grill the burgers directly over the smoldering packet of wood chips, as this will impart harsh flavors to the meat.

- 2 pounds 85 percent lean ground beef, broken into small pieces
- 3 tablespoons barbecue sauce
  Salt and pepper
- 2 teaspoons onion powder
- 2 teaspoons garlic powder
- 2 cups wood chips
- 4 rolls, for serving

1. Using your hands, gently knead the beef, barbecue sauce, ½ teaspoon salt, and 1 teaspoon pepper in a large bowl until well incorporated. Shape the meat mixture into four 1-inch-thick patties. Combine the onion powder, garlic powder, ½ teaspoon salt, and 1 teaspoon pepper in a small bowl; sprinkle the spice mixture evenly over both sides of the patties.

2. Soak the wood chips in water to cover for 15 minutes; drain. Following the photo on page 161, seal the wood chips in a foil packet and cut vent holes in the top.

3. About 20 minutes before grilling, light a large chimney starter filled with charcoal briquettes (about 100 pieces) and allow it to burn until the charcoal is partially covered in a thin layer of fine gray ash, about 15 minutes. Spread the coals in an even layer over half of the grill bottom, leaving the other half with no coals. Arrange the foil packet directly on the coals. Set the cooking grate in place and heat covered, with the lid vent opened completely, until the wood chips begin to smoke heavily, about 5 minutes. Use a grill brush to scrape the cooking grate clean. Lightly dip a wad of paper towels in vegetable oil; holding the wad with tongs, wipe the cooking grate. The grill is ready when the coals are hot (you can hold your hand 5 inches above the grate for 2 seconds).

4. Place the burgers on the hot side of the grill but

not directly over the foil packet. Cook the burgers, covered, until well browned, about 4 minutes per side. Move the burgers to the cooler side of the grill and continue to cook, covered, to the desired doneness, 3 to 5 minutes longer. Transfer to a plate, tent with foil, and let rest for 5 minutes. Serve on the rolls.

VARIATION

GAS-GRILLED SMOKEHOUSE BURGERS

Follow the recipe for Charcoal-Grilled Smokehouse Burgers through step 2. Position the foil packet directly on the primary burner of a gas grill. Turn all the burners to high, close the cover, and heat until very hot and the wood chips begin to smoke heavily, about 15 minutes. Leave the primary burner on high and turn the remaining burner(s) off. Use a grill brush to scrape the cooking grate clean. Lightly dip a wad of paper towels in vegetable oil; holding the wad with tongs, wipe the cooking grate. Continue with the recipe from step 4, grilling with the lid down.

NOTES FROM THE TEST KITCHEN

SMOKEHOUSE, NOT SMOKE OUT
Grilling the burgers directly over the smoking packet of wood chips can result in harsh smoke flavor. On most grills you can simply position the burgers and packet away from each other over the flame. But on small gas grills where there isn't enough room for four burgers above the primary burner but slightly removed from the foil packet, we suggest turning all burners to high and searing the burgers over high heat away from the chips for the first stage of cooking. Once the burgers are well browned, simply turn off the burner below the burgers while they finish cooking via indirect heat.

WRAPPING WOOD CHIPS IN FOIL
To get wood chips to slowly produce aromatic smoke, soak them in water for 15 minutes and then spread the soaked, drained chips in the center of a 15 by 12-inch piece of heavy-duty aluminum foil. Fold the foil and seal the edges of the packet, then cut several slits to allow smoke to escape.

CRUNCHY BAKED PORK CHOPS

WHEN DONE RIGHT, baked breaded pork chops are the ultimate comfort food: tender cutlets surrounded by a crunchy coating that crackles apart with each bite. But all too often, baked chops fall short of that ideal. Opt for the convenience of a shaky packaged product from the supermarket for your breading and you wind up with a bland-tasting chop with a thin, sandy crust. Make your own breading with fresh crumbs and the flaws are different—a soggy, patchy crust that won't stick to the meat. My goal was clear: to cook a juicy, flavorful chop with a crisp, substantial crust that would stay on the meat from fork to mouth.

My first task was choosing the best cut of meat. Though bone-in chops retain moisture better, I decided on a boneless cut for this dish, so I wouldn't have to bread the bone and there would be no distraction from the crunchy crust. This gave me two options: sirloin or center-cut. I settled on center-cut boneless loin chops, which were not only easier to find in the supermarket but also cooked more evenly.

Next I needed to determine the chop size. The ½-inch-thick chops generally used for pan-frying were too easily overwhelmed by the kind of crust I wanted, and the 1½-inch-thick chops usually reserved for barbecuing or stuffing proved to be too thick, giving me too much meat and not enough crust. Pork chops that fell in between— ¾ to 1 inch thick—were my tasters' top choice.

The test kitchen's standard breading method (dusting with flour, dipping in beaten egg, and rolling in toasted breadcrumbs) was sufficient as I figured out the best cooking technique. Simply baking the breaded chops on a baking sheet, the most obvious method and one used in many recipes, made the bottoms soggy. I tried breading just the top and sides, and while this quick fix worked, tasters felt cheated. What if I let air circulation keep the bottom crumbs crisp? Placing the chops on a wire rack set inside the baking sheet definitely helped. Upping the oven temperature from 350 to 425 degrees helped even more. The coating crisped up more readily, and the excess moisture evaporated by the time the pork reached the requisite 150-degree serving temperature.

I had figured out the right chops to use and the proper way to cook them. Now I could concentrate on the breading. Tasters deemed panko too fine-textured and bland. Crushed Melba toast was crunchier but didn't stick together. Ultimately, tasters preferred the fresh flavor and slight sweetness of crumbs made from white sandwich bread.

I tossed the fresh crumbs with a little salt, pepper, and oil; then I spread them on a baking sheet and toasted them until they were golden brown. The resulting crust was decently crisp but still not as good as I knew it could be. What if I took a cue from the supermarket coating and toasted the crumbs to a deeper brown? Though boxed crumbs produce a crust that is thin and sandy, the processed coating does have one thing going for it—a true crispness that I'd yet to achieve. For my next test, I left the crumbs in the oven until they looked danger-ously overtoasted and was pleasantly surprised that this worked—the breading didn't burn when baked again on the chops, and my crumb coating was now seriously crisp. To add even more flavor, I stirred in some minced garlic and shallot with the crumbs before they went into the oven and tossed in some grated Parmesan cheese and minced herbs after they cooled. These chops tasted great. Everything would be perfect if I could just ensure one thing: that the crumbs stuck onto the pork evenly, rather than peeling off in patches.

With crumbs as thick and coarse as these, I knew I'd need something with more holding power than a typical egg wash to glue them to the pork. I recalled a cookbook recipe that used mustard instead of eggs to stick crumbs on chops. A straight swap made the taste too intense, but keeping the eggs and adding a few tablespoons of Dijon mustard thickened the mixture nicely and brought just enough new flavor to the mix. But while the crumbs stuck onto the baked chops better than they had with a simple egg wash, a few areas still flaked off.

A fellow test cook wondered aloud what would hap-pen if I got rid of the egg wash altogether and dipped the floured chops into a thick batter before breading them. I laughed. After all, batter is for fried food. Who ever heard of using it for baking? I did it anyway, using a basic fritto misto batter of flour, cornstarch, water, oil, and eggs as my base. Fully expecting this experiment to tank, I was surprised when the pork chops came out with a crust that was crunchier than before and stayed on like a protective sheath. This batter, though, requires

resting and seemed too fussy for a weeknight dish. But what if I made a quick egg wash that was more like a batter?

I whisked enough flour into the egg and mustard mixture to give it the thick consistency of mayonnaise. This adhering agent was now more of a spackle than a watery glue. After flouring the chops, I coated them evenly in the egg wash–batter hybrid, covered them in breadcrumbs, and baked them again. Much better, but there was a soft, puffy layer directly beneath the crumbs. Replacing the whole eggs with egg whites, which have less fat but enough protein to lend sticking power, pro-vided just the crisp, dry crust I was looking for. But even more impressive, the crumbs clung firmly onto the meat even during some heavy knife-and-fork action. This pork finally had some real chops.

—SANDRA WU, *Cook's Illustrated*

CRUNCHY BAKED PORK CHOPS

SERVES 4

This recipe was developed using natural pork, but enhanced pork (injected with a salt solution) will work as well. If using enhanced pork, eliminate the brining in step 1. The breadcrumb mixture can be prepared through step 2 up to 3 days in advance. The breaded chops can be frozen for up to 1 week. They don't need to be thawed before baking; simply increase the cooking time in step 5 to 35 to 40 minutes.

Salt
4 (6 to 8-ounce) boneless, center-cut pork chops, ¾ to 1 inch thick, trimmed of excess fat (see note)
4 slices high-quality white sandwich bread, torn into 1-inch pieces
1 shallot, minced (about 3 tablespoons)
3 garlic cloves, minced
2 tablespoons vegetable oil
Pepper
2 tablespoons grated Parmesan cheese
½ teaspoon minced fresh thyme
2 tablespoons minced fresh parsley
¼ cup plus 6 tablespoons unbleached all-purpose flour
3 large egg whites
3 tablespoons Dijon mustard
Lemon wedges, for serving

1. Adjust an oven rack to the middle position and heat the oven to 350 degrees. Dissolve ¼ cup salt in 1 quart water in a medium container or gallon-sized zipper-lock bag. Submerge the chops, cover with plastic wrap, and refrigerate for 30 minutes. Rinse the chops under cold water and dry thoroughly with paper towels.

2. Meanwhile, pulse the bread in a food processor until coarsely ground, about eight 1-second pulses (you should have about 3½ cups crumbs). Transfer the crumbs to a rimmed baking sheet and add the shallot, garlic, oil, ¼ teaspoon salt, and ¼ teaspoon pepper. Toss until the crumbs are evenly coated with oil. Bake until deep golden brown and dry, about 15 minutes, stirring twice during baking time. (Do not turn off the oven.) Cool to room temperature. Toss the crumbs with the Parmesan, thyme, and parsley.

3. Place ¼ cup of the flour in a pie plate. In a second pie plate, whisk the egg whites and mustard until combined; add the remaining 6 tablespoons flour and whisk until almost smooth, with pea-sized lumps remaining.

4. Increase the oven temperature to 425 degrees. Spray a wire rack with vegetable oil spray and place in a rimmed baking sheet. Season the chops with pepper. Dredge 1 pork chop in the flour; shake off the excess. Using tongs, coat with the egg mixture; let the excess drip off. Coat all sides of the chop with the breadcrumb mixture, pressing gently so that a thick layer of crumbs adheres to the chop. Transfer the breaded chop to the prepared wire rack. Repeat with the remaining 3 chops.

5. Bake until an instant-read thermometer inserted into the center of the chops registers 140 degrees, 17 to 25 minutes. Let rest on the rack until the chops register 150 degrees on an instant-read thermometer, about 5 minutes. Serve with the lemon wedges.

VARIATION

CRUNCHY BAKED PORK CHOPS WITH PROSCIUTTO AND ASIAGO CHEESE

Follow the recipe for Crunchy Baked Pork Chops through step 3, omitting the salt added to the breadcrumb mixture in step 2. Before breading, place a ⅛-inch-thick slice Asiago cheese on top of each chop. Wrap each chop with a thin slice prosciutto, pressing on the prosciutto so that the cheese and meat adhere to one another. Proceed with the recipe from step 4, being careful when handling the chops so that the cheese and meat do not come apart during breading.

NOTES FROM THE TEST KITCHEN

THE SECRETS TO A CRISP COATING

1. DIP: A thick batter of flour, mustard, and egg whites grips the breadcrumbs like glue.

2. COAT: Coating the chops with well-toasted fresh breadcrumbs results in a crust with flavor and crunch.

3. ELEVATE: Baking the chops on a rack set in a baking sheet allows greater air circulation and prevents the bottoms from turning soggy.

THE 30-MINUTE BRINE

Center-cut chops are quite lean, and left untreated they will be very dry and chewy, even when cooked to medium (an internal temperature of 150 degrees). The salt in the brine changes the structure of the muscle proteins and allows them to hold on to more moisture when exposed to heat. Tasters had no trouble picking out the brined chops versus chops left untreated.

Making the brine superconcentrated (with ¼ cup of table salt dissolved in 1 quart of water) gets the job done in just 30 minutes—the time it will take you to prepare the fresh breadcrumb coating. And this potent brine fits, along with four chops, in a medium container or gallon-sized zipper-lock bag. No brining bucket needed.

One exception: If you've purchased enhanced chops injected with a salt solution, don't brine them. The injected solution will make the chops moist, even spongy, and brining will make the meat way too salty. We prefer the flavor of natural chops and find that 30 minutes in a strong brine makes them plenty juicy.

SKILLET-BARBECUED PORK CHOPS

SKILLET-BARBECUED PORK CHOPS

TO ENJOY THE CHARRED, SALTY-SWEET FLAVOR of grilled pork chops coated with spicy barbecue sauce in the off-season, I have two options: go to a restaurant with an indoor grill or attempt to make them in my own kitchen. Getting smoky flavor into the chops is almost assured when cooking over a live fire outdoors. Back inside, it can be more elusive.

The first order of business was to find a way of giving the pork a nice, evenly charred surface without overcooking the interior. I tried searing the chops in a blazing hot skillet and then turning the heat way down once they developed a good crust, a method I've used to good effect with steak and lamb chops. Aside from the fact that this technique filled the test kitchen with billowing smoke and splattered oil, the pork ended up stringy by the time a well-charred crust had developed. The problem? Pork chops are leaner than steaks and lamb chops and therefore more prone to drying out. Brining improved matters a bit, but it was clear that my technique was going to need an overhaul. Since I've successfully cooked charred, juicy pork chops on an outdoor grill, I wondered what was so different about cooking in a skillet.

For one thing, a piece of meat elevated above the heat source on a grill doesn't remain in contact with the juices released during cooking. In a pan, pork chops end up simmering in their own juices, which lowers the temperature of the cooking surface, leading to meat that overcooks before it can brown properly. If I couldn't get the pork itself to char, why not add another element that would char instead? I realized that there was already an outdoor technique that would accomplish this exact goal—the dry spice rub.

Though standard fare for a grill, a spice rub is rarely applied to meat cooked in a skillet—in a hot skillet, the rub (which darkens more readily than the pork proteins) doesn't just char, it blackens. But by starting with medium heat rather than high, I found I could let the spice rub char while the pork cooked at a gentler pace, which resulted in chops that were perfectly cooked both inside and out. Lowering the heat serendipitously solved my smoky kitchen problem, as well.

I turned my attention to the barbecue sauce. Starting with the requisite ketchup and molasses, I ran through a battery of taste tests. Hits of Worcestershire sauce and Dijon mustard gave the sauce complexity and heat, and onions and cider vinegar added a pungent kick. A spoonful of brown sugar helped mellow out and blend the sharper flavors. I figured a couple of teaspoons of my dry spice rub added to my sauce could only improve its flavor. Tasters confirmed my hunch.

Although my sauce was now balanced, I felt it needed more outdoor flavor. Without the benefit of a live fire with smoldering hickory chips, I had only one place to turn: liquid smoke. In the test kitchen, we generally shun artificial or synthetic ingredients, so I was pleased to learn that liquid smoke is a completely natural product. All suspicions were laid to rest when a batch of sauce to which I had surreptitiously added a teaspoon of liquid smoke swept the next blind tasting. The key to keeping liquid smoke palatable is moderation.

Now I had my charred pork and my smoky sauce, but I also had a problem. I had been ignoring something every good outdoor cook knows: The sauce is not merely an accompaniment to the meat—it's an essential part of the cooking process. I had been treating the chops and the sauce as two discrete elements rather than parts of the same entity, applying the sauce only after the meat had been fully cooked. On an outdoor grill, the sauce caramelizes and intensifies, lacquering the chops in a sticky glaze. Could I re-create this process on my stovetop without ruining my pans and splattering hot barbecue sauce all over the kitchen?

Brushing the sauce directly onto the chops while they were still in the pan produced a sticky, burnt mess and a stovetop splattered with sauce. What if instead of bringing the sauce to the pork, I brought the pork to the sauce? I cooked up a new batch of chops, this time removing them from the pan a few minutes early. After transferring the pork chops to a baking sheet, I brushed them with a thin coat of barbecue sauce and wiped out the skillet so I could finish cooking with a clean, hot surface. When the pork chops sizzled vigorously as they went back into the hot pan for their second sear, my hopes were high.

I flipped the chops and saw that the sauce had reduced to a sticky, smoky, caramelized glaze that firmly adhered to the meat. Served with the remaining reduced sauce, these skillet-barbecued pork chops with a rib-sticking sauce finally tasted like the real deal.

—J. KENJI ALT, *Cook's Illustrated*

SKILLET-BARBECUED PORK CHOPS

SERVES 4

We prefer natural to enhanced pork (pork that has been injected with a salt solution to increase moistness and flavor) for this recipe, though enhanced pork can be used. If using enhanced pork, skip the brining in step 1 and add ½ teaspoon salt to the spice rub. Grate the onion on the large holes of a box grater. In step 5, check your chops after 3 minutes. If you don't hear a definite sizzle and the chops have not started to brown on the underside, increase the heat to medium-high and continue cooking as directed (follow the indicated temperatures for the remainder of the recipe).

PORK CHOPS

  ½ cup table salt

  4 (8 to 10-ounce) bone-in pork rib chops, ¾ to 1 inch thick, trimmed of excess fat, sides slit following the photo on page 167 (see note)

  4 teaspoons vegetable oil

SPICE RUB

  1 tablespoon paprika

  1 tablespoon brown sugar

  2 teaspoons ground coriander

  1 teaspoon ground cumin

  1 teaspoon pepper

SAUCE

  ½ cup ketchup

  3 tablespoons light or mild molasses

  2 tablespoons grated onion (see note)

  2 tablespoons Worcestershire sauce

  2 tablespoons Dijon mustard

  1 tablespoon cider vinegar

  1 tablespoon brown sugar

  1 teaspoon liquid smoke

1. FOR THE PORK CHOPS: Dissolve the salt in 2 quarts water in a large bowl or container. Submerge the chops in the brine, cover with plastic wrap, and refrigerate 30 minutes.

2. FOR THE SPICE RUB: Combine all of the ingredients in a small bowl. Measure 2 teaspoons of the mixture into a medium bowl and set aside for the sauce. Transfer the remaining spice rub to a pie plate or large plate.

3. FOR THE SAUCE: Whisk all of the ingredients into the bowl with the reserved spice mixture; set aside.

4. TO COOK THE CHOPS: Remove the chops from the brine and pat dry with paper towels. Coat both sides of the chops with the spice rub, pressing gently so the rub adheres. Pat the chops to remove any excess rub; discard the excess rub.

5. Heat 1 tablespoon of the oil in a 12-inch heavy-bottomed nonstick skillet over medium heat until just smoking. Following the photo on page 167, place the chops in the skillet in a pinwheel formation; cook until charred in spots, 5 to 8 minutes. Flip the chops and continue to cook until the second side is browned and charred and an instant-read thermometer inserted into the center of the chops registers 130 degrees, 4 to 8 minutes. Remove the skillet from the heat and transfer the chops to a clean plate or baking sheet. Lightly brush the top side of each chop with 2 teaspoons of the sauce.

6. Wipe out the pan with paper towels and return to medium heat. Add the remaining 1 teaspoon oil and heat until just smoking. Add the chops to the pan, sauce-side down, and cook without moving until the sauce has caramelized and charred in spots, about 1 minute. While cooking, lightly brush the top side of each chop with 2 teaspoons sauce. Turn the chops and cook until the second side is charred and caramelized and an instant-read thermometer inserted into the center of the chops registers 140 degrees, 1 to 1½ minutes.

7. Transfer the chops back to the plate or baking sheet, tent with foil, and let rest until the center of the chops registers 150 degrees on an instant-read thermometer, about 5 minutes. Meanwhile, add the remaining sauce to the pan and cook, scraping the pan bottom, until thickened to ketchuplike consistency and reduced to ⅔ cup, about 3 minutes. Brush each chop with 1 tablespoon of the reduced sauce and serve, passing the remaining sauce at the table.

WHAT'S IN THE PACKAGE?

Given the number of chops we went through to develop this recipe, we thought purchasing "family size" packs of pork chops would be the logical choice, but we ran into some unpleasant surprises at the bottom of the package. The chops they don't want you to see are gristly and unevenly butchered.

LOOKS LIKE A GOOD VALUE

The chops on top look good, but beware of what lies beneath.

BEST BET

Choose a smaller package in which the meat is laid in a single layer so you can see what you are paying for.

SEARING CHOPS

1. To get pork chops to lie flat and cook evenly, cut two slits about 2 inches apart through the fat and connective tissue.

2. Arrange the chops in a pinwheel pattern with the tips of the ribs pointing toward the pan edge. When searing the chops, don't move them until charred black spots develop.

GRILLED PORK CUTLETS

CHICKEN CUTLETS ARE A WEEKNIGHT STANDBY, but pork cutlets—a relatively new addition to the meat case—are not as well known. Although they are the same size as chicken cutlets, pork cutlets (cut from the blade end of the ribs) are not as tender. My first attempts at cooking pork cutlets on the grill taught me that they become leathery very quickly, and they cooked so fast that they didn't have time to char or develop much grill flavor. This wasn't going to be an easy fix.

The problems start at the market. Prepackaged cutlets often have shredded edges and irregular thicknesses that lead to uneven cooking. Returning to the meat case, I noticed thin-cut pork chops (cut from the loin)—they were almost as thin as the cutlets, and their shape and thickness were much more consistent. I brought the thin-cut boneless chops home and gave them a few quick whacks with my meat pounder to make homemade cutlets. After a few minutes over high heat, they came off the grill evenly cooked, tender, and moist but still a little pale and bland.

Most recipes call for flipping the cutlets halfway through the cooking time, but they cook so quickly that this doesn't give the meat a chance to brown. Since increasing the cooking time would lead to dried-out cutlets, I left them on one side for most of the cooking time (about 2 minutes) to develop a nice char, then finished them for 30 seconds on the other side.

With the cooking method settled, I could focus on infusing the pork with flavor. Pungent spice rubs overwhelmed the thin cutlets, but marinating worked well. While larger cuts are only superficially seasoned by a marinade, these thin cutlets were flavored to the core. Bottled Italian dressing received poor marks for its dull dried-herb flavor, so I used Italian ingredients to make my own vinaigrette. Balsamic vinegar, olive oil, garlic, and thyme formed the base, and a last-minute addition of sugar softened the acidity of the vinegar and helped produce even more caramelization on the cutlets. This simple marinade lent itself to easy variations, making pork cutlets an interesting (and quick-to-prepare) option for the grill.

—CALI RICH, *Cook's Country*

CHARCOAL-GRILLED PORK CUTLETS

SERVES 4 TO 6

Marinating for more than 2 hours will make the chops rubbery.

- ⅓ cup balsamic vinegar
- ⅓ cup olive oil
- 2 garlic cloves, minced
- 1 teaspoon minced fresh thyme
- ¾ teaspoon sugar
- ¾ teaspoon salt
- ¼ teaspoon pepper
- 12 thin-cut boneless pork chops (about 2 pounds), trimmed and pounded into ¼-inch-thick cutlets (see note)

1. Combine the vinegar, oil, garlic, thyme, sugar, salt, and pepper in a large zipper-lock plastic bag. Transfer the pork cutlets to the bag and refrigerate 30 minutes or up to 2 hours.

2. About 20 minutes before grilling, light a large chimney starter filled with charcoal briquettes (about 100 pieces) and allow it to burn until the charcoal is partially covered in a thin layer of fine gray ash, about 15 minutes. Spread the coals in an even layer over half of the grill bottom, leaving the other half with no coals. Set the cooking grate over the coals, cover the grill, and heat until hot, about 5 minutes. Use a grill brush to scrape the cooking grate clean. Lightly dip a wad of paper towels in vegetable oil; holding the wad with tongs, wipe the cooking grate. The grill is ready when the coals are hot (you can hold your hand 5 inches above the grate for 2 seconds).

3. Remove the cutlets from the bag and discard the marinade. Place the cutlets on the grate directly over the coals and grill until the bottoms begin to turn opaque around the edges, about 2 minutes. Flip the cutlets and grill until just cooked through, about 30 seconds. Transfer to a platter, tent with foil, and let rest for 5 minutes. Serve.

VARIATIONS
GAS-GRILLED PORK CUTLETS

Follow the recipe for Charcoal-Grilled Pork Cutlets through step 1. Turn all the burners to high, close the cover, and heat until very hot, about 15 minutes. Use a grill brush to scrape the cooking grate clean. Lightly dip a wad of paper towels in vegetable oil; holding the wad with tongs, wipe the cooking grate. Continue with the recipe from step 3, cooking the cutlets with the lid down.

GRILLED PORK CUTLETS WITH ROSEMARY AND RED WINE VINEGAR

Follow the recipe for Grilled Pork Cutlets, substituting ⅓ cup red wine vinegar for the balsamic vinegar, 1 teaspoon minced fresh rosemary for the thyme, and ¾ teaspoon honey for the sugar. Proceed with the recipe as directed.

GRILLED PORK CUTLETS WITH CILANTRO AND LIME

Follow the recipe for Grilled Pork Cutlets, adding ½ teaspoon ground cumin to the marinade and substituting ⅓ cup lime juice (from 3 limes) for the balsamic vinegar, 3 tablespoons minced fresh cilantro for the thyme, and ¾ teaspoon brown sugar for the granulated sugar. Proceed with the recipe as directed.

NOTES FROM THE TEST KITCHEN

TURNING CHOPS INTO CUTLETS
Thin-cut boneless pork chops can be quickly turned into cutlets ready for the grill. Here's how:

Place two chops on the work surface and cover them with plastic wrap. Using a meat pounder, pound the chops into ¼-inch-thick cutlets. Repeat with the remaining chops.

THIN-CUT CHOPS VS. CUTLETS
Prepackaged pork cutlets are often cut from the blade end of the ribs and can be ragged and uneven, which results in uneven cooking. We prefer to make our own cutlets from thin-cut pork chops (see above), which are cut from the loin and generally have a much more uniform shape.

THIN-CUT PORK CHOP POUNDED OUT
Our homemade cutlets have a uniform shape and cook evenly.

RAGGED PREPACKAGED PORK CUTLET
Prepackaged cutlets look sloppy and cook unevenly.

HERBED ROAST PORK TENDERLOIN

RECIPES ABOUND for herb-flavored pork tenderloin, employing techniques such as crusting, marinating, and stuffing the pork with sundry combinations of herbs. Like other test cooks, I also had poor luck with herb crusts—the herbs came close to combusting on the outside of the meat. Marinating in an herb-infused oil took a long time, and the herb payout was minimal. Stuffing was the most promising method, and since a single tenderloin only feeds about three people, I decided to proceed using two tenderloins so that the dish would be more substantial.

I butterflied the roasts and rubbed the inside of each with a simple herb paste of parsley and olive oil. I rolled them back up, tied them for even cooking, and roasted them side-by-side in a 450-degree oven. The herbs stayed bright green but had a dull flavor, and the roasts weren't browning much on the outside. I had a lot of work to do, and I decided to start with the stuffing.

After trying several herbs alone and in combination, I discovered that soft herbs like parsley, basil, and tarragon (which have a high moisture content) all tasted washed out because they were steaming inside the meat. Turning to heartier (and drier) fresh herbs, my tasters rejected rosemary as being too potent, but they liked a combination of fragrant thyme and sage. Mustard, garlic, and lemon juice and zest added more bold flavors. The final step was replacing the olive oil with rich butter; tasters liked the herb butter so much that I made extra to brush on the finished roasts.

In an attempt to promote browning, I coated the exterior of the roasts with a rub of sugar, salt, and pepper (a little olive oil helped the rub adhere), but these 1½-pound roasts weren't in the oven long enough for the sugar to caramelize by the time the interior had cooked through. Browning the roasts in a skillet and then transferring them to the oven was the only reliable way to create a good crust without overcooking the meat—but I wanted a good crust with less work.

It was then that I remembered seeing two pork tenderloins tied together into one big roast at the butcher shop. Since this "double wide" tenderloin would take longer to cook, I hoped it would give the sugar-rubbed exterior a chance to brown in the oven. After butterflying and rubbing the roasts, I overlapped them by a couple of inches and folded them up lengthwise into a cylinder. I tied the double roast and cooked it in a 450-degree oven, flipping it once to ensure even cooking. When the supersized tenderloin came out of the oven, my efforts were rewarded with a crisp, browned roast that, when sliced, revealed a juicy spiral of herb-infused meat.

—KELLEY BAKER, *Cook's Country*

HERBED ROAST PORK TENDERLOIN

SERVES 6

Pork tenderloins can vary greatly in weight; we prefer to use larger tenderloins here. When purchasing a two-pack of tenderloins, look for a gross weight of about 3 pounds, or buy individual tenderloins weighing about 1½ pounds each.

- 3 tablespoons unsalted butter, at room temperature
- 2 tablespoons whole-grain mustard
- 1 teaspoon grated lemon zest
- 1 teaspoon fresh lemon juice
- 1 garlic clove, minced
- 1 tablespoon minced fresh sage
- 1 tablespoon minced fresh thyme
  Salt and pepper
- 1 teaspoon sugar
- 2 pork tenderloins (about 3 pounds total) (see note)
- 1 tablespoon olive oil

1. Adjust an oven rack to the middle position and heat the oven to 450 degrees. Beat the butter, mustard, lemon zest and juice, garlic, herbs, ¼ teaspoon salt, and ¼ teaspoon pepper in a bowl until combined. Reserve 3 tablespoons of the butter mixture. Combine the sugar, ¼ teaspoon salt, and ¼ teaspoon pepper in a small bowl.

2. Pat the tenderloins dry with paper towels and, following photos on page 170, butterfly the tenderloins, spread the interiors evenly with the herb-butter mixture, interlock the tenderloins, and tie securely with kitchen twine at 1½-inch intervals. Rub the pork with the oil and sprinkle the sugar mixture evenly over the exterior.

3. Roast the meat on a rimmed baking sheet until the

exterior is golden brown and an instant-read thermometer inserted into the center of the tenderloin registers 140 degrees, about 35 minutes, flipping the pork halfway through cooking. Transfer to a cutting board and brush the top of the pork with the reserved herb-butter mixture. Tent with foil and let rest until the center of the tenderloin registers 150 degrees on an instant-read thermometer, about 15 minutes. Remove the twine. Slice and serve.

NOTES FROM THE TEST KITCHEN

PREPARING THE TENDERLOINS
Butterflying the tenderloins exposes more surface area of the meat for better herb flavor penetration.

1. Butterfly the tenderloins by laying them flat on a cutting board and slicing down the middle of each. Leave about ¼ inch of meat intact, then open like a book.

2. Spread the interior of each tenderloin with the butter mixture.

3. Arrange the tenderloins so that the thick and thin ends are opposite one another, then overlap the tenderloins halfway. Fold to interlock the cut sides of the tenderloins.

4. Tie the folded tenderloins securely with kitchen twine at 1½-inch intervals.

PEPPER-CRUSTED PORK LOIN

PEPPER-CRUSTED BEEF WORKS SO WELL because beef has enough richness to offset some of the pepper's sharp heat, but lean pork doesn't have enough flavor to stand up to the same peppery bite. I wanted to find a way to deeply infuse a pork loin with spicy pepper flavor while eliminating the harsh burn.

To get a substantial crust on the entire surface of the pork loin, I started by rubbing 5 tablespoons of cracked peppercorns over the roast. After browning the pork on the stovetop and finishing it in the oven (the test kitchen's technique for most roasts), the jolt of pepper was way too harsh. Cutting back on the amount of peppercorns resulted in a speckled, uneven crust. I hoped the test kitchen trick of gently heating the peppercorns in oil to bloom their flavor and mellow their heat would work, but the resulting roast still had too much pepper burn.

Since the bite of the cracked pepper was proving to be too strong no matter how I handled it, I wondered if I could temper the pepper's heat, while keeping most of its flavor, by using a finer grind. After testing several grinds from barely cracked to finely ground, my tasters and I settled on a middle ground that allowed for a thinner, milder crust with plenty of pepper flavor. Two tablespoons of coarsely ground pepper gave me the right amount of spice, but it didn't yield enough rub to fully coat the roast.

To stretch the rub, I tried supplementing the pepper with other ingredients; strong spices like mustard, coriander, and cumin overwhelmed the mellow pork, but my tasters appreciated the piney tang of fresh rosemary as a complement to the pepper. Adding brown sugar and salt worked to further extend the rub; the sugar tamed the heat even more, and the salt helped carry all the flavors into the meat, especially when I let the rubbed roast sit for an hour.

There was still one problem: The pepper crust was burning during the initial sear on the stovetop. Simply switching the searing from the stovetop to a hot oven solved the problem. Finishing the roast at a more moderate temperature ensured juicy pork with bold flavor both inside and out. I'd finally made a Pepper-Crusted Pork Loin to be proud of.

—DIANE UNGER, *Cook's Country*

PEPPER-CRUSTED PORK LOIN WITH CHERRY BRANDY SAUCE

SERVES 6

If you prefer, serve the pork loin with fruit chutney or applesauce instead of the Cherry Brandy Sauce. And, if you can't find frozen cherries, substitute one 14.5-ounce can of pitted tart red cherries in water, drained.

PORK

- 3 tablespoons light brown sugar
- 2 tablespoons coarsely ground black pepper
- 2 tablespoons minced fresh rosemary
- 1½ teaspoons salt
- 1 (3-pound) boneless center-cut pork loin

CHERRY BRANDY SAUCE

- 4 tablespoons (½ stick) unsalted butter
- 2 onions, chopped (about 2 cups)
- 3 cups low-sodium chicken broth
- ½ cup brandy
- 1 (8-ounce) bag frozen pitted sweet cherries, thawed (see note)
- 1 cup dried cherries
- 2 tablespoons balsamic vinegar
  Salt

1. FOR THE PORK LOIN: Combine the sugar, pepper, rosemary, and salt and rub all over the pork. Let the roast sit at room temperature for 1 hour or refrigerate for up to 24 hours.

2. FOR THE SAUCE: Meanwhile, melt 2 tablespoons of the butter in a large saucepan over medium heat. Cook the onions until golden, about 8 minutes. Stir in the broth, brandy, and cherries and simmer until thick and syrupy, about 15 minutes. Off the heat, stir in the vinegar and the remaining 2 tablespoons butter. Cover and set aside to keep warm. Season with salt to taste. (The sauce can be refrigerated for up to 2 days.)

3. Adjust an oven rack to the upper-middle position and heat the oven to 450 degrees. Arrange the pork on a V-rack set in a roasting pan. Roast for 15 minutes, then lower the oven temperature to 375 degrees and cook until an instant-read thermometer inserted into the thickest part of the meat registers 140 degrees, about 50 minutes longer. Transfer the pork to a cutting board and tent with foil. Let rest until the center of the roast

registers 150 degrees on an instant-read thermometer, about 15 minutes. Slice and serve, passing the sauce at the table.

NOTES FROM THE TEST KITCHEN

THE RIGHT GRIND

A crunchy, fiery crust of cracked peppercorns may work well with an assertively flavored cut of beef, but when it comes to pork, moderation is essential. To give a nice spicy kick without overwhelming the mild taste of the pork, we found that we had to grind the pepper just right—and not use too much of it.

CRACKED PEPPER
Packs a scorching heat

COARSELY GROUND PEPPER
Lends welcome heat, spice, and texture

THE BEST PEPPER MILLS

There is nothing more frustrating than grinding a pepper mill 30 times to yield a measly teaspoon of pepper. We already had a favorite pepper mill from our testing back in 2001, but had come across some models that justified our retesting them. We tested eight pepper mills looking for efficiency, and the quality and uniformity of the grind. We were pleased to find that our winning model from 2001, the **Unicorn Magnum Plus**, $45, was still our favorite. (See page 333 for more information about our testing results.)

THE BEST CUTTING BOARD

No kitchen is complete without a good solid cutting board. But, with so many cutting boards on the market—everything from bamboo to glass—it's hard to know what to buy. We tested 13 cutting boards to determine which ones held up the best. After cutting, washing, and dropping each board, the winner was the **Totally Bamboo Congo**, $39.99. (See page 335 for more information about our testing results.)

GRILLED STUFFED PORK LOIN

I'M FOND OF THE MEATY TEXTURE and moderate price of pork loin, but I'm annoyed by its tendency toward dryness. Most grilled pork loin recipes try to compensate with some combination of brining (soaking the meat in a salt-and-sugar solution prior to cooking), rubs, sauces, or condiments, but I was intrigued by something a little different: a stuffing. In theory, a rich filling could keep the loin moist and add aesthetic appeal to the otherwise plain-Jane cut of meat.

In the test kitchen, we typically favor the blade-end pork roast for grilling because of its abundant fat. However, this asset became a liability when I tried to stuff a blade roast. As soon as I split it open, the meat fell apart into a lumpy mess of muscle, sinew, and fat. A center-cut loin roast proved the better choice because this solid muscle cut cleanly, but its leanness worried me.

I explored a variety of approaches to the stuffing, including recipes based on cheeses, cured meats, breadcrumbs, and herbs. Most of the fillings oozed free of the roast, turned mushy, or were bland, but a chutney-like blend of dried fruits, spices, sugar, and vinegar caught my attention. Its flavor was unbalanced and its texture was dusty from dried spices, but the fruits' dense, chewy consistency and deep flavor were well suited to the pork, and the stuffing stayed put.

After testing various combinations of dried fruits, my tasters proclaimed apples and cranberries the perfect pairing. I poached the fruit in a blend of apple cider and apple cider vinegar until tender, then added cayenne, allspice, and grated fresh ginger. Brown sugar trumped white sugar and honey, and sliced shallot and mustard seeds added just the right zip to both the fruit and the pork. I strained off the excess poaching liquid to prevent the filling from being too wet, then ground the mixture to a coarse paste in the food processor.

How, exactly, do you stuff a pork loin? One popular method involves slicing the meat into a broad sheet onto which the filling is spread before the pork is rolled up tightly, like a jellyroll. Butchers call this a roll cut, and it sounds easy enough, but I found the knife work tricky. My early attempts looked amateurish, so I rethought the approach. I regarded the loin as more square than cylindrical and saw that just three or four straight, short cuts, like a triple butterfly, could produce the same results. Gentle persuasion with a meat pounder evened out any nicks and unevenness to give me a long, flat sheet that was easy to fill and roll up. Snugly tying up the rolled roast ensured a compact shape that cooked evenly and sliced easily.

To this point, I'd yet to try brining the roast. I hoped the filling would make brining redundant, and tests proved this to be the case. In fact, a stuffed and brined roast was, if possible, too moist. Turns out I'd made an unexpected scientific discovery, one our science editor confirmed. His analysis: Because the meat was sliced so thin (just ½ inch thick), the acids in the filling were denaturing the proteins in the meat and helping them hold onto moisture. The effects of acids on meat are limited to the area near the surface, so they don't usually do much for a thick pork loin. However, in this recipe, the entire roast was "surface," so I was essentially marinating the meat from the inside out.

To coax even more flavor out of the roast, most recipes sear the meat before or after cooking it, but my attempts to sear this leaner cut of pork left me with a tough exterior. I tried a variety of spice rubs but found them overpowering. A liberal coating of salt and pepper was more than sufficient.

Finally, I considered glazing as a finishing touch. Didn't I have leftover liquid from preparing the filling? I reduced the sticky-sweet, spiced blend of sugar, cider, and vinegar down to a thick, spreadable consistency and lacquered the loin during its last few minutes on the grill. The mahogany glaze not only improved the look of the roast, it sharpened the flavor of the pork and filling alike.

—MATTHEW CARD, *Cook's Illustrated*

CHARCOAL-GRILLED PORK LOIN WITH APPLE-CRANBERRY FILLING
SERVES 6

This recipe is best prepared with a loin that is 7 to 8 inches long and 4 to 5 inches wide. To make cutting the pork easier, freeze it for 30 minutes. If mustard seeds are unavailable, stir an equal amount of whole-grain mustard into the filling after the apples have been processed. The pork loin can be stuffed and tied a day ahead of time, but don't season the exterior until you are ready to grill.

GRILLED STUFFED PORK LOIN

FILLING

- 1 cup apple cider
- ½ cup cider vinegar
- ¾ cup (5¼ ounces) packed light brown sugar
- 1 large shallot, halved lengthwise and sliced thin crosswise (about ¼ cup)
- 1½ cups packed dried apples
- ½ cup packed dried cranberries
- 1 tablespoon grated fresh ginger
- 1 tablespoon yellow mustard seeds (see note)
- ½ teaspoon ground allspice
- ⅛–¼ teaspoon cayenne pepper

PORK

- 2 (3-inch) wood chunks
- 1 (2½-pound) boneless center-cut pork loin roast (see note)
  Kosher salt and pepper

1. FOR THE FILLING: Bring all of the ingredients to a simmer in a medium saucepan over medium-high heat. Cover, reduce the heat to low, and cook until the apples are very soft, about 20 minutes. Push the mixture through a fine-mesh strainer to extract as much liquid as possible. Return the liquid to the saucepan and simmer over medium-high heat until reduced to ⅓ cup, about 5 minutes; reserve the glaze. Meanwhile, pulse the apple mixture in a food processor until uniformly coarsely chopped, about fifteen 1-second pulses. Transfer the filling to a bowl and refrigerate while preparing the pork.

2. FOR THE PORK: Soak the wood chunks in water to cover for 1 hour; drain. Meanwhile, following the photos on page 175, cut the meat to an even ½-inch thickness. Season the inside liberally with salt and spread the apple filling in an even layer, leaving a ½-inch border. Roll tightly and tie with kitchen twine at 1-inch intervals. Season the exterior liberally with salt and pepper.

3. About 20 minutes before grilling, open the bottom grill vent. Light a large chimney starter filled with 5 quarts of charcoal briquettes (about 85 pieces) and allow it to burn until the charcoal is partially covered in a thin layer of fine gray ash, about 15 minutes. Spread the coals over half of the grill bottom, leaving the other half with no coals. Place the drained wood chunks on the coals. Set the cooking grate over the coals, cover the grill, and heat until hot, about 5 minutes. Use a grill brush to scrape the cooking grate clean. Lightly dip a wad of paper towels in vegetable oil; holding the wad with tongs, wipe the cooking grate. The grill is ready when the coals are hot (you can hold your hand 5 inches above the grate for 2 seconds).

4. Place the roast, fat-side up, on the grate over the cool side of the grill. Cover the grill and position the vent, halfway open, over the roast to draw smoke through the grill. Grill-roast until an instant-read thermometer inserted into the thickest part of the roast registers 130 to 135 degrees, 55 to 70 minutes, flipping once halfway through the cooking time. Brush the roast with half of the reserved glaze; flip and brush with the remaining glaze. (You may need to reheat the glaze briefly to make it spreadable.) Continue to cook until the glaze is glossy and sticky and the center of the roast registers 140 degrees on an instant-read thermometer, about 5 minutes longer.

5. Transfer the roast to a cutting board, loosely tent with foil, and let rest until the roast registers 150 degrees on an instant-read thermometer about 15 minutes. Cut into ½-inch-thick slices, removing the twine as you cut. Serve.

VARIATION

GAS-GRILLED PORK LOIN WITH APPLE-CRANBERRY FILLING

Follow the recipe for Charcoal-Grilled Pork Loin with Apple-Cranberry Filling through step 2, substituting 2 cups wood chips for the wood chunks, soaking them for 30 minutes. Place the wood chips in a small disposable aluminum pan. About 20 minutes before grilling, position the pan over the primary burner of a gas grill (the burner that will remain on during cooking). Position the cooking grate over the burners. Turn all the burners to high, close the cover, and heat until very hot, about 15 minutes. Use a grill brush to scrape the cooking grate clean. Lightly dip a wad of paper towels in vegetable oil; holding the wad with tongs, wipe the cooking grate. Leave the primary burner on high and turn the remaining burner(s) off. Place the roast, fat-side up, on the side opposite the primary burner and proceed with the recipe from step 4.

NOTES FROM THE TEST KITCHEN

NOT ALL PORK LOINS CAN BE STUFFED

Center-cut roasts come in various shapes, some of which are not suited to stuffing. Here's what to look for (and what to avoid).

LONG AND THIN
This roast is 12 inches long and just 3 inches wide . . .

TOO LITTLE ROOM
. . . so there's not much surface area for the stuffing.

SHORT AND WIDE
This roast is just 8 inches long and nearly 5 inches wide . . .

PLENTY OF ROOM
. . . so there's more surface area once the roast is opened up.

PROPANE LEVEL INDICATORS

You never want to run out of gas midway through grilling. To that end, we tested three propane level indicators, which are designed to show how much fuel you have in your tank. Our favorite, which we vastly preferred over the other models, is the **Original Grill Gauge**, $13.99, which looks like a car gas gauge. You hook the indicator to the collar of the tank; when you lift the tank three inches off the ground, it registers the gas level by weight.

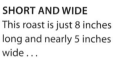

HOW TO STUFF A PORK LOIN

1. Position the roast fat-side up. Insert a knife ½ inch from the bottom of the roast and cut horizontally, stopping ½ inch before the edge. Open this flap up.

2. Cut through the thicker half of the roast about ½ inch from the bottom, stopping about ½ inch before the edge. Open this flap up.

3. Repeat until the pork loin is an even ½ inch thickness throughout. If uneven, cover with plastic wrap and use a meat pounder to even it out.

4. With the long side of the meat facing you, season the meat and spread the filling, leaving a ½-inch border on all sides.

5. Starting from the short side, roll the pork loin tightly.

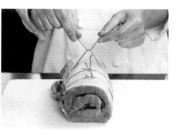

6. Tie the roast with twine at 1-inch intervals.

SOUTH CAROLINA PULLED PORK

THROUGHOUT AMERICA'S BARBECUE BELT, pit masters balance the meaty richness of pulled pork by dressing it with all manner of barbecue sauces. On a recent trip to South Carolina—to Columbia and Charleston, to be exact—I discovered a mustard-based sauce I'd never tried before. Nicknamed "Carolina gold," this sauce originated in the state's midlands area, with historians at the South Carolina Barbecue Association attributing it to the mustard-loving German immigrants who settled there in the 1700s. This savory, tangy barbecue was so good I ate it for lunch, mid-afternoon snack, and dinner for two days running on my trip.

I was determined to re-create this barbecue in the test kitchen. After years of testing, we've perfected an easy cooking technique where boneless pork shoulder is rubbed with dry spices (to help it develop a flavorful crust) before being slow-smoked on the grill for a few hours. Once the pork has taken on plenty of smoke, it's wrapped in foil and allowed to gently steam to tenderness in the convenience of a low oven before being shredded and sauced.

There was one issue to address before I figured out how to re-create the sauce—the spice rub. Since Carolina gold is largely about mustard, I wanted to see if I could use the rub to jump-start the mustard flavor. To a basic mixture of sugar, salt, pepper, paprika, and cayenne I added a tablespoon of dry mustard. Tasters approved, but wanted more mustard. It took a full three tablespoons to get a solid mustard punch from the rub, which cooked into a rich, spicy crust on the grill.

Most authentic South Carolina sauces use yellow mustard, the cheap stuff you slather on hot dogs, but I wanted to see if another kind of mustard might work better. Tasters found the German, English, Dijon, and powdered mustards too overpowering. Spicy brown mustard was deemed "murky tasting," while honey mustard introduced an unwelcome extra sweetener to the mix. Yellow mustard was the clear favorite, with tasters praising its bright, assertive tang.

For the other sauce ingredients, tasters preferred rich brown sugar to white sugar, honey, or molasses. Distilled vinegar lent an uncomplicated sharpness that augmented the tang of the mustard. While most barbecue sauces are built on a foundation of onions and garlic, I was surprised that tasters thought their distinct flavor competed with the mustard, and preferred the sauce without them. A little savory Worcestershire and hot sauce rounded out the flavors of the sauce. As if my streamlined formula wasn't easy enough, tasters preferred the brasher uncooked, "dump-and-stir" sauces to those that mellowed while simmering on the stove.

The sauce was such a success that I wondered if I could get additional mileage from it. I increased the proportions to yield a little extra, which I then spread on the meat before putting it into the oven. The spicy, smoky crust was good to begin with, but now it was even thicker, sweeter, and more deeply flavored. This barbecued pulled pork really struck gold—Carolina gold!

—ADAM RIED, *Cook's Country*

SOUTH CAROLINA–STYLE PULLED PORK ON A CHARCOAL GRILL
SERVES 8

Pork shoulder (usually labeled pork butt or Boston butt) can be found both boneless (almost always wrapped in netting) or on the bone. The boneless roast is a bit easier to handle but either can be used in this recipe. If your pork roast is more than 5 pounds, plan on an extra 30 to 60 minutes of oven cooking time. If you prefer pork with a more uniform texture, chop the meat fine rather than pulling it into shreds.

PORK
- 3 tablespoons dry mustard
- 1½ tablespoons light brown sugar
- 2 tablespoons salt
- 2 teaspoons ground black pepper
- 2 teaspoons paprika
- ¼ teaspoon cayenne pepper
- 1 (4 to 5-pound) boneless pork shoulder roast (see note)
- 4 cups wood chips

SOUTH CAROLINA PULLED PORK

MUSTARD BARBECUE SAUCE

- ½ **cup yellow mustard**
- ½ **cup packed light brown sugar**
- ¼ **cup white vinegar**
- 2 **tablespoons Worcestershire sauce**
- 1 **tablespoon hot sauce**
- 1 **teaspoon salt**
- 1 **teaspoon pepper**

- 8 **sandwich rolls, split**

1. FOR THE PORK: Combine the dry mustard, sugar, salt, pepper, paprika, and cayenne, breaking up any lumps. Pat the pork dry with paper towels and rub all over with the spice mixture. (The roast can be wrapped tightly in plastic and refrigerated for 24 hours.)

2. Soak the wood chips in water to cover for 15 minutes; drain. Seal the wood chips in a foil packet and, following the photos on page 161, cut vent holes in the top.

3. About 20 minutes before grilling, open the bottom grill vent. Light a large chimney starter filled halfway with charcoal briquettes (about 50 pieces) and allow it to burn until the charcoal is partially covered in a thin layer of fine gray ash, about 15 minutes. Arrange the coals in a pile on half of the grill bottom, leaving the other half with no coals. Arrange the foil packet directly on the coals. Set the cooking grate over the coals, cover the grill with the lid vent open halfway, and heat until hot and the wood chips begin to smoke heavily, about 5 minutes. Use a grill brush to scrape the cooking grate clean. Lightly dip a wad of paper towels in vegetable oil; holding the wad with tongs, wipe the cooking grate. The grill is ready when the coals are hot (you can hold your hand 5 inches above the grate for 2 seconds).

4. Place the pork on the cool side of the grill and barbecue, covered, until the exterior of the pork has a rosy crust, about 2 hours.

5. FOR THE BARBECUE SAUCE AND TO FINISH: Adjust an oven rack to the lower-middle position and heat the oven to 325 degrees. Whisk the mustard, sugar, vinegar, Worcestershire, hot sauce, salt, and pepper

in a bowl until smooth. Transfer the pork to a roasting pan and brush ½ cup of the sauce over the meat. Cover the roasting pan tightly with foil and bake until a fork inserted into the pork can be removed with no resistance, 2 to 3 hours. Remove from the oven and rest, still wrapped in foil, for 30 minutes. Unwrap the pork and, when cool enough to handle, pull the meat into thin shreds, discarding the fat if desired. Toss the pork with the remaining sauce. Serve on the rolls.

VARIATION

SOUTH CAROLINA–STYLE PULLED PORK ON A GAS GRILL

Follow the recipe for South Carolina–Style Pulled Pork on a Charcoal Grill through step 2. Position the foil packet directly on the primary burner of a gas grill. Turn all the burners to high, close the cover, and heat until very hot and the wood chips begin to smoke heavily, about 15 minutes. Use a grill brush to scrape the cooking grate clean. Lightly dip a wad of paper towels in vegetable oil; holding the wad with tongs, wipe the cooking grate. Leave the primary burner on high and turn the remaining burner(s) off. Continue with the recipe from step 4, grilling with the lid down.

NOTES FROM THE TEST KITCHEN

SMOKY PULLED PORK

Indirect heat is the key to smoky, low-and-slow barbecue. Place the foil packet containing the drained soaked wood chips directly on the heat source on the opposite side of the grill from the pork shoulder, and give the meat plenty of time—about 2 hours—to absorb the smoke and form a flavorful crust before bringing it indoors to finish cooking to complete tenderness.

CHICAGO-STYLE BARBECUED RIBS

THEY BOAST ABOUT THEIR BARBECUE pretty loudly in Chicago, where baby back ribs are slow-smoked to fall-apart tenderness and slathered with a spicy sauce. To understand what makes Chicago ribs the source of so much pride, I hopped on a plane to eat my way through a half dozen of the Windy City's finest rib joints.

Aside from discovering that I can eat 65 ribs in two days, I learned that Chicago ribs are typically smoked at about 200 degrees for at least eight hours (and sometimes for up to a day). This slow-and-low cooking method ensures the moist, tender meat that helps define Chicago ribs.

Back home, I hoped to shorten the cooking time by using a slightly hotter fire, but the resulting ribs were tough and chewy. I had better luck starting the ribs on the grill (so they picked up good color and smoke flavor) and finishing them in a 250-degree oven for another two hours or so. Ribs made this way weren't tough, but they weren't really tender or moist, either.

Some recipes suggested precooking the ribs by poaching them in simmering water, but this made them bloated and bland. Other recipes called for mopping or spraying water on the ribs to ensure moistness. The extra humidity helped, but every time I opened the grill lid to apply water, I also allowed heat to escape. Placing a pan of water in the grill during cooking moistened the ribs without lengthening the cooking time. To create really moist ribs, I took this method one step further and steamed the ribs in the oven as well. After just a few hours, these smoky ribs were so tender that I had trouble picking them up.

I smuggled several bottles of Chicago barbecue sauce back to the test kitchen; their labels revealed a few unusual ingredients, namely celery salt and allspice. The other thing that makes this sauce stand out is the heat, which comes from plenty of cayenne. Since Chicago sauce is supposed to be brash and assertive, no simmering was necessary—I just mixed all the sauce ingredients together in a bowl and brushed it on the ribs at the end. These moist, tender, and spicy ribs were just as good as any I had in Chicago.

—MEREDITH BUTCHER, *Cook's Country*

CHICAGO-STYLE BARBECUED RIBS ON A CHARCOAL GRILL

SERVES 4 TO 6

The dry spices are used to flavor both the rub and the barbecue sauce. When removing the ribs from the oven, be careful not to spill the hot water in the bottom of the baking sheet.

RIBS

- 1 tablespoon dry mustard
- 1 tablespoon paprika
- 1 tablespoon dark brown sugar
- 1½ teaspoons garlic powder
- 1½ teaspoons onion powder
- 1½ teaspoons celery salt
- 1 teaspoon cayenne pepper
- ½ teaspoon ground allspice
- 2 (1½-pound) racks baby back ribs, membranes removed (see the photo on page 181)
- 1 cup wood chips
  Disposable 13 by 9-inch aluminum roasting pan

SAUCE

- 1¼ cups ketchup
- ¼ cup molasses
- ¼ cup cider vinegar
- ¼ cup water
- ⅛ teaspoon liquid smoke

1. FOR THE RIBS: Combine the mustard, paprika, sugar, garlic and onion powders, celery salt, cayenne, and allspice. Measure 2 tablespoons of the mixture into a medium bowl and set aside for the sauce. Pat the ribs dry with paper towels and massage the remaining spice rub into both sides of the ribs. (The ribs can be wrapped in plastic and refrigerated for up to 24 hours.)

2. Soak the wood chips in water to cover for 15 minutes; drain.

3. About 20 minutes before grilling, open the bottom grill vent. Light a large chimney starter filled with charcoal briquettes (about 100 pieces) and allow it to burn until the charcoal is partially covered in a thin layer of fine gray ash, about 15 minutes. Place the disposable aluminum pan filled with 2 cups water on one side of the grill, and arrange the coals in a pile on the opposite

CHICAGO-STYLE BARBECUED RIBS

side. Scatter the drained chips over the coals. Set the cooking grate over the coals, cover the grill with the lid vent open halfway, and heat until hot and the wood chips begin to smoke heavily, about 5 minutes. Use a grill brush to scrape the cooking grate clean. Lightly dip a wad of paper towels in vegetable oil; holding the wad with tongs, wipe the cooking grate.

4. Position the ribs over the water-filled pan and cook, covered with the grill lid vent open halfway, rotating and flipping the racks once, until the ribs are deep red and smoky, about 1½ hours.

5. Adjust an oven rack to the middle position and heat the oven to 250 degrees. Set a wire rack inside a rimmed baking sheet and add just enough water to cover the pan bottom. Arrange the ribs on the wire rack, cover tightly with foil, and cook until the ribs are completely tender, 1½ to 2 hours. Transfer to a serving platter, tent with foil, and let rest for 10 minutes.

6. FOR THE SAUCE: Meanwhile, whisk all of the ingredients into the bowl with the reserved spice rub. Brush the ribs with 1 cup of the barbecue sauce. Serve, passing the remaining sauce at the table.

VARIATION
CHICAGO-STYLE BARBECUED RIBS ON A GAS GRILL

Follow the recipe for Chicago-Style Barbecued Ribs on a Charcoal Grill through step 2. Place the chips in a small disposable aluminum pan and position the pan directly on the primary burner of a gas grill. Place another disposable aluminum pan filled with 2 cups water on the secondary burner(s) and set the cooking grate in place. Turn all the burners to high and heat, covered, until the chips are smoking heavily, about 15 minutes. Use a grill brush to scrape the cooking grate clean. Lightly dip a wad of paper towels in vegetable oil; holding the wad with tongs, wipe the cooking grate. Turn the primary burner to medium and turn the remaining burner(s) off. Continue with the recipe from step 4, grilling with the lid down.

NOTES FROM THE TEST KITCHEN

SECRETS TO TENDER RIBS
Adding steam on the grill and in the oven makes these ribs especially moist and tender.

1. To remove the chewy membrane on the bone side of the ribs, loosen it with the tip of a paring knife and, with the aid of a paper towel, pull it off slowly in one big piece.

2. Place a disposable aluminum pan on the bottom of the grill and fill it with 2 cups of water. The water creates steam that keeps the ribs from drying out.

3. After smoking, place a wire rack in a rimmed baking sheet and add water to cover the bottom of the baking sheet. Place the ribs on the rack, wrap the pan in foil, and bake until tender.

GRILL GRATE LIFTER
Replenishing coals is a must for many slow-cooked barbecue recipes, but dealing with a blazing hot grill can be a dicey task. As an alternative to grasping the grate with a mitt, the Barr Brothers Company offers its **Grill Grabber Grate Lifter**, $6.99. It looks like a skillet handle and measures just under 10 inches from polypropylene grip to stainless steel tip. Its curved, notched prongs securely hooked under the bars of the grate and steadily held its weight (it can support up to five pounds) as we poured more coals into the kettle. It also works indoors as an oven rack puller.

GRILLED BRATS AND BEER

BURGERS AND DOGS may be the tailgating staples in the rest of the country, but in the Midwest the pregame ritual is not complete without grilled bratwurst and beer. A disposable aluminum pan filled with cheap lager and sliced onions is placed on one half of the grill, with the sausages on the other half. Some people cook the sausages in the beer first before finishing them on the grill, while others grill and then simmer. The idea is that the beer and onions flavor the bratwurst, which is then nestled into a bun, smothered with the beer-soaked onions, and doused with plenty of mustard. It sounds foolproof, but my first attempts resulted in gray, soggy sausages and bland onions floating in hot beer.

I began by setting all the burners to high and placing a pan full of beer and onions on one side. I discovered that first braising the bratwurst in the beer and onions resulted in that unappealing gray color, which persisted even after grilling. I had better luck by first browning the sausages over medium-high heat (they burned over high heat) to give them good seared flavor and color before finishing them in the beer and onion mixture. Brats prepared this way picked up nice flavor, but they also became soggy. The solution to perfect texture was simple: throw the grilled-then-braised brats back over the flames for a final crisping.

The bratwurst tasted great, but the pale onions didn't. While most recipes simply add raw onions to the beer, I saw the hot grill as a tool to add serious flavor. I sliced the onions into rounds and threw them on the grill to acquire a nice char before adding them to their beer bath; the seared flavor of the onions enhanced the beer and, by extension, the sausages. Looking to add even more flavor, I tried dark ales and expensive lagers, but I quickly discovered that their big flavors become overly harsh and bitter when reduced. Cheap, mild lagers remained mellow when simmered for half an hour.

Once the bratwurst and onions have been cooked, the braising liquid is normally dumped on the ground. But because the grilled onions and brats had infused the beer with so much flavor, I couldn't bear to see it go to waste. I tried adding the mustard to this liquid instead of saving it for the bun. When reduced in the beer and

onion mixture, the mustard lent brightness and body to the liquid, which was now more like a sauce. A little bit of sugar, black pepper, and some caraway seeds added richness and complexity.

Now my recipe has it all: crisp, charred, and flavorful bratwurst nestled onto a bun and slathered with my beer-onion-mustard sauce. All I need now are tickets to the big game.

—MEREDITH BUTCHER, *Cook's Country*

CHARCOAL-GRILLED BRATS AND BEER

SERVES 10

Depending on the size of your grill, you may need to cook the onions in two batches in step 3. Standard hot dog buns will be too small for the bulky brats. We prefer a mellow beer like Budweiser or Miller Genuine Draft for this recipe; imported beers will be too bitter when reduced.

4 onions, sliced into ½-inch rounds
3 tablespoons vegetable oil
  Pepper
2 (12-ounce) beers (see note)
⅔ cup Dijon mustard
1 teaspoon sugar
1 teaspoon caraway seeds
  Disposable 13 by 9-inch aluminum roasting pan
10 bratwurst sausages
10 (6-inch) sub rolls

1. Arrange 50 charcoal briquettes over the bottom of the grill. Light a large chimney starter filled with charcoal briquettes (about 100 pieces) and allow it to burn until the charcoal is partially covered with a thin layer of fine gray ash, about 15 minutes. Pour the coals evenly over the cold coals. Set the cooking grate over the coals, cover the grill, and heat with the lid vent open completely until hot, about 5 minutes. Use a grill brush to scrape the cooking grate clean. Lightly dip a wad of paper towels in vegetable oil; holding the wad with tongs, wipe the cooking grate. The grill is ready when the coals are medium hot (you can hold your hand 5 inches above the grate for 3 to 4 seconds).

2. Brush the onions with the oil and season to taste

with pepper. Whisk the beer, mustard, sugar, caraway seeds, and 1 teaspoon pepper in the disposable aluminum roasting pan.

3. Following the photos, arrange the disposable aluminum roasting pan on one side of the grill and grill the onions on the other side of the grill until lightly charred, 6 to 10 minutes. Transfer the onions to the pan and grill the sausages until browned, 6 to 10 minutes. Transfer the sausages to the pan, cover the grill, and simmer until the sausages are cooked through, about 15 minutes. Remove the cooked sausages from the pan and grill until lightly charred, about 4 minutes. Transfer the sausages to a platter and tent with foil.

4. Continue to simmer the beer mixture, with the grill covered, until the onions are tender and the sauce is slightly thickened, about 5 minutes. Place the bratwurst in the rolls and spoon the sauce and onions over them. Serve.

VARIATION

GAS-GRILLED BRATS AND BEER

Turn all the burners on a gas grill to medium-high, close the cover, and heat for 15 minutes. Use a grill brush to scrape the cooking grate clean. Lightly dip a wad of paper towels in vegetable oil; holding the wad with tongs, wipe the cooking grate. Continue with the recipe for Charcoal-Grilled Brats and Beer from step 2.

NOTES FROM THE TEST KITCHEN

THE BEST GRILL BRUSH

Anyone who has grilled a rack of sticky barbecued ribs has had to deal with the task of removing the sugary, burned-on mess that gets left behind. We set out to find a grill brush that could make the tedious task of cleaning a gunked-up cooking grate more efficient. What did we find? Brushes with stiffer bristles fared better than their softer counterparts, but none of them worked very well. The bristles on most bent after a few strokes and trapped large quantities of gunk, thereby decreasing their efficiency. Our favorite—the **Grill Wizard Grill Brush,** $11.98—has no brass bristles to bend, break, or clog with unwanted grease and grime. Instead, this brush has one large woven mesh stainless steel scrubbing pad, which is able to conform to any cooking grate's spacing, size, and material. Best of all, the pad is detachable, washable, and replaceable (a spare is included).

FOUR STEPS TO BETTER BRATWURST

Whether you're tailgating at the game or just grilling in your backyard, here's how to get great grilled brats and perfectly cooked onions every time.

1. Simmer the beer, mustard, and spices in a disposable aluminum pan over one side of the grill. Grill the sliced onions on the opposite side.

2. Transfer the grilled onions to the simmering beer mixture and grill the bratwurst until just browned.

3. Submerge the browned bratwurst in the simmering beer mixture to finish cooking.

4. Once the sausages are cooked through, return them to the grill to crisp up while the beer mixture finishes reducing.

THE BEST DIJON MUSTARD

Dijon mustard is a staple here in the test kitchen, and we wanted to find out which nationally available brands were the best. We rounded up eight Dijon mustards and tasted them plain and in a simple mustard vinaigrette. The result: Our tasters preferred the spicier mustards, and the most important taste factor was balance of flavor. Mustards that were too acidic or too salty or muddied with other flavors were downgraded by our tasters. Our favorite Dijon mustard was **Grey Poupon Dijon Mustard,** $3.79 for 10 ounces, which tasters described as a "nice balance of sweet, tangy, and sharp." (See page 331 for more information about our testing results.)

POULTRY

STUFFED CHICKEN BREASTS

CHEESY, BREADY STUFFING is the first thing an American cook falls back on to fill chicken breasts. This approach is fine but ho-hum. The French, however, take the concept in a different direction: a stuffing of force-meat made from the chicken itself. The idea derives from a classic preparation known as a ballottine. This complex method involves skinning and boning a whole chicken, stuffing the breasts, and wrapping them back up in the skin. The real deal is usually made only by professional chefs in four-star restaurants; French home cooks take shortcuts. Could we follow suit?

Since I wanted to make things as simple as possible, boning a whole chicken was out of the question. I decided to start with boneless, skinless breasts, which meant I'd have to come up with a stuffing that didn't rely on the traditional dark meat. I tried simply using vegetables as a base. The meatless stuffing tasted great (tasters preferred mushrooms accented by leeks and herbs), but as soon as I cut into the chicken, the filling fell out onto the board. I needed a binder. I tried a wide assortment, including cubed white bread, ricotta cheese, and corn bread. A few of these variations tasted fine, but they took me back to producing a more pedestrian style of stuffed chicken breast.

I thought of buying one extra chicken breast to use in the filling, but most supermarkets sell them in packages of two and four. What if I bought larger breasts and trimmed a little meat off each to use in the stuffing? I hoped the trimmings, used in conjunction with the mushroom and leek stuffing I'd already developed, would make a filling that was both tasty and cohesive.

I began with a new batch of breasts that weighed 8 ounces each. I trimmed 1½ ounces off each, pureed the trimmings to a fine paste in the food processor, then folded in the sautéed mushrooms and leeks. Success! With just a small amount of meat as a binder, the filling firmed up enough to stay in place during cooking and stayed together even when I sliced the chicken into thin medallions.

I started off using the simple slit-and-tuck method of stuffing: cutting a pocket in the chicken, inserting the filling, and securing it with toothpicks. This technique, however, exposed the chicken's entire surface to the heat, which caused it to overcook and become dry and fibrous. The original ballottine method, in which the stuffing is spread over the pounded breast before being rolled into a roulade, produced much better results. The chicken and stuffing were more uniformly distributed, allowing them to cook evenly and guaranteeing that each bite contained a mixture of both.

I was having difficulty pounding out whole breasts to exactly the right thickness (they tended to tear apart or develop leaky holes) until I followed a technique for a Chicken Kiev recipe developed by a colleague in which the breast is opened up, or butterflied, before pounding. Now I could easily pound the breasts to a uniform ¼-inch thickness. But no matter how carefully you pound chicken, it inevitably comes out unevenly shaped, making it difficult to roll into a neat roulade. But there was an easy and elegant solution: instead of trimming meat for the stuffing before pounding the chicken, I reversed the order. I first pounded the breasts, then trimmed them to form perfect, easy-to-roll rectangles, reserving the trimmings for the stuffing. Now all I had to do was spread the stuffing mixture on each breast, roll up the chicken, and tie it with twine.

With both the stuffing and assembly method resolved, I shifted my attention to the cooking technique. A classical ballottine is generally cooked in one of two ways: pan-roasting or poaching. Pan-roasting nicely browns the exterior but can produce leathery results. Poaching, on the other hand, produces meat that's very tender and moist but also bland. What if I combined the high-heat browning of a hot skillet with a gentler cooking method to finish it off? A quick braise might do the trick.

For my next test, I browned my chicken on all sides, added chicken broth and wine to the pan, covered it, and brought it to a simmer. I'd unwittingly killed two birds with one stone: I had the most flavorful, evenly cooked chicken yet and also a braising liquid that could form a great base for a pan sauce. When the chicken was cooked through, I removed it from the pan, stirred in some mustard, and reduced the contents of the pan to create a concentrated sauce.

Sliced into thin medallions and drizzled with the pan sauce, my stuffed chicken breasts had all the hallmarks of the French original: moist chicken wrapped around a cohesive stuffing, all enhanced with an intense pan sauce. Even with shortcuts, it was definitely a meal worthy of four stars.

—J. KENJI ALT, *Cook's Illustrated*

STUFFED CHICKEN BREASTS

STUFFED CHICKEN BREASTS

SERVES 4 TO 6

If your 8-ounce chicken breasts come with the tenderloin still attached, pull them off with your hands and reserve them to make the chicken puree in step 1. If necessary, trim these breasts slightly to make uniform rectangles and to yield 1½ to 2 ounces total trimmings per breast.

- 4 boneless, skinless chicken breasts (8 ounces each), tenderloins removed and reserved and breasts trimmed (see note)
- 3 tablespoons vegetable oil
- 10 ounces white mushrooms, sliced thin
- 1 small leek, white part halved lengthwise, washed, and chopped (about 1 cup)
- 2 garlic cloves, minced
- ½ teaspoon minced fresh thyme
- 1 tablespoon fresh lemon juice
- ½ cup dry white wine
- 1 tablespoon minced fresh parsley
  Salt and pepper
- 1 cup low-sodium chicken broth
- 1 teaspoon Dijon mustard
- 2 tablespoons unsalted butter

1. Use the tip of a sharp chef's knife to cut each breast horizontally, starting at the thinnest end and stopping the knife tip ½ inch away from the edge so that the halves remain attached. Open up the breasts to create 4 cutlets. Place 1 cutlet at a time in a heavy-duty zipper-lock bag and pound to ¼-inch thickness. (The cutlet should measure about 8 by 6 inches.) Trim about ½ inch from the long sides of the cutlets (about 1½ to 2 ounces of meat per cutlet, or a total of ½ cup from all 4 cutlets); each cutlet should be a rectangle that measures about 8 by 5 inches. Process all the trimmings in a food processor until smooth, about 20 seconds. Transfer the puree to a medium bowl and set aside. (Do not wash out the processor bowl.)

2. Heat 1 tablespoon of the oil in a 12-inch skillet over medium-high heat until shimmering. Add the mushrooms and cook, stirring occasionally, until all the moisture has evaporated and the mushrooms are golden brown, 8 to 11 minutes. Add 1 more tablespoon

of the oil and the leek; continue to cook, stirring frequently, until softened, 2 to 4 minutes. Add the garlic and thyme, and cook, stirring frequently, until fragrant, about 30 seconds. Add 1½ teaspoons of the lemon juice and cook until all the moisture has evaporated, about 30 seconds. Transfer the mixture to the bowl of the food processor. Return the pan to the heat; add the wine and scrape the pan bottom to loosen any browned bits. Transfer the wine to a small bowl and set aside. Rinse the skillet clean and dry with paper towels.

3. Pulse the mushroom mixture in the food processor until roughly chopped, about 5 one-second pulses. Transfer the mushroom mixture to the bowl with the pureed chicken. Add 1½ teaspoons of the parsley, ¾ teaspoon salt, and ½ teaspoon pepper. Using a rubber spatula, fold together the stuffing ingredients until well combined (you should have about 1½ cups stuffing).

4. With the thinnest ends of the cutlets pointing away from you, spread one-quarter of the stuffing evenly over each cutlet with a rubber spatula, leaving a ¾-inch border along the short sides of the cutlet and a ¼-inch border along the long sides. Roll each breast up as tightly as possible without squeezing out any stuffing and place seam-side down on a cutting board. Evenly space 3 pieces of kitchen twine (each about 12 inches long) beneath each breast and tie, trimming any excess.

5. Season the chicken with salt and pepper. Heat the remaining 1 tablespoon oil in the skillet over medium-high heat until just smoking. Add the chicken bundles and brown on 4 sides, about 2 minutes per side. Add the broth and reserved wine to the pan and bring to a boil. Reduce the heat to low, cover the pan, and cook until an instant-read thermometer registers 160 degrees when inserted into the thickest part of the chicken, 12 to 18 minutes. Transfer the chicken to a cutting board and tent loosely with foil.

6. While the chicken rests, whisk the mustard into the cooking liquid. Increase the heat to high and simmer the liquid, scraping the pan bottom to loosen any browned bits, until dark brown and reduced to ½ cup, 7 to 10 minutes. Off the heat, whisk in the butter and remaining 1½ teaspoons parsley and 1½ teaspoons lemon juice; season to taste with salt and pepper.

Remove the twine and cut each chicken bundle on the bias into 6 medallions. Transfer the chicken to individual plates; spoon the sauce over the chicken and serve.

NOTES FROM THE TEST KITCHEN

ASSEMBLING STUFFED CHICKEN BREASTS

1. Slice each breast horizontally, stopping ½ inch from the edges so the halves remain attached.

2. Open up each breast, place it in a plastic bag, and pound it to ¼-inch thickness.

3. Trim ½ inch from each long side of each cutlet and reserve the trimmings for the stuffing.

4. Spread one-quarter of the stuffing evenly over each cutlet, leaving a ¾-inch border along the short sides and ¼-inch border along the long sides.

5. Roll up each cutlet and secure it snugly with three pieces of twine.

GLAZED CHICKEN BREASTS

ON A FLIGHT ONCE TO PARIS, I chose the glazed chicken meal option. The flight attendant set down a plastic tray displaying a pale chicken breast with flabby skin smothered by a cloying glaze. I made it through two bites. That evening I found myself at an upscale restaurant ordering the house specialty: duck à l'orange. A silver platter arrived bearing carved duck pieces clad with deep-amber skin coated in a shiny, glazy sauce. The meat was perfectly moist, and each bite revealed the satisfying combination of roasted poultry and a citrus sauce balanced by sweet and sour flavors.

These contrasting experiences got me to thinking about glazed chicken's status in the American culinary repertoire. At best it's a humdrum weeknight dinner. I wanted a glazed chicken breast with perfectly rendered skin and moist meat sufficiently coated with a complexly flavored glaze; one worthy of fine china but still something I could make after work during the week.

When I got back home, I searched for glazed chicken recipes on the Internet, where I mostly found simple "dump-and-bake" versions. The instructions: Pour a jar of fruit preserves over raw chicken breasts and bake. I wasn't surprised when my attempt at one of these recipes emerged from the oven looking much like my airplane meal. Browning the skin was an easy fix. I could brown the chicken in an ovenproof skillet on the stovetop before transferring the skillet to the oven to finish cooking (our standard test kitchen method for cooking bone-in, skin-on breasts). I could add a glaze to the pan just after the chicken breasts were sufficiently browned.

But first I would have to fix the glaze. Every recipe I dug up in my research used a good deal of sticky, sweet ingredients for the base: fruit preserves, molasses, maple syrup, and brown sugar. How was it that my duck à l'orange sauce in Paris was glazy yet not cloying? My hunch was that it was some sort of reduction sauce. Flipping through French cookbooks, I found my answer: reduced orange juice. Orange juice is sticky, and its acidity helps balance the sugar—another key ingredient in the duck sauce. I wasn't interested in creating a recipe for chicken à l'orange, but using orange juice in my glaze seemed like a good place to start.

The recipes I found for classic orange sauce offered me enough guidance to piece together a working recipe. After browning some chicken breasts, I transferred the meat to a plate while I reduced orange juice and sugar in the empty skillet. I then returned the chicken breasts to the skillet, rolled them in the glaze, and finished them off in the oven. Tasters complained that the glaze was "too thin," "irresponsibly sweet," and "did not adhere to the chicken." More sugar would have been the ideal solution to the textural issue but was inappropriate for a glaze that was already too sweet.

Then I remembered a technique a colleague in the test kitchen used for her cake frosting recipe. She mixed in a small amount of light corn syrup to add luster and body—but, curiously, not sweetness. I'd always assumed corn syrup was super-sweet, but when I tasted a lineup of sugar, brown sugar, maple syrup, and honey against corn syrup, I discovered otherwise. Nutrition labels on the sweeteners confirmed my palate's accuracy: Corn syrup contains half (and sometimes less than half) as much sugar as other sweeteners.

Excited by the prospect that corn syrup might help my cause, I immediately trimmed some chicken breasts, heated a skillet, and whipped up a new batch of glaze. Not only did this corn syrup–enhanced glaze cook up perfectly, the meat seemed juicier, almost as if I had brined the chicken. This warranted a quick call to our science editor, who told me that the concentrated glucose in corn syrup has a high affinity for water, which means it helps to hold moisture in the glaze, making the overall dish seem juicier. That same glucose also thickens and adds a gloss to the glaze.

However, as much as tasters liked the glaze's clean flavor, they now thought it wasn't sweet enough. A little honey instead of sugar gave the glaze just the right level of sweetness. And minced shallot, vinegar, Dijon mustard, and a pinch of pepper flakes created complexity.

Despite these improvements, there was one complaint—from me. I still felt the glaze should cling even more to the chicken. From past tests, I knew that adding cornstarch or flour to the glaze only made it gloppy. Maybe the problem wasn't with the glaze but with the chicken. What if I added a thin layer of flour to the outside of the meat before browning it? In the test kitchen, we don't typically coat meat with flour before browning it, but it gave the chicken breasts a thin, crispy crust that

served as a good grip for the glaze. (Cornstarch also held the glaze, but it turned the skin a bit slimy.)

I added a small amount of orange juice just before serving to brighten the glaze flavors even further. This finishing touch made all the difference. Now I had elevated glazed chicken to an elegant new height—far beyond 30,000 feet.

—CHARLES KELSEY, *Cook's Illustrated*

ORANGE-HONEY GLAZED CHICKEN BREASTS

SERVES 4

When reducing the glaze in step 4, remember that the skillet handle will be hot; use an oven mitt. To make sure the chicken cooks evenly, buy breasts that are similar in size—about 12 ounces apiece. If the glaze looks dry during baking, add up to 2 tablespoons of juice to the pan. If your skillet is not ovenproof, brown the chicken breasts and reduce the glaze as instructed, then transfer the chicken and glaze to a 13 by 9-inch baking dish and bake (don't wash the skillet). When the chicken is fully cooked, transfer it to a plate to rest and scrape the glaze back into the skillet to be reduced.

- 1½ cups plus 2 tablespoons orange juice
- ⅓ cup light corn syrup
- 3 tablespoons honey
- 1 tablespoon Dijon mustard
- 1 tablespoon distilled white vinegar
- ⅛ teaspoon red pepper flakes
  Salt and pepper
- ½ cup unbleached all-purpose flour
- 4 bone-in, skin-on chicken breast halves (about 12 ounces each; see note), ribs removed, trimmed of excess fat and skin
- 2 teaspoons vegetable oil
- 1 shallot, minced (about 3 tablespoons)

1. Adjust an oven rack to the middle position and heat the oven to 375 degrees. Whisk the 1½ cups orange juice, corn syrup, honey, mustard, vinegar, pepper flakes, ⅛ teaspoon salt, and ⅛ teaspoon pepper together in a medium bowl. Place the flour in a pie plate, then season the chicken on both sides with salt and pepper. Working with one chicken breast at a time, coat the chicken with the flour, patting off the excess.

2. Heat the oil in an ovenproof 12-inch skillet over medium heat until shimmering. Add the chicken breasts skin-side down; cook until well browned and most of the fat has rendered from the skin, 8 to 14 minutes. (If after 3 minutes you don't hear definite sizzling, increase the heat to medium-high. If after 6 minutes the chicken is darker than lightly browned, reduce the heat slightly.) Turn the chicken and lightly brown the other side, about 5 minutes longer. Transfer the chicken to a plate.

3. Pour off all but 1 teaspoon fat from the pan. Add the shallot and cook until softened, 1 to 2 minutes. Increase the heat to high and add the orange juice mixture. Simmer, stirring occasionally, until syrupy and reduced to 1 cup (a heatproof spatula should leave a slight trail when dragged through the glaze), 6 to 10 minutes. Remove the skillet from the heat and tilt it to one side so the glaze pools in one corner of the pan. Using tongs, roll each chicken breast in the pooled glaze to coat evenly and place skin-side down in the skillet.

4. Transfer the skillet to the oven and bake the chicken until the thickest part of the breasts registers 160 degrees on an instant-read thermometer, 25 to 30 minutes, turning the chicken skin-side up halfway through cooking. Transfer the chicken to a platter and let rest 5 minutes. Return the skillet to high heat (be careful—the handle will be very hot) and cook the glaze, stirring constantly, until thick and syrupy (a heatproof spatula should leave a wide trail when dragged through the glaze), about 1 minute. Remove the pan from the heat and whisk in the remaining 2 tablespoons orange juice. Spoon 1 teaspoon of the glaze over each breast and serve, passing the remaining glaze at the table.

VARIATIONS

APPLE-MAPLE GLAZED CHICKEN BREASTS

Follow the recipe for Orange-Honey Glazed Chicken Breasts, substituting apple cider for the orange juice and 2 tablespoons maple syrup for the honey.

PINEAPPLE–BROWN SUGAR GLAZED CHICKEN BREASTS

Follow the recipe for Orange-Honey Glazed Chicken Breasts, substituting pineapple juice for the orange juice and 2 tablespoons brown sugar for the honey.

CHICKEN SALTIMBOCCA

I CAN NEVER FIND ENOUGH quick and easy chicken dishes for my weeknight repertoire. So when I came across a new chicken spin on an old Italian classic—veal saltimbocca—I was immediately intrigued. The traditional version has long been a standard menu item in the trattorias of Italy as well as Italian restaurants in this country. Made by sautéing veal cutlets with prosciutto and sage, this simple yet elegant dish promises, literally, to "jump in your mouth" with its distinctive blend of flavors.

But as happens all too often when cooks start to meddle with a perfectly good thing, most chicken adaptations I found took the dish too far from its roots, wrapping the cutlet around stuffing or adding unnecessary breading or cheese. Others fiddled with the proportions, allowing a thick slab of prosciutto to share equal billing with the chicken and knock the balance of flavors out of whack. Perfecting chicken saltimbocca, then, would be a matter of avoiding the temptation to overcomplicate the dish with extraneous ingredients and figuring out how to give each of the three key elements—chicken, prosciutto, and sage—its due.

Though we generally prefer to make our own cutlets to ensure that pieces are of uniform size and shape, I decided to forgo butchering and buy commercially prepared cutlets to keep the process as streamlined as possible. I opted for mass-produced supermarket cutlets and trimmed their edges to remove any thin, tattered pieces.

Most of the simpler chicken saltimbocca recipes I came across followed the traditional practice of threading a toothpick through the prosciutto and a whole sage leaf to attach them to the cutlet, then dredging the entire package in flour before sautéing it on both sides. I found this method to be problematic. Flour got trapped in the small gaps where the ham bunched up around the toothpick, leaving sticky, uncooked spots. I wondered if I could skip the flouring and sauté the chicken and prosciutto without any coating. This worked fine for the ham, which crisped nicely without help from the flour. The chicken, on the other hand, browned unevenly and tended to stick to the pan. Surprisingly, flouring only the cutlet—before attaching the ham—proved to be the solution. And by sautéing the cutlet prosciutto-side down first, I was able to keep the flour under the prosciutto from turning gummy.

With my flouring method under control, it was time to turn my attention to proportions. While we liked high-end prosciutto for the rich flavor it added to the overall dish, if the slice was too thick, the taste overwhelmed everything else and the ham had trouble staying put. If the slice was ultrathin, however, it fell apart too easily. The ideal slice was just thick enough to hold its shape—about the thickness of two or three sheets of paper. Though some recipes folded the slice to make it fit on the cutlet, this resulted in ham that was only partially crisped and overpowered the chicken with its flavor. I found trimming the ham to fit the cutlet in a single layer worked best on all counts.

While the prosciutto needed to be tamed, the sage flavor needed a boost. In the traditional dish, each cutlet features a single sage leaf (fried in oil before being attached), so that the herbal flavor imparted is very subtle. Perhaps the sage of yore boasted far bigger leaves than are grown today, but this was one aspect of the original that I found lacking. Tethering additional leaves to the cutlet with the toothpick, however, was cumbersome and still resulted in adding flavor only to bites that actually contained sage.

I wanted a more even distribution of herbal flavor. Would infusing the cooking oil with sage be a way to diffuse—and heighten—its flavor? I tossed a handful of leaves into the cooking oil before sautéing the cutlets, removing the herbs before they burned. Tasters, however, detected only a very slight flavor boost in the finished dish. The way to more intense and evenly distributed sage flavor turned out to be as simple as chopping the leaves and sprinkling them over the floured cutlet before adding the ham. The only thing missing was the pretty look of the whole sage leaf. While not necessary, frying extra sage leaves to place on the cooked cutlets is an elegant finishing touch.

The only aspect of the dish I had not yet examined was the toothpick. After skewering prosciutto to 150 cutlets in the course of my testing, I decided enough was enough. What would happen if I just omitted the toothpick? After flouring the cutlet, sprinkling it with sage, and placing the prosciutto on top, I carefully lifted the bundle and placed it as I had been doing, prosciutto-side down, in the hot oil. Once the edges of the chicken on the bottom had browned, I flipped the cutlet, revealing ham that seemed almost hermetically sealed to the chicken. A quick pan sauce made from vermouth, lemon juice, butter, and parsley was all I needed to accentuate the perfect balance of flavors. I now had a quick Italian food fix with all the jumping in my mouth, not the kitchen.

—DAVID PAZMIÑO, *Cook's Illustrated*

CHICKEN SALTIMBOCCA

SERVES 4

Buy cutlets that are approximately 5 to 6 inches long. If the tip is too thin, trim back 1 to 2 inches to make the cutlet of uniform thickness. If cutlets are unavailable, you can make your own by slicing four (8-ounce) boneless, skinless chicken breasts in half horizontally. Although whole sage leaves make a beautiful presentation, they are optional and can be left out of step 3. Make sure to buy prosciutto that is thinly sliced, not shaved; also avoid slices that are too thick, as they won't stick to the chicken.

CHICKEN SALTIMBOCCA

½ cup unbleached all-purpose flour
Pepper
8 thin boneless, skinless chicken breast cutlets (about 2 pounds), trimmed of ragged edges as necessary (see note)
1 tablespoon minced fresh sage leaves, plus 8 large leaves (optional)
8 thin slices prosciutto, cut into 5 to 6-inch-long pieces to match chicken (about 3 ounces) (see note)
4 tablespoons olive oil
1¼ cups dry vermouth or white wine
2 teaspoons fresh lemon juice
4 tablespoons (½ stick) unsalted butter, cut into 4 pieces and chilled
1 tablespoon minced fresh parsley
Salt

1. Adjust an oven rack to the middle position and heat the oven to 200 degrees. Combine the flour and 1 teaspoon pepper in a shallow dish.

2. Pat the cutlets dry with paper towels. Dredge the chicken in the flour, shaking off any excess. Lay the cutlets flat and sprinkle evenly with the minced sage. Place 1 prosciutto slice on top of each cutlet, pressing lightly to adhere; set aside.

3. Heat 2 tablespoons of the oil in a 12-inch skillet over medium-high heat until beginning to shimmer. Add the sage leaves (if using) and cook until the leaves begin to change color and are fragrant, about 15 to 20 seconds. Using a slotted spoon, remove the sage to a paper towel–lined plate; reserve. Add half of the cutlets to the pan, prosciutto-side down, and cook until light golden brown, 2 to 3 minutes. Flip and cook on the other side until light golden brown, about 2 minutes more. Transfer to a wire rack set over a rimmed baking sheet and keep warm in the oven. Repeat with the remaining 2 tablespoons oil and cutlets, then transfer to the oven to keep warm while preparing the sauce.

4. Pour off the excess fat from the skillet. Stir in the vermouth, scraping up any browned bits, and simmer until reduced to about ⅓ cup, 5 to 7 minutes. Stir in the lemon juice. Turn the heat to low and whisk in the butter, 1 tablespoon at a time. Off the heat, stir in the parsley and season to taste with salt and pepper. Remove the chicken from the oven and place on a platter. Spoon the sauce over the cutlets before serving.

NOTES FROM THE TEST KITCHEN

SALTIMBOCCA MADE SIMPLE

1. Flour just the chicken—not the prosciutto—before sautéing.

2. Sprinkle the cutlets evenly with the minced sage, then top each with a slice of prosciutto.

3. Cook the cutlets, prosciutto-side down, to help the ham adhere to the cutlets.

CAN ANY PROSCIUTTO BE WORTH $60 PER POUND?
Americans have long looked to Italy for the best prosciutto. So when we heard about a new prosciutto on the market crafted not in Italy but in Iowa, we were more than curious.

Tasted side-by-side with prosciutto di Parma and prosciutto San Daniele, the newcomer from Iowa, La Quercia Prosciutto Americana, $18.99 per pound, was the hands-down winner. Tasters marveled at the deep, earthy flavor and creamy texture of this prosciutto. The other domestic brands we tasted simply aren't worth buying.

MEAT POUNDERS
To find a meat pounder that could produce thin cutlets of uniform thickness in the fewest number of strokes, we bought five models in a variety of shapes and weights. Our previous favorite, the middleweight **Norpro Meat Pounder**, $23.99, beat the new contenders by pounding out clean, even cutlets in a reasonable 35 strokes, with an offset handle that distributes its weight comfortably.

CRISPY GARLIC CHICKEN CUTLETS

OVER THE YEARS, THE TEST KITCHEN has perfected a method for making crispy chicken cutlets: We coat the cutlets in flour, dip them in egg wash, then coat them with fresh breadcrumbs before pan-frying. But when you add fresh garlic to the mix for more flavor, you also get more problems. Overcooked garlic tastes harsh and bitter, and too much garlic can give you breath that will peel paint. I wanted crispy cutlets with an intensely sweet, sharp—but not overpowering—garlic bite.

My first test was to try a minced garlic-and-oil marinade for the cutlets. Determined to keep the marinating time to under 30 minutes, I kept upping the garlic until I got to four minced cloves, which provided good garlic punch to the breaded and fried chicken (better than when I tried adding fresh garlic to the egg wash). This thick paste of minced garlic, safely tucked under the flour, egg, and breadcrumbs, cooked gently and lent a caramelized (rather than burnt) garlic flavor.

The whole eggs I was using in my egg wash helped the breadcrumbs stick to the chicken, but they made for soggy crumbs when combined with the oil paste. I tried replacing the eggs with mayonnaise and mustard, but both imparted too much flavor. Egg whites, whisked until foamy to increase their sticking power, made the perfect glue, getting the coating to adhere to the chicken without adding competing flavor or grease.

As for the breading, the test kitchen prefers toasted homemade breadcrumbs to supermarket crumbs, which can be stale-tasting and gritty. Looking to add another layer of garlic flavor, I tried making my crumbs from garlic-flavored croutons and pita chips and supermarket garlic bread. Unfortunately, every product either tasted artificial or made the coating soggy. Returning to white bread, I tried infusing the crumbs with fresh garlic, garlic salt, and garlic powder. The fresh garlic burned on the outside of the cutlets, and the garlic salt didn't provide enough kick; the garlic powder, however, added a welcome and distinct flavor.

Tasters wanted even more garlic flavor, but where else could I add it? The chicken was marinated in garlic, and the breadcrumbs were garlic-flavored. The only thing left to flavor was the cooking oil. Throwing whole garlic cloves into hot oil while cooking the chicken brought back the burnt flavor. So rather than cooking the garlic with the chicken, I simply added cloves (smashed to release more flavor) to the cold oil and heated them up together. When it was time to add the chicken, I removed the garlic cloves from the hot oil. This batch had it all—mellow, caramelized garlic flavor from the chicken on the inside and a crispy, garlicky crust on the outside.

—LYNN CLARK, *Cook's Country*

CRISPY GARLIC CHICKEN CUTLETS
SERVES 3 TO 4

Look for cutlets that are between ¼ inch and ½ inch thick, or make your own by slicing 3 boneless, skinless chicken breasts in half horizontally.

- 1 cup plus 3 tablespoons vegetable oil
- 4 garlic cloves, minced, plus 6 cloves peeled and smashed
- 6 thin boneless, skinless chicken cutlets (about 1½ pounds), trimmed (see note)
- 3 slices high-quality white sandwich bread, torn into large pieces
- 1 cup unbleached all-purpose flour
- 3 large egg whites
- 1 tablespoon garlic powder
- 4 teaspoons cornstarch
- Salt and pepper

1. Adjust an oven rack to the middle position and heat the oven to 200 degrees. Combine 3 tablespoons of the oil, the minced garlic, and cutlets in a zipper-lock bag and refrigerate while preparing the remaining ingredients. Pulse the bread in a food processor until coarsely ground. Bake the breadcrumbs on a baking sheet until dry, about 20 minutes.

2. Spread the flour in a shallow dish. In another shallow dish, whisk the egg whites until foamy. Combine the breadcrumbs, garlic powder, and cornstarch in a third shallow dish. Remove the cutlets from the bag and season with salt and pepper. One at a time, coat the cutlets lightly with flour, dip in the egg whites, and dredge in the crumbs, pressing to adhere. Place the cutlets on a wire rack set over a baking sheet and let dry 5 minutes.

3. Heat ½ cup of the oil and 3 of the smashed garlic cloves in a large nonstick skillet over medium heat until the garlic is lightly browned, about 4 minutes. Discard the garlic and fry 3 of the cutlets until crisp and deep golden, about 2 minutes per side. Transfer to a paper towel–lined plate and place in the warm oven. Discard the oil, wipe out the skillet, and repeat with the remaining oil, garlic, and cutlets. Serve.

NOTES FROM THE TEST KITCHEN

BUILDING BALANCED GARLIC FLAVOR
We used three hits of garlic to pump up the flavor in our chicken cutlets while avoiding any bitter, raw, or burnt garlic taste.

MINCED GARLIC
A quick minced or pressed garlic marinade gets the flavor started.

GARLIC POWDER
For a garlicky coating, garlic powder (mixed with breadcrumbs) holds up well in the hot skillet.

SMASHED GARLIC
For a final hit of garlic, we tossed smashed cloves into the skillet to infuse the oil with garlic flavor.

PISTACHIO-CRUSTED CHICKEN BREASTS

A SIMPLE BREADED CHICKEN BREAST can be quickly transformed into a richer dish with the addition of nuts to the breading. Too bad this easy-sounding recipe is so problematic. Ground nuts don't readily adhere to the chicken, and, when they do, they usually burn long before the chicken is cooked through. For the transformation from straight breadcrumbs to nuts to be a success, I had to uncover a few key tricks.

Using boneless, skinless chicken breasts, I began by adapting our standard breading technique: dredging the chicken in flour and then an egg wash, and, finally, breadcrumbs. I first tried replacing the crumbs with sliced almonds, but the thin almond slices refused to stick to the chicken. I had more success when the almonds were processed into fine crumbs in the food processor, but even then the crust tasted dense, oily, and sodden after it was cooked or, worse, they burned to an inedible mess.

Unlike breadcrumb crusts, which need a fair amount of time in a hot skillet to crisp up, nut crusts brown quickly because of their high oil content. Some recipes solve this burning issue by baking the coated chicken breasts, but no one in the test kitchen liked the pallid, soggy results. For a really crisp coating, pan-frying seemed to be our only option.

To keep the nuts from burning, and to cut their somewhat dense nature, I tried mixing them with some fresh breadcrumbs. Their flavor was neutral (other options, such as crushed crackers and cereal, were too distracting) and the crumbs did indeed help to keep the nuts from burning. Testing various ratios of nuts to breadcrumbs, I landed on equal parts freshly ground nuts and crumbs. I found that light Japanese-style breadcrumbs, panko, worked especially well. And a teaspoon of moisture-absorbing cornstarch further ensured an ultracrisp crust.

As for flavor, I was surprised to find that the nut crust tasted relatively mild. To spruce it up, I added potent Dijon mustard and minced garlic to the eggs. I also found that flavoring the nuts with 2 teaspoons cinnamon was an easy and effective way to bring out their character.

The pan-fried chicken was delicious on its own, but some tasters felt that a brightly flavored chutney or relish was in order to balance the richness of the nutty crust. Factoring that in, I developed an easy peach chutney to serve alongside. Holding the chicken warm in a 200-degree oven, I wiped the oil out of the pan and returned it to the stove. All of the relish ingredients (except the cilantro and vinegar) are added to the pan and simmered together—no sautéing aromatics or long simmering times required.

—SUZANNAH MCFERRAN, *America's Test Kitchen Books*

PISTACHIO-CRUSTED CHICKEN BREASTS WITH PEACH CHUTNEY

SERVES 4

Don't process the nuts longer than directed or they will turn pasty and oily. Regular store-bought dried bread-crumbs taste very disappointing here; if you cannot find panko, process 2 slices of high-quality white sandwich bread to coarse crumbs in a food processor, then spread them out on a baking sheet and let them dry in a 250-degree oven for about 20 minutes.

CHICKEN

- 4 boneless, skinless chicken breasts (5 to 6 ounces each), tenderloins removed and breasts trimmed
   Salt and pepper
- ¾ cup shelled pistachios (see note)
- ¾ cup panko (Japanese breadcrumbs; see note)
- 2 teaspoons curry powder
- 1 teaspoon cornstarch
- 1 cup unbleached all-purpose flour
- 2 large eggs
- 4 teaspoons Dijon mustard
- 3 garlic cloves, minced
- ¾ cup vegetable oil

CHUTNEY

- ¾ cup peach preserves
- ½ cup raisins

- ½ cup water
- 1 teaspoon minced or grated fresh ginger
- ⅛ teaspoon cayenne pepper
- 2 tablespoons minced fresh cilantro
- 2 teaspoons white vinegar
   Salt and pepper

1. FOR THE CHICKEN: Adjust an oven rack to the middle position and heat the oven to 200 degrees. Pound each breast between 2 sheets of plastic wrap to a uniform ½-inch thickness. Pat the chicken dry with paper towels and season with salt and pepper.

2. Process the pistachios in a food processor to fine crumbs, about 25 seconds (do not overprocess). Toss the nuts with the panko, curry powder, and cornstarch in a shallow dish. Combine the flour, ½ teaspoon salt, and ¼ teaspoon pepper in a second shallow dish and whisk the eggs, mustard, and garlic in a third shallow dish. Working with 1 chicken breast at a time, dredge in the flour mixture, shaking off the excess, then coat with the egg mixture, allowing the excess to drip off. Finally, coat with the nut mixture, pressing gently so that the crumbs adhere. Place the nut-crusted chicken in a single layer on a wire rack set over a rimmed baking sheet and let sit 5 minutes.

3. Meanwhile, heat 6 tablespoons of the oil in a 12-inch nonstick skillet over medium heat until shimmering. Add 2 of the chicken breasts and cook until browned on both sides, 4 to 6 minutes total. Drain the chicken briefly on a paper towel–lined plate, then transfer to a clean wire rack set over a rimmed baking sheet and keep warm in the oven. Discard the oil and wipe out the skillet with paper towels. Repeat with the remaining 6 tablespoons oil and nut-crusted chicken.

4. FOR THE CHUTNEY: Discard the oil and wipe out the skillet with paper towels. Add the peach preserves, raisins, water, ginger, and cayenne to the skillet and simmer over medium-high heat until thick and glossy, 3 to 5 minutes. Off the heat, stir in the cilantro and vinegar and season to taste with salt and pepper. Serve, passing the peach chutney separately.

KOREAN FRIED CHICKEN

KOREAN FRIED CHICKEN

FRIED CHICKEN HAS, UNTIL RECENTLY, always been considered a Western delicacy. But in recent years as Western culture has migrated east so too has its penchant for fast food and, with it, fried chicken. The Koreans, however, have completely transformed the thick-crusted fried chicken of the American South into chicken with a paper-thin, crisp coating (*yang-nyum tong dak*)—each piece painted with a tangy, saucy glaze.

While fried foods play only a minimal role in the Korean diet, I wanted to find out what all the hype was about. Korean-style fried chicken is purportedly twice-fried to give it its super-crispy skin. Twice-frying involves frying the chicken pieces for an initial period, typically 3 to 5 minutes, removing the chicken from the oil and allowing it to rest for about 5 to 7 minutes, then returning it to the oil to finish cooking. I was curious to see how well this technique actually worked, so I built a recipe from existing information gathered from Korean cookbooks and headed into the test kitchen.

To begin, I tested twice-fried chicken against our conventional fried chicken. For these initial tests I left off any coating so I could fully judge the results of the frying method. The twice-fried chicken had an initial fry time of 5 minutes, followed by a 5-minute rest, and concluded with a 3 to 5-minute fry until the chicken was cooked. The conventional fried chicken was fried straight through for 8 to 10 minutes until cooked.

After tasting both versions side by side it was clear that the twice-fried method resulted in a crispier, thinner-skinned chicken. But why does twice-frying yield crispier chicken? I consulted our science editor for the answer.

To explain, our science editor began with the problem of traditional fried chicken. Hold a piece of crisp Southern fried chicken in your hand and peel back the crisp breading. What do you find underneath? Flabby skin. Skin is composed of 50 percent water, 40 percent fat, and 10 percent connective tissue and other matter. During the process of frying the chicken, the meat cooks and the moisture in the skin begins to evaporate and the fat begins to melt, or render. But by the time the chicken is cooked through, there is still a significant amount of water remaining in the skin, as well as fat. In order to crisp the skin, one could continue to fry the chicken, but then the meat would overcook and the skin would start to burn. Twice-frying, however, slows down the cooking process to allow for more moisture to evaporate and more fat to render. Here's how it works: In the first fry, the meat begins to cook and the moisture in the skin—specifically the outer layer of the skin—begins to evaporate and the fat begins to render. The chicken is then removed from the oil and rested, which brings down the temperature of both the meat and the skin. This resting period serves two purposes: first, it allows time for more moisture to evaporate from the skin, and second, it helps prevent the meat from overcooking. In the second fry the relatively dry outer layer of skin can quickly become very hot and crisp, while retaining moisture within the deepest layers of skin and the meat. During this process more fat is rendered, providing an ultrathin crisp skin. With a clear explanation of the twice-frying process, I moved on to determining the best coating for the chicken.

Many of the recipes I found called for dusting the chicken with cornstarch before frying, while other recipes took it a step further and dipped their chicken into a thin mixture of cornstarch and water or into a batter of eggs, cornstarch, and water. I tested our fried chicken with all three techniques. The chicken that was coated with only cornstarch fried up crispier than without the coating, gaining a golden brown color. But the skin was only moderately crisp and the cornstarch seemed to weigh the skin down in some spots. The two batter tests yielded lackluster results, as both slid immediately off the chicken when it hit the hot oil. It was clear that I needed to prepare the surface of the chicken in a manner that would allow the batter to stick. The solution was coating the chicken pieces with a thin layer of cornstarch before dipping them into the batter.

Now that the batter was adhering to the chicken, I tried our test again. The egg batter turned into a heavy, dense crust. The cornstarch and water batter, however, yielded chicken with a light, crisp, and beautifully golden crust. This was unlike any fried chicken I'd ever eaten.

With our chicken fried, I shifted our attention to our sauces. Proper Korean fried chicken is coated very lightly with a pungent sauce. But before you think along the lines of Buffalo wings, think again. The coating is light, not a thick slather. The two most popular Korean fried chicken sauces are a sweet soy-garlic sauce and a spicy chili sauce. I made our sweet soy-garlic sauce by combining sugar, soy sauce, water, and garlic in a saucepan and reducing it to a glaze. I balanced the sauce with a splash of rice vinegar and a shot of hot sauce. The chili sauce was also simple, composed of ketchup, sugar, chili-garlic sauce, and a touch of lemon juice. Once the chicken was fried, I tossed it lightly with the sauce until coated and sprinkled it with sliced scallions and minced cilantro. Tasters grabbed plenty of napkins before stepping up to enjoy this fried chicken feast.

—BRYAN ROOF, *America's Test Kitchen Books*

KOREAN FRIED CHICKEN

SERVES 4

The chicken must be fried in two batches. To make the best use of your time, batter the second batch of chicken while the first batch is resting. If using both light and dark meat (breasts and thighs or drumsticks), divide them into separate batches since the dark meat requires a few extra minutes to cook through on the second fry in step 5.

    3   quarts vegetable oil
    1½ cups cornstarch
    3½ pounds bone-in, skin-on chicken pieces (split breasts
        cut in half, drumsticks, and/or thighs)
        Salt and pepper
    1   cup water
    1   recipe sauce (recipes follow)
    2   scallions, sliced thin on the bias
    1   tablespoon minced fresh cilantro

1. Adjust an oven rack to the middle position and heat the oven to 200 degrees. Measure 2 inches of oil into a large Dutch oven and heat over medium-high heat to 350 degrees. (Use an instant-read thermometer that registers high temperatures or clip a candy/deep-fat thermometer onto the side of the pan.) Line 2 rimmed baking sheets with wire racks; set aside.

2. Sift ½ cup of the cornstarch into a wide, shallow dish. Set a large mesh strainer over a large bowl. Pat the chicken dry with paper towels and season with salt and pepper. Working with several pieces of chicken at a time, coat the chicken thoroughly with the cornstarch, then transfer to the strainer and shake vigorously to remove all but a thin coating of cornstarch. Transfer the chicken to one of the wire racks.

3. Whisk the remaining 1 cup cornstarch, water, and 1 teaspoon salt together in a large bowl to form a smooth batter. When the oil is hot, finish coating the chicken by adding half of the chicken to the batter and turn to coat well. Using tongs, remove the chicken from the batter, one piece at a time, allowing any excess batter to drip back into the bowl. Add to the hot oil.

4. Fry the chicken, stirring to prevent the pieces from sticking together and adjusting the heat as necessary to maintain an oil temperature of 350 degrees, until the chicken begins to crisp, turn slightly golden, and registers about 90 degrees on the thermometer, about 5 minutes. Transfer the fried chicken to the second prepared wire rack, and set aside for 5 to 6 minutes. Batter and fry the remaining chicken during this time.

5. Line a baking sheet with several layers of paper towels, and return the oil to 350 degrees (if necessary) over medium-high heat. Return the first batch of fried chicken to the oil and continue to fry until the exterior is very crisp, deep golden brown, and an instant-read thermometer inserted into the center of the chicken registers about 160 degrees for breasts, or 175 degrees for thighs or drumsticks, 3 to 6 minutes. Transfer the chicken to the paper towel–lined baking sheet to drain, and keep warm in the oven. Repeat with the second batch; let the second batch drain for about 1 minute. (The unsauced fried chicken can be held for up to an hour in a 200-degree oven.)

6. Transfer all the chicken to a large bowl, drizzle with the sauce, and gently toss until evenly coated. Transfer the chicken to a platter, sprinkle with the scallions and cilantro, and serve.

KOREAN FRIED CHICKEN WINGS

Follow the recipe for Korean Fried Chicken, substituting 3½ pounds chicken wings, separated into sections,
wingtips discarded, for the chicken pieces; fry in 2 batches
as directed in steps 4 and 5 (the cooking times will be
about the same).

SWEET SOY-GARLIC SAUCE

MAKES ABOUT ⅔ CUP

To make the sauce spicier, stir in additional chili-garlic
sauce to taste.

- ½ cup sugar
- ¼ cup soy sauce
- ¼ cup water
- 3 garlic cloves, minced
- 1 tablespoon rice vinegar
- 1 teaspoon Thai chili-garlic sauce, such as sriracha
  (see page 18)

Simmer all of the ingredients together in a small saucepan over medium heat until syrupy, about 5 minutes. Let
cool to room temperature before serving. (The sauce can
be refrigerated in an airtight container for up to 1 day.)

TOMATO CHILI-GARLIC SAUCE

MAKES ABOUT ⅔ CUP

To make the sauce spicier, stir in additional chili-garlic
sauce to taste.

- 5 tablespoons sugar
- ¼ cup ketchup
- 1 tablespoon Thai chili-garlic sauce, such as sriracha
  (see page 18)
- 1 teaspoon fresh lemon juice

Whisk the sugar, ketchup, chili sauce, and lemon juice
together and let sit to blend the flavors, about 15 minutes, before serving. (The sauce can be refrigerated in an
airtight container for up to 1 day.)

CHICKEN TIKKA MASALA

IT IS SAID THAT IN THE 1970s, a plateful of
overcooked chicken tikka—boneless, skinless chicken
chunks, skewered and cooked in a tandoor oven—was
sent back to the kitchen of a London curry house by
a disappointed patron. The Bangladeshi chef acted
quickly, heating canned tomato soup with cream, sprinkling in Indian spices, and pouring it over the chicken
before sending it back out to the dining room. His
inventive creation of chicken tikka masala satisfied the
demanding customer, and as the recipe was perfected,
diners worldwide (including India) fell in love with the
tender, moist pieces of chicken napped in a lightly spiced
tomato cream sauce.

Despite its popularity in restaurants, recipes for
chicken tikka masala are absent from some of my favorite
Indian cookbooks, a testament to its lack of authenticity in Indian cuisine. The recipes I did find had much in
common. They all called for marinating chicken breast
chunks in yogurt, often for 24 hours, then skewering
them, kebab-style, for cooking. The tandoor oven was
replaced with a broiler or grill. The masala ingredients
varied, but the sauces were all as easy to prepare as a
quick Italian tomato sauce.

But the similarities didn't end there: In all of the recipes, the chicken was either mushy or dry and the sauces
were unbearably rich and overspiced. The good news is
that these problems did not seem impossible to over-
come, and the promise of a new way to cook chicken
with exotic flavors held plenty of appeal. I just needed a
decent recipe.

I wanted a four-season dish, so I chose the broiler
(not the grill). Cooking the boneless breasts whole and
cutting them into pieces only after they were broiled was
a step in the right direction. The larger pieces of chicken
didn't dry out as quickly under the searing heat of the
broiler. It also got rid of the fussy step of skewering raw,
slippery chicken pieces. But the chicken still wasn't juicy
enough.

The yogurt marinade is meant to tenderize the meat
and infuse it with the essence of spices and aromatics.
While overnight marinades did adequately flavor the

chicken, they also made the texture too tender, bordering on mushy. Given enough time, the lactic acid in yogurt breaks down the protein strands in meat.

I was tempted to abandon the yogurt marinade altogether. But yogurt is so fundamental to this recipe that excluding it felt like a mistake. Could I find a different way to use it? I considered salting, a technique we have used for steaks, roasts, chicken parts, and whole turkeys. Salt initially draws moisture out of protein; then the reverse happens and the salt and moisture flow back in. What if I salted the chicken first, then dipped it in yogurt right before cooking?

I rubbed the chicken with a simple mixture of salt and everyday spices common in Indian cookery: coriander, cumin, and cayenne. I waited 30 minutes, which gave me time to prepare the masala sauce, then dunked the chicken in yogurt and broiled it. The result was the best tikka yet—nicely seasoned with spices and tender but not soft. In just half an hour's time, the salt rub had done its job of flavoring the chicken and keeping it moist, and the yogurt mixture acted as a protective barrier, shielding the lean meat from the powerful heat of the broiler.

To encourage gentle charring on the chicken, I fattened up the yogurt with two tablespoons of oil. I also took advantage of the yogurt's thick texture, mixing it with minced garlic and freshly grated ginger. The aromatics clung to the chicken as it cooked, producing tikka that was good enough to eat on its own.

Masala means "hot spice," and the ingredients in a masala sauce depend largely on the whims of the cook. When the masala is to be served as part of chicken tikka masala, however, tomatoes and cream always form the base. Working with a mixture of sautéed aromatics (onions, ginger, garlic, and chiles) simmered with tomatoes (crushed tomatoes were favored over diced canned or fresh because of their smoother consistency) and cream, I tested combination after combination of spices. With plenty of winners and no real losers, I eventually settled on the simplest choice of all: commercial garam masala. Garam masala blends warm spices such as cardamom, black pepper, cinnamon, and coriander in one jar. To bloom the flavor of the garam masala, I sautéed it in oil along with the aromatics instead of adding it to the

simmering sauce, as some recipes suggest. There was just one problem: Many commercially prepared masala sauces contain tartrazine, an artificial coloring. Without it, the spices lent my sauce an ugly gray cast. A tablespoon of tomato paste easily restored a pleasant shade of red.

My recipe was getting rave reviews, but I had the nagging feeling that something was missing. I scanned through a flavor checklist in my mind: Salt? No. Acidity? No. Heat? No. Sweetness? That was it. I stirred a teaspoon of sugar into the pot, then another. My work was done, the sugar having successfully rounded out the flavors of the sauce. When I spooned the chicken over basmati rice and sprinkled it with cilantro, I knew I had a dish worth staying home for.

—REBECCA HAYS, *Cook's Illustrated*

CHICKEN TIKKA MASALA

SERVES 4 TO 6

This dish is best when prepared with whole-milk yogurt, but low-fat yogurt can be substituted. For a spicier dish, do not remove the ribs and seeds from the chile. If you prefer, substitute 2 teaspoons ground coriander, ¼ teaspoon ground cardamom, ¼ teaspoon ground cinnamon, and ½ teaspoon ground black pepper for the garam masala. The sauce can be made ahead, refrigerated for up to 4 days in an airtight container, and gently reheated before adding the hot chicken. Serve with basmati rice.

CHICKEN TIKKA

- ½ teaspoon ground cumin
- ½ teaspoon ground coriander
- ¼ teaspoon cayenne pepper
- 1 teaspoon salt
- 2 pounds boneless, skinless chicken breasts, trimmed
- 1 cup plain whole-milk yogurt (see note)
- 2 tablespoons vegetable oil
- 2 garlic cloves, minced
- 1 tablespoon grated fresh ginger

MASALA SAUCE

- 3 tablespoons vegetable oil
- 1 onion, minced (about 1 cup)

2 garlic cloves, minced

2 teaspoons grated fresh ginger

1 serrano chile, ribs and seeds removed, chile minced (see note)

1 tablespoon tomato paste

1 tablespoon garam masala (see note)

1 (28-ounce) can crushed tomatoes

2 teaspoons sugar

½ teaspoon salt

⅔ cup heavy cream

¼ cup chopped fresh cilantro

1. FOR THE CHICKEN: Combine the cumin, coriander, cayenne, and salt in a small bowl. Sprinkle both sides of the chicken with the spice mixture, pressing gently so the mixture adheres. Place the chicken on a plate, cover with plastic wrap, and refrigerate 30 to 60 minutes. In a large bowl, whisk together the yogurt, oil, garlic, and ginger; set aside.

2. FOR THE SAUCE: Heat the oil in a large Dutch oven over medium heat until shimmering. Add the onion and cook, stirring frequently, until light golden, 8 to 10 minutes. Add the garlic, ginger, chile, tomato paste, and garam masala; cook, stirring frequently, until fragrant, about 3 minutes. Add the tomatoes, sugar, and salt; bring to a boil. Reduce the heat to medium-low, cover, and simmer 15 minutes, stirring occasionally. Stir in the cream and return to a simmer. Remove the pan from the heat and cover to keep warm.

3. While the sauce simmers, adjust an oven rack to the upper-middle position (about 6 inches from the heating element) and heat the broiler. Using tongs, dip the chicken into the yogurt mixture (the chicken should be coated with a thick layer of yogurt) and arrange on a wire rack set in a foil-lined rimmed baking sheet or broiler pan. Discard the excess yogurt mixture. Broil the chicken until the thickest parts register 160 degrees on an instant-read thermometer and the exterior is lightly charred in spots, 10 to 18 minutes, flipping the chicken halfway through cooking.

4. Let the chicken rest 5 minutes, then cut into 1-inch chunks and stir into the warm sauce (do not simmer the chicken in the sauce). Stir in the cilantro, season to taste with salt, and serve.

GENERAL TSO'S CHICKEN

THERE'S A GOOD REASON General Tso's chicken, a Chinese restaurant staple named for an imposing 19th-century Hunan military officer, hardly resembles the fiery cuisine of that Chinese province—it was invented in New York City in the early 1970s. The appeal of this dish (which is also known as General Gau's, Cho's, and Tsang's) is easy to see: Boneless chicken pieces are marinated in soy sauce, battered, and deep-fried to a crispy brown before being coated with a sweet-hot sauce made with dried chiles, more soy, sugar, vinegar, hoisin sauce or tomato paste, garlic, and ginger.

I gathered several recipes and headed into the test kitchen to try to make a General Tso's chicken as good as my favorite Chinese restaurant's. My tasters and I were very disappointed with the results, as most of these recipes produced gummy, soggy chicken coated in a saccharine-sweet sauce.

I started on the ground floor, with the chicken. While many recipes use boneless thighs, in side-by-side tests my tasters preferred the milder white meat of boneless breasts. Marinating the chicken in soy sauce for 30 minutes added moisture and flavor, but the coating and frying were trickier. Most recipes call for the chicken to be dipped in egg whites, coated in cornstarch, and deep-fried. The resulting crust, though crispy when just out of the oil, was pale in color and quickly turned soft when sauced. Adding baking soda to the cornstarch helped the chicken brown better, and fortifying this mixture with flour kept the coating crisp, even when doused with sauce.

As for the sweet and spicy sauce, dried chiles were hard to find and had unpredictable levels of heat—some batches of sauce were searingly hot, others meek. Red pepper flakes were the perfect substitute, especially when I sautéed them with fresh garlic and ginger to round out their heat. My tasters never warmed to the tomato paste used in many recipes, but they loved sweet and spicy hoisin, a fermented bean sauce that's sometimes referred to as Chinese barbecue sauce. Soy sauce, white vinegar, and sugar enhanced the other flavors.

This sauce was so flavorful I wondered if it could double as a marinade in place of the traditional soy-only marinade. My tasters responded enthusiastically to the supercharged flavor of chicken marinated in the sweet and spicy sauce.

I thought my work was done, but then an astute colleague pointed out that the second batch of fried chicken (with 1½ pounds of chicken, my recipe required frying the meat in two batches) had a darker, crunchier crust than the first. I realized that when the first batch of chicken was passing through the cornstarch coating mixture, it was leaving traces of the marinade behind; those craggy pieces created extra crunch when they were picked up and fried on the second batch. Wanting to increase this effect, I added some marinade to the cornstarch mixture before I coated the first batch of chicken. The result was crunchy, flavorful coating on every piece. With that signature sweet and spicy flavor infused into the chicken, coating, and sauce, this was a General Tso's Chicken worth saluting.

—KELLEY BAKER, *Cook's Country*

GENERAL TSO'S CHICKEN

SERVES 4

In step 4, the fried chicken pieces can be held in a 200-degree oven for up to 30 minutes before being added to the sauce (if held any longer, they will lose their crispness). If the sauce is too thick in step 5, whisk in 1 tablespoon of water before adding the crispy chicken. Serve with Chinese-Style Sticky Rice (page 77).

MARINADE AND SAUCE

- ½ cup hoisin sauce
- ¼ cup white vinegar
- 3 tablespoons soy sauce
- 3 tablespoons sugar
- 2 tablespoons cornstarch
- 1½ cups water
- 4 boneless, skinless chicken breasts (about 1½ pounds), cut into 1-inch pieces
- 1 tablespoon vegetable oil
- 4 garlic cloves, minced
- 2 tablespoons grated fresh ginger
- ½ teaspoon red pepper flakes

COATING AND FRYING

- 3 large egg whites
- 1½ cups cornstarch
- ½ cup unbleached all-purpose flour
- ½ teaspoon baking soda
- 4 cups vegetable oil

1. FOR THE MARINADE AND SAUCE: Whisk the hoisin, vinegar, soy sauce, sugar, cornstarch, and water in a bowl. Combine 6 tablespoons of the hoisin mixture and the chicken in a zipper-lock bag; refrigerate 30 minutes.

2. Heat the oil in a large skillet over medium heat until shimmering. Cook the garlic, ginger, and pepper flakes until fragrant, about 1 minute. Add 2 cups of the hoisin mixture and simmer, whisking constantly, until dark brown and thickened, about 2 minutes. Cover and keep the sauce warm.

3. FOR COATING AND FRYING: Whisk the egg whites in a shallow dish until foamy. Combine the cornstarch, flour, baking soda, and remaining hoisin mixture in a second

GENERAL TSO'S CHICKEN

shallow dish until the mixture resembles coarse meal. Remove the chicken from the marinade and pat dry with paper towels. Toss half of the chicken with the egg whites until well coated, then dredge the chicken in the cornstarch mixture, pressing to adhere. Transfer the coated chicken to a plate and repeat with the remaining chicken.

4. Heat the oil in a Dutch oven over medium-high heat until the oil registers 350 degrees. (Use an instant-read thermometer that registers high temperatures or clip a candy/deep-fat thermometer onto the side of the pan.) Fry half of the chicken until golden brown, about 3 minutes, turning each piece halfway through cooking. Transfer the chicken to a paper towel–lined plate. Return the oil to 350 degrees and repeat with the remaining chicken.

5. TO SERVE: Warm the sauce over medium-low heat until simmering, about 1 minute. Add the crispy chicken and toss to coat. Serve.

SKILLET BAKED RICE WITH CHICKEN AND LEMONY MEATBALLS

THIS BAKED RICE DISH, known as *arroz con costra*, is Spain's answer to a skillet supper. An array of meats such as chicken and pork mingle with lemony meatballs and chickpeas amid red pepper–infused rice, topped off with an egg crust. This dish might sound odd, but its variety of textures and layers of flavor is ultimately very satisfying. With so many ingredients, especially the choice of meat (some recipes include rabbit, chicken, pork, sausages, and meatballs), I knew I had to narrow them down to a manageable few. And keeping in mind that this is a one-pan meal, I aimed to streamline the recipe where possible, without compromising flavor or texture.

To streamline ingredient options, I first cooked several batches using various combinations of meat. I felt rabbit wasn't worth the bother and chose chicken instead. Meatballs were a must—any batch made without them elicited thumbs-down from tasters. With these two decided, the dish had plenty of heft, so pork and sausages were struck from the list. As a compromise,

I chose to use ground pork in our meatballs and add bacon to the dish to further reinforce the rich pork flavor that is traditional.

For the meatballs, I combined ground pork with bread moistened with milk to ensure tenderness. I also added an egg for richness and structure. With the basic mixture in order, I turned my attention to flavor. Some recipes for this dish include ground almonds in the meatballs, and tasters loved the richness and texture they added. And lemon, in the form of grated lemon zest, added a citrusy kick that made these meatballs truly stand out. Minced fresh parsley was the only herb necessary for a hit of freshness.

With the meatball mixture formed into 1-inch balls ready to be browned, I focused on the chicken, bacon, and chickpeas. For convenience and ease, I chose boneless, skinless chicken breasts and canned chickpeas. Many authentic recipes call for slab bacon cut into chunks, but with the limited availability of slab bacon in our supermarkets I opted for thick-cut sliced bacon, cut into medium-small dice. With our meats (and meatballs) prepped and assembled, it was time to start cooking. First, I cooked the bacon and then browned the chicken in its rendered fat. The meatballs were browned next. I then removed all the meat to a plate to work on the rice.

Bomba and Calasparra are medium-grain Spanish rices traditional to this dish, although you can use another medium-grain rice. (Long-grain rice can also be used, although the dish's texture won't be as creamy.) I added the rice to the skillet, along with a garlicky red pepper puree (whirred together in a blender), which provided just enough liquid to scrape the fond from the bottom of the skillet. I then added more chicken broth to the skillet and nestled the browned meats and chickpeas into the rice, so that the whole dish could finish cooking together. At this point, I transferred the skillet to the oven for gentle, even cooking.

The final element to the dish, the egg crust, is somewhat like a souffléed omelet. Once the rice had absorbed the liquid, I removed the skillet from the oven and poured a mixture of whisked eggs and milk evenly over the top of the dish. Once back in the oven, the egg mixture puffs slightly and turns golden brown. At last—a skillet supper worth writing home about.

—SARAH WILSON, *America's Test Kitchen Books*

SKILLET-BAKED RICE WITH CHICKEN AND LEMONY MEATBALLS

SERVES 6

Spanish medium-grain rices such as Bomba or Calasparra are traditional in this dish, but you can substitute another medium-grain rice. Or, use an equal amount of long-grain rice, although the dish will be less creamy. An ovenproof 12-inch skillet is essential to this recipe.

MEATBALLS

- 1 slice high-quality white sandwich bread, torn into small pieces
- 1 tablespoon milk
- 8 ounces ground pork
- ¼ cup slivered almonds, chopped fine
- 3 tablespoons minced fresh parsley
- 1 large egg
- 1 tablespoon grated lemon zest
  Salt and pepper

RICE

- 6 tablespoons olive oil
- 3 garlic cloves
- 4 cups low-sodium chicken broth
- 1 jarred roasted red pepper (about 4 ounces), rinsed and patted dry
- 3 slices thick-cut bacon , cut into ½-inch cubes
- 12 ounces boneless, skinless chicken breasts, cut into 1-inch pieces
  Salt and pepper
- 2 cups medium-grain rice (see note)
- 1 cup canned chickpeas, drained and rinsed

EGG CRUST

- 7 large eggs
- ¼ cup whole milk
- 1 teaspoon salt

1. FOR THE MEATBALLS: In a large bowl, mash the bread and milk together to form a smooth paste. Add the pork, almonds, parsley, egg, lemon zest, ½ teaspoon salt, and ¼ teaspoon pepper and mix until uniform. Shape the mixture into 1-inch-round meatballs (1 generous tablespoon per meatball; you should have about

18 meatballs). Refrigerate the meatballs on a large platter or baking sheet until needed. (The meatballs can be prepared up to this point, covered, and refrigerated for up to 2 days.)

2. FOR THE RICE: Heat the oil and garlic cloves in a 12-inch ovenproof skillet over low heat until the garlic cloves are fragrant and softened, about 3 minutes. Using a slotted spoon, transfer the garlic to a blender (or food processor), leaving the oil in the skillet. Add ½ cup of the broth and the red pepper, and process until smooth, about 20 seconds; set aside.

3. Add the bacon to the skillet and cook until the fat is rendered and the bacon is browned, 4 to 6 minutes. Transfer to a medium bowl, leaving the fat in the skillet.

4. Pat the chicken dry with paper towels and season with salt and pepper. Heat the fat in the skillet over high heat until shimmering and brown the chicken on all sides, about 5 to 8 minutes. Using a slotted spoon, transfer the chicken to the bowl with the bacon, leaving the fat in the skillet.

5. Adjust an oven rack to the middle position and heat the oven to 350 degrees. Add the meatballs to the fat in the skillet and cook over medium-high heat until browned on all sides, 7 to 10 minutes. Using a slotted spoon, transfer the meatballs to the bowl with the chicken.

6. Add the rice and red pepper puree to the skillet and cook over medium heat, scraping up any browned bits, until the liquid reduces and the rice starts to look creamy, 2 to 3 minutes. Stir in the remaining 3½ cups broth, bring to a simmer, and cook, stirring often, until the rice swells and the liquid thickens, about 5 minutes. Stir in the reserved chicken, meatballs, and bacon, and the chickpeas and return to a simmer, stirring often. Transfer the skillet to the oven (do not cover) and continue to cook until the liquid is absorbed, 8 to 10 minutes.

7. FOR THE EGG CRUST: Meanwhile, whisk the eggs, milk, and salt together in a medium bowl. When the rice has absorbed most of the liquid in the skillet, pour the egg mixture evenly over the rice. Increase the oven temperature to 500 degrees and continue to bake until the top is browned, about 10 minutes. Remove the skillet from the oven and let it sit for 10 minutes before serving.

GRILLED LEMON-PARSLEY CHICKEN BREASTS

LEFT TO THEIR OWN DEVICES, boneless, skinless chicken breasts don't stand a chance on the backyard grill. Because they have no skin and little fat, untreated chicken breasts invariably turn out dry and leathery, with a mild—some might say bland—flavor. A quick and easy "solution" that millions of outdoor cooks commonly resort to is soaking the breasts in a store-bought marinade. Nice idea, but in a taste test we couldn't find one brand we could stomach, let alone recommend. Taking a few minutes to make my own marinade would yield better results.

I knew, though, that nothing else mattered if I couldn't produce perfectly grilled chicken breasts—moist, tender, and able to stand on their own flavor-wise. I didn't want to have to pound the chicken breasts or lose the tenderloin, which recipes usually recommend saving for "another use" (such as taking up permanent residence in the freezer). I wanted to keep things as simple as possible.

Cooked as most recipes suggest—that is, over a hot, single-level fire—the outsides of the breasts did what I expected: They turned into black shoe leather by the time the internal temperature reached 160 degrees. When cooked solely over indirect heat on the cooler side of a modified two-level fire (all the coals banked on one side of the grill), the interiors were noticeably moister, but the tough exteriors lacked color and true grilled flavor. Although searing the meat over the hotter side of the grill before moving it to the cool side to finish cooking offered a slight improvement, the chicken still wasn't where I wanted it to be.

Were my conventional methods holding me back? Several test cooks suggested using a "hobo pack": wrapping the chicken up into a tight foil pouch to keep it moist while cooked over the grill. But without periodically opening the foil and risking a steam burn, I had no way of knowing when the chicken was ready. And when it was, it still lacked grilled texture and flavor. I needed a gentler cooking method. Since stovetop poaching does wonders for chicken, I wondered if I could make it work on the grill. I placed a disposable aluminum pan filled halfway with chicken broth over the grates, let it come up to a simmer, and added the chicken breasts. Once they reached 140 degrees, I finished them on the hot grates. Tasters complained that the texture was neither poached nor grilled but "weird."

Had I gone too far? Maybe not if I looked at things from a different perspective. Suppose I inverted the disposable pan over the chicken to trap the heat? Creating less temperature fluctuation would allow the breasts to cook more evenly. I started by searing the breasts on the hot side of the grill before moving them to the cooler side, where I covered them with the pan (I flipped them halfway through). Tasters noticed improved flavor and texture that were closer to what I wanted, but still no cigar. What if I tried reversing the cooking order, starting the covered breasts on the cooler side of the grill until they were nearly done (140 degrees), then giving them a quick sear afterward? The result was perfectly cooked boneless, skinless chicken breasts.

I could now pursue my original goal of injecting some real flavor into the breasts by creating a marinade that could take the place of the test kitchen's standard practice of brining chicken. Lemon and garlic immediately came to mind, so I mixed together a combination of olive oil, lemon juice, garlic, salt, and pepper. I added some sugar to cut the acidity and help with browning. I quickly found that too much lemon juice caused the exterior of the chicken breasts to turn white. No good—I wasn't cooking seviche. But cutting the lemon juice down to 1 tablespoon made the interior bland and dry.

I knew from past brining experiences that without enough liquid, osmosis—the flow of water across a barrier from a place with a higher water concentration (the brine or marinade) to a place with a lower one (the chicken)—is inhibited. The liquid moving into the chicken should have carried with it some of the dissolved salt and flavor, but these molecules were too concentrated to penetrate the tissue. Adding 2 tablespoons of water diluted the concentration of salt and flavor molecules in the marinade enough for an exchange of dissolved molecules to flow in and out of the chicken. A 30-minute marinade did the trick.

I thought I was finished, but tasters weren't ready to let me off the hook. I wanted to keep things simple, but they wanted a sauce. No problem: I could use the ingredients from the marinade—plus chopped parsley for color and Dijon mustard for extra flavor and emulsification—to spoon over the cooked chicken. This new complementary sauce added more moisture as well as another layer of flavor. These grilled chicken breasts

were easy enough to make for myself on a weeknight (I could save the extras to top a salad the next day) and fancy enough to serve to guests at my next dinner party.
—SANDRA WU, *Cook's Illustrated*

CHARCOAL-GRILLED LEMON-PARSLEY CHICKEN BREASTS

SERVES 4

This chicken can be served with a simply prepared vegetable for a light dinner. It can also be used in a sandwich or tossed with greens for a salad. The chicken should be marinated no less than 30 minutes and no more than 1 hour.

    1   teaspoon Dijon mustard
    2   tablespoons fresh lemon juice
    6   tablespoons olive oil
    1   tablespoon minced fresh parsley
    1¼ teaspoons sugar
        Salt and pepper
    3   garlic cloves, minced
    2   tablespoons water
    4   boneless, skinless chicken breasts (6 to 8 ounces each), trimmed
        Disposable 13 by 9-inch aluminum roasting pan

1. Whisk together the mustard, 1 tablespoon of the lemon juice, 3 tablespoons of the oil, parsley, ¼ teaspoon of the sugar, ¼ teaspoon salt, and ¼ teaspoon pepper in a small bowl; set aside.

2. Whisk together the remaining 1 tablespoon lemon juice, remaining 3 tablespoons oil, remaining 1 teaspoon sugar, 1½ teaspoons salt, ½ teaspoon pepper, garlic, and water in a medium bowl. Place the marinade and chicken in a gallon-size zipper-lock bag and toss to coat; press out as much air as possible and seal the bag. Refrigerate 30 minutes, flipping the bag after 15 minutes.

3. Meanwhile, light a large chimney starter filled with charcoal briquettes (about 100 pieces) and allow it to burn until the charcoal is partially covered in a thin layer of fine gray ash, about 20 minutes. Spread the coals over half of the grill bottom, leaving the other half with no coals. Set the cooking grate over the coals, cover the grill, and heat until hot, about 5 minutes. Use a grill brush to scrape the grate clean. Lightly dip a wad

of paper towels in vegetable oil; holding the wad with tongs, wipe the cooking grate. The grill is ready when the side with the coals is medium-hot (you can hold your hand 5 inches above the grate for 3 to 4 seconds).

4. Remove the chicken from the bag, allowing the excess marinade to drip off. Place the chicken on the cooler side of the grill, smooth-side down, with the thicker side facing the coals. Cover with the disposable pan and cook until the bottom of the chicken just begins to develop light grill marks and is no longer translucent, 6 to 9 minutes. Using tongs, flip the chicken and rotate so that the thinner side faces the coals. Cover with the disposable pan and continue to cook until the chicken is opaque and firm to the touch and an instant-read thermometer inserted into the thickest part of the chicken registers 140 degrees, 6 to 9 minutes longer.

5. Move the chicken to the hotter side of the grill and cook, uncovered, until dark grill marks appear, 1 to 2 minutes. Using the tongs, flip the chicken and cook until dark grill marks appear and an instant-read thermometer inserted into the thickest part of the chicken registers 160 degrees, 1 to 2 minutes longer. Transfer the chicken to a cutting board, let rest, tented with foil, 5 minutes. Slice each breast on the bias into ¼-inch-thick slices and transfer to individual plates. Drizzle with the reserved sauce and serve.

VARIATIONS

GAS-GRILLED LEMON-PARSLEY CHICKEN BREASTS

Follow the recipe for Charcoal-Grilled Lemon-Parsley Chicken Breasts through step 2. Turn all the burners to high and heat with the lid down until very hot, about 15 minutes. Use a grill brush to scrape the grate clean. Lightly dip a wad of paper towels in vegetable oil; holding the wad with tongs, wipe the cooking grate. Leave the primary burner on high and turn off the other burner(s). Proceed with the recipe from step 4, grilling with the lid down and omitting the disposable pan. Increase the browning times in step 5 by 1 to 2 minutes.

GRILLED CHIPOTLE-LIME CHICKEN BREASTS

Follow the recipe for Grilled Lemon-Parsley Chicken Breasts, substituting lime juice for the lemon juice and using an extra teaspoon juice in the reserved sauce in step 1. Substitute 1 teaspoon minced chipotle chile in adobo sauce for the mustard and cilantro for the parsley. Proceed with the recipe as directed.

GRILLED ORANGE-TARRAGON CHICKEN BREASTS

Follow the recipe for Grilled Lemon-Parsley Chicken Breasts, substituting orange juice for the lemon juice and tarragon for the parsley. Add ¼ teaspoon orange zest to the reserved sauce in step 1. Proceed with the recipe as directed.

NOTES FROM THE TEST KITCHEN

GRILLING BONELESS, SKINLESS CHICKEN BREASTS

1. Place the chicken on the cool side of the grill, with the thicker ends facing the coals.

2. Cover the chicken with a disposable aluminum roasting pan; cook 6 to 9 minutes.

3. Flip the chicken so that the thinner ends face the coals and continue grilling, covered, 6 to 9 minutes.

4. Finish the chicken over the coals until dark grill marks appear, 1 to 2 minutes on each side.

CHICKEN TAGINE

A NORTH AFRICAN SPECIALTY, a tagine is an exotically spiced, assertively flavored stew slow-cooked in an earthenware vessel of the same name. Tagines can include all manner of meats, vegetables, and fruit, though our hands-down favorite combines chicken with richly flavored figs and fragrant honey.

While tagine is a hit in the test kitchen, it's not a dish I ever thought was suited for American home-cooking. Why? Most traditional recipes require time-consuming, labor-intensive cooking methods, a special pot (the tagine), and hard-to-find ingredients. Could I make this dish accessible to the home cook?

A little research proved that I wasn't the first to take a stab at making tagine more accessible. While most of the recipes I tried lacked the depth of an authentic tagine, they did hold promise, proving that a Western cooking method (braising in a Dutch oven) was a serviceable substitute for stewing in a tagine. I also discovered that the flavors we associated with Moroccan cooking weren't necessarily "exotic"—they were a strategic blending of fairly common ingredients.

Almost all of the recipes I collected specified a whole chicken, cut into pieces, and I soon found out why. Batches made entirely with white meat lacked the depth and character of those made with a blend of dark and white. But when I cooked the white and dark meat in the same way—simmered partially submerged in broth— the white meat turned dry and stringy.

Noting that the dark meat—drumsticks and thighs— takes roughly one hour of simmering time to become tender, I found that the breasts (cut in half for easier serving) took only 20 minutes. Giving the dark meat a 40-minute head start in the pot took care of the different cooking times and ensured that all of the chicken was perfectly cooked and ready at the same time.

Some recipes called for rubbing the chicken with lemon and salt and letting the meat marinate before cooking; others employed salt alone or salt blended with spices. I found that adding spices at this point resulted in a muddy-flavored broth.

Some carrots, a large sliced onion, and a few minced garlic cloves rounded out the basic flavors of the stew.

I was ready to tackle the defining ingredients: spices, figs, and honey. Many recipes called for a spice blend called *ras el-hanout*, which translates loosely as "top of the shop" and may contain upward of 30 spices. I experimented with a broad range of spices until I landed on a blend that was short on ingredients but long on flavor. Cumin and ginger lent depth, cinnamon brought warmth that tempered a little cayenne heat, and coriander boosted the stew's lemon flavor. Paprika added sweetness but, perhaps more important, colored the broth a deep, attractive red. Thoroughly blooming the spices in hot oil brought out the full depth of their flavors.

Finding the right fig proved harder than I had anticipated. Sweet, fresh, juicy figs were the obvious choice for the stew, but they are seasonal and thus a rarity at our local markets. Other options included dried figs, and, after tasting several varieties in the tagine, I concluded that Turkish figs were our favorite type. But when I added the dried figs to the stew too soon, they lost some of their deep flavor and turned mushy. Stirring in the figs just a few minutes before serving proved a better approach, as they retained their flavor and softened only slightly.

The lemon flavor in authentic tagines comes from preserved lemon, a long-cured Moroccan condiment that's hard to find outside of specialty stores. "Quick" preserved lemons can be produced at home in a few days, but I wanted to keep our recipe as simple as possible. Part tart citrus, part pickled brine, traditional preserved lemon has a unique flavor that's tough to imitate. So I chose not to try; instead, I aimed for a rich citrus back-note in the dish. I added a few broad ribbons of lemon zest along with the onions, and the high heat coaxed out the zest's oils and mellowed them. Adding a lemon's worth of juice just before serving reinforced the bright flavor.

For the honey, I found that adding it with the broth balanced things out. Chopped cilantro freshened the flavors of the stew, but I felt it still lacked a certain spark. A last-minute addition of raw garlic, finely chopped lemon zest, and a spoonful of honey seemed to clinch it, as the sharpness and sweetness brought out the best in each of the stew's components.

—MATTHEW CARD, *America's Test Kitchen Books*

CHICKEN TAGINE WITH DRIED FIGS AND HONEY

SERVES 4 TO 6

Use a vegetable peeler to remove wide strips of zest from the lemon before juicing it; be sure to trim away the bitter-tasting white pith from the zest before using. The breasts and thighs/drumsticks do not cook at the same rate; if using both, note that the breast pieces are added partway through the cooking time. Most markets carry three types of dried figs: Turkish, Calimyrna (a California-grown variety of Turkish Smyrna figs), and Mission. After trying each, we found that we preferred the softer, silkier texture of the Turkish or its close cousin, Calimyrna. Serve with couscous.

- 5   garlic cloves, minced
- 1¼ teaspoons sweet paprika
- ½   teaspoon ground cumin
- ¼   teaspoon ground ginger
- ¼   teaspoon ground coriander
- ¼   teaspoon ground cinnamon
- ⅛–¼ teaspoon cayenne pepper
- 3   (2-inch-long) strips lemon zest from 1 to 2 lemons (see note)
- 2   tablespoons honey
- 4   pounds bone-in, skin-on chicken pieces (split breasts cut in half, drumsticks, and/or thighs), trimmed
     Salt and pepper
- 2   tablespoons olive oil, plus more as needed
- 1   large onion, halved and sliced ¼ inch thick
- 2   carrots, peeled and cut crosswise into ½-inch-thick coins, very large pieces cut into half-moons (about 2 cups)
- 2   cups low-sodium chicken broth
- 1   cup dried Turkish figs, stemmed and quartered (see note)
- 2   tablespoons minced fresh cilantro
- 3   tablespoons fresh lemon juice

1. Combine 4 teaspoons of the garlic, the paprika, cumin, ginger, coriander, cinnamon, and cayenne together in a small bowl; set aside. Mince 1 strip of the lemon zest and mix with the remaining teaspoon of minced garlic and 1 tablespoon of the honey in a separate small bowl; set aside.

2. Pat the chicken dry with paper towels and season with salt and pepper. Heat the oil in a large Dutch oven over medium-high heat until just smoking. Brown half of the chicken on both sides, 5 to 8 minutes per side, reducing the heat if the pan begins to scorch. Transfer the chicken to a plate, leaving the fat in the pot. Return the pot to medium-high heat and repeat with the remaining chicken; transfer the chicken to the plate.

3. Pour off all but 1 tablespoon fat from the pot. (Add additional oil to equal 1 tablespoon, if needed.) Add the onion, the remaining 2 lemon zest strips, and ¼ teaspoon salt to the pot and cook over medium heat, stirring occasionally, until softened, 5 to 7 minutes. Stir in the garlic-spice mixture and cook until fragrant, about 30 seconds. Stir in the carrots, broth, and the remaining 1 tablespoon honey, scraping up any browned bits.

4. Nestle the chicken, along with any accumulated juices, into the pot and bring to a simmer. Cover, turn the heat to medium-low, and simmer until the chicken is fully cooked and tender, about 20 minutes for the breasts (160 to 165 degrees on an instant-read thermometer) or 1 hour for the thighs and drumsticks (170 to 175 degrees on an instant-read thermometer). (If using both white and dark meat of chicken, simmer the dark meat, the thighs and drumsticks, for 40 minutes before adding the breasts.)

5. Transfer the chicken to a serving dish, tent loosely with foil, and let rest while finishing the sauce. Skim as much fat as possible off the surface of the sauce, add the figs, and return to a simmer until the sauce has thickened slightly and the carrots are tender, 4 to 6 minutes. Stir in the garlic/lemon-zest/honey mixture, cilantro, and lemon juice. Season with salt and pepper to taste. Pour the sauce over the chicken and serve.

VARIATIONS

CHICKEN TAGINE WITH SAFFRON AND MINT

Follow the recipe for Chicken Tagine with Dried Figs and Honey, substituting ¼ teaspoon saffron threads, crumbled, for the cumin, ginger, coriander, cinnamon, and cayenne pepper, and orange zest for the lemon zest. Omit the honey. Substitute ½ cup Moroccan oil-cured olives, pitted, for the figs, mint for the cilantro, and ⅓ cup orange juice for the lemon juice.

CHICKEN TAGINE WITH DATES AND YOGURT

Follow the recipe for Chicken Tagine with Dried Figs and Honey, substituting pitted dates, halved, for the dried figs and ½ cup plain whole-milk yogurt for the lemon juice. Omit the honey.

NOTES FROM THE TEST KITCHEN

KEEPING YOUR KNIVES SAFE

If you store your knives loose in a drawer, you're putting the sharp edge of your blades—and your reaching hands—in danger. Blade sheaths are designed to protect against both risks, and we wondered if one style protected better and was easier to use than another. After some scary moments, we can safely say, yes. Our favorite model was the **Forschner Blade-Safe Case,** $4.95, for 8 to 10-inch knives. We liked its snap closure and its 2½-inch depth, which accommodated a variety of chef's, slicing, and paring knives. While it was a bit hard to open, it kept sharp blades safely covered.

FRENCH CHICKEN IN A POT

MY FIRST ENCOUNTER with *poulet en cocotte* occurred in a Parisian bistro. Recommended to me by the waiter as a specialty of the house, the dish featured a whole chicken baked with a smattering of root vegetables in a covered pot. At first glance, the chicken was nothing to rave about—it had pale, soft skin very unlike the crisp exterior of the roasted poultry I was used to—but its deep aroma was better than that of any roast chicken I could remember. My first bite confirmed that the dish was very special, indeed—the meat was incredibly tender and juicy, with a rich, soul-satisfying flavor.

As I continued to savor each bite, I began to think about the American obsession with crisp chicken skin. I'd certainly be willing to give up a crisp exterior if it meant I could have tender, succulent meat bursting with concentrated chicken flavor.

The basic method for poulet en cocotte is simple: place a seasoned chicken in a pot, scatter in a small handful of chopped vegetables, cover, and bake. Unlike

FRENCH CHICKEN IN A POT

braising, little to no liquid is added to the pot, resulting in a drier cooking environment. Many of the recipes I found called for auxiliary ingredients such as bacon, mushrooms, or tomatoes. But when I tried these extras, I found they served only to cover up what I was really after: great chicken flavor, pure and simple, like I'd had in Paris. I would stick with the chunks of potatoes, onions, and carrots I remembered from that meal.

Though most recipes did nothing to the chicken except season it before placing it in the pot to bake, I decided extra measures were necessary. I tried basting the bird, but going to the oven every 20 minutes was a hassle that had little impact on the taste. Next I tried lightly browning the top and bottom of the chicken on the stovetop before baking. Now I was getting somewhere—the flavor was beginning to deepen. But how could I get even more intense chicken flavor? I remembered earlier tests in which I'd added a splash of wine or broth to the pot at the start of cooking. These versions resulted in meat that was very juicy, but the steamier environment created a washed-out flavor. What if I actually decreased the humidity inside the pot?

Eager for answers, I prepped a new chicken and a batch of vegetables, drying each thoroughly with paper towels before adding them to the pot. This had little effect. And then it dawned on me that the vegetables were releasing liquid and making the pot too steamy. To create something close to a one-pot meal, I had been using more vegetables and in larger chunks than I remembered from my bistro dish. But I'd gladly sacrifice the veggies if it meant a bird with better flavor.

My next go-round, I cooked a chicken by itself save for a little oil to prevent it from sticking. This was a bird with great flavor that won over tasters and reminded me of my meal in Paris. And with no vegetables to soak them up, the flavorful juices remained in the pot. After defatting the liquid, I had a simple, richly flavored jus to accompany my chicken—a huge bonus. Still, the bird was not perfect. Tasters complained that the breast meat was a tad tough and fibrous, and I had to agree. I wondered what a lower oven temperature would do.

Setting up a half dozen chickens in pots, I tested a range of oven temperatures below 400 degrees. To account for pots with poorly fitting lids, I sealed each with foil before adding the top, ensuring that as much

of the chicken juices as possible would stay inside. Temperatures from 300 to 375 degrees produced better results, but even lower temperatures—between 250 and 300 degrees—yielded chickens with incredibly tender breast meat. And while these birds took much longer than average to cook (about an hour and a half—all walk-away time, mind you), tasters raved about the meat's rich, concentrated flavor, which was all thanks to the technique: slow-cooking the chicken in nothing more than its own juices.

The last cooking hurdle to clear was the matter of the dark meat not cooking quickly enough. By the time the breast meat was perfectly cooked to 160 degrees, the dark meat (which needs to be cooked to 175 degrees) still wasn't ready. Placing the oven rack on the lowest position, so it was closer to the heat source, combined with browning the dark meat for an extra minute or two, solved the problem.

With the cooking process under control, it was time to finesse the flavors. Two teaspoons of kosher salt was enough to season the chicken without making the jus too salty. And I discovered that I could get away with adding a small amount of potently flavored aromatic vegetables—chopped onion, celery, whole garlic cloves—to the pot. Lightly browning them along with the chicken helped wick away any excess moisture, and the caramelization added rich color and flavor to the jus. Stirring in a little fresh lemon juice to finish the jus brightened and balanced all of its flavors.

My French chicken in a pot will never place first in a beauty contest, if a browned roast bird is the standard. But its tender, juicy, intensely flavored meat is sure to be a winner every time.

—CHARLES KELSEY, *Cook's Illustrated*

FRENCH CHICKEN IN A POT

SERVES 4

The cooking times in the recipe are for a 4½ to 5-pound bird. A 3½ to 4½-pound chicken will take about an hour to cook, and a 5 to 6-pound bird will take close to 2 hours. This recipe requires a 5 to 8-quart Dutch oven with a tight-fitting lid to work. If using a 5-quart pot, do not cook a chicken larger than 5 pounds. Use the best chicken available, such as a Bell & Evans. If using a kosher chicken, reduce the kosher salt to 1 teaspoon (or

½ teaspoon table salt). If you choose not to serve the skin with the chicken, simply remove it before carving. The amount of jus will vary depending on the size of the chicken; season it with about ¼ teaspoon lemon juice for every ¼ cup.

1 **(4½ to 5-pound) roasting chicken, giblets discarded, wingtips tucked under the chicken (see note)**

2 **teaspoons kosher salt or 1 teaspoon table salt (see note)**

¼ **teaspoon pepper**

1 **tablespoon olive oil**

1 **small onion, chopped (about ½ cup)**

1 **celery rib, chopped**

6 **garlic cloves, peeled and trimmed**

1 **bay leaf**

1 **medium fresh rosemary sprig (optional)**

½–1 **teaspoon fresh lemon juice**

1. Adjust an oven rack to the lowest position and heat the oven to 250 degrees. Pat the chicken dry with paper towels and season with the salt and pepper. Heat the oil in a large Dutch oven over medium heat until just smoking. Add the chicken, breast-side down; scatter the onion, celery, garlic, bay leaf, and rosemary (if using) around the chicken. Cook until the breast is lightly browned, about 5 minutes. Using a wooden spoon inserted into the cavity of the bird, flip the chicken breast-side up and cook until the chicken and vegetables are well browned, 6 to 8 minutes. Remove the Dutch oven from the heat; place a large sheet of foil over the pot and cover tightly with the lid. Transfer the pot to the oven and cook until an instant-read thermometer registers 160 degrees when inserted in the thickest part of the breast and 175 degrees in the thickest part of the thigh, 80 to 110 minutes.

2. Transfer the chicken to a carving board, tent with foil, and rest 20 minutes. Meanwhile, strain the chicken juices from the pot through a fine-mesh strainer into a fat separator, pressing on the solids to extract the liquid; discard the solids (you should have about ¾ cup juices). Allow the liquid to settle 5 minutes, then pour into a saucepan and set over low heat. Carve the chicken, adding any accumulated juices to the saucepan. Stir the lemon juice into the jus to taste. Serve the chicken, passing the jus at the table.

NOTES FROM THE TEST KITCHEN

HOW TO MAKE FRENCH CHICKEN IN A POT

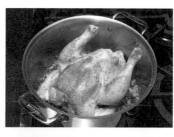

1. Sear the chicken on both sides to enhance flavor.

2. Cover the pot with foil before adding the lid to trap the chicken juices inside.

3. Cook the chicken at 250 degrees for 80 to 110 minutes.

4. Transfer the chicken to a carving board to rest so that the juices can redistribute.

IS A CLAY COOKER BETTER?

Clay pot roasters have garnered fame for coaxing remarkable flavor from few ingredients and minimal work: You simply soak the cooker in water for 15 minutes, add the raw ingredients, and place the covered pot in a cold oven. You then crank the heat up to at least 400 degrees. Theoretically, the steam released from the water-soaked clay and the gradual temperature increase should yield tender, juicy meat.

Can a clay cooker outperform a Dutch oven? To find out, we compared two batches of our French Chicken in a Pot, one cooked in a Dutch oven and the other adapted for a clay roaster. We preferred the Dutch oven method. Though both chickens cooked up equally moist and fall-apart tender, clay cookers are not stovetop-safe, so we needed to brown the chicken in a skillet before transferring it to the clay pot. We'll stick with the Dutch oven.

CRISP ROAST CHICKEN

WHEN IT COMES TO ROAST CHICKEN, we've always put juiciness and evenly cooked meat first and have simply made do with so-so skin. Could we develop a method that would deliver both juicy meat and really crisp, flavorful skin?

In order to isolate all the variables that contribute to skin crisping, I decided to work with skin alone. To this end, I removed the skin from a few dozen chickens. Because I knew that meat (or skin) can't brown until all its surface moisture has evaporated, I decided to see what would happen if I dried out the skin before cooking—a standard method in recipes for Peking duck. I stretched a piece of skin on a wire rack and left it overnight in the refrigerator to dry out. The next day, I roasted it side by side with a moist piece of skin I had just removed from the chicken. The difference was striking: After 20 minutes, the dried skin had turned golden brown and crisp, while the fresh skin remained pale and limp. Could I dry out the skin even more with salt? I rubbed a new piece with salt and again left it to dry overnight. The next day, the skin looked shriveled as it came out of the refrigerator but cooked up even crisper than before.

Encouraged by this success, I pushed on with my experiments. I recalled a technique I'd witnessed for cooking chicharrónes—crisp pieces of deep-fried pork belly—during a trip to South America. To get these pieces to crisp to the point of brittleness, they are coated with baking soda and allowed to rest before cooking. I got to thinking about why such a thing would work. The Maillard reaction that occurs during browning (in which proteins denature and recombine with sugar molecules to create hundreds of new flavor compounds) is speeded up in an alkaline environment. When I tried mixing baking soda into my salt rub, it left a bitter aftertaste. Baking powder (which is also alkaline, though less so than baking soda), however, produced a markedly crisper skin without otherwise announcing its presence. A bit of research revealed two more effects this leavening agent produces on chicken skin: Baking powder helps chicken skin dehydrate more readily, enhancing the effects of overnight air-drying. In addition, it reacts with the proteins in chicken skin to produce a crunchier texture.

I was ready to try this technique on the whole bird. I combined baking powder with salt and rubbed the mixture evenly over a chicken, then let it rest overnight in the refrigerator. The next day I put the chicken in the oven and cooked it according to our Easy Roast Chicken recipe. It was a qualified success: The skin came out much crisper than usual for this recipe, but it was nowhere near as crisp as it had been when I roasted it on its own.

As I cooked another chicken, I peered through the oven's glass door for ideas. Thirty minutes into the roast, I got an important clue: Juices and rendered fat were accumulating beneath the chicken's skin with nowhere to go, turning my once-dry skin wet and flabby. Clearly, for maximum crispness, the skin would need more than just an overnight rub to dry out; it would need a way for liquid to escape during cooking. For my next test, I used a metal skewer to poke about 20 holes in the fat deposits of each breast half and thigh, then proceeded to roast the chicken. The total amount of fat under the skin was now greatly reduced, but stubborn pockets remained, which led to flabby spots on the finished bird.

Would kicking up the oven temperature correct this? I upped it from 350 degrees to 450 for the majority of the cooking time, then increased it all the way to 500 for the last few minutes. I was worried that the high heat would dry out the breast, but I found that by starting the chicken breast-side down and flipping it midway through cooking, the breast meat was amply protected and cooked gently enough to come out tender and juicy.

And the skin? Better than before, but still not perfect. I was nearly tempted to remove the skin from the chicken and cook the two separately. Then I realized the answer: To allow fat to flow freely from my roasting chicken, I would have to separate the skin from the meat over much of the bird. For my next test, I carefully ran my hand between the meat and the skin all over the bird (making sure not to tear it). I also cut a few holes in the skin near the back of the bird to provide extra-large channels for the rendering fat to drip down and escape. When I pulled the chicken out, the proof was in the pan: a large amount of rendered fat, far more than before. There was so much fat that I couldn't help wondering if the meat would be less flavorful. But the skin was now better than anything I could have hoped for: deep, even brown and cracklingly crisp to the touch. And underneath this crisp exterior, the meat was tender, juicy, and flavorful to the bone.

—J. KENJI ALT, *Cook's Illustrated*

CRISP ROAST CHICKEN

SERVES 3 TO 4

For best flavor, use a high-quality chicken, such as one from Bell & Evans. Do not brine the bird; it will prohibit the skin from becoming crisp. The sheet of foil between the roasting pan and V-rack will keep the drippings from burning and smoking.

1   (3½ to 4½-pound) chicken, giblets discarded (see note)
1   tablespoon kosher salt or 1½ teaspoons table salt
1   teaspoon baking powder
½   teaspoon pepper

1. Place the chicken breast-side down on the work surface. Following the photos, use the tip of a sharp knife to make four 1-inch incisions along the back of the chicken. Using your fingers or the handle of a wooden spoon, carefully separate the skin from the thighs and breast. Using a metal skewer, poke 15 to 20 holes in the fat deposits on top of the breast halves and thighs. Tuck the wingtips underneath the chicken.

2. Combine the salt, baking powder, and pepper in a small bowl. Pat the chicken dry with paper towels and sprinkle all over with the salt mixture. Rub the mixture in with your hands, coating the entire surface evenly. Set the chicken breast-side up in a V-rack set on a rimmed baking sheet and refrigerate, uncovered, for 12 to 24 hours.

3. Adjust an oven rack to the lowest position and heat the oven to 450 degrees. Using a paring knife, poke 20 holes about 1½ inches apart in a 16 by 12-inch piece of foil. Place the foil loosely in a large roasting pan. Flip the chicken so that the breast side faces down, and set the V-rack in the roasting pan on top of the foil. Roast the chicken 25 minutes.

4. Remove the roasting pan from the oven. Using 2 large wads of paper towels, rotate the chicken breast-side up. Continue to roast until an instant-read thermometer inserted in the thickest part of the breast registers 135 degrees, 15 to 25 minutes.

5. Increase the oven temperature to 500 degrees. Continue to roast until the skin is golden brown and crisp and an instant-read thermometer inserted in the thickest part of the breast registers 160 degrees and 175 degrees in the thickest part of the thigh, 10 to 20 minutes.

6. Transfer the chicken to a cutting board and let rest, uncovered, for 20 minutes. Carve and serve immediately.

NOTES FROM THE TEST KITCHEN

ARE HIGH-PRICED CHICKENS WORTH THE SPLURGE?

We compared three specialty birds with our favorite supermarket chicken, from Bell & Evans ($2.29 per pound). Our favorite was the **D'Artagnan Heritage Blue Foot** bird ($20.99 for a 3¼ to 4-pound chicken) that tasters praised for its exceptional flavor and sweet, tender meatiness. Tasters also liked the chicken flavor of the **Joyce Foods Poulet Rouge Fermier du Piedmont** ($15 to $17 per bird depending on size). These winning birds bested the Bell & Evans chicken and are highly recommended—for those with unlimited chicken budgets.

CRISP-SKIN MAKEOVER

A little advance prep and a high-heat roast render our chicken skin so crisp it crackles.

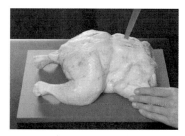

1. Incisions cut in the skin along the chicken's back create openings for the fat to escape.

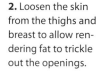

2. Loosen the skin from the thighs and breast to allow rendering fat to trickle out the openings.

3. Poke holes in the skin of the breast and thighs to create additional channels for fat and juices to escape.

4. Rub a mixture of baking powder and salt into the skin and air-dry the chicken in the refrigerator to help the skin crisp and brown.

ULTIMATE GARLIC ROAST CHICKEN

FLAVORING A ROAST CHICKEN with garlic sounds easy, but while testing existing garlic chicken recipes I learned that the garlic flavor was either nonexistent or so strong the birds were inedible. Some recipes sprinkled powdered or granulated garlic over the chicken, but the garlic burned and turned bitter by the time the meat was done. Garlic butter rubbed under the skin tasted steamed and overly pungent. I wanted the sweet, nutty garlic flavor to be strong but not overpowering, with a pan sauce that would enhance the garlic in the chicken.

I started by using the test kitchen's method for roasting a whole chicken: breast-side down, elevated on a wire rack, at 375 degrees for 35 minutes, then breast-side up at 450 degrees for another 30 to 40 minutes. This ensures that the dark meat has more exposure to high heat, promoting even cooking and crispier skin.

The most promising recipe from my initial tests included instructions for roasted garlic, which was pureed and rubbed over the skin of the chicken during the last 15 minutes of cooking. This chicken exhibited pronounced but not overpowering garlic flavor. Roasted garlic was a good place to start, but roasting whole heads of garlic takes over an hour in the oven. Was there a faster way to roasted garlic flavor?

The test kitchen sometimes cooks garlic in oil to tame its bite and draw out its sweetness. Following this path, I cut garlic cloves in half (to speed their cooking), covered the garlic with olive oil, and cooked them over low heat for just 10 minutes. Then I pureed the softened cloves and olive oil to a smooth paste and carefully slid the paste under the skin of the breast, thighs, and legs (the paste burned on the exterior of the bird) and rubbed some reserved garlic-infused oil over the outside of the chicken to help crisp the skin. The resulting chicken had moist meat, crisp skin, and a nice garlic punch.

In the test kitchen, we typically add water to the roasting pan to keep the drippings from scorching. I saw this as an opportunity to add more garlic puree and flavorful liquids (tasters liked chicken broth and white wine) that could cook down in the oven and form the foundation of a simple pan sauce. I was now making 8 tablespoons of garlic puree and needed 50 cloves of garlic. For cooks who can't imagine working with so much fresh garlic, I found that prepeeled garlic cloves were just fine in this recipe.

The pan sauce was perfumed with sweet garlic flavor, but the actual bits of garlic were pretty spent; I strained them out. A little cornstarch thickened the sauce, and butter and fresh tarragon added the finishing touches. I finally had a chicken and pan sauce with ultimate garlic flavor.

—DIANE UNGER, *Cook's Country*

ULTIMATE GARLIC ROAST CHICKEN
SERVES 3 TO 4

You will need one 8-ounce jar of peeled garlic cloves or 3 to 4 whole heads of garlic.

- 50 garlic cloves, peeled and halved (see note)
- ¼ cup extra-virgin olive oil
- 1 (3½ to 4-pound) chicken, giblets discarded
  Salt and pepper
- 1¾ cups low-sodium chicken broth
- ¾ cup dry white wine
- ½ cup plus 1 tablespoon water
- 1 teaspoon cornstarch
- 2 tablespoons cold unsalted butter, cut into pieces
- 2 teaspoons minced fresh tarragon

1. Adjust an oven rack to the lower-middle position and heat the oven to 375 degrees. Combine the garlic and oil in a small saucepan. Cook, covered, over medium-low heat, stirring occasionally, until the garlic is softened and straw-colored, 10 to 15 minutes. Reserve 1 tablespoon of the oil and transfer the remaining garlic mixture to a food processor; puree until smooth. Let cool.

2. Pat the chicken dry inside and out with paper towels. Combine ¼ cup of the garlic puree, ¼ teaspoon salt, and ½ teaspoon pepper in a small bowl. Tuck the wings under the chicken. Following the photos on page 219, spread the garlic mixture under the skin of the chicken and rub the reserved oil over the outside of the chicken. Tie the legs together with kitchen twine. Season the chicken with salt and pepper and arrange, breast-side down, on a V-rack set inside a roasting pan. Roast until just golden, about 35 minutes.

3. Remove the chicken from the oven and, using a wad of paper towels, flip the chicken breast-side up. Raise the oven temperature to 450 degrees. Whisk the broth, wine, ½ cup water, and remaining garlic puree in a measuring cup, then pour into the roasting pan. Return the chicken to the oven and roast until an instant-read thermometer inserted in the thickest part of the breast registers 160 degrees and the thickest part of the thigh registers 175 degrees, 30 to 40 minutes. Transfer the chicken to a cutting board and let rest 20 minutes.

4. Meanwhile, transfer the pan juices and any accumulated chicken juices to a saucepan; skim the fat. Whisk the remaining 1 tablespoon water and cornstarch in a small bowl, then add to the saucepan. Simmer until the sauce is slightly thickened, about 2 minutes. Whisk in the butter, then strain into a serving bowl. Stir in the tarragon and season to taste with salt and pepper. Carve the chicken and serve, passing the sauce at the table.

NOTES FROM THE TEST KITCHEN

ROASTED GARLIC THREE WAYS
Getting great roasted garlic flavor into the chicken and pan sauce meant cooking halved garlic cloves in oil until their flavor had mellowed—and enhanced the oil. The mixture was then pureed (reserving some of the oil) to create a paste. Here's how we flavored the chicken and sauce with those elements.

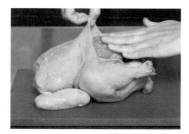

1. Use your hands to evenly distribute the garlic puree under the skin of the chicken. Be sure that the puree coats not only the breast meat but the thigh and leg meat as well.

2. For garlicky, crisp skin, rub the entire exterior of the chicken, front and back, with the reserved garlic oil.

3. Add the reserved garlic puree (along with chicken broth and white wine) to the roasting pan halfway through cooking; this will serve as the foundation for the pan sauce.

EASY ROAST TURKEY BREAST

ROASTING A WHOLE TURKEY BREAST should be easy. The biggest challenge with the holiday bird is that the dark meat takes longer to cook than the white meat; this is neatly avoided by the all-white breast. And the stuffing, which slows down the whole process and makes it much more cumbersome, is a nonissue. You have no choice but to bake the holiday dressing separately. So why have I had such trouble with this seemingly easy recipe?

I like turkey and roast a whole breast several times a year. Sometimes the meat is moist and juicy, but more often than not the lean white meat comes out chalky and dry. The layers closest to the skin get especially parched as the meat near the bone takes its time coming up to temperature, and the skin is never as crisp as I'd like.

Over the years, the test kitchen has discovered that brining (soaking in a saltwater solution for several hours) makes turkey moister. The salt changes the protein structure in the meat and helps it hold on to more moisture. Brining is especially helpful with delicate white meat, so it came as no surprise that brined turkey breasts were clearly juicier than unbrined turkey breasts. But brining is not enough. The right roasting technique is a must, too.

Thinking that a turkey breast is little more than a giant chicken breast, I looked to a method the test kitchen developed several years ago for roasting whole bone-in, skin-on chicken breasts. For this recipe, the skin on the whole chicken breasts is loosened and the meat is rubbed with softened butter. Loosening the skin helps it to lift and separate from the meat, which promotes even browning and creates crisper skin. The fat in the butter also keeps the breast meat moist and adds much-needed flavor. We found that roasting the chicken breasts skin-side up in a 450-degree oven delivered excellent results. Could I apply the same technique to a whole turkey breast that weighed four times as much?

I brined a turkey breast, loosened the skin, rubbed the meat with butter, and set the breast skin-side up in a V-rack placed inside a roasting pan. (While chicken breasts can be roasted on a broiler-pan top, larger cuts like a bone-in turkey breast do better in a V-rack, which promotes better air circulation.) At 450 degrees, the skin scorched and the meat was much too dry. I tried the opposite approach and reduced the oven temperature to 325 degrees. After a couple of hours in the oven, my turkey breast emerged with flabby, straw-colored skin—certainly not the look I was going for. The meat, however, was a different story: It was tender and flavorful.

Desiring browner, crisper skin meant trying higher oven temperatures. I hoped that starting the turkey breast out at 325 degrees would conserve moisture in the meat and that a last-minute blast of heat would crisp the skin. But it was difficult to know when to crank up the heat. More worrisome, I found it hard to control the amount of browning, and the meat had a slightly leathery exterior. Not the best results, but I felt like I was getting somewhere using dual oven temperatures.

After testing several more oven temperature combinations, I finally found the best method: Starting the turkey breast in a 425-degree oven for the first half hour of cooking and then reducing the heat to 325 degrees for the remaining hour. The initial blast of heat kick-starts the browning, ensuring the skin is beautifully golden by the end of the cooking time. And the low temperature gently finishes the turkey meat, helping it stay moist and tender.

One minor problem, though: During the high-heat roasting, the minimal drippings in the pan burned, smoking up the oven and, eventually, the test kitchen. A quick solution was to add water to the roasting pan before cooking. A cup was the perfect amount; any more and too much steam formed, prohibiting parts of the skin from browning properly.

I had one last round of tests to conduct. I was adding salt and pepper to the 4 tablespoons of butter I was rubbing over the turkey meat, and I wondered what other flavors might work. Fresh herbs, citrus zest, garlic, and even ground spices were easy to incorporate into the softened butter mixture and gave the turkey a significant flavor boost. In order to make sure these flavors didn't overwhelm small patches of the turkey breast, I found it imperative to massage the butter evenly into the meat. Dividing the butter mixture in half and working each portion over one side of the breast guaranteed that the butter and seasonings were evenly applied.

My final recipe isn't any harder to make than the less successful recipes I had tried in my research. The butter rub and dual oven temperatures, though, ensure that the skin is really crisp and the meat flavorful and moist. This is a turkey breast that I can now look forward to making several times a year.

—CHARLES KELSEY, *Cook's Illustrated*

EASY ROAST TURKEY BREAST

SERVES 8 TO 10

This recipe works equally well with any type of turkey breast. We recommend brining (see page 221) if using a natural turkey breast (no salt added). Using a kosher turkey breast (soaked in saltwater during processing) or self-basting turkey breast (injected with salt and water) eliminates the need for brining. The ingredient list on the turkey breast's package will say whether it's been treated with salt. If brining the turkey, omit the salt from the recipe. If the breast has a pop-up timer, do not remove it. Just ignore it (they pop too late) and follow the times and temperatures in the recipe. A turkey breast doesn't yield much in the way of drippings, so a classic pan gravy recipe is not an option.

- 4 tablespoons (½ stick) unsalted butter, at room temperature
- ¾ teaspoon salt
- ¼ teaspoon pepper
- 1 (6 to 7-pound) whole, bone-in, skin-on turkey breast, trimmed and patted dry with paper towels (see note)
- 1 cup water

1. Adjust an oven rack to the middle position and heat the oven to 425 degrees. Mix the butter, salt, and pepper in a medium bowl with a rubber spatula until thoroughly combined. Carefully separate the turkey skin from the meat over the breast; avoid breaking the skin.

2. Work the butter mixture under the skin on both sides of the breast and rub the skin of the turkey to evenly distribute the butter over the breast. Spray a V-rack with vegetable oil spray and set inside a large roasting pan. Place the turkey in the rack with the skin side facing up; pour the water into the roasting pan.

3. Roast the turkey 30 minutes. Reduce the oven temperature to 325 degrees. Continue to roast the turkey until an instant-read thermometer inserted into the thickest part of the breast registers 160 degrees, about 1 hour longer. Transfer the turkey to a carving board and let rest 20 minutes. Carve and serve.

VARIATIONS

EASY ROAST TURKEY BREAST WITH LEMON AND THYME

Follow the recipe for Easy Roast Turkey Breast, adding 3 minced garlic cloves, 2 tablespoons minced fresh thyme, and 1 teaspoon grated lemon zest to the butter mixture in step 1.

EASY ROAST TURKEY BREAST WITH ORANGE AND ROSEMARY

Follow the recipe for Easy Roast Turkey Breast, adding 3 minced garlic cloves, 1 tablespoon minced fresh rosemary, 1 teaspoon grated orange zest, and ¼ teaspoon red pepper flakes to the butter mixture in step 1.

EASY ROAST TURKEY BREAST WITH SOUTHWESTERN FLAVORS

Follow the recipe for Easy Roast Turkey Breast, adding 3 minced garlic cloves, 1 tablespoon minced fresh oregano, 2 teaspoons ground cumin, 2 teaspoons chili powder, ¾ teaspoon cocoa powder, and ½ teaspoon cayenne pepper to the butter mixture in step 1.

NOTES FROM THE TEST KITCHEN

HOW TO BRINE A TURKEY BREAST

A natural turkey breast works just fine for this recipe; however, to ensure that the meat turns out moist and well seasoned, we suggest that you brine a natural turkey breast following the directions below. Do not brine a kosher or self-basting turkey breast.

Dissolve ½ cup of table salt (or ¾ cup of kosher salt) in 4 quarts of cold water in a large container; submerge the turkey breast in the brine, cover it with plastic wrap, and refrigerate it for 3 to 6 hours. (Do not brine the turkey breast any longer, or it will be too salty.) Rinse the turkey breast under cold water and dry it thoroughly with paper towels before proceeding with the recipe.

CARVING A TURKEY BREAST

1. Run a chef's knife along one side of the breastbone. Use your other hand (with a towel) to pry the entire breast half from the bone while cutting.

2. Slice the breast meat on the bias. Repeat the process with the meat on the other side of the breastbone.

DOUBLE-DUTY THERMOMETER

Holiday cooking means constantly opening your refrigerator and freezer, which can cause the temperatures to rise. To monitor the safety of our cold storage, we use refrigerator and freezer thermometers. We recently tested six models and ranked the **Maverick Cold Check Digital Refrigerator/Freezer Thermometer,** $34.95, first. Though relatively pricey, it is the only model that simultaneously monitors the temperature in both the freezer and refrigerator, thanks to a 75-inch wire probe that runs from the display (which you keep in the refrigerator) to the freezer.

A GOOD ROASTING PAN IS ESSENTIAL

We think a quality roasting pan is a key piece of kitchen equipment. The pan must be sturdy enough to support the weight of a large bird and must have handles that are easily accessible and a bottom that is heavy enough to prevent burning. We tested models ranging in price from $8.99 to $180. Our favorite was the **Calphalon Contemporary Stainless Steel Roasting Pan,** $100. It had all the features of more expensive pans (including its own V-rack), was hefty enough for even the biggest bird, easy to get in and out of the oven, and widely available.

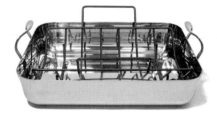

SEAFOOD

POACHED SALMON

SEEMINGLY THE IDEAL STOVETOP RECIPE, poached salmon is fast, requires just one pot, and there's no splattering oil to burn yourself on or strong odors to permeate the house. And, when done right, the fish has an irresistibly supple, velvety texture delicately accented by the flavors of the poaching liquid. Add a simple sauce and the dish is even more flavorful. But when done wrong, which seems to be the usual case, the fish has a dry, chalky texture and washed-out taste that not even the richest sauce can redeem.

The classic French method for poaching salmon is to simmer an entire side of the fish gently in a highly flavored broth called *court-bouillon*. The salmon is cooled and served cold, often as part of a buffet. But I wasn't looking for a make-ahead method for cold salmon to serve a crowd. I wanted to produce perfectly cooked, individual portions of hot salmon and a sauce to go with them—all in under half an hour.

My first objective was to achieve great texture and flavor in the salmon itself; after that I'd focus on the sauce. First consideration: the cooking liquid. A classic court-bouillon is made by filling a pot with water, wine, herbs, vegetables, and aromatics, then boiling it all very briefly (court-bouillon literally means "short-boiled stock"). After straining the solids, you're left with an intensely flavored liquid in which to poach your fish. The broth's strong flavors are absorbed by the fish, which helps compensate for all the salmon flavor that leaches out into the liquid.

This method certainly did produce flavorful results. However, there was just one annoying little problem: To cook dinner for four, I'd just prepped a slew of ingredients (onions, carrots, celery, leeks, parsley) and bought still others (bay leaves, tomato paste, peppercorns, and white wine), only to dump them and the stock down the drain at the end. This waste isn't bothersome when you're preparing a side of fish to feed a group, but it's hardly worth it for a simple Tuesday night supper at home.

What if I used less liquid? At the very least, this would mean I'd have to buy and prep (and waste) fewer ingredients, plus using less liquid would likely mean less flavor leaching out of the salmon. I poached the salmon in just enough liquid to come half an inch up the side of the fillets. Regarding flavor only, this was my most successful attempt yet. In fact, the salmon retained so much of its own natural flavor that I wondered if I could cut back even more on the quantity of vegetables and aromatics I was using in the liquid. A couple of shallots, a few herbs, and some wine proved to be all I needed. But nailing the flavor issue brought another problem into sharp relief—dry texture.

Like all animal flesh, salmon has a certain temperature range at which it is ideal to eat. The proteins in salmon begin coagulating at around 120 degrees, transforming it from translucent to opaque. At around 135 degrees, the flesh is completely firm and will start to force moisture out from between its protein fibers. Any higher, and the salmon becomes dry as cardboard (like a well-done steak). I had been using an instant-read thermometer to ensure that the centers of my salmon fillets were exactly 125 degrees (medium) before removing them from the poaching liquid. But testing the temperature of various parts of the fillet showed that by the time the center was 125 degrees, most of the other thinner sections registered higher temperatures. I was concerned that the texture of these thinner areas would be dry, but found their higher fat content kept them moist.

With high cooking temperatures, the exterior of a piece of meat will cook much faster than the interior. This is great when pan-searing the skin of a salmon fillet or a beef steak, when you want a browned exterior and rare interior, but it's no good for poaching, where the goal is to have an evenly cooked piece all the way through. The most obvious solution was to lower the cooking temperature. For the next batch, I placed the salmon in the cold pan with poaching liquid and brought the liquid barely up to a simmer, then reduced the heat to its lowest possible setting and covered the pan until the salmon cooked through. Then I realized a new problem that I'd unwittingly introduced when I reduced the amount of cooking liquid: Since the salmon wasn't totally submerged in liquid, it relied on steam to deliver heat and flavor. At such a low temperature, even with a lid on, not enough steam was being created to efficiently cook the parts of the fish sticking out above the liquid. Was there a way to create more steam without increasing the temperature?

Thinking back to high school chemistry, I remembered that adding alcohol to water lowers its boiling temperature: The higher the concentration of alcohol, the more vapor will be produced as the liquid is heated.

More vapor, in turn, means better heat transfer, which leads to faster cooking, even at temperatures below a simmer. I also knew that alcohol could increase the rate at which proteins denature. Therefore, if I used more alcohol in the cooking liquid, it would theoretically be able to cook the fish faster and at a lower temperature. I increased the ratio of wine to water, going from a few tablespoons of wine to ½ cup. Acid also helps fish protein denature (in addition to improving flavor), so I squeezed a little lemon juice into the liquid before adding the salmon. My hopes were high as I opened the lid to a burst of steam and salmon that appeared perfectly cooked. Everything was fine until my fork got to the bottom of the fillet. Even though the top, sides, and center were now just right, the bottom, which had been in direct contact with the pan, was still overcooked.

I knew I wasn't the first person to ever have this problem—in fact, a solution already exists: a fish poacher. This specialized pan comes with a perforated insert that elevates the fish, allowing it to cook evenly on all sides. But I wasn't about to go out and buy an expensive new pan for a technique that I'd only use a few times a year. Then I realized that I had the solution literally in my hand. Instead of squeezing lemon juice into the poaching liquid, I sliced the fruit into thin disks and lined the pan with them. By resting the salmon fillets on top of the lemon slices, I was able to insulate the fish from the pan bottom while simultaneously flavoring it. This time the salmon came out evenly cooked all the way through.

It was time to focus on the sauce. Ticking off the list of ingredients in my super-concentrated poaching liquid, I realized I had the foundation of a *beurre blanc*. (This classic French sauce is made by reducing wine flavored with vinegar, shallots, and herbs and then finishing it with butter.) I would need only to reduce my poaching liquid and whisk in the butter. But since a few tablespoons of butter per serving would push this dish out of the "everyday" category, I developed a vinaigrette-style variation in which I used olive oil instead of butter; tasters liked the oil version as much as the original.

This salmon-poaching method guarantees moist and delicately flavored fish and produces just the right amount of poaching liquid for a great-tasting sauce—all without boiling away any flavor or pouring ingredients down the drain.

—J. KENJI ALT, *Cook's Illustrated*

POACHED SALMON WITH HERB AND CAPER VINAIGRETTE

SERVES 4

If a skinless whole fillet is unavailable, follow the recipe as directed with a skin-on fillet, adding 3 to 4 minutes to the cooking time in step 2. Remove the skin after cooking. This recipe will yield salmon fillets cooked to medium. If you prefer rare salmon (translucent in the center), reduce the cooking time by 2 minutes, or until the salmon registers 110 degrees in the thickest part.

- 1 (1¾ to 2-pound) skinless salmon fillet, about 1½ inches at the thickest part (see note)
- 2 lemons
- 2 tablespoons minced fresh parsley, stems reserved
- 2 tablespoons minced fresh tarragon, stems reserved
- 1 large shallot, minced (about 4 tablespoons)
- ½ cup dry white wine
- ½ cup water
- 2 tablespoons capers, rinsed and roughly chopped
- 1 tablespoon honey
- 2 tablespoons extra-virgin olive oil
  Salt and pepper

1. Following the photos on page 230, use a sharp knife to remove any whitish fat from the belly of the fillet and cut the fillet into 4 equal pieces.

2. Cut the top and bottom off 1 lemon; cut into 8 to ten ¼-inch-thick slices. Cut the remaining lemon into 8 wedges and set aside. Arrange the lemon slices in a single layer across the bottom of a 12-inch skillet. Scatter the herb stems and 2 tablespoons of the minced shallots evenly over the lemon slices. Add the wine and water.

3. Place the salmon fillets in the skillet, skinned-side down, on top of the lemon slices. Set the pan over high heat and bring the liquid to a simmer. Reduce the heat to low, cover, and cook until the sides are opaque but the center of the thickest part is still translucent (or until an instant-read thermometer inserted in the thickest part registers 125 degrees), 11 to 16 minutes. Remove the pan from the heat and, using a spatula, carefully transfer the salmon and the lemon slices to a paper towel–lined plate and tent loosely with foil.

4. Return the pan to high heat and simmer the cooking liquid until slightly thickened and reduced to 2 tablespoons, 4 to 5 minutes. Meanwhile, combine the remaining 2 tablespoons shallots, chopped herbs, capers, honey, and oil in a medium bowl. Strain the reduced cooking liquid through a fine-mesh strainer into the bowl with the herb-caper mixture, pressing on the solids to extract as much liquid as possible. Whisk to combine; season with salt and pepper to taste.

5. Season the salmon lightly with salt and pepper. Using a spatula, carefully lift and tilt the salmon fillets to remove the lemon slices. Place the salmon on a serving platter or individual plates and spoon the vinaigrette over the top. Serve, passing the reserved lemon wedges separately.

VARIATION

POACHED SALMON WITH DILL AND SOUR CREAM SAUCE

Follow the recipe for Poached Salmon with Herb and Caper Vinaigrette through step 3, substituting 8–12 dill stems for the parsley and tarragon stems. Strain the cooking liquid through a fine-mesh strainer into a medium bowl; discard the solids. Return the strained liquid to the skillet. Omit the capers, honey, and olive oil and whisk 1 tablespoon Dijon mustard and the remaining 2 tablespoons shallots into the liquid. Simmer over high heat until slightly thickened and reduced to 2 tablespoons, 4 to 5 minutes. Whisk in 2 tablespoons sour cream and the juice from 1 reserved lemon wedge; simmer for 1 minute. Remove from the heat; whisk in 2 tablespoons unsalted butter and 2 tablespoons minced fresh dill. Season with salt and pepper to taste. Continue with the recipe from step 5, spooning the sauce over the salmon before serving.

NOTES FROM THE TEST KITCHEN

THE BENEFITS OF BELLY FAT
A center-cut salmon fillet typically tapers down on one side to the fattier belly of the fish. The belly's fattiness helps keep this section of the fish moist, despite its thinner profile. The belly area is sometimes covered with a chewy white membrane, which should be trimmed away before cooking. Finally, if needed, neaten up any ragged edges that can dry out and fray during cooking.

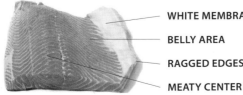

WHITE MEMBRANE

BELLY AREA

RAGGED EDGES

MEATY CENTER

MISO-GLAZED SALMON

ORIGINALLY A METHOD OF PRESERVATION before refrigeration, fish marinated in *miso* (a fermented bean paste with a salty, rich, savory flavor) has long been a part of Japanese cuisine. And its salty-sweet flavor has made it a popular addition to restaurant menus worldwide. Traditionally, after an extensive marinade (usually a blend of white miso paste, sugar, and rice wine), the fish is then grilled or broiled to produce a dark brown crust and a candylike coating of nutty miso flavor. The texture of the fish becomes firm and pleasantly chewy. The miso and sugar essentially cure the fish, with the miso lending saltiness and the sugar sweetness. Determined to get to the bottom of this centuries-old technique-turned-recipe, I headed into the kitchen with two goals: to make the preparation balanced in both saltiness and sweetness, and to replicate the expected firmness of the finished fish, something that only comes from days of curing. But could I do it without leaving the fish in the marinade for three days—the typical time cited in recipes uncovered in my research?

To start, I chose salmon for its high fat content and widespread availability. But before I invested the time marinating the fish, I needed an appropriate marinade. After reviewing several recipes from Japanese cookbooks, I built a simple recipe of white miso, sugar, and sake. Whisking all the marinade ingredients together, I submerged my salmon fillets in the mixture for an hour, then cooked them and tasted.

The results were disappointing. The salmon was more sweet than salty and the flavor was largely unbalanced. I thought about decreasing the sugar and increasing the miso to boost the saltiness. But upon closer inspection, I noticed that there were two problems with my initial recipe. First off, I had inadvertently purchased "light" miso from a local natural foods market. Light miso is an American product that is meant as a low-sodium substitute to authentic miso. It just tastes like salt, without the maltiness and nuttiness of authentic Japanese miso. The next issue stemmed from the viscosity of the marinade. About the consistency of heavy cream, it just wasn't thick enough to cling to the fish and have much of an impact.

Going back into the kitchen with the right miso (purchased from an Asian market), I tweaked amounts of all the ingredients to yield a thicker marinade. The results?

Fish with a wonderful salty, sweet flavor. I next turned my attention to the marinade time.

I began testing the marinade times in one-hour increments up to 12 hours, and then skipped to one day, two days, and three days. But as I tested these traditional two- and three-day marinating times, I felt that this was just not practical. Instead I decided to focus on two marinating times. One, a minimum duration for marinating the fish—long enough to flavor the fish adequately, and two, a modified traditional marinade for when you want to take the time to impart more flavor.

Salmon that was cured for only one hour had little marinade flavor. While the crust of the fish was very flavorful, the interior was largely bland. My testing eventually led me to a minimum marinade time of five hours. This was enough to flavor the interior of the salmon and firm it up as well. And for a longer marinade time, 24 hours or one full day produced fish with deep, slightly sweet flavor, and tasters loved the way the fish firmed up once cooked.

Creating some flavorful caramelization on the flesh of the fish was a key goal, so I focused right away on high-heat cooking. Grilling was doomed from the start. Because of the high sugar content of the marinade, the fish stuck to the grill and broke apart when I tried to flip it.

I next tried roasting, but this method resulted in pale fish that tasted dry. But with broiling, I met with success. The salmon browned nicely under the intense broiler heat and, as a result, also developed better flavor. Best of all, the fish remained juicy and moist.

—BRYAN ROOF, *America's Test Kitchen Books*

MISO-GLAZED SALMON

SERVES 4

Although white miso is preferred here, you can substitute brown, red, barley, or brown rice miso; do not use "light" miso because its flavor is too mild to impart sufficient flavor to the fish. When removing the salmon from the marinade, do not wipe away any excess marinade clinging to the fish; the excess marinade will turn to a sweet-salty crust during cooking. If portions of the salmon begin to burn while cooking, shield those areas from the heat with aluminum foil. Cod or mackerel can be substituted for the salmon.

1 (1¾ to 2-pound) skin-on salmon fillet, about 1½ inches at the thickest part
1 cup white miso (see note)
1 cup sugar
½ cup sake

1. Following the photos on page 230, use a sharp knife to remove any whitish fat from the belly of the fillet and cut the fillet into 4 equal pieces.

2. Whisk the miso, sugar, and sake together in a medium bowl to dissolve the sugar and miso (the mixture will be quite thick). Gently lay the salmon in a 1-gallon zipper-lock bag and pour the marinade into the bag. Seal the bag, pressing out as much air as possible, and refrigerate for at least 5 hours and up to 24 hours, flipping the bag occasionally to ensure that the fish marinates evenly. (Do not overmarinate.)

3. Adjust an oven rack 6 inches from the broiler element and heat the broiler. Line a broiler pan bottom with foil and top with the slotted broiler pan top. Remove the fish from the marinade, lay on the broiler pan top skin-side down, and spoon 1 tablespoon of the marinade out of the bag over each fillet; discard the remaining marinade.

4. Broil the salmon until nicely browned and the flesh is opaque and flakes apart when gently prodded with a paring knife, 6 to 9 minutes. Transfer the salmon to a platter and serve.

OVEN-ROASTED SALMON

STEAMING AND POACHING are two of the best methods for achieving the silky, almost buttery, texture that is salmon's signature trait; pan-searing is the best way to exploit its high fat content to produce a flavorful, caramelized crust. But what if you want both qualities—moist, succulent flesh inside, and, if not a crust, at least a contrasting texture on the outside? Recipes for roasting salmon promise just that.

I knew that roasting at a high temperature (from 400 to 475 degrees) can create browning on the exterior of the fish, but by the time that point is reached, you've got a well-done piece of salmon. Slow-roasting at a very gentle oven temperature, between 250 and 300 degrees, seemed like a better place to start. To ensure uniform pieces that would cook evenly, I bought a whole center-cut fillet and divided it into four pieces that I cooked at 275 degrees for about 20 minutes. This method resulted in moist, near-translucent flesh through and through, but the fish was a little mushy, and there was no contrast in texture whatsoever. Cranking the temperature higher would definitely create a more golden exterior, but it would also sacrifice some of the medium-rare flesh inside.

Perhaps a hybrid cooking technique combining high and low heat, as I often use for roasting chicken with crisp skin and tender, juicy meat, would work. After a bit of experimentation, I settled on a starting temperature of 500 degrees, which I reduced to 275 degrees immediately upon placing the fish in the oven. The initial blast of high heat firmed the exterior of the salmon and helped render some of the excess fat that had made the slower-roasted fish mushy. To prevent the oven temperature from dropping too rapidly, I also preheated the baking sheet. This necessitated cooking the fish with its skin on, so the fillets could be placed skin-side down in the pan to protect the flesh. The fish tasted a little too fatty on my first try with this new approach, but making several slits through the skin before placing it in the pan allowed most of the fat residing directly beneath the skin to render off onto the baking sheet.

The fish then gently cooked while the oven temperature slowly dropped. Though the temperature was never really in a range that I would consider true slow-roasting, this technique did rely on the declining ambient temperature, as opposed to constant heat, to slowly cook the fish. It worked beautifully: I now had salmon with a little firmness on the outside and a lot of moist, succulent meat on the inside.

I was inspired to dress up this perfectly cooked salmon to make it more of a company meal. I dismissed spice rubs and glazes, which require sustained high heat to fully flavor the fish. And marinades were just too subtle. Quick salsas and easy, no-cook relishes were the answer. I found that those with an acidic element worked best to balance the richness of the fish. Tasters liked a tomato-basil relish, a spicy cucumber version, a tangy tangerine and ginger combo, and a tart grapefruit-basil pairing. In addition to bright flavor, each relish provided a further contrast in texture to complement the salmon's silkiness.

—KEITH DRESSER, *Cook's Illustrated*

OVEN-ROASTED SALMON WITH TANGERINE AND GINGER RELISH
SERVES 4

It is important to keep the skin on during cooking; remove it afterward if you choose not to serve it. If tangerines are unavailable, substitute 3 medium oranges.

RELISH
- 4 tangerines, rind and pith removed and segments cut into ½-inch pieces (about 1 cup) (see note)
- 1 scallion, sliced thin
- 2 teaspoons fresh lemon juice
- 2 teaspoons extra-virgin olive oil
- 1½ teaspoons minced or grated fresh ginger
  Salt and pepper

SALMON
- 1 (1¾ to 2-pound) skin-on salmon fillet, about 1½ inches at the thickest part
- 2 teaspoons olive oil
  Salt and pepper

1. FOR THE RELISH: Place the tangerine pieces in a fine-mesh strainer set over a medium bowl and drain for 15 minutes. Pour off all but 1 tablespoon tangerine juice from the bowl and whisk in the scallion, lemon juice, extra-virgin olive oil, and ginger. Stir in the tangerine pieces and season with salt and pepper to taste; set aside.

2. FOR THE SALMON: Adjust an oven rack to the lowest position, place a rimmed baking sheet on the rack, and heat the oven to 500 degrees. Following the photos on page 230, use a sharp knife to remove any whitish fat from the belly of the fillet and cut the fillet into 4 equal pieces. Make 4 or 5 shallow slashes about an inch apart along the skin side of each piece, being careful not to cut into the flesh.

3. Pat the salmon dry with paper towels. Rub the fillets evenly with the oil and season liberally with salt and pepper. Reduce the oven temperature to 275 degrees and remove the baking sheet. Carefully place the salmon skin-side down on the baking sheet. Roast until the centers of the thickest part of the fillets are still translucent when cut into with a paring knife or an instant-read thermometer inserted in the thickest part of the fillets registers 125 degrees, 9 to 13 minutes. Transfer the fillets to individual plates or a platter. Top with the relish and serve.

OVEN-ROASTED SALMON WITH TANGERINE AND GINGER RELISH

OVEN-ROASTED SALMON WITH SPICY CUCUMBER RELISH

Combine 1 peeled, seeded, and diced cucumber (about 2 cups), 1 tablespoon minced shallot, 1 minced serrano chile, 2 tablespoons chopped fresh mint, 1 tablespoon fresh lime juice, and ¼ teaspoon salt in a medium bowl. Let stand at room temperature to blend the flavors, 15 minutes. Season with additional lime juice and salt to taste. Follow the recipe for Oven-Roasted Salmon with Tangerine and Ginger Relish, substituting the cucumber mixture for the Tangerine and Ginger Relish.

OVEN-ROASTED SALMON WITH FRESH TOMATO RELISH

Combine ¾ pound ripe tomatoes, cored, seeded, and cut into ¼-inch dice (about 1½ cups), 2 tablespoons chopped fresh basil, 1 tablespoon extra-virgin olive oil, 1 tablespoon minced shallot, 1 teaspoon red wine vinegar, and 1 small garlic clove, minced, in a medium bowl. Season with salt and pepper to taste. Follow the recipe for Oven-Roasted Salmon with Tangerine and Ginger Relish, substituting the tomato mixture for the Tangerine and Ginger Relish.

OVEN-ROASTED SALMON WITH GRAPEFRUIT AND BASIL RELISH

Remove the rind and pith from 2 red grapefruits and cut the segments into ½-inch pieces (about 1 cup). Place the pieces in a fine-mesh strainer set over a medium bowl and drain for 15 minutes. Pour off all but 1 tablespoon grapefruit juice from the bowl; whisk in 1 tablespoon minced shallot, 2 tablespoons chopped fresh basil, 2 teaspoons fresh lemon juice, and 2 teaspoons extra-virgin olive oil. Stir in the grapefruit pieces and season with salt and pepper to taste. Follow the recipe for Oven-Roasted Salmon with Tangerine and Ginger Relish, substituting the grapefruit mixture for the Tangerine and Ginger Relish.

NOTES FROM THE TEST KITCHEN

PREPARING SALMON FOR ROASTING

1. Hold a sharp knife at a slight downward angle to the flesh and cut off the whitish, fatty portion of the belly.

2. Cut the salmon fillet into four pieces of equal size to help ensure that they cook at the same rate.

3. Make four or five shallow slashes along the skin side of each piece of fish, being careful not to cut into the flesh.

SALMON PRIMER

In season, we've always preferred the more pronounced flavor of wild-caught salmon to farmed Atlantic salmon, which has traditionally been the main farm-raised variety for sale in this country. But with more species of wild and farmed salmon available these days, we decided to see what distinguishes one from the next. We tasted three kinds of wild Pacific salmon alongside two farmed kinds; they ranged in price from $9 to $20 per pound.

Farmed Atlantic salmon ($9/lb., year round) was bland and had a texture that divided tasters. Farmed king salmon ($12/lb., year round) had a richer yet still mild flavor and a custardy texture, but it is not widely available. Wild coho salmon ($12/lb., July through September) had a balanced flavor, but its texture was unimpressive. Boasting a strong flavor and a meaty texture, wild king salmon ($20/lb., May through September) often winds up on the menus of top restaurants, which pushes the retail price up. Our favorite is wild sockeye salmon ($13/lb., May through September). Characterized by a deep reddish color, the sockeye had a smooth, firm texture and an assertive flavor with clean, briny notes.

While we loved the generally stronger flavor of the wild-caught fish, our tasting confirmed: If you're going to spend the extra money on wild salmon, make sure it looks and smells fresh, and realize that high quality is available only from late spring through the end of summer.

SOLE MEUNIÈRE

A DECEPTIVELY EASY FRENCH RESTAURANT DISH, *sole meunière* features a browned butter sauce seasoned with lemon and parsley, which is poured over the fish just before serving. What could be simpler or more delicious? But when I cooked a few test batches to get a handle on the technique for making this dish, what I got were plates of pale, soggy fillets in pools of greasy sauce—that is, if the fish hadn't stuck to the pan or fallen apart as I tried to plate it. Despite these failures (or maybe because of them), two things did become clear. The simplicity of this dish makes it imperative that everything be prepared and cooked just so, and the four-star flavor of this dish made it worthwhile to fix these problems.

Taking a closer look at my initial meunière recipes, it was no wonder that I had found little success at the stove. Some recipes called for almost two sticks of butter for two pounds of fish. Who wants to eat fish literally swimming in fat? Other recipes resulted in fish that were soggy and white. It was time to go back to basics.

Whole Dover sole—a variety of white flatfish—is the most authentic choice for preparing fish "à la meunière," but it is hard to come by even in the best of fish markets and prohibitively expensive when it can be had. I settled instead on a filleted white flatfish that would be available in most markets, such as sole or flounder. After cooking 20 pounds of flatfish, I discovered that the variety of sole or flounder didn't much matter; what counted was the thickness of the fillet and its freshness. If the fillet was thinner than ⅜ inch, it was nearly impossible to brown it without overcooking it. Fillets that were ⅜ inch thick or slightly more were perfect. Those that weighed 5 to 6 ounces each fit easily in a large skillet. Fillets weighing 7 to 10 ounces were also acceptable, although they required cutting and trimming.

A thin coat of flour speeds up the browning, which is a particularly useful thing to know when you've got thin fillets that cook quickly. Straight from the fishmonger's wrapping paper, fillets are typically wet. They must be patted dry or the flour will become thick and gluey. Simply dredging the dried fillets in flour presented problems. Excess flour fell off the fish and into the pan, where it burned. Shaking off the extra flour before cooking solves this problem. Still, even after a quick shake, the fillets cooked up with blotchy brown crusts that did nothing for the flavor.

I then tried a technique used by Julia Child, who recommends seasoning the fillets with salt and pepper and letting them sit before dredging. The salt extracts just enough water from the fish to give it a thin coating of moisture that helps to ensure a perfectly even coating of flour. Without "bald spots" in the coating, the fish browns uniformly and tastes better. After five minutes, the fillets had begun to glisten with moisture. I dredged them with flour, shook off the excess, and cooked them. "Perfectly seasoned and evenly coated" was the thumbs-up response from tasters.

The technique of pan-frying necessitates a heavy skillet and a good amount of fat. Food is cooked in a single layer and you must wait patiently for it to brown, turning it once and then waiting again. Stifle the temptation to lift the food and take a peek. For maximum browning (and to keep the fish from falling apart), the fish must be left undisturbed as it cooks.

I found that traditional skillets did not work well. No matter how much fat I used, the fish had a tendency to stick. A nonstick skillet worked well every time, producing beautifully browned fillets without sticking. A 12-inch skillet is a must and even then only two fillets would fit at a time without overlapping. Rather than using two skillets side by side, I chose to cook the fish in two batches, using a warmed plate in a preheated 200-degree oven to keep the first batch hot.

Clarified butter (butter with the milk solids removed) is the traditional fat used by the French. Not only does clarified butter lend a rich flavor to the fish, but it has a higher smoking point (and thus burns less easily) than whole butter. Clarifying butter is easy, but it is too lengthy a process for a quick midweek entrée. I cooked one batch with canola oil and another with clarified butter, and even the least discerning tasters noticed the difference. Whole butter burned, but a mixture of oil and butter, a classic combination, did the trick.

Next I experimented with the amount of fat. Although recipes ranged from 1 to 6 tablespoons (for two fillets), I found that 2 tablespoons were ample, especially in a nonstick skillet. I began by cooking the fillets over low heat, but the results were mediocre at best; the fillets did not brown but instead poached in the fat, and the taste was lackluster. High heat turned out to be equally problematic. By the time the interior of each fillet had cooked, some of the exterior had scorched, resulting in a bitter and unappealing taste. Next, I heated the pan over high heat, then lowered the heat to medium-high as soon as I added the fish. The exterior browned beautifully, while the inside remained succulent.

For ⅜-inch-thick fillets, three minutes on the first side and about two minutes on the second side achieved both a flavorful, nutty-tasting exterior and a moist, delicate interior. Because the side that is cooked first is the most attractive, I found it best to stick to the hard-and-fast rule of cooking for three minutes on the first side and then adjusting the time for the second side. (With flatfish, the side of the fillet that is cooked first also matters—it should be the side that was cut from the bones, not the skin side.) How could I tell when a thin fillet was done? Restaurant chefs press the fillets with their fingers—a reliable technique but one that requires practice. Observation eventually indicated that the fillet was done when opaque. Because the fish continues to cook off the heat of the stovetop (and in the gentle heat of the preheated oven), it is imperative to remove it before it's fully cooked. Instead of using the tip of a knife, a method that tends to damage the fillet, I found that a toothpick inserted into a thick edge worked well.

One last cooking consideration remained to be resolved. Traditionally, the sauce served with meunière is *beurre noisette*, or browned butter, with lemon and parsley added. Crucial to the flavor of the sauce, which adds a rich nuttiness to the fish, is proper browning of the milk solids in the butter, a task not easily accomplished in a nonstick skillet because the dark surface of the pan makes it nearly impossible to judge the color of the butter. Instead I browned the butter in a medium stainless steel skillet; its shiny bottom made it easy to monitor the color. I then added lemon juice to the browned butter, sprinkled the fish with parsley, and poured the sauce over the fish.

—ELIZABETH GERMAIN, *Cook's Illustrated*

SOLE MEUNIÈRE

SERVES 4

Try to purchase fillets that are of similar size, and avoid those that weigh less than 5 ounces because they will cook too quickly. A nonstick skillet ensures that the fillets will release from the pan, but for the sauce a traditional skillet is preferable because its light-colored surface will allow you to monitor the color of the butter

as it browns. Laying the fish in the skillet "bone" side down is beneficial for browning, though not crucial.

FISH

4 sole or flounder fillets (5 to 6 ounces each and ⅜ inch thick) (see note)
Salt and pepper
½ cup (2½ ounces) unbleached all-purpose flour
2 tablespoons vegetable oil
2 tablespoons unsalted butter, cut into 2 pieces

BROWNED BUTTER

4 tablespoons (½ stick) unsalted butter, cut into 4 pieces
1½ tablespoons fresh lemon juice
Salt and pepper
1 tablespoon minced fresh parsley

1 lemon, cut into wedges, for serving

1. FOR THE FISH: Adjust the oven racks to the lower- and upper-middle positions, set 4 heatproof dinner plates on the racks, and heat the oven to 200 degrees. Pat the fish dry with paper towels and season both sides with salt and pepper; let stand until the fillets are glistening with moisture, about 5 minutes.

2. Spread the flour into a wide, shallow dish. Coat both sides of the fillets with flour, shake off the excess, and lay in a single layer on a baking sheet. Heat 1 tablespoon of the oil in a 12-inch nonstick skillet over high heat until shimmering. Add 1 tablespoon of the butter and swirl to melt and coat the pan bottom. Carefully place 2 fillets in the skillet, "bone" side down, and immediately reduce the heat to medium-high, and cook, without moving the fish, until the edges of the fillets are opaque and the bottom is golden brown, about 3 minutes.

3. Following the photo on page 233, use 2 spatulas to gently flip the fillets, then continue to cook on the second side until the thickest part of the fillet easily separates into flakes when a toothpick is inserted, about 2 minutes longer. Transfer each of the fillets to a heated dinner plate in the oven. Wipe out the skillet and repeat with the remaining 1 tablespoon oil, 1 tablespoon butter, and the remaining fillets; transfer each fillet to a plate in the oven.

4. FOR THE BROWNED BUTTER: While the fillets rest in the oven, melt the butter in a 10-inch skillet over medium-high heat and cook, swirling the pan constantly, until the butter is golden brown and has a nutty aroma, 2 to 3 minutes. Off the heat, stir in the lemon juice and season with salt and pepper to taste. Remove the fillets from the oven, spoon the sauce over each fillet, and sprinkle with the parsley. Serve immediately with the lemon wedges.

VARIATIONS

SOLE MEUNIÈRE WITH TOASTED SLIVERED ALMONDS

Follow the recipe for Sole Meunière, adding ¼ cup slivered almonds to the skillet when the butter has melted in step 4.

SOLE MEUNIÈRE WITH CAPERS

Follow the recipe for Sole Meunière, adding 2 tablespoons rinsed capers to the butter with the lemon juice in step 4.

NOTES FROM THE TEST KITCHEN

SAUTÉING DELICATE FISH FILLETS

Sautéing delicate fish fillets such as sole or flounder can be tricky because the tender fish is apt to stick to the pan and break apart. Some recipes coat the fillets with egg and flour, which does create a barrier against sticking, but its thick texture and rich flavor overwhelm the fish. Other recipes dredge the fish in flour, but the flour tends to stick in some places and not others, resulting in "bald" spots and uneven browning. The solution is simple: Sprinkle the fillets with salt and pepper and let them stand for 5 minutes. The salt draws out moisture in the fish, creating a thin, wet sheen—just enough for the flour to evenly adhere to. This method produces a crust thin enough to protect the fish without overwhelming the fillets' texture or flavor.

FLIPPING FISH FILLETS

To turn fish fillets without breaking them, use 2 spatulas; a regular model and an extra-wide version especially designed for fish work best. Using the regular spatula, gently lift the long side of the fillet. Then, supporting the fillet with the extra-wide spatula, flip it so that the browned side faces up.

FISH EN PAPILLOTE

A CLASSIC FRENCH METHOD, cooking fish *en papillote* involves baking fish in a tightly sealed parchment paper packet. The fish steams in its own juices, developing a flaky, delicate texture and an intense, clean flavor. It's naturally light and, with the addition of vegetables, the fish becomes a well-rounded main course. Best of all, this dish takes little work outside of assembly; there's no stovetop cooking and little mess. So what's the rub? Most traditional recipes are a bit fussy regarding preparation and require origami-like folding of the parchment paper to insure an airtight seal (and dramatic presentation: The packets puff up like balloons). I wanted to make fish en papillote easy and contemporary, with perfectly moist and tender pieces of fish, well-seasoned vegetables, and flavorful juices.

First things first: I ditched the parchment paper (rare in most kitchens) in favor of foil—I'll take ease of preparation over presentation any day. Instead of intricate folding, I crimped the foil together into simple "hobo packs" to seal it tight.

While I knew I wanted to use white fish fillets, such as cod, haddock, red snapper, sole, halibut, and tilapia, determining when it was done took some work, as there's no way to sneak a peek at the fish when it's sealed tightly in foil. The antiquated rule of thumb for cooking fish—10 minutes of cooking time per inch of thickness—failed in this case: The fish was barely opaque within that period. After experimenting with oven temperatures, I found that 1-inch-thick fillets cooked best at 450 degrees for 20 minutes. While this seemed like an excessive length of time at such high heat, the fish was well insulated within the sealed packets and became flaky without drying out. Cooking the packets for this amount of time at a relatively high temperature also helped concentrate the exuded liquid so that neither the fish nor the vegetables became waterlogged.

Because the vegetables have to cook at the same rate as the fish, I knew there would be certain limitations. Dense vegetables such as potatoes were immediately out of the running because they took too long to cook through, and I knew that any other vegetables I did choose would have to be cut thin. Light, clean-tasting zucchini was a crowd-pleaser, and it took little work to slice the squash into thin rounds. For sweetness and body, I added diced tomatoes. As for flavoring the zucchini and tomatoes, I turned to garlic, crushed red pepper flakes, and oregano for an assertive kick and to intensify the mild flavor of the fish. All are traditional Provençal flavorings.

Despite the clear flavors of fish and vegetables alike, tasters felt the dish tasted a bit lean, so I searched for a way to add a little more flavor and fullness. Butter was thought to be too rich for the delicate en papillote method. Olive oil, however, was welcomed for its clean flavor; extra-virgin olive oil in particular was praised for the light and summery notes it lent to the dish. The oil mixed with the juices in the packet to create a delicious broth that could be sopped up with bread. For a finishing touch of flavor and color, I sprinkled chopped basil over each plate just before serving.

—RACHEL TOOMEY, *America's Test Kitchen Books*

FISH EN PAPILLOTE WITH ZUCCHINI AND TOMATOES

SERVES 4

This recipe calls for haddock, but cod, red snapper, thick sole fillets, halibut, and tilapia also work well here. Ask your fishmonger to remove the skin from the fillets. The packets may be assembled several hours ahead of time and refrigerated, but they should be baked just before serving. Because the fish is sealed tightly in the packets, it will continue to cook out of the oven. To prevent overcooking, open each packet promptly after baking.

- 1 (1½-pound) haddock fillet, about 1 inch at the thickest part (see note)
- 2 tablespoons extra-virgin olive oil
- 2 garlic cloves, minced
- 1 teaspoon minced fresh oregano
- ⅛ teaspoon red pepper flakes
  Salt and pepper
- 3 plum tomatoes, cored, seeded, and chopped into ½-inch pieces
- 2 zucchini, sliced ¼ inch thick
- ¼ cup minced fresh basil

1. Adjust an oven rack to the middle position and heat the oven to 450 degrees. Use a sharp knife to cut the fillet into 4 equal pieces.

2. Combine the oil, garlic, oregano, pepper flakes, ¼ teaspoon salt, and ⅛ teaspoon pepper in a medium bowl. Measure half of the oil mixture into a second medium bowl and toss gently with the tomatoes. Add the zucchini to the remaining oil mixture and toss to coat.

3. Cut four 12-inch squares of heavy-duty foil and lay them flat on a work surface. Shingle a quarter of the zucchini slices in the center of each piece of foil. Season the fillets with salt and pepper and place one on top of each zucchini portion. Following the photos, top the fish with tomatoes, then tightly crimp the foil into packets.

4. Set the packets on a rimmed baking sheet and bake until the fish just flakes apart, about 20 minutes. Carefully open the packets, allowing the steam to escape away from you, and let cool briefly. Smooth out the edges of the foil and, using a spatula, gently push the fish, vegetables, and any accumulated juices out onto warmed serving plates. Sprinkle with the basil before serving.

NOTES FROM THE TEST KITCHEN

MAKING FOIL PACKETS

1. Arrange the vegetables and seasoned fish in the center of a 12-inch square of heavy-duty aluminum foil.

2. Crimp the edges together in a ¼-inch fold, then fold over three times. Fold the open edges at either end of the packet together in a ¼-inch fold, and then fold over twice more to seal.

3. After baking, open the packets carefully. Using a spatula, gently slide the fish, vegetables, and any accumulated juices out onto warmed serving plates.

OVEN-FRIED FISH

THERE'S AN ALLURE TO FRIED FISH that few foods can match. But the addictive nature of deep-fried fish comes with a price: Its high calorie count can make a bacon cheeseburger look like diet fare. So how do you lighten up fried fish? You remove the frying—or, more to the point, the fat. The test kitchen has had great luck with oven-frying chicken, and I wondered if the lessons I learned there could be applied to fried fish. I wanted my fish to be low in calories—but I wanted fried flavor, too.

Starting with the coating made the most sense—technique would follow. Deep-fried fish is often dipped in a thick batter before frying, but I would need some sort of breading for my oven-fried fish. Determined to investigate every imaginable crust alternative, I gathered a host of ingredients, including fresh and dried breadcrumbs, jagged Japanese panko, handfuls of different breakfast cereals, cornmeal, and crackers of all stripes. Using a standard breading procedure, I tested each choice. The breadcrumbs came across as stale and boring; panko failed to crisp much in the oven; the cereals exhibited too many distinct flavors (I didn't want my fish to taste like Grape-Nuts); and the crackers were a complete bust, both greasy and sweet.

Back at the store, I found something I hadn't initially considered: Melba toast. Crisp as can be, subtly flavored, and containing zero fat, it held some promise. I pulverized a box of toast, then diligently coated and baked a few fillets. This batch of oven-fried fish was good—really good. The Melba crumbs crisped up surprisingly well and added a pleasant wheaty flavor that nicely complemented the mild fish.

That said, the crumb coating lacked the fried flavor of a regular deep-fried coating. Clearly it needed a bit of fat. After a misguided test or two, I realized that all I needed to do was toss the crumbs with a bit of oil—just enough to coat them lightly. A finishing spritz of vegetable oil spray over the coated fillets proved the coup de grâce. Once baked, the coating tasted on par with any deep-fried crust.

To this point, I used standard breading protocol: I dipped the fish in flour, then a beaten egg, and finally the Melba crumbs. While this is a tried-and-true method for coating pan-fried foods, I wondered if it was really necessary for oven-frying. I first tried omitting the base layer of flour and found little difference between fish coated with flour and that without. Out went the flour. The egg, however, was a must: The crumbs fell from the fish without it. Hoping to trim a few calories, I tried a whites-only "dip" and was quite pleased. The sticky egg whites tenaciously gripped the crumbs—and I couldn't tell the difference in flavor between whole egg and whites-only coatings.

To crisp the crumbs without drying out the thin fish fillets, I assumed a hot oven was a necessity. I tested temperatures ranging from a moderate 400 degrees to a blistering 500 degrees and most liked the results found by splitting the difference. At 450 degrees, the fish just cooked through—remaining quite moist—in the time it took for the coating to brown. I used a technique from our oven-fried chicken recipe and cooked the fillets on a wire rack liberally coated with vegetable spray to prevent sticking.

Now I had achieved the requisite crunch, but my tasters still clamored for more flavor. Borrowing ideas from the oven-fried chicken recipe, I added Dijon mustard, garlic powder, and cayenne to the egg wash. Tasters unanimously approved.

Finally, I'd been using cod for the sake of testing, but was curious what other types of fish might work as well. After testing everything I could find locally, I was pleased with how haddock, catfish, trout, tilapia, and sole fillets turned out when oven-fried. I do recommend against using very thin and/or delicate fish fillets, however, as they had a tendency to break apart. Thick, meaty fillets, such as tuna, failed to cook through and aren't recommended either.

Fried fish without tartar sauce just doesn't seem right, but what about all that mayonnaise? Fortunately, I found that reduced-fat mayonnaise is a perfectly acceptable substitute for the real stuff, especially when boosted with the tanginess and surprisingly rich flavor of low-fat sour cream. Into this base, I mixed traditional tartar sauce flavorings: minced cornichons (along with a splash of their pickling juice), red onion, and piquant capers. Sure, with only 45 calories and 2.5 grams of fat per tablespoon, it tasted a little leaner than the higher-fat traditional sauce, but I thought the flavorings came through more clearly, being less obscured by full-fat mayonnaise. Now I could satisfy my craving for fried fish for only 300 calories and 7 grams of fat per serving—plus sauce, of course.

—RACHEL TOOMEY, *America's Test Kitchen Books*

OVEN-FRIED FISH WITH LIGHT TARTAR SAUCE

OVEN-FRIED FISH WITH LIGHT TARTAR SAUCE

SERVES 4

Catfish, trout, haddock, thick sole fillets, or tilapia can be substituted for the cod. Stay away from very delicate fillets or thick, meaty fish such as swordfish or tuna. If some of the pieces have thin, tapered ends, tuck them under before breading to prevent them from overcooking and drying out. Generously coat the fish with the Melba crumbs, but do not pile them on or they will not adhere to the fish; there will be crumbs left over.

TARTAR SAUCE

- ¼ cup reduced-fat mayonnaise
- 2 tablespoons low-fat sour cream
- 3 large cornichons, minced (about 1½ tablespoons)
- 2 teaspoons cornichon pickling juice
- 2 tablespoons minced red onion
- 1 tablespoon capers, rinsed and minced
  Salt and pepper
  Water

FISH

- Vegetable oil spray
- 1 (1½-pound) cod fillet, about 1 inch at the thickest part (see note)
- 1 (5-ounce) box plain Melba toast, broken into 1-inch pieces (see note)
- 2 tablespoons vegetable oil
- 3 large egg whites
- 1 tablespoon Dijon mustard
- 2 teaspoons minced fresh thyme
- ¼ teaspoon garlic powder
- ⅛ teaspoon cayenne pepper
  Salt and pepper
- 1 lemon, cut into wedges, for serving

1. FOR THE TARTAR SAUCE: Mix all of the sauce ingredients together, adding water as needed to thin the sauce. Cover and refrigerate until the flavors blend, about 30 minutes. Season with salt and pepper to taste. (The sauce can be refrigerated in an airtight container for several days.)

2. FOR THE FISH: Adjust an oven rack to the upper-middle position and heat the oven to 450 degrees. Line a rimmed baking sheet with foil, place a wire rack on the sheet, and coat the rack with vegetable oil spray. Use a sharp knife to cut the fillet into 4 equal pieces.

3. Pulse the Melba toast into coarse crumbs in a food processor, about twelve 1-second pulses. Spread the crumbs in a shallow dish and toss with the oil. In a separate shallow dish, whisk the egg whites, mustard, thyme, garlic powder, and cayenne together.

4. Pat the fish dry with paper towels, then season with salt and pepper. Working with one piece of fish at a time, dip it into the egg white mixture, then coat with Melba crumbs. Press on the Melba crumbs to make sure they adhere to the fish. Lay the coated fish on the prepared wire rack and spray the tops with vegetable oil spray.

5. Bake until the coating is golden and the fish just flakes apart, 12 to 15 minutes. Serve with the lemon wedges and tartar sauce.

NOTES FROM THE TEST KITCHEN

FINDING THE RIGHT COATING

Here is a summary of some of the many coating candidates:

CORNFLAKES: TOO SWEET
Cornflakes gave the coating a good crunch and color, but too much corn flavor. In general, most cereals had a distinct flavor that overpowered the dish.

CRACKERS: TOO SOFT
Many of the crackers failed to make a crisp, crunchy coating; some were too sweet. In addition, many were high in fat and calories.

FRESH BREADCRUMBS: TOO CHEWY
A coating made with fresh breadcrumbs had a beautiful color and tasted great, but the finished product came out of the oven slightly soggy and chewy.

MELBA TOAST: THE WINNER
The coating made with Melba toast was crisp, crunchy, and flavorful and baked up to a rich copper-brown color. As an added bonus, Melba toast is completely fat-free.

CRISPY WEST LAKE FISH

A FRESHWATER LAKE located in central Hangzhou in eastern China, West Lake has been famous for its exquisite beauty for more than a thousand years. The source of inspiration for many poets and artists, West Lake has also inspired various dishes, including West Lake fish, a whole freshwater fish, either poached or fried, and served with a spicy sweet and sour sauce. I've had a couple of versions of West Lake fish at my local Chinese restaurant and was very impressed. Gently poached or crisply fried, a white fish, often catfish, is presented to the table still whole, looking as though it's swimming across the plate, yet it falls easily into ready-to-eat portions with barely an effort. Theatrics aside, the sweet, moist flesh of the fish pairs perfectly with the sweet and sour sauce that defines this dish. I set out to see if I could create a home version.

While West Lake fish is traditionally cooked and served whole, I wanted an easier approach to this dish, so off the bat I decided to use fish fillets. Traditional recipes are divided into two camps when it comes to the cooking method: poached and pan-fried. Poaching the fillets was a bit tricky as they had a tendency to fall apart during cooking. The poached fillets also tasted uninteresting when compared to the pan-fried version with its golden, crisp crust, so I settled on pan-fried. Many of the pan-fried recipes I found dredged the fish in cornstarch before cooking to give it an extra-crisp coating and I thought that this was a good idea. There is no need to coat the fish with egg or oil before coating with the cornstarch, because the natural moisture within the fish provides a tacky texture to which a thin, even coating of cornstarch can stick. I encouraged this by salting the fish and letting it sit for a few minutes before coating it with the cornstarch.

With my cooking method in order, it was time to address the sauce. I started with the sweet and sour elements, namely sugar and vinegar. Many of the recipes I consulted recommend Chinese red vinegar, but this product is difficult to find. I turned to red wine vinegar as a viable substitute. An equal amount of sugar brought the right balance to this sauce. I stumbled across an interesting recipe in my research where the sugar is caramelized first with the aromatics (garlic and ginger) before the liquid ingredients are added. I tested it and tasters were sold. The caramelized sugar mixture added a depth of flavor that was clearly missing in previous versions of the sauce. I also found that fresh red chiles benefited from this caramelization. One chile was enough to give my sauce a bit of fire, while the bright red color lent the dish a fresh appearance.

Sweet and sour sauces always include soy sauce—it adds a necessary saltiness and savory element to this dish. But other similar sauces use as much soy sauce as they do vinegar or sugar. In this case, the soy was far too overpowering for the fish and I ultimately brought it all the way down to just a tablespoon, or one-third of the sweet or sour element for the right balance of flavors. A modest amount of rice wine rounded out the potent acid and sweet elements of the sauce, and a cup of water took this sweet and sour sauce from too intense to just right.

Finally, my sauce was in harmony with the fish—except that the sauce was thin and watery. Again cornstarch came to the rescue, thickening the sauce to the right consistency, so that it clung to the crispy, tender fish.

—SARAH WILSON, *America's Test Kitchen Books*

CRISPY WEST LAKE FISH

SERVES 4

You can use either skinless or skin-on fillets here; most tasters liked the crisp texture of the cooked skin. Any thin, medium-firm white fish fillets can be substituted for the catfish, including haddock, tilapia, flounder, snapper, trout, orange roughy, tilefish, and arctic char. Keep the sauce and the fish separate until ready to serve to help preserve the crisp exterior of the fish.

SAUCE
- 1 tablespoon minced or grated fresh ginger
- 2 garlic cloves, minced
- 1 small Thai red, serrano, or red or green jalapeño chile, seeds and ribs removed, chile chopped
- 3 tablespoons sugar
- 1 cup water
- 3 tablespoons red wine vinegar
- 1 tablespoon soy sauce
- 1 tablespoon Chinese rice wine or dry sherry

1 tablespoon cornstarch

3 scallions, sliced thin

FISH

4 catfish fillets (about 6 ounces each) (see note)

Salt and pepper

3 tablespoons cornstarch

¼ cup vegetable oil

1. FOR THE SAUCE: Combine the ginger, garlic, chile, and sugar together in a small heavy-bottomed saucepan and cook over medium-high heat until the sugar melts and turns golden brown, 5 to 7 minutes. Whisk the water, vinegar, soy sauce, rice wine, and cornstarch together, then carefully whisk into the saucepan—the sugar mixture will be extremely hot. Continue to simmer, stirring constantly, until the sauce is thickened, 2 to 4 minutes. Cover and set aside off the heat.

2. FOR THE FISH: Adjust the oven racks to the lower- and upper-middle positions, set 4 heatproof dinner plates on the racks, and heat the oven to 200 degrees. Pat the fish dry with paper towels and season both sides with salt and pepper; let stand until the fillets are glistening with moisture, about 5 minutes.

3. Spread the cornstarch into a wide, shallow dish. Coat both sides of the fillets with cornstarch, shake off the excess, and lay in a single layer on a baking sheet. Heat 2 tablespoons of the oil in a 12-inch nonstick skillet over high heat until shimmering. Carefully place 2 fillets in the skillet, skin-side down, and immediately reduce the heat to medium-high. Cook, without moving the fish, until the edges of the fillets are opaque and the bottom is golden and crisp, about 4½ minutes.

4. Use 2 spatulas to gently flip the fillets, then continue to cook on the second side until the thickest part of the fillet easily separates into flakes when a toothpick is inserted, about 3 minutes longer. Transfer each of the fillets to a heated dinner plate in the oven. Wipe out the skillet and repeat with the remaining 2 tablespoons oil and the remaining fillets; transfer each fillet to a plate in the oven. (The fish can be held in the oven for up to 10 minutes before continuing.)

5. Return the sauce to a brief simmer over medium-high heat. Stir in the scallions, pour the sauce over the fish, and serve immediately.

BAKED STUFFED SHRIMP

FOR A SPECIAL OCCASION MEAL, baked stuffed shrimp certainly sounds like a winner. Colossal shrimp are spread open, packed with a buttery stuffing, and baked until the stuffing is crisp and the shrimp are just cooked through. But after preparing several cookbook recipes, I realized that there are two big problems—mushy, bland stuffing and shrimp as chewy as rubber bands. I wanted crisp, flavorful stuffing and perfectly cooked shrimp without heading to a restaurant.

Most stuffing recipes simply stir melted butter and seasonings into bread or cracker crumbs. After sampling several recipes, my tasters preferred the sweeter flavor of fresh breadcrumbs. More surprising was that they preferred mayonnaise to butter (which was too greasy) as a binder. Seasoned with mustard, lemon, garlic, cayenne pepper, and a splash of briny clam juice, the stuffing was now very flavorful. Toasting the crumbs before baking helped ensure a crispy baked stuffing.

After peeling, deveining, and butterflying the largest shrimp I could find (about 12 shrimp per pound), I divided the stuffing among the shrimp and popped them into a hot oven. Shrimp shrink and curl as they cook, and as a result the stuffing got forced out like a pilot in an ejector seat. To solve this problem, I turned the shrimp over and pressed the stuffing into them. Instead of pushing the stuffing out, this time the shrimp curled around to cradle it. But when I transferred the shrimp from the baking pan to the serving platter, the stuffing rolled right off. It was only when I accidentally cut clear through one shrimp in the prep stage that I found a way to keep the stuffing in place. As the shrimp contracted in the oven, the stuffing was sealed in place.

The cardinal rule of most shrimp recipes is to cook them quickly, otherwise they will overcook and become tough. I tried a range of temperatures from 350 to 475 degrees to crisp the stuffing and cook the shrimp; I was able to get the stuffing crisp, but I couldn't seem to avoid tough, rubbery shrimp—even with short cooking times. Thinking of how the test kitchen gently poaches shrimp for shrimp cocktail, I wondered what would happen if I broke the rule and baked the shrimp for a longer time at a lower temperature.

I arranged my shrimp on the pan and gave it a try.

Sure enough, after a full 20 minutes at 275 degrees, the shrimp were moist and perfectly cooked—and they actually shrank less in the gentle heat. After a quick flash under the broiler to crisp up the stuffing, I finally had baked stuffed shrimp that were special enough for any occasion.

—DIANE UNGER, *Cook's Country*

BAKED STUFFED SHRIMP

SERVES 4 TO 6

If you can't find clam juice, chicken stock will work in a pinch. Any sturdy rimmed baking sheet can be used in place of the broiler pan bottom.

4	slices high-quality white sandwich bread, torn into pieces
½	cup mayonnaise
¼	cup bottled clam juice (see note)
¼	cup minced fresh parsley
4	scallions, minced
2	garlic cloves, minced
2	teaspoons grated zest and 1 tablespoon fresh lemon juice
1	tablespoon Dijon mustard
⅛	teaspoon cayenne pepper
	Salt
1¼	pounds colossal shrimp (about 12 per pound), peeled and deveined (see page 244)

1. Adjust an oven rack to the upper-middle position and heat the oven to 375 degrees. Pulse the bread in a food processor to coarse crumbs. Transfer the crumbs to a broiler pan bottom and bake until golden and dry, 8 to 10 minutes, stirring halfway through the cooking time. Remove the crumbs from the oven and reduce the temperature to 275 degrees.

2. Combine the toasted breadcrumbs, mayonnaise, clam juice, parsley, scallions, garlic, lemon zest and juice, mustard, cayenne, and ¼ teaspoon salt in a large bowl.

3. Pat the shrimp dry with paper towels and season with salt. Grease the empty broiler pan bottom. Following photos, butterfly and cut a hole through the center of each shrimp and arrange cut-side down on the

prepared pan. Divide the breadcrumb mixture among the shrimp, pressing to adhere. Bake until the shrimp are opaque, 20 to 25 minutes.

4. Remove the shrimp from the oven and heat the broiler. Broil the shrimp until the crumbs are deep golden brown and crispy, 1 to 3 minutes. Serve.

NOTES FROM THE TEST KITCHEN

PERFECT STUFFED SHRIMP

Cutting a hole clear through the center of each butterflied shrimp may seem like a mistake, but it actually gives the shrimp a way of holding on to the stuffing. The shrimp are butterflied on the convex side before being flipped over onto the pan.

1. Use a sharp paring knife to cut along (but not through) the vein line, then open up the shrimp like a book.

2. Using the tip of the paring knife, cut a 1-inch opening all the way through the center of the shrimp.

3. After the shrimp have been butterflied and the opening has been cut, flip the shrimp over onto the broiler pan so that they will curl around the stuffing.

4. Divide the stuffing among the shrimp, firmly pressing the stuffing into the opening and to the edges of the shrimp.

KUNG PAO SHRIMP

THE CLASSIC SICHUAN STIR-FRY of meat or shellfish with peanuts and chiles in a rich brown sauce, kung pao is now a Chinese restaurant standard, although its origins date back to 19th-century central-western China in the Sichuan province. While most of the original versions of this dish I found use chicken, we've found more modern versions of kung pao dishes that use beef, seafood, tofu, or just vegetables, and shrimp is a popular variation. Unfortunately, the kung paos I sampled in half a dozen well-reputed restaurants were hopeless. The first one was dismal, with tough, tiny little shrimp drenched in a quart of pale, greasy, bland sauce, and things just got worse from there.

Like most stir-fries, kung pao cooks quickly, so it is well suited for a weeknight meal. Moreover, I thought that by carefully examining the key cooking issues—the type and preparation of both the shrimp and the nuts along with the composition and texture of the sauce—I could come up with something akin to what the Chinese cook at home.

Most Chinese stir-fries go heavy on the vegetables, but kung pao dishes are different. The quantity of vegetables is limited, with the emphasis instead on the shrimp and the nuts. The restaurant versions I tried often included green pepper, and some added bamboo shoots, carrots, celery, scallions, and zucchini. I worked my way through these choices and more and settled on a modest amount of red pepper for sweetness and scallion for freshness, bite, and color. Kung pao needs nothing else from the vegetable kingdom.

Taking a step up the food chain, I looked at the shrimp next. While some recipes call for small or medium shrimp, I felt that larger shrimp made a more satisfying kung pao, and large shrimp were easier to peel, too. After checking out jumbo, extra-large, and large, I selected extra-large (21 to 25 per pound) for their combination of succulence and generous appearance.

The best way to prepare the shrimp was a matter of some debate. Traditionally, they are coated with egg white, cornstarch, and seasonings, and then fried in a generous quantity of oil in order to create a softly crisp coating that will help the sauce adhere. However, the egg coating tended to cook up in unattractive clumps, which would later float about in the dish, and the two to three cups of oil required to deep-fry seemed both cumbersome and wasteful. Dealing with all that oil edged the dish out of the realm of simple weeknight cooking. Instead, I chose to quickly stir-fry the shrimp in a film of oil and to thicken the sauce slightly to help it coat the shrimp.

The nuts help define kung pao. In most of the restaurant dishes I tried, the flavor of the nuts was too subtle, so they acted more as a garnish than a key element. I wanted to better integrate the nuts into the dish and to deepen their flavor, and one move accomplished both goals. Whereas most recipes add the nuts near the end of the cooking time, I stir-fried them right along with the shrimp at the beginning. This way, they toasted briefly in the pan, intensifying in flavor, which they then contributed to the sauce. Most kung pao recipes rely on either peanuts or cashews, and I appreciated the former for their savory flavor and crisp texture. By comparison, cashews seemed both sweet and a little soft.

The test kitchen has conducted extensive investigations into stir-frying technique, so I knew that a wide, heavy skillet, preheated until the oil smokes, is a better mate with the flat American stovetop burner than a deeply curved wok. With all that heat, though, it would be easy to overcook, and therefore toughen, the shrimp and to burn the aromatic garlic and ginger that are part of the sauce. Two simple tricks helped me to avoid both problems. First, I learned not to cook shrimp all the way through at first because they would finish cooking in the sauce later; an initial stay in the pan of just under two minutes was ideal. Second, while most stir-fry recipes add garlic and ginger near the beginning, I prefer to add them near the end of cooking to prevent burning and preserve their fresh flavors.

When it came to the sauce, I pictured it deep brown, syrupy in texture, and glistening, with balanced elements of sweet, savory, salty, garlicky, and hot. I tried both chicken broth and water as a base and preferred the broth for the savory underpinning it provided. For a bit of sweetness I added sugar in amounts from one tablespoon down to one teaspoon, but even a mere teaspoon was overkill. Instead, I chose to add the classic Asian trio of hoisin sauce, oyster sauce, and sesame oil, all available in the supermarket and all good sources of color, flavor depth, and subtle sweetness. An ample supply of garlic—three cloves—gave the sauce authority, and ginger and rice vinegar added brightness. I liked Chinese black rice vinegar (also called Chinkiang vinegar) even better because it was more complex—smoky, salty, plumlike, and slightly sweet. Cornstarch is the thickener of choice for Asian sauces and 1½ teaspoons reliably gelled the sauce to a soft, glazy, shrimp-coating consistency.

For heat, I chose whole dried chiles, which are traditional for this dish (although red pepper flakes work well also). I altered the technique with which they are generally used, however, by stir-frying them with the shrimp and peanuts at the beginning of the cooking. This extra bit of pan time toasted the chiles, deepening their flavor noticeably.

Sichuan peppercorns are the other defining flavor in authentic kung pao dishes, as I discovered from my cursory research on this dish, but I had trouble finding recipes that use them. Curious, I dug a bit deeper to find that from 1968 to 2005, it was illegal to bring Sichuan peppercorns into the U.S. (they are carriers of a tree disease that can potentially harm citrus crops). Since they're now available (mostly at Asian markets and specialty spice purveyors), I tested different amounts and was amazed to realize that some recipes include handfuls of this potent spice. I found that a teaspoon, crushed and added with the peanuts and chiles to bloom in the hot pan, was just the right amount to tingle my palate and give this kung pao shrimp the authenticity it demanded.

—SARAH WILSON, *America's Test Kitchen Books*

KUNG PAO SHRIMP

SERVES 4

You can substitute plain rice vinegar for the black rice vinegar (available in Asian markets), but I prefer the latter for its fruity, salty complexity. Don't eat the whole chiles in the final dish; if you can't find small dried red chiles, substitute 1 teaspoon red pepper flakes. Serve with steamed white rice.

SAUCE

- ¾ cup low-sodium chicken broth
- 1 tablespoon oyster sauce
- 1 tablespoon hoisin sauce
- 2 teaspoons black rice vinegar or plain rice vinegar (see note)
- 2 teaspoons toasted sesame oil
- 1½ teaspoons cornstarch

STIR-FRY

- 1 pound extra-large shrimp (21 to 25 per pound), peeled and deveined
- 2 teaspoons soy sauce
- 2 teaspoons Chinese rice wine or dry sherry
- 3 garlic cloves, minced
- 1 teaspoon minced or grated fresh ginger
- 2 scallions, minced
- 2 tablespoons plus 1 teaspoon vegetable oil
- 6 small whole dried red chiles (each about 2 inches long) (see note)
- ½ cup roasted unsalted peanuts
- 1 red bell pepper, stemmed, seeded, and cut into ½-inch pieces
- 1 teaspoon Sichuan peppercorns, crushed

1. FOR THE SAUCE: Whisk all of the ingredients together; set aside.

2. FOR THE STIR-FRY: Toss the shrimp with the soy sauce and rice wine in a small bowl and let marinate for 10 minutes, or up to 1 hour. In a separate bowl, mix together the garlic, ginger, scallions, and 1 teaspoon of the vegetable oil; set aside. In a third bowl, crumble half of the chiles coarsely, then toss with the remaining whole chiles and peanuts; set aside.

3. Heat 1½ teaspoons of the remaining vegetable oil in a 12-inch nonstick skillet over high heat until just smoking. Add half of the shrimp and cook, without stirring, until the shrimp are browned at the edges, about 1 minute. Stir in the chiles and peanuts and cook until the shrimp are almost completely opaque and the peanuts have darkened slightly, about 30 seconds longer. Transfer the mixture to a medium bowl and repeat with 1½ teaspoons more vegetable oil and the remaining shrimp; transfer to the bowl and set aside.

4. Add the remaining 1 tablespoon vegetable oil to the skillet and return to high heat until just smoking. Add the red bell pepper and Sichuan peppercorns and cook until the bell pepper is slightly softened and the peppercorns are fragrant, about 1 minute.

5. Clear the center of the skillet, add the garlic mixture, and cook, mashing the mixture into the pan, until fragrant, 15 to 20 seconds. Stir the garlic mixture into the peppers. Stir in the shrimp mixture with any accumulated juices. Whisk the sauce to recombine, then add to the skillet and cook, tossing constantly, until the sauce is thickened, about 30 seconds. Transfer to a platter and serve.

SIZING SHRIMP

Shrimp are sold by size (small, medium, large, and so on) as well as by the number needed to make 1 pound, usually given in a range. Choosing shrimp by the numerical rating is more accurate than choosing by a size label, which varies from store to store. Here's how the two systems line up.

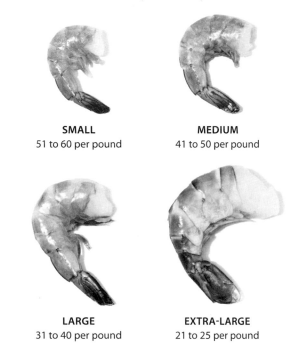

SMALL
51 to 60 per pound

MEDIUM
41 to 50 per pound

LARGE
31 to 40 per pound

EXTRA-LARGE
21 to 25 per pound

SHRIMP SALAD

MAYBE IT'S A GOOD THING that most shrimp salads are drowning in a sea of gloppy mayonnaise. The dressing might be bland, but at least it helps camouflage the sorry state of the rubbery, flavorless boiled shrimp. I wanted to find a cooking technique that would deliver perfectly cooked shrimp without the extra work of grilling, roasting, or sautéing. Was it too much to ask that the shrimp have some flavor of their own?

To begin, I rounded up some creamy-style shrimp salad recipes. Most call for boiling a flavorful liquid of white wine, lemon juice, herbs, spices, and water (called a *court-bouillon* by the French). After the shrimp are submerged into this hot liquid, the pot is removed from the heat and covered for about 10 minutes. Many of the recipes call for quickly shocking the shrimp in an ice bath to prevent overcooking. Although they looked perfect, shrimp prepared this way were in fact flavorless and tough. Reducing the time the shrimp spent in the liquid did make them more tender, but it did nothing to improve their flavor.

But I had a trick up my sleeve: a technique practiced in the 1970s by the French chef Michel Guérard. He poached proteins by starting them in cold liquid. The cold proteins and broth would heat simultaneously, unlike the traditional poaching technique in which the shrimp proteins immediately turn opaque (and rubbery) upon submersion in hot water. In this way the shrimp would better absorb flavors from the poaching liquid—a kind of turbocharged flavor injection.

In the test kitchen I took the court-bouillon ingredients—leaving out the white wine, which tasters found overwhelming—and added the shrimp. I then heated the liquid to various temperatures. Too low and the shrimp were mushy; too high and they turned tough. Eventually, I discovered that heating the liquid to a near simmer (165 degrees) was ideal. The shrimp were actually flavorful and their texture was so firm and crisp that several tasters compared them to lobster.

All I needed now was the perfect deli-style dressing. While mayonnaise provides creamy cohesiveness, I didn't want it to mask the shrimp flavor or drown out the other ingredients. After testing several amounts, tasters felt a perfect coating was ¼ cup per 1 pound of shrimp. Diced celery, minced shallots, chopped herbs, and fresh lemon juice added unifying aromatic and herbal notes and a pleasant vegetal crunch and acidity. With less mayo, I also found that variations, using bolder flavors like chipotle chile, orange, and roasted red pepper, were not only possible, but delicious, too.

—DAVID PAZMIÑO, *Cook's Illustrated*

SHRIMP SALAD

SERVES 4

This recipe can also be prepared with large shrimp (31 to 40 per pound); the cooking time will be 1 to 2 minutes less. The shrimp can be cooked up to 24 hours in advance, but hold off on dressing the salad until ready to serve. The recipe can be easily doubled; cook the shrimp in a 7-quart Dutch oven and increase the cooking time to 12 to 14 minutes. Serve the salad on a bed of greens or on a buttered and grilled bun.

1   pound extra-large shrimp (21 to 25 per pound), peeled and deveined

¼   cup plus 1 tablespoon juice from 2 to 3 lemons, spent halves reserved

5   sprigs plus 1 teaspoon minced fresh parsley

3   sprigs plus 1 teaspoon minced fresh tarragon

1   teaspoon whole black peppercorns plus ground pepper

1   tablespoon sugar

    Salt

¼   cup mayonnaise

1   small shallot, minced (about 2 tablespoons)

1   small celery rib, minced (about ⅓ cup)

1. Combine the shrimp, the ¼ cup lemon juice, reserved lemon halves, parsley sprigs, tarragon sprigs, whole peppercorns, sugar, and 1 teaspoon salt with 2 cups cold water in a medium saucepan. Place the saucepan over medium heat and cook the shrimp, stirring several times, until pink and firm to the touch and the centers are no longer translucent, 8 to 10 minutes (the water should be just bubbling around the edge of the pan and register 165 degrees on an instant-read thermometer). Remove the pan from the heat, cover, and let the shrimp sit in the broth for 2 minutes.

2. Meanwhile, fill a medium bowl with ice water. Drain the shrimp into a colander, and discard the lemon halves, herbs, and spices. Immediately transfer the shrimp to the ice water to stop the cooking and chill thoroughly, about 3 minutes. Remove the shrimp from the ice water and pat dry with paper towels.

3. Whisk together the mayonnaise, shallot, celery, remaining 1 tablespoon lemon juice, 1 teaspoon minced parsley, and 1 teaspoon minced tarragon in a medium bowl. Cut the shrimp in half lengthwise and then each half into thirds; add the shrimp to the mayonnaise mixture and toss to combine. Season with salt and pepper to taste and serve.

VARIATIONS

SHRIMP SALAD WITH ROASTED RED PEPPER AND BASIL

Follow the recipe for Shrimp Salad, omitting the tarragon sprigs from the cooking liquid. Replace the celery, minced parsley, and minced tarragon with ⅓ cup thinly sliced jarred roasted red peppers, 2 teaspoons rinsed capers, and 3 tablespoons chopped fresh basil.

SHRIMP SALAD WITH AVOCADO AND ORANGE

Follow the recipe for Shrimp Salad, omitting the tarragon sprigs from the cooking liquid. Replace the celery, minced parsley, and minced tarragon with 4 halved and thinly sliced radishes; 1 large orange, peeled and cut into ½-inch pieces; ½ ripe avocado, cut into ½-inch pieces; and 2 teaspoons minced fresh mint.

SPICY SHRIMP SALAD WITH CORN AND CHIPOTLE

Follow the recipe for Shrimp Salad, substituting the juice from 3 to 4 limes (save spent halves) for the lemon juice and omitting the tarragon sprigs from the cooking liquid. Replace the celery, minced parsley, and minced tarragon with ½ cup cooked corn kernels, 2 minced chipotle chiles in adobo sauce (about 2 tablespoons), and 1 tablespoon minced fresh cilantro.

SHRIMP SALAD WITH WASABI AND PICKLED GINGER

Follow the recipe for Shrimp Salad, omitting the tarragon sprigs from the cooking liquid. Replace the shallot, minced parsley, and minced tarragon with 2 teaspoons wasabi powder, 2 scallions, white and green parts sliced thin, 2 tablespoons chopped pickled ginger, and 1 tablespoon toasted sesame seeds.

NOTES FROM THE TEST KITCHEN

DEVEINING SHRIMP

1. After removing the shell, use a paring knife to make a shallow cut along the back of the shrimp so that the vein is exposed.

2. Use the tip of the knife to lift the vein out of the shrimp. Discard the vein by wiping the blade against a paper towel.

CLAMS AND CHORIZO

TWO OF PORTUGAL'S PRIZED INGREDIENTS—spicy pork sausage and plump clams—steamed in a spicy tomato broth, *amêijoas na cataplana*, is a classic combination. Sometimes called *cataplana* for short (the word refers to the hinged, clam-shaped vessel in which the dish is traditionally cooked), the dish makes a hearty supper served with crusty bread to soak up the flavorful broth. But just because something is simple in composition doesn't mean it is always prepared well. This was obvious after I tested a handful of authentic cataplana recipes. Some included a plethora of ingredients such as bell peppers and mushrooms, which only served to muddy the flavors. I wanted to pare this appealing twosome back to its simple roots to highlight the briny clams and spicy sausage.

To start my testing, I steamed two different batches of clams: soft-shell clams (known as steamers) and littlenecks (hard shells). I quickly ruled out the steamers; their shells were brittle and prone to breaking in the broth. The littlenecks were perfect—plump and flavorful.

On to the all-important sausage. Most recipes called for a dried sausage such as chorizo (spicy cured sausage) or linguiça (garlicky Portuguese sausage). After testing batches of each cooked side by side on the stove, I found that I preferred the spicy meatiness of the chorizo. (Chorizo comes in two varieties, Mexican and Spanish; respectful of the Iberian connection, I opted for the Spanish.) Half a pound of sausage added heady flavor to the dish without overpowering the clams. Upping the textural contrast, I cut the sausage into larger pieces than most recipes suggested. Last but hardly least was the broth. Off the bat, I included onion and garlic, traditional ingredients in the dish. Tomatoes serve as the base of the broth, and I decided on canned whole tomatoes. They required a quick chop, but held up better than canned diced tomatoes. To finish the broth, I added white wine for acidity; ¾ cup was enough to brighten the flavors without leaving an alcohol aftertaste. Finally, a number of recipes in my research added a dusting of minced fresh parsley to the finished dish just before serving—just a coda that lends color and a freshness to this comforting rustic dish.

—SARAH WILSON, *America's Test Kitchen Books*

CLAMS AND CHORIZO
SERVES 4

Tasters preferred Spanish-style chorizo to Portuguese linguiça sausage in this recipe, but linguiça can be substituted if desired. Serve with garlic toast or crusty bread to sop up the heady broth.

- 1 tablespoon extra-virgin olive oil
- ½ pound chorizo sausage, sliced in half lengthwise, then sliced crosswise into ½-inch-wide pieces (see note)
- 1 onion, minced (about 1 cup)
- 3 garlic cloves, minced
- 1 (28-ounce) can whole tomatoes, tomatoes chopped, and juice reserved
- ¾ cup dry white wine
- 4 pounds littleneck clams, scrubbed
- 2 tablespoons minced fresh parsley

1. Heat the oil in a large Dutch oven over medium heat until shimmering. Add the chorizo and cook, stirring occasionally, until browned and slightly rendered, about 4 minutes. Transfer the chorizo to a paper towel–lined plate, leaving the fat in the pot.

2. Add the onion to the fat in the pot and cook over medium-high heat until softened, 5 to 7 minutes. Stir in the garlic and cook until fragrant, about 30 seconds. Stir in the tomatoes with their juice and wine and simmer until thickened slightly, about 3 minutes.

3. Increase the heat to high and stir in the clams and reserved chorizo. Cover and cook, stirring once, until the clams have opened, 4 to 8 minutes.

4. Use a slotted spoon to transfer the clams and chorizo to a large serving bowl or individual bowls; discard any clams that haven't opened. Stir the parsley into the broth, then pour the broth over the clams and serve.

NOTES FROM THE TEST KITCHEN

CANNED WHOLE TOMATOES
Overall, we found that whole tomatoes packed in juice have a livelier flavor than those packed in puree. Our favorite, **Progresso Italian-Style Whole Peeled Tomatoes with Basil**, earned comments such as "bright, lively flavor" and "the perfect balance of acidic and fruity notes." Progresso sells whole tomatoes packed in juice and packed in puree, so be sure to read the fine print and buy the ones packed in juice.

DESSERTS

PEANUT BUTTER AND JELLY BARS

BAR COOKIES COME IN COUNTLESS VARIETIES and, if one is to judge by Internet chatter and Google searches, the most popular might just be peanut butter and jelly bars (PB & J hereafter). Sweet and salty, crunchy and chewy, the bars hit all the right buttons and should make just about anyone happy. I say "should" because the existing recipes I've prepared largely produced cookies plagued by bland flavors (both crust and filling) and a soggy bottom crust. I wanted to develop a perfect rendition of this cookie-jar favorite, and to make it easy enough to make with kids—perhaps the prime audience for this simple cookie.

PB & J bars have three components: crust, jelly filling, and nut-studded topping. And as is common practice with many varieties of bar cookies, a portion of the crust is reserved for the topping (and, in this case, combined with chopped peanuts). In almost all the versions I found, the crust contains just flour, butter, sugar, either baking powder or soda, and, most important, peanut butter.

Virtually every recipe I collected for the bars blended the batter via the creaming method and I could find no reason to break with tradition. The sugar and softened butter are creamed together, after which eggs, vanilla, and peanut butter are whipped in before the dry ingredients are added.

The smallest variation in volume of the crust's ingredients had a pronounced effect on its flavor and texture. Between the butter and peanut butter there was plenty of fat, which I needed to keep in check with flour; otherwise the crust baked up greasy. As for sugar, the more of it I added, the crunchier and harder the crust grew—more like a dense shortbread than a short and sandy crust. With too little sugar, however, the crust tasted bland and the texture dried out. A couple of eggs contributed moistness and bound the dough together, while a little baking powder helped to keep the crust from being too dense. I added everywhere from ½ cup to triple that of peanut butter and preferred the rich flavor and short texture of crust prepared with one cup—and chunky peanut butter at that, which seemingly contributed more flavor.

While jelly may suffice for a PB & J sandwich, I thought its bland flavor bombed in a bar cookie, contributing little to the cookie besides a generic, fruity sweetness. Jam, which contains more fruit and so has a thicker texture than jelly, proved to be a far better choice.

The topping couldn't have been easier to pull together: a blending of reserved crust dough and chopped nuts crumbled over the jam. Salted and roasted peanuts tasted far, far better than raw or unsalted nuts. The salt really helped to bring out the best in the nut flavor and cut through the jam's sweetness.

While most of the recipes I found baked the bars in one fell swoop, I found this approach all but guaranteed a soggy base as the hot jam seeped into the porous crust. How could the crust turn crisp and crunchy without direct exposure to the oven's heat? For previously developed bar cookie recipes, the test kitchen prebaked the bottom crust until lightly browned before layering on the topping. It makes good common sense and worked beautifully in this instance: The peanut-flavored crust was as crunchy as I could have hoped for and stayed that way for days, despite the moist topping. These bar cookies are easy to make and are sure to please both kids and adults alike.

—BRYAN ROOF, *America's Test Kitchen Books*

PEANUT BUTTER AND JELLY BARS

MAKES 24

Feel free to use any flavor of jam here, but stay away from jelly, which has a weaker fruit flavor.

- 2 cups (10 ounces) unbleached all-purpose flour
- 1 teaspoon baking powder
- ¾ teaspoon salt
- 12 tablespoons (1½ sticks) unsalted butter, softened
- 1½ cups (10½ ounces) sugar
- 2 large eggs
- 1 cup chunky peanut butter
- 1 teaspoon vanilla extract
- ½ cup roasted, salted peanuts, chopped coarse
- 1½ cups raspberry jam (see note)

1. Adjust an oven rack to the middle position and heat the oven to 350 degrees. Following the photos on page 249, line a 13 by 9-inch baking pan with a foil sling and grease the foil. Whisk the flour, baking powder, and salt together in a medium bowl.

2. In a large bowl, beat the butter and sugar together with an electric mixer on medium speed until light and fluffy, 3 to 6 minutes. Beat in the eggs, one at a time. Beat in the peanut butter and vanilla until combined, scraping down the bowl and beaters as needed. Reduce the mixer speed to low and slowly add the flour mixture until just incorporated, about 30 seconds.

3. Reserve 1 cup of the dough for the topping. Press the remaining dough evenly into the prepared baking pan. Bake the crust until just beginning to turn golden, about 15 minutes. Meanwhile, stir the peanuts into the reserved dough for the topping.

4. Spread the jam evenly over the hot crust, then drop small pieces of the topping evenly over the jam. Bake the bars until the jam is bubbling and the topping is golden, about 45 minutes, rotating the pan halfway through baking.

5. Let the bars cool completely in the pan, set on a wire rack, about 2 hours. Remove the bars from the pan using the foil, cut into squares, and serve. (The bars will keep in an airtight container for 2 days.)

NOTES FROM THE TEST KITCHEN

MAKING A FOIL SLING

With their gooey fillings and high sugar content, brownies and bar cookies and often snack cakes can be nearly impossible to remove from their baking pans—no matter how well the pan is greased. Here's a method that works every time.

1. Fold two long sheets of foil so they are as wide as the baking pan. Lay them in the pan, perpendicular to one another, with the extra foil overhanging the edges.

2. Push the foil into the corners and up the sides of the pan. Grease the sides and bottom before adding the batter.

LOW-FAT PEANUT BUTTER COOKIES

MOST COOKIES GET THEIR FAT and calories from sugar, eggs, and a whole lot of butter. Peanut butter cookies go a step further by adding at least a cup of the fatty main ingredient to the mix. That's why a single peanut butter cookie weighs in at 200 calories and 12 grams of fat. Could I find a way to lose the fat and keep the peanut flavor?

Many peanut butter cookie recipes contain 2 cups of granulated sugar and a whopping 16 tablespoons of butter. In addition to adding sweetness, sugar also makes cookies pleasantly chewy. When I reduced the amount of sugar, the flavor was fine (peanut butter cookies shouldn't be achingly sweet), but the cookies were too dry. By switching to moister brown sugar, I was able to get away with using just 1¼ cups. I found recipes that replaced the butter with ingredients like mashed pears, prunes, and applesauce, but the resulting cookies were dry and too fruity. Other recipes cut back on butter by melting it (to make it more easily absorbed into the dough), but too much melted butter made the cookies greasy. A combination of 2 melted tablespoons and 4 softened tablespoons produced good results with much less fat.

I'd saved the big challenge for last: the peanut butter. Simply decreasing the peanut butter left the cookies devoid of flavor. Reduced-fat peanut butter, which replaces some of the peanuts with stabilizers, is wetter and looser than full-fat, and its moisture actually improved the texture of my cookies. The peanut pieces in chunky low-fat peanut butter added an extra layer of flavor.

I searched the supermarket for products to boost the nutty flavor. Sesame oil, tahini (sesame paste), and roasted soy nut butter all lacked peanut punch. Ground peanut butter sandwich cookies, peanut brittle, and peanut granola bars all had off-flavors; in desperation, I'd also grabbed a box of Cap'n Crunch's Peanut Butter Crunch cereal. After I ground it down and incorporated it into the flour, the cereal added so much big peanut flavor— with minimal fat—that I had to use only 5 tablespoons of reduced-fat peanut butter. One of my cookies has only 130 calories and 4 grams of fat, while a traditional peanut butter cookie has 200 calories and 12 grams of fat, and my tasters actually preferred these cookies to the full-fat version.

—MEREDITH BUTCHER, *Cook's Country*

LOW-FAT PEANUT BUTTER COOKIES

MAKES 24

Skippy Reduced Fat Super Chunk is the test kitchen's favorite brand of low-fat peanut butter.

1½ cups Cap'n Crunch's Peanut Butter Crunch cereal
⅓ cup (1⅔ ounces) plus 1½ cups (7½ ounces) unbleached all-purpose flour
¼ teaspoon baking soda
¼ teaspoon salt
4 tablespoons (½ stick) unsalted butter, softened; plus 2 tablespoons unsalted butter, melted
5 tablespoons reduced-fat chunky peanut butter (see note)
1¼ cups packed (8¾ ounces) light brown sugar
2 large egg whites
1 teaspoon vanilla extract
1 tablespoon water

1. Adjust an oven rack to the middle position and heat the oven to 350 degrees. Line 2 baking sheets with parchment paper. Pulse the cereal and ⅓ cup flour in a food processor until finely ground. Add the remaining flour, baking soda, and salt and pulse to combine. With an electric mixer on medium speed, beat the softened butter, peanut butter, and sugar together until fluffy, about 2 minutes. Beat in the melted butter, egg whites, and vanilla until combined. Add the flour mixture and mix on low until incorporated. Add the water and mix until absorbed.

2. Roll 1½ tablespoons dough into 1½-inch balls and space 2 inches apart on the prepared baking sheets. Following the photos, press and crosshatch the dough. Bake one sheet of cookies until the edges are lightly browned but the centers are still soft, 10 to 12 minutes, rotating the baking sheet halfway through baking. Let the cookies cool on the baking sheet for 5 minutes, then transfer to a wire rack to cool completely before serving. Repeat with the remaining dough. (The cookies will keep in an airtight container for 3 days.)

NOTES FROM THE TEST KITCHEN

SURE SPREADING

Because these cookies contain less fat, they will not spread as easily as full-fat versions. Pressing each dough ball into a ½-inch-thick disk gives the cookies a jump start on spreading in the oven.

1. With the back of a measuring cup or a flat-bottomed glass, press each dough ball into a ½-inch-thick disk.

2. Using a fork, make a crosshatch pattern on top of each cookie.

BETTER FOR BAKING THAN FOR BREAKFAST

An unlikely ingredient—Cap'n Crunch's Peanut Butter Crunch cereal—can be ground and used in place of some of the flour to increase peanut butter flavor with a minimum of fat.

REDUCED-FAT PEANUT BUTTER

In our recipe makeover for Peanut Butter Cookies, we found that using reduced-fat peanut butter (which replaces 25 percent of regular peanut butter's fat with stabilizers such as corn syrup solids) allowed us to cut down on fat without sacrificing flavor. But which brand is best? To find out, we tasted chunky versions of three of the most popular reduced-fat brands (Skippy, Jif, and Smart Balance Omega) three different ways: straight from the jar, spread on white bread, and baked into peanut butter cookies. Although each brand performed admirably, **Skippy Reduced Fat Super Chunk**, $2.39 for 18 ounces, won top honors for its well-balanced peanut flavor and extra-chunky texture.

LOW-FAT PEANUT BUTTER COOKIES

THIN AND CRISPY OATMEAL COOKIES

MOST PEOPLE'S DEFINITION of the perfect oatmeal cookie is something big, hearty, and chewy, with raisins and nuts in every bite. That has never been my ideal. When I crave an oatmeal cookie, I look for something thin, crisp, and delicate that allows the simple flavor of buttery oats to really stand out. I want the refinement of a lace cookie combined with the ease of a drop cookie. The test kitchen has an excellent recipe for Big Chewy Oatmeal-Raisin Cookies. Could I get the crisp, delicate cookie I wanted by simply adjusting the ingredients in this recipe?

Thick, chewy oatmeal cookies get their texture from generous amounts of sugar and butter (usually melted to lend even greater chewiness), a high ratio of oats to flour, and a modest amount of leavener. Most recipes beat in a couple of eggs and vanilla and finish with raisins and nuts, ingredients I knew wouldn't work in a thin, crisp cookie. Because I wanted rich, buttery flavor, I rejected the idea of shortening from the get-go (even though it typically provides a crisper texture) and used the same amount of butter called for in chewy cookie recipes. The sugar would take more finessing.

Most recipes use a combination of brown and granulated sugars. Brown sugar lends rich flavor and moisture, and granulated provides crispness and encourages exterior browning. Since the greater the amount of sugar in a cookie, the chewier it is, I began by scaling the sugar down, using equal amounts of light brown and granulated. But the cookies still had too much chew. When I switched to all granulated sugar, the cookies became hard and crunchy, with a one-dimensional, overly sweet flavor. Adding ¼ cup of light brown sugar back added subtle caramel notes without compromising the texture.

To contribute better structure and richer flavor to the cookies, an egg or two is beaten in next. One egg held the cookies together nicely without giving them a cakey texture. Along with the one egg, I added a teaspoon of vanilla to round out the flavor. Now that the wet ingredients were all set, I was ready to tackle the dry stuff.

Drawing on past experience baking cookies, I speculated that using less flour would likely yield a final product that was crisper rather than chewier, flatter rather than puffier. But without enough flour, the oatmeal cookies spread too much, becoming formless, gossamer-thin lace cookies. A fairly standard amount of flour gave the cookies a thicker, oat cake–like texture. I slowly cut down the amount until I ended up with 1 cup of flour. Though these cookies emerged from the oven with enough structure and were crisper than their predecessors, they still weren't on the mark. Because they didn't spread enough, they lacked the thinness I was looking for, and the dry edges and slightly chewy centers were obviously wrong. Replacing some of the flour with ground-up oats—a technique I'd seen in some recipes—didn't work: The cookies became even chewier. Using quick or instant oats in lieu of old-fashioned oats made them dense and bland. What if I used less oats instead? It was worth a try.

I tried reducing the amount of oats to get rid of some of the unwanted bulk. As I watched them bake, I noticed that the balls of dough spread fairly quickly along the edges, which became dark and crisp, while the thicker, paler middles took much longer to catch up. Pressing the dough down into flat-topped cylinders helped the cookies bake more evenly, but they still weren't spreading enough. Could the leavener be the problem?

Baking powder—the leavener used in our Big Chewy Oatmeal-Raisin Cookies—is a mixture of baking soda and two kinds of acid salts. These components react to create gas bubbles that help baked goods expand. I'd been using ½ teaspoon of baking powder, which clearly wasn't working too well. I tried taking it out completely, but that left me with leaden rocks that barely eased out of their initial raw dough form. To get the cookies to at least brown better, I replaced the baking powder with baking soda: They spread even less.

The only thing left to try was using what seemed like too much leavener. The basic principles of leavener are as follows: Use too little and there won't be enough bubbles to help the dough rise; use too much and you end up with excess carbon dioxide, which causes the bubbles to get too big. These big bubbles eventually combine with one another, rise to the top of the dough, and burst, resulting in a flat product. But since what I wanted was a thin, flat cookie, perhaps I could make this "mistake" work to my advantage. After testing varying amounts and combinations of baking powder and baking soda, I found that ¾ teaspoon of baking powder coupled with ½ teaspoon of baking soda gave me exactly what I wanted. This time, the cookies puffed up in the oven, collapsed, and spread out, becoming a much thinner version of their former selves. Even better, they had no trace of the soapy aftertaste that is often a by-product of too much leavener. I was finally getting somewhere.

Now the cookies were thin and had a nice buttery, oaty flavor. To address their slightly greasy aftertaste, I reduced the amount of butter. Two issues remained: They were baking unevenly—the top tray was often darker than the bottom one, even after being rotated halfway through—and had a tendency to bend into nearly a U shape before breaking in half. They just weren't snappy enough.

To guard against the tough, dry cookies that can result from overbaking, most recipes for thick and chewy cookies say to remove them from the oven when they still look slightly raw. Suspecting this was an unnecessary precaution here, I tried baking my cookies all the way through until they were fully set and evenly browned from center to edge. Since the cookies were now thin, they didn't become tough. Instead, they were crisp throughout. Baking the cookies one sheet at a time ensured that they cooked evenly. And rather than transferring them warm from the baking sheet to a cooling rack, I accidentally discovered that the cookies got crisper when left to cool completely on the baking sheet. I'd finally achieved my goal: a thin, delicate oatmeal cookie with buttery flavor and just the right amount of crunch. A cookie this good might even convert the fans of chewiness over to my side.

—SANDRA WU, *Cook's Illustrated*

THIN AND CRISPY OATMEAL COOKIES

MAKES 24

To ensure that the cookies bake evenly and are crisp throughout, bake them 1 tray at a time. Place them on the baking sheet in 3 rows, with 3 cookies in the outer rows and 2 cookies in the center row. If you reuse a baking sheet, allow the cookies on it to cool at least 15 minutes before transferring them to a wire rack, then reline the sheet with fresh parchment before baking more cookies. I developed this recipe using Quaker Old Fashioned Rolled Oats. Other brands of old-fashioned oats can be substituted but may cause the cookies to spread more. Do not use instant or quick-cooking oats.

1 cup (5 ounces) unbleached all-purpose flour
¾ teaspoon baking powder
½ teaspoon baking soda
½ teaspoon salt
14 tablespoons (1¾ sticks) unsalted butter, softened
1 cup (7 ounces) granulated sugar
¼ cup packed (1¾ ounces) light brown sugar
1 large egg
1 teaspoon vanilla extract
2½ cups old-fashioned rolled oats (see note)

1. Adjust an oven rack to the middle position and heat the oven to 350 degrees. Line 3 large (18 by 13-inch) baking sheets with parchment paper. Whisk the flour, baking powder, baking soda, and salt in a medium bowl.

2. In a standing mixer fitted with a paddle attachment, beat the butter and sugars at medium-low speed until just combined, about 20 seconds. Increase the speed to medium and continue to beat until light and fluffy, about 1 minute longer. Scrape down the bowl with a rubber spatula. Add the egg and vanilla and beat on medium-low until fully incorporated, about 30 seconds. Scrape down the bowl again. With the mixer running at low speed, add the flour mixture and mix until just incorporated and smooth, 10 seconds. With the mixer still running on low, gradually add the oats and mix until well incorporated, 20 seconds. Give the dough a final stir with the rubber spatula to ensure that no flour pockets remain and the ingredients are evenly distributed.

3. Divide the dough into 24 equal portions, each about 2 tablespoons (or use a #30 cookie scoop), then roll between the palms of your hands into balls. Place the cookies on the prepared baking sheets, spacing them about 2½ inches apart, 8 dough balls per sheet (see note). Using your fingertips, gently press each dough ball to ¾-inch thickness.

4. Bake 1 sheet at a time until the cookies are a deep golden brown, the edges are crisp, and the centers yield to a slight pressure when pressed, 13 to 16 minutes, rotating the baking sheet halfway through baking. Transfer the baking sheet to a wire rack; let the cookies cool completely on the baking sheet before serving. (The cookies will keep in an airtight container for 3 days.)

THIN AND CRISPY COCONUT-OATMEAL COOKIES

Follow the recipe for Thin and Crispy Oatmeal Cookies, decreasing the oats to 2 cups and adding 1½ cups sweetened flaked coconut to the batter with the oats in step 2.

THIN AND CRISPY ORANGE-ALMOND OATMEAL COOKIES

Follow the recipe for Thin and Crispy Oatmeal Cookies, creaming 2 teaspoons finely grated orange zest with the butter and sugars in step 2. Decrease the oats to 2 cups and add 1 cup coarsely chopped toasted almonds to the batter with the oats in step 2.

SALTY THIN AND CRISPY OATMEAL COOKIES

We prefer the texture and flavor of a coarse-grained sea salt, like Maldon or fleur de sel, but kosher salt can be used. If using kosher salt, reduce the amount sprinkled over the cookies to ¼ teaspoon.

Follow the recipe for Thin and Crispy Oatmeal Cookies, reducing the amount of salt in the dough to ¼ teaspoon. Lightly sprinkle ½ teaspoon coarse sea salt evenly over the flattened dough balls before baking.

NOTES FROM THE TEST KITCHEN

MORE LEAVENER FOR THINNER COOKIES

It may sound counterintuitive, but doubling the usual amount of leavener in oatmeal cookies is the key to crispness. The amplified dose creates big bubbles that first help the dough rise, then combine and burst, resulting in a flat cookie.

MORE LEAVENER = CRISPER COOKIES

MERINGUE COOKIES

A CLASSIC MERINGUE COOKIE consists of just two ingredients—egg whites and sugar—whipped together, then baked. If all goes right, the cookie that emerges from the oven is glossy and white, with a shatteringly crisp texture that dissolves instantly in your mouth. But when things go wrong, you wind up with meringues as dense as Styrofoam or weepy, gritty, and cloyingly sweet. How can a cookie with so few ingredients produce such unreliable results?

Almost every meringue recipe I found fell into one of two categories: French meringue, in which egg whites are whipped with sugar, and fussier Italian meringue that calls for pouring hot sugar syrup into the whites as they are being beaten. The Italian meringue produced cookies that were dense and candy-like, so I decided to go with the French version. Though the French method was the simpler of the two, these meringues proved just as finicky. Add sugar too soon and the meringue doesn't fully expand, resulting in flat, dense cookies. Add sugar too late and you get a meringue that is voluminous when raw but weepy and gritty when cooked. Why such different results? It turns out that with egg whites, it's all about timing.

As an egg white is beaten, its proteins unfold and cross-link to create a network of bonds that reinforce the air bubbles produced in a sea of water (egg whites are composed mainly of water). Early in the process, the proteins have not completely unfurled and linked together, so the bubbles can't hold a firm shape. Sugar added at this stage will grab water molecules from the egg whites, lending stability to the bubbles. Sugar, however, interferes with the ability of proteins to cross-link; if it's added too early, fewer proteins will bond and trap air, resulting in a meringue that is less voluminous.

If, on the other hand, you continue to beat the whites without adding sugar, more air bubbles will form, more proteins will bond to reinforce them, and the meringue will puff up and take on the firm texture of shaving cream. Sugar added after this stage has been reached will have less water to dissolve in, giving the finished meringues a gritty texture and a tendency to weep out drops of sugar syrup during baking.

So the key is to add sugar only when the whites have been whipped enough to gain some volume but still have enough free water left in them for the sugar to dissolve completely. After some experimentation, I discovered that the best time to add sugar is just before the soft peak stage, when the meringue is very frothy and bubbly but not quite firm enough to hold a peak (see "Stabilizing Meringue with Sugar," page 257). Adding the sugar in a slow stream down the side of the bowl of a running standing mixer helped distribute the sugar more evenly, which created a smoother meringue.

Many recipes call for adding an acid such as cream of tartar before whipping the whites. In theory, acid helps the egg proteins unwind faster and bond more efficiently. But I got the best results when I left the acid out. Without acid, the whites formed peaks more slowly, giving me a wider time frame in which to add the sugar, leading to a more stable meringue.

Now that I had a smooth and stable meringue, I was ready to shape it into cookies and bake. I figured the simplest approach would be to scoop a small amount of meringue with a spoon and use a second spoon to drop the dollop onto a baking sheet. After much effort, however, I ended up with two baking sheets of misshapen blobs that didn't bake properly. Some came out browned and crumbly; others were wet in the center. To guarantee uniform shape and proper cooking, I would have to pipe them. A pastry bag produced perfectly shaped meringues, and a zipper-lock bag with a corner cut off worked nearly as well.

Traditionally, meringues are baked at a very low temperature and then left in the turned-off oven, sometimes for as long as overnight. The idea is to completely dry out the cookies while allowing them to remain snow-white. I tried baking at temperatures as low as 175 degrees, but our ovens had trouble maintaining this temperature, leading to inconsistent results. An hour in a 225-degree oven followed by another hour in the turned-off oven produced perfectly cooked meringues every time.

It was time to shift my attention to flavor. There was one complaint common to every cookie I'd made so far: They were too sweet. My working recipe used 1 cup of sugar for 4 egg whites (the lowest amount I could find in any recipe). Could I cut back the sugar to ¾ cup with no adverse effects? I made up a new batch of meringues with less sugar, and everything was fine until I put them into the oven. Then disaster struck. The meringues, which up to now had been holding their shape perfectly,

started collapsing and shrinking. Why would reducing the amount of sugar suddenly ruin my cookies?

It turns out that beyond its stabilizing role in the mixing bowl, sugar also plays a stabilizing role in the oven. Without sufficient sugar, the meringues lose moisture too rapidly as they bake, causing them to collapse. In order to solve this problem, I needed to find something with the hygroscopic (water-clinging) property of sugar, but without the sweetness. My first thought was to swap some of the sugar with corn syrup, which is made from glucose and is about 75 percent as sweet as the sucrose in table sugar. This trick works—as long as you don't mind brown meringues. I had forgotten that corn syrup browns much more easily than regular sugar, and my meringues emerged from the oven a light amber color instead of the pure white I wanted. I decided to try another corn product that is also hygroscopic and would add no sweetness to the meringues: cornstarch. Moderation was key; too much cornstarch and tasters complained the cookies left a starchy aftertaste. With 2 teaspoons of cornstarch and ¾ cup of sugar, complaints disappeared.

All that remained to complete my cookies were a little vanilla and a pinch of salt (both found in many recipes that my tasters liked). Finally I had snow-white meringues that were light and crisp, with just the right amount of sweetness. And, as a final measure, I decided to develop a few flavor variations—namely, chocolate, nut, and citrus.

—J. KENJI ALT, *Cook's Illustrated*

MERINGUE COOKIES

MAKES 4 DOZEN

The meringues may be a little soft immediately after being removed from the oven but will stiffen as they cool. To minimize stickiness on humid or rainy days, allow the meringues to cool in a turned-off oven for an additional hour (for a total of 2) without opening the door, then transfer them immediately to airtight containers and seal.

¾ cup (5¼ ounces) sugar
2   teaspoons cornstarch
4   large egg whites
¾ teaspoon vanilla extract
⅛ teaspoon salt

MERINGUE COOKIES

1. Adjust the oven racks to the upper-middle and lower-middle positions and heat the oven to 225 degrees. Line 2 baking sheets with parchment paper. Combine the sugar and cornstarch in a small bowl.

2. In a standing mixer fitted with a whisk attachment, beat the egg whites, vanilla, and salt at high speed until very soft peaks start to form (the peaks should slowly lose their shape when the whisk is removed), 30 to 45 seconds. With the mixer running at medium speed, slowly add the sugar mixture in a steady stream down the side of the mixer bowl (the process should take about 30 seconds). Stop the mixer and scrape down the sides and bottom of the bowl with a rubber spatula. Return the mixer to high speed and beat until glossy, and stiff peaks have formed, 30 to 45 seconds.

3. Working quickly, place the meringue in a pastry bag fitted with a ½-inch plain tip or a large zipper-lock bag with ½ inch of the corner cut off. Pipe meringues into 1¼-inch-wide mounds about 1 inch high on the prepared baking sheets, 6 rows of 4 meringues on each sheet. Bake 1 hour, rotating the baking sheets front to back and top to bottom halfway through baking. Turn off the oven and let the meringues cool in the oven for at least 1 hour. Remove from the oven and let cool to room temperature before serving, about 10 minutes. (The cookies will keep in an airtight container for up to 2 weeks.)

VARIATIONS

CHOCOLATE MERINGUE COOKIES

Follow the recipe for Meringue Cookies, gently folding 2 ounces finely chopped bittersweet chocolate into the meringue mixture at the end of step 2.

TOASTED ALMOND MERINGUE COOKIES

Follow the recipe for Meringue Cookies, substituting ½ teaspoon almond extract for the vanilla extract. In step 3, sprinkle the meringues with ⅓ cup coarsely chopped toasted almonds and 1 teaspoon coarse sea salt, such as Maldon (optional), before baking.

ORANGE MERINGUE COOKIES

Follow the recipe for Meringue Cookies, stirring 1 teaspoon finely grated orange zest into the sugar mixture in step 1.

NOTES FROM THE TEST KITCHEN

STABILIZING MERINGUE WITH SUGAR
The key to glossy, even-textured meringue is adding sugar at just the right time.

TOO SOON
After 15 seconds, the egg whites begin to get foamy, but it's too early to add the sugar.

JUST RIGHT
Adding sugar just as the foam starts to gain volume yields a stable, voluminous meringue.

TOO LATE
Adding sugar once the egg whites form stiff peaks will result in a gritty meringue.

PASTRY BAGS
In our testing of pastry bags, we found that size and material were the two key factors. We preferred larger models of about 18 inches, which give you enough length to grip and twist the top. While canvas is traditional, we liked materials such as plastic and coated canvas that are easier to clean. Finding the apertures of our bags sometimes too large or too small to work with tips bought separately, we learned that pastry bags have larger openings for handling jobs such as meringues or mashed potatoes, while decorating bags' smaller openings fit the tiny piping tips for fine scrollwork and writing. If your pastry-tip set didn't come with a coupler to help adapt tips to your bag, you can buy one at any kitchen store.

Our favorite? We ultimately preferred the more durable, reusable **Ateco 18-Inch Plastic Coated Pastry Bag,** $4.45.

HOMEMADE GRAHAM CRACKERS

AN ORDAINED PRESBYTERIAN MINISTER born in Connecticut, Sylvester Graham invented graham crackers in the 19th century. He was best known for his advocacy of dietary reform—he was well ahead of his time in certain respects—and his eponymous coarse-grain whole-wheat flour, which was used in the cornerstones of his diet, graham bread and graham crackers. Graham bread may have gone by the wayside, but his flour is still commonplace and graham crackers live on, though in a form far, far removed from the original. Once touted by Graham as a tool for fighting wantonness and vice, graham crackers are now the stuff of after-school snacks, campfire s'mores, and quick piecrusts. Made largely with refined flour, they taste bland and have a mealy, soulless texture. But let's say there's a middle ground between Graham's ascetic cracker and the modern iteration: a crisp cracker made with both wholesome graham and white flours, that's moderately sweet, and tastes great—with or without marshmallows and chocolate. A cracker that parents and children alike could enjoy?

While store-bought graham crackers are a largely similar lot, I was surprised to find recipes for homemade crackers that varied a good deal in content and mixing method. Some cleaved close to Graham's original (i.e., healthy to the extreme), while others were as rich as shortbread and included a variety of spices. Tasters found elements to love in both styles and I hoped to find a middle ground.

Some recipe development revolves around the technique, some around the ingredients. In this case, nearly every recipe I found employed the same method for making the dough: The dry ingredients are blended, the fat is cut in, and then the wet ingredients are added and stirred until it forms a cohesive mass. In the food processor, it took a couple of minutes to pull together and I could find little with which to quibble. Sometimes easy really is best.

With the mixing method being a nonissue, I cobbled together a working recipe and set to work figuring out the ideal flour mixture. While some of the recipes I had found excluded graham flour altogether—relying, instead, on milder whole-wheat flour (cheating!)—those with graham flour blended it with a bit of all-purpose

flour for good reason: structure. Without the white flour, the crackers fell apart when I tried to lift them from the baking sheet. I experimented with varying ratios and grew to like crackers made with just enough all-purpose flour to hold the cracker together, but by no means mellow the graham flour's assertive flavor. Some of the recipes I had found included rye flour or bran in addition to the graham flour, but I found these flavors distracting. For a bit of lift, I followed convention and blended baking powder with a little baking soda. Surprisingly, most of the recipes I gathered employed water as the dough's liquid component, but it worked well; dairy made the crackers too soft and delicate.

Graham may have gone apoplectic at the thought of sugar in his crackers, but modern crackers are always made with sugar, honey, molasses, or a combination thereof. I made batches with each independently and in conjunction and while none of the three impressed me— each tasting flat or possessing a dubious texture—I liked the earthy flavor and crisp snap of crackers made with a combination of sugar and molasses best of all.

Be it butter, shortening, or oil, fat was included in every recipe I found. Tasting crackers made with each side by side, I much preferred the crackers made with butter for their rich flavor; shortening and oil contributed little flavor and made the texture greasy. As with most baked goods, the more butter I added, within reason, the better the crackers tasted. After trying batches with up to 1½ sticks of butter, I settled on 1 stick as perfect: The crackers tasted rich and had a pleasantly crisp crunch and tender crumb without being the least bit greasy.

Some of the recipes I found piled on the spices, but I thought that these complicated the otherwise clear graham flavor. Testing small amounts of spices independently, tasters responded well to cinnamon and a small spoonful found its way into the recipe. As for the oven temperature, I'd been baking the crackers at 350 degrees for the sake of testing, but wondered if lower or higher temperatures might improve my results. While lower temperatures only made them take longer to cook, 375 degrees made the crackers a bit crisper and lighter.

They tasted proper and looked almost right, although a bit motley. Despite my best efforts, I couldn't roll the dough out evenly into a thin sheet. Dividing the dough into two smaller, manageable pieces helped, but my real salvation came in the form of parchment paper. I sandwiched the dough between two sheets and rolled away with little fear of the dough sticking to the rolling pin or work surface. Pricked with a fork and scored into squares, the crackers looked store-bought but tasted far, far better.

—SARAH WILSON, *America's Test Kitchen Books*

HOMEMADE GRAHAM CRACKERS

MAKES 36

If you can't find graham flour, you can substitute whole-wheat flour but the cookies will be slightly less flavorful.

- 1¾ cups (8¾ ounces) graham flour (see note)
- ½ cup (2½ ounces) unbleached all-purpose flour
- ½ cup (3½ ounces) sugar
- 1 teaspoon baking powder
- ½ teaspoon baking soda
- ½ teaspoon salt
- ¼ teaspoon ground cinnamon
- 8 tablespoons (1 stick) unsalted butter, cut into ½-inch pieces and chilled
- 5 tablespoons water
- 2 tablespoons light molasses
- 1 teaspoon vanilla extract

1. Adjust the oven racks to the upper-middle and lower-middle positions and heat the oven to 375 degrees.

2. Process the flours, sugar, baking powder, baking soda, salt, and cinnamon in a food processor until combined, about 3 seconds. Add the butter and process until the mixture resembles coarse meal, about 15 seconds. Add the water, molasses, and vanilla and process until the dough comes together, about 20 seconds.

3. Divide the dough into 2 even pieces. Roll each piece of dough out between 2 pieces of parchment paper to a 16 by 8-inch rectangle, ⅛ inch thick. Remove the top sheet of parchment and trim the dough into a tidy 15 by 7½-inch rectangle with a knife, then score it into eighteen 2½-inch squares. Prick each square several times with a fork.

4. Slide each piece of dough and parchment onto separate baking sheets. Bake the cookies until golden brown, 10 to 15 minutes, switching and rotating the baking sheets halfway through baking. Let the cookies cool completely on the baking sheets, then break them apart along the scored lines and serve. (The cookies will keep in an airtight container for 3 days.)

VARIATION

HOMEMADE CINNAMON GRAHAM CRACKERS

Increase the amount of cinnamon in the dough to ½ teaspoon. Toss ¼ cup sugar with 1 teaspoon ground cinnamon, then sprinkle over the scored cookies just before baking.

NOTES FROM THE TEST KITCHEN

INEXPENSIVE STANDING MIXERS

The $500 standing mixers in our test kitchen are powerful enough to work all day. Can the home cook who needs less muscle buy a good standing mixer for less money? To find out, we rounded up eight models priced under $200 and whipped cream, creamed butter and sugar, made chunky cookie dough, and kneaded pizza dough. Our test cooks aren't ready to trade in their $500 mixers, but the **KitchenAid Classic Plus Stand Mixer**, $199, offers good value and performance for the average home cook. It aced every test and testers found it easy to operate. (See page 338 for more information about our testing results.)

BAKING SHEETS

We tested 11 baking sheets (a standard size is 18 by 13 inches) in a variety of materials and came to some interesting conclusions. First of all, shiny, light-colored baking sheets do a better job of evenly browning the bottoms of cookies than dark baking sheets do. Most of the dark sheets are nonstick, and we found that these pans tend to overbrown cookies. It also turns out that a nonstick surface (whether light or dark) is highly water-repellent and speeds evaporation by driving moisture away, which can make cookies too dry. Shiny, silver-colored sheets heat much more evenly; if sticking is a concern, there is always parchment paper, which also helps prevent the bottoms of the cookies from overbrowning. After baking over 2,900 cookies, the **Lincoln Food Service Half-Size Heavy Duty Sheet Pan** (left), $15.40, and the **Norpro Heavy Gauge Aluminum Jelly Roll Pan** (right), $17.99, came out on top. (See page 334 for more information about our testing results.)

PALMIERS

WHETHER YOU CALL THEM *palmiers (à la française),* elephant ears, butterflies, pig's ears, Prussians, or angel wings, they are all the same thing: flat heart-shaped sheets of coiled puff pastry coated thickly with a crunchy glaze. The best are crisp, dry, and lightly caramelized, tasting of nothing but pure butter, browned wheat, and golden sugar.

While palmiers themselves aren't particularly labor intensive to prepare, puff pastry is. Puff pastry is a multi-layered dough (what the professionals call "laminated") in which an elastic dough is wrapped tightly around a thin sheet of butter and folded time and time again, which exponentially develops alternating layers of dough and butter. When baked, the moisture in the butter evaporates into steam, causing the layers of dough to puff and separate into the hundreds of flaky, friable layers that mark proper puff pastry. The dough is typically prepared in a standing mixer and requires a good deal of time—and patience—to make.

Many palmiers recipes make do with store-bought commercial puff pastry, but I'm not a fan of the greasy texture and chemical aftertaste of the stuff (vegetable oil or shortening is typically substituted for some, if not all, of the butter). Could I create an "easy" version of puff pastry from which to make homemade palmiers? Of course I wasn't the first cook to want an easy version of puff pastry as I found a folder's worth of viable-looking recipes. Out of those I prepared, several held promise—quick dough, whipped up in the food processor, could be good dough.

Working with a rough master recipe, I tested my way through the dough's variables—all-purpose flour, water, sugar, and salt—until I was pretty pleased with the results. However, a drawback to using the food processor became clear: toughness. The machine blended the dough so quickly that it was hard to prevent overprocessing and, consequently, the dough turned tough and intractable. Cutting back on the water to minimize gluten development seemed to help a little, though it made the dough too dry and harder to roll. I found greater success by adding a couple of teaspoons of lemon juice, the acid content of which inhibited gluten development to keep the dough tender without making it unduly dry. That, and the juice's bright flavor also improved the flavor of the dough.

I chilled the dough, then wrapped it around the butter square (sticks of butter dusted with flour and pounded into a wafer-thin sheet) and began the process of "turning" the dough, or folding the dough to create the countless layers. Most professionals suggest that six turns are ideal and we found that to be the case here. Preparing the dough was still a multihour affair, however, as the dough required plenty of time to rest between turns. That said, the dough was definitely easy to put together and, considering it could be made well ahead of schedule, convenient.

So once you have the dough, how do you make palmiers? Plenty of sugar and a rolling pin. The dough is rolled out thin on a bed of sugar to completely coat it, after which it is fashioned into a heart-like shape by rolling each side of the rectangle inwards to meet in the middle. I quickly realized that it was imperative to freeze the dough log until firm before slicing crosswise into cookies; otherwise the cookies lost definition.

Puff pastry is typically baked hot to prompt a high rise, but in this case, high temperatures caused the sugar to burn before the dough was fully set, leaving it flabby and chewy. Lower temperatures precluded any chance of the sugar burning, but made for dense, tough, and flat pastry. The ideal baking temperature, then, was a compromise between texture and flavor. After ruining several sheet pans of palmiers, I decided that 375 degrees was the best temperature as it generated a good rise and a flaky texture in the time it took for the sugar to melt and slightly caramelize.

While most palmier recipes flip the cookies midway through baking, I found that the cookies were quite fragile at this point and easy to damage unless I was extremely careful. I thought the cookies might fare better if allowed to bake longer (and become firmer textured) before flipping and my hunch paid off. In fact, the longer I let them cook, the sturdier they were and the richer the caramelization—both sides needn't be equally cooked for great flavor. While my palmiers took a bit of time to make, there was really quite little hands-on effort; and the kitchen agreed that every minute was worth it: These tasted every bit as good as those at any bakery in town.

—SARAH WILSON, *America's Test Kitchen Books*

PALMIERS

PALMIERS

MAKES 24

If the dough becomes too warm and sticky to work with, cover it with plastic wrap and let it chill in the refrigerator until firm. The log of palmier dough can be wrapped tightly in plastic wrap and frozen for up to 1 month. Slice the frozen dough into cookies and bake as directed. Once baked, the palmiers can be stored in an airtight container at room temperature for up to 3 days.

DOUGH

- 3 cups (15 ounces) unbleached all-purpose flour, plus extra for the work surface
- 1½ tablespoons sugar
- 1½ teaspoons salt
- 2 teaspoons fresh lemon juice
- 1 cup ice water

BUTTER SQUARE

- 3 sticks unsalted butter, chilled
- 2 tablespoons unbleached all-purpose flour

PALMIERS

- 1 cup (7 ounces) sugar

1. FOR THE DOUGH: Pulse the flour, sugar, and salt together in a food processor to combine. With the machine running, add the lemon juice, followed by ¾ cup of the ice water, in a slow steady stream. Add the remaining ¼ cup water as needed, 1 tablespoon at a time, until the dough comes together and no floury bits remain.

2. Turn the dough onto a sheet of plastic wrap and flatten into a 6-inch square. Wrap the dough tightly in the plastic wrap and refrigerate for about 1 hour.

3. FOR THE BUTTER SQUARE: Lay the 3 sticks of butter side by side on a sheet of parchment paper. Sprinkle the flour over the butter and cover with a second sheet of parchment paper. Pound the butter with a rolling pin until the butter is softened and the flour is fully incorporated, then roll it into an 8-inch square. Wrap the butter square in plastic wrap and refrigerate until chilled, about 1 hour.

4. Roll the dough into an 11-inch square on a lightly floured work surface. Following the photos on page 110, place the chilled butter square diagonally in the center of the dough. Fold the corners of the dough up over the butter square so that the corners meet in the middle, and pinch the dough seams to seal.

5. Using a rolling pin, gently tap the dough, starting from the center and working outward, until the square becomes larger and the butter begins to soften. Gently roll the dough into a 14-inch square, adding extra flour as needed to prevent sticking. Fold the dough into thirds to form a rectangle, then fold the rectangle in thirds to form a square. Wrap the dough in plastic wrap and let rest in the refrigerator for 2 hours.

6. Repeat step 5 twice and let the dough rest in the refrigerator for 2 more hours. (The dough can be wrapped tightly in plastic wrap and refrigerated for up to 2 days or frozen for up to 1 month. Let the dough thaw completely in the refrigerator, about 12 hours, before using.)

7. FOR THE PALMIERS: Sprinkle ½ cup of the sugar over the counter and lay the puff pastry dough on top of the sugar. Roll the dough into a 24 by 12-inch rectangle, about ¼ inch thick, dusting with extra sugar as needed to prevent sticking.

8. Following the photos on page 263, roll both of the short sides of the dough towards the center, so that they meet in the middle. Wrap the log of dough in plastic wrap, transfer to a baking sheet, and freeze until firm, about 20 minutes.

9. Adjust an oven rack to the middle position and heat the oven to 375 degrees. Line a large baking sheet with parchment paper.

10. Slice half of the log of dough into ½-inch-thick cookies with a long, thin-bladed slicing knife; wrap the remaining, unsliced dough and keep frozen until ready to bake. Lay the cookies on the prepared baking sheet, spaced about 1 inch apart. Bake the cookies until they begin to brown and firm up, 15 to 20 minutes.

11. Flip the cookies over, rotate the baking sheet, and continue to bake until golden and crisp, 5 to 10 minutes longer. Immediately transfer the cookies to a wire rack and let cool completely, about 20 minutes, before serving. Repeat with the remaining dough, using a cool, freshly lined baking sheet.

SHAPING PALMIERS

1. Roll both of the short sides of the dough towards the center so that they meet in the middle.

2. After the dough has been frozen for 20 minutes to firm it up, slice it into ½-inch-thick cookies with a long, thin-bladed slicing knife.

WHEN TO FLIP

In order to achieve the crackly glazed exterior of a palmier, each cookie needs to bake on both sides. But flipping the cookies too early could yield misshapen palmiers. Rather than flipping the palmiers at the halfway point, wait until the sugar coating on the palmiers has started to caramelize before carefully flipping each cookie over. That way they hold their shape and bake up golden brown and crackly.

APRICOT-ALMOND BUNDT CAKE

OTHER THAN THE UNIQUE PAN, what makes a Bundt cake a Bundt cake? While there are no absolutes, they are typically richer than a sheet cake, but not quite as buttery (or dense) as a pound cake. They come in countless flavors, from plain-Jane vanilla, chocolate, or lemon to gussied-up with all manner of fruits and nuts. A favorite of mine combines the tart flavor of apricots with crunchy bittersweet almonds. It's a classic match, though not the easiest to pull off: Both ingredients have a subtle, fleeting flavor that can be hard to capture. So how do you do it?

I baked off a cross-section of Bundt cake recipes and found that most of them were either too dense or too light; none had the balanced texture that, to me, represents the real charm of a perfect Bundt cake. As for flavor, most recipes added a handful of chopped fresh or dried apricots to a vanilla-flavored cake or brushed a sticky flavored glaze across the top of the cake and called it a day. Clearly I had some work to do.

After cobbling together a basic working recipe, I set to testing the batter's variables in pursuit of the perfect texture; flavorings would follow. A fairly high ratio of fat to flour combined with a large number of eggs proved to be a good start. As for liquid, most Bundt cakes include something acidic to balance the cake's sweetness. Sour cream and yogurt are the most common options, but, in this case, I thought buttermilk did a great job of making the crumb tangy without weighing it down. The creaming process contributed some leavening, but not enough for the texture I was after. I tested the usual leaveners and thought the best results came from a combination of both baking powder and soda in a 2-to-1 ratio. Baked at a moderate 350 degrees, the cake had the firm but not overly dense texture I sought.

On to flavoring the cake. Given their short season, limited availability, and mild flavor, fresh apricots were out of the equation. Dried apricots were the best choice, though when chopped fine and mixed into the batter, their chewy texture marred the otherwise tender crumb of the cake. Reconstituting the chopped apricots in boiling water helped a great deal and, once folded into the batter, lent an appealing speckled appearance and a solid apricot flavor to the cake.

Pretty good, but not great, my cake seemed to need an additional flavor boost. The aforementioned buttermilk provided some acid, but tasters thought it could use more to boost the apricot's fruitiness. Lemon juice seemed like the logical choice and it worked well, providing a welcome brightness. While I was at it, I wondered if lemon zest might help and added what I could scrape off the lemon I had juiced. Tasters loved the results: not lemony per se, the citrus effectively galvanized the apricot's flavor.

I thought the cake had as rich an apricot flavor as I could get, but then I reviewed my recipes and found an unexpected ingredient in one recipe: apricot preserves. Intrigued, I added a few spoonfuls to the blended batter, baked the cake, and had the best results to date. I hadn't thought I could have possibly loaded the cake with any more apricot flavor, but the preserves clinched it. Unfortunately, the addition of the preserves weighed down the batter and made the crumb perceptibly denser. A colleague suggested creaming the preserves with the butter and sugar to lighten its texture and the tip paid off, making the cake even lighter than before the jam was added.

As for the almonds, I tested all the different types of almonds the store had to offer and thought that slivered packed the biggest flavor, especially once toasted, chopped, and dispersed through the batter. Additional almond flavorings, like almond extract or amaretto liqueur, came across as too strong in this instance. Some of us in the kitchen thought it tasted perfect at this point, others thought a glaze would bring it there; I'll leave that up to you, the cook, to decide.

—BRYAN ROOF, *America's Test Kitchen Books*

APRICOT-ALMOND BUNDT CAKE WITH ORANGE GLAZE

SERVES 12

This cake tastes great on its own, but topping it with orange-flavored glaze makes it even better. If time is a factor, a dusting of confectioners' sugar works, too.

CAKE

1	cup (5 ounces) dried apricots, chopped
3	cups (15 ounces) unbleached all-purpose flour
1	teaspoon salt
1	teaspoon baking powder
½	teaspoon baking soda
½	cup buttermilk, at room temperature
1	tablespoon vanilla extract
1	tablespoon grated lemon zest
1	tablespoon fresh lemon juice
2¼	sticks unsalted butter, cut into chunks and softened
1½	cups (10½ ounces) granulated sugar
½	cup apricot preserves
3	large whole eggs, at room temperature
1	large egg yolk, at room temperature
½	cup slivered almonds, toasted and chopped

ORANGE GLAZE

1¾	cups (7 ounces) confectioners' sugar
1	teaspoon grated orange zest
¼	cup fresh orange juice
	Pinch salt

1. FOR THE CAKE: Adjust an oven rack to the lower-middle position and heat the oven to 350 degrees. Carefully grease and flour a 12-cup Bundt pan.

2. In a small bowl, cover the apricots with boiling water and let sit until softened and plump, about 5 minutes; drain off the water and pat the apricots dry. In a medium bowl, whisk the flour, salt, baking powder, and baking soda together. In another medium bowl, whisk the buttermilk, vanilla, lemon zest, and lemon juice together.

3. In a large bowl, beat the butter, granulated sugar, and preserves together with an electric mixer on medium speed until light and fluffy, 3 to 6 minutes. Beat in the whole eggs and egg yolk, one at a time, until incorporated, about 1 minute.

4. Reduce the speed to low and beat in one-third of the flour mixture, followed by half of the buttermilk mixture. Repeat with half of the remaining flour mixture and the remaining buttermilk mixture. Beat in the remaining flour mixture until just incorporated. Stir in the apricots and almonds.

5. Scrape the batter into the prepared pan and smooth the top. Wipe any drops of batter off the sides of the pan and gently tap the pan on the counter to settle the batter. Bake the cake until a wooden skewer inserted into the center comes out with a few moist crumbs attached, 50 to 60 minutes, rotating the pan halfway through baking.

6. Let the cake cool in the pan for 10 minutes, then flip it out onto a wire rack. Let the cake cool completely, about 2 hours, before glazing.

7. FOR THE GLAZE: Whisk all of the glaze ingredients together in a medium bowl until smooth and let sit until thickened, about 25 minutes. Pour the glaze over the top of the cake after it has cooled completely, letting the glaze drip down the sides. Let the glaze set before serving, about 25 minutes. (The cake can be stored in an airtight container at room temperature or wrapped in plastic wrap for up to 2 days.)

DOUBLING UP ON APRICOTS

To really fortify the apricot flavor of our cake we used both dried apricots and apricot preserves. We first chopped the dried apricots, then reconstituted them in hot water to soften them. The chopped apricots gave the cake crumb an appealing speckled appearance, and rehydrating the apricots kept them from interrupting the delicate texture of the cake. We also added a healthy measure of apricot preserves. The preserves further built up the apricot flavor and made the cake deliciously moist. Creaming the preserves with the butter helped to make the cake even lighter.

THE BEST BUNDT PAN

Bundt pans come in a wide variety of shapes, finishes, and sizes and can cost anywhere from $9 to $30 or more. We decided to find out which pan would deliver a nicely shaped, evenly browned cake that would also release easily. We tested eight 12-cup Bundt pans, baking our Classic Yellow Bundt Cake in each, and our favorite was

the **NordicWare Platinum Series 12-Cup Classic Bundt Pan**, $29.95. Made of thick, durable cast aluminum, this Bundt pan produced the absolute best cake with even browning every time.

COLD-OVEN POUND CAKE

YEARS AGO, WHEN MY GRANDMOTHER ran a small baked goods business out of her home, her most popular item was cold-oven pound cake. It had the buttery richness of a traditional pound cake, but instead of the typical dense texture, it was very light, with a tender yet sturdy crumb and a surprisingly crisp crust. What Grandma never told her customers was how easy it was to make: She beat eggs into the creamed butter and sugar, mixed in cream and flour, and poured the batter—absent chemical leavener—into a tube pan that went into a stone-cold oven. The cake magically emerged tall and golden about an hour later. Since her recipe was misplaced long ago, I set out to record my own version.

My hunt for the origin of this curious recipe took me back over a hundred years. At the turn of the 20th century, gas lighting was being phased out in favor of newer electric technology. Looking to replace lost revenue, gas companies set their sights on the oven business. One of their marketing gimmicks was to push easy and "thrifty" recipes, like cold-oven pound cake, that didn't require preheating. This cake became popular throughout the South and was later reported to be Elvis Presley's favorite pound cake.

I gathered several existing recipes and headed to the kitchen. While most of the cakes lacked the lift and tenderness of Grandma's, one contemporary recipe showed promise; it did, however, contain a nontraditional ingredient—baking powder. The addition of just ½ teaspoon of this leavener (less than half the amount used for standard pound cake) produced a consistently lofty, even rise. I was able to get away with using so little because baking powder is double-acting (it produces carbon dioxide bubbles—and thus rise—when mixed with liquid and then again in the heat of the oven), and putting the cake into a cold oven meant that the gluten did not set up as quickly, allowing the carbon dioxide more time to produce greater rise.

Though grand in stature, the cake was still too dense. To create a lighter crumb, I exchanged the heavy cream from the working recipe for leaner whole milk and I swapped out all-purpose flour for cake flour. Baking the cake on the lower-middle rack of an oven turned to 325 degrees ensured an evenly cooked cake with a crisp, golden crust that would have made Grandma proud.

—CALI RICH, *Cook's Country*

COLD-OVEN POUND CAKE

SERVES 12

You'll need a 16-cup tube pan or angel food cake pan for this recipe; if not using a nonstick pan, make sure to thoroughly grease a traditional pan. In step 2, don't worry if the batter looks slightly separated.

- 3 cups (12 ounces) cake flour
- ½ teaspoon baking powder
- 1 teaspoon salt
- 1 cup whole milk
- 2 teaspoons vanilla extract
- 2½ sticks unsalted butter, softened
- 2½ cups (17½ ounces) sugar
- 6 large eggs, at room temperature

1. Adjust an oven rack to the lower-middle position. Grease and flour a 16-cup tube pan. Combine the flour, baking powder, and salt in a bowl. Whisk the milk and vanilla in a measuring cup.

2. With an electric mixer on medium speed, beat the butter and sugar until fluffy, about 2 minutes. Beat in the eggs, one at a time, until combined. Reduce the speed to low and add the flour mixture in 3 additions, alternating with 2 additions of the milk mixture. Mix on low until smooth, about 30 seconds. Use a rubber spatula to give the batter a final stir.

3. Pour the batter into the prepared pan and smooth the top. Place the cake in a cold oven. Adjust the oven temperature to 325 degrees and bake, without opening the oven door, until the cake is golden brown and a toothpick inserted into the center comes out clean, 65 to 80 minutes.

4. Let the cake cool in the pan for 15 minutes, then turn it out onto a wire rack. Let the cake cool completely, about 2 hours. Serve. (The cooled cake can be stored in an airtight container at room temperature or wrapped in plastic wrap for up to 2 days.)

NOTES FROM THE TEST KITCHEN

THE BEST TUBE PAN

Whether you are making an old-fashioned tube cake, angel food cake, or chiffon cake, you need a tube pan—the center tube conducts heat and helps the cake bake faster and more evenly. Among the models available we found pans made with a range of materials and with features like removable bottoms, cooling feet, and tubes taller than the rim of the pan, so you can upturn cooling cakes without the usual aid of a narrow-necked bottle. We discovered in our testing that pans with removable bottoms made in lightweight materials (under 1 pound) allowed batter to seep under the bottom. Poor browning was the other flaw for most pans, especially those with pale, tinny finishes. We found that pans with a dark, nonstick coating delivered tall and evenly burnished cakes—and they even worked with angel food cakes too, which we worried would slip down the nonstick sides. Our favorite all-purpose tube pan? The **Chicago Metallic Angel Food Cake Pan with Feet**, $19.95.

This 16-cup tube pan is heavy, and has a dark, nonstick finish, and handy feet on the rim that elevate the upturned pan for cooling when you're making an angel food cake.

TRES LECHES CAKE

TO FIND THE SECRET to great *tres leches*—a sponge cake soaked with a mixture of "three milks" (heavy cream, evaporated milk, and sweetened condensed milk), then topped with whipped cream—I went to south Texas, where the Mexican-American community has been making this cake for generations. After eating my way through dozens of cakes and talking to several pastry chefs and cooks, I determined that a good tres leches cake should be moist (but not mushy) and not overly sweet.

Most of the cakes I sampled failed in one or both of those regards, but one I had in a San Antonio restaurant stood out for being incredibly moist but not soggy, with the added twist of a caramel topping called dulce de leche. This was a cake worth trying to re-create in the test kitchen.

Everyone in Texas told me that the open crumb of a sponge cake did the best job of absorbing the milk mixture, so I started with the test kitchen's sponge cake recipe, which gets its lift from beaten egg whites. It emerged from the oven puffed and golden but sank in the center when I poured on the milk mixture. In search of a sturdier sponge cake, I tried several other recipes, with no success. A colleague finally suggested a "hot milk" sponge, made by heating milk and butter and then pouring the mixture into whipped whole eggs (which are sturdier than just whites). This cake baked up tall and sturdy enough to handle the milk mixture.

Most recipes use one can each of evaporated and sweetened condensed milk and an equal amount of cream. Cutting back the cream to just 1 cup produced a thicker mixture that didn't oversaturate the cake. After many tests, I found that pouring room-temperature milk over warm cake worked best.

I thought back to the dulce de leche–topped tres leches I'd had in San Antonio. This type of caramel is traditionally made by boiling an unopened can of sweetened condensed milk for about an hour; since I was already using sweetened condensed milk, I wondered if I could cook it down a little to get the dulce de leche flavor inside my cake. So I poured the milk into a bowl and microwaved it until it became slightly thickened and straw-colored. I mixed this with the other milks and poured it over the cake. With a hint of rich caramel in each custard-laden bite, this was the Tres Leches Cake I had been looking for: one worthy of the Lone Star State.

—CALI RICH, *Cook's Country*

TRES LECHES CAKE

SERVES 12

If using a standing mixer to beat the eggs in step 3, be sure to use the whisk attachment. The cake becomes more moist and dense as it sits.

MILK MIXTURE

- 1 (14-ounce) can sweetened condensed milk
- 1 (12-ounce) can evaporated milk
- 1 cup heavy cream
- 1 teaspoon vanilla extract

CAKE

- 2 cups (10 ounces) unbleached all-purpose flour
- 2 teaspoons baking powder
- 1 teaspoon salt
- ½ teaspoon ground cinnamon
- 8 tablespoons (1 stick) unsalted butter
- 1 cup whole milk
- 4 large eggs, at room temperature
- 2 cups (14 ounces) sugar
- 2 teaspoons vanilla extract

FROSTING

- 1 cup heavy cream
- 3 tablespoons light corn syrup
- 1 teaspoon vanilla extract

1. FOR THE MILK MIXTURE: Pour the condensed milk into a large microwave-safe bowl and cover tightly with plastic wrap. Microwave on low power, stirring and replacing the plastic every 3 to 5 minutes, until slightly darkened and thickened, 9 to 15 minutes. Remove from the microwave and slowly whisk in the evaporated milk, cream, and vanilla. Let cool to room temperature.

2. FOR THE CAKE: Adjust an oven rack to the middle position and heat the oven to 325 degrees. Grease and flour a 13 by 9-inch baking pan. Whisk the flour, baking powder, salt, and cinnamon in a bowl. Heat the butter

and milk in a small saucepan over low heat until the butter is melted; set aside off the heat.

3. With an electric mixer on medium speed, beat the eggs in a large bowl for about 30 seconds, then slowly add the sugar until incorporated. Increase the speed to medium-high and beat until the egg mixture is very thick and glossy, 5 to 7 minutes. Reduce the speed to low and slowly mix in the melted butter mixture and vanilla. Add the flour mixture in 3 additions, scraping down the bowl as necessary, then mix on medium speed until fully incorporated, about 30 seconds. Using a rubber spatula, scrape the batter into the prepared pan and bake until a toothpick inserted into the center comes out clean, 30 to 35 minutes. Transfer the cake to a wire rack and let cool for 10 minutes.

4. Using a skewer, poke holes at ½-inch intervals in the top of the cake. Slowly pour the milk mixture over the cake until completely absorbed. Let sit at room temperature 15 minutes, then refrigerate uncovered 3 hours or up to 24 hours.

5. FOR THE FROSTING: Remove the cake from the refrigerator 30 minutes before serving. With an electric mixer on medium speed, beat the cream, corn syrup, and vanilla to soft peaks, 1 to 2 minutes. Frost the cake and slice into 3-inch squares. Serve. (The assembled cake can be refrigerated for up to 3 days.)

NOTES FROM THE TEST KITCHEN

DELUXE LIQUID MEASURING CUP

To use a liquid measuring cup, you typically set it on a level surface, pour in the ingredient, and crouch down to see if the liquid meets the line at eye level. Then you adjust. But the new **Cuisipro Deluxe Liquid Measuring Cup**, $8.95 for the 2-cup and $11.95 for the 4-cup, streamlines this process; it can be read from above. The clear plastic measure is dishwasher- and microwave-safe and features a removable clip fitted with a magnetized, dual-sided red plastic marker. When you slide the outer marker to the desired measurement line, the inner tab moves with it. Then you fill to the level of the inside marker. We measured and weighed 1 cup of water to test for accuracy, then compared results with our favorite Pyrex 2-cup glass measure. The Cuisipro, read from a standing position, measured even more accurately than the Pyrex, and we like its durability and easy-to-read markings.

TUNNEL OF FUDGE CAKE

IN 1966, ELLA HELFRICH of Houston, Texas, won second place—and $5,000—in the annual Pillsbury Bake-Off for her Tunnel of Fudge Cake recipe. Ella's glazed, nutty, and brownie-like cake was baked in a Bundt pan, but its most distinguishing feature was the ring (or "tunnel") of creamy fudge that formed inside the cake as it baked. More important, it was my birthday cake from the time I was eight years old.

Wanting to bake this cake for my son on his birthday, I dusted off my mother's old Pillsbury recipe, in which three sticks of butter were creamed with 1½ cups of white sugar, and then eggs, flour, and nuts were mixed in along with a secret ingredient: a package of powdered Pillsbury Two Layer Double-Dutch Fudge Buttercream Frosting mix. This mix was the key to the cake, as it contained large amounts of cocoa powder and confectioners' sugar, which separated out during baking—this cake was always slightly underbaked—and came together to help form the fudgy center. Pillsbury no longer sells this frosting mix, but they do offer an updated recipe (which includes lots of cocoa powder and confectioners' sugar) on their Web site.

I had high hopes as I pulled the new Pillsbury recipe out of the oven. Sadly, it was lacking in chocolate flavor, and even worse, it had no fudgy center. Other modern recipes attempt to replace the frosting mix with ingredients like instant chocolate pudding and homemade chocolate ganache hardened into a ring and set in the middle of the batter, but they also failed to create the signature tunnel. Some recipes plant chunks of chocolate inside the batter, but they baked up with a liquid interior that gushed when the cake was sliced. A proper Tunnel of Fudge Cake has a creamy, frosting-like filling that holds its shape when the cake is cut. I decided to return to the updated Pillsbury recipe and see if I could fix it.

To add more chocolate flavor, I switched from natural cocoa powder (which can be sour) to less-acidic Dutch-processed cocoa and added melted chocolate to the batter. As for the tunnel, I knew that slightly underbaking the cake was a big part of it. But even when underbaked, the interior of my cake was still too dry and decidedly nonfudgy.

To add moisture (and flavor), I swapped out almost half of the granulated sugar with brown sugar. But the big key was adjusting the amounts of two base ingredients: flour and butter. Cutting back on the flour made the cake much more moist, and using less butter helped the cakey exterior set more quickly; together these changes created the perfect environment for the fudgy interior to form. Finally, after two dozen failed cakes, the "tunnel" was back.

—BRIDGET LANCASTER, *Cook's Country*

TUNNEL OF FUDGE CAKE

SERVES 12

Do not use a cake tester, toothpick, or skewer to test the cake—the fudgy interior won't give an accurate reading. Instead, remove the cake from the oven when the sides just begin to pull away from the pan and the surface of the cake springs back when pressed gently with your finger.

CAKE

¾ cup (2¼ ounces) Dutch-processed cocoa powder, plus extra for the pan
½ cup boiling water
2 ounces bittersweet chocolate, chopped
2 cups (10 ounces) unbleached all-purpose flour
2 cups pecans or walnuts, chopped fine
2 cups (8 ounces) confectioners' sugar
1 teaspoon salt
5 large eggs, at room temperature
1 tablespoon vanilla extract
1 cup (7 ounces) granulated sugar
¾ cup packed (5¼ ounces) light brown sugar
2½ sticks unsalted butter, softened

CHOCOLATE GLAZE

¾ cup heavy cream
¼ cup light corn syrup
8 ounces bittersweet chocolate, chopped
½ teaspoon vanilla extract

1. FOR THE CAKE: Adjust an oven rack to the lower-middle position and heat the oven to 350 degrees. Grease a 12-cup Bundt pan and dust with cocoa powder. Pour the boiling water over the chocolate in a medium bowl and whisk until smooth. Cool to room temperature. Whisk the cocoa, flour, nuts, confectioners' sugar, and salt in a large bowl. Beat the eggs and vanilla in a large measuring cup.

2. With an electric mixer on medium-high speed, beat the granulated sugar, brown sugar, and butter until light and fluffy, about 2 minutes. On low speed, add the egg mixture until combined, about 30 seconds. Add the chocolate mixture and beat until incorporated, about 30 seconds. Beat in the flour mixture until just combined, about 30 seconds.

3. Scrape the batter into the prepared pan, smooth the batter, and bake until the edges are beginning to pull away from the pan, about 45 minutes. Cool upright in the pan on a wire rack for 1½ hours, then invert onto a serving plate and cool completely, at least 2 hours.

4. FOR THE GLAZE: Cook the cream, corn syrup, and chocolate in a small saucepan over medium heat, stirring constantly, until smooth. Stir in the vanilla and set aside until slightly thickened, about 30 minutes. Drizzle the glaze over the cake and let set for at least 10 minutes. Serve. (The cake can be stored in an airtight container at room temperature or wrapped in plastic wrap for up to 2 days.)

NOTES FROM THE TEST KITCHEN

BIRTH OF THE BUNDT PAN

Metallurgical engineer H. David Dalquist invented the Bundt pan in 1950 at the request of bakers in Minneapolis who were using old-fashioned ceramic pans of the same design. Dalquist turned to cast aluminum to produce a pan that was much lighter and easier to use. Sales of his Bundt pan (a name he trademarked) were underwhelming until the Tunnel of Fudge Cake made its debut. To meet demand, Dalquist's company, NordicWare, went into 24-hour production. Over 50 million Bundt pans have been sold worldwide.

THE TRUTH ABOUT DARK CHOCOLATE

We've tasted and cooked with lots of chocolate that falls into the "gourmet" category, and although many brands have distinctive flavors that tasters liked in particular desserts, two chocolates consistently produced great results in all types of baked goods, **Callebaut Intense Dark Chocolate** (left), 53 cents per ounce, and **Ghirardelli Bittersweet Chocolate Baking Bar** (right), 75 cents per ounce. We liked these better than more expensive dark chocolates and they are widely available. Tasters praised both for rich, complex flavor and a creamy texture. (See page 324 for more information about our testing results.)

RUSTIC PLUM CAKE

THE INSPIRATION FOR THIS RECIPE came from *Zwetschgenkuchen*, an Austrian specialty in which ripe, sweet plums (the regional variety Zwetschgen) are nestled into rich cake, or *Kuchen*. It is a simple way to enjoy a summertime fruit at its peak, but finding a promising recipe wasn't so easy. I consulted numerous cookbooks and even talked to Austrians who grew up on the dessert, and I learned that, depending on which country or region claimed credit, plum cake could be anything from an Alsatian tart to a German yeasted bread. One friend recalled her grandmother shaking plums from a tree, then baking them into a cake, pits and all.

To get my bearings, I tried a variety of recipes. In most, the plums sank into the cake and created a sodden center. To get around this, some recipe writers placed a scant layer of thinly sliced plums on top, leaving behind mouthfuls of plain cake. Others mixed up a cake batter so dry and pancakey that the plums, having no choice but to be sponged up, did little to improve the cake's texture. What, I wondered, was the secret to this quintessential rustic treat?

It wasn't until a fellow test cook suggested I try a plum cake recipe that the *New York Times* ran every August from 1981 to 1996 that I found a style of cake I liked. This recipe was easy to make (a creamed cake batter spread into a springform pan, topped with plums, and baked), and it had a hefty plum presence. It called for Italian plums, which are well suited to baking. Although this buttery yellow cake was sturdy enough to support all the fruit, tasters criticized it for being on the dry side. And the fruit was rather bland, needing embellishment beyond the uninspired sprinkling of cinnamon and sugar. I set out to add some finesse to this recipe.

With its simple ingredient list of butter, sugar, flour, eggs, salt, and baking powder, my working recipe didn't contain any liquid dairy element, which explained why the batter was strong enough to support all those plums and also the dryness my tasters had complained about. I tried adding a little milk, but the cake turned light and fluffy, and the fruit plummeted to the bottom of the pan. This cake needs to be dense and sturdy.

Many rich European cakes replace some of the flour with ground nuts. I tried hazelnuts, walnuts, and almonds and found that in addition to a welcome flavor

RUSTIC PLUM CAKE

dimension (almonds were the preferred choice with plums), the nuts also added both bulk and richness. So rich was the cake, in fact, I had to cut back on the butter to avoid a greasy texture. The extra structure added by the nuts enabled me to both decrease the flour (making the cake even moister) and omit an egg white (making it more tender).

Adding nuts to the recipe also led me to reexamine the mixing method for this cake. I decided to try melting the butter and mixing everything in the food processor, which I was already using to grind the nuts, instead of the standard creaming method (whipping the sugar and butter together before adding the other ingredients). Not only was the food processor method more streamlined, but it also gave the cake a denser, chewier quality—a little too dense, even. A switch to softened butter, added to the dry ingredients before the eggs, made the cake lighter; this cake now offered the right textural contrast to the tender fruit.

The small Italian prune plums used in my working recipe are prized for baking due to their relatively dry, firm flesh and thin skin. But miss those few weeks when they're in season and you are plumb out of luck. I wanted a way to prepare this cake with any variety of fresh plum.

I found that even Italian prune plums needed some help to realize their full potential. I tried tossing the plum halves in sugar alone and then in melted butter and sugar, to little success. Realizing something more drastic was going to be necessary to get more than adequate plum flavor, I started with a battery of plum precooking methods. I tried roasting the plums (tossed in melted butter and sugar) and poaching them in sugar syrup. These methods intensified the flavor of the plums, but the fruit baked up overcooked and mushy.

Needing a quicker cooking method, I sautéed the plums, cut-side down, in butter and sugar in a skillet on the stovetop. Although the plums developed a nice golden color and caramelized flavor, the high heat caused the skins to peel back and the flesh to blow out—mushy fruit once again. I tried making caramel in the pan and then adding the fruit, but the caramel was still so hot that the fruit became overcooked. Cooling the caramel first caused it to harden, making it impossible to combine with the plums.

I was almost ready to give up on the skillet altogether when I decided to rethink how I was using it. What if I kept the plums in the skillet but cooked them over a gentler heat? True, I was forfeiting any chance of caramelizing the plums, but perhaps I could still coax more flavor without sacrificing texture. With just a sprinkling of sugar in the pan under the plums, I started them on medium heat. They slowly began to release their juices, which formed a syrup with the sugar. Effectively poached in their own juices, the plums were intensely flavored without being overcooked. And once in the cake, their syrupy surfaces stayed moist even after a spell in the oven. Best of all, this technique worked with every variety of plum I tested.

Excited about this solution, I explored other flavoring options, wondering if there was something more interesting to add than plain sugar. I tried brown sugar and cinnamon, but these both dumbed down the bright flavors of the fruit. Lemon juice gave a nice kick but was too assertive. I found red fruit jams enhanced the fruitiness of the plums better than plain sugar, and a shot of brandy added a nice tartness. Reducing the brandy with the jam first eliminated any harsh booziness. Finally, I had landed on a plum cake true to its name, and I knew eating it would be *the* highlight of my summer.

—ERIKA BRUCE, *Cook's Illustrated*

RUSTIC PLUM CAKE

SERVES 6 TO 8

This recipe works best with Italian plums, which are also called prune plums. If substituting regular red or black plums, use an equal weight of plums, cut them into eighths, and stir them a few times while cooking. Arrange the slices, slightly overlapped, in two rings over the surface of the cake. Do not use canned Italian plums. Blanched whole almonds can be used but must be processed 30 seconds longer until finely ground. The brandy can be omitted, but then you will need to melt the jam with 1 tablespoon water before adding the plums. Don't add the leftover plum cooking liquid to the cake before baking; reserve it and serve with the finished cake or over ice cream. The cake can be served with lightly sweetened whipped cream.

2 tablespoons red currant jelly or seedless raspberry jam

3 tablespoons brandy (see note)

1 pound (about 10 large or 14 small) Italian prune plums, halved and pitted (see note)

¾ cup (5¼ ounces) granulated sugar

⅓ cup slivered almonds (see note)

¾ cup (3¾ ounces) unbleached all-purpose flour

½ teaspoon baking powder

¼ teaspoon salt

6 tablespoons (¾ stick) unsalted butter, cut into 6 pieces, and softened

1 large whole egg, at room temperature

1 large egg yolk, at room temperature

1 teaspoon vanilla extract

¼ teaspoon almond extract (optional)
    Confectioners' sugar, for serving

1. Cook the jelly or jam and brandy in a 10-inch non-stick skillet over medium heat until reduced to a thick syrup, 2 to 3 minutes. Remove the skillet from the heat and place the plums cut-side down in the syrup. Return the skillet to medium heat and cook until the plums shed their juices and a thick syrup is again formed, about 5 minutes, shaking the pan to prevent the plums from sticking. Cool the plums in the pan, about 20 minutes.

2. Adjust an oven rack to the middle position and heat the oven to 350 degrees. Grease and flour a 9-inch springform pan. Process the granulated sugar and almonds in a food processor until the nuts are finely ground, about 1 minute. Add the flour, baking powder, and salt; pulse to combine. Add the butter and pulse until the mixture resembles coarse sand, about ten 1-second pulses. Add the whole egg, egg yolk, vanilla, and almond extract (if using) and process until smooth, about 5 seconds, scraping the bowl once if needed (the batter will be very thick and heavy).

3. Transfer the batter to the prepared pan; using a spatula, spread the batter evenly to the pan edges and smooth the surface. Stir the plums to coat with the syrup. Arrange the plum halves, skin-side down, evenly over the surface of the batter. Bake until the cake is golden brown and a wooden skewer inserted into the center comes out with a few crumbs attached, 40 to 50 minutes. Run a paring knife around the sides of the cake to loosen. Let the cake cool in the pan on a wire

rack until just warm or to room temperature, at least 30 minutes. Remove the sides of the pan and dust the cake with confectioners' sugar. Cut into slices and serve.

NOTES FROM THE TEST KITCHEN

A TRULY RELIABLE SPRINGFORM PAN

A springform pan is an essential piece of equipment for Rustic Plum Cake and other cakes impossible to remove from a standard cake pan. In addition to a smooth-working buckle, we found the most crucial feature on a reliable springform pan to be its ability to resist leakage—either batter out or water in (for those cakes that are baked in a water bath). Of the six pans we tested, we favored the **Frieling Handle-It Glass Bottom 9-inch Springform Pan**, $31.95, for its sturdy, rimless glass bottom (which allows you to monitor the browning progress of a crust) and its convenient handles.

SECRETS TO A PERFECT PLUM CAKE

COOK THE PLUMS: Gently heating plums in a few tablespoons of jam and brandy heightens their flavor without overcooking them.

USE THICK, RICH CAKE BATTER: The batter must be thick enough to support the fruit, without being dry. The secret? Ground nuts.

PACK WITH FRUIT: You want fruit in every bite, so place the plums (skin-side down and not touching the pan edges) over the entire surface of the batter.

TEXAS SHEET CAKE

THE OFFICIAL STATE CAKE OF TEXAS, Texas sheet cake is a huge, pecan-topped chocolate cake with three distinct layers of chocolaty goodness. A diverse range of textures is created when a sweet chocolate icing is poured over a cake that's still hot out of the oven; when the cake cools, you're left with an icing layer, a fudgy layer where the icing and hot cake have mixed together, and a bottom layer of moist cake. The cake is easy to make (no mixer is required) and great to take to potlucks and barbecues because, as its name implies, it's baked in a sheet pan and serves a crowd. But recipes I found all had one big problem: They didn't pack much chocolate wallop.

Most Texas sheet cake recipes start by blooming cocoa powder in water with margarine, oil, butter, vegetable shortening, or a combination thereof. The cocoa mixture is then combined with flour, sugar, baking soda, eggs, dairy (milk, buttermilk, or sour cream), and vanilla in a single bowl. I baked up cakes with different combinations of margarine, oil, butter, and shortening, and my tasters agreed that margarine imparted an unpleasant artificial flavor. The cake made with all butter tasted great, but the texture was too light and cakey. The cake made with a combination of butter (for flavor) and vegetable oil (to keep the cake moist) was the best overall, producing a cake with a dense, brownie-like texture.

All of the recipes I found had a skimpy ¼ cup of cocoa, which accounted for the measly chocolate flavor. Doubling the amount of cocoa certainly helped, but adding 8 ounces of melted semisweet chocolate gave me the strong chocolate flavor my tasters were craving. The semisweet chocolate also contributed moisture and fat to the batter, which made for a fudgier cake. As for the dairy, tasters preferred rich, tangy sour cream over buttermilk or milk.

Standard recipes for the icing call for a stick of butter, milk, another ¼ cup of cocoa, and 4 cups of confectioners' sugar. My tasters deemed this formula too sweet, so I took the amount of sugar down to 3 cups and doubled the cocoa (as I had done in the cake) to ½ cup. To give the icing more body, I replaced the milk with heavy cream, and I added a tablespoon of corn syrup to give the frosting a lustrous finish.

Since my cake was already pretty moist, I was curious as to whether the icing absolutely had to be poured over the cake while it was hot. I baked up two sheet cakes, icing one directly out of the oven and icing the other after it had cooled. The results were clear—the cake iced while hot had that characteristic moist, gooey, fudgy layer under the frosting, while the other cake was an ordinary frosted cake. This sheet cake may come from Texas, but I think the rest of the country deserves to share its big chocolate flavor.

—DIANE UNGER, *Cook's Country*

TEXAS SHEET CAKE

SERVES 24

Toast the pecans in a dry skillet over medium heat, shaking the pan occasionally, until golden and fragrant, about 5 minutes.

CAKE

- 2 cups (10 ounces) unbleached all-purpose flour
- 2 cups (14 ounces) granulated sugar
- ½ teaspoon baking soda
- ½ teaspoon salt
- 2 large whole eggs, at room temperature
- 2 large egg yolks, at room temperature
- 2 teaspoons vanilla extract
- ¼ cup sour cream
- 8 ounces semisweet chocolate, chopped
- 4 tablespoons (½ stick) unsalted butter
- ¾ cup vegetable oil
- ¾ cup water
- ½ cup (1½ ounces) Dutch-processed cocoa powder

CHOCOLATE ICING

- 8 tablespoons (1 stick) unsalted butter
- ½ cup heavy cream
- ½ cup (1½ ounces) Dutch-processed cocoa powder
- 1 tablespoon light corn syrup
- 3 cups (12 ounces) confectioners' sugar
- 1 tablespoon vanilla extract
- 1 cup toasted pecans, chopped (see note)

1. FOR THE CAKE: Adjust an oven rack to the middle position and heat the oven to 350 degrees. Grease an 18 by 13-inch rimmed baking sheet. Combine the flour, sugar, baking soda, and salt in a large bowl. Whisk the whole eggs, egg yolks, vanilla, and sour cream in another bowl until smooth.

2. Heat the chocolate, butter, oil, water, and cocoa in a large saucepan over medium heat, stirring occasionally, until smooth, 3 to 5 minutes. Whisk the chocolate mixture into the flour mixture until incorporated. Whisk the egg mixture into the batter, then pour into the prepared baking sheet. Bake until a toothpick inserted into the center of the cake comes out clean, 18 to 20 minutes. Transfer to a wire rack.

3. FOR THE ICING: About 5 minutes before the cake is done, heat the butter, cream, cocoa, and corn syrup in a large saucepan over medium heat, stirring occasionally, until smooth. Off the heat, whisk in the confectioners' sugar and vanilla. Spread the warm icing evenly over the hot cake and sprinkle with the pecans. Let the cake cool to room temperature on the wire rack, about 1 hour, then refrigerate until the icing is set, about 1 hour longer. Cut into 3-inch squares. Serve. (The cake can be wrapped in plastic and refrigerated for up to 2 days. Bring to room temperature before serving.)

NOTES FROM THE TEST KITCHEN

TIMING IS EVERYTHING
The key to perfectly moist Texas Sheet Cake is to let the warm icing soak into the hot cake. As soon as the cake comes out of the oven, pour the warm icing over the cake and use a spatula to spread the icing to the edges of the cake. This creates the signature fudgy layer between the icing and the cake.

ICING WITH EASE
Unlike a regular spatula, the blade of an offset spatula dips down at the handle, keeping your fingers and knuckles out of the way. Though they come in many sizes, we prefer the **8½-inch Ateco Offset Spatula** (top), $5, because it's also perfect for spreading cake and brownie batter—and even transferring cookies from baking sheets. For smaller jobs, such as cupcakes, the **4½-inch Wilton Angled Comfort Grip Spatula** (bottom), $4.50, scored ahead of the pack.

INDIVIDUAL BANANAS FOSTER CAKES

INVENTED DURING THE 1950s at Brennan's, one of New Orleans's most storied restaurants, Bananas Foster is an ingenious confection composed of bananas caramelized in a butterscotch sauce and flambéed with rum. While many desserts of this age—and genre—have faded from popularity, Bananas Foster has faultless flavor and remains relevant. I've recently come across a number of cakes—from small bakeries and large megastores alike—that use the dessert as a launching pad for an upside-down cake: The dessert's trademark bananas and sauce are baked beneath a rich, moist yellow cake that is inverted before serving. While the cakes I've tasted haven't been particularly exciting—sweet, bland, and mushy textured—the concept of the cake was inspiring enough that I wanted to make my own version with a complex flavor and a compelling crumb.

Apparently, Bananas Foster cake really hasn't hit the mainstream as my research uncovered few recipes (and those I did gather generally started off with a box of yellow cake mix or bottle of caramel sauce). That said, I found plenty of recipes for Bananas Foster itself, so I decided to focus first on the fruit and sauce; the cake would follow. For most Bananas Foster recipes, the butter and brown sugar are simply blended together in the skillet and brought to a simmer before the bananas are added. I tested a half-dozen recipes and, in most cases, the sauce turned out greasy and a couple "broke," or the butter separated from the grainy sugar. Following the recommendation of the most successful recipe I tried, I constantly whisked the ingredients together until they were completely and irrevocably emulsified—no more problems.

Few recipes I found specified the best type of brown sugar to use, but a side-by-side comparison of batches made with each type made it clear: Dark brown sugar produced a sauce that tasted earthier and far more satisfying. As for the rum, recipes typically specified spicy, deep-flavored dark rum, and I had to agree as light rum tasted much milder and contributed a meek flavor to the sauce. While traditional recipes flambé the rum to burn off the excess alcohol (and as a bit of showmanship), I found the step unnecessary (and it actually diminished the sauce's flavor). The alcohol's bitterness was tempered by the cake's turn in the oven. Simply stirring the rum into the sauce, off the heat, worked just fine.

When I sautéed and caramelized the bananas in the sauce—as I would for the traditional dessert—the bananas turned mushy and virtually dissolved into the sauce as the cake cooked. Clearly, if the bananas were to be baked, they should be added to the cake while still raw. I poured the sauce into the pan and shingled the sliced bananas across the bottom. It looked great and I hoped it would remain that way once baked.

As for the cake, I gathered a few upside-down cake recipes, baked a selection of these, and found that cakes prepared via the reverse creaming method (where the butter is beaten into the flour) yielded the best crumb and sturdiest cake—enough to support the banana and caramel topping once the cake was flipped. I fiddled with the basic ratio of ingredients and tweaked them in subsequent batches until I was pleased with the results.

With this basic batter, I next looked for flavors that best complemented the bananas and sauce. First of all, I replaced a portion of the granulated sugar used to sweeten the cake with dark brown sugar, which contributed an earthy flavor to complement that of the topping. To maximize the sauce's rum flavor, I added a splash to the batter along with a spoonful of cinnamon. And finally, the acidic bite of lemon zest clarified the cake's flavors and accented the banana's fruitiness.

While the cake tasted good at this point, there were structural issues. No matter what type of dish I baked the cake in, be it square or round, metal or glass, a baking dish or a tall-sided springform pan, nothing cooked the cake evenly through to the center, making it nearly impossible to invert the cake without making a mess of the shingled bananas. After chasing one too many red herrings involving the batter, rack placement, and oven temperature, I had the solution: individual cakes. I divided the sauce equally among ovensafe ramekins, shingled banana slices on top, and spooned the batter over the bananas. They looked great fresh from the oven, and, after a brief cooling period to allow the molten sugar to set a little, the little cakes were easy to invert and released readily from their ramekins. The cakes looked beautiful and tasted even better, especially when paired with the natural accompaniment for cake or Bananas Foster: vanilla ice cream.

—RACHEL TOOMEY, *America's Test Kitchen Books*

INDIVIDUAL BANANAS FOSTER CAKES
SERVES 8

These cakes get their inspiration from the classic New Orleans dessert known as Bananas Foster, in which bananas are cooked in a caramel-butter sauce, then flambéed with rum and served over vanilla ice cream. These are great served with or without the ice cream.

- 14 tablespoons (1¾ sticks) unsalted butter, cut into 14 pieces and softened
- ⅔ cup packed (4⅔ ounces) dark brown sugar
- 6 tablespoons dark rum
- 3 ripe, firm bananas, peeled and sliced ¼ inch thick
- ½ cup whole milk
- 3 large eggs, at room temperature
- 2 teaspoons vanilla extract
- 1¾ cups (8¾ ounces) unbleached all-purpose flour
- 1 cup (7 ounces) granulated sugar
- 2 teaspoons baking powder
- ¾ teaspoon salt
- ¾ teaspoon ground cinnamon
- ½ teaspoon grated lemon zest

Vanilla ice cream, for serving (optional)

1. Adjust an oven rack to the middle position and heat the oven to 325 degrees. Grease eight 6-ounce ramekins, then set on a large rimmed baking sheet.

2. Melt 6 tablespoons of the butter in a small saucepan over medium heat. Add ⅓ cup of the brown sugar and cook, whisking constantly, until the mixture is thoroughly combined, about 2 minutes. Off the heat, whisk in 2 tablespoons of the rum. Spoon a generous tablespoon of the sauce into the bottom of each ramekin.

3. Following the photo on page 276, shingle the banana slices on top of the sauce inside each ramekin. Whisk the remaining ¼ cup rum, the milk, eggs, and vanilla together in a medium bowl.

4. In a large bowl, whisk the remaining ⅓ cup brown sugar, the flour, granulated sugar, baking powder, salt, cinnamon, and zest together. Using an electric mixer on medium-low speed, beat the remaining 8 tablespoons butter into the flour mixture and continue to beat the mixture until it resembles moist crumbs, 1 to 3 minutes.

5. Beat in all but ¼ cup of the milk mixture, then increase the speed to medium and beat the batter until smooth, light, and fluffy, 1 to 3 minutes. Reduce the speed to low and slowly beat in the remaining ¼ cup milk mixture until the batter looks slightly curdled, about 15 seconds.

6. Give the batter a final stir with a rubber spatula to make sure it is thoroughly combined. Spoon the batter evenly into the prepared ramekins, smooth the tops, and gently tap the ramekins on the counter to settle the batter. (At this point you can wrap the ramekins tightly with plastic wrap and refrigerate for up to 24 hours. Let the ramekins sit at room temperature for 30 minutes, then bake as directed.) Bake the cakes on the rimmed baking sheet until a toothpick inserted into the centers comes out with a few crumbs attached, 25 to 30 minutes, rotating the baking sheet halfway through baking.

7. Immediately run a small knife around the edges of the cakes, gently invert each ramekin onto an individual serving plate, and let sit until the cakes release themselves from the ramekins, about 5 minutes. Remove the ramekins and serve with vanilla ice cream, if desired.

NOTES FROM THE TEST KITCHEN

MAKING BANANAS FOSTER CAKES

Shingle the banana slices in a circle over the sauce.

WHAT'S THE SCOOP?
To find the perfect dipper, we scooped up six models, both traditional and innovative, plus our favorite portion scoop from Fantes. The perfect orbs of ice cream made by the thin-rimmed stainless **Rosle Ice Cream Scoop**, $19.95, impressed us most—especially when it came to loading up a brittle sugar cone. Testers liked its slim handle and the thin edge cut through hard ice cream easily.

TIRAMISÙ

DESPITE TIRAMISÙ'S SIMPLICITY, there is a lot that can go wrong. If it's soggy or parched, ponderously dense, sickly sweet, or fiery with alcohol, it's not worth the caloric cost.

The word *tiramisù* means "pick me up," a reference to the invigorating qualities of the dish's espresso, sugar, and alcohol. Store-bought ladyfingers (spongecake-like cookies) are dipped into alcohol-spiked espresso and then layered into a dish along with buttery mascarpone (a thick cream) that has been enriched with sugar and eggs. The dish is dusted with cocoa or sprinkled with chocolate and served chilled.

A good tiramisù is a seamless union of flavors and textures—it's difficult to tell where cookies end and cream begins, where bitter espresso gives over to the bite of alcohol, and whether unctuous or uplifting is the better adjective to describe it. Rather than lament all the unworthy tiramisùs out there, I decided to make a batch . . . or two . . . or 40 . . . to get to the bottom of a good one.

The most complicated recipes I found involved making a zabaglione, a frothy custard, as the base of the mascarpone filling. This required a double boiler, vigilance, and a lot of whisking. I made six recipes and determined that a zabaglione base was not worth the trouble.

As such, the mechanics of making the mascarpone filling became quite simple: I combined raw egg yolks and sugar, mixed in the spirits, and finished with the mascarpone. My early tests taught me that a 13 by 9-inch dish was the right size and that the pound of mascarpone called for in most recipes was inadequate—the ladyfinger-to-cream ratio was off, and the tiramisù was slight in stature. Another ½ pound made the filling generous but not fulsome.

With too few yolks, the filling wasn't as rich as tasters liked, a problem that plagued several of the recipes I initially tested. Six yolks made the filling silky and suave, with a round, rich flavor. (For those wary of desserts made with raw eggs, I also created a slightly more involved variation that cooks the yolks.)

Next, I tested different amounts of sugar and decided that ⅔ cup provided the perfect amount of sweetness. I also added an ingredient—salt—that isn't found in most tiramisù recipes. It greatly heightened all the flavors and made the most remarkable difference.

Tiramisù recipes fall into three camps: those that call for the addition of whipped egg whites to the filling; those that call for the addition of whipped cream; and those that call for neither. Without whipped whites or whipped cream, the filling was too heavy. Whipped egg whites watered down the flavor of the filling and made it too airy. Whipped cream lightened the texture without affecting the mascarpone's delicate flavor. I found that ¾ cup of cream (half the amount in many other recipes) was sufficient.

To make tiramisù, ladyfingers are dipped into espresso spiked with alcohol so that the rather dry, bland cookies are moistened and flavored. Brewed espresso is not practical for many home cooks, so I tried three things in its stead: strong coffee made from espresso-roast beans; espresso made from instant espresso granules; and a rather wicked potion made by dissolving instant espresso in strong brewed coffee. Though it wasn't palatable straight from a cup, this last concoction tasted best in tiramisù.

I found that the technique for dipping or soaking the ladyfingers greatly affects the outcome. A quick in-and-out dip wasn't adequate for moistening the cookies, and the result was a dry tiramisù. Fully submerging or otherwise saturating the ladyfingers yielded a wet, squishy tiramisù. Eventually, I found a method that worked reliably. One at a time, I dropped each ladyfinger into the liquid so that it floated on the surface, then without further ado I rolled it over to moisten the other side.

The only thing left to determine was the best spirit with which to spike the filling and the coffee-soaking mixture. Marsala gave the tiramisù a syrupy, citrusy overtone without appreciable alcohol character. Brandy gave it a lightly fruity flavor and good kick. Dark rum, with its caramel notes, complemented the rich, deep, toasty qualities of the coffee; it was the undisputed favorite.

My tiramisù was assembled like any other. I arranged half of the dipped ladyfingers in the dish and covered them with half of the mascarpone. I followed the lead of others and dusted the mascarpone with cocoa. The layering was repeated, and cocoa finished the tiramisù. (A sprinkling of grated chocolate was a nice addition.) The last detail: Tiramisù requires at least six hours in the fridge for the flavors and textures to meld.

Simple to prepare but grand enough to serve the most discerning *famiglia,* this tiramisù is an ideal holiday dessert.

—DAWN YANAGIHARA, *Cook's Illustrated*

TIRAMISÙ

SERVES 10 TO 12

Brandy and even whiskey can stand in for the dark rum. The test kitchen prefers a tiramisù with a pronounced rum flavor; for a less potent rum flavor, halve the amount of rum added to the coffee mixture in step 1. Do not allow the mascarpone to warm to room temperature before using it; it has a tendency to break if allowed to do so.

- 2½ cups strong brewed coffee, at room temperature
- 1½ tablespoons instant espresso granules
- 9 tablespoons dark rum (see note)
- 6 large egg yolks
- ⅔ cup (4⅔ ounces) sugar
- ¼ teaspoon salt
- 1½ pounds mascarpone (see note)
- ¾ cup cold heavy cream
- 14 ounces (42 to 60, depending on size) dried ladyfingers
- 3½ tablespoons Dutch-processed cocoa powder
- ¼ cup grated semisweet or bittersweet chocolate (optional)

1. Stir the coffee, espresso, and 5 tablespoons of the rum in a wide bowl or baking dish until the espresso dissolves; set aside.

2. In the bowl of a standing mixer fitted with a whisk attachment, beat the yolks at low speed until just combined. Add the sugar and salt and beat at medium-high speed until pale yellow, 1½ to 2 minutes, scraping down the bowl with a rubber spatula once or twice. Add the remaining 4 tablespoons rum and beat at medium speed until just combined, 20 to 30 seconds; scrape the bowl. Add the mascarpone and beat at medium speed until no lumps remain, 30 to 45 seconds, scraping down the bowl once or twice. Transfer the mixture to a large bowl and set aside.

3. In the now-empty mixer bowl (no need to clean the bowl), beat the cream at medium speed until frothy, 1 to 1½ minutes. Increase the speed to high and continue to beat until the cream holds stiff peaks, 1 to 1½ minutes longer. Using a rubber spatula, fold one-third of the whipped cream into the mascarpone mixture to lighten, then gently fold in the remaining whipped cream until no white streaks remain. Set the mascarpone mixture aside.

4. Working one at a time, drop half of the ladyfingers

into the coffee mixture, roll, remove, and transfer to a 13 by 9-inch glass or ceramic baking dish. (Do not submerge the ladyfingers in the coffee mixture; the entire process should take no longer than 2 to 3 seconds for each cookie.) Following the photos, arrange the soaked cookies in a single layer in the baking dish, breaking or trimming the ladyfingers as needed to fit neatly into the dish.

5. Spread half of the mascarpone mixture over the ladyfingers; use a rubber spatula to spread the mixture to the sides and into the corners of the dish and smooth the surface. Place 2 tablespoons of the cocoa in a fine-mesh strainer and dust the cocoa over the mascarpone mixture.

6. Repeat the dipping and arrangement of the lady-fingers; spread the remaining mascarpone mixture over the ladyfingers and dust with the remaining 1 ½ table-spoons cocoa. Wipe the edges of the dish with a dry paper towel. Cover with plastic wrap and refrigerate 6 to 24 hours. Sprinkle with the grated chocolate, if using; cut into pieces and serve chilled.

VARIATION
TIRAMISÙ WITHOUT RAW EGGS

This recipe involves cooking the yolks in a double boiler, which requires a little more effort and makes for a slightly thicker mascarpone filling, but the results are just as good as with our traditional method. You will need an additional ⅓ cup heavy cream.

Follow the recipe for Tiramisù through step 1. In step 2, add ⅓ cup cream to the yolks after the sugar and salt; do not whisk in the rum. Set the bowl with the yolks over a medium saucepan containing 1 inch gently simmering water; cook, constantly scraping along the bottom and sides of the bowl with a heatproof rubber spatula, until the mixture coats the back of a spoon and registers 160 degrees on an instant-read thermometer, 4 to 7 minutes. Remove from the heat and stir vigorously to cool slightly, then set aside to cool to room temperature, about 15 minutes. Whisk in the remaining 4 tablespoons rum until combined. Transfer the bowl to a standing mixer fitted with a whisk attachment, add the mascarpone, and beat at medium speed until no lumps remain, 30 to 45 seconds. Transfer the mixture to a large bowl and set aside. Continue with the recipe from step 3, using the full amount of heavy cream specified (¾ cup).

NOTES FROM THE TEST KITCHEN

ASSEMBLING TIRAMISÙ

1. Arrange soaked ladyfingers snugly in a single layer in a baking dish.

2. Spread half of the mascarpone mixture over the ladyfingers.

3. Dust half of the cocoa over the mascarpone mixture. Repeat the layering and dusting.

DIP, DON'T SUBMERGE
Both of the ladyfingers below were in the coffee mixture for the same amount of time, but different soaking techniques yielded very different results.

PERFECTLY SOAKED
This ladyfinger was dropped into the coffee mixture, rolled, and removed within 2 to 3 seconds. The coffee mixture has not completely saturated this cookie.

OVERSOAKED
This ladyfinger was fully submerged in the coffee mixture for 2 to 3 seconds. The coffee mixture has penetrated all the way to the center of the cookie.

SHOPPING FOR LADYFINGERS
Ladyfingers, also called *savoiardi*, are spongecake-like cookies and an essential ingredient in tiramisù. The crisp, dry cookies can normally be found in the international or cookie aisle of the supermarket. Some supermarket bakeries also sell fresh ladyfingers with a soft, cakelike texture. Fresh ladyfingers will become mushy when soaked and aren't an option in our recipe for Tiramisù.

FOOLPROOF PIE DOUGH

PIE CRUST IN A NUTSHELL: Mix flour, salt, and sugar together, cut in some fat, add water just until the dough sticks together, roll it out, and bake it. A study in simplicity. Yet it can all go wrong so easily. The dough is almost always too dry and crumbly to roll out successfully. The crust is either flaky but leathery or tender with no flakes. And the results are seemingly random: The recipe that gave you a perfect crust last month resulted in a tough-as-nails crust when you followed it this week.

I wanted to figure out exactly where a crust goes south, so I set out to sort through all the dubious science, purported secret ingredients, and perennial pie crust theories to separate fact from fiction and create a recipe that not only bakes up tender and flaky every single time, but also rolls out easily.

The first question was what type of fat to use. The test kitchen likes the rich flavor of an all-butter crust. Problem: Butter starts to soften at around 50 degrees and fully melts at around 100 degrees, which means the crust has to be worked very quickly. Also, butter's high water content (about 20 percent; the rest is fat) can lead to leathery crusts, as too much water will stimulate the formation of gluten, the protein matrix that provides structure in baked goods. Enter hydrogenated vegetable shortening, a soft fat that doesn't melt until a relatively high temperature and contains no water, just fat. But although crusts made with shortening are very tender, they have virtually no flavor. I ultimately found that a combination of butter and shortening provided the best balance of flavor and tenderness.

I moved on to the next step: cutting the fat into the flour. Of all the methods I tried (food processor, standing mixer, pastry blender, and by hand), the food processor was the fastest and most consistent. Even so, I ran into my first major hurdle—some recipes call for cutting the butter into walnut-sized pieces, and others say to incorporate the fat until it resembles wet sand. Which approach is better? And once you determine which method to use, is it possible to produce same-sized pieces of butter time after time?

What if I ran the food processor until the flour and fat were completely combined? This is simple to repeat every time, and there's no way to overprocess it. But dough is supposed to have pockets of fat in it, which melt upon baking to leave behind the gaps that create flaky layers. By fully incorporating the fat, I was left with no pockets, and sure enough, my dough baked up with no flakes. My next attempt was to process only a portion of the fat completely into the flour, freeze the rest of the fat, and grate it into the mixed dough to create those fat pockets. Consistent? Yes. But despite the fact that there were plenty of pockets of unmixed fat, my crust still came out flake-free.

While I was testing methods for incorporating the fat into the flour, I had been dealing with the frustrating issue of how much water to add to the dough. Some recipes call for a range of water that can vary by as much as 100 percent, claiming that a hot or humid day can throw measurements off. This excuse seemed a little suspicious, and I was eventually able to dismiss the theory by measuring the effects of humidity on flour. It was time to step back and examine the structure of a pie crust.

When fat is being cut into flour, the flour is separated into two groups; some of the flour is coated with a layer of fat, which protects it from absorbing any water, while the uncoated flour will absorb water and form gluten. When the dough is rolled out, this gluten stretches into sheets separated by pockets of unmixed fat that melt upon baking, leaving behind crisp, separated sheets. The problem is that depending on who's making the crust, the exact temperature of the fat, and even the type of food processor being used, the ratio of fat-coated flour to uncoated flour can change drastically from batch to batch. This means a pie crust recipe that barely absorbed ¼ cup of water one time might readily absorb ½ cup the next. It also explains why the same recipe is flaky one day but not the next: For consistent flakiness, you need the same ratio of fat-coated flour to uncoated flour.

It's not just the chunks of fat that create flakiness. It's also the uncoated flour that mixes with water and forms gluten that guarantees a flaky crust. This explained the failure of the test in which I combined all the flour with some of the butter, then added grated butter to the dough. You need at least some flour that hasn't been coated with butter in the dough in order to create the gluten layers that form flakes. When processing the fat in a traditional crust, leaving some chunks of butter in the dough is a good sign that the dough hasn't been overprocessed (that is, chunks of butter in the dough are an indication that there is enough uncoated flour left to combine with water and create a flaky crust).

FOOLPROOF PIE DOUGH

What if I measured out the two types of flour—the portion I wanted coated with fat and the portion I wanted to remain uncoated—separately? Rather than starting with all the flour in the processor, I put aside 1 cup of flour, then placed the remaining 1½ cups of flour in the food processor with all of the fat and processed it until it formed a unified paste. I then added the cup of reserved flour back to the bowl and pulsed it just until it was evenly distributed around the bowl. This would guarantee the dough had a constant amount of uncoated flour to mix with the water. After mixing in the water and rolling out the dough, I now theoretically had a dough with two distinct parts: long sheets of gluten separated by a flour-fat paste.

The dough baked up as flaky as could be. And since the stage in which the fat gets processed into the flour was no longer ambiguous, my new crusts came out identically, time and again.

I had guaranteed flakiness, but tenderness was still a crapshoot. Most recipes with 2½ cups of flour call for 6 to 8 tablespoons of ice water. If I kept the water at the lower end of this range, the dough baked up very tender but was dry and hard to roll out. When I used the full 8 tablespoons, the dough was smooth and easy to roll out but baked up tough—too much gluten was forming. I had to figure out a way to tenderize the finished crust without reducing the amount of water I used.

Scanning through recipes turned up a common "miracle ingredient"—acid. Many recipes say that a teaspoon of vinegar or lemon juice can tenderize dough, claiming that gluten formation is inhibited at lower pH values. But after consulting our science editor, I learned that gluten formation is actually increased in slightly acidic environments (a pH of between 5 and 6) and doesn't begin to decrease until the pH drops below 5. This required replacing nearly half the water with lemon juice, by which point the crust was inedibly sour.

What about using lower-protein cake or pastry flour? No good. The crusts baked up sandy and too short. What about adding cream cheese or sour cream? Although this made the crust more tender, it had a strange, soft chewiness.

Let's review: In order to roll easily, dough needs more water, but more water makes crusts tough. Therefore, I needed something that's not water but is still wet. As the aromas from a nearby pan of reducing wine reached my nose, the answer hit me like a bottle to the head: alcohol.

Eighty-proof vodka is essentially 40 percent ethanol and 60 percent water. As it happens, gluten cannot form in alcohol, which means that for every tablespoon of vodka I added, only 60 percent of it contributed to gluten development. I made a batch of pie dough with 4 tablespoons each of cold vodka and water. The resulting dough was as smooth as Play-Doh, and I couldn't have made it crack even if I'd wanted to. I was tempted to toss it, thinking it would bake up tough as leather, but giving good science the benefit of the doubt, I baked it anyway. It was an unparalleled success. The dough baked up every bit as tender and flaky as any crust I'd ever had, without a hint of booziness to give away its secret. One hundred forty-eight pie crusts later, I'd finally come up with a recipe that is 100 percent reliable.

—J. KENJI ALT, *Cook's Illustrated*

FOOLPROOF PIE DOUGH FOR A DOUBLE-CRUST PIE

MAKES ENOUGH FOR ONE 9-INCH PIE

Vodka is essential to the texture of the crust and imparts no flavor—do not substitute. This dough will be moister and more supple than most standard pie doughs and will require more flour to roll out (up to ¼ cup).

- 2½ cups (12½ ounces) unbleached all-purpose flour
- 1 teaspoon salt
- 2 tablespoons sugar
- 12 tablespoons (1½ sticks) unsalted butter, cut into ¼-inch slices and chilled
- ½ cup vegetable shortening, cut into 4 pieces and chilled
- ¼ cup cold vodka (see note)
- ¼ cup cold water

1. Pulse 1½ cups of the flour, salt, and sugar in a food processor until combined, about 2 one-second pulses. Add the butter and shortening and process until a homogenous dough just starts to collect in uneven clumps, about 15 seconds (the dough will resemble cottage cheese curds and there should be no uncoated flour). Scrape the bowl with a rubber spatula and redistribute the dough evenly around the processor blade. Add the remaining 1 cup flour and pulse until the mixture is evenly distributed around the bowl and the mass of dough has been broken up, 4 to 6 quick pulses. Empty the mixture into a medium bowl.

2. Sprinkle the vodka and water over the mixture. With a rubber spatula, use a folding motion to mix, pressing down on the dough until the dough is slightly tacky and sticks together. Divide the dough into two even balls and flatten each into a 4-inch disk. Wrap each in plastic wrap and refrigerate at least 45 minutes or up to 2 days.

FOOLPROOF PIE DOUGH FOR A SINGLE-CRUST PIE

MAKES ENOUGH FOR ONE 9-INCH PIE

- 1¼ cups (6¼ ounces) unbleached all-purpose flour, plus extra for the work surface
- ½ teaspoon salt
- 1 tablespoon sugar
- 6 tablespoons (¾ stick) unsalted butter, cut into ¼-inch slices and chilled
- ¼ cup vegetable shortening , cut into 2 pieces and chilled
- 2 tablespoons cold vodka
- 2 tablespoons cold water

1. Pulse ¾ cup of the flour, salt, and sugar together in a food processor until combined, about 2 one-second pulses. Add the butter and shortening and process until a homogenous dough just starts to collect in uneven clumps, about 10 seconds (the dough will resemble cottage cheese curds and there should be no uncoated flour). Scrape the bowl with a rubber spatula and redistribute the dough evenly around the processor blade. Add the remaining ½ cup flour and pulse until the mixture is evenly distributed around the bowl and the mass of dough has been broken up, 4 to 6 quick pulses. Empty the mixture into a medium bowl.

2. Sprinkle the vodka and water over the mixture. With a rubber spatula, use a folding motion to mix, pressing down on the dough until it is slightly tacky and sticks together. Flatten the dough into a 4-inch disk. Wrap in plastic wrap and refrigerate at least 45 minutes or up to 2 days.

3. Adjust an oven rack to the lowest position, place a rimmed baking sheet on the rack, and heat the oven to 425 degrees. Remove the dough from the refrigerator and roll out on a generously floured (up to ¼ cup) work surface to a 12-inch circle about ⅛ inch thick.

Roll the dough loosely around a rolling pin and unroll into a 9-inch pie plate, leaving at least a 1-inch overhang on each side. Ease the dough into the plate by gently lifting the edge of the dough with one hand while pressing into the plate bottom with the other hand. Leave the overhanging dough in place; refrigerate until the dough is firm, about 30 minutes.

4. Trim the overhang to ½ inch beyond the lip of the pie plate. Fold the overhang under itself; the folded edge should be flush with the edge of the pie plate. Flute the edges using your thumb and forefinger or press the tines of a fork against the dough to flatten it against the rim of the pie plate. Refrigerate the dough-lined plate until firm, about 15 minutes.

5. Remove the pie plate from the refrigerator, line the crust with foil, and fill with pie weights or pennies. Place the pie plate on the preheated baking sheet and bake for 15 minutes (for a partially baked crust). Remove the foil and weights, rotate the plate, and bake for 5 to 10 additional minutes (for a fully baked crust).

NOTES FROM THE TEST KITCHEN

KEY STEPS TO FOOLPROOF PIE DOUGH

1. MAKE A FAT AND FLOUR PASTE: Completely blending part of the flour with all of the butter ensures a consistent amount of fat-coated flour in the final dough.

2. ADD MORE FLOUR: Pulsing in the remaining flour ensures a consistent amount of uncoated flour in the finished dough.

3. ADD WATER AND VODKA: Sprinkling the dough with water and vodka ensures even distribution. No need to skimp—unlike water, vodka won't make the dough tough.

BANOFFEE PIE

THE NAME MAY SOUND STRANGE at first, but banoffee pie is exactly what it sounds like: banana and toffee pie. Thick drifts of coffee-scented whipped cream cover a crisp pastry shell filled with fresh banana and silky caramel-flavored "cream." Odd, perhaps, but each component perfectly balances one another and this pie tastes good—really good.

Banoffee pie is British by birth, though its lineage is subject to some controversy. The most vocal claimants are the owners of the Hungry Monk Restaurant, of East Sussex, England, who first listed it on their menu in 1972 as "banoffi pie"; it still resides there, as well as on thousands of other British menus. While it is not a particularly complicated pie to prepare, we found a few issues that can make or break the pie's success and we wanted to make a perfect and easy version.

First things first, we needed a crust. While some versions employ a cookie-crumb or graham cracker crust, the Hungry Monk version uses a flaky, butter-rich pastry and, after tasting pies with each of the different crusts, we agreed that the flaky crust better suited the texture and flavor of the filling. Our natural choice for a crust of this style was our recently developed Foolproof Pie Dough (see page 282).

The traditional "toffee" filling is prepared by boiling a can of condensed milk for hours to caramelize its natural sugars and thicken its texture. Sure, the filling prepared in this fashion tastes great, but the time involved and the inherent danger of boiling a sealed can left me skeptical. An exploded mess and flying metal? Hours trapped in the kitchen? No thanks. Could we find a faster or easier filling? Some recipes we found suggested substituting *cajeta*, a Latin caramel sauce (made with either cow's or goat's milk), which is actually quite similar to the boiled condensed milk filling (and was likely its inspiration). Once we eventually found a jar of cajeta, it did make a great replacement, but its availability is spotty in many parts of the country, which ruled it out. American-style caramel sauce didn't taste quite right and was far looser textured than ideal—it oozed out beneath the banana slices once the pie was cut.

Trying the store-bought sauce led us to consider making a thick caramel sauce from scratch. After a few attempts, we achieved a texture and flavor approximating that of the boiled condensed milk, but the recipe was tricky, requiring a keen eye and split-second timing. Realizing that many cooks might not feel confident playing with molten sugar, we decided to continue the search for a simpler solution.

Fishing for further options, a colleague suggested using chewy store-bought caramel candies. Obviously, they needed to be melted, which we first tried to do in the microwave with disastrous results. The candies melted far more smoothly in a saucepan over a mild flame and, once spread into the pie crust, looked like the real deal. However, once the caramel cooled, it was as sticky and tough as taffy. To soften that texture, we heated the caramels with a bit of water, which worked perfectly and the cooled "caramel" was as smooth and creamy as the boiled condensed milk.

Over the caramel went the bananas, followed by the espresso whipped cream. Instant espresso powder is the usual flavoring agent and we could find little fault with it. Some recipes stabilize the whipped cream with gelatin or cornstarch to facilitate slicing, but we found the additions to be not only unnecessary, but also detrimental to the cream's unctuousness. If chilled for a couple of hours, the cream set up firm enough to be sliced cleanly. Once on the plate, it softened a bit to a seductively smooth texture to offset the crisp pastry. This banoffee pie would become a staple in our repertoire.
—SUZANNAH MCFERRAN, *America's Test Kitchen Books*

BANOFFEE PIE

SERVES 8

We like to use either Kraft Caramels or Brach's Milk Maid Caramels for this recipe, but any brand of soft caramels will do. For a more child-friendly version of this classic pie, omit the espresso powder and add 1 teaspoon vanilla extract. Once filled with caramel and bananas, the pie can be covered loosely with plastic wrap and refrigerated for up to 6 hours before being topped with the whipped cream and placed in the freezer.

1   recipe Foolproof Pie Dough for a Single-Crust Pie, fully baked and cooled (page 282)

7   ounces (about 26) soft caramels (see note)

¼ cup water

3 ripe, firm bananas, peeled and sliced ½ inch thick

1½ cups heavy cream, chilled

2 tablespoons sugar

2 teaspoons instant espresso or instant coffee (see note)

1. Cook the caramels and water together in a small saucepan over medium-high heat, stirring occasionally, until melted and smooth, 8 to 10 minutes. Spread the caramel evenly into the cooled crust. Shingle the banana slices in concentric rings on top of the caramel. Cover the pie with plastic wrap and refrigerate until the caramel is cold, about 1 hour.

2. Whip the cream, sugar, and instant espresso together with an electric mixer on medium-low speed until frothy, about 1 minute. Increase the speed to high and continue to whip until the cream forms soft peaks, 1 to 3 minutes. Spread the whipped cream attractively over the top of the chilled pie, then freeze the pie until the whipped cream is very stiff but the pie is not fully frozen, about 2 hours, before serving. (Do not let the pie freeze completely.)

APPLE-CRANBERRY PIE

SWEET AND TART, TENDER AND CRISP—apple pie is a balance. Adding cranberries upsets that delicate balance—the tart berries overwhelm the subtle perfume of the apples and shed a lot of liquid that makes the bottom crust soggy. My goal was to find a way to combine these two classic fall fruits in such a way that the full flavor of both came through and the crust remained crisp.

At first I thought it might be a simple matter of fine-tuning the proportion of cranberries to apples. I was wrong. No matter how few cranberries I used, adding them whole inevitably led to wincing when cranberries burst in tasters' mouths.

Thinking how cooking transforms whole cranberries into a stiff, sweet jelly, I assumed that precooking would at least solve the problem of excess juice from the cranberries. True, but it did little for their mouth-puckering flavor.

Most traditional apple pie recipes call for a balanced mix of sweet and tart apples. Instead, I tried using only sweet apples, figuring the cranberries would add plenty of tartness to this pie. Likewise, replacing the standard lemon juice with orange juice helped, but not enough. No matter what I tried, it seemed impossible to get the more subtle flavor of the apples to come through when combined with the cranberries. The solution? Don't combine them. I arranged the cooked cranberries and the apples in two distinct layers within the pie. This time, the flavor of both elements came through clearly.

I had one last test to run. The apple layer was mushier than I wanted, especially in comparison to the thick cranberry layer. When making Deep-Dish Apple Pie, I discovered that precooking the apples actually made them firmer in the finished pie. It turns out that cooking apples over low heat converts the pectin within their cells to a more heat-stable form. As a result, the apples can tolerate nearly an hour in the oven without becoming excessively soft. Only one problem: Heating the apples on the stovetop released a lot of juice that made the crust soggy, and straining the apples and reducing their juice were extra steps I wanted to avoid.

I wondered if the microwave would be easier. Sure enough, 10 minutes in the microwave did the trick, making the apples firm but not soupy, with nicely thickened juices (thanks to a tablespoon of cornstarch). With distinct layers of pale yellow apples and deep-red cranberries, I had a pie that looked good and tasted even better.

—J. KENJI ALT, *Cook's Illustrated*

APPLE-CRANBERRY PIE

SERVES 8

Use sweet, crisp apples, such as Golden Delicious, Jonagold, Fuji, or Braeburn. The two fillings can be made ahead, cooled, and stored separately in the refrigerator for up to 2 days.

2 cups frozen or fresh cranberries

¼ cup orange juice

1   **cup (7 ounces) sugar plus extra for sprinkling**
½   **teaspoon ground cinnamon**
½   **teaspoon salt**
¼   **cup water**
1   **tablespoon cornstarch**
3½ **pounds sweet apples (about 8 medium), peeled, cored, and cut into ¼-inch-thick slices (see note)**
1   **recipe Foolproof Pie Dough for a Double-Crust Pie (page 281)**
1   **large egg white, beaten lightly**

1. Bring the cranberries, juice, ½ cup of the sugar, ¼ teaspoon of the cinnamon, and ¼ teaspoon of the salt to a boil in a medium saucepan over medium-high heat. Cook, stirring occasionally and pressing the berries against the side of the pot, until the berries have completely broken down and the juices have thickened to a jam-like consistency (a wooden spoon scraped across the bottom should leave a clear trail that doesn't fill in), 10 to 12 minutes. Remove from the heat, stir in the water, and cool to room temperature, about 30 minutes.

2. Meanwhile, mix the remaining ½ cup sugar, the remaining ¼ teaspoon cinnamon, remaining ¼ teaspoon salt, and cornstarch in a large microwave-safe bowl; add the apples and toss to combine. Microwave on high power, stirring with a rubber spatula every 3 minutes, until the apples are just starting to turn translucent around the edges and the liquid is thick and glossy, 10 to 14 minutes. Cool to room temperature, about 30 minutes.

3. While the fillings cool, adjust an oven rack to the lowest position, place a rimmed baking sheet on the oven rack, and heat the oven to 425 degrees. Remove 1 disk of the dough from the refrigerator and roll out on a generously floured (up to ¼ cup) work surface to a 12-inch circle about ⅛ inch thick. Roll the dough loosely around the rolling pin and unroll into a 9-inch pie plate, leaving at least a 1-inch overhang. Ease the dough into the plate by gently lifting the edge of the dough with one hand while pressing into the plate bottom with the other hand. Leave the dough that overhangs the plate in place; refrigerate until the dough is firm, about 30 minutes.

4. Transfer the cooled cranberry mixture to the dough-lined pie plate and spread into an even layer. Place the apple mixture on top of the cranberries, mounding slightly in the center; push down any sharp apple edges.

5. Roll the remaining disk of dough on a generously floured work surface (up to ¼ cup) to a 12-inch circle about ⅛ inch thick. Roll the dough loosely around the rolling pin and unroll over the pie, leaving at least a 1-inch overhang on each side.

6. Using kitchen shears, cut evenly through both layers of the overhanging dough, leaving a ½-inch overhang. Fold the dough under itself so that the edge of the fold is flush with the outer rim of the pie plate. Flute the edges using your thumb and forefinger or press with the tines of a fork to seal. Brush the top and edges of the pie with the egg white and sprinkle with sugar. Using a sharp paring knife, cut four 1½-inch slits in the top of the dough in a cross pattern.

7. Place the pie on the preheated baking sheet and bake until the top is a light golden brown, 20 to 25 minutes. Reduce the oven temperature to 375 degrees, rotate the baking sheet, and continue to bake until the crust is a deep golden brown, 25 to 30 minutes longer. Transfer the pie to a wire rack to cool for at least 2 hours. Cut into wedges and serve.

NOTES FROM THE TEST KITCHEN

THE BEST APPLE CORER
Rather than slicing an apple into quarters and then removing the core and seeds from each piece, we'd rather reach for an apple corer, which does the job in one fell swoop. We tested five models and found out the task wasn't always so cut-and-dried. Models with narrow blade diameters (less than ¾ inch) struggled to cut through firmer apples, and stubby metal tubes (less than 3½ inches) came up short when asked to plow through large apples. We had much better results with the reasonably priced **OXO Good Grips Corer,** $6.50, and testers appreciated its comfortable grip.

APPLE SLAB PIE

TRADITIONAL APPLE PIE and apple slab pie are both two-crusted affairs filled with spiced apples—but that's where the similarities end. Unlike a traditional pie, slab pie is made in a baking sheet and can feed 20 people. It is short in stature, its filling is thickened to ensure neat slicing, and it's topped with a sugary glaze. I was excited to give this pie a try.

I have no problem making homemade pie dough for a regular pie, but I wasn't thrilled to learn I needed to make a quadruple batch to cover the bottom and top of this mammoth pie. Rolling the dough out to such a big size was very difficult; all the required stretching, rolling, and flipping was ripping my delicate homemade pie dough beyond repair.

It was easier to start with sturdier store-bought pie dough rounds. By gluing two of them together with water and then rolling the double-dough out into a large rectangle, I was able to get the crust into the pan without a tear. Now that I had the shaping down, I needed to find a way to improve the bland flavor of the store-bought dough. Using an old test kitchen trick, I tried rolling the dough in crushed cookie crumbs. Gingersnaps lent too much spice, but crushed animal crackers contributed a welcome sweet and buttery flavor. Brushing the rolled dough with melted butter added even more richness.

For the filling I chose two kinds of apples: a firm variety (Granny Smith) that would hold its shape and a softer one (Golden Delicious) that would cook down to create a saucy filling. I needed eight of each to adequately fill my pie. I added cinnamon, sugar, lemon juice, and a little flour (to help thicken the filling) to the sliced apples, filled and covered the pie, and baked it. The flavor was great, but the filling was too soupy to cut into neat squares. I tried adding more flour, but because a slab pie filling needs to be more cohesive than regular apple pie filling, it took a lot of flour, and the result was too pasty. Cornstarch made the filling slimy, but tapioca thickened the filling without making it starchy.

But even with this thickened filling, the bottom crust was getting soggy—especially in the middle. I'd been making the filling right before assembling the pie, but for one test I got pulled away from the kitchen and left a batch of apples sitting for about 30 minutes. When I returned, I noticed a pool of juice in the bottom of the bowl, so I drained away the juice and baked the pie as usual. This time the filling was much firmer, and the crust wasn't soggy at all.

As for the glaze, the traditional combination of confectioners' sugar and milk tasted a little flat. Remembering the pool of apple juice that had drained from the filling, I reduced it in a saucepan to concentrate its flavor, then mixed the reduced juice with confectioners' sugar and lemon juice. Spread over the cooled top crust, this glaze offered just the right finish for my crisp and buttery giant of a pie.

—DIANE UNGER, *Cook's Country*

APPLE SLAB PIE

SERVES 18 TO 20

An 18 by 13-inch nonstick baking sheet works best for this pie. If using a conventional baking sheet, coat it lightly with vegetable oil spray. You will need 4 ounces of animal crackers. The pie can be made up to 24 hours in advance and refrigerated. Bring to room temperature before serving.

PIE

- 3½ pounds Granny Smith Apples (about 8 medium), peeled, cored, and sliced thin
- 3½ pounds Golden Delicious apples (about 8 medium), peeled, cored, and sliced thin
- 1½ cups (10½ ounces) granulated sugar
- ½ teaspoon salt
- 1½ cups animal crackers (see note)
- 2 (15-ounce) boxes Pillsbury Ready to Roll Pie Crust
- 4 tablespoons (½ stick) unsalted butter, melted and cooled
- 6 tablespoons Minute tapioca
- 2 teaspoons ground cinnamon
- 3 tablespoons fresh lemon juice

GLAZE

- ¾ cup reserved apple juice (from the filling)
- 2 tablespoons fresh lemon juice
- 1 tablespoon unsalted butter, softened
- 1¼ cups (5 ounces) confectioners' sugar

1. FOR THE PIE: Combine the apples, 1 cup of the granulated sugar, and salt in a colander set over a large bowl. Let sit, tossing occasionally, until the apples release their juices, about 30 minutes. Press gently on the apples to extract liquid and reserve ¾ cup juice.

2. Adjust an oven rack to the lower-middle position and heat the oven to 350 degrees. Pulse the crackers and remaining ½ cup granulated sugar in a food processor until finely ground. Dust the work surface with half of the cracker mixture, brush half of one pie round with water, overlap with the second pie round, and dust the top with the remaining cracker mixture. Roll out the dough to 19 by 14 inches and transfer to a rimmed baking sheet. Brush the dough with the butter and refrigerate; roll out the top crust in the same way.

3. Toss the drained apples with the tapioca, cinnamon, and lemon juice and arrange evenly over the bottom crust, pressing lightly to flatten. Brush the edges of the bottom crust with water, and arrange the top crust on the pie. Press the crusts together and use a paring knife to trim any excess dough. Use a fork to crimp and seal the outside edge of the pie, then to pierce the top of the pie at 2-inch intervals. Bake until the pie is golden brown and the juices are bubbling, about 1 hour. Transfer to a wire rack and let cool 1 hour.

4. FOR THE GLAZE: While the pie is cooling, simmer the reserved apple juice in a saucepan over medium heat until syrupy and reduced to ¼ cup, about 6 minutes. Stir in the lemon juice and butter and let cool to room temperature. Whisk in the confectioners' sugar and brush the glaze evenly over the warm pie. Let the pie cool completely, at least 1 hour longer before serving.

NOTES FROM THE TEST KITCHEN

THE BEST MULTIPURPOSE PEELER

Different peelers (straight, serrated, and julienne) suit different requirements. A new gadget, the **Prepara Trio Three Blade Peeler,** $14.95, does it all. This three-in-one peeler stores two blades in its grip-covered shaft while the third pops up for use. Switching blades is as simple as a click of the release button and a turn of the wheel on the base of the handle. We found each blade performed well on a range of produce and, thankfully, the blade cartridge is dishwasher-safe. A great option for those looking to save drawer space.

HOW TO MAKE APPLE SLAB PIE

1. Use water to "glue" together the two pie crusts.

2. Add flavor to the store-bought crust by rolling it out in a mixture of crushed cookie crumbs and sugar.

3. Transfer the dough to a rimmed baking sheet and brush with melted butter for extra richness.

4. Top the filled pie with a second "double" crust.

5. Use a fork to tightly seal the edges of the crust.

A NEW USE FOR AN OLD FAVORITE

Grind animal crackers (and sugar) to a powder in the food processor and then use this mixture—instead of flour—to facilitate rolling out the dough. The animal cracker–sugar mixture lends much-needed flavor to bland store-bought pie dough.

APPLE GALETTE

APPLE GALETTE

I WAS INTRODUCED TO APPLE GALETTE on my first visit to a French *pâtisserie*. One bite and I knew I had found a tart that I loved as much as apple pie. Galettes come in various shapes and sizes—from ones in which the dough is folded over a pile of apples to others that feature layers of sweet pastry, almond filling, and meticulously layered apples. I wanted to re-create the one I first fell in love with: This galette features a thin, crispy, flaky, sugary crust topped with a generous layer of apples sliced a mere ⅛ inch thick. There's not much to this galette besides flour, sugar, butter, and fruit, and you don't even need a fork to eat it. When baked properly, the pieces are sturdy enough to eat out of hand, just like a slice of pizza.

What I thought would be a simple task proved to be surprisingly tricky. Nearly all the recipes I tried were made from a simple dough (flour, sugar, salt, butter, and ice water) that claimed to produce the texture I was after. But in nearly every case, the dough was tough, cracker-like, and bland. I did learn a few things. Because of their size and thinness, round galettes were difficult to roll out and transfer to a baking sheet. I decided to stick with rectangular galettes. From the way even my mediocre attempts were being devoured by tasters, I knew that this dessert had to feed a crowd.

For my early tests, I used a food processor to cut the butter completely into the dry ingredients. Although this is the test kitchen's preferred technique for classic American pie dough, I thought that a French dough might require a French technique. A few years ago, one of my colleagues experimented with *fraisage*. This technique calls for partially cutting the butter into the dry ingredients, leaving large pea-sized pieces of fat unmixed. But what makes fraisage truly unique is how the dough is combined. Small bits of the barely mixed dough are pressed firmly against the counter with the heel of the hand to create a uniform dough. As a result, the chunks of butter are pressed into long, thin sheets that create lots of flaky layers when the dough is baked.

Fraisage did indeed produce a flakier crust than had my initial tests, but tasters said it was tougher than they would have thought. Something wasn't making sense. Upon closer examination of our Freeform Fruit Tart

recipe, it dawned on me. That recipe called for piling juicy summer fruit onto the dough and then folding the edges of the dough over the fruit. My recipe called for shingling a single layer of fairly dry apples on top. Without a mound of fruit to keep the dough moist, my crust was drying out before the apples could brown and caramelize. Adding a bit more butter to the dough increased tenderness slightly, but not enough.

I wondered if using a different flour could be the answer. Until now, I had been using all-purpose flour, even though many recipes for French pastry call for pastry flour. It was time to give this flour a try. Basically, the difference between these two flours is protein content. When mixed with water, the proteins (gliadin and glutenin) in flour create a stronger, more elastic protein called gluten. The higher the gluten content, the stronger and tougher the dough. Pastry flour has a protein content of 9 percent, and the protein content of all-purpose flour ranges from 10 percent to 12 percent. This difference might not seem like much, but when I made galettes from each type of flour the results were dramatic. The galette made with all-purpose flour was tough, and the one with pastry flour was flaky, tender, and sturdy. The only problem is that pastry flour is not widely available.

Looking for a more practical alternative, I tried cake flour, which is sold in supermarkets and has a protein content of just 8 percent. But when I substituted 1 cup, ½ cup, and even ¼ cup of cake flour for the equivalent amount of all-purpose flour, the dough—though tender—crumbled. It turns out that cake flour goes through a bleaching process (with chlorine gas) that affects how its proteins combine with water. As a result, weaker gluten is formed—perfect for a delicate cake but not for a pastry that must be both tender and sturdy.

Casting a wider net, I looked through numerous French cookbooks. Although most recipes were nearly identical in ingredients, there were two that stood out. Tart doughs in Julia Child's *From Julia's Kitchen* and André Soltner's *Lutèce Cookbook* both touted instant flour (also called quick-mixing flour) as the essential ingredient for flaky yet tender tart crusts. I keep instant flour in the back of my cabinet to make lump-free gravies, but I had never thought of it for pastry-making. Instant flour is made by slightly moistening all-purpose flour with water. After being spray-dried, the tiny flour granules look like small clusters of grapes. Since these preclumped flour granules are larger than those of finer-ground all-purpose flour, they absorb less water, making it harder for the proteins to form gluten.

I replaced some of the all-purpose flour with various amounts of instant flour. I found that ½ cup of instant flour kept the dough tender yet sturdy enough to cut neat slices of galette that could be eaten out of hand. An unlikely supermarket ingredient, along with a classic French mixing technique, had helped me create a remarkable crust.

The ideal galette should have both a crust and apples that are a deep golden-brown color. After several tests, most tasters felt that 400 degrees struck the right balance between intensely caramelized and simply burnt. Now the galette was perfect—almost. Although not all galette recipes called for it, many brush the hot-out-of-the-oven tart with apricot preserves. This glaze provided an attractive sheen and fruity tartness that tasters praised as they picked up another slice.

—DAVID PAZMIÑO, *Cook's Illustrated*

APPLE GALETTE

SERVES 8 TO 10

The galette can be made without instant flour, using 2 cups of all-purpose flour and 2 tablespoons of corn-starch. However, you might have to increase the amount of ice water. Although any apple will work in this recipe, Golden Delicious, Granny Smith, and Empire are pre-ferred. If you don't have an apple corer, halve the peeled apples and then use a melon baller or paring knife to remove the core from each half. Make sure to cut the apples as thinly as possible. If they are cut thicker than ⅛ inch, they will be hard to shingle. If the dough has chilled longer than 1 hour, let it stand at room tem-perature for 15 to 20 minutes to soften. If the dough becomes soft and sticky while being rolled, transfer it to a baking sheet and refrigerate it for 10 to 15 minutes. Check the bottom of the galette halfway through bak-ing—it should be a light golden brown. If it is darker, reduce the oven temperature to 375 degrees. Serve with vanilla ice cream, lightly sweetened whipped cream, or crème fraîche.

DOUGH

1½ cups (7½ ounces) unbleached all-purpose flour, plus extra for the work surface
½ cup (2½ ounces) instant flour (see note)
½ teaspoon salt
½ teaspoon sugar
12 tablespoons (1½ sticks) unsalted butter, cut into ¼-inch pieces and chilled
7–9 tablespoons ice water

APPLE FILLING

1½ pounds (about 3 medium) apples (see note)
2 tablespoons unsalted butter, cut into ¼-inch pieces
¼ cup (1¾ ounces) sugar
2 tablespoons apricot preserves
1 tablespoon water

1. FOR THE DOUGH: Combine the flours, salt, and sugar in a food processor with three 1-second pulses. Scatter the butter pieces over the flour, pulse to cut the butter into the flour until the butter pieces are the size of large pebbles, about ½ inch, about six 1-second pulses.

2. Sprinkle 1 tablespoon water over the mixture and pulse once quickly to combine; repeat, adding water 1 tablespoon at a time and pulsing, until the dough begins to form small curds that hold together when pinched with your fingers (the dough should look crumbly and should not form a cohesive ball).

3. Empty the dough onto the work surface and gather into a rough rectangular mound about 12 inches long and 5 inches wide.

4. Following the photos on page 291 and starting at the farthest end, use the heel of your hand to smear a small amount of dough against the surface, pushing firmly down and away from you, to create a separate pile of dough (the flattened pieces of dough should look shaggy). Continue the process until all the dough has been worked. Gather the dough into a rough 12 by 5-inch mound and repeat the smearing process. The dough will not have to be smeared as much as the first time and should form a cohesive ball once the entire portion is worked. Form the dough into a 4-inch square, wrap in plastic, and refrigerate until cold and firm but still malleable, 30 minutes to 1 hour.

5. FOR THE FILLING: About 15 minutes before baking, adjust an oven rack to the middle position and heat the oven to 400 degrees. Peel, core, and halve the apples. Cut the apple halves lengthwise into ⅛-inch-thick slices.

6. Place the dough on a floured 16 by 12-inch piece of parchment paper and dust with more flour. Roll the dough until it just overhangs all four sides of the parchment and is about ⅛ inch thick, dusting the top and bottom of the dough and rolling pin with flour as needed to keep the dough from sticking. Trim the dough so the edges are even with the parchment paper.

7. Roll up 1 inch of each edge and pinch firmly to create a ½-inch-thick border. Transfer the dough and parchment to a large rimmed baking sheet.

8. Starting in one corner, shingle the sliced apples into the crust in tidy, diagonal rows, overlapping them by a third. Dot the apples with the butter and sprinkle evenly with the sugar. Bake until the bottom of the tart is a deep golden brown and the apples have caramelized, 45 to 60 minutes, rotating the baking sheet halfway through baking.

9. While the galette is cooking, combine the apricot preserves and water in a medium microwave-safe bowl. Microwave on medium power until the mixture begins to bubble, about 1 minute. Pass through a fine-mesh strainer to remove any large apricot pieces. Brush the baked galette with the warm glaze, transfer the galette to a wire rack, and let cool for 15 minutes. Transfer to a cutting board. Cut in half lengthwise and then crosswise into individual portions. Serve.

NOTES FROM THE TEST KITCHEN

THE BEST MANDOLINE

A mandoline can make quick work of turning out piles of identically sliced vegetables. Testing a range of 13 models being marketed to home cooks, we were shocked by the assortment of sizes and prices (anywhere from $25 to $400). We preferred models with a V-shaped blade, and rimmed, long-pronged hand guards. We found our winner in the **OXO Good Grips V-Blade Mandoline Slicer,** $49.99. Testers liked its wide, sturdy gripper guard, and its razor-sharp blade made short work of a variety of fruits and vegetables. (See page 337 for more information about our testing results.)

PREPARING APPLE GALETTE

1. Starting at the farthest end of the rectangular pile of dough, smear the dough against the surface. Repeat until the rest of the crumbs have been worked.

2. Gather the smeared bits into another rectangular pile and repeat the smearing process until all the crumbs have been worked again.

3. Cut a piece of parchment to measure exactly 16 by 12 inches, flour the paper, then roll the dough out on top until it just overhangs the edge and is ⅛ inch thick.

4. Trim the dough so that the edges are even with the parchment paper.

5. Roll up 1 inch of each edge to create a ½-inch-thick border.

6. Slide the parchment and dough onto a rimmed baking sheet. Carefully shingle the apples across the tart on a diagonal, overlapping each row by a third.

EASY FRESH FRUIT TART

WITH GLISTENING, RIPE SUMMER FRUIT nestled atop smooth pastry cream and a buttery pastry crust, a fresh fruit tart seems like the perfect summer dessert, until you try to make one from scratch. First there's making and baking the pastry shell. The pastry cream seems easier by comparison, until it curdles or burns. And having to arrange the berries with the precision of a mosaic artist is nobody's idea of fun. Could I reengineer this classic summer dessert and make it much simpler?

Starting at the bottom, I knew that making homemade pastry would be too much work. Store-bought pie crust was too delicate to hold the filling and berries, but frozen puff pastry was surprisingly strong. I baked the shell unfilled, and it puffed up light and crisp; but when I assembled the tart, the berries rolled off the sides. Folding in the edges of the unbaked puff pastry created a barrier to keep the fruit in place.

I tried replacing homemade pastry cream with instant vanilla pudding, but tasters immediately rejected the artificial flavor. Softened cream cheese (flavored with sugar and vanilla) was a much better approximation of pastry cream, but it was too thick and pasty. To play off the fruit topping, I tried thinning the cream cheese with jams, jellies, and preserves. The jams and preserves were too chunky, but the jelly (strawberry was the tasters' favorite) gave the cheese a silky texture and sweet berry flavor.

Instead of meticulously arranging each piece of fruit on top of the tart and then glazing them all, I put a mixture of blueberries, raspberries, and strawberries into a bowl and poured a little heated strawberry jelly over them. This glazed the fruit before it was assembled on the tart, meaning I could just spoon the berries over the creamy filling. Once piled on the filling, the glazed fruit looked like stained glass.

Unfortunately, after an hour in the refrigerator to set the glaze (which glues the berries in place), the bottom of the pastry shell became soggy. It turned out that a little sugar sprinkled over the pastry before cooking formed a moisture-proof barrier that kept the crust nice and crisp. Now I had all of the great flavor, texture, and stunning appearance of a fancy fruit tart—with almost none of the work.

—DIANE UNGER, *Cook's Country*

EASY FRESH FRUIT TART
SERVES 4 TO 6

Turbinado, a coarse raw sugar, works especially well in place of the granulated sugar sprinkled on the pastry. Although I liked a mix of berries, virtually any ripe fruit—alone or in combination—will work here. Smooth jelly (rather than chunky jam or preserves) is a must for this recipe.

1   (9½ by 9-inch) sheet puff pastry, thawed overnight in the refrigerator
2   teaspoons sugar (see note)
⅛   teaspoon ground cinnamon
4   ounces cream cheese, softened
½   cup plus 2 tablespoons strawberry jelly
1   teaspoon vanilla extract
3   cups fresh berries (see note)

1. Adjust an oven rack to the upper-middle position and heat the oven to 425 degrees. Line a baking sheet with parchment paper. Unfold the puff pastry onto the prepared baking sheet and, following the photos on page 293, prepare the pastry shell.

2. Combine the sugar and cinnamon and sprinkle the mixture over the inside of the tart shell. Transfer to the oven and bake until the pastry and sugar are a deep golden brown, 15 to 22 minutes. Transfer to a wire rack and let cool at least 1 hour.

3. While the crust is baking, stir the cream cheese, 2 tablespoons jelly, and vanilla in a bowl until smooth. Refrigerate until ready to use. (The mixture can be made up to 2 days in advance; stir well before using.)

4. Spread the cream cheese mixture over the inside of the cooled tart shell. Place the remaining jelly in a large microwave-safe bowl and microwave on high power until the jelly melts, about 30 seconds. Add the berries to the bowl and toss gently until coated with the jelly. Spoon the berries over the cream cheese mixture and refrigerate until the jelly is set, at least 1 hour and up to 4 hours. Let sit at room temperature for 30 minutes. Serve.

TURNING PUFF PASTRY INTO A TART SHELL

1. Brush a ½-inch border along the edges of the pastry with water. Fold the long edges of the pastry over by ½ inch, then fold the short edges over by ½ inch.

2. Working lengthwise, lightly score the outer edge of all folded edges of the tart shell with a paring knife.

3. To prevent the center of the tart from puffing up in the oven, poke the dough repeatedly with a fork.

CRANBERRY-PECAN TART

PECAN PIE MAY BE MY FAVORITE of the classic holiday offerings, but not everyone is quite so fond of its frank flavor or unmitigated sweetness—even the best of the bunch are sugary enough to make your teeth ache. I've come across a few variations that add tart fresh cranberries for balance and while I enjoyed the blend of flavors, the juxtaposition of juicy, chewy cranberries with the pie's eggy custard and crunchy nuts left me cold. The combination, however, was inspiring: Why not take the flavors and finesse them into something more refined, like a thin, sophisticated tart in which the cranberries and pecans are glazed with a bittersweet caramel, skipping the custard altogether?

Classic tart pastry, what the French call *pâte sablée*, differs from flaky, neutral-flavored American-style pie crust on three counts: it is crunchy and crisp (like a cookie), moderately sweet, and rich—typically including eggs and/or heavy cream along with plenty of butter. Tart dough is also blessedly easier to make than pie dough, requiring nothing more than a quick turn in the food processor to blend the ingredients together. With all the fat and minimal water (only from the eggs and butter), there's little fear of toughness.

The test kitchen previously developed a foolproof tart dough that I could use here. While most tart dough recipes require hard-to-find superfine sugar and pastry flour, the kitchen found that pantry staples confectioners' sugar and all-purpose flour work just fine, as long as the dough's fat content is kept high enough. In this case, the dough contains a full stick of butter in addition to a tablespoon of heavy cream and an egg yolk, both of which moisten the dough with little risk of gluten development—the real danger in using higher protein all-purpose flour instead of pastry flour. Being softer and more malleable than pie dough, tart dough is quite easy to roll out and fit to the pan. If it rips, it can simply be patted back together with little fear of the dough turning tough or cracking once baked. That being said, the test kitchen found it important that the dough be well rested—at least an hour after preparation—and chilled once again after being fitted to the pan to prevent the shell from shrinking while in the oven (pie weights provide further insurance).

With a crisp prebaked tart shell, I could move on to the filling. While traditional pecan pie filling is a sticky blend of brown sugar, corn syrup, and eggs, I wanted the cleaner flavor and silkier texture of pure caramel sauce—just caramel, cream, and butter. Making caramel simply involves melting and cooking sugar until it reaches a rich, golden brown—about 350 degrees; if cooked past 355 degrees, the sugar will burn and taste quite bitter. A keen eye and close attention are important in judging the subtle shifts in the caramel's rapidly changing color.

After trying several of the most promising methods for preparing caramel, I found my favorite involved dissolving the sugar in a little water, then simmering the syrup in a saucepan until the sugar begins to color, after which the sugar is closely monitored.

Once the cooking sugar reaches the desired tawny color of perfect caramel, it's crucial to prevent it from cooking any further at the risk of burning. This is where the cream comes into play: It cools the sugar enough to prevent it from burning. The addition also prompts ferocious sputtering, but the tall sides of the saucepan easily contain it.

I wanted a smooth and creamy caramel in which to suspend the nuts and cranberries, but I found if I added too much cream or butter to it, it became impossible to slice the tart—the caramel oozed out of the crust and puddled on the plate. After numerous rounds of varying the ratios of both the cream and butter, I finally settled on an ideal combination. Tasters, however, thought its flavor fell flat. A little vanilla extract helped on this count, as did a splash of lemon juice and a little salt to counter the sweetness of the sauce.

I tossed toasted pecans and fresh cranberries in the caramel, poured it into the shell, and chilled the filling until firm. While it looked great, the cranberries came across as too sour and raw flavored—they needed to be cooked. I slid the whole, assembled tart into the oven and baked it until set, which took the bite out of the cranberries and brought the flavors of the filling together. The tart sliced beautifully, looked elegant, and tasted every bit as good as I had hoped.

—MEGAN WYCOFF, *America's Test Kitchen Books*

CRANBERRY-PECAN TART

SERVES 8 TO 10

Tart crust is crisper and less flaky than pie crust—it is more similar in texture to a cookie. Serve with lightly sweetened whipped cream or vanilla ice cream. Once baked and cooled, the tart can be wrapped loosely with plastic wrap and held at room temperature for up to a day before serving.

TART SHELL

- 1 large egg yolk
- 1 tablespoon heavy cream

½ teaspoon vanilla extract

1¼ cups (6¼ ounces) unbleached all-purpose flour, plus extra for the work surface

⅔ cup (2⅔ ounces) confectioners' sugar

¼ teaspoon salt

8 tablespoons (1 stick) unsalted butter, cut into ¼-inch pieces and chilled

TART FILLING

¼ cup water

1 cup (7 ounces) granulated sugar

⅔ cup heavy cream

3 tablespoons unsalted butter, cut into ½-inch pieces

½ teaspoon vanilla extract

½ teaspoon fresh lemon juice

⅛ teaspoon salt

1¼ cups pecans, toasted and chopped

1½ cups cranberries, fresh or frozen (thawed)

1. FOR THE TART SHELL: Whisk the egg yolk, cream, and vanilla together in a small bowl. Process the flour, confectioners' sugar, and salt together in a food processor until combined. Scatter the butter over the top and pulse until the mixture resembles coarse cornmeal, about 15 pulses.

2. With the machine running, add the egg mixture through the feed tube and continue to process until the dough just comes together around the processor blade, about 12 seconds.

3. Turn the dough onto a sheet of plastic wrap and flatten into a 6-inch disk. Wrap the dough tightly in the plastic wrap and refrigerate for 1 hour. Before rolling the dough out, let it sit on the work surface to soften slightly, about 10 minutes.

4. Roll the dough out to an 11-inch circle on a lightly floured surface, then, following the photos on page 295, fit it into a 9-inch tart pan with a removable bottom. Set the dough-lined tart pan on a large plate and freeze for 30 minutes.

5. Adjust an oven rack to the middle position and heat the oven to 375 degrees. Set the tart pan on a large baking sheet. Press a large piece of foil into the tart shell and over the edges of the pan, and fill with pie weights. Bake until the tart shell is set, about 30 minutes, rotating the baking sheet halfway through baking. Transfer the baking sheet to a wire rack and carefully remove the weights and foil. Let the tart shell cool on the baking sheet while making the filling.

6. FOR THE TART FILLING: Reduce the oven temperature to 325 degrees. Measure the water into a medium saucepan, then pour the granulated sugar into the center of the pan (don't let it hit the pan sides). Gently stir the sugar with a clean spatula to wet it thoroughly. Bring to a boil over medium-high heat and cook, without stirring, until the sugar has dissolved completely and the liquid has a faint golden color (about 300 degrees on a candy thermometer), 6 to 10 minutes.

7. Reduce the heat to medium-low and continue to cook, stirring occasionally, until the caramel has an amber color (about 350 degrees on a candy thermometer), 1 to 3 minutes. Off the heat, slowly whisk in the cream until combined (the mixture will bubble and steam vigorously). Stir in the butter, vanilla, lemon juice, and salt until combined. Stir in the pecans and cranberries and mix gently to coat. Pour the caramel mixture into the tart shell. Bake the tart on the baking sheet until the filling is set (it should not jiggle when shaken), 25 to 30 minutes.

8. Let the tart cool completely on the baking sheet, about 1½ hours. To serve, remove the outer metal ring of the tart pan, slide a thin metal spatula between the tart and the tart pan bottom, and carefully slide the tart onto a serving platter or cutting board.

NOTES FROM THE TEST KITCHEN

HOW TO TOAST NUTS
In order for nuts and seeds to contribute the most flavor, they need to be toasted. If the nuts are to be stirred into the batter, they need to be toasted beforehand. To toast a small amount (under 1 cup) of nuts or seeds, put them in a dry skillet over medium heat. Simply shake the skillet occasionally to prevent scorching and toast until they are lightly browned and fragrant, 3 to 8 minutes. Watch the nuts closely because they can go from golden to burnt very quickly. To toast a large quantity of nuts, spread the nuts in a single layer on a rimmed baking sheet and toast in a 350-degree oven, shaking the baking sheet every few minutes, until the nuts are lightly browned and fragrant, 5 to 10 minutes.

MAKING A TART SHELL

1. After rolling the dough out into an 11-inch circle on a lightly floured work surface, wrap it loosely around the rolling pin and unroll it over the tart pan.

2. Lifting the edge of the dough, gently ease the dough into the pan. Press the dough into the fluted sides of the pan and into the corners.

3. Run the rolling pin over the top of the tart pan to remove any excess dough and make a clean edge.

4. If parts of the edge are too thin, reinforce them by pressing in some of the excess dough. If it is too thick, press some of the dough up over the edge of the pan and trim it away.

5. Set the dough-lined tart pan on a large plate and freeze for 30 minutes.

6. Set the dough-lined tart pan on a large baking sheet. Press a large piece of foil inside the frozen tart crust and up over the edges of the pan. Fill the tart shell with pie weights.

SKILLET PEACH COBBLER

ANYONE WHO HAS BITTEN into an impeccably ripe peach knows just how juicy peaches can be. Unfortunately, so does anyone who's ever made a peach cobbler. The peaches typically shed those juices in the oven, leaving the filling watery and the cobbles soggy. I wanted tender peaches and a crisp, buttery biscuit topping. How was I going to get there?

Most recipes attempt to solve the soupy peach problem by loading them up with starchy thickeners, but this left the fruit as gluey and gummy as canned peach pie filling. Other recipes draw moisture out of the sliced peaches by sprinkling them with sugar and letting them drain in a colander. Although this technique prevented a watery filling, I couldn't help but think that a lot of flavor was draining away with all that peach juice.

Searching for a way to thicken my peach filling without running off any of its flavorful juice, I turned to my skillet. I first sautéed the peaches in butter and sugar to release their juices and then cooked them down until all their liquid had evaporated. The resulting peaches were buttery-sweet, with a concentrated taste, but their texture was reminiscent of baby food. I decided to withhold some of the peaches from the sautéing process and add them to the skillet just before baking. Prepared in this manner, the filling had a deep, concentrated flavor (from the sautéed peaches) and a tender, but not at all mushy, texture (from the second addition of peaches). To finish, a splash of lemon juice brought out the sweet-tart taste of the fruit, and a dusting of cornstarch brought the filling together.

As for the cobbles, my tasters liked the flavor of buttermilk biscuits, but their texture was too delicate—the biscuits fell apart on top of the juicy peach filling. Buttermilk biscuits get their light and flaky texture from having cold butter cut into the dry ingredients. Using melted butter made my biscuits sturdier, and they held up much better on top of the fruit. These biscuits were also easier to prepare, since they require no gentle handling—in fact, this dough must be briefly kneaded by hand. With a final sprinkling of cinnamon sugar, I had a reliable recipe for peach cobbler.

—JEREMY SAUER, *Cook's Country*

SKILLET PEACH COBBLER
SERVES 6 TO 8

Four pounds of frozen sliced peaches can be substituted for fresh; there is no need to defrost them. Start step 2 when the peaches are almost done.

FILLING
- 4 tablespoons (½ stick) unsalted butter
- 5 pounds peaches, peeled, pitted, and cut into ½-inch wedges (see note)
- 6 tablespoons (2⅔ ounces) sugar
- ⅛ teaspoon salt
- 1 tablespoon fresh lemon juice
- 1½ teaspoons cornstarch

TOPPING
- 1½ cups (7½ ounces) unbleached all-purpose flour, plus extra for the work surface
- 6 tablespoons (2⅔ ounces) sugar
- 1½ teaspoons baking powder
- ¼ teaspoon baking soda
- ¼ teaspoon salt
- ¾ cup buttermilk
- 4 tablespoons (½ stick) unsalted butter, melted and cooled
- 1 teaspoon ground cinnamon

1. FOR THE FILLING: Adjust an oven rack to the middle position and heat the oven to 425 degrees. Melt the butter in a large ovensafe nonstick skillet over medium-high heat. Add two-thirds of the peaches, sugar, and salt and cook, covered, until the peaches release their juices, about 5 minutes. Remove the lid and simmer until all the liquid has evaporated and the peaches begin to caramelize, 15 to 20 minutes. Add the remaining peaches and cook until heated through, about 5 minutes. Whisk the lemon juice and cornstarch in a small bowl, then stir into the peach mixture. Cover the skillet and set aside off the heat.

2. FOR THE TOPPING: Meanwhile, whisk the flour, 5 tablespoons of the sugar, baking powder, baking soda, and salt in a medium bowl. Stir in the buttermilk and butter until the dough forms. Turn the dough out onto a lightly floured work surface and knead briefly until smooth, about 30 seconds.

3. Combine the remaining 1 tablespoon sugar and cinnamon. Break the dough into rough 1-inch pieces and space them about ½ inch apart on top of the hot peach mixture. Sprinkle with the cinnamon sugar and bake until the topping is golden brown and the filling is thickened, 18 to 22 minutes. Let cool on a wire rack for 10 minutes. Serve. (Although best eaten the day it is made to maintain the texture of the cobbles, leftovers may be refrigerated for up to 1 day. Individual portions may be removed from the skillet and reheated in the microwave.)

BERRY FOOL

HERETICAL AS IT MAY SOUND, apple pie was not always the quintessential American dessert. Centuries ago, fruit fool held that honor. Brought to America by British colonists in the 1700s, this dessert was made by folding pureed stewed fruit (traditionally gooseberries) into a sweet custard. Gooseberry fool was important enough to show up in the recipes of Martha Washington. Two hundred years later, it was still enough of a classic to earn a place in James Beard's classic cookbook, *American Cookery.* The origin of the dessert's name, however, remains a mystery. Some believe it comes from the French verb *fouler* (to crush or pound). Others think the etymology points to the idea that as a dessert, this concoction was a bit of sweet foolishness.

Traditional recipes call for gently heating milk, cream, sugar, and egg yolks until thickened and then folding in cooked, pureed fruit once the custard has cooled. The resulting dessert has a deep, fruity flavor and a wonderfully silken creaminess. But cooking custard is a fussy endeavor. Overheat the yolks and you produce scrambled eggs; neglect to bring the mixture up to a high enough temperature and you've made eggnog.

Modern recipes skip the custard and use whipped cream. But most of the whipped-cream versions I tested, including one from Beard's *American Cookery,* blunted the flavor of the fruit and seemed too light and insubstantial when compared with fool made with custard. Worse, if the recipe departed from the traditional fruit choice—gooseberries—the dessert turned soupy and loose. I knew I wasn't going to be using gooseberries unless I grew them in my backyard. And I definitely didn't want to cook up custard. Could I concoct a dessert with the intense fruitiness and rich body of a traditional fool just the same?

The reason fool made with gooseberries has a firmer texture is that this hard-to-find heritage fruit is naturally high in pectin. When exposed to heat, sugar, and acid, pectin breaks down and causes the fruit to thicken. I wanted to use raspberries and strawberries, but they contain very little pectin and remain loose when cooked. Would adding a little commercially made pectin help? It did—but I needed to add so much extra sugar for the pectin to work that my puree was transformed into a super-sweet jam.

Some fool recipes I found cooked low-pectin fruits such as raspberries and strawberries with egg yolks to thicken them up, in essence creating a fruit curd. Not surprisingly, a yolk-based fruit puree turned out to be just as temperamental as custard, requiring lots of attention to keep the fruit from turning lumpy. Furthermore, when I folded the curd into the whipped cream, the dessert no longer tasted fresh and fruity; it had an eggy flavor that superseded everything else. Cornstarch proved equally unhelpful in achieving the results I wanted. Though I used less than typically called for in a fruit pie filling, the cooked berries still lost some of their fresh, vibrant flavor, and the mixture had a slight chalkiness my tasters didn't like.

The idea of using gelatin had been percolating in the back of my mind—recipes for desserts such as mousse and Bavarian crème often use it to firm up texture. But adding it to fruit? Wouldn't that turn my puree into Jell-O? For gelatin to work, I would need to use a judicious hand. I added just 2 teaspoons, softening the gelatin in some uncooked berry puree and then combining the softened mixture with some heated puree to help melt and distribute the gelatin. After setting for a couple of hours in the refrigerator, the puree thickened to the consistency of a loose pie filling: perfect. Once I tasted the puree, I knew I had hit the jackpot—it had a far fresher and more intense fruit flavor than anything

I'd managed to produce yet. And, unlike the other methods I'd tried, I didn't need to actually cook the fruit. I only needed to get the puree hot enough to melt the gelatin.

All that remained was to create a richer, sturdier cream base to partner with the fruit puree. Making custard was out. But why not try to make whipped cream more custard-like? I rounded up a bunch of candidates to add density to the billowy cream: whole-milk yogurt, mascarpone cheese, crème fraîche, and sour cream. Whipped together with heavy cream, each worked surprisingly well in creating a mixture that was airy yet more substantial than plain whipped cream. Sour cream won out for adding just the right degree of richness, along with a mildly tangy undertone.

My tasters, however, were clamoring for a bit more fruit flavor, as well as contrasting fruit texture. Layering the fruit puree and cream base with fresh berries tasted great but left pools of juice in the mixture. Letting the berries stand in a sugar mixture solved the problem by drawing out excess juice that could be strained off.

I could have left the fool well enough alone, but I had encountered several recipes that sprinkled the dessert with crumbled cookies or sweet crackers. I tried a range of these, including graham crackers and gingersnaps. Tasters' favorite was sweet wheat crackers, for the pleasant contrast their nuttiness added to the cream and fruit.

With its fruity flavor and creamy texture, I now had a modern, reliable recipe that kept only the best traits of this old-fashioned dessert.

—DAVID PAZMIÑO, *Cook's Illustrated*

BERRY FOOL

SERVES 6

Blueberries or blackberries can be substituted for raspberries in this recipe. You may also substitute frozen fruit for fresh, but there will be a slight compromise in texture. If using frozen fruit, reduce the amount of sugar in the puree by 1 tablespoon. The thickened fruit puree can be made up to 4 hours in advance; just make sure to whisk it well in step 4 to break up any clumps before combining it with the whipped cream. For the best results, chill your beater and bowl before whipping the cream. I like the granular texture and nutty flavor of Carr's Whole Wheat Crackers, but graham crackers or gingersnaps will also work.

- 2 quarts strawberries (about 2 pounds), washed, dried, and hulled
- 1 pint raspberries (about 12 ounces) (see note)
- ½ cup (3½ ounces) plus 4 tablespoons sugar
- 2 teaspoons unflavored gelatin
- 1 cup heavy cream
- ¼ cup sour cream
- ½ teaspoon vanilla extract
- 4 Carr's Whole Wheat Crackers, finely crushed (about ¼ cup) (see note)
- 6 sprigs fresh mint, for serving (optional)

1. Process 1 quart of the strawberries, ½ pint of the raspberries, and ½ cup sugar in a food processor until the mixture is completely smooth, about 1 minute. Strain the berry puree through a fine-mesh strainer into a 4-cup liquid measuring cup (you should have 2½ cups puree; reserve any excess for another use). Transfer ½ cup puree to a small bowl and sprinkle the gelatin over the top; stir until the gelatin is incorporated and let stand at least 5 minutes. Heat the remaining 2 cups puree in a small saucepan over medium heat until it begins to bubble, 4 to 6 minutes. Remove the pan from the heat and stir in the gelatin mixture until dissolved. Transfer the gelatin-puree mixture to a medium bowl, cover with plastic wrap, and refrigerate until cold, about 2 hours.

2. Meanwhile, chop the remaining 1 quart strawberries into rough ¼-inch pieces. Toss the strawberries, remaining ½ pint raspberries, and 2 tablespoons of the sugar together in a medium bowl. Set aside for 1 hour.

3. Place the heavy cream, sour cream, vanilla, and remaining 2 tablespoons sugar in the chilled bowl of a standing mixer. Beat on low speed until bubbles form, about 30 seconds. Increase the speed to medium and continue beating until the beaters leave a trail, about 30 seconds. Increase the speed to high; continue beating until the mixture has nearly doubled in volume and holds stiff peaks, about 30 seconds. Transfer

BERRY FOOL

⅓ cup of the whipped-cream mixture to a small bowl and set aside.

4. Remove the thickened berry puree from the refrigerator and whisk until smooth. With the mixer running at medium speed, slowly add two-thirds of the puree to the whipped-cream mixture; mix until incorporated, about 15 seconds. Using a spatula, gently fold in the remaining thickened puree, leaving streaks of puree.

5. Transfer the uncooked berries to a fine-mesh strainer; shake gently to remove any excess juice. Divide two-thirds of the berries evenly among 6 tall parfait or sundae glasses. Divide the creamy berry mixture evenly among the glasses, followed by the remaining uncooked berries. Top each glass with the reserved plain whipped-cream mixture. Sprinkle with the crushed crackers and garnish with the mint sprigs, if using. Serve immediately.

NOTES FROM THE TEST KITCHEN

A SWEET FINISH
Though not traditional, a sprinkling of crushed sweet wheat crackers (gingersnaps and graham crackers will also work) adds subtle crunch and nutty notes that complement the berry flavors in our fool.

BALLOON WHISKS
When only a cup or so of whipped cream is needed, is it really necessary to haul out a standing mixer? Manufacturers claim the bulbous design of balloon-style whisks makes short work of whisking air into cream. We timed how long five different models took to whip a cup of heavy cream to stiff peaks, comparing the whipping times and user-friendliness of each. Our all-around winner was the **OXO Steel 11-Inch Balloon Whisk,** $9.99, for its quick whip time, comfy handle, lightweight design, and slim price tag.

CHERRY CLAFOUTI

FEW DISHES EXEMPLIFY homey French cooking quite as well as cherry *clafouti*, a creamy and light baked custard studded with whole fruit. Originally from the Limousin region of central France, hard against the foothills of the Massif Central, the dessert sounds simple—just fruit and batter—but is in fact notoriously finicky and can suffer from all manner of problems with both its flavor and texture. The perfect clafouti could be considered one of French cooking's greatest mysteries and one I was willing to take a stab at unravelling.

Clafouti batter typically contains little but eggs, flour, either milk or cream, sugar, and a flavoring or two. The ratios of those ingredients, however, can vary a great deal from recipe to recipe, producing clafouti with textures ranging from moist, airy, and delicate like an omelet to dense, squat, and chewy like a torte, and everywhere in between. After whipping up a half-dozen different recipes, I preferred clafouti that was rich and full flavored yet light textured; I didn't take to those that tasted particularly eggy or starchy.

The basic structure of a clafouti is a balancing act between starch, eggs, and dairy—either milk or cream. Testing, then, involved identifying the best ratio of each component and how they interacted. Eggs and dairy are the primary components of the batter so this is where I chose to commence testing. Eggs contribute structure, moisture, and flavor to clafouti and recipes typically include anywhere from four to eight eggs for a clafouti serving six to eight people. Recipes with too many eggs possessed a rubbery texture; with too few eggs, the clafouti was too soft to cut neatly and the flavor was overly mild. Not pleased with the flavor or texture of any recipe using only whole eggs, I tried varying amounts of whole eggs and egg yolks and found a happy middle ground with a combination of two whole eggs and two yolks. Firm-textured yet not rubbery and rich but not eggy, the clafouti was progressing in the right direction.

As for dairy, clafouti recipes typically use milk, cream, or a combination thereof. I thought milk alone tasted lean and much preferred a richer blend of milk and cream. Cream alone, however, proved to make the best clafouti, rich tasting with a satisfyingly hefty—but not dense—texture. This was dessert after all and a little bit of cream was fine by me.

Flour binds the batter and creates the structure necessary to support the fruit. The more flour I added, the stiffer and stickier the batter became as the flour's protein developed into tough gluten, great for bread but not so for tender custard. Adding less flour to the batter kept the texture tender, but a certain gumminess persisted. Revisiting the initial testing recipes, I found a few that cut or completely replaced the flour with cornstarch. After experimenting a little, I was pleased with a half-and-half blend of flour and cornstarch, though an all-cornstarch clafouti proved the best yet: light, creamy, and not the least bit gummy.

Few of the clafoutis I prepared were particularly sweet and those that were weren't very enjoyable. Sugar is used in a clafouti to accent and define the fruit flavor, not overpower it. While cherries aren't particularly sweet, I still found any more than ⅓ cup of sugar made the clafouti cloying and dull.

Finally pleased with the batter, I could now address the star of the show: the cherries. Authentic recipes claim that unpitted tart cherries are a must as the pits intensify the fruit's flavor. However, I didn't find that to be the case, and picking the pits out of each mouthful— and the accompanying risk of a cracked tooth—took some of the joy out of the dessert. Pitted cherries tasted just fine, especially when the batter's flavor was boosted by a stiff shot of vanilla and a splash of amaretto liqueur (some recipes go as far as to make almond milk with which to flavor the batter, but this seemed like a lot of work for such a simple dessert).

While some recipes insist on a cast-iron baking pan, I wanted to find another option, one more accessible to all cooks. I tested a few possibilities and found a basic 9-inch pie plate worked just fine. While "perfect" might be in the eye of the beholder, I like to think that my clafouti turned out pretty close.

—BRYAN ROOF, *America's Test Kitchen Books*

CHERRY CLAFOUTI

SERVES 6 TO 8

The simple flavors of this dish make using fresh fruit a must; the texture and flavor of jarred, canned, or frozen cherries are very disappointing here.

⅓ cup (2⅓ ounces) granulated sugar
2 tablespoons cornstarch
   Pinch salt
1¼ cups heavy cream
2 large whole eggs, at room temperature
2 large egg yolks, at room temperature
1 tablespoon amaretto
2 teaspoons vanilla extract
1½ cups (12 ounces) fresh sour cherries, pitted
   and halved (see note)
   Confectioners' sugar, for dusting

1. Adjust an oven rack to the lower-middle position and heat the oven to 350 degrees. Whisk the granulated sugar, cornstarch, and salt together in a large bowl until combined. Whisk in the cream, whole eggs, egg yolks, amaretto, and vanilla, until smooth and thoroughly combined.

2. Arrange the cherries in a single layer in a 9-inch pie plate and pour the cream mixture over the top. Bake the clafouti until a toothpick inserted in the center comes out clean, 35 to 40 minutes, rotating the pie plate halfway through baking.

3. Let the clafouti cool until the custard has set up, about 15 minutes. Dust with confectioners' sugar before serving.

VARIATION
PLUM CLAFOUTI

For a nice presentation, fan the plum slices out attractively over the bottom of the dish before pouring in the custard.

Follow the recipe for Cherry Clafouti, substituting 2 plums, pitted and sliced into ¼-inch wedges, for the cherries, and 1 tablespoon cognac for the amaretto.

NOTES FROM THE TEST KITCHEN

CORNSTARCH FOR LIGHTNESS
Many clafouti recipes call for flour to act as a binder, but flour produced a thick, overly heavy clafouti. Cornstarch, a mere 2 tablespoons, was the answer. The relatively small amount was enough to bind the custard without weighing it down, yielding a light and creamy texture.

TEST KITCHEN RESOURCES

THE YEAR'S BEST TIPS, TECHNIQUES,
AND EQUIPMENT AND INGREDIENT RATINGS

BEST KITCHEN QUICK TIPS

KEEPING SUMMER SALADS COLD

Crystal Fouch of Clearfield, Ky., uses her enameled cast-iron Dutch oven for more than just cooking—it's also one of her favorite serving vessels for cold foods.

1. Fill an enameled cast-iron Dutch oven with ice water and let it stand until the pot is thoroughly chilled, about five minutes. Dump out the water and dry the pot.

2. Transfer chilled food, such as potato or macaroni salad, into the pot for serving. The pot will retain the cold temperature much longer than would a glass or plastic serving bowl.

MEASURING SHORTENING SHORTCUT

If you need to measure shortening in a recipe that also calls for an egg, Shirley Ryle of Big Spring, Texas, recommends breaking the egg into the measuring cup that you'll use for the shortening. Swirl the egg around and then empty the measuring cup. When you pack the shortening into the measuring cup, the shortening will slide right out—no more scraping to get every last bit.

CLEVER OLIVE PITTING

The most common way to remove pits from olives without an olive pitter is to smash them on a cutting board. Marci Abbrecht of Wellesley, Mass., came up with a more elegant—and equally effective—alternative. Place a funnel upside down on the work surface. Stand one end of the olive on the spout and press down, allowing the pit to fall through the funnel.

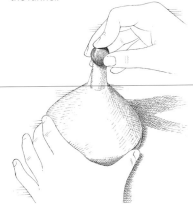

DECORATE WITH EASE

When Tracey Witham of Braintree, Mass., serves ice-cream cones to her kids, she puts sprinkles in a muffin tin. Then her kids can dip their cones into the sprinkles without any mess.

SIMPLIFIED SEED REMOVAL

Splitting a pumpkin or winter squash is easy enough, but removing the tangled mess of seeds and pulp is another matter. Instead of using a spoon, Katie Graf of Lincoln, Neb., reaches for a round metal cookie cutter. The sharp edges conform to the curves of the squash, making it easy to remove the seeds and stringy pulp.

FREE UP YOUR FREEZER

Space is an issue in nearly everyone's freezer, especially if you tend to store already-assembled casseroles in their baking dish. Joan Vogan of Sugarland, Texas, came up with a smart solution. She lines her casserole dish with aluminum foil before starting the assembly. When completed, she puts the whole thing in the freezer for several hours, then removes the frozen casserole from the baking dish and rewraps it, and puts it back into the freezer without the dish. When the time comes to bake it, she simply removes the foil and puts the casserole into the original dish to thaw. This not only gives her the use of the baking dish during the time the casserole is in the freezer, it also frees up space in the freezer.

NO-MESS MIXING

Splattering food all over the kitchen is not an uncommon occurrence when using an electric mixer. To avoid the mess, Kathy Parker Hoge of Houston, Texas, sticks a paper plate through the beaters: The paper plate stops any food that splatters up.

AN EASIER SQUEEZE

Pressing all the juice from a lemon or lime with a citrus juicer can be tricky. To ensure he gets every last drop, Fred Dunayer of Sarasota, Fla., employs the following technique:

1. Using a paring knife, cut the lemon peel from pole to pole, making four ¼-inch-deep slits. Next, cut the lemon in half crosswise.

2. Place the lemon half in the juicer and squeeze to remove all of the juice.

TESTING FRYING OIL TEMPERATURE

Amy Malek of Houston, Texas, has a trick that takes the guesswork out of determining when frying oil is hot. She simply places a kernel of popcorn in the oil as it heats up. The kernel will pop when the oil is between 350 and 365 degrees, just the right temperature for deep-frying.

GRILLING SMALL ITEMS

There's nothing worse than watching perfectly grilled vegetables slip through the grill grates and scorch on the hot coals below. Kim Thom of Vancouver, B.C., uses a cooling rack to protect vegetables.

Place the wire cooling rack perpendicular to the grill grates. Heat for about five minutes, then rub the rack lightly with oil before grilling.

PERFECT WAFFLES

Searching for picture-perfect waffles for every batch, Jessica Anderson of Galloway, Ohio, experimented with measuring cups to find out the right amount of batter to pour on her iron. Now they always look great, and there's no more messy cleanup from excess batter oozing out the sides. So you won't forget, she suggests writing the amount on a small label and posting it on the handle of your waffle iron.

SMART SAFFRON HANDLING

Barbara Soldano of Ridgefield, Conn., began using saffron in a few dishes recently, but had trouble getting small pinches out of the jar: The strands would get stuck on her fingers or would fall on the counter or floor, and she didn't want to waste a single strand of this expensive spice. Her solution? Use tweezers to gently pick out what she needs. It takes just a little bit longer, but now she doesn't waste anything.

PERFECT PIE PASTRY

Rolling pie dough into an even circle requires deft hands and experience. Joy Lillie of San Jose, Calif., uses parchment paper and a pencil to make the process less daunting.

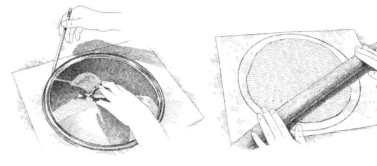

1. Place a 12-inch skillet lid on a sheet of parchment paper. Using a pencil, trace a circle around the lid.

2. Roll out a disk of lightly floured dough on the parchment, using the tracing as a guide and stopping when the dough reaches the line.

PROOFING BREAD DOUGH

Laura Liu of Brooklyn, N.Y., had trouble telling when her bread dough had properly risen inside a sloped bowl, so she came up with the following trick. Lightly spray a slow-cooker insert with nonstick cooking spray. Place the dough in the insert and cover until it has risen. The straight sides and glass lid of the insert allow the baker to easily gauge the dough's progress.

OILING THE GRILL EFFICIENTLY

Instead of wasting paper towels every time he oils the grates on his grill, Justin Fahey of Newton, Mass., came up with a new way to get the job done. He simply cuts an onion in half and sticks a fork in the top of the pole end. Then he dips the flat end of the onion into the oil and rubs the grates. Once he is finished, he cuts the onion into rings and grills them up to go along with his steaks.

SAFER CHILE HANDLING

Mincing fresh chiles can lead to hand burns that last for hours. Tired of fiery fingers, Ellen Watson of Sacramento, Calif., found protection in a grater and a zipper-lock bag. Using the bag as a glove, hold the chile and grate it along the surface of a box or Microplane grater. This method doesn't allow you to remove the seeds, so you will get maximum heat from chiles prepared this way.

BEST KITCHEN QUICK TIPS

KEEPING GRILLED VEGETABLES WARM

Whenever Greg Hockert of Melbourne, Fla., uses his gas grill to prepare meat and vegetables for dinner, the vegetables always get done first and turn cold on the serving platter while he waits for the meat to finish. To remedy this, he keeps a metal bowl on top of the grill lid, where it heats up during cooking. Once the vegetables are done, he transfers them to the warm bowl and puts it back on top of the grill lid. The grill keeps the bowl heated, which keeps the vegetables warm until serving time.

TIDY CHOCOLATE CHOPPING

When chopped into chunks for cookies or bars, chocolate often shatters, leaving behind shavings and powder. Todd Nystul of Baltimore, Md., uses his microwave to solve the problem.

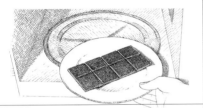

1. Place the chocolate bar on a microwave-safe plate and microwave on the lowest setting for about one minute, turning the chocolate halfway through. When the chocolate softens and begins to melt at the corners, remove it from the microwave. (If the chocolate bar is very thick, it may take longer to soften.)

2. Place the warm chocolate on a cutting board and chop it into chunks.

QUICK TOASTED BREADCRUMBS

Instead of toasting crumbs in the oven or in a skillet, Grier Hickman of Hong Kong recommends toasting the bread in the toaster first and then pulsing it a few times in the food processor.

HASSLE-FREE BACON CHOPPING

Patti Merrell of Baytown, Texas, makes slippery bacon a cinch to mince with the following tip.

1. Wrap the bacon in plastic wrap and freeze for 15 minutes.

2. The bacon will harden just enough so that, using a chef's knife, it can be chopped as finely as needed with nary a slip.

NO MORE SOGGY CHEESECAKE

After refrigerating a baked and cooled cheesecake, Lori Johnson of Nordland, Wash., always found that unwanted moisture collected on the top of the cake, ruining her creation. Her solution is to arrange a layer of paper towels over the cheesecake before covering it with plastic wrap and refrigerating.

NO-SLIP STRAINER

When straining vegetables or broths, Kristi Shawl of Spreckels, Calif., always found it difficult to keep the lip of her fine-mesh strainer from falling into the bowl or pot she was straining into. Her solution? She wraps a thick rubber band around the balancing loop of the strainer to create a no-slip grip that stays in place.

SMART GUACAMOLE PREP

Cubing avocados for a big batch of guacamole is incredibly labor intensive. To speed things up, Diane Conn of Sonora, Calif., slices them in half and removes the pits. Then she presses the avocados into a grid-style cooling rack and slides the peel off, leaving perfect ½-inch cubes of avocado in no time.

EASY BUTTER CUBES

Carolyn Winslow of Bellingham, Wash., uses an egg slicer to quickly and precisely cut butter into small pieces for pie dough and biscuits.

1. Place up to 4 tablespoons of butter into an egg slicer and push down on the slicing blades to create planks.
2. Rotate the butter a quarter turn, then push down on the slicing blades to create small pieces.

FAST MUSTARD VINAIGRETTE

Ramzey Kiyali of Alpharetta, Ga., came up with a solution to using every last drop from jars of mustard. Instead of throwing the jars away, add some oil, vinegar, and seasonings, put the top back on, and shake away. You'll have mustard vinaigrette in a flash.

SLIPPERY CHICKEN SOLUTION

Halving a chicken breast horizontally to form thin cutlets is a slippery proposition. Looking for a safer way to accomplish this task, Manny Landron of Raleigh, N.C., came up with the following approach: Using tongs, hold a chicken breast that has been frozen for 15 minutes perpendicular to the work surface. Cut through the chicken to make two even cutlets.

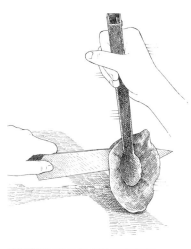

EASIER STIR-FRIES

When prepping vegetables for a stir-fry, instead of putting them in individual bowls, Linda Borders of Plano, Texas, layers them in one big bowl by separating them with plastic wrap. The vegetables that will be added last to the skillet go into the bowl first. When she is ready to cook, she removes each layer individually before adding it to the skillet. That way there is only one bowl to wash instead of a lot of little ones.

REMOVING PESKY FRUIT STICKERS

Fruit and vegetable stickers can be difficult to remove, especially from soft produce, such as plums and tomatoes. Misty Dawn Gaubatz of Missoula, Mont., came up with the following solution.

1. Dip the corner of a paper towel in vegetable oil. Rub the oiled towel over the sticker and let sit for about five minutes.

2. Peel off the offending sticker without damaging the fruit.

DISPOSABLE VEGETABLE SCRUBBER

Finding herself in a kitchen without a vegetable scrubber, Carol Alexander of Charlottesville, Va., designed a homemade substitute.

1. Fold an empty perforated onion or citrus bag to form a compact shape, then secure it with a rubber band.

2. Use the scrubber to clean vegetables under cool running water, then discard the scrubber.

THIN SPATULA STAND-IN

If you have only a thick plastic spatula, it can be difficult to remove warm cookies from a baking sheet without breaking them. Finding herself in such a situation, Olga Marino of Baltimore, Md., reached for a metal cheese slicer. With its thin, sharp blade, it's the perfect tool for sliding under warm cookies and transferring them to a cooling rack without breaking or tearing.

PREVENTING DOUGH FROM STICKING

Gina Colby of Austin, Texas, found that lightly spraying her dough hook with nonstick cooking spray before mixing bread dough prevented dough from edging up the hook and made cleanup a breeze.

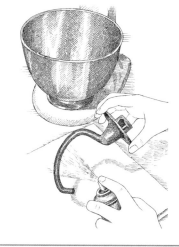

NICELY WHIPPED

Chilling your mixing bowl and beaters can make it easier (and faster) to achieve billowy whipped cream, but rarely does anyone have enough room in their freezer for a mixing bowl. So whenever she needs to whip some cream, Amy Parker of Cypress, Texas, fills her mixing bowl with ice cubes and waits about 10 minutes. Once the bowl is chilled, she empties the cubes, wipes the bowl dry, and starts whipping. Within minutes, she has perfectly whipped cream.

STEWS 101

CHOOSING THE RIGHT CUT

Choosing the proper cut of meat is the single most important part of making a great stew. For beef, pork, and lamb, we prefer cuts from the shoulder area, because they are well marbled with fat and have the best combination of flavor and texture. And in chicken stews, thigh meat is the preferred choice.

BEEF
We love the beefy taste and exceptional tenderness of chuck-eye roast. Another good option: the chuck 7-bone roast.

CHUCK EYE ROAST

LAMB
Roasts from the lamb shoulder can be hard to find, so we rely on shoulder-cut chops such as the round-bone for our stews. An alternative choice is the blade chop.

ROUND-BONE LAMB CHOP

CHICKEN
The extra fat and connective tissue in thigh meat make it better suited than breast meat for stew; it also separates more easily from the bone than does drumstick meat. We use skin-on thighs to protect the meat and keep it from over-cooking and drying out during browning.

BONE-IN CHICKEN THIGH

PORK
We like pork butt (also called Boston shoulder or Boston butt) for its great flavor, but the less-expensive and slightly fattier picnic shoulder is also a fine choice.

PORK BUTT

COOKING TIMES FOR MEAT

MEAT	CUBE SIZE	APPROX. COOKING TIME
Beef, Pork, and Lamb	1 to 1½ inches	2 to 2½ hours
Beef, Pork, and Lamb	1½ to 2 inches	2½ to 3 hours
Chicken Thighs	whole	30 to 60 minutes

COOKING TIMES FOR VEGETABLES

VEGETABLE	PREPARATION	COOKING TIME
Potatoes	1- to 1½-inch cubes	1 hour
Carrots	sliced ¼ to ½ inch thick	1 hour
Parsnips	sliced ¼ to ½ inch thick	1 hour
Sweet Potatoes	quartered and sliced ¼ inch thick	1 hour
Turnips	½-inch dice	45 minutes
Peppers	½-inch dice	45 minutes
Frozen Vegetables	do not thaw	15 to 20 minutes
Hearty Greens	washed and chopped	20 to 30 minutes
Tender Greens	washed and chopped	1 to 2 minutes

KEY EQUIPMENT

DUTCH OVEN
A Dutch oven is essential for making stew. Look for one that is twice as wide as it is high, with a minimum capacity of 6 quarts (7 or 8 is even better). The bottom should be thick, so food browns evenly and the pot retains heat during cooking. The pot should also have a tight-fitting lid.

TEST KITCHEN FAVORITE
▶ LE CREUSET 7¼-Quart Round French Oven, $229.95

BEST BUY
▶ TRAMONTINA 6.5 Quart Cast Iron Dutch Oven, $40

TONGS
Our favorite pair of tongs handily picks up the smallest pieces of meat without tearing or mashing.

TEST KITCHEN FAVORITE
▶ OXO GOOD GRIPS 12-Inch Locking Tongs, $10.39

LADLE
A ladle is the best tool for skimming fat and portioning stew.

TEST KITCHEN FAVORITE
▶ RÖSLE Ladle with Pouring Rim & Hook Handle, $26.95

1. CUT YOUR OWN MEAT: It is best to cut your own stew meat to guarantee same-sized chunks that share the same flavor and cooking time.

2. BROWN THE MEAT PROPERLY: Crowding the pan with too much meat or using inadequate heat can cause meat to steam (rather than brown) and ultimately lose flavor. To avoid this problem, add the meat only after the oil begins to smoke and leave plenty of space between pieces (this means no more than 1 pound of meat per batch).

3. SAUTÉ THE AROMATICS TO ENHANCE FLAVOR: Recipes that call for dumping spices and aromatics, such as garlic and onion, into the pot at the same time as the liquid fail to maximize their flavor. So hold the liquid and sauté these flavor-enhancing ingredients first.

4. FLOUR THE AROMATICS TO THICKEN THE STEW: Many recipes call for thickening a stew at the end of cooking by leaving the lid off, but this method risks overcooking. Thicken stew at the beginning of the cooking process by sprinkling flour over the sautéed aromatics. Cook the flour for a minute or two to remove any raw flour taste.

5. SIMMER THE STEW IN THE OVEN: Cooking stew in a covered Dutch oven at 300 degrees allows the internal temperature of the meat to rise slowly, ensures that the meat is tender, and eliminates scorching.

6. COOK THE MEAT UNTIL FALL-APART TENDER: When meat is undercooked, its fat and connective tissue have not had the chance to break down sufficiently, and it will taste rubbery and tough. Cook meat to the point where collagen has melted down into gelatin. This yields tender meat that separates easily when pulled apart with two forks.

7. DEFAT BEFORE SERVING: Pour stew liquid into a narrow container before defatting. This will create a thicker layer of fat that's easier to remove. Alternatively, refrigerate the stew overnight. When the fat solidifies, it can be lifted right off.

FLAVOR ENHANCERS

BEEF BROTH

While broth is not as central to the flavor of stew as it is to soup, choosing a high-quality brand is still important. And using a low-sodium broth is essential; as the liquid in a stew reduces, regular full-sodium broth can turn the stew too salty and ruin the flavor.

TEST KITCHEN FAVORITES
▶ SWANSON Certified Organic Free Range Chicken Broth and PACIFIC Beef Broth

TOMATO PASTE

A small amount of tomato paste added to a stew along with the aromatics brings depth and color.

TEST KITCHEN FAVORITE
▶ AMORE Tomato Paste

ROASTING MEAT 101

ESSENTIAL EQUIPMENT

INSTANT-READ THERMOMETER

An instant-read thermometer is by far the best way to gauge when a roast is done. We prefer digital to dial-face models for their speed, accuracy, and ease of reading.

TEST KITCHEN FAVORITE
▸ THERMOWORKS Super-Fast Thermapen, $85

BEST BUY
▸ CDN ProAccurate DTQ450, $17.95

ROASTING PAN AND RACK

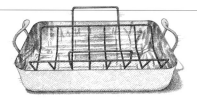

A roasting pan and rack (which elevates the roast above the drippings and grease) are essential pieces of equipment for roasting. Size and construction are the most important factors to consider when selecting a roasting pan. Because we often sear meat before we roast it, we like a flameproof pan that can be used on the stovetop. We avoid pans with nonstick finishes, because they can't handle high oven temperatures. The perfect pan should accommodate a big holiday turkey with ease, so 15 by 11 inches is our preferred size. For a roasting rack, we prefer a sturdy-handled V-rack that holds a roast snugly in place and can be easily removed from the pan.

TEST KITCHEN FAVORITE
▸ CALPHALON Contemporary Stainless Steel Roasting Pan, $100 (comes with a roasting rack)

CHOOSING THE RIGHT CUT AND THE RIGHT METHOD

Choosing a roast can be a confusing endeavor, and once you've made a selection it's important to use the right roasting method. We've developed two categories of roasting that work best for different kinds and cuts of meat: fast and high and slow and low.

FAST, HIGH-TEMPERATURE ROASTING

Though lower oven temperatures generally guarantee more evenly cooked meat, small, narrow roasts like beef tenderloin and rack of lamb depend on a relatively quick cooking time to ensure juicy, tender meat. Roast these cuts at an oven temperature of 450 degrees.

FAVORITE CUTS

BEEF TENDERLOIN
The most tender cut of beef money can buy, but the flavor is mild.

TOP SIRLOIN BEEF ROAST
As flavorful and juicy (though not as tender) as a rib roast at a fraction of the cost.

RACK OF LAMB
The extreme tenderness of this mild-tasting cut commands a high price tag. It usually contains eight or nine ribs, depending on how the meat has been butchered.

SLOW, LOW-TEMPERATURE ROASTING

Heat takes a long time to penetrate into the center of large cuts of meat such as prime rib, leg of lamb, and rack of pork, making them susceptible to a thick outer swath of gray, overcooked meat. To prevent this problem, roast large cuts slowly at 250 degrees for beef, 250 degrees for lamb, and 325 degrees for pork.

FAVORITE CUTS

BEEF RIB ROAST, FIRST CUT
The standard for roast beef. This cut is extremely tender and flavorful, albeit on the expensive side.

BONELESS BLADE PORK ROAST
The most flavorful cut from the loin, with a fair amount of fat that allows it to remain juicy when roasted. Though not as juicy as a blade roast, a center rib roast is a great alternative because it is flavorful and widely available.

LEG OF LAMB
This cut is not as tender as the rack, but it boasts fuller flavor. It may be sold with the bones in but is more commonly found butterflied and boneless.

5 STEPS TO A GREAT ROAST

1. SEASON AND LET STAND: Sprinkle the exterior of the roast with salt (preferably kosher) and let it stand at room temperature for at least an hour. As the roast sits, the salt draws out its juices, which then combine with the salt before being reabsorbed into the meat. The result: a roast that is flavorful both inside and out.

2. TIE BEFORE COOKING: Tying a roast forces it into a more even shape, ensuring that the thin, narrow ends won't overcook before the thick middle part is done. Tying also makes for a nicer presentation and easier slicing.

3. SEAR BEFORE ROASTING: Browning meat produces new flavor compounds that are essential to the success of a roast. To guarantee a well-caramelized crust, sear the roast in 1–2 tablespoons of oil for two to three minutes per side, either in the roasting pan or a skillet, before putting it into the oven.

4. CHOOSE THE APPROPRIATE ROASTING METHOD: Most recipes call for cooking roasts in a moderately hot (350- to 400-degree) oven, but this method can lead to an overcooked exterior and unevenly cooked interior. Depending on the meat's size and shape, we prefer to roast at temperatures as high as 450 degrees or as low as 250 degrees. (See "Choosing the Right Cut and the Right Method," left.)

5. LET THE MEAT REST: All roasts should rest under a foil tent for 10 to 20 minutes before being carved. As the protein molecules in the meat cool, they will reabsorb any accumulated juices and redistribute them throughout the roast.

OUTDOOR ROASTING ON THE GRILL

The oven isn't your only option for roasting meat. For tender cuts that don't require slow cooking over low heat, such as beef tenderloin, the grill works just as well. Grill-roasting relies on indirect heat between 300 and 400 degrees (in contrast to true grilling, which occurs at temperatures in excess of 500 degrees). Coals are banked on one side of the grill, and meat roasts on the "cool" side, with the lid kept down to trap heat and create an environment much like the oven. With a gas grill, the primary burner is kept on and the others are turned off.

1. SEASON, LET THE MEAT STAND 1 HOUR, AND TIE BEFORE GRILL-ROASTING: (See steps 1 and 2 in "5 Steps to a Great Roast," left.) For lean cuts of pork, skip the salt and brine the meat before placing it on the grill.

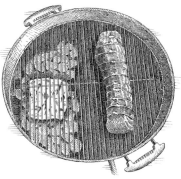

2. USE WOOD CHUNKS OR CHIPS TO ENHANCE THE SMOKY FLAVOR: While charcoal will impart some flavor to the meat, wood chunks or chips are necessary to achieve true smokiness (especially with a gas grill). Place soaked, drained chunks directly on charcoal; wrap wood chips in a foil packet poked with holes (or place in a foil tray for a gas grill). To keep the fire burning as long as possible, we also prefer to use briquettes rather than hardwood charcoal.

3. BANK THE COALS ON ONE SIDE OF THE GRILL: Many recipes recommend banking coals on both sides of the grill. We find the edges of large roasts can burn with this method. We prefer to transfer all coals to one side of the grill, leaving half of the grill free of coals so the meat can cook without danger of burning. To ensure even cooking, it is a good idea to rotate the meat halfway through cooking.

4. USE VENTS TO REGULATE THE HEAT: To help regulate heat, adjust the vents on both the lid and grill bottom. We prefer to close the vents partially to keep the coals from burning up too fast and to help the grill retain heat.

WHEN IS IT DONE?

A thermometer takes the guesswork out of knowing when a roast is done. To ensure that the probe stays in the roast, insert the thermometer at an angle. To get an accurate reading, push the probe deep into the roast and then slowly draw it out until you locate the center of the meat (indicated by the lowest temperature). Avoid bones and pan surfaces. And take more than one reading.

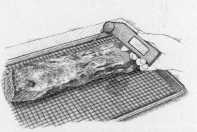

The ideal serving temperatures for optimal flavor and juiciness are listed below. If food safety is your primary concern, cook all meat until well-done. Note: The meat should come off the heat 5 to 10 degrees below the desired final temperature, as the internal temperature will continue to rise as the meat rests.

TYPE OF MEAT	RARE	MEDIUM-RARE	MEDIUM	WELL-DONE
beef and lamb	125	130	140	160
pork	*	*	150	160

* not recommended

FISH 101

Many people find fish intimidating—both to buy and to cook. But the truth is, once you're armed with basic guidelines, fish is no more complicated to buy and cook than vegetables. The keys are learning to recognize good quality, keeping the preparation simple, and avoiding overcooking.

BUYING AND STORING BASICS

AT THE STORE

- Whether it's a specialty seafood shop or a neighborhood supermarket, make sure the source is one with a high volume. High volume means high turnover, which ensures freshness. The store should smell like the sea, not fishy or sour.

- The fish should be stored on ice or well refrigerated. If stored on ice, the fish shouldn't be sitting in water.

- The flesh of fish should appear moist and shiny, not dull, and with even coloring. It should feel firm, not mushy. If possible, ask the fishmonger to press the flesh with his finger to confirm its texture.

- Try to have the fishmonger slice steaks or fillets to order; it's best to avoid precut fish.

AT HOME

Fish stored at 32 degrees will keep twice as long as fish stored at the typical home refrigerator temperature of 40 degrees. To create the optimum storage conditions, place the fish in a zipper-lock bag on ice (or cover with ice packs) and store it at the back of the refrigerator, where it's coldest. And remember to chill the fish immediately upon getting it home.

PRECOOKING PREP

THAWING FROZEN FISH

Frozen fish should be fully thawed before cooking, ideally defrosted overnight in the refrigerator. Remove the fish from its packaging, lay it in a single layer on a rimmed plate (to catch any released water), and cover it with plastic wrap. Thoroughly dry fish before cooking. Alternatively, defrost fish under cold running water in its original packaging.

REMOVING PIN BONES

Pin bones are small white bones that run through the center of a fillet. Most fish is sold with the pin bones removed, but it pays to check before cooking (especially with salmon or trout). To locate pin bones, run your fingers gently over the fillet's surface, feeling for hard, tiny bumps. Use tweezers or needle-nose pliers to grasp and remove the bones.

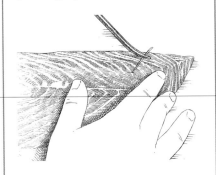

ENSURING EVEN COOKING

Fish fillets often come in odd-sized pieces of uneven thickness. If your fillet has a thin, wide tailpiece, tuck it under before cooking to allow it to cook at the same rate as the thicker portion.

1. With a sharp knife, cut halfway through the flesh crosswise, 2 to 3 inches from the tail end.

2. Fold the tail end under the cut seam to create a fillet of relatively even thickness.

JUDGING DONENESS

An instant-read thermometer is a useful tool to check doneness in thick fillets, but with thin fillets you have to resort to a more primitive test—nicking the fish with a paring knife and then peeking into the interior to judge the color and flakiness. Whitefish, such as cod, should be cooked to medium (about 140 degrees)—that is, the flesh should be opaque but still moist and just beginning to flake; salmon is best cooked to medium-rare (about 125 degrees), with the center still translucent; and tuna is best when rare (about 110 degrees), with only the outer layer opaque and the rest of the fish translucent.

FIVE FAVORITE METHODS FOR COOKING FISH

PAN-SEARING

This method uses less fat than sautéing and calls for starting the fish in an even hotter pan. The result: a flavorful, deeply golden crust, even without the aid of flour.

Heat 1 tablespoon vegetable oil in a nonstick skillet over high heat until just smoking. Add the fish and cook for 30 seconds. Reduce the heat to medium-high and cook the fish until it's well browned, 3 to 5 minutes. Using tongs, flip the fish. Remove the fish when it is still slightly translucent; the residual heat will continue to cook the flesh.

GRILLING

Grilling is a great way to accentuate flavor. Superheating the grill is the secret to preventing fish from sticking.

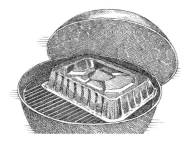

1. Place a disposable aluminum pan upside down over the grill. Cover for five minutes to superheat the grill and help prevent sticking. Scrape the grate clean with the grill brush, then wipe it with oil-dipped paper towels.

2. Place the fish on the grill perpendicular to the grates. Grill the fish on the first side until browned, 2 to 3 minutes (if the fish has skin, place it skin-side up). Slide one spatula underneath the fillet to lift; use another spatula to support the fish. Continue to cook to the desired doneness.

SAUTÉING

Dredging fish in flour and then sautéing it in a combination of butter and oil creates a crispy, delicate crust you can't get with other techniques. This method is best for thin fillets such as sole or flounder.

1. Pat the fish dry and season with salt. Let the fish stand until it glistens with moisture, about 5 minutes. Place ½ cup flour in a pie plate and dredge the fish in the flour. Shake off any excess.

2. Heat 1 tablespoon vegetable oil in a skillet over high heat; add 1 tablespoon butter and heat until the foaming subsides. Reduce the heat to medium-high and add the fish to the pan. When the bottoms are golden brown, use two spatulas to gently flip the fish. Continue to cook to the desired doneness.

BRAISING

Braising can either add flavor to mild-flavored fish or mellow assertively flavored fish. The keys are to use low heat and a skillet with a tight-fitting lid.

In a skillet over medium heat, sauté 1 sliced onion and 4 minced garlic cloves in 2 tablespoons olive oil until softened. Stir in ½ cup white wine and a 14-ounce can diced tomatoes and bring the mixture to a simmer. Season the fish with salt and pepper. Nestle the fish into the sauce and spoon a little sauce over it. Cover the skillet, reduce the heat to medium-low, and cook the fish to the desired doneness.

POACHING

Poaching keeps fish moist. The flavorful liquid in which the fish is cooked can be strained, reduced, and served as a sauce.

Bring 6 cups water, 1 cup white wine, juice of 1 lemon, 1 teaspoon salt, ½ chopped onion, and 1 chopped carrot to a simmer in a large Dutch oven. A few whole peppercorns, bay leaf, and several sprigs of fresh parsley or thyme can be added. Simmer until the flavors have blended, about 20 minutes. Reduce the heat to the lowest setting and place the fish into the liquid. Cover the pot and poach to the desired doneness, 6 to 10 minutes. Remove the fish using a slotted spoon or spatula.

COOKING VEGETABLES 101

BROCCOLI

SHOPPING NOTES: The stalks are just as tasty as the florets, so make sure they aren't dry or cracked.

PREPARATION: Cut the florets into 1½-inch pieces; peel the stalks and cut on the bias into ¼-inch-thick pieces.

BASIC COOKING METHOD: Pan-roasting brings out broccoli's sweet rather than sulfurous flavors. Sauté peeled stalks from 1¾ pounds broccoli in a 12-inch nonstick skillet filmed with 2 tablespoons vegetable oil for 2 minutes. To promote browning, cook over medium-high heat and do not stir. Add the florets and cook until they start to brown (1 to 2 minutes), then add 3 tablespoons water, cover, and cook for 2 minutes. Remove the lid and cook until the water evaporates and the broccoli is tender, another 2 minutes.

PREPARING BROCCOLI

1. Hold a bunch of broccoli upside down on a work surface. Using a chef's knife, trim off the florets very close to their heads. Cut florets into 1½-inch pieces.

2. Place each stalk on a cutting board and square it off with a chef's knife. Remove the outer ⅛ inch of stalk, which is quite tough.

3. Cut the peeled stalk on the bias into ¼-inch-thick slices about 1½ inches long.

COMMON COOKING METHODS

Here is what you need to know about the most common vegetable cooking techniques.

BOILING allows you to season vegetables as they cook (use 1 tablespoon table salt per 4 quarts water). Boiled vegetables need further embellishment, such as a compound butter or vinaigrette. **Try with nonporous green vegetables, such as green beans and snap peas.**

STEAMING washes away less flavor than boiling and leaves vegetables crisper. Doesn't allow for seasoning vegetables and only works with small batches (1 pound or less). **Try with porous or delicate vegetables such as asparagus, broccoli, and cauliflower.**

SAUTÉING allows for the addition of everything from garlic to herbs but requires constant attention and a non-stick pan. **Try with peas and zucchini.**

PAN-ROASTING caramelizes natural sugars in vegetables and promotes browning. Doesn't work if the pan is overloaded, and most recipes rely on a tight-fitting lid to capture steam and help cook the vegetables through. **Try with asparagus and broccoli.**

ROASTING concentrates flavors by driving off excess moisture and makes vegetables crisp. Requires at least 30 minutes (including time to heat the oven). **Try with asparagus, carrots, cauliflower, green beans, and zucchini.**

BROILING browns vegetables quickly and deeply. Broilers require constant attention; keep food at least 4 inches from the heating element to prevent flare-ups. **Try with asparagus and zucchini.**

ZUCCHINI

SHOPPING NOTES: Zucchini weighing less than 8 ounces are more flavorful and less watery than larger ones.

PREPARATION: Shred, discarding the seeds and core, then salt and squeeze dry.

BASIC COOKING METHOD: Shredding, salting (use 1½ teaspoons salt with 2½ pounds zucchini), and squeezing removes moisture from this watery vegetable, as does a dry-heat cooking method, like sautéing. Toss the dried zucchini with 2 teaspoons olive oil and then cook in a 12-inch nonstick skillet filmed with 2 teaspoons additional oil over high heat for 4 minutes. Stir infrequently as the zucchini cooks to promote browning.

SHREDDING AND SALTING ZUCCHINI

1. Cut the zucchini into 3-inch pieces. Shred on the large holes of a box grater, rotating the zucchini as needed to avoid shredding the seeds and core.

2. Toss the zucchini with salt in a colander and drain for 10 minutes. Wrap the zucchini in a kitchen towel, in batches, and wring out excess moisture.

PEAS

SHOPPING NOTES: Frozen peas are almost always better than fresh shell peas, which tend to be starchy.

PREPARATION: Frozen peas can be used without thawing.

BASIC COOKING METHOD: Add frozen peas directly to the pan with sautéed aromatics (garlic and/or shallots cooked in a few tablespoons of butter until fragrant) and cover the pan to trap steam and heat the peas through (this will take about 4 minutes). Add 2 teaspoons sugar to 1 pound frozen peas to boost flavor.

GREEN BEANS

SHOPPING NOTES: Slender, crisp green beans are best boiled. Older, tougher green beans are best roasted.

PREPARATION: Trim ends.

BASIC COOKING METHOD: Roasting promotes the conversion of starches to sugars, thus improving flavor. Toss 1 pound trimmed beans with 1 tablespoon olive oil and roast on a foil-lined baking sheet in a 450-degree oven for 20 minutes. Turn the beans once for even browning.

TRIMMING THE ENDS FROM GREEN BEANS

Line up the beans on a board and trim all the ends with just one slice.

CAULIFLOWER

SHOPPING NOTES: Buy heads of cauliflower with tight, firm florets without any discoloration.

PREPARATION: Trim the leaves and stem, then cut into large wedges.

BASIC COOKING METHOD: Roasting avoids the sulfurous cauliflower smell. Toss the wedges from 1 head cauliflower with 4 tablespoons olive oil and roast on a foil-lined baking sheet in a 475-degree oven for 25 to 35 minutes. Cover the pan with foil for the first 10 minutes of the cooking time to ensure that the cauliflower cooks through. Also, place the baking sheet on the bottom oven rack to maximize browning. Flip the wedges once the bottom has browned nicely (after about 20 minutes).

CUTTING UP CAULIFLOWER

1. Pull off the outer leaves and cut the stem flush to the base of the cauliflower.

2. Cut the head into 8 equal wedges so that the core and florets remain intact.

CARROTS

SHOPPING NOTES: Avoid extra-large carrots, which are often woody and bitter. Baby carrots are fine for roasting but too thick for glazing.

PREPARATION: Peel regular carrots and slice on the bias.

BASIC COOKING METHODS: Roasting intensifies sweetness without requiring other ingredients. Toss 1 pound baby carrots with 1 tablespoon olive oil in a broiler-pan bottom and roast in a 475-degree oven for 20 minutes, shaking the pan several times to promote even browning. Glazing makes carrots even sweeter. Cook 1 pound sliced carrots with 1 tablespoon sugar and ½ cup chicken broth in a covered 12-inch nonstick skillet for 5 minutes. Uncover and cook until the liquid reduces to 2 tablespoons, 1 to 2 minutes. Add 1 tablespoon butter and an additional 2 tablespoons sugar and cook, stirring frequently, until the carrots are tender and evenly glazed, about 3 minutes.

SLICING CARROTS ON THE BIAS

Cut carrots on the bias into pieces ¼ inch thick and 2 inches long.

THREE COMMON COOKING MISTAKES (AND HOW TO AVOID THEM)

OVERCOOKING

Vegetables will continue to soften as they make their way to the table. To keep vegetables crisp and tender, remove them from the heat when slightly underdone.

UNEVEN COOKING

Make sure vegetables are cut uniformly. This is particularly important when steaming and sautéing.

SLOW COOKING

Overloaded pans will cook very slowly. When roasting and sautéing, give vegetables room to brown. Piled on top of each other, they will steam and won't taste as good.

ASPARAGUS

SHOPPING NOTES: Pencil-thin asparagus are easily overcooked and thick spears are woody; choose asparagus ½ to ⅝ inch thick.

PREPARATION: Trim the tough ends.

BASIC COOKING METHODS: Broiling and pan-roasting concentrate flavors in delicate asparagus. Toss 2 pounds trimmed asparagus with 1 tablespoon olive oil on a baking sheet and broil, shaking the pan once, for 8 to 10 minutes. Or heat 1 tablespoon each vegetable oil and butter in a 12-inch nonstick skillet. Add 2 pounds trimmed asparagus, with half of the tips pointing in one direction and other half pointing in the opposite direction. Cover and cook over medium-high heat for 5 minutes. Uncover and cook over high heat until tender and browned, 5 to 7 minutes.

TRIMMING ASPARAGUS

With one hand, hold the asparagus about halfway down the stalk; with the thumb and index finger of your other hand, hold the spear about an inch from the bottom. Bend the stalk until it snaps.

FREEZING SUMMER PRODUCE 101

We froze freshly picked summer fruits and vegetables last summer, then thawed them in the middle of winter to find out which methods of freezing work best. If you follow our suggestions, you should be able to freeze produce for about six months.

SCIENCE OF FREEZING

When fruits and vegetables freeze, the water that is contained in each cell turns into ice crystals. The size of these ice crystals depends on how rapidly the produce is frozen: Quick freezing yields smaller crystals; slow freezing creates larger crystals. As these ice crystals form, they rupture cell walls and internal cell organelles, which release enzymes from their locked compartments. When produce thaws, these enzymes cause produce to develop off-flavors and turn brown and soggy.

In vegetables, these enzymes can be deactivated by blanching. Because fruits are too delicate to blanch, sugar or sugar syrup is used to reduce the formation of ice crystals during freezing. In high concentrations, sugar acts as a barrier between fruit and oxygen. We also found it necessary to add ascorbic acid to peaches and nectarines when freezing, which deactivates the molecules that cause browning.

HOW TO FREEZE FRUIT

We learned it's best to freeze fruit with sugar syrup or sugar to reduce the formation of damaging ice crystals.

FRUIT PREP

Fruits are best frozen in individual bags containing no more than 2 cups of fruit. The chart below gives the amount of syrup or sugar that should be added to every 2 cups of fruit. To avoid lowering your freezer's temperature by overcrowding, freeze no more than 8 cups of fruit at a time. Wash and dry fruits before freezing.

SYRUP PACK: For every 2 cups of fruit, cover with the listed amount of syrup. To make 6 cups of syrup, heat 3 cups of sugar and 4 cups of water in a medium saucepan over medium-high heat, stirring occasionally, until the sugar has dissolved, about 5 minutes. Cool to room temperature.

SUGAR PACK: Toss 2 cups of fruit with the listed amount of sugar before bagging and freezing. For peaches and nectarines, add 1½ teaspoons of Fruit Fresh (or similar ascorbic acid–based product) to the sugar.

MASTER STEPS FOR FREEZING FRUIT

1. FILL THE BAG: Fit a labeled and dated quart-sized zipper-lock freezer bag into a 2-cup liquid measuring cup. Spoon 2 cups prepared fruit into the bag.

2. ADD THE SYRUP: If using sugar syrup, pour the syrup over the fruit to cover. If using sugar, toss the sugar with the fruit to coat.

3. SEAL: Remove as much air as possible from the bag before sealing. Place the bag into a second zipper-lock bag.

4. FREEZE: Lay bags flat in a single layer on a baking sheet. Freeze until solid, at least 24 hours, then store anywhere in the freezer.

FRUIT PREP

FRUIT	AMOUNT	PREPARATION	FREEZING METHOD	AMOUNT OF SUGAR OR SYRUP
strawberries	2 cups	hulled and halved	syrup	1¼ cups
raspberries	2 cups	picked over	syrup	1¼ cups
blueberries	2 cups	picked over	sugar	⅓ cup
peaches or nectarines	2 cups	pitted and cut into ½-inch-thick slices	sugar	½ cup

THAWING FRUIT

After much testing, we found slow thaws preserved more of the fruit's original flavor and texture. Once the fruit is thawed, transfer it to a colander and gently rinse it to remove excess syrup and sugar. Because the fruit's resiliency will have decreased, we prefer to use frozen fruit in applications where the fruit will be cooked.

HOW TO FREEZE VEGETABLES

When freezing vegetables, blanching and shocking is critical (see "Science of Freezing," on page 316). Work quickly and keep vegetables as cold as possible after they have been blanched and shocked. Freezing warm vegetables takes longer and creates large, damaging ice crystals.

VEGETABLE PREP

Blanch all vegetables in 6 quarts of water seasoned with 1 tablespoon of salt. Transfer to a bowl filled with ice water and cool for 1 minute. While we had success freezing corn, green beans, snow peas, snap peas, shell peas, and greens, we found tomatoes, cucumbers, zucchini, and eggplant didn't freeze well, due to their high water content and delicate cell structure. If you have an abundance of these vegetables, we suggest cooking them first, such as in a sauce, then freezing them.

MASTER STEPS FOR FREEZING VEGETABLES

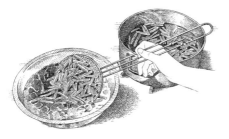  

1. BLANCH AND SHOCK: Cook the prepared vegetables until their color has brightened but the vegetables are still very crisp (see the times in the chart at bottom). Transfer to a bowl filled with ice water and cool for 1 minute. If needed, add more ice to the water to keep it cold.

2. DRY WELL AND FREEZE: Transfer to a rimmed baking sheet covered with 3 layers of paper towels. Cover with another 2 layers and gently dry. Place in a single layer on a baking sheet lined with parchment paper and freeze until solid, 1 to 2 hours.

3. PACKAGE AND STORE: Once frozen, transfer 2 cups into a labeled, dated zipper-lock freezer bag, squeezing out as much air as possible. Place the bag into another zipper-lock freezer bag and store in the coldest part of the freezer.

VEGETABLE PREP

VEGETABLE	AMOUNT	PREPARATION	BLANCHING TIME
asparagus	1 pound	tough ends snapped off and discarded	2 minutes
corn (whole)	6 ears	husks and silks removed	3 ears at a time for 6 minutes
corn (kernels)	6 ears	kernels removed from cob	4 minutes
green beans	1 pound	ends trimmed and cut into 1½-inch pieces	2 minutes
snow peas	1 pound	strings removed	1 minute
snap peas	1 pound	strings removed	2 minutes
shell peas	2 pounds	shelled	2 minutes
tender greens (spinach, chard)	8 cups lightly packed (about 2 large bunches)	stemmed and washed	1 minute
tough greens (kale)	8 cups lightly packed (about 2 large bunches)	stemmed and washed	2 minutes

THAWING VEGETABLES

When cooking with frozen vegetables, we mostly found it better to use the vegetables without thawing. This was the case with moist-heat cooking methods, such as steaming and boiling, or when the vegetables were added to soups, stews, and sauces. However, we did find cooking times for frozen vegetables were half as long as for their fresh counterparts. With dry-heat cooking methods such as sautéing, we found it best if the vegetables were partially thawed; again, they were done in about half the time. To partially thaw vegetables, allow them to slowly thaw in the refrigerator for about 4 hours. In a pinch, thaw the bag of frozen vegetables in cold water for 15 to 20 minutes.

STOCKING A BAKING PANTRY 101

SUGARS AND OTHER SWEETENERS

GRANULATED SUGAR

White, or granulated, sugar is commonly derived from either sugarcane or sugar beets, though flavor differences are imperceptible.

CONFECTIONERS' SUGAR

To prevent clumping, this pulverized sugar contains a small amount of cornstarch.
TO REPLACE: **1 cup confectioners' sugar**
• 1 cup granulated sugar + 1 teaspoon cornstarch ground in a blender

BROWN SUGAR

When we want cookies with a serious chew, we use brown sugar, which is white sugar combined with molasses. Dark brown sugar contains 6.5 percent molasses as compared with light brown's 3.5 percent.
SPECIAL STORAGE NOTE: Airtight containers keep moisture at bay, but brown sugar can still dry out. To revive hardened brown sugar, place it in a bowl with a slice of bread. Cover the bowl with plastic wrap and microwave it on high power for 10 to 20 seconds.
TO REPLACE: **1 cup light brown sugar**
• 1 cup granulated sugar + 1 tablespoon molasses (use 2 tablespoons for dark brown sugar)

MOLASSES

For most baking, we prefer light (or mild) molasses to dark (or robust). But if you want a fuller flavor, opt for the latter. Stay away from blackstrap; it can be bitter.
SPECIAL STORAGE NOTE: To prevent sticky lids on molasses or honey jars, dip a small piece of paper towel into vegetable oil and wipe the threads of the jar. The bare film of oil prevents the lid from sticking.

HONEY

In baking, we prefer a mild-flavored honey, such as orange blossom or clover.
SPECIAL STORAGE NOTE: All honey will harden and crystallize over time, but that doesn't mean you have to throw it away. Place the open container of honey in a saucepan filled with 1 inch of water and stir over low heat until liquefied.

MAPLE SYRUP

For most baking, we prefer to use darker, grade B maple syrup because of its assertive flavor. Grade A dark amber is a close second.
SPECIAL STORAGE NOTE: Maple syrup is susceptible to the growth of yeasts, molds, and bacteria. Once opened, store it in the refrigerator, where it will keep for six months to a year.

FATS AND OILS

OIL

We rarely use oil in baking, but when we do, we call for neutral-tasting canola or vegetable oil.

SHORTENING

We frequently use shortening in pie crust for extra flakiness. Because shortening doesn't contain water, it can add a desirable crispness to some cookies. Avoid butter-flavored shortening, which will give baked goods an unpleasant chemical flavor.

BAKING SPRAY

Baking spray—nonstick cooking spray with flour—creates an impenetrable nonstick surface without the mess of buttering and flouring pans. And baking sprays don't pool in pan corners like regular sprays.

FLOURS

Most baking recipes call for all-purpose flour. But some recipes call for cake flour or bread flour. Why? In most cases, it's due to differences in protein level. More protein leads to more gluten, which translates to coarseness, chewiness, toughness, or crispness.

ALL-PURPOSE FLOUR

We prefer unbleached to bleached flour, as we find bleaching imparts a slight chemical flavor that is detectable in very simple recipes such as biscuits.

CAKE FLOUR

This low-protein flour is sold in boxes and yields cakes with an especially fine, delicate crumb. It's our first choice for angel food, pound, and yellow layer cakes.

TO REPLACE: 1 cup cake flour
- ⅞ cup all-purpose flour + 2 tablespoons cornstarch

BREAD FLOUR

This high-protein flour (sometimes labeled "made for bread machines") is a must for rustic breads with a chewy crumb and crisp crust.

OTHER INGREDIENTS

BAKING POWDER AND SODA

Although both are chemical leaveners, they react under different conditions and are not interchangeable.

SPECIAL STORAGE NOTE: Keep baking powder and baking soda sealed in a cool, dry place. Baking powder will lose its effectiveness within a year.

TO REPLACE: **1 teaspoon baking powder**
- ¼ teaspoon baking soda + ½ teaspoon cream of tartar

YEAST

We use instant yeast (or rapid-rise yeast) exclusively in the test kitchen. It doesn't need to be proofed and can be added directly to dry ingredients.

SPECIAL STORAGE NOTE: Store yeast in the refrigerator or the freezer. Because yeast is a living organism, the expiration date on the package should be observed.

CHOCOLATE

Unadulterated chocolate is sold as unsweetened or baking chocolate and packs the boldest chocolate punch. Most bittersweet and semisweet chocolates contain 50 percent to 70 percent chocolate; the rest is mostly sugar. We rely on both chocolates in many recipes. We generally use milk chocolate for snacking.

SPECIAL STORAGE NOTE: Wrap chocolate tightly in plastic and store it in a cool, dry place. Milk and white chocolates will keep for at least six months; dark chocolates will be fine for a few years.

SALT

We use table salt in baking recipes. Its fine grains dissolve and distribute more readily than kosher or sea salt.

VANILLA

We have tasted pure and imitation extracts side by side and have been shocked to find that we couldn't tell the difference between the two. (Custards are an exception; imitation extract will taste a bit off.) That said, imitation extract isn't all that cheap, and we prefer to buy the real thing; imitation vanilla is derived from wood pulp.

THINKING OUTSIDE THE PANTRY

While not necessarily pantry staples, there are a handful of ingredients in the test kitchen refrigerator—like butter, eggs, and milk—that are crucial for baking. When baking, we use unsalted butter exclusively in the test kitchen. And for consistency, all of our recipes call for large eggs. Unless specified, we always bake with whole milk, although we find that buttermilk often gives a lighter, fluffier texture to cakes and biscuits. If you don't use a lot of buttermilk, there are some options: You can use powdered buttermilk (which can be stored in the pantry and reconstituted with water) or make clabbered or soured milk. To make clabbered milk, add 1 tablespoon of lemon juice, white vinegar, or cream of tartar per 1 cup of milk and let stand for 10 minutes.

SUPERMARKET TEA

While you can find black, green, and even white tea on the shelves these days, we focused our tasting on 10 black teas because 87 percent of all tea drunk in America is black. We tasted the teas plain and with milk added. Brands that showed well when tasted plain were generally quite dull when tasted with milk; likewise, brands that showed well when milk was added were generally too strong. Teas are listed in order of preference.

RECOMMENDED PLAIN

TWININGS ENGLISH BREAKFAST TEA
STYLE: Loose tea
ORIGIN: India, Kenya
PRICE: $9.95 for 7.05-ounce tin ($1.41 per ounce)
COMMENTS: "Fruity and smooth," "floral, fragrant, nice and balanced," agreed tasters, who liked that this tea was "not too strong" but packed "a lot of flavor." "A good, bold cup of tea. Cheerio and all that."

PG TIPS
STYLE: Pyramid paper tea bags
ORIGIN: India, Kenya, Sri Lanka
PRICE: $12.50 for 240 bags ($.47 per ounce)
COMMENTS: "Not too astringent—clean-tasting and very nice," most tasters agreed, with a "lovely woodsy smell" and "a nice balance that matches the aroma," with hints of "citrus" and "tropical fruit."

BIGELOW NOVUS KENILWORTH CEYLON
STYLE: Pyramid nylon mesh tea bags
ORIGIN: Sri Lanka
PRICE: $6.30 for 15 bags ($3.99 per ounce)
COMMENTS: Tasters appreciated an "earthy" quality in this tea, with a "lightly floral aroma and a super-smooth, almost honeyed flavor" and "moderate body."

LIPTON BLACK PEARL
STYLE: Pyramid nylon mesh tea bags
ORIGIN: Sri Lanka
PRICE: $3.39 for 20 bags ($2.42 per ounce)
COMMENTS: "Good and smooth," this tea was "fruity, pleasant, and mild," with a "clean taste" that "builds in the mouth," with a "surprisingly good aftertaste" and "slight astringency." Some, however, found it "nothing special."

STASH ENGLISH BREAKFAST TEA
STYLE: Loose tea
ORIGIN: Sri Lanka, India, and China
PRICE: $5.95 for 3.5 ounces ($1.70 per ounce)
COMMENTS: "A strong smoky flavor and low astringency. I love it," said one taster, and others agreed—"quite smooth," "woodsy, floral, and sweet-smelling." However, a few found it "hoppy" and "musty like a barn."

RECOMMENDED WITH MILK

TAZO AWAKE
STYLE: Loose tea
ORIGIN: Sri Lanka, India
PRICE: $21.58 for 17.6 ounces ($1.23 per ounce)
COMMENTS: "Wow! Extremely smoky, with a strong, clean taste. Very good." "Fruity, delicious, and smooth, with a most pleasant aroma; perfumed but not overly precious." Tasters liked its spicy notes of clove, cinnamon, and vanilla. "Great balance of flavor and intensity."

TETLEY SPECIALTY TEA ENGLISH BREAKFAST
STYLE: Disk-shaped paper tea bags
ORIGIN: India, Sri Lanka, Kenya
PRICE: $3.19 for 20 bags ($2.28 per ounce)
COMMENTS: "Balanced; stands up to milk," with a "big flavor" that is "full-bodied" and "good and complex," with a "rich, steeped aroma."

RED ROSE
STYLE: Loose tea
ORIGIN: Sri Lanka, India, Kenya, Indonesia
PRICE: $3 for 8 ounces ($.38 per ounce)
COMMENTS: "Tea flavor comes through the milk," with an "almost savory," "strong," "complex and assertive" taste that has notes of "pumpkin" and "clove."

LIPTON TEA
STYLE: Folded dual paper tea bags
ORIGIN: A changing blend from many countries around the world, such as Sri Lanka, India, Kenya, Indonesia, China, Brazil, Argentina, Ecuador, Malawi, Vietnam, and New Guinea
PRICE: $4.99 for 100 bags ($.62 per ounce)
COMMENTS: Smelling "sweet," like "honey," and "yeasty, like dough," it came across as "plain-tasting," "not jarring," "strong but flavorful—very drinkable."

NOT RECOMMENDED

CELESTIAL SEASONINGS DEVONSHIRE ENGLISH BREAKFAST
STYLE: Square paper tea bags
ORIGIN: India, Kenya
PRICE: $2.99 for 20 bags ($2.14 per ounce)
COMMENTS: "Light aroma, light flavor, light everything" was the consensus here, with a few tasters liking its "roundness," but others calling it "one-note" or "dull and boring," adding that "nothing stands out." This tea ranked last in both tastings.

ORANGE JUICE

A growing number of fresh-squeezed orange juices have been popping up in the produce department. The industry term for these brands is "super-premium juice," and they're often packaged in fancier bottles that cultivate this image. We wanted to know whether these high-end juices tasted better and fresher than their not-from-concentrate cousins, so we tested five upscale juices with ordinary Tropicana Pure Premium, the winner of our previous, middle-market tasting. We sent samples of the juice to an independent laboratory to test brix (sugar content) and percentage of acidity. We also tasted and retasted the juices. Our favorite juices were made with a combination of Florida's Valencia, Pineapple, and Hamlin oranges (Florida oranges tend to be sweeter than California oranges due to a warmer, more humid climate). Other brands bragged that they used all or predominately Valencia oranges, considered the best oranges for juice, but our tasters weren't impressed. In the end, our tasters preferred the sweeter juices made with Florida oranges. Juices are listed in order of preference.

HIGHLY RECOMMENDED

NATALIE'S ORCHID ISLAND JUICE COMPANY GOURMET PASTEURIZED ORANGE JUICE
ACIDITY: 0.86 percent
BRIX: 14 percent
ORIGIN: Florida
TYPES OF ORANGES: Includes Valencia, Hamlin, and Pineapple
PRICE: $4.99 for 64-ounce jug (8 cents per ounce)
COMMENTS: The only juice to give fresh-squeezed a run for its money, Natalie's was deemed "very sweet and fruity" with "nice bits of pulp" and a "strong floral smell." Tasters praised its "well-balanced and fresh-tasting" flavors with notes of "tropical fruit."

RECOMMENDED

TROPICANA PURE PREMIUM 100% PURE AND NATURAL ORANGE JUICE WITH SOME PULP
ACIDITY: 0.81 percent
BRIX: 13.6 percent
ORIGIN: Florida
TYPES OF ORANGES: Includes Valencia, Hamlin, and Pineapple
PRICE: $3.99 for 64-ounce carton (6 cents per ounce)
COMMENTS: While its scores were a notch down from Natalie's, this dairy-case staple and winner of our previous orange juice tasting came in above the rest of the fresh-squeezed–style pack. Tasters admired its "bright, clean" taste with a "nice amount of pulp and good balance of sweet to acidic flavor." "Good overall flavor."

TROPICANA PURE VALENCIA ORANGE JUICE
ACIDITY: 0.82 percent
BRIX: 13.2 percent
ORIGIN: Florida
TYPES OF ORANGES: Valencia, with a blend of other varietals (at the time of our tasting)
PRICE: $3.50 for 33.8-ounce bottle (10 cents per ounce)
COMMENTS: "Tastes more like tangerine than orange," "perfumy and flowery," with a "low acidity." Some liked its "nice, sweet flavor," others called it "sugary" and "supersweet" like "orange candy or Tang."

RECOMMENDED WITH RESERVATIONS

BOLTHOUSE FARMS 100% VALENCIA ORANGE JUICE
ACIDITY: 1.01 percent
BRIX: 14.2 percent
ORIGIN: California
TYPE OF ORANGES: Valencia
PRICE: $3.99 for 33.8-ounce bottle (12 cents per ounce)
COMMENTS: This high-acid, high-sugar juice "tastes like the oranges were slightly unripe" and has an "unpleasant, acidic taste—makes my mouth pucker." Tasters were split on the texture: "If you don't want pulp, this is good: has body and density," though some deemed it "a bit thick," asking, "Is this from concentrate?" A few really disliked it: "I wouldn't waste vodka on this." "Overall, not fresh."

NOT RECOMMENDED

NAKED ALL NATURAL JUST JUICE 100% ORANGE JUICE
ACIDITY: 0.87 percent
BRIX: 12.8 percent
ORIGIN: California (supplemented with Florida oranges if crops are diminished by natural disasters such as frost or wildfire)
TYPE OF ORANGES: Valencia
PRICE: $9.99 for 64-ounce jug (16 cents per ounce)
COMMENTS: This juice was "not fresh-tasting." Some said it was "floral, without much orange flavor." Others called it "thin" and "smooth, with no pulp." A few tasters found it "bleh." "Very plain. Nothing stood out." "It puckers up your mouth." Some disliked its "cooked-cardboard taste."

ODWALLA ORANGE JUICE
ACIDITY: 0.89 percent
BRIX: 12.4 percent
ORIGIN: California (supplemented with oranges from around the world)
TYPES OF ORANGES: Mostly Navel and Valencia, but all Valencia in summer and fall (label changes accordingly)
PRICE: $7.59 for 64-ounce jug (12 cents per ounce)
COMMENTS: "Tastes like orange rind," "thin," "piney and pithy," and "not overpowering in sweetness." One taster said it "tastes strangely of cardamom." Most disliked its "acidic" character, but a few found it "refreshing."

TURKEY

Does roasting the best holiday bird start before you ever step foot in the kitchen? With the cost of turkeys ranging from $1.29 per pound for common supermarket turkeys to $7.14 per pound for a gourmet heritage turkey, we suspected the cost, quality, and flavor of Thanksgiving dinner were all related. So we tested eight turkeys, including supermarket, kosher, organic, pasture-raised, and heritage birds. Modern commercial turkeys have been bred to grow bigger faster and to have more white meat, which means less fat when they are fully grown—not so good for the home cook. Turkey growers have resorted to alternative means to return flavor—and fat—to the turkey, including injecting "basting" solutions during processing or through koshering the turkey. Our top two winners split the difference in terms of cost and processing—Rubashkin's Aaron's Best is an affordable frozen kosher bird, while Walters Hatchery Heritage Breed was a pricey, yet flavorful, turkey. Turkey brands are listed in order of preference.

HIGHLY RECOMMENDED

RUBASHKIN'S AARON'S BEST
Frozen kosher
PRICE: $1.99 per pound
COMMENTS: Lab tests revealed that this bird had the most salt and one of the highest levels of fat among the birds in our lineup; tasters noticed, finding this kosher turkey "very moist, with excellent texture" and boasting "both white and dark meat that are moist and flavorful."

WALTERS HATCHERY HERITAGE BREED
Frozen
PRICE: $7.14 per pound (plus shipping)
COMMENTS: Virtually tied for first place, this heritage bird had nearly three times as much fat as the leanest turkeys. It offered "robust turkey flavor" and was "very tender." "What I expect a turkey to be: mild, sweet, flavorful." Both the light and dark meat were juicy.

RECOMMENDED

BUTTERBALL
Frozen basted
PRICE: $1.49 per pound
COMMENTS: Tasters generally liked this self-basting turkey, calling it "nice and moist, with fairly good, unremarkable flavor," though some found it "too salty," "almost wet rather than moist," and "rather bland." Lab tests showed it had the second-highest salt level in the lineup.

JENNIE-O
Fresh basted
PRICE: $1.49 per pound
COMMENTS: Tasters dubbed this self-basting turkey "middle-of-the-road," with "mild flavor, but it's good." A few described it as tasting "more like chicken," calling the white meat "a bit dry and chewy." Its salt level was quite low, closer to the natural birds than to the self-basting Butterball.

RECOMMENDED WITH RESERVATIONS

EMPIRE KOSHER
Fresh kosher
PRICE: $2.69 per pound
COMMENTS: "A good consistency, with good moisture and texture, but lacking flavor" was the consensus on this kosher turkey. "White meat tastes like nothing: What am I eating?" A few noted a "metallic," "almost bitter" aftertaste. Lab tests revealed that this kosher bird had just over half the salt of the top-rated Aaron's bird.

SHADY BROOK FARMS
Fresh
PRICE: $1.29 per pound
COMMENTS: "Bland-o-rama" white meat, with a "chewy" texture that was "too dry." "Like my mother used to make, unfortunately." Tasters were divided on the dark meat, with some finding it good and others complaining of a "gamy" taste and "stringy" texture.

GOOD EARTH FARMS ORGANIC PASTURE-RAISED
Shipped frozen from Wisconsin farm
PRICE: $2.49 per pound (plus shipping)
COMMENTS: Tasters found this organic bird "tough," with a "dense, chewy quality." They noted its "clear turkey flavor," which was "very good," but felt it "needs gravy!" "Not a good stand-alone turkey." It had the lowest salt level in the lineup.

DIESTEL FAMILY TURKEY RANCH
Frozen
PRICE: $1.99 per pound
COMMENTS: "Even the dark meat is dry," tasters said of this California-raised bird, noting the dark meat was "rubbery, dark, and funky," with a "fishy flavor." The light meat fared better, with "great turkey flavor," but again, it was "too chewy."

SUPERMARKET PARMESAN CHEESE

Recently, many more brands of shrink-wrapped, wedge-style, American-made Parmesan have been appearing in supermarkets. They're sold at a fraction of the price of the authentic Parmigiano-Reggiano, which can cost up to $33 a pound. To see how they stacked up, we bought eight nationally distributed brands at the supermarket, six domestic Parmesans and two imported Parmigiano-Reggianos. Our tasters easily picked out the imports from the lineup; Boar's Head and Il Villaggio Parmigiano-Reggianos were the clear winners. Why the international divide? The taste differences can partly be attributed to the diet of American cows versus that of Italian cows and the raw milk (not pasteurized milk) Italians use to make Parmesan. Cheeses are listed in order of preference.

RECOMMENDED

BOAR'S HEAD PARMIGIANO-REGGIANO
PRICE: $17.17 per pound
ORIGIN: Imported from Italy, aged 24 months
SALT: 1.65 g.
MOISTURE: 32.46 g.
COMMENTS: Tasters deemed this sample "best in show" and "authentic," praising its "good crunch" and "nice tangy, nutty" flavor. "Rich" and "complex," this cheese had a "very good balance of acid/fruit/nutty/creamy."

IL VILLAGGIO PARMIGIANO-REGGIANO
PRICE: $16.99 per pound
ORIGIN: Imported from Italy, aged 24 months
SALT: 2.21 g.
MOISTURE: 31.11 g.
COMMENTS: "Nutty, granular, tangy, and tasty" was the verdict, with tasters noting its "good, sharp flavor," "craggy" texture, "nice aroma," and "melt-on-your-tongue feel." In polenta, this cheese was "rich and bold."

BELGIOIOSO PARMESAN
PRICE: $8.99 per pound **BEST BUY**
ORIGIN: Domestic, aged at least 10 months
SALT: 3.19 g.
MOISTURE: 34.78 g.
COMMENTS: "Mild but complex," this cheese was a little "soft and creamy for a Parmesan," with a "too moist" texture. Grated, it had a "nice and tangy" aroma and "lovely, delicate flavor." In polenta, it was "nutty, well balanced, very good."

SARVECCHIO PARMESAN (FORMERLY STRAVECCHIO)
PRICE: $11.99 per pound
ORIGIN: Domestic, aged 20 months
SALT: 2.59 g.
MOISTURE: 29.85 g.
COMMENTS: "Good, interesting flavor; almost has a sharp, lemony note," according to one taster. Another praised the "rich nuttiness" in this "crumbly" cheese "with a slight crunch." One taster summed up: "A Parm with guts!"

RECOMMENDED WITH RESERVATIONS

ROSALIA'S TRATTORIA PARMESAN
PRICE: $8.49 per pound
ORIGIN: Domestic, aged at least 10 months
SALT: 2.40 g.
MOISTURE: 39.01 g.
COMMENTS: Tasters disliked its "plastic," "dense and rubbery" texture: "It's like I bit into food from a dollhouse." Grated, it had "nutty flavor and fresh aroma" but was "a bit one-dimensional." In polenta, it was "very cheesy," with "flavorful bite."

NOT RECOMMENDED

KRAFT GRATE-IT FRESH PARMESAN
PRICE: $11.40 per pound (sold in plastic grater, 7 ounces for $4.99)
ORIGIN: Domestic, aged 10 months
SALT: 3.57 g.
MOISTURE: 32.82 g.
COMMENTS: The high salt content showed: "I felt like a deer at a salt lick." Shredded with its own grater, this cheese had a texture "like dental floss," with flavor that was "artificial." One unhappy taster asked, "Was this grated from a Parm-scented candle?"

STELLA PARMESAN
PRICE: $8.98 per pound
ORIGIN: Domestic, aged 10 months
SALT: 2.90 g.
MOISTURE: 33.48 g.
COMMENTS: In chunks, tasters were not impressed: "Soapy, fake, rubbery. Yuck." Grated, this sample fared better, with a "nutty, buttery aroma and flavor," though several deemed it "nothing special." In polenta, it was "very bland."

DIGIORNO PARMESAN
PRICE: $8.49 per pound
ORIGIN: Domestic, aged at least 6 months
SALT: 2.50 g.
MOISTURE: 34.67 g.
COMMENTS: "Rubbery" came up over and over in tasters' comments. "Like eating candle wax, and the flavor's not much better." Grated, it was "blandsville." In polenta, it was "too mild." "Did you forget to put the cheese in here?"

DARK CHOCOLATE

Just a few years ago, selecting dark chocolate for your dessert recipe was an easy task. Now there are dozens of choices. We sampled the following chocolates plain, in chocolate pots de crème, and baked into brownies. In the end, we preferred the one that achieved the best balance of cocoa butter, cocoa solids, and sugar. Chocolates are listed in order of preference.

RECOMMENDED

CALLEBAUT INTENSE DARK CHOCOLATE, L-60-40NV
CACAO: 60 percent
PRICE: 53 cents per ounce
COUNTRY OF ORIGIN: Belgium
COMMENTS: "Complex flavor, creamy and thick," "dark and earthy," with a "rich cocoa flavor" and "a nice balance of sweetness and bitterness." Tasters picked up "caramel, smoke, and espresso" in the plain tasting. It baked into "what a brownie should be."

GHIRARDELLI BITTERSWEET CHOCOLATE BAKING BAR
CACAO: 60 percent
PRICE: 75 cents per ounce
COUNTRY OF ORIGIN: USA
COMMENTS: Tasters discerned "coffee, smoke, and dried fruit" in this "creamy, rich, glossy" chocolate, with a "slight sour after-taste." In brownies, it had "quintessential brownie flavor" that was "assertive," "like dark chocolate but not cocoa-y or bitter like some others; a really good blend of tastes."

DAGOBA ORGANIC SEMISWEET DARK CHOCOLATE
CACAO: 59 percent
PRICE: $1.30 per ounce
COUNTRY OF ORIGIN: USA
COMMENTS: "Fairly sweet" (a few said "cloy-ingly" so), with "great chocolate flavor," it had "hints of fruit" and "apricot and almond." In pots de crème, it was "very buttery and chocolaty, with a silky texture" and a flavor that was "smooth yet strong." In brownies: "a good one all-around," "malty, sweet, rich, slightly floral."

MICHEL CLUIZEL NOIR DE CACAO DARK CHOCOLATE
CACAO: 60 percent
PRICE: $1.43 per ounce
COUNTRY OF ORIGIN: France
COMMENTS: "Creamy, not bitter. Nice for an eating chocolate," "complex and earthy," but tasters were reminded of "olive oil" or "mayonnaise." In brownies, it was "very smooth and well balanced," if a bit "bland"; in pots de crème, it was "supercreamy," "like milk chocolate."

VALRHONA LE NOIR SEMISWEET CHOCOLATE
CACAO: 56 percent
PRICE: $1.37 per ounce
COUNTRY OF ORIGIN: France
COMMENTS: "A nondark-chocolate-lover's dark chocolate," this was "well balanced" and "creamy," with "a sharp chocolate flavor" and "not much aftertaste." In pots de crème, it was "supersmooth and cushiony" and "almost too creamy"; "fudgy" brownies were "very sweet."

RECOMMENDED WITH RESERVATIONS

E. GUITTARD TSARATANA PURE SEMISWEET DARK CHOCOLATE
CACAO: 61 percent
PRICE: $1.45 per ounce
COUNTRY OF ORIGIN: USA
COMMENTS: "Fruity, spicy," "sweet and smoky," this "very creamy" chocolate had slightly "odd" flavors, including banana, tobacco, beef, and leather, along with caramel and honey. While it had some fans, others observed that it made drier, cakier brownies and slightly "chalky" pots de crème.

HERSHEY'S ALL-NATURAL EXTRA DARK PURE DARK CHOCOLATE
CACAO: 60 percent
PRICE: 63 cents per ounce
COUNTRY OF ORIGIN: USA
COMMENTS: A "chalky" texture was decried by many tasters, both when eaten plain and in brownies, though the brownies were praised for "rich, roasted chocolate flavor." In pots de crème, it was "dark and glossy," but "very gloppy" and "too gummy and dense—flavor is good, though."

EL REY MIJAO DARK CHOCOLATE, VENEZUELAN SINGLE BEAN, CARENERO SUPERIOR
CACAO: 61 percent
PRICE: 50 cents per ounce
COUNTRY OF ORIGIN: Venezuela
COMMENTS: "Not very complex" and "mild," with a slightly "sour" aftertaste, it was "sweet and buttery" in pots de crème and "kinda flat" and "dull" in brownies, where it was also deemed "tooth-achingly sweet." "Solid, if unspectacular."

SCHARFFEN BERGER FINE ARTISAN SEMISWEET DARK CHOCOLATE
CACAO: 62 percent
PRICE: $1.03 per ounce
COUNTRY OF ORIGIN: USA
COMMENTS: "Lots of fruit" here: Tasters noted cherry (some said "cough syrup"), grape, raspberry, raisins, and prunes. "Complex, but I didn't care for it," said one. "Gluey" in pots de crème, it had a "roasty" quality in brownies, but "lacked choco-oomph."

BAKER'S SEMI-SWEET BAKING CHOCOLATE SQUARES (USA)
CACAO: 54 percent
PRICE: 44 cents per ounce
COUNTRY OF ORIGIN: USA
COMMENTS: "Very sweet, you can almost taste the sugar granules," with a "bitter coffee flavor." "Very cocoa-y, but otherwise pretty boring." "Tastes like cheap chocolate." It rated poorly when tasted plain and in pots de crème due to its granular texture, but shone in brownies as "very moist, chewy," and "fudgy."

VEGETABLE BROTH

Just 10 years ago, vegetable broth was hard to find in the supermarket. Now you can find it canned, boxed, and in cubes, powders, and pastes. Some use fresh vegetables, while others use dehydrated or powdered vegetable content, or numerous flavor enhancers, like monosodium glutamate (MSG) or disodium inosinate—the broths with these additives did not rate as highly with our tasters. We sampled several brands, first heated and served plain, then cooked into soup and risotto. Our tasters had a distinct preference for the fresher taste of broths, which are quick-cooked liquids, with the longer-cooked stocks falling to the bottom half of the lineup. Broths are listed in order of preference.

RECOMMENDED

SWANSON VEGETARIAN VEGETABLE BROTH
PRICE: $1.50 for 14-ounce can
SODIUM: 940 milligrams
COMMENTS: "Good balance of veggie flavors—carrot and celery are distinguishable, but not overwhelming." "I'd have this as plain soup if I had a cold." The fact that it had the highest sodium level in the lineup didn't escape our tasters ("mega-salty"). With a host of chemical additives, many noted that it tasted like poultry; we had to reassure a vegetarian taster that we hadn't slipped in a chicken broth. Even when we corrected the salt levels of all of the other broths to match, this one still came out on top.

RECOMMENDED WITH RESERVATIONS

COLLEGE INN GARDEN VEGETABLE BROTH
PRICE: $1.09 for 14.5-ounce can
SODIUM: 590 milligrams
COMMENTS: Offering "decent, well-balanced vegetable flavor," this broth had "mostly tomato flavor," yet was still deemed "one of the best." Plain, it had a "slightly sour, tangy" taste, though cooked into risotto, it was "a good background," and in soup, "neutral."

KNORR VEGETARIAN VEGETABLE BOUILLON CUBES
PRICE: $1.49 for 2.1-ounce box (makes 12 cups)
SODIUM: 830 milligrams
COMMENTS: "A bit salty, but good flavor," agreed tasters, noting that this broth made from pressed cubes "seems beefy, not vegetable-y." Again and again, tasters were reminded of the broth that comes with packaged ramen noodles.

IMAGINE ORGANIC VEGETABLE BROTH
PRICE: $3.59 for 32-ounce box
SODIUM: 550 milligrams
COMMENTS: With a "body more like soup than broth" and a flavor described as mostly "carrot—in color and flavor" (others, less flatteringly, called it "gross" and "murky"), this broth was "quite sweet," "thick," and "flat and flavorless" in soup, with only "a slight vegetable taste—but of canned vegetables." In risotto: "SO yellow" and "pretty darned bland. It's like a flavor eraser."

NOT RECOMMENDED

BETTER THAN BOUILLON VEGETABLE BASE
PRICE: $5.99 for 8-ounce jar (makes 38 cups)
SODIUM: 710 milligrams
COMMENTS: Tasters agreed that broth made from this paste-style base was "a salt lick!" "metallic," and "musty," with a "smoke flavor reminiscent of a Slim Jim." The broth's origins were easily detected in every application.

EMERIL'S ALL NATURAL ORGANIC VEGETABLE STOCK
PRICE: $4.29 for 32-ounce box
SODIUM: 570 milligrams
COMMENTS: "Sickeningly sweet, with a sour aftertaste." Like "weak V8" or "dirty carrot peels." It reminded tasters of "frozen onion rings that got freezer burn" and had a "weird, gelatinous texture." In soup, it was so "bland" that one taster asked: "Did you make this with water instead of broth?"

SWANSON CERTIFIED ORGANIC VEGETARIAN VEGETABLE BROTH
PRICE: $4 for 32-ounce box
SODIUM: 570 milligrams
COMMENTS: "Brackish," "thin," "bitter," and "vegetal," with a "horrible" flavor. One taster wrote, "Celery! Celery! Celery!" while another, recalling the gruel in *Oliver Twist*, called it "orphan water."

IMAGINE ORGANIC VEGETABLE COOKING STOCK
PRICE: $3.29 for 32-ounce box
SODIUM: 580 milligrams
COMMENTS: Tasters reacted to this broth's strong flavor, described variously as "dirty tamarind water," "bitter celery leaves," "weirdly sweet and sour," and "fermented." "This is just wrong," one taster complained. "An acid punch with a carrot aftertaste," summed up another. "So this is what lighter fluid and sugar taste like."

KITCHEN BASICS NATURAL VEGETABLE COOKING STOCK
PRICE: $2.99 for 32-ounce box
SODIUM: 330 milligrams
COMMENTS: "Tastes like rotten vegetables." "Gross and grassy—Is this houseplant broth?" Its brown color made risotto look muddy, with "watered-down caramel," "old date," "maple," "pumpkin," and "molasses" notes. In sum, it "doesn't taste anything like vegetables."

POTATO CHIPS

With annual sales topping $30 billion, potato chips beat out pretzels and tortilla chips as America's favorite snack food. There are endless chip varieties and flavors, but which bag of plain chips should the purist reach for? We grabbed eight national brands and started snacking. Potato chips are made with three basic ingredients—potatoes, oil, and salt. According to our tasters, starchy white russets and Idahos are the only way to go; Terra's "flaky," "vegetal" Yukon Golds left tasters wondering if they were made from real potatoes. The type of oil used for frying turned out to be very important too. Our top four chips were fried in safflower, sunflower, corn, and cottonseed oils, which have much lower concentrations of unsaturated fatty acids (unsaturated fatty acids can break down at high temperatures and take on a fishy flavor and odor). Kettle-style chips finished first and fourth in our tasting. These thick-cut chips are cooked in small batches and spend more time in the cooking oil. A thicker cut means more potato flavor, and longer cooking times result in crunchier chips. Potato chips are listed in order of preference.

HIGHLY RECOMMENDED

LAY'S KETTLE COOKED ORIGINAL
PRICE: $2.89 for 9 ounces
COMMENTS: The classic lunchbox chip, only better—or, as one taster wrote, "thick, salty goodness." Another noted, "These have some body" and "big potato flavor."

RECOMMENDED

HERR'S CRISP 'N TASTY POTATO CHIPS
PRICE: $2.99 for 11.5 ounces
COMMENTS: These "shatteringly crisp" spuds actually "tasted like potatoes" and were relatively sturdy compared with other thin chips.

UTZ POTATO CHIPS
PRICE: $2.99 for 12 ounces
COMMENTS: Though some snackers found these "very light and crisp" chips a bit greasy, most thought the balance of salt and potato flavor was right on.

KETTLE CHIPS LIGHTLY SALTED
PRICE: $2.69 for 5 ounces
COMMENTS: If you like that "well-done," "earthy" flavor, these are the chips for you. Some tasters found them too dark, while others appreciated their lower salt level and "pure potato flavor."

RECOMMENDED WITH RESERVATIONS

WISE ALL NATURAL POTATO CHIPS
PRICE: $5.39 for 20 ounces
COMMENTS: "Brittle to a fault," one taster noted. These super-salty, super-greasy chips satisfied some tasters' classic chip cravings but came off as "cheap" and "Styrofoamy" to others.

LAY'S CLASSIC POTATO CHIPS
PRICE: $2.50 for 13.7 ounces
COMMENTS: Not surprisingly, these archetypal chips from the yellow bag were described as "right down the middle" and "run-of-the-mill: first grease, then salt, minimal potato."

CAPE COD POTATO CHIPS
PRICE: $3.19 for 9 ounces
COMMENTS: Despite the pleasing crunch and lack of grease on this classic kettle chip, the "fishy," "off" flavors from canola oil and prevalence of green-tinged potatoes were off-putting.

NOT RECOMMENDED

TERRA GOLDS ORIGINAL POTATO CHIPS
PRICE: $2.79 for 5 ounces
COMMENTS: The only sample made from Yukon Gold potatoes also had the lowest fat and salt content. The golden color and crunchy texture of these chips were, as one taster noted, "deceiving," given their "stale" yet "raw potato" flavor.

WHOLE WHEAT BREAD

Every major commercial producer of bread now sells at least one type of wheat bread. To determine which brand is best, we rounded up nine types of 100-percent whole wheat bread (breads made with only whole wheat—and not refined white—flour) and sampled them plain and toasted with butter. Overall, our tasters had a preference for breads with a distinct, clean, and nutty wheat flavor that was balanced by just a hint of sweetness. How is this achieved? A look at the ingredients lists reveals two very important factors: the presence (or absence) of chemical preservatives and high-fructose corn syrup. Many manufacturers add chemical preservatives that inhibit the growth of microbes and mold. The preservatives can lend a slight off-flavor to the breads, which our tasters detected in several of the low-rated brands. To mask those off-flavors, most of these low-rated breads use high-fructose corn syrup as their primary sweetener; the corn syrup is powerfully sweet and can make desirable wheat flavor less apparent. Our top three brands do not contain high-fructose corn syrup, and tasters praised them for stronger wheat flavor. As for texture, our tasters liked breads that were heartier, chewier, and denser than white bread. Breads are listed in order of preference.

HIGHLY RECOMMENDED

PEPPERIDGE FARM 100% NATURAL WHOLE WHEAT BREAD
PRICE: $3.39 for 24 ounces
COMMENTS: This bread, which had a low level of sugars and no corn syrup, was praised for its "whole-grain, earthy flavor" and "nuttiness." The "dense, chewy" texture was lauded as being "grainy but moist."

RECOMMENDED

RUDI'S ORGANIC BAKERY HONEY SWEET WHOLE WHEAT BREAD
PRICE: $3.79 for 22 ounces
COMMENTS: This bread earned high marks for its "dense and wholesome" texture. It also had the lowest total sugars of any brand in the lineup. "Closest to traditional wheat bread in taste and texture," said one taster.

ARNOLD NATURAL 100% WHOLE WHEAT BREAD
PRICE: $2.50 for 20 ounces
COMMENTS: "Nutty and wheaty," said tasters, who appreciated this bread's "complex" and "strong, healthy" flavor. Its texture was praised as "hearty." A few panelists complained about a "bitter" aftertaste.

RECOMMENDED WITH RESERVATIONS

FREIHOFER'S STONEGROUND 100% WHOLE WHEAT BREAD
PRICE: $2.99 for 24 ounces
COMMENTS: This "middle-of-the-road" bread had a "soft and gummy" texture. Its very "sweet" flavor (courtesy of high-fructose corn syrup) led a few tasters to comment that it "doesn't taste like real wheat bread."

RECOMMENDED WITH RESERVATIONS (CONT.)

J.J. NISSEN CANADIAN 100% WHOLE WHEAT PREMIUM BREAD
PRICE: $2.99 for 24 ounces
COMMENTS: This bread was deemed "halfway between white and wheat" and "less wholesome-tasting" than most. It had a "very soft," "gummy" texture.

ARNOLD WHOLE GRAINS 100% WHOLE WHEAT BREAD
PRICE: $3.19 for 24 ounces
COMMENTS: This bread had "nutty" wheat flavor, but several tasters complained about "rancid" or "sour" notes. Texture was deemed "chewy."

OROWEAT WHOLE GRAINS 100% WHOLE WHEAT BREAD
PRICE: $3.49 for 24 ounces
COMMENTS: This bread contains high-fructose corn syrup and a relatively high amount of total sugars, and our tasters noticed, saying it was "sweet and almost fruity."

NOT RECOMMENDED

WONDER STONEGROUND 100% WHOLE WHEAT BREAD
PRICE: $2.99 for 24 ounces
COMMENTS: With "sour" and "bitter" flavors and "no wheat flavor," this bread scored lowest in the plain tasting. "Soft" and "springy" texture didn't win fans, either.

OROWEAT COUNTRY 100% WHOLE WHEAT BREAD
PRICE: $3.49 for 24 ounces
COMMENTS: "Very sweet, with little wheat flavor" was a common complaint about this bread, which had the most total sugars of any bread in the tasting.

EXTRA-SHARP CHEDDAR CHEESE

So, what is extra-sharp cheddar? It depends on whom you ask. The USDA's only requirement regarding cheddar is that the final product contain at least 50 percent milk-fat solids and no more than 39 percent moisture by weight. As for what distinguishes different varieties of cheddar—mild, medium, sharp, extra-sharp, and beyond—that is left in the hands of the cheese makers. This much we do know for sure: As cheddar ages, new flavor compounds are created, and the cheese gets firmer in texture and more concentrated in flavor—and it gets sharper. But does more sharpness make for better cheddar? To find out which supermarket extra-sharp cheddar cheese our tasters liked best, we purchased eight varieties (plus Cabot Sharp Cheddar, the winner of our previous tasting of regular sharp cheddars) and tried them plain (at room temperature to fully appreciate their nuances) and melted into grilled cheese sandwiches. Our tasters generally liked the older, sharper cheeses best. Our three top-rated cheeses—Cabot Private Stock, Cabot Extra Sharp, and Grafton Village—are all aged for at least 12 months, and tasters rated them the three sharpest. Cheeses are listed in order of preference.

HIGHLY RECOMMENDED

CABOT PRIVATE STOCK CHEDDAR CHEESE
PRICE: $3.99 for 8 ounces ($7.98 per pound)
AGED: 16 to 18 months
COMMENTS: "One great cheese," commented one taster. "The flavor is balanced—salty, pleasantly bitter, creamy, sweet. This is what I expect from an extra-sharp cheddar," said another. Tasters rated this cheese second-sharpest overall.

CABOT EXTRA SHARP CHEDDAR CHEESE
PRICE: $3.29 for 8 ounces ($6.58 per pound)
AGED: 12 to 18 months
COMMENTS: "This is a substantial cheese," stated one impressed taster; the panel agreed, as it rated a close second overall. "Supersharp" was a common refrain, while "sharp and smelly, like I like it" was a more unique perspective.

RECOMMENDED

GRAFTON VILLAGE CHEESE COMPANY PREMIUM CHEDDAR
PRICE: $4.99 for 8 ounces ($9.98 per pound)
AGED: 12 months
COMMENTS: Our panel rated this cheese the sharpest. "It explodes with tanginess," wrote one taster. "Really nice crumbly texture; complex flavor, with an aftertaste that is sharp and tangy—yum," said another taster. "Very funky and delicious."

CABOT SHARP CHEDDAR CHEESE
PRICE: $3.29 for 8 ounces ($6.58 per pound)
AGED: 8 to 12 months
COMMENTS: Winner of our prior tasting of sharp cheddars, this sample was judged as the sharpest cheese outside of our top three.

RECOMMENDED (CONT.)

TILLAMOOK SPECIAL RESERVE EXTRA SHARP CHEDDAR CHEESE
PRICE: $4.99 for 8 ounces ($9.98 per pound)
AGED: at least 15 months
COMMENTS: "Decent sharpness and good flavor" was the general opinion about this orange cheddar (tinted with annatto); a few tasters found it "a little sour."

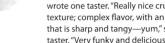

CRACKER BARREL EXTRA SHARP WHITE CHEDDAR CHEESE
PRICE: $3.49 for 8 ounces ($6.98 per pound)
AGE: not disclosed by manufacturer
COMMENTS: Tasters appreciated the "soft and creamy texture" of this Kraft product but complained about "pedestrian" flavor that "lacked complexity."

LAND O'LAKES EXTRA SHARP CHEDDAR CHEESE
PRICE: $2.99 for 8 ounces ($5.98 per pound)
AGED: at least 9 months
COMMENTS: "Pleasant but unremarkable" was our tasters' consensus on this "mild," "not very sharp" cheddar from Wisconsin.

HELUVA GOOD NEW YORK STATE EXTRA-SHARP CHEDDAR
PRICE: $3.29 for 8 ounces ($6.58 per pound)
AGED: at least 9 months
COMMENTS: "Lacking in complexity, but decent flavor" summarizes our tasters' opinions of this cheese. Some complaints about "gummy" texture, but cheese did melt nicely.

RECOMMENDED WITH RESERVATIONS

CRACKER BARREL NATURAL EXTRA SHARP CHEDDAR 2% MILK REDUCED FAT
PRICE: $3.49 for 8 ounces ($6.98 per pound)
AGE: not disclosed by manufacturer
COMMENTS: "Texture is rubbery and not cheddarlike," said one displeased taster. "Are you sure this is cheddar?" asked another. The flavor was best described as "sour, not sharp."

PASTA SAUCE

If you're going to buy pasta sauce—and Americans spend $1.7 billion a year on jarred sauces—you should know which one tastes best. We assembled a lineup of nine national brands of marinara or tomato and basil sauce and told our testers to "mangia." All of the sauces listed reconstituted tomato paste (water and tomato paste) and tomatoes as their first two ingredients, so we thought texture might differentiate them. The sauces ranged from perfectly smooth to quite chunky. To measure the relative chunkiness of each sauce, we portioned an equal weight of each into a fine-mesh strainer, rinsed it under running water for 20 seconds, and then weighed the remains. Our tasters' favorite sauce, Bertolli, was the chunkiest, with 44 percent of its initial weight remaining after rinsing. After good tomato flavor and chunky consistency were established as desirable qualities, overwhelming dried herb flavor was identified as not desirable in the least. Our top three sauces were more subtly seasoned than some others, and they compare favorably with homemade sauces. Sauces are listed in order of preference.

RECOMMENDED

BERTOLLI TOMATO AND BASIL SAUCE
PRICE: $1.99 for 24 ounces
COMMENTS: This sauce had a "good balance of flavors" and "a nice chunky texture." Because it wasn't overseasoned with dried herbs, tasters thought this sauce tasted "the most like fresh-cooked tomatoes."

FRANCESCO RINALDI TRADITIONAL MARINARA
PRICE: $1.69 for 24 ounces
COMMENTS: This brand's "mild sweetness and spice" helped to bring out its "tangy," "bright and tomatoey" qualities. Tasters appreciated its "thick" consistency and "good texture."

PREGO MARINARA ITALIAN SAUCE
PRICE: $2.79 for 25 ounces
COMMENTS: Our tasters didn't love this sauce's "too smooth" texture, noting that it "looks like ketchup." But they were impressed that it "actually tastes like tomatoes" and "doesn't have that fake herb flavor."

BARILLA MARINARA SAUCE
PRICE: $1.99 for 24 ounces
COMMENTS: Tasters liked the "chunkiness" of this sample, but they complained that it was "candy-sweet" and overwhelmed by too much herb flavor. As one taster noted, "Tomato flavor is lost to oregano."

NEWMAN'S OWN MARINARA
PRICE: $3.19 for 24 ounces
COMMENTS: This sauce was praised for being "spicy" and "peppery" without too many dried herb "distractions." "Good texture," said one taster of this "thick and pasty" sauce, "but not much tomato flavor."

RECOMMENDED (CONT.)

MUIR GLEN ORGANIC TOMATO BASIL PASTA SAUCE
PRICE: $3.69 for 25.5 ounces
COMMENTS: Familiar refrains: "I like the chunky texture, but the dried basil is overwhelming" and "pleasantly chunky, but overpowering stale dried herb taste." Tomatoes "seemed more roasted" than other samples.

RECOMMENDED WITH RESERVATIONS

EMERIL'S ALL NATURAL ITALIAN STYLE TOMATO & BASIL PASTA SAUCE
PRICE: $4.99 for 25 ounces
COMMENTS: Astute tasters noted that this sauce "tastes artificial and sweet" and had a "funky aftertaste that tastes artificial"; it is the only sauce in our lineup that contains corn syrup.

NOT RECOMMENDED

CLASSICO TOMATO & BASIL PASTA SAUCE
PRICE: $2.59 for 26 ounces
COMMENTS: "Who can taste anything other than those terrible dried herbs?" bemoaned one wincing taster. "Major spice overload: I hardly detect tomato in here," said another.

RAGÚ OLD WORLD STYLE TRADITIONAL PASTA SAUCE
PRICE: $1.59 for 26 ounces
COMMENTS: "What did you do with the SpaghettiO's that came with this?" asked one taster about this "thin and flat" sauce. One of the few samples that tasters thought "could use more spice."

JARRED HOT SALSA

We don't like jarred salsa. Yes, we know it's now America's favorite condiment, but previous taste tests have been disappointing. Almost no jarred salsas have reached "recommended" status, and none have come close to homemade fresh salsa. Our prior taste tests have focused on mild and medium varieties, so maybe hot salsas would be more interesting than their timid siblings. When we sampled nine national brands, we were surprised that most tasters didn't need to quell the burn with cold milk or water as they nibbled. Only the Pace, Frontera Hot Habanero, and Green Mountain Gringo salsas were considered sufficiently hot, and none were excessively incendiary. These hot salsas were livelier and better than the mild salsas we've tasted in the past, with eight of the nine receiving passing grades. But even the best were merely good, not great, and didn't approach the quality of fresh salsa. Why? Good salsa relies on the interplay of fresh vegetable flavors and textures. Jarred salsas have the freshness and crispness cooked out of them. Our advice: If you're buying jarred salsa, go for the hot stuff. Salsas are listed in order of preference.

RECOMMENDED

PACE HOT CHUNKY SALSA
PRICE: $2.49 for 16 ounces
COMMENTS: Most tasters were impressed by this spicy salsa's "bright tomato and chile" and "vegetal" flavors, as well as its "chunky," "crunchy" texture. There is a "quick hit of tomato flavor, then fire" from the big burn.

FRONTERA HOT HABANERO SALSA WITH ROASTED TOMATOES AND CILANTRO
PRICE: $4.69 for 16 ounces
COMMENTS: The roasted tomatoes in this brand were clearly identifiable. "Smoky and complex, yet still has fresh zing," said one taster. "Exciting to eat," said another. This was also the hottest salsa in our tasting.

NEWMAN'S OWN ALL NATURAL CHUNKY HOT SALSA
PRICE: $2.79 for 16 ounces
COMMENTS: This salsa is seasoned with plenty of garlic, cilantro, and black pepper. One taster made note of an "herby flavor I like, but that isn't typical for salsa." "Could be hotter" was a common comment.

HERDEZ HOT SALSA CASERA
PRICE: $3.49 for 16 ounces
COMMENTS: This salsa was the saltiest of the lot—and tasters noticed, saying, "Less of a cooked taste, but too salty." With the shortest ingredient list in our lineup, several tasters praised this brand as "fresh-tasting" and "clean and crisp."

RECOMMENDED WITH RESERVATIONS

TOSTITOS HOT CHUNKY SALSA
PRICE: $2.99 for 15.5 ounces
COMMENTS: This "basic and inoffensive," "ordinary" salsa had average scores for heat level, flavor, and texture.

OLD EL PASO THICK N'CHUNKY HOT SALSA
PRICE: $2.79 for 16 ounces
COMMENTS: Many tasters commented on the "cloyingly sweet" nature of this salsa. The "strong tomato flavor" comes from the wealth of tomato chunks—this salsa had more solids (65 percent) than any other in our test.

EMERIL'S KICKED UP CHUNKY HOT SALSA
PRICE: $3.79 for 16 ounces
COMMENTS: "Another bland, tomatoey salsa" that was "not very interesting" but had "decent flavor." "Not hot enough," said one uninspired taster; "tastes like canned tomato puree," said another.

GREEN MOUNTAIN GRINGO HOT SALSA
PRICE: $3.79 for 16 ounces
COMMENTS: This brand received some very high marks but also some dreadfully low ones. One thing is not debatable—it has a "fierce," "lingering" heat. The only brand to include tomatillos, which might have polarized tasters.

NOT RECOMMENDED

CHI-CHI'S HOT FIESTA SALSA
PRICE: $2.79 for 16 ounces
COMMENTS: "I wouldn't dip into this twice," said one wincing taster. Many detected "soapy," "musty," "funky," "sour," or "bitter" flavors. "Just all-around bad," and thin, too—this salsa had the lowest solid content of the brands tasted. "Tastes stale, but if you had beer and chips you might not notice," cracked another.

DIJON MUSTARD

To be labeled Dijon, a mustard must adhere to the formula developed more than 150 years ago in Dijon, France. Finely ground brown or black mustard seeds are mixed with vinegar, wine, and/or grape must, and lightly seasoned with salt and sometimes a hint of spice, creating a smooth Dijon mustard with nose-tingling heat. We rounded up eight nationally available brands and tasted them plain and in a simple mustard vinaigrette. The three hottest mustards—Grey Poupon, Maille, and Roland—were our tasters' overall favorites. Interestingly, when we measured the pH level of each brand, this hot trio also proved to be the least acidic (a higher pH value means lower acidity). When mustard seeds are ground, the enzyme that is released activates the mustard's dormant heat-producing chemicals (called glucosinolates), but the addition of acid retards this reaction. So less acid produces a mustard with more heat-producing chemicals. But these heat-producing chemicals dissipate over time. For this reason, we recommend checking "use by" dates, buying fresher mustards when possible, and never storing Dijon for more than six months. Mustards are listed in order of preference.

HIGHLY RECOMMENDED

GREY POUPON DIJON MUSTARD
PRICE: $3.79 for 10 ounces
pH: 3.64
COMMENTS: This "potent," "bold" American-made mustard was deemed the hottest by tasters. It "gets you in the nose like a Dijon should." A "nice balance of sweet, tangy, and sharp" sealed the deal for one happy taster, who declared, "I want this on my ham and cheese sandwich."

MAILLE DIJON ORIGINALE TRADITIONAL DIJON MUSTARD
PRICE: $3.99 for 7.5 ounces
pH: 3.68
COMMENTS: This French brand is made in Canada, where the bulk of the mustard seeds for the French mustard industry are grown. It had a "nice balance of heat and complexity," with tasters calling out "perfume-y" flavors of "smoke," "butter," "fruit," and "pepper." It was the second hottest mustard in our lineup.

ROLAND EXTRA STRONG DIJON MUSTARD
PRICE: $4.79 for 13 ounces
pH: 3.80
COMMENTS: This French mustard features a "sharp horseradish bite" and "nasal heat" and was the third hottest mustard overall. Tasters loved the "smoky," "oaky," and "meaty" flavors. "Surprising complexity."

RECOMMENDED

JACK DANIEL'S STONE GROUND DIJON MUSTARD
PRICE: $3.49 for 9 ounces
pH: 3.58
COMMENTS: Tasters didn't detect much heat in this "mild and sweet" sample when tasting it plain, but its heat bloomed in the vinaigrette, where it was deemed "robust" and "salty" (it had the most salt of any sample).

RECOMMENDED WITH RESERVATIONS

ANNIE'S NATURALS ORGANIC DIJON MUSTARD
PRICE: $3.49 for 9 ounces
pH: 3.45
COMMENTS: This sample's "warm spice flavor" hurt its overall scores: "weird sweet and spicy notes" was a common complaint. Tasters thought this mustard was too acidic, noting its "tart" character.

FRENCH'S DIJON MUSTARD
PRICE: $2.99 for 9 ounces
pH: 3.47
COMMENTS: "Highly acidic—almost tastes pickled," "way too much vinegar," and "overly tangy without balance" were common complaints. Still, some tasters thought it was passable, calling this supermarket standard "not remarkable, but not terrible" and "like ballpark mustard."

WESTBRAE NATURAL DIJON STYLE MUSTARD
PRICE: $2.50 for 8 ounces
pH: 3.45
COMMENTS: This mustard tied for the most acidic and had the least amount of salt, prompting tasters to describe it as "lacking depth," "with no interesting dance of flavors." A few did like its "mellow, building heat."

NOT RECOMMENDED

PLOCHMAN'S PREMIUM DIJON MUSTARD
PRICE: $2.99 for 9 ounces
pH: 3.46
COMMENTS: Tasters were disappointed that this "watery," "sour," "fruity and weak" sample had "no heat or complexity." "Sissy mustard" sums up its performance.

GARLIC PRESSES

We have a crush on garlic in the test kitchen—it appears in more than one-quarter of our recipes. Having cooked so much garlic, we've learned a thing or two about preparing it. For example, we've learned that for the average home cook, a garlic press is faster, easier, and more effective than trying to get a fine, even mince with a chef's knife. Also, a finely processed clove of garlic makes for a better distribution of garlic and fuller garlic flavor throughout a dish. Though the garlic press has been around since the 1950s, our testing revealed that there are still many less-than-stellar versions on the market today. Garlic presses are listed in order of preference.

RECOMMENDED | PERFORMANCE | TESTERS' COMMENTS

KUHN RIKON 2315 EPICUREAN GARLIC PRESS
PRICE: $34.95
MATERIAL: Stainless steel

CONSISTENCY OF GARLIC: ★★★
PRESSING PERFORMANCE: ★★★
DESIGN: ★★★
CLEANUP: ★★★

Heavy, solid gliding mechanism, with comfortably curved handles and hopper that lifts for easy cleaning. Mince is "very fine" and unpeeled garlic was "no problem." Overall, testers noted, "It pressed—and cleaned—like a dream."

RECOMMENDED WITH RESERVATIONS | PERFORMANCE | TESTERS' COMMENTS

RÖSLE GARLIC PRESS
PRICE: $34.95
MATERIAL: Stainless steel

CONSISTENCY OF GARLIC: ★★
PRESSING PERFORMANCE: ★★★
DESIGN: ★★
CLEANUP: ★★★

Solid, heavy press has pop-up hopper for cleaning. Straight, cylindrical, shiny handles "didn't feel perfectly ergonomic," but the press was "surprisingly easy to use and clean."

TRUDEAU GARLIC PRESS
PRICE: $11.99 **BEST BUY**
MATERIAL: Chrome-plated metal with nonslip rubber handles

CONSISTENCY OF GARLIC: ★★
PRESSING PERFORMANCE: ★★
DESIGN: ★★★
CLEANUP: ★★★

"Good press" with a "solid" feel produced garlic pieces that were "uniform but a little chunky." Press was "very easy to clean," with flip handles and "generous" hopper.

MESSERMEISTER PRO-TOUCH JUMBO GARLIC PRESS WITH SANTOPRENE HANDLES
PRICE: $9.95
MATERIAL: Zinc alloy, satin finished, with rubber handles

CONSISTENCY OF GARLIC: ★★
PRESSING PERFORMANCE: ★★
DESIGN: ★★★
CLEANUP: ★★★

"Sturdy and easy to squeeze," except for unpeeled cloves, which required more muscle. Garlic came out slightly "chunky" and "coarse." Construction is solid and heavy. "Jumbo" hopper no bigger than average.

ZYLISS SUSI 2 GARLIC PRESS
PRICE: $14.99
MATERIAL: Aluminum base with nonstick coating

CONSISTENCY OF GARLIC: ★★★
PRESSING PERFORMANCE: ★★★
DESIGN: ★
CLEANUP: ★★

Tapered holes shaped like tiny funnels gave "huge yield" of "fine-textured garlic" that was "super-easy" to press. "Effortless" with unpeeled cloves. Some testers preferred this lightweight model, but nonstick finish began to peel around the hopper.

ZYLISS JUMBO GARLIC PRESS
PRICE: $16.99
MATERIAL: Aluminum base with nonstick coating

CONSISTENCY OF GARLIC: ★★★
PRESSING PERFORMANCE: ★★★
DESIGN: ★
CLEANUP: ★★

"Jumbo" press held four to five cloves; handled unpeeled cloves well, producing a "very good mince." Cleaning tool stores in the handle, but some found it "hard to figure out." Nonstick finish began to peel.

NOT RECOMMENDED | PERFORMANCE | TESTERS' COMMENTS

OXO STEEL 58181 GARLIC PRESS
PRICE: $16.99
MATERIAL: Stainless steel with rubber handles, plastic cleaning spikes

CONSISTENCY OF GARLIC: ★
PRESSING PERFORMANCE: ★★
DESIGN: ★★
CLEANUP: ★★★

Plunger couldn't be fully depressed to bottom of hopper. "Inefficient," complained testers. Flip-handled model cleaned up easily. Testers deemed the sieve holes too large, producing "coarse," "chunky" pieces.

OXO GOOD GRIPS 28181 GARLIC PRESS
PRICE: $14.50
MATERIAL: Die-cast zinc, rubber handles, plastic cleaning spikes

CONSISTENCY OF GARLIC: ★★
PRESSING PERFORMANCE: ★
DESIGN: ★★
CLEANUP: ★★★

Plunger couldn't quite get to the bottom of the hopper, leaving some garlic unprocessed. Couldn't handle unpeeled cloves. Traditional flip-handled model rinsed out easily. Handles were comfortable and easy to press.

GIANT GARLIC PRESS
PRICE: $14
MATERIAL: Stainless steel

CONSISTENCY OF GARLIC: ★★
PRESSING PERFORMANCE: ★★
DESIGN: ★★
CLEANUP: ★

Shaped like a potato ricer, this press struck testers as "flimsy." Hopper is "huge" but could press only three cloves, because plunger couldn't get into position with more. Press was "a pain to clean."

CUISINART RED GARLIC PRESS
PRICE: $14.95
MATERIAL: Steel with plastic handles

CONSISTENCY OF GARLIC: ★★
PRESSING PERFORMANCE: ★
DESIGN: ★★
CLEANUP: ★★

Testers disliked "tiny hopper," which removes for cleaning. "I'd lose this in a second," complained one, "and it's too easy to put in backward." Unpeeled garlic "spattered and squished up the sides."

AMCO HOUSEWORKS GARLIC PRESS
*Also sold as the Crate and Barrel Garlic Slicer and Press
PRICE: $19.95
MATERIAL: Die-cast aluminum

CONSISTENCY OF GARLIC: ★★
PRESSING PERFORMANCE: ★
DESIGN: ★
CLEANUP: ★

Fell completely apart in dishwasher after six washes. Press "left a lot behind," and pieces were somewhat uneven. Slices "too thick"; garlic looked "chewed-up" and stuck in the blades.

PEPPER MILLS

We rounded up four new models of pepper mills and one classic wooden mill to see if they could compete with the two top competitors (the Unicorn Magnum Plus and East Hampton Industries Peppermate) from our last pepper mill tests. Output, level of grind, and easy adjustability were our main concerns. We use a lot of pepper, so output had to be consistent. In the kitchen, we regularly need fine-, medium-, and coarse-ground pepper, so our mills had to produce uniform grinds at all settings. Plus, the mills had to be easy to operate and switch between grind settings in an uncomplicated fashion. Mills are listed in order of preference.

HIGHLY RECOMMENDED	PERFORMANCE	TESTERS' COMMENTS
UNICORN MAGNUM PLUS **PRICE:** $45	GRIND QUALITY: ★★★ GRIND QUANTITY: ★★★ ADJUSTABILITY: ★★	Our defending champ wins again for producing an abundance of perfectly ground pepper with minimal effort. "Prodigious," said one impressed tester. Its grind adjuster (attached to the grinding mechanism on the bottom of the mill) is easy to use, though it does not have fixed settings.
WILLIAM BOUNDS PROVIEW PEPPER MILL **PRICE:** $39.95	GRIND QUALITY: ★★★ GRIND QUANTITY: ★★ ADJUSTABILITY: ★★★	Testers loved the "intuitive" grind adjuster with fixed settings and the window at the bottom of the hopper, which allows you to see when you need to refill. While this mill couldn't keep pace with the output of the Magnum Plus, it produced perfectly uniform pepper at the coarse, medium, and fine settings.

RECOMMENDED	PERFORMANCE	TESTERS' COMMENTS
PEUGEOT CHATEAUNEUF ADJUSTABLE PEPPER MILL **PRICE:** $80	GRIND QUALITY: ★★ GRIND QUANTITY: ★★ ADJUSTABILITY: ★★★	This mill produced a good volume of very uniform pepper at all six fixed settings, but our testers wanted the finely ground pepper to be finer and the coarsely ground to be coarser. At more than twice the price of most other models, it's a good thing this "straight shooter" mill felt "heavy and solid" and was easy to operate.
EAST HAMPTON INDUSTRIES PEPPERMATE CERAMIC BLADE PEPPER MILL (MODEL 723) **PRICE:** $34.95	GRIND QUALITY: ★★★ GRIND QUANTITY: ★★★ ADJUSTABILITY: ★	This unique mill produces an ample quantity of perfectly ground pepper through a range of settings. Its side-twisting lever is "efficient" and minimizes fatigue. Its one drawback is the adjuster mechanism, which is awkwardly located inside the hopper. Testers especially liked the snap-on clear plastic reservoir that catches pepper as you grind.

RECOMMENDED WITH RESERVATIONS	PERFORMANCE	TESTERS' COMMENTS
VIC FIRTH GOURMET SIERRA CHERRY PEPPER MILL **PRICE:** $38.95	GRIND QUALITY: ★★ GRIND QUANTITY: ★★ ADJUSTABILITY: ★★	This model offers a few improvements to the basic finial-topped design: Its finial has fixed stops, which ensure that you won't lose your setting—and that the finial won't fall off when grinding. The directional guide points users to coarse or fine pepper. However, the hopper is small, and the coarse pepper was not very coarse.
OLDE THOMPSON WOOD SENATOR 8-INCH PEPPER MILL **PRICE:** $15.95	GRIND QUALITY: ★★ GRIND QUANTITY: ★★★ ADJUSTABILITY: ★	This is your classic, no-frills, finial-topped pepper mill—a design we've never loved, because, as one tester said, "It's hard to grind when you tighten [the finial], and it falls off when you loosen it." This mill's finely ground pepper was very nice, but the grind was not uniform at medium and coarse settings.

NOT RECOMMENDED	PERFORMANCE	TESTERS' COMMENTS
TRUDEAU ONE HAND PEPPER MILL **PRICE:** $24.95	GRIND QUALITY: ★★ GRIND QUANTITY: ★ ADJUSTABILITY: ★★	This is not an efficient pepper mill. The one-hand action looked promising, but the mechanism was "physically tiring" and "annoying." It produced acceptably uniform pepper at fine and medium settings.

BAKING SHEETS

The baking sheets in our test kitchen aren't just used for baking. We use ours for everything from baking cookies and jellyroll cakes to roasting oven fries, to broiling and roasting meats (with the help of an inserted wire cooling rack). We tested eight brands of rimmed baking sheets, noting how they handled these tasks, and how they held up—whether they warped during cooking. Known as a "half-sheet pan" in restaurant supply stores and as a "jellyroll pan" in retail stores, the ideal baking sheet is thick and solidly constructed; a too-flimsy pan warps under high heat, and a light-weight pan can transfer heat too intensely, leading to burnt cookies. Baking sheets are listed in order of preference.

HIGHLY RECOMMENDED | PERFORMANCE | TESTERS' COMMENTS

LINCOLN FOODSERVICE HALF-SIZE HEAVY DUTY SHEET PAN
PRICE: $15.40
MATERIAL: Aluminum alloy (13-gauge)
SIZE: 18" x 13" x 1"
WEIGHT AND THICKNESS: 1 lb., 14 oz.; 1.8 mm.

COOKIES: ★★★
JELLYROLL: ★★★
OVEN FRIES: ★★★
PORK: ★★★
WIGGLE AND WARP: ★★★
DESIGN: ★★★

"Perfect" cookies, oven fries, and jellyroll in this "flawless" pan. Pork produced "lots of fat but no worries about spilling—pan is solid as a rock." Jellyroll browned and released perfectly. Pan can't be twisted, did not warp. "The search is over."

RECOMMENDED | PERFORMANCE | TESTERS' COMMENTS

NORPRO HEAVY GAUGE ALUMINUM JELLY ROLL PAN
PRICE: $17.99
MATERIAL: Aluminum
SIZE: 18" x 12" x 1"
WEIGHT AND THICKNESS: 1 lb., 15 oz.; 1.0 mm.

COOKIES: ★★★
JELLYROLL: ★★★
OVEN FRIES: ★★★
PORK: ★★★
WIGGLE AND WARP: ★★
DESIGN: ★★★

Oven fries were evenly browned, as were cookies and jellyroll cake, and pan felt solid when we barbecued pork. However, while it felt sturdy, pan could be wiggled and had warped slightly by end of testing.

GOURMET STANDARD TRI-PLY STAINLESS STEEL JELLY ROLL PAN
PRICE: $59.95
MATERIAL: Two layers of stainless steel sandwiching a layer of aluminum
SIZE: 16" x 13" x 1"
WEIGHT AND THICKNESS: 3 lb., 5 oz.; 1.8 mm.

COOKIES: ★★★
JELLYROLL: ★★★
OVEN FRIES: ★★★
PORK: ★★★
WIGGLE AND WARP: ★★
DESIGN: ★★

Performed all cooking tests well, but this "pretty but pricey" pan's nonstandard size was a handicap: At just 16 inches long (15 inches once rims are discounted), it's too short for standard wire rack to fit inside, and parchment sheets must be trimmed.

ANOLON COMMERCIAL BAKEWARE JELLY ROLL PAN
PRICE: $14.95
MATERIAL: Aluminized steel
SIZE: 18" x 13" x 1"
WEIGHT AND THICKNESS: 2 lb., 6 oz.; 0.5 mm.

COOKIES: ★★
JELLYROLL: ★★★
OVEN FRIES: ★★★
PORK: ★★★
WIGGLE AND WARP: ★★★
DESIGN: ★★

"Sturdy" pan produced crisp, evenly cooked fries, released jellyroll easily, and was steady with hot pan full of barbecued pork and drippings. However, cookies baked up too dark, due to thinness of pan.

VOLLRATH JELLY ROLL PAN
PRICE: $9.95
MATERIAL: Aluminum alloy
SIZE: 18" x 13" x 1"
WEIGHT AND THICKNESS: 1 lb., 11 oz.; 1.02 mm.

COOKIES: ★★★
JELLYROLL: ★★★
OVEN FRIES: ★★
PORK: ★★
WIGGLE AND WARP: ★★
DESIGN: ★★★

Cookies baked well, as did jellyroll, but fries were "a little uneven and not very crisp." Pan bent when full of hot barbecued pork, but did not spill. Was slightly warped after testing.

NORDICWARE NATURAL COMMERCIAL BAKEWARE BAKER'S HALF SHEET
PRICE: $14.99
MATERIAL: Aluminum
SIZE: 18" x 13" x 1"
WEIGHT AND THICKNESS: 1 lb., 10 oz.; 0.8 mm.

COOKIES: ★★
JELLYROLL: ★★★
OVEN FRIES: ★★
PORK: ★★★
WIGGLE AND WARP: ★★★
DESIGN: ★★

While cookies baked evenly, they were too dark. Oven fries in middle of pan were "soggy, wimpy," and underdone, but those around edges of pan were too dark. Pan was stable with hot drippings. Soft surface scratched too easily: Butter knife used to loosen cake left deep hatches all around pan.

RECOMMENDED WITH RESERVATIONS | PERFORMANCE | TESTERS' COMMENTS

CHICAGO METALLIC COMMERCIAL COOKIE/JELLY ROLL PAN
PRICE: $15.25
MATERIAL: Aluminized steel
SIZE: 18" x 13" x 1"
WEIGHT AND THICKNESS: 2 lb., 7 oz.; 0.5 mm.

COOKIES: ★★
JELLYROLL: ★★★
OVEN FRIES: ★★
PORK: ★★
WIGGLE AND WARP: ★★
DESIGN: ★

Cookies and fries browned unevenly. Oil pooled at one end of pan after it warped under high heat while making fries; pan buckled a bit with pork, causing some hot fat to splash out as we moved pan. Rolled rim trapped dishwater.

WILTON JELLY ROLL AND COOKIE PAN
PRICE: $13.99
MATERIAL: Aluminum
SIZE: 18" x 12" x 1"
WEIGHT AND THICKNESS: 1 lb.; 0.8 mm.

COOKIES: ★
JELLYROLL: ★★
OVEN FRIES: ★
PORK: ★★
WIGGLE AND WARP: ★
DESIGN: ★

Light and "flimsy, bendy" ("It's flapping like a sail") pan transferred heat too rapidly: Cookies burned; jellyroll baked very quickly; oven fries were still uncooked inside when exteriors were deeply brown. Pan was "quite warped" by end of testing.

CUTTING BOARDS

A basic cutting board was once an easy purchase, but now we have choices galore—plastic, wood, bamboo, wood composite, glass. Not to mention the varying sizes and, therefore, weights to choose from. The heaviest board we whacked into was the impressive 10-pound John Boos Chopping Block. Substantial, yes; easy to clean, no. Bamboo boards, which are lightweight and attractive, have recently flooded the field, so we thought they might run away with first place in our testing. But in our testing, we found our top picks cut across material distinctions, displaying similar features of comfort, durability, and solid construction. Boards are listed in order of preference.

HIGHLY RECOMMENDED

	PERFORMANCE	TESTERS' COMMENTS
TOTALLY BAMBOO CONGO **PRICE:** $39.99 **MATERIAL:** Butcher-block-style bamboo **WEIGHT:** 5 pounds	CUTTING: ★★★ DURABILITY: ★★★ CLEANUP: ★★★ USER-FRIENDLINESS: ★★★	Solid and cushy surface of a wooden butcher block, but lightweight, with nicely rounded edges that are easy to grasp. Perfect score in every test.
J.K. ADAMS TAKES TWO **PRICE:** $22 **MATERIAL:** Hard rock sugar maple **WEIGHT:** 3.7 pounds	CUTTING: ★★★ DURABILITY: ★★★ CLEANUP: ★★ USER-FRIENDLINESS: ★★★	Classic plank board is solid but light enough to be convenient for frequent use. Knife felt cushioned during use; board showed few marks of cuts; blade stayed sharp after 750 cuts. Chipotle stain hung on.
ARCHITEC GRIPPER NONSLIP **PRICE:** $14.99 **MATERIAL:** Polypropylene (plastic) **WEIGHT:** 0.9 pounds	CUTTING: ★★ DURABILITY: ★★★ CLEANUP: ★★★ USER-FRIENDLINESS: ★★★	Nonslip "gripper" underside keeps board extremely stable but makes it one-sided. Pleasant cutting surface, but it slightly dulled a new knife.

RECOMMENDED

	PERFORMANCE	TESTERS' COMMENTS
TOTALLY BAMBOO KAUAI **PRICE:** $28 **MATERIAL:** Vertical-grain bamboo **WEIGHT:** 2.7 pounds	CUTTING: ★★★ DURABILITY: ★★ CLEANUP: ★★★ USER-FRIENDLINESS: ★★★	This pretty board was easy to handle, felt solid and well cushioned under the knife, and was tough enough to handle the cleaver. Surface became deeply incised in one area after 750 cuts, but it didn't stain.
JOHN BOOS CHOPPING BLOCK **PRICE:** $74.95 **MATERIAL:** Northern hard rock maple **WEIGHT:** 10.4 pounds	CUTTING: ★★★ DURABILITY: ★★ CLEANUP: ★ USER-FRIENDLINESS: ★★★	This deluxe cutting board is mighty heavy to hoist around the kitchen. Feels great under the knife, keeping blade sharp after 750 cuts; definitely needs oiling and careful drying to keep its good looks and avoid splitting, as our first sample did.
TRUBAMBOO PALM BEACH **PRICE:** $39.99 **MATERIAL:** Flat-grain bamboo **WEIGHT:** 5.2 pounds	CUTTING: ★★★ DURABILITY: ★★ CLEANUP: ★★ USER-FRIENDLINESS: ★★	Board did the job but was unremarkable. Surface showed faint cuts and became increasingly fuzzy, with tiny raised fibers, as we used and cleaned it.

RECOMMENDED WITH RESERVATIONS

	PERFORMANCE	TESTERS' COMMENTS
THE CUTTING BOARD COMPANY **PRICE:** $11.35 **MATERIAL:** Polypropylene (plastic) **WEIGHT:** 3.7 pounds	CUTTING: ★★ DURABILITY: ★★ CLEANUP: ★★ USER-FRIENDLINESS: ★★	Surface was too slick when new—onion skidded as we cut. Cleaver made deep cuts, raised ridges on surface. This board slipped around if we didn't use a mat underneath, and it stained deeply.
EPICUREAN CUTTING SURFACES, KITCHEN SERIES **PRICE:** $24.95 **MATERIAL:** Wood-laminate composite **WEIGHT:** 1.9 pounds	CUTTING: ★★ DURABILITY: ★★ CLEANUP: ★★ USER-FRIENDLINESS: ★★	Hard board clacked loudly under the knife; surface gave off sawdust after repeated cuts. Board smells like a wet dog when washed (it's the glue).
ARCHITEC GRIPPER BAMBOO **PRICE:** $14.99 **MATERIAL:** Vertical-grain bamboo **WEIGHT:** 2.4 pounds	CUTTING: ★★ DURABILITY: ★★ CLEANUP: ★ USER-FRIENDLINESS: ★★	Four rubber feet trapped wetness and gave board a hollow feel. More difficult to cut across planks than along them. Showed every cut, and stains hung on.

NOT RECOMMENDED

	PERFORMANCE	TESTERS' COMMENTS
OXO GOOD GRIPS FOLDING UTILITY **PRICE:** $24.99 **MATERIAL:** Polypropylene (plastic) **WEIGHT:** 3.8 pounds	CUTTING: ★★ DURABILITY: ★ CLEANUP: ★★★ USER-FRIENDLINESS: ★	Rubbery surface of board felt pleasant, but center-fold ridge got in the way of cutting. Board ripped in two at fold when swept off counter.

SERRATED KNIVES

In the kitchen, we've seen serrated knives with scalloped edges that provide too little grip, and knives with pointed serrations that were either too long or too small, creating snags on food or not cutting it at all. We found that for a knife to be a great all-purpose tool, it had to have a slightly flexible blade with serrations that are both uniformly spaced and moderate in length. To test our serrated knives, we used them to slice bread and tomatoes, quarter a club sandwich, split a cake round horizontally, and cut sticky-bun dough into pieces for baking. Knives are listed in order of preference.

HIGHLY RECOMMENDED

	PERFORMANCE	TESTERS' COMMENTS
WÜSTHOF CLASSIC BREAD KNIFE, 10 INCHES **PRICE:** $79.95 **STYLE:** Forged construction, pointed serrations	BREAD & TOMATOES: ★★★ CLUB SANDWICH: ★★★ CAKE: ★★★ STICKY DOUGH: ★★★	Well-balanced knife with deeply tapered pointed serrations handled every task with exceptional ease and control, even for our left-handed tester. Not as good for large hands.
VICTORINOX FORSCHNER 10¼-INCH CURVED BLADE BREAD KNIFE, BLACK FIBROX HANDLE **PRICE:** $24.95 **BEST BUY** **STYLE:** Stamped construction, pointed serrations	BREAD & TOMATOES: ★★★ CLUB SANDWICH: ★★★ CAKE: ★★★ STICKY DOUGH: ★★★	Comfortable, sharp blade and pointed serrations performed almost as well as our top knife, struggling a tad more with crusty bread. Taller blade was easier on large-handed testers. Good for lefties.

RECOMMENDED

	PERFORMANCE	TESTERS' COMMENTS
VIKING 10-INCH SERRATED SLICER **PRICE:** $108 **STYLE:** Forged construction, pointed serrations	BREAD & TOMATOES: ★★★ CLUB SANDWICH: ★★★ CAKE: ★★★ STICKY DOUGH: ★★★	Lethally sharp forged blade with deeply tapered pointed serrations was easy to control during delicate tasks. Feels (and is) expensive and isn't good for lefties or cooks with large hands.

RECOMMENDED WITH RESERVATIONS

	PERFORMANCE	TESTERS' COMMENTS
VICTORINOX FORSCHNER 14-INCH BREAD/SERRATED SLICING KNIFE, BLACK FIBROX HANDLE **PRICE:** $30.95 **STYLE:** Stamped construction, pointed serrations	BREAD & TOMATOES: ★★ CLUB SANDWICH: ★★★ CAKE: ★★★ STICKY DOUGH: ★★★	Extra-long blade excelled at tackling a large, crusty loaf and splitting a cake round. But its length kept us poking at the back of the kitchen counter when cutting smaller foods such as tomatoes.
MAC BREAD/ROAST KNIFE, SUPERIOR SERIES, 10½ INCHES **PRICE:** $28 **STYLE:** Stamped construction, scalloped ("reverse") serrations	BREAD & TOMATOES: ★★ CLUB SANDWICH: ★★★ CAKE: ★★★ STICKY DOUGH: ★★★	Comfortable, fairly lightweight, sharp knife, but scallop-shaped serrations slid over bread crust and tomato skin for several strokes before biting in. But for its rounded edges, it would be a winner.
F. DICK UTILITY SERRATED EDGE KNIFE, 1905 SERIES, 10 INCHES **PRICE:** $74.95 **STYLE:** Forged construction, pointed serrations	BREAD & TOMATOES: ★★ CLUB SANDWICH: ★★ CAKE: ★★ STICKY DOUGH: ★★★	Thick, forged knife weighed nearly twice as much as the top-ranked knives. It glided through bread but was described as feeling "like an ax" cutting a tomato or splitting a cake.
GLOBAL 10-INCH BREAD KNIFE, SERRATED **PRICE:** $122.95 **STYLE:** Forged construction, pointed serrations	BREAD & TOMATOES: ★★ CLUB SANDWICH: ★★★ CAKE: ★ STICKY DOUGH: ★★★	Priciest knife in the lineup looks and feels like a chef's knife with serrations. The alleged 10-inch blade is only 9½ inches. Acceptable, but not stellar, performance.

NOT RECOMMENDED

	PERFORMANCE	TESTERS' COMMENTS
WARTHER SERRATED KNIFE, 9-INCH **PRICE:** $48.50 **STYLE:** Stamped construction, microserrations	BREAD & TOMATOES: ★★ CLUB SANDWICH: ★★★ CAKE: ★ STICKY DOUGH: ★★★	Saw-toothed serrations and too-short blade (just 8¾ inches) were not up to tackling big bread loaves or cake rounds. Praised for paper-thin slices of tomato.
MESSERMEISTER 10-INCH PARK PLAZA BREAD/SERRATED SLICING KNIFE **PRICE:** $39.95 **STYLE:** Stamped construction, mixed-shape serrations	BREAD & TOMATOES: ★★ CLUB SANDWICH: ★★★ CAKE: ★★ STICKY DOUGH: ★	An odd mix of wavy, pointed, and rounded serrations lacked bite and held this knife back, particularly when trying to slice through thick, leathery bread crust.
LAMSONSHARP FORGED OFFSET BREAD KNIFE WITH EBONY HANDLE, 9 INCHES **PRICE:** $67.95 **STYLE:** Forged construction, tiny pointed serrations	BREAD & TOMATOES: ★★ CLUB SANDWICH: ★★★ CAKE: ★★ STICKY DOUGH: ★	While this knife felt solidly built, its blade was too short and its pointed serrations too tiny, making it struggle through both hard bread and sticky dough.

MANDOLINE SLICERS

Part of the challenge in selecting a mandoline is the tester; mandoline slicers can be confusing to use, have multiple parts, and, occasionally, require time spent with cryptic instructions just to figure out how to change the blade. Clearly, user-friendliness would play a major role in our ratings, as would safety, considering that these tools have hand guards for a reason. To test, we had both novice and experienced testers try out several mandolines by slicing russet potatoes and beefsteak tomatoes and assessing the models on safety features and usability. Where applicable, we also tested julienne and crinkle- or waffle-cutting blades. Mandolines are listed in order of preference.

HIGHLY RECOMMENDED	PERFORMANCE	TESTERS' COMMENTS
OXO GOOD GRIPS V-BLADE MANDOLINE SLICER **PRICE:** $49.99	STRAIGHT CUTS: ★★★ JULIENNE CUTS: ★★★ WAFFLE CUTS: ★★★ USER-FRIENDLINESS: ★★★	Razor-sharp V-blade made short work of a variety of fruits and vegetables, with a wide, sturdy gripper guard that felt exceptionally safe. Extra blades conveniently store beneath the frame. Measurement-marked dial sets slice thickness.
KYOCERA ADJUSTABLE CERAMIC MANDOLINE SLICER **PRICE:** $24.95 BEST BUY	STRAIGHT CUTS: ★★★ JULIENNE CUTS: N/A WAFFLE CUTS: N/A USER-FRIENDLINESS: ★★★	"It looks like a toy, but it works like crazy!" exclaimed one tester, who pledged to go out immediately and buy one. No julienne or waffle blades, but this slicer is razor-sharp, adjusts easily, and fits in a drawer. Plus the price is right.
JOYCE CHEN BENRINER ASIAN MANDOLINE PLUS **PRICE:** $39.96	STRAIGHT CUTS: ★★★ JULIENNE CUTS: ★★★ WAFFLE CUTS: N/A USER-FRIENDLINESS: ★★	Reasonably priced model comes close to the performance range of the top-rated OXO minus the safety perks. Some testers argued its julienne was the best, if you could brave the supersharp blade with the dinky hand guard.
OXO MANDOLINE SLICER **PRICE:** $69.99	STRAIGHT CUTS: ★★ JULIENNE CUTS: ★★★ WAFFLE CUTS: ★★★ USER-FRIENDLINESS: ★★★	A close relative of the winning slicer, this model was intuitive, simple, and an all-around solid performer. Testers loved the "idiot-proof" dial to set slice thickness and change blades, and the sturdy, soft-grip handle and feet. Would have been the winner, but its straight blade struggled to slice tomatoes.

RECOMMENDED	PERFORMANCE	TESTERS' COMMENTS
BORNER V-SLICER PRIMA STAINLESS STEEL MANDOLINE **PRICE:** $99.95	STRAIGHT CUTS: ★★★ JULIENNE CUTS: ★★ WAFFLE CUTS: N/A USER-FRIENDLINESS: ★★	V-blade made "beautiful, intact" tomato slices, as well as juli-enned carrots testers called so "professional" you could "make log cabins with them." But waste was considerable, especially with harder vegetables that the guard couldn't grip.
ZYLISS EASY SLICE 2 FOLDING MANDOLINE **PRICE:** $34.99	STRAIGHT CUTS: ★★★ JULIENNE CUTS: ★★ WAFFLE CUTS: N/A USER-FRIENDLINESS: ★★	The other model with a click-wheel to set slice thickness, this slicer would have shared user-friendliness points with the OXO had it not been for its "flimsy" plastic frame. And as cleanly as the microserrated blade sliced the tomatoes, some testers didn't appreciate hairline scrapes on the food.

NOT RECOMMENDED	PERFORMANCE	TESTERS' COMMENTS
SHUN MANDOLINE **PRICE:** $379.95	STRAIGHT CUTS: ★★ JULIENNE CUTS: ★★ WAFFLE CUTS: N/A USER-FRIENDLINESS: ★★	A colossal disappointment with an equally colossal price tag. Testers who were quick to compare this "beast" to a "deli machine on steroids" at first sight were shocked when the spring-loaded gripper "destroyed" tomatoes and required more than a little effort to slide across the blade. It produced "crisp, beautiful potato slices" but was an overall "pain in the neck."
BRON COUKE STAINLESS STEEL SUPER PRO MANDOLINE **PRICE:** $179.95	STRAIGHT CUTS: ★★ JULIENNE CUTS: ★★ WAFFLE CUTS: ★★ USER-FRIENDLINESS: ★	Everyone agreed that "after the setup, the results are pretty nice." Directions were "cryptic" and "confusing," and though it could make all the cuts in the book, it was "not very intuitive for novice users." Tomatoes "smeared" and "pulped" on its straight blade.
MICROPLANE V-SLICER **PRICE:** $39.99	STRAIGHT CUTS: ★★ JULIENNE CUTS: N/A WAFFLE CUTS: N/A USER-FRIENDLINESS: ★★	Some testers appreciated the thickness-adjusting wheel, others felt it brought fingers too close to the blade. Tomato slices were "translucent," but the heavy, juicy fruit was too weighty for the gripper. "A bit wobbly" and food "tends to get trapped" on the underside.
DE BUYER V-PRO MANDOLINE **PRICE:** $199.99	STRAIGHT CUTS: ★★ JULIENNE CUTS: ★★ WAFFLE CUTS: ★ USER-FRIENDLINESS: ★	"Completely unintuitive," "uncomfortable," and "overbuilt," this brawny French model's only saving grace was its incred-ibly sharp V-blades. The spring-loaded guard "boinged" food across the counter.

INEXPENSIVE STANDING MIXERS

The $500 standing mixers in our test kitchen are powerful enough to work all day, but home cooks need a more affordable option. With standing mixers priced under $200, we whipped cream, made chunky cookie dough (with chocolate chunks, pecans, oatmeal, and dried cherries), and kneaded pizza dough—tasks that larger, pricier mixers can do effortlessly. Most mixers handled the whipped cream and cookie dough with ease, but the pizza dough was another story; some mixers struggled because they weren't powerful enough to knead for a prolonged period of time. While we're not quite ready to trade in our $500 mixers, the first three listed below offer good value and performance for the average home cook. Mixers are listed in order of preference.

HIGHLY RECOMMENDED	PERFORMANCE	TESTERS' COMMENTS
KITCHENAID CLASSIC PLUS STAND MIXER **PRICE:** $199 **FEATURES:** 4.5-quart bowl, enameled metal dough hook and paddle, metal whisk	PIZZA DOUGH: ★★★ COOKIE DOUGH: ★★★ WHIPPED CREAM: ★★★	This mixer aced every test. Testers praised the "intuitive" controls and "solid" feel. While not as powerful as more expensive KitchenAid models, this mixer is a great value.

RECOMMENDED	PERFORMANCE	TESTERS' COMMENTS
BOSCH COMPACT KITCHEN MACHINE **PRICE:** $129 **FEATURES:** 4-quart bowl; metal dough hook, paddle/whisk hybrid, and whisk; plastic splatter guard	PIZZA DOUGH: ★★★ COOKIE DOUGH: ★★ WHIPPED CREAM: ★★★	Despite a few mechanical quirks (the beater hits the bowl when you raise the arm, and the bowl doesn't feel securely locked in), this mixer performed at a high level. It was even faster than the KitchenAid in the tough pizza dough test.
HAMILTON BEACH ECLECTRICS STAND MIXER **PRICE:** $179.95 **FEATURES:** 4.5-quart bowl, enameled metal dough hook and paddle, metal whisk, plastic splatter guard	PIZZA DOUGH: ★★ COOKIE DOUGH: ★★★ WHIPPED CREAM: ★★★	Testers praised the design of this mixer, especially the head-tilt button, which was "easy to engage by feel, without looking." It creamed butter and sugar "effortlessly" and whipped cream with "impressive efficiency."

RECOMMENDED WITH RESERVATIONS	PERFORMANCE	TESTERS' COMMENTS
EUROPRO CONVERTIBLE HAND/STAND MIXER **PRICE:** $59.99 **FEATURES:** 3.5-quart bowl, 2 metal beaters, 2 metal dough hooks, spatula, plastic bowl with cover, motorized bowl	PIZZA DOUGH: ★★ COOKIE DOUGH: ★ WHIPPED CREAM: ★★	This mixer allows you to select speeds for both the beaters and the bowl. While some users found this confusing, it helped keep the pizza dough moving around the bowl. This model struggled with the cookie dough, "really fighting" the heavy mix-ins.
SUNBEAM HERITAGE MIXMASTER, LEGACY EDITION **PRICE:** $159.99 **FEATURES:** 4.5-quart and 2.2-quart bowls, 2 metal beaters, 2 metal beater/whisk hybrids, 2 metal dough hooks, motorized bowl	PIZZA DOUGH: ★ COOKIE DOUGH: ★★★ WHIPPED CREAM: ★★	This mixer (and the two that follow) had a damning flaw: It couldn't effectively knead the pizza dough. This "sturdy" mixer had no trouble working the heavy mix-ins into the cookie dough, and testers liked the "simple" dial control.
FARBERWARE SELECT SERIES ELECTRONIC STAND MIXER **PRICE:** $99.99 **FEATURES:** 4-quart bowl, 2 metal beaters, 2 metal dough hooks, 1 metal whisk	PIZZA DOUGH: N/A COOKIE DOUGH: ★★ WHIPPED CREAM: ★★	This machine whipped cream acceptably, but labored to produce good cookie dough. Manual warns against kneading more than 8 ounces of dough (a ridiculously small amount), so we skipped this test. A few testers disliked the "involved" 3-step sequence of turning the mixer on, but others liked how each speed automatically ramped up to minimize spillage.
SUNBEAM HERITAGE MIXMASTER **PRICE:** $129 **FEATURES:** 4.6-quart and 2.2-quart bowls, 2 metal beaters, 2 metal dough hooks	PIZZA DOUGH: ★ COOKIE DOUGH: ★★ WHIPPED CREAM: ★★	This mixer "felt less powerful" than the Legacy Edition. Also, its bowl is not motorized, which contributed to its poorer (but still acceptable) showing with the cookie dough.

CAST-IRON SKILLETS

The first cast-iron cookware was reportedly made in China in the 6th century B.C.—quite an exotic origin for a humble pan that helps us cook eggs. Its humility is apparent in its pricing too: you can buy four good cast-iron pans for the price of one good nonstick pan. Other perks include the durability of cast iron (it will last a lifetime) and its versatility—a cast-iron skillet can be used to sear a steak or bake corn bread. One hitch: You have to know how to care for your skillet. It must be seasoned to prevent it from rusting or reacting with the foods you cook. Nowadays, unlike in the 6th century, you have the option of buying a preseasoned cast-iron skillet. Skillets are listed in order of preference.

HIGHLY RECOMMENDED	PERFORMANCE	TESTERS' COMMENTS
LODGE LOGIC 12-INCH SKILLET **MATERIAL:** Cast iron, preseasoned **PRICE:** $26.95 **COOKING SURFACE:** diameter 10"; bottom thickness 5.66 mm. **WEIGHT:** 7.2 lb.	 EGGS: ★★★ STEAK: ★★★ CORN BREAD: ★★★ CHICKEN: ★★★ DESIGN: ★★	Classic shape provided "plenty of room" in steak and chicken tests, but small handle made pan feel heavy when lifted. Eggs stuck "considerably" and took "tons of scrubbing" to clean the first time around but barely stuck and cleaned up easily the second time. Corn bread was crusty, with perfect release.
THE CAMP CHEF SK-12 CAST IRON SKILLET **MATERIAL:** Cast iron, preseasoned **PRICE:** $24.99 **COOKING SURFACE:** diameter 9¾"; bottom thickness 10.37 mm. **WEIGHT:** 9.2 lb.	 EGGS: ★★★ STEAK: ★★★ CORN BREAD: ★★★ CHICKEN: ★★★ DESIGN: ★★	Heaviest and thickest pan in the lineup was "a beast" to handle, but its heft made it shine in our cooking tests, where a consistent heat and deep sear were desirable. Right out of the box, we made scrambled eggs that didn't stick and corn bread that browned well and released perfectly.

RECOMMENDED	PERFORMANCE	TESTERS' COMMENTS
LODGE PRO-LOGIC 12-INCH SKILLET **MATERIAL:** Cast iron, preseasoned **PRICE:** $29.95 **COOKING SURFACE:** diameter 9¼"; bottom thickness 5.44 mm. **WEIGHT:** 7.4 lb.	 EGGS: ★★★ STEAK: ★★★ CORN BREAD: ★★★ CHICKEN: ★★★ DESIGN: ★★	"Gorgeous" browning on the fried chicken and steak. Eggs improved dramatically, from "horrible sticking" to "very easy to clean" by the end of testing. Handle is wide and well balanced, and loop-shaped helper handle is easy to grasp. Curved (rather than angled) sides make sauces easier to scrape up.
LE CREUSET ROUND SKILLET, 11-INCH **MATERIAL:** Enameled cast iron with matte-finish black enamel interior **PRICE:** $109.95 **COOKING SURFACE:** diameter 9¾"; bottom thickness 10.26 mm. **WEIGHT:** 6.5 lb.	 EGGS: ★★★ STEAK: ★★★ CORN BREAD: ★★★ CHICKEN: ★★★ DESIGN: ★★	"Pretty" pan was well proportioned and easier to handle than others. Sloping sides made eggs and sauce easier to scrape up. Achieved "beautiful crust" on steak and corn bread. On first test, eggs stuck ferociously, but results improved dramatically in second round, with minimal sticking. Can't use metal utensils or stack anything inside without damaging enamel finish.
OLVIDA 13-INCH SKILLET **MATERIAL:** Cast iron covered with nickel plate **PRICE:** $98.95 **COOKING SURFACE:** diameter 10¾"; bottom thickness 9.87 mm. **WEIGHT:** 8.65 lb.	 EGGS: ★★ STEAK: ★★★ CORN BREAD: ★★★ CHICKEN: ★★★ DESIGN: ★★	Chicken and steak browned beautifully in this heavy, roomy, silver-colored pan with "steady heating." The fond for pan sauce was a little light on flavor, almost like the nonstick skillet. Eggs stuck a moderate amount, without much change as testing progressed; pan cleaned up easily. Dishwasher-safe.

RECOMMENDED WITH RESERVATIONS	PERFORMANCE	TESTERS' COMMENTS
WAGNER COLLECTION SKILLET, 11¾-INCH **MATERIAL:** Cast iron, unseasoned **PRICE:** $19 **COOKING SURFACE:** diameter 9¾"; bottom thickness 5.82 mm. **WEIGHT:** 6.8 lb.	 EGGS: ★★ STEAK: ★★★ CORN BREAD: ★★ CHICKEN: ★★★ DESIGN: ★★	Slightly less steady heating than higher-ranked pans, but good results shallow-frying chicken and searing steak. Eggs stuck moderately, even as testing progressed, and pan always required some scrubbing. Corn bread browned well but stuck to pan. Thumb-hold on handle is nice feature.
CAJUN CLASSIC 12-INCH CAST IRON SKILLET **MATERIAL:** Cast iron, unseasoned **PRICE:** $16 **COOKING SURFACE:** diameter 9½"; bottom thickness 8.15 mm. **WEIGHT:** 5.85 lb.	 EGGS: ★★ STEAK: ★★ CORN BREAD: ★★★ CHICKEN: ★★★ DESIGN: ★★	Straight-sided pan was crowded while shallow-frying two chicken breasts and when searing a pair of steaks. Steak pan sauce had a slight metallic taste, indicating the acid had reacted with pan. Eggs continued to stick in second round but cleaned up easily.
BAYOU CLASSIC HEAVY DUTY CAST IRON SKILLET, 12 INCHES **MATERIAL:** Cast iron, unseasoned **PRICE:** $11 **COOKING SURFACE:** diameter 9½"; bottom thickness 4.06 mm. **WEIGHT:** 6.15 lb.	 EGGS: ★ STEAK: ★★ CORN BREAD: ★★★ CHICKEN: ★★ DESIGN: ★★	Thin bottom caused steep temperature drop when chicken was added to hot oil. Steaks cooked unevenly and with unsteady temperatures (too hot, then too cool). Pan was crowded and began steaming steaks. Scrambled eggs stuck considerably throughout testing. Cooking surface was roughest of the lineup.

INEXPENSIVE 12-INCH NONSTICK SKILLETS

In the realm of nonstick skillets, All-Clad's $135 skillet is dear to our hearts (and burners). But we wanted to see if any models priced under $60 would work as well or better than our prized pan. So we sautéed onions, cooked fish fillets, and made omelets in eight inexpensive pans. The first thing we noticed was size does matter—unless the pan was too heavy for users, bigger is better. Also, testers preferred handles made entirely of metal, which are securely riveted to the pan and can withstand higher temperatures in the oven. To gauge durability, we administered some abuse tests, such as washing with an abrasive metal scrubber. Skillets are listed in order of preference.

RECOMMENDED	PERFORMANCE	TESTERS' COMMENTS
WEAREVER PREMIUM HARD ANODIZED 12-INCH NONSTICK SKILLET **PRICE:** $28.03 **WEIGHT:** 2.35 pounds **COOKING SURFACE:** 9 inches **CAPACITY:** 12.8 cups	HANDLE: ★★★ DURABILITY: ★★★	This light pan was a breeze to maneuver and sautéed at a rapid pace. Testers "liked the feel" of the "comfortable" handle, which stayed cool on the stovetop. We wish the cooking surface and capacity were a tad larger.
CIRCULON ELITE HARD ANODIZED 12-INCH NONSTICK DEEP SKILLET **PRICE:** $59.95 **WEIGHT:** 2.95 pounds **COOKING SURFACE:** 9.5 inches **CAPACITY:** 19.2 cups	HANDLE: ★★ DURABILITY: ★★★	This "heavy" pan aced the durability test; the signature raised concentric ridges really do seem to improve longevity. One tester was especially impressed by the huge volume: "You could make stock in this." A few testers were put off by its straight sides, which made manipulating food a little tricky.
CALPHALON SIMPLY CALPHALON NONSTICK 12-INCH SKILLET **PRICE:** $54.95 **WEIGHT:** 2.85 pounds **COOKING SURFACE:** 9 inches **CAPACITY:** 13.8 cups	HANDLE: ★★ DURABILITY: ★★★	This pan performed well, thanks in part to its light weight and the even, gentle slope of the sides. The "nicely angled" handle stayed cool, but many testers disliked the "awkward" molded ridge on the grip. This pan has a relatively small capacity.
CUISINART CHEF'S CLASSIC NON-STICK HARD ANODIZED 12-INCH SKILLET **PRICE:** $49.95 **WEIGHT:** 3.15 pounds **COOKING SURFACE:** 9.5 inches **CAPACITY:** 15 cups	HANDLE: ★★ DURABILITY: ★	This heavy pan cooked well, and testers liked the nicely flared lip and overall shape. The handle stayed cool in the kitchen but was considered to be "too thin" for a perfect grip, and the helper handle was deemed "completely unnecessary."
FARBERWARE MILLENNIUM SOFT TOUCH STAINLESS 12-INCH NONSTICK SKILLET **PRICE:** $39.99 **WEIGHT:** 3.95 pounds **COOKING SURFACE:** 10 inches **CAPACITY:** 14.9 cups	HANDLE: ★★ DURABILITY: ★★	This "nicely shaped" pan felt "very sturdy" and sautéed very slowly. Some testers praised this pan as "heavy and big," but others thought it too "awkward," "too heavy," and "not well balanced." The handle was comfortable but "not balanced perfectly."

RECOMMENDED WITH RESERVATIONS	PERFORMANCE	TESTERS' COMMENTS
KITCHENAID GOURMET DISTINCTIONS STAINLESS STEEL 12-INCH NONSTICK SKILLET **PRICE:** $49.95 **WEIGHT:** 4.40 pounds **COOKING SURFACE:** 9 inches **CAPACITY:** 14.2 cups	HANDLE: ★★ DURABILITY: ★★	As the heaviest pan in our lineup, this drew mixed reviews. Some testers called it "beastly" and "ridiculously" heavy, but a few praised its "hefty" construction. The helper handle just "got in the way." A few testers felt the "cooking surface seems small for such a heavy pan."
RACHAEL RAY PORCELAIN ENAMEL NONSTICK 12-INCH FRENCH SKILLET **PRICE:** $29.95 **WEIGHT:** 2.15 pounds **COOKING SURFACE:** 9 inches **CAPACITY:** 14.4 cups	HANDLE: ★★ DURABILITY: ★	This "woklike" pan has a "comfortable" metal-and-silicone handle—but the exposed metal closest to the pan got dangerously hot. The cooking surface became significantly scratched up during our abuse tests; even before that, a few testers were asking, "Will it last?"

NOT RECOMMENDED	PERFORMANCE	TESTERS' COMMENTS
T-FAL SOLANO HARD ENAMEL 12-INCH SAUTÉ PAN **PRICE:** $24.99 **WEIGHT:** 2.40 pounds **COOKING SURFACE:** 10.5 inches **CAPACITY:** 14.6 cups	HANDLE: ★ DURABILITY: ★	"Bad ergonomics" and "handles awkwardly" were typical complaints from testers. We liked the large cooking surface, but this pan finished at the bottom of all our other criteria, and its screw-on plastic handle loosened considerably during testing.

STOVETOP GRIDDLES

Nonstick skillets are perfect for smaller breakfasts, but if you need to feed a crowd, a griddle that can span two burners is the way to go. We tested eight models, all priced under $100, to see how they'd handle bacon and pancakes. Only the Anolon and All-Clad models provided consistent, even heat across the entire griddle, producing perfectly crisp bacon and golden pancakes. We also examined the griddle handles—flat handles made it hard to move the griddle, and metal handles got too hot too quickly. Griddles are listed in order of preference.

RECOMMENDED | PERFORMANCE | TESTERS' COMMENTS

ANOLON ADVANCED DOUBLE BURNER GRIDDLE
PRICE: $48.95
MATERIAL: Nonstick anodized aluminum
WEIGHT: 3.7 pounds
COOKING SURFACE: 17 by 9.25 inches

BACON: ★★
PANCAKES: ★★★
HEAT DISTRIBUTION: ★★★
HANDLE HEAT RESISTANCE: ★★★

This griddle cooked up golden-brown pancakes every time. Bacon crisped quickly, and a convenient pour spout made grease disposal easy. Light construction makes this griddle cool down quickly (only 14 minutes) and easy to wash—convenient enough for everyday use.

ALL-CLAD LTD GRANDE GRIDDLE
PRICE: $99.95
MATERIAL: Nonstick anodized aluminum
WEIGHT: 5.9 pounds
COOKING SURFACE: 17.5 by 9 inches (excluding well)

BACON: ★★★
PANCAKES: ★★
HEAT DISTRIBUTION: ★★★
HANDLE HEAT RESISTANCE: ★★

Pancakes were golden brown, but trying to fit six large ones on the surface was a challenge—as the batter spread into the well, the round pancakes warped into odd shapes. The bacon was crisp, and most of the fat ended up in the large well, making the strips less greasy.

RECOMMENDED WITH RESERVATIONS | PERFORMANCE | TESTERS' COMMENTS

KITCHEN ESSENTIALS FROM CALPHALON PRO SERIES DOUBLE GRIDDLE
PRICE: $59.99
MATERIAL: Nonstick anodized aluminum
WEIGHT: 4.95 pounds
COOKING SURFACE: 17.25 by 10 inches

BACON: ★★
PANCAKES: ★★
HEAT DISTRIBUTION: ★★
HANDLE HEAT RESISTANCE: ★★

This griddle had the greatest width, letting us use a large spatula to flip the pancakes. While the bacon cooked right over the burners crisped in a short time, strips in the middle of the pan took a few extra minutes—a minor flaw.

CIRCULON 2 DOUBLE BURNER GRIDDLE
PRICE: $49.99
MATERIAL: Nonstick anodized aluminum
WEIGHT: 3.7 pounds
COOKING SURFACE: 17.25 by 9.25 inches

BACON: ★★
PANCAKES: ★★
HEAT DISTRIBUTION: ★
HANDLE HEAT RESISTANCE: ★★★

The circular ridges on the griddle surface kept food from sticking, but tasters weren't crazy about the ringed pattern these ridges imprinted on the pancakes. The bacon, which did not pick up the circular marks, crisped quickly and evenly.

KITCHENAID GOURMET ESSENTIALS DOUBLE BURNER GRIDDLE
PRICE: $39.95
MATERIAL: Nonstick aluminum with enamel exterior
WEIGHT: 3.95 pounds
COOKING SURFACE: 17.25 by 7.25 inches

BACON: ★
PANCAKES: ★★★
HEAT DISTRIBUTION: ★
HANDLE HEAT RESISTANCE: ★★★

This griddle cooked pancakes pretty evenly, but bacon didn't fare as well. Slices arranged across its narrow 7.25-inch width hung over the edges and didn't crisp properly. The bacon began smoking after 3 minutes, which did not happen on the other griddles.

NOT RECOMMENDED | PERFORMANCE | TESTERS' COMMENTS

NORDICWARE PRO CAST FLAT-TOP REVERSIBLE GRILL/GRIDDLE
PRICE: $53.85
MATERIAL: Nonstick cast aluminum
WEIGHT: 5.05 pounds
COOKING SURFACE: 17 by 9.14 inches (excluding well)

BACON: ★★
PANCAKES: ★
HEAT DISTRIBUTION: ★★
HANDLE HEAT RESISTANCE: N/A

The lack of lip and slippery surface made flipping pancakes almost impossible, with most of them sliding off the griddle. The bacon cooked more easily, but the prospect of cleanup scared off testers, who, given the lack of handles, feared that hot grease would splash onto their hands when they tried to pour it off.

LODGE LOGIC PRO GRID IRON GRIDDLE
PRICE: $42.99
MATERIAL: Preseasoned cast iron
WEIGHT: 14 pounds
COOKING SURFACE: 16.81 by 8.44 inches (excluding well)

BACON: ★
PANCAKES: ★
HEAT DISTRIBUTION: ★★
HANDLE HEAT RESISTANCE: ★

This griddle is a challenge to maneuver, clean, and store. Controlling the heat was difficult, with both pancakes and bacon scorching within seconds—even with the burner on medium-low. With a 35-minute cool-down time, this 14-pound griddle is a beast.

KITCHEN ESSENTIALS FROM CALPHALON CAST IRON REVERSIBLE GRILL/GRIDDLE
PRICE: $39.99
MATERIAL: Preseasoned cast iron
WEIGHT: 11.6 pounds
COOKING SURFACE: 13.25 by 8.75 inches (excluding well)

BACON: ★
PANCAKES: ★
HEAT DISTRIBUTION: ★★
HANDLE HEAT RESISTANCE: ★

This griddle should come with a warning to keep a fire extinguisher close by. So small that it barely covered both burners, it also has flat handles that let flames from the stove reach the surface of the griddle, igniting a small grease fire. Only four pancakes fit at once, and batter spilled into the hard-to-clean well.

SLOW COOKERS

In recent years, manufacturers have started adding new features—and higher price tags—to slow cookers. We tested seven models, paying special attention to modern updates, such as stovetop-safe inserts, programmable timers, and insert handles, which make it easy to remove the insert. Our slow cookers are ranked for features, evaporation (excess moisture is often a problem in slow-cooker dishes; the less evaporation, the better), and cooking ability. They all did well in our cooking tests—pot roast and chili. Slow cookers are listed in order of preference.

HIGHLY RECOMMENDED	PERFORMANCE	TESTERS' COMMENTS
ALL-CLAD STAINLESS STEEL SLOW COOKER WITH CERAMIC INSERT **PRICE:** $149.95 **FEATURES:** 6.5-quart capacity, digital timer, "keep warm" mode	CORE FEATURES: ★★★ EVAPORATION TEST: ★★★ COOKING: ★★★	This cooker aced the evaporation test and all the cooking tests, and it has every feature we want, including insert handles and a clear lid. Provided a steady, slow heat that is ideal for breaking down the collagen in tough cuts of meat without overcooking them.

RECOMMENDED	PERFORMANCE	TESTERS' COMMENTS
KITCHENAID STAINLESS STEEL SLOW COOKER **PRICE:** $129.95 **FEATURES:** 7-quart capacity, digital timer, "keep warm" mode, "auto" setting starts on high for two hours then shifts to low, "cooking" and "keep warm" indicator lights, capacity markings on inside of insert	CORE FEATURES: ★★★ EVAPORATION TEST: ★ COOKING: ★★★	This model cooked slightly hotter than the other contenders, but none of the finished food suffered as a result. The slightly squared insert shape was praised for being "easy to pour out of."
CUISINART SLOW COOKER **PRICE:** $99.95 **FEATURES:** 6.5-quart capacity; analog timer; "keep warm" mode; automatically starts on "high" (even when set to "low") when timer is in use until contents reach 140 degrees, then switches to "low"; cooking rack; "cook" and "warm" indicator lights	CORE FEATURES: ★★★ EVAPORATION TEST: ★★ COOKING: ★★★	This machine did very well in all cooking tests. Several testers were surprised that the bulky, boxy exterior of this cooker got very hot during long cooking. "It looks like it should be insulated," said one.
HAMILTON BEACH PROGRAMMABLE SLOW COOKER WITH TEMPERATURE PROBE **PRICE:** $59.95 **FEATURES:** 6-quart capacity, digital timer, programmable temperature probe, "keep warm" mode	CORE FEATURES: ★★ EVAPORATION TEST: ★★ COOKING: ★★★	While the temperature probe itself wasn't a lure for testers ("slow cooking shouldn't be that temperature-specific"), this model passed the evaporation test and performed well in the cooking tests. This cooker was downgraded for being the only one without handles on the insert, which made removing it difficult—especially when hot.

RECOMMENDED WITH RESERVATIONS	PERFORMANCE	TESTERS' COMMENTS
HAMILTON BEACH OVAL STAY OR GO SLOW COOKER **PRICE:** $39.95 **FEATURES:** 6-quart capacity, clips that lock lid in place for travel, recipe name tag on front of base, analog dial controls	CORE FEATURES: ★ EVAPORATION TEST: ★★★ COOKING: ★★★	The gimmicky travel clips and recipe name tag were not part of this model's appeal, but testers did appreciate its solid performance in the kitchen and the "straightforward, no frills" ease of operation. This inexpensive cooker does not have a timer, which is a serious drawback.
RIVAL OVAL VERSAWARE CROCK POT **PRICE:** $54.95 **FEATURES:** 6-quart capacity, insert is stovetop-safe to medium heat, detachable cord	CORE FEATURES: ★ EVAPORATION TEST: ★★★ COOKING: ★★★	"No timer?" asked testers. "No 'on' light?" The opaque lid was another strike against this cooker, but it did perform well in the cooking tests. Several testers complained about the "overhanging lip" on the insert, which necessitates complete inversion to pour out contents.

NOT RECOMMENDED	PERFORMANCE	TESTERS' COMMENTS
WEST BEND OVAL VERSATILITY SLOW COOKER **PRICE:** $64.95 **FEATURES:** 6-quart capacity, insert/pot is stovetop-safe to medium heat, base functions as a griddle, detachable cord	CORE FEATURES: ★ EVAPORATION TEST: ★★★ COOKING: ★	Testers complained about the lack of an "on" light, especially since this machine begins heating as soon as it's plugged in—there is no "off" setting. This model was also downgraded for heating faster on "low" than "high" and for having an awkward-fitting lid that "falls into the pot easily."

LIQUID DISH DETERGENTS

Most of us buy whatever dish detergent is on sale or whichever product looks or smells the best, but do they all work the same? To find out, we tested seven brands by systematically burning portions of several classic hard-to-clean foods—beef and bean chili, béchamel sauce, and skin-on chicken thighs marinated in teriyaki sauce—onto stainless-steel skillets. Then we measured out equal ratios of each dish detergent and water, submerged the dirty pans, and started scrubbing, counting our strokes for each pan. Our ratings reflect the detergents that performed best at scrubbing off each stuck-on mess (and conserved the most elbow grease). Detergents are listed in order of preference.

HIGHLY RECOMMENDED	PERFORMANCE	TESTERS' COMMENTS
METHOD GO NAKED ULTRA CONCENTRATED DISH DETERGENT **PRICE:** $2.99 for 25 fluid ounces (12 cents per ounce) **TIMES MORE EFFECTIVE THAN PLAIN WATER:** 5.3 **AVERAGE SCRUB STROKES:** 36.0	CHILI: ★★★ BÉCHAMEL: ★★★ CHICKEN TERIYAKI: ★★★	This eco-friendly detergent comes in a sleek bottle, but we were impressed by the contents—this detergent aced all of our scrubbing tests.
SEVENTH GENERATION FREE & CLEAR NATURAL DISH LIQUID **PRICE:** $3.19 for 25 fluid ounces (13 cents per ounce) **TIMES MORE EFFECTIVE THAN PLAIN WATER:** 5.0 **AVERAGE SCRUB STROKES:** 34.3	CHILI: ★★★ BÉCHAMEL: ★★★ CHICKEN TERIYAKI: ★★★	This eco-friendly detergent did the best job on the nasty mess of burnt chicken teriyaki. While it is the most expensive detergent in our lineup, it performed admirably in all tests.

RECOMMENDED	PERFORMANCE	TESTERS' COMMENTS
DAWN ULTRA ORIGINAL SCENT CONCENTRATED DISHWASHING LIQUID **PRICE:** $2.69 for 25 fluid ounces (11 cents per ounce) **TIMES MORE EFFECTIVE THAN PLAIN WATER:** 4.7 **AVERAGE SCRUB STROKES:** 38.3	CHILI: ★★ BÉCHAMEL: ★★ CHICKEN TERIYAKI: ★★	This bright blue detergent proved its worth by finishing just a tier below our two winners (it scored well in each washing test), making it our top choice among mass-market brands.
AJAX LEMON SUPER DEGREASER DISH LIQUID **PRICE:** $1.99 for 38 fluid ounces (5 cents per ounce) **BEST BUY** **TIMES MORE EFFECTIVE THAN PLAIN WATER:** 4.7 **AVERAGE SCRUB STROKES:** 44.0	CHILI: ★★ BÉCHAMEL: ★★ CHICKEN TERIYAKI: ★★	This inexpensive, "very lemony-smelling" detergent performed well in cleaning tests. A few testers commented on the high volume of suds this detergent produced.
IVORY ULTRA CLASSIC SCENT CONCENTRATED DISHWASHING LIQUID **PRICE:** $2.99 for 25 fluid ounces (12 cents per ounce) **TIMES MORE EFFECTIVE THAN PLAIN WATER:** 4.0 **AVERAGE SCRUB STROKES:** 42.0	CHILI: ★★ BÉCHAMEL: ★★ CHICKEN TERIYAKI: ★★	This detergent has no dyes but a strong "fresh baby" smell. It did an especially good job cutting through the burnt chili residue.
PALMOLIVE ULTRA ORIGINAL CONCENTRATED DISH LIQUID **PRICE:** $2.49 for 25 fluid ounces (10 cents per ounce) **TIMES MORE EFFECTIVE THAN PLAIN WATER:** 4.0 **AVERAGE SCRUB STROKES:** 42.7	CHILI: ★★ BÉCHAMEL: ★★ CHICKEN TERIYAKI: ★★	Although a few testers were turned off by the bright green color, others liked the "old-time," "fresh laundry" scent.
JOY ULTRA CONCENTRATED LEMON DISHWASHING LIQUID **PRICE:** $2.29 for 25 fluid ounces (9 cents per ounce) **TIMES MORE EFFECTIVE THAN PLAIN WATER:** 3.9 **AVERAGE SCRUB STROKES:** 46.0	CHILI: ★ BÉCHAMEL: ★ CHICKEN TERIYAKI: ★	This detergent finished last or second-to-last in all of our tests. Its lemon scent was deemed "pleasing" and "clean-smelling."

CONVERSIONS & EQUIVALENCIES

Some say cooking is a science and an art. We would say that geography has a hand in it, too. Flour milled in the United Kingdom and elsewhere will feel and taste different from flour milled in the United States. So, while we cannot promise that the loaf of bread you bake in Canada or England will taste the same as a loaf baked in the States, we can offer guidelines for converting weights and measures. We also recommend that you rely on your instincts when making our recipes. Refer to the visual cues provided. If the bread dough hasn't "come together in a ball," as described, you may need to add more flour—even if the recipe doesn't tell

you so. You be the judge. For more information on conversions and ingredient equivalents, visit our Web site at www.cooksillustrated.com and type "conversion chart" in the search box.

The recipes in this book were developed using standard U.S. measures following U.S. government guidelines. The charts below offer equivalents for U.S., metric, and Imperial (U.K.) measures. All conversions are approximate and have been rounded up or down to the nearest whole number. For example:

1 teaspoon	=	4.929 milliliters, rounded up to 5 milliliters
1 ounce	=	28.349 grams, rounded down to 28 grams

VOLUME CONVERSIONS

U.S.	METRIC
1 teaspoon	5 milliliters
2 teaspoons	10 milliliters
1 tablespoon	15 milliliters
2 tablespoons	30 milliliters
¼ cup	59 milliliters
⅓ cup	79 milliliters
½ cup	118 milliliters
¾ cup	177 milliliters
1 cup	237 milliliters
1¼ cups	296 milliliters
1½ cups	355 milliliters
2 cups	473 milliliters
2½ cups	592 milliliters
3 cups	710 milliliters
4 cups (1 quart)	0.946 liter
1.06 quarts	1 liter
4 quarts (1 gallon)	3.8 liters

WEIGHT CONVERSIONS

OUNCES	GRAMS
½	14
¾	21
1	28
1½	43
2	57
2½	71
3	85
3½	99
4	113
4½	128
5	142
6	170
7	198
8	227
9	255
10	283
12	340
16 (1 pound)	454

CONVERSIONS FOR INGREDIENTS COMMONLY USED IN BAKING

Baking is an exacting science. Because measuring by weight is far more accurate than measuring by volume, and thus more likely to achieve reliable results, in our recipes we provide ounce measures in addition to cup measures for many ingredients. Refer to the chart below to convert these measures into grams.

INGREDIENT	OUNCES	GRAMS
1 cup all-purpose flour*	5	142
1 cup cake flour	4	113
1 cup whole wheat flour	5½	156
1 cup granulated (white) sugar	7	198
1 cup packed brown sugar (light or dark)	7	198
1 cup confectioners' sugar	4	113
1 cup cocoa powder	3	85
Butter†		
4 tablespoons (½ stick, or ¼ cup)	2	57
8 tablespoons (1 stick, or ½ cup)	4	113
16 tablespoons (2 sticks, or 1 cup)	8	227

* U.S. all-purpose flour, the most frequently used flour in this book, does not contain leaveners, as some European flours do. These leavened flours are called self-rising or self-raising. If you are using self-rising flour, take this into consideration before adding leavening to a recipe.
† In the United States, butter is sold both salted and unsalted. We generally recommend unsalted butter. If you are using salted butter, take this into consideration before adding salt to a recipe.

OVEN TEMPERATURES

FAHRENHEIT	CELSIUS	GAS MARK (IMPERIAL)
225	105	¼
250	120	½
275	130	1
300	150	2
325	165	3
350	180	4
375	190	5
400	200	6
425	220	7
450	230	8
475	245	9

CONVERTING TEMPERATURES FROM AN INSTANT-READ THERMOMETER

We include doneness temperatures in many of our recipes, such as those for poultry, meat, and bread. We recommend an instant-read thermometer for the job. Refer to the table above to convert Fahrenheit degrees to Celsius. Or, for temperatures not represented in the chart, use this simple formula:

Subtract 32 degrees from the Fahrenheit reading, then divide the result by 1.8 to find the Celsius reading.

EXAMPLE:

"Roast until the juice runs clear when the chicken is cut with a paring knife or the thickest part of the breast registers 160 degrees on an instant-read thermometer." To convert:

160° F – 32 = 128°
128° ÷ 1.8 = 71° C (rounded down from 71.11)

INDEX

Note: *Italicized* page references indicate color photographs.

D